Ta Tsing Leu Li Being The Fundamental Laws, And A Selection From The Supplementary Statutes Of The Penal Code Of China

George Thomas Staunton

Nabu Public Domain Reprints:

You are holding a reproduction of an original work published before 1923 that is in the public domain in the United States of America, and possibly other countries. You may freely copy and distribute this work as no entity (individual or corporate) has a copyright on the body of the work. This book may contain prior copyright references, and library stamps (as most of these works were scanned from library copies). These have been scanned and retained as part of the historical artifact.

This book may have occasional imperfections such as missing or blurred pages, poor pictures, errant marks, etc. that were either part of the original artifact, or were introduced by the scanning process. We believe this work is culturally important, and despite the imperfections, have elected to bring it back into print as part of our continuing commitment to the preservation of printed works worldwide. We appreciate your understanding of the imperfections in the preservation process, and hope you enjoy this valuable book.

TA TSING LEU LEE;

BEING

THE FUNDAMENTAL LAWS,

AND A SELECTION FROM THE

SUPPLEMENTARY STATUTES,

OF THE

PENAL CODE OF CHINA;

ORIGINALLY PRINTED AND PUBLISHED IN PEKIN,
IN VARIOUS SUCCESSIVE EDITIONS,
UNDER THE SANCTION, AND BY THE AUTHORITY, OF THE SEVERAL
EMPERORS OF THE *TA TSING,* OR PRESENT DYNASTY.

TRANSLATED FROM THE CHINESE;
AND ACCOMPANIED WITH AN APPENDIX,
CONSISTING OF AUTHENTIC DOCUMENTS, AND A FEW OCCASIONAL NOTES,
ILLUSTRATIVE OF THE SUBJECT OF THE WORK;

BY SIR GEORGE THOMAS STAUNTON, BART. F.R.S.

Mens, et animus, et consilium, et sententia civitatis, posita est in *LEGIBUS.*
CICERO PRO CLUENTIO.

LONDON:
PRINTED FOR T. CADELL AND W. DAVIES, IN THE STRAND.
1810.

OF BIBL

Strahan and Prefton,
Printers-Street, London.

TO

JOHN BARROW, ESQ. F.R.S.

&c. &c. &c.

IN TESTIMONY OF SINCERE REGARD AND ESTEEM,

THIS VOLUME IS INSCRIBED,

BY

HIS OBLIGED AND ATTACHED FRIEND,

THE TRANSLATOR.

TRANSLATOR's PREFACE.

IN undertaking the work which is now ſubmitted to the eye of the Public, the Tranſlator was not unconſcious of the difficulties and diſadvantages he would have to contend with in ſo novel an attempt. He was however encouraged to proceed by the perſuaſion that the work was in itſelf amply deſerving of the labour which it might be neceſſary to beſtow upon it; that the intrinſic value, the unqueſtionable authenticity of the materials, and the general importance and curioſity of the ſubject, would fully compenſate thoſe particular defects and imperfections which, in an undertaking of this nature, were foreſeen to be unavoidable, and, upon the whole, make amends for the too conciſe and almoſt obſcure brevity of the text, in ſome places, its tedious and uninſtructive prolixity in others, and its general unſuitableneſs for tranſlation into an Engliſh idiom. Under all circumſtances he flattered himſelf, that a faithful verſion of the Fundamental Laws of the Penal Code of China might, with the addition of ſome ſupplementary matter, not only prove intereſting as far as regards its immediate ſubject, but likewiſe afford a more compendious and ſatisfactory illuſtration, than any other Chineſe work that could have been ſelected, of the peculiar ſyſtem and conſtitution of the Government, the principles of its internal policy, its connection with the national habits and character, and its influence upon the general ſtate and condition of the people in that country.

 To

To account for the limited and defective nature of our information upon these interesting subjects, notwithstanding the number and variety of the literary communications concerning the Chinese empire, which we already possess in Europe, through the medium of the European languages, it will be requisite to advert particularly to the circumstances under which these communications have been made, and to the sources from which they have, for the most part, been derived.

It will not be necessary, in the course of this enquiry, to trace back the subject to any very remote period. It is well known that the Empire of China, bounded on one side by the ocean, and on the other by ranges of inaccessible mountains, or vast and seemingly impervious desarts, continued, until about the commencement of the 13th century of our era, to be effectually secluded by these natural barriers from any direct and regular intercourse with the rest of the inhabited globe. The various inquisitive and enlightened nations, which successively flourished in ancient times, both in Western Asia and in Europe, scarcely appear to have even suspected its existence.

In the mean while, however, the people who, at a remote period of antiquity, first colonized this fertile and extensive region, were gradually emerging from primeval barbarism. Without either receiving assistance, or encountering opposition, from their less fortunate neighbours, they slowly but regularly advanced upon the strength of their own internal resources and local advantages, nearly, if not entirely, to their present state of civilization and improvement.

The commencement of the 13th century is the period at which the Chinese first submitted in a body to the sway of a foreign conqueror; and although the dynasty, established by the successful invaders, was not of any long duration, it must have had a material, and even in some degree a permanent effect, upon the relations between China and contemporary Powers; more especially, as this revolution in the East was, it will be perceived, at no considerable interval of time, seconded

ſeconded in the Weſt, by the fortunate era of the reſtoration of letters, and of the introduction of the moſt important of the improvements in navigation in modern Europe.

As a new ſpirit of curioſity and enterprize had been thus excited, and means apparently adequate to its complete gratification diſcovered, it might naturally be ſuppoſed that one of the firſt objects would have been that of taking advantage of the additional facilities which ſeemed to have been afforded for a communication with the Chineſe empire; that the early accounts, however vague and imperfect, which had been given by caſual travellers, of its extent, magnificence, and political importance, would have ſoon led, in the ordinary courſe of events, to an intimate acquaintance and a regularly eſtabliſhed intercourſe with that remote and recently diſcovered, but, at the ſame time, highly intereſting portion of the civilized world.

At the end, however, of ſeveral centuries, theſe expectations are ſtill but very imperfectly realized. This Great Empire, too well aſſured of the competency of its own natural and artificial reſources, to be induced to ſeek, and, if not too powerful, at leaſt too diſtant and compactly united, to be liable to be compelled to enter into alliances and cloſe connections with the Powers of Europe, has never as yet, except in a precarious and limited degree, admitted of any ſpecies of intercourſe with them. It continues to this day wholly regardleſs and independent of thoſe nations of the Weſt, whoſe general ſuperiority in policy and in arms has triumphantly extended their power and influence over almoſt every other exiſting ſociety of mankind.

A conſiderable portion of the intercourſe which actually ſubſiſts between China and the Nations of Europe owes its origin, as is well known, to the influence of religious motives; and was eſtabliſhed under rather favourable auſpices, by the indefatigable zeal and appropriate talents of the early miſſionaries of the Catholic church. Theſe eccleſiaſtics, having been for the moſt part of the Society of Jeſus, were not wanting in the ſagacity, or neglectful of the policy, which had, on ſo many other occaſions, crowned the projects of their ſociety with ſucceſs. It is difficult indeed to ſay how far, under ſuch circumſtances, even the moſt ancient of the inſtitutions, upon which the fabric of the Chineſe government is founded, or the moſt deeply rooted of the prejudices and attachments, by which it continues to be ſuſtained, could have withſtood their powerful and undermining influence, had they not happened to have loſt the ſupport and countenance both of the head of the Catholic church, and of their reſpective temporal ſovereigns.

The conſequent extinction of their order having ſubverted the ſyſtem of politics, which until then the Miſſionaries in China had ſucceſsfully obſerved, having cauſed the adoption of a plan of converſion more ſtrict, and probably more orthodox, but, in the ſame proportion, more unaccommodating to the prejudices of the people, and more alarming to the jealouſy of the government, and having alſo, generally ſpeaking, thrown the profeſſion into leſs able hands, the cauſe of Chriſtianity and of Europe neceſſarily loſt much of its temporary luſtre and influence. In addition to this unfavourable change of circumſtances, the French revolution has ſubſequently had the effect of conſiderably reducing both the amount of the funds which ſupport, and the number of the labourers who cultivate the Chriſtian vineyard in China; under which accumulated diſadvantages the intercourſe with Europeans, as far as the Miſſionaries are concerned, it will eaſily be conceived, muſt of late years, in ſpite of every exertion, have been gradually on the decline.

Although, among the few Miſſionaries whom the Emperor of China ſtill retains in his ſervice at Pekin, and among the larger number who are clandeſtinely employed in maintaining and propagating the Chriſtian faith in the provinces, there are, no doubt, many amiable and reſpectable, and perhaps even ſome learned men, they can ſcarcely be expected

expected to make any material addition, under their present difficulties, to the stock of useful and valuable information which Europe has already derived from the same quarter.

The literary labours of the Missionaries, consisting of original descriptions and of translations, are, however, already numerous and extensive. Their works seem, at first sight, to have been penned with such diligence, and formed upon plans so comprehensive, as to promise satisfaction on every subject connected with the Chinese empire, in which European curiosity can be interested. But, on a closer examination, we find reason to lament that their attention had not been more directed to the objects that were principally desirable, and we begin to suspect that their situation, or some other circumstances, must have had a tendency to disqualify them from representing those objects with all the accuracy and fidelity of disinterested and impartial observers. At the same time, it is impossible to conceive any set of persons more advantageously placed for the purpose of collecting and communicating the information that was most required. Having devoted themselves to a residence for life among the people of that empire, it was naturally one of their first objects to acquire a knowledge of their manners, habits, and language. The active duties of their profession necessarily led them to cultivate the favour of the rich, to conciliate the affections of the poor, and to associate generally with every class of the inhabitants. As they appeared exclusively in the character either of artists or of men of science, they were in no danger of becoming objects of jealousy to any rank, or to any party; they had generally a free communication with every department of the court and of the government, and at times were admitted to a familiar intercourse even with the sovereign himself.

It is, however, to be recollected, on the other hand, that, with the Missionaries, science and literature were objects only of a secondary consideration, infinitely inferior in their estimation to that sacred

cause

caufe in which they were united, which they were bound to fupport, and to which all others were to be made fubfervient; that they were perfons who had all of them profeffedly renounced the world, and who, having abftracted themfelves accordingly from its various purfuits, had been in great meafure incapacitated from acquiring that particular experience which is neceffary towards appreciating the merits and characteriftic features of other countries, by the moft obvious and indifpenfable of tefts, a comparifon with their own. It was alfo inevitable, that perfons thus fituated fhould be, generally fpeaking, under the influence of a ftrong pre-difpofition in favour of a people, for the fake of whofe converfion they had renounced their country, and devoted their lives; and of a government, from whom, at one period, they had received extraordinary kindnefs and indulgence, and upon the continuance of whofe protection the fuccefs of their future undertakings was forefeen almoft entirely to depend.

Although having, perfonally, accefs to all the principal objects of curiofity, and chief fources of information, and poffeffing fufficiently the requifite talents of defcription, we too often find that a want of fubftantial impartiality and difcriminating judgment in their writings, has tended to throw a falfe colouring on many of the objects which they delineate, and has fometimes produced thofe inconfiftencies by which errors and mifreprefentations of this defcription are often found to contribute to their own detection.

In like manner, although an intimate knowledge of the language of China enabled the Miffionaries to explore and illuftrate the antiquities of the empire, by the perufal and tranflation of the obfcure and difputed texts of its moft ancient poets, hiftorians, and philofophers, an extreme anxiety to place thefe productions in the moft favourable and pleafing light, has led them, in fome inftances, to engraft fo much of the European character and ftyle upon the Chinefe originals, that the authenticity of their verfions has, however unjuftly, been in thofe cafes more than fufpected.

Other

Other works again, ſuch as the Chineſe preſs abundantly affords, concerning the preſent ſtate of the empire, its civil, political, and legal inſtitutions, they have, it muſt be acknowledged, in great meaſure neglected, either as comparatively unimportant in their eſtimation, or as inſufficient and ill-ſuited for conveying thoſe highly favourable ideas, with which they ſeem themſelves to have been impreſſed, of the character of the Chineſe people, and the principles of the Chineſe government.

By the foregoing obſervations, it is by no means intended to detract from the real merits of the learned and pious writers of this claſs, either by denying, that they have afforded to the European world a vaſt collection of uſeful and intereſting information, or by aſſerting, that they have, in any particular inſtances, been guilty of wilful deception or miſrepreſentation. It is merely wiſhed to point out ſome of the cauſes which render it unſafe to rely implicitly on their authority, to ſtate the particular bias under which they wrote, and to notice ſome of the effects of which that bias was neceſſarily productive.

The communications between European ſtates and the dominions of China, which a ſpirit of commercial enterprize gave riſe to, although they have been, at times, of conſiderable importance to ſeveral of the Continental nations, and are at preſent, with reſpect to Great Britain, of ſuch a nature and extent, as to be very eſſentially contributive to her national proſperity, yet they did not, until a very late period, produce any fruits deſerving of particular notice, either to ſcience or literature.

With the exceptions of the Travels of Mr. Bell of Antermony, and the Tranſlation of a Chineſe Novel, by an obſcure hand, but illuſtrated by the name of its Editor, ſcarcely any thing of importance reſpecting China, derived from a commercial origin, appeared in England until the period of the Embaſſy of the late Earl of Macartney. His Lordſhip's miſſion was certainly an important ſtep towards obtaining a more accurate and intimate

intimate knowledge of the Chinefe empire. That empire was, on that occafion, in fome degree laid open to the view of perfons, whofe talents and judgment were worthy of their country, and of an enlightened age; and who, it was natural to expect, would be difpofed to defcribe the country and its inhabitants, as they really found them, and to ftate the opinions they might be led to form on the different objects which occurred, with candour and fincerity. — If, in eftimating the credit due to their impartiality, fome allowance for the national prejudices of Englifhmen fhould be deemed requifite, the tendency of thofe prejudices would, at all events, be very diffimilar to that of the bias which had influenced their predeceffors in the fame field of enquiry. When alfo it is confidered that, in paffing rapidly over the narrow path to which they were confined, the opportunities of obfervation muft have been comparatively few and limited, it will juftly be deemed a fubject of pride and fatisfaction, and a very material addition to the immediate advantages which that expedition produced to this country, that it has, in fo fhort a time, and under fuch unfavourable circumftances, been the means of throwing an entire new light upon, and of correcting and extending our ideas of that extraordinary and interefting empire; that, in fhort, if it has not led to the difcovery of a new world, it has, as it were, enabled us to recover a portion of the old, by removing, in a confiderable degree, thofe obftacles by which our contemplation of it had been intercepted.

The fhort refidence in China of Lord Macartney's Embaffy, although it fcarcely afforded any opportunity of either confirming or difproving the various geographical, hiftorical, and ftatiftical details, with which we had been furnifhed by the Miffionaries, was amply fufficient to difcover that the fuperiority over other nations, in point of knowledge and of virtue, which the Chinefe have long been accuftomed to affume to themfelves, and which fome of their European hiftorians hiſtorians have too readily granted them, was in great meaſure fallacious; their knowledge was perceived to be defective in thoſe points in which we have, in Europe, recently made the greateſt progreſs, and to which we are therefore proportionately partial. Their virtues were found to conſiſt more in ceremonial obſervances, than in moral duties; more in profeſſion, than in practice; and their vices, when traced and diſcovered upon occaſions where they were the leaſt expected, ſeemed to deſerve a more than ordinary degree of reprobation.

The firſt impreſſions occaſioned by a diſcovery, that the Chineſe people and government were in many reſpects the converſe of that which, agreeably to the moſt authentic accounts, they might have been expected to be found, were naturally unfavourable.

But if the Engliſh viſitors at the court of Pekin had been permitted to remain any conſiderable time, and with a ſufficient degree of freedom in the interior of the empire, they might gradually have acquired a more direct and extenſive knowledge of the governors and of the governed in China; they might, by conſtant and familiar intercourſe with the ſeveral claſſes of the inhabitants, have learned more of their manners, habits, and ordinary conduct, and have been enabled to judge of, and to characterize, their influencing motives on different occaſions, upon ſurer grounds.

If they had poſſeſſed equal opportunities with the miſſionaries, who preceded them, of exerting their judgment upon the Chineſe character, though they certainly would not have coincided in all their ſentiments and opinions, they might, perhaps, have found ſomething to compenſate the evils they had juſtly reprobated and lamented, and they might even have at laſt determined, that a conſiderable proportion of the opinions moſt generally entertained by Chineſe and Europeans of each other was to be imputed either to prejudice, or to miſinforma-

tion;

tion; and that, upon the whole, it was not allowable to arrogate, on either ſide, any violent degree of moral or phyſical ſuperiority.

In regard to the diffuſion of knowledge among the natives, they might not indeed meet with ſuch illuſtrious inſtances as thoſe of a Newton, a Locke, or a Bacon; nor even, perhaps, generally, find any tolerable proficiency in the ſciences, which in Europe the writings of thoſe great men have contributed ſo much to advance and to eſtabliſh; but, neverthelefs, ſuch a ſufficiency, in all ranks and conditions, of the information eſſential or moſt uſeful to each; ſuch a competency and ſuitableneſs of the means to the end, as might, upon a general view of the whole population, fairly entitle the Chineſe to be put in competition with ſome, at leaſt, of the nations of Europe, in reſpect to all the eſſential characteriſtics of civilization.

The virtues of the Chineſe, although very inferior, no doubt, to their profeſſions, and of a lower order than thoſe which Chriſtianity has happily implanted, or invigorated, in the European world, they might alſo have found as little alloyed, either with the ſanguinary or the ſelfiſh vices, as among any people for whoſe guidance the ſalutary light of revelation has not yet penetrated.

Even the crime of infanticide, for inſtance, which has been conſidered ſuch an indelible ſtain upon the Chineſe character, might be found to admit of ſome extenuation, if it was diſcovered to be rarely if ever practiced, except in the anguiſh of hopeleſs poverty, or in caſes of ſuch unhappy and defective formation, as might be conceived to render life a painful burden. The criminality of the Chineſe, in this reſpect, might alſo be ſafely contraſted with the legalized cruelty and unnatural indifference of Roman fathers under ſimilar circumſtances. Paſſing from the people to the government, the obvious and undeniable defects of the latter might juſtly be compared with the acknowledged corruptions and imperfections of thoſe of Europe; and it might perhaps

perhaps be found, upon a general view, that the happineſs of the people was not more frequently neglected or interrupted, upon the one ſyſtem than upon the other.

There would ſtill, no doubt, remain, both in the habits of the people, and the principles of the government, ſome exceptionable traits, which are happily not to be exactly paralleled in Europe; but, on the other hand, ſome very conſiderable and poſitive moral and political advantages might be found peculiar to the Chineſe; attributable to the ſyſtem of early and univerſal marriage, except indeed, as far as that ſyſtem may be conſidered to conduce to the misfortune of a redundant population; to the ſacred regard that is habitually paid to the ties of kindred; to the ſobriety, induſtry, and even intelligence of the lower claſſes; to the almoſt total abſence of feudal rights and privileges; to the equable diſtribution of landed property; to the natural incapacity and indiſpoſition of the government and people to an indulgence in ambitious projects and foreign conqueſts; and laſtly, to a ſyſtem of penal laws, if not the moſt juſt and equitable, at leaſt the moſt comprehenſive, uniform, and ſuited to the genius of the people for whom it is deſigned, perhaps of any that ever exiſted.

The foregoing conjectures reſpecting the degree of eſtimation in which the Chineſe government and people will be held by the other civilized nations of the world, when the veil is more completely withdrawn, which has hitherto intercepted their view, and balked their curioſity, although they neither have been nor can be verified, under preſent circumſtances, by adequate perſonal enquiry, yet their reaſonableneſs and probability may even now be inveſtigated with advantage, and tried upon almoſt every point, by the intereſting evidence which the Chineſe, in their own numerous and reſpectable literary productions, have themſelves afforded.

After making every allowance for national partialities, prejudices, and defects, whatever they may be, it will generally be found, that the beſt and moſt authentic information of the ſtate of any country, having pretenſions to civilization, is contained in the works of the natives, and in the vernacular language.

Although the character of the Chineſe government, in common with that of thoſe of all other Aſiatics nations, neceſſarily prevents the preſs from becoming, in any conſiderable degree, a vehicle for the inveſtigation of political queſtions, or for the introduction of innovations of any kind, yet there are no previous licenſes demanded, or reſtrictive regulations enforced; nor in the caſe of publications upon ordinary ſubjects, any checks whatever impoſed upon their number or variety. On the contrary, the encouragement given to purſuits which are purely literary, has always been conſidered as one of the remarkable features of Chineſe policy. Theſe purſuits are profeſſedly the ſole channel of introduction to political advancement in the ſtate, to offices, rank, and honours of almoſt every deſcription. With the proſpect of ſuch rewards, the number of competitors in the paths of literature muſt neceſſarily be infinite; and, in point of fact, the firſt rudiments, at leaſt, of literary knowledge, are almoſt univerſally diffuſed among the natives of every claſs and denomination. — Through the concurrence of theſe cauſes the productions of the preſs in China not only open a wide field of inveſtigation to the literary and philoſophical enquirer, but are, in a much greater degree than could otherwiſe have been expected, calculated to ſupply that ſpecies of information which the preſent ſyſtem of our intercourſe with the Chineſe, affords ſo little proſpect of obtaining by perſonal communication.

It is not, indeed, to be expected, that an acquaintance with Chineſe literature, however intimate, can materially add to our preſent ſtock of theore-

theoretical knowledge upon natural and philoſophical ſubjects; and in reſpect to the Ethics and Antiquities of the Chineſe, it may perhaps be conſidered that the tranſlations already effected by the Miſſionaries afford a ſufficient ſpecimen: but there are many other objects of reſearch, which ſurely are neither unintereſting nor unimportant. As men of ſcience, we have yet much to learn reſpecting the arts, which, with the advantage of long and uninterrupted experience, and a proportionate degree of practical ſkill, are ſucceſsfully cultivated by an eminently induſtrious and ingenious people. As men of letters, we have yet to comprize, within the circle of our philology, the various branches of a new ſpecies of Belles Lettres, contained in a highly refined and moſt ſingular language; we have, laſtly, as ſtateſmen and philoſophers, to examine more cloſely, and to dive more deeply into the principles, operation, and conſequences, of the civil policy, characteriſtic laws, and general ſyſtem of a government and conſtitution, not indeed the beſt or the pureſt, but certainly the moſt anciently, and, if we may judge from its duration, the moſt firmly eſtabliſhed, and the moſt conformable to the genius and character of the people, of any of which mankind has had experience.

The great, and indeed almoſt the only obſtacle, which exiſts to inquiries of this nature, is the circumſtance of the literature of China being buried in a language by far the leaſt acceſſible to a foreign ſtudent of any that was ever invented by man. Among the languages of Europe, ſeveral agree to a conſiderable extent, even in their phraſeology, and all are connected by various analogies. The languages of the Aſiatic nations are indeed radically different from thoſe Europe, and their ſtudy is, to Europeans, proportionately difficult; but in one point at leaſt, all the written languages of the world coincide, that of the Chineſe only excepted. — In all, ideas are expreſſed by a combination of letters, repreſenting, not the ideas themſelves, but certain

particular

particular ſounds with which theſe ideas, either by accident or convention, have become identified. It is excluſively in the Chineſe language, that the ſeemingly viſionary ſcheme of a philoſophical character, immediately expreſſive, according to an eſtabliſhed and received claſſification, of the ideas as they ariſe in the mind, under an entire diſregard of the ſounds employed to give them utterance, has ever been generally adopted as the univerſal medium of communication; a plan of which it may juſtly be ſaid, that the practice is no leſs inconvenient and perplexing, than the theory is beautiful and ingenious.

Experience has nevertheleſs in various inſtances proved, that theſe difficulties, however great, are by no means inſurmountable, even by ordinary zeal and application. It is alſo to be conſidered, that they would be more ſeriouſly felt by thoſe, by whom the firſt ſteps ſhould be taken towards introducing and recommending the knowledge of the Chineſe language in this country, than by thoſe who might afterwards follow in the ſame path of literature. The modes of acting and thinking peculiar to a people who have ſcarcely ever been placed in circumſtances tending in any reſpect towards an aſſimilation with the reſt of mankind, eſpecially when conveyed in a language whoſe ſtyle and idioms are frequently as little conformable to our received notions of propriety, as they are reconcileable to our ordinary rules and diſtinctions of grammar, cannot indeed be expected to prove in any form of tranſlation, altogether agreeable to the taſte of European readers. It ſeems requiſite that the ſtudents in this branch of oriental literature ſhould become numerous, that its peculiarities ſhould be traced and explained by a more correct knowledge of the people themſelves, and that the minds of the readers ſhould be ſomewhat habituated to them, as they already are in a conſiderable degree, to the peculiarities in the ſtyle and idioms of other Eaſtern languages. Yet, even in the preſent ſtate of our knowledge of the Chineſe people, and of our political relations with the Chineſe empire, it is not unreaſonable to hope, that communications derived from

authentic

authentic ſources in the original language, may have ſome effect in drawing attention to, and exciting an intereſt in, the hitherto neglected literature of that country; — it is neceſſary indeed, that the work ſelected ſhould, in one eſſential point at leaſt, be unexceptionable, however defective in others; that its tranſlation ſhould combine as many advantages, and as few objections as poſſible, and in particular, that the excellence of the matter, ſhould render the manner in which it was expreſſed a conſideration of comparatively little importance.

Among the multifarious publications of the Chineſe, ancient as well as modern, which are ſtill extant, and hitherto untranſlated into any European language, the *TA-TSING-LEU-LEE*, or Imperial Code of Penal Laws, certainly ranks with thoſe of the firſt claſs, in reſpect to the importance of the ſubject of which it treats, and the pre-eminence of the authority by which it was originally eſtabliſhed, as well as, at different periods down to the preſent time, ſucceſſively ſanctioned and confirmed. As in this work alſo, the two very deſirable qualities of a comparatively ſimple ſtyle, and a compendious form, happen fortunately to be united, its contents are certainly, in many reſpects, leſs difficult of acceſs, than thoſe of moſt other publications of a ſimilar extent in the Chineſe language and character.

It has juſtly been obſerved by Mr. Gibbon, that "the laws of a "nation form the moſt inſtructive portion of its hiſtory." But the laws of the Chineſe, if taken in the moſt comprehenſive ſenſe of the term, framed, as they have been, by the wiſdom and experience of a long ſeries of ages, and ſuitably provided, as they are, for the government of an empire, unparalleled in the hiſtory of the world, in extent and population, muſt, it will readily be imagined, be proportionally numerous and complicated. They are alſo, which is ſtill more embarraſſing, generally intermingled in ſuch a degree with details concerning the ancient hiſtory and actual condition, of the civil, political, and ceremonial inſtitutions of the empire, that individual works on theſe ſubjects

ſubjects are ſometimes extended to the extraordinary length of upwards of an hundred volumes, and the aggregate is, of courſe, enormous in proportion.

From ſuch a vaſt and heterogeneous maſs of materials, to attempt any thing like a compendious illuſtration of the true ſpirit and character of their legal inſtitutions, would be a very preſumptuous, if not abſolutely a hopeleſs undertaking. The *TA-TSING-LEU-LEE*, however, happily renders, in this reſpect, any ſuch laborious and indefinite reſearch unneceſſary, as, in fact, no ſelection could be made, however judiciouſly, that would not be ſuperſeded by the authority, as far as it extends, of the authenticated compendium.

The Chineſe government, according to one of the fundamental principles of its conſtitution, is, it is to be obſerved, divided into ſeveral diſtinct, though not altogether independent, branches or departments. The civil and military eſtabliſhments, the public revenue and expenditure, the national rites and ceremonies, the public works, and the adminiſtration of public juſtice, are each of them regulated by a particular code of laws and inſtitutions; but the laws of the empire, in the ſtricteſt and moſt appropriate ſenſe of the term, and which may be denominated Penal Laws, by way of contradiſtinction, are the peculiar and excluſive province of the laſt of theſe departments. All regulations which are either directly penal, by the denunciation of puniſhment in the event of diſobedience, or indirectly, by their coercive operation, have evidently a diſtinct character, though neceſſarily connected, more or leſs, with every branch of that conſtitution which is upheld and protected by their ſanction.

Accordingly, the *TA-TSING-LEU-LEE*, although originating with one, treats indirectly and incidentally of all the branches of the Chineſe conſtitution; and the information it thus imparts, upon a comparatively reduced ſcale, of the adminiſtration of the civil and military affairs of the empire, of the public revenue and public works, and of the

the ceremonial inſtitutions and obſervances, though not altogether ſo clear or ſo comprehenſive, as it might have been in a work having theſe for its profeſſed objects, will not, probably, to a European reader, be the leaſt acceptable of its contents.

In China, the ſucceſſion of a new line, or dynaſty of princes, has been, as it muſt be in moſt regular and profeſſedly abſolute monarchies, invariably attended, not only with an entire diſſolution of the government, but nominally, at leaſt, with an abrogation of the conſtitution eſtabliſhed by the preceding family; though in moſt caſes the neceſſity muſt already have been apparent of afterwards rebuilding the fabric of ſimilar materials, and upon ſimilar principles. None, therefore, of the laws and inſtitutions now in force in the Chineſe empire, bear a more remote date than that of the laſt Tartar conqueſt: notwithſtanding which, this code, as well as indeed almoſt every thing in which the Chineſe people is concerned, carries with it, it is important to remark, an internal evidence of the antiquity of its origin and prototype, not leſs convincing and unqueſtionable, perhaps, than the moſt ſolid monuments, or the beſt authenticated records by which the paſt periods of the exiſtence of any nation are at preſent atteſted.

A conſiderable portion of the intereſt, to which enquiries into the preſent ſtate of the Chineſe empire are entitled, neceſſarily depends upon the credibility of its extraordinary pretenſions to antiquity; and theſe pretenſions have, it muſt be acknowledged, been ſometimes diſputed as not ſufficiently ſupported, either by remains or veſtiges, actually exiſting in China, of very remote ages, or by the corroborative teſtimony of any other than their own native hiſtorians. It may be proper, therefore, to ſtate in this place, ſome of the grounds upon which the ſubſtantial accuracy and authenticity of the accounts given us in theſe reſpects by the Chineſe themſelves, are nevertheleſs aſſumed as points, which may now be conſidered as almoſt beyond the reach of controverſy.

It is, in the firſt place, a material conſideration, that although the annals of the Chineſe, like thoſe of almoſt all other nations, are prefaced with incredible, and confeſſedly fabulous accounts of their primitive ſtate, and of the circumſtances which attended their firſt eſtabliſhment, yet the period at which that part of their hiſtory which is profeſſed to be authentic commences, early as it is, is completely reconcileable with the data concerning the re-peopling of the world, which we derive from the inſpired writings.

As, therefore, no direct objection can be maintained on this ground to the antiquity claimed by the Chineſe, it ſeems impoſſible by any indirect objection, drawn from the want of ſpecific external or internal evidence, to reſiſt the inference, that a people, whoſe written language, conſiſting of ſymbolical characters, is founded on the moſt ancient of principles, and the frame of whoſe government is eſſentially conformable to the patriarchal ſyſtem of the firſt ages, muſt have ſegregated themſelves (if the expreſſion may be allowed) from the reſt of mankind before the period at which the ſymbolical was ſuperceded by the alphabetical character, and the patriarchal, by other ſyſtems and forms of government.

We do not indeed recognize in the Chineſe conſtitution, which the lapſe of ſo many ages has refined and conſolidated, and which has been neceſſarily moulded to the various purpoſes of a great and powerful monarchy, that original form of the patriarchal government which ſubſiſted in detached families, and among wandering tribes, in the rude and ſimple ages of antiquity.

But there is every reaſon to conſider the foundation to be the ſame in both caſes. The vital and univerſally operating principle of the Chineſe government is the duty of ſubmiſſion to parental authority, whether veſted in the parents themſelves, or in their repreſentatives, and which, although uſually deſcribed under the pleaſing appellation of filial piety, is much more properly to be conſidered as a general rule

of

of action, than as the expression of any particular sentiment of affection. It may easily be traced even in the earliest of their records; it is inculcated with the greatest force in the writings of the first of their philosophers and legislators; it has survived each successive dynasty, and all the various changes and revolutions which the state has undergone; and it continues to this day powerfully enforced, both by positive laws, and by public opinion.

A government, constituted upon the basis of parental authority, thus highly estimated and extensively applied, has certainly the advantage of being directly sanctioned by the immutable and ever-operating laws of Nature, and must thereby acquire a degree of firmness and durability to which governments, founded on the fortuitous superiority of particular individuals, either in strength or abilities, and continued only through the hereditary influence of particular families, can never be expected to attain. Parental authority and prerogative seem to be, obviously, the most respectable of titles, and parental regard and affection the most amiable of characters, with which sovereign or magisterial power can be invested, and are those under which, it is natural to suppose, it may most easily be perpetuated.

By such principles the Chinese have been distinguished ever since their first existence as a nation; by such ties, the vast and increasing population of China is still united as one people, subject to one supreme government, and uniform in its habits, manners, and language. In this state, in spite of every internal and external convulsion, it may possibly very long continue.

In conclusion of the subject of the antiquity of the Chinese it may be sufficient to answer the objections arising from the want of external evidence and internal monuments, by one or two general remarks.

The peculiar site of the region inhabited by the Chinese has been already noticed. The variety of soil and climate which it comprehends, its fertility and productiveness, are equally well known. Under ſuch circumſtances the Chineſe were neither neceſſitated by want, nor tempted by curioſity, to croſs thoſe barriers of ſea and land to which they owed ſo much of their internal ſecurity and proſperity. Having no natural enemies to contend with, they ſoon loſt that warlike character which their primitive anceſtors might have poſſeſſed in the wilds of Tartary. The art of navigating ſhips at a diſtance from land, and the adventurous purſuits of trade with foreign nations, being wholly unneceſſary to them, they generally deſpiſed as well as neglected.

With little opportunity of becoming generally acquainted with the ſtate of the reſt of the inhabited world, and with the unfavourable and uninviting ſpecimen of it, which the wretchedneſs and barbariſm of their immediate neighbours preſented, it was almoſt impoſſible that they ſhould not look back with peculiar complacency upon their own undiſputed ſuperiority, and gradually acquire much of that high degree of national vanity and arrogance for which they are remarkable.

Thus the Chineſe, although they certainly became at a very early period a rich, populous, and, comparatively, an enlightened nation, have not been at any time enterprizing, warlike, or commercial, and therefore have been in fact deficient in thoſe qualities which, of all others, are the moſt conducive to the extenſion of the fame of any people among diſtant countries.

The want of ancient monuments, were it even without exception to be admitted, might, in great meaſure, be accounted for by the proneneſs to decay of all their buildings, owing to the unſubſtantial ſyſtem and principles of their architecture; but they have at leaſt one monument of antiquity, which, in point of magnitude and extent, certainly eclipſes thoſe of all other nations and ages.

There are, perhaps, few facts in hiſtory more inconteſtably proved than the conſtruction, in the third century before the Chriſtian era, of the great wall which ſtill continues to ſeparate and form a barrier between China and that tract of country, now denominated Chineſe Tartary.

This

This ſtupendous effort of human labour is not indeed, viewing its object, any proof of the bravery, nor viewing its inefficacy, any proof of the ſagacity, of the nation which produced it, but it will not be denied to be a deciſive evidence that the Chineſe formed even at that remote period a conſiderable empire, were united under a ſtrong and regular government, and certainly in no very low ſtate of civilization.

This digreſſion relative to the antiquity of the Chineſe empire, as far as it may be inferred from general conſiderations, has been conceived neceſſary to the introduction of the few following remarks, applicable more particularly to the origin and hiſtory of their laws, ſuch as they now appear to us in the code of the preſent dynaſty.

On this ſubject it is to be preſumed the Miſſionaries might have given us ample and authentic details, as they expreſsly inform us (Memoires ſur les Chinois, vol. viii. p. 220.) that there exiſts in China an "Hiſtoire des Loix de Chine, en 74 volumes, en remontant de "dynaſtie en dynaſtie, juſqu'a *Yao* et *Chun*;" which emperors are univerſally admitted by the Chineſe to be the founders of their laws, if not alſo of their monarchy. In the numerous quartos however, which are occupied by the tranſlations of Moyriac de Mailla, the compilations of Du Halde and Groſier, and the miſcellaneous work entitled "Memoires concernant les Chinois," very little is to be found concerning the laws which can be conſidered in the light of hiſtorical deduction, and that little, it is to be regretted, is in a great meaſure contradictory, or looſe and inconcluſive.

In the Memoires ſur les Chinois, vol. i. p. 180, it is ſtated that "Les interpretes du *Chou-King* s'accordent aſſez à dire qu'il n'y avoit "point de ſupplices ſous le regne de *Yao*, et qu'ils n'etoient pas néceſ-"ſaires. La vertu et la douceur de ce bon prince ſuffiſoient, diſent-"ils, pour empêcher les fautes, ou du moins en prévenir les ſuites. "Son exemple perſuadoit l'amour de la vertu, et conſervoit l'inno-"cence des mœurs publiques." Yet it is admitted in the ſame page, that

that the aſſociate and ſucceſſor of the abovementioned monarch, and the emulator of his virtues, was ſuppoſed by ſome of the commentators to have eſtabliſhed the following terrible puniſhments, which equal in ſeverity any thing which is even now recognized, and in ordinary practice in China:—" 1. Une marque ineffaçable ſur le " front: 2. l'amputation du bout du nez: 3. l'amputation du bout " des pieds: 4. la caſtration: 5. la mort."

Theſe commentators are indeed imagined to have been miſtaken; but in page 20, of the 3d volume, and 56, of the 4th volume of the ſame work, the fact is re-aſſerted without any other reſervation than that, although ſuch laws had really been eſtabliſhed at the period ſtated, the innocence and virtues of the people were ſuch, that many centuries elapſed before it became neceſſary to enforce them.

The truth, it is moſt probable, lies between the two extremes; and while we may agree with the Miſſionaries, that the practice of ſuch cruelties in the ordinary adminiſtration of juſtice is improbable, and inconſiſtent with the high character which is given of the wiſdom of the ſovereign and the mildneſs of the people at that era, we ſhall ſcarcely be ſo extravagant as to ſuppoſe that puniſhments, and even ſevere ones, could have been at any time, altogether unneceſſary.

The notices which are interſperſed throughout the above works, of the alterations and improvements which afterwards took place in the ſyſtem of the Chineſe penal law, under the princes of the ſeveral ſucceſſive dynaſties, contain unfortunately, as has been obſerved, nothing preciſe or circumſtantial; and all the information, which, in addition to the communications of the Miſſionaries, the Tranſlator of the preſent work feels himſelf juſtified in offering as authentic, is compriſed in a ſhort note, attached to the Chineſe original.

The firſt regular code of penal laws is, in that note, attributed to a perſon named *Lee-Quee*, and is denominated after him, *Lee-Quee-Fa-King*. It ſeems to have been ſimple in its arrangement and conſtruction,

ſtruction, having been confined to ſix books only, two of which appear to have been introductory, the third relative to priſons, the fourth to the adminiſtration of the police, the fifth to the leſſer or miſcellaneous offences, and the ſixth to all the great and capital crimes againſt public juſtice.

The character of *Lee-Quee*, as well as the age in which he lived, are left in great meaſure to conjecture; but there is reaſon to infer that the code which bears his name, was firſt put in force under the dynaſty of *Tſin*, which ſucceeded to the throne of China B. C. 249; but it is evident, from the ſlight mention that is made of this perſonage, that ſo far from having been a legiſlator, he was not even a compiler of any conſiderable celebrity.

There can in fact be little doubt, that the principal characteriſtics, not only of the code publiſhed by *Lee-Quee*, but alſo of that in force at this day, originated at periods far more remote than that under conſideration; but a new compilation, at leaſt, of the Chineſe laws muſt neceſſarily have formed a part of the plan of that celebrated Emperor of the race of *Tſin*, who is ſaid to have been ſo ambitious of the reputation of having been the actual founder of the monarchy, as to have ſought it by a vain and abſurd attempt at the deſtruction of all the books, records, and other exiſting memorials, of preceding ages.

The Chineſe note already quoted likewiſe deſcribes, generally, the alterations and enlargements which took place in the plan and diviſions of the code upon the ſucceſſive elevation to power of each of the ſeveral dynaſties of *Han*, *Wee*, *Tſin*, *Tſe*, *Swee*, *Tang*, *Sung*, *Yuen*, and *Ming*, until it aſſumed, ſhortly after the acceſſion, A. D. 1644, of the dynaſty of *Tſing*, now reigning, that form in which it ſtill continues to be promulgated and obſerved throughout the empire.

Having thus been able to trace back the preſent code with certainty, to conſiderably remote ſources, it will not be deemed extraordinary that, as even in our European codes, although the ſtructure is comparatively

paratively of a recent date, it is often rendered intricate and inconvenient from an adherence to a plan, which, owing to its antiquity, is in ſome places altogether inapplicable to the ſtate of things as they at preſent exiſt; and yet, out of reſpect to its origin, is only cautiouſly, and perhaps awkwardly, modified, inſtead of being wholly ſet aſide or fundamentally altered, as often as new circumſtances and events had rendered it expedient. Another, and a no leſs conſiderable ſource of obſcurity, is, it muſt be acknowledged, the very artificial and complex conſtruction of the code itſelf; however much the ingenuity of the contrivance, and the labour beſtowed in the adaptation of the means to the end, may at the ſame time be deſerving of being admired.

It may indeed be almoſt invariably remarked, in reſpect to the inſtitutions of civilized, and particularly anciently civilized, nations, that although the ends of ſubſtantial juſtice may in general be really conſulted, it is almoſt in vain to expect to find a ſuitable proviſion for the attainment of thoſe ends by the ſhorteſt and ſimpleſt means. This deſideratum, however its attainment may be held out in the ſpeculations of theoriſts, ſeems to be reſerved to be accompliſhed by the wiſdom of future ages. How far, in the formation of the laws of the Chineſe, the ends of ſubſtantial juſtice are even conſulted, there muſt, alſo, no doubt, be ſome variety of ſentiment. There are certainly many points upon which theſe laws are altogether indefenſible. We ſhall look in vain, for inſtance, for thoſe excellent principles of the Engliſh law, by which every man is preſumed innocent until he is proved guilty; and no man required to criminate himſelf. Such maxims the Chineſe ſyſtem neither does nor indeed could recognize. But it will ſcarcely eſcape obſervation, that there are other parts of the code which, in a conſiderable degree, compenſate theſe and ſimilar defects, are altogether of a different complexion, and are perhaps not unworthy of imitation, even among the fortunate and enlightened nations of the Weſt. It is ſufficiently obvious, indeed, that the intrinſic merits of of any code of laws, which is not profeſſed to be, either the reſult of the meditations of a philoſopher, or the untried theory of a legiſlator, but which, on the contrary, actually is in force, forms the baſis of the government of a nation, and as ſuch, has been fairly ſubmitted to the important teſt of experience, are not to be eſtimated by any imaginary ſtandard of perfection. Such a Code can be juſtly compared only with thoſe other codes of law, whoſe practicability and expediency have already been tried by a ſimilar ordeal; and in making the eſtimate, the conſideration of thoſe local circumſtances and peculiarities, upon a conformity to which, the excellence of the national laws in every country ſo greatly depend, is certainly leaſt of all to be omitted.

This is, upon the whole, very juſtly deſcribed, as well as happily illuſtrated, by the Preſident de Monteſquieu, in his "Eſprit des "Loix;" and is ſo important to the right underſtanding of the laws of the extraordinary people under conſideration, that the following ſhort quotation from that work, it is hoped, will not be unacceptable.

"Les loix politiques et civiles de chaque nation," he obſerves, "doi-"vent être tellement propres au peuple pour lequel elles ſont faites, que "c'eſt un très grand haſard ſi celles d'une nation peuvent convenir à "une autre. Il faut qu'elles ſe rapportent à la nature et au principe "du gouvernement qui eſt établi, ou qu'on veut établir; ſoit quelles "le forment, comme font les loix politiques; ſoit qu'elles le main-"tiennent, comme font les loix civiles. Elles doivent êtres relatives "au *phyſique* du pays, au climat glacé, brûlant ou tempéré; à la qua-"lité du terrain, à ſa ſituation, à ſa grandeur; au genre de vie des "peuples, laboureurs, chaſſeurs, ou paſteurs: elles doivent ſe rappor-"ter au degré de liberté que la conſtitution peut ſouffrir; à la religion "des habitans, à leurs inclinations, à leur richeſſes, à leur nombre, à "leur commerce, à leurs mœurs, à leurs manieres. Enfin, elles ont "des rapports entr'elles; elles en ont avec leur origine, avec l'objet du

 "legiſlateur,

" legiflateur, avec l'ordre des chofes fur lefquelles elles font établies.
" C'eſt dans toutes ces vues qu'il faut les confiderer."

To this may be added, from the high authority of Sir William Jones, the more concife and equally appropriate remark which he makes on the fame fubject, in his Preface to the Laws of *Menu*; " That the beft " intended legiflative provifions would have no beneficial effect, even " at firft, and none at all in a fhort courfe of time, unlefs they were " congenial to the difpofition and habits, to the religious prejudices, " and approved immemorial ufages, of the people, for whom they " were enacted."

After expreffing a wifh, that the reader fhould form his judgment of the Chinefe Laws by thefe criteria, it feems preferable to refer directly to the tranflation of the Code itfelf, and to the illuftrations fubjoined to it, than to attempt in this place any detailed anticipation of its peculiarities and characteriftics. A few general obfervations refpecting their application and practice, may, neverthelefs, until clearer lights can be thrown on the fubject by clofer and more capable obfervers, be of fome utility, in as much as they may contribute to that juft conception of the facts themfelves, without which the moft accurately drawn conclufions would, of courfe, be nugatory.

It may be noticed, in the firft place, that although the ingenious M. Pauw, in his Philofophical Refearches, has not exceeded the truth in obferving, that " les principaux refforts du gouvernement Chinois " font le fouet et le batôn;" neither thefe, nor any other corporal punifhments, are in fuch univerfal ufe, or adminiftered with fuch undiftinguifhing feverity, as has fometimes been imagined.

Thus, in a book of drawings, copied apparently from Chinefe originals, and publifhed in England under the title of " *Punifhments of* " *China*;" the fancy of the painter has given, in fome inftances, a reprefentation of cruelties, and of barbarous executions, which it would be be very erroneous to ſuppoſe have a place in the ordinary courſe of juſtice, although ſomething of ſuch a nature may, no doubt, have been practiſed heretofore under ſome tyrannical and ſanguinary Emperors; and even perhaps in the preſent age, upon ſome particular and extraordinary occaſions.

Thus, alſo, although every page of the following tranſlation may ſeem at firſt ſight to bear teſtimony to the univerſality of corporal puniſhments in China, a more careful inſpection will lead to a diſcovery of ſo many grounds of mitigation, ſo many exceptions in favour of particular claſſes, and in conſideration of particular circumſtances, that the penal ſyſtem is found, in fact, almoſt entirely to abandon that part of its outward and apparent character.

The acts which the laws of China enforce, and thoſe which they prohibit, are indeed, in ſome caſes, ſuch as are more uſually left in Europe to the deciſion of cuſtom and individual feeling; but, in a country in which the laws have not in any conſiderable degree, the active concurrence, either of a ſenſe of honour, or of a ſenſe of religion, it may perhaps be abſolutely requiſite that they ſhould take ſo wide a range. Experience may have dictated the neceſſity of their interfering in this direct manner in the enforcement of all thoſe national habits and uſages, whoſe preſervation, as far as they are of a moral or prudential tendency, muſt undoubtedly be of eſſential importance both to the ſecurity of the government and to the happineſs of the people.

Another object which ſeems to have been very generally conſulted, is that of as much as poſſible combining, in the conſtruction and adaptation of the ſcale of crimes and puniſhments throughout the Code, the oppoſite advantages of ſeverity in denunciation and lenity in execution.

The exceſſive ſeverity of the puniſhments actually inflicted in caſes of treaſon, rebellion, breach of duty to parents and huſbands, and in ſome others, is ſcarcely any exception to this rule; as, even in ſuch inſtances,

 the

the execution of the law is lenient in comparifon to its literal and *prima facie* interpretation. One confiderable inconvenience, indeed, refults from this fyftem: in confequence of its adoption, although the place intended to be affigned to each tranfgreffion againft the laws, in the general fcale of criminality, is certainly very readily difcoverable by the number of blows of the bamboo, or by the extent of the punifhment, in other refpects, nominally denounced againft the tranfgreffor, the punifhment which he is in any particular cafe actually liable to fuffer, is rarely if ever to be afcertained without various references and confiderable refearch. The fections of the Chinefe Code may thus, perhaps, not unaptly be compared to a collection of confecutive mathematical problems, with this additional circumftance of perplexity, that a juft and entire comprehenfion of each fection individually, requires a general knowledge of thofe that follow, no lefs than of thofe which precede it.

With all its defects, however, and with all its intricacy, this Code of Laws is generally fpoken of by the natives with pride and admiration; all they feem in general to defire is, its juft and impartial execution, independent of caprice, and uninfluenced by corruption.

That the laws of China are, on the contrary, very frequently violated by thofe who are their adminiftrators and conftitutional guardians, there can, unfortunately, be no queftion; but to what extent, comparatively with the laws of other countries, muft at prefent be very much a matter of conjecture; at the fame time, it may be obferved as fomething in favour of the Chinefe fyftem, that there are very fubftantial grounds for believing, that neither flagrant, nor repeated acts of injuftice, do, in point of fact, often, in any rank or ftation, ultimately efcape with impunity.

The foregoing obfervations have either had relation to the peculiar fubject of the original of the prefent work, or to the circumftances which

which have been conceived to render it not altogether unworthy of the attention of the learned and curious in Europe.

It ſtill remains for the Tranſlator to explain in what manner, and to what extent, it has been his endeavour to transfuſe the original Chineſe text into the idiom of the Engliſh language. And this he feels it his duty to do more fully and circumſtantially than if he had been purſuing a well known and beaten track, which might not only have juſtified a greater degree of confidence, but have likewiſe rendered explanations for the ſatisfaction of his readers leſs neceſſary.

In reſpect to the plan, the moſt obvious conſideration which occurred, at the very commencement of the undertaking, was, that a tranſlation at length, of every thing contained under the title of *TA-TSING-LEU-LEE*, a work occupying, in ſo conciſe a language as the Chineſe, no leſs than 2906 octavo pages, was, if not abſolutely impracticable, certainly altogether inexpedient.

If, in order to reduce the work into a compendious form, the Tranſlator had permitted himſelf the liberty of making an abſtract or abridgment of the text, he might, at the ſame time have endeavoured to have adopted a more ſyſtematic arrangement, a more pleaſing ſtyle, and a more harmonious phraſeology; but he was ſenſible that he ſhould in the ſame proportion have impaired the two recommendations moſt eſſential to the value of the work, its authenticity, and its originality. He, therefore, determined upon a ſelection, not, indeed, according to any conjectural eſtimate of the ſuperior importance of any particular part of the Code over another, but according to the rule, which, by the diviſion of the laws into fundamental and ſupplementary, the Code itſelf afforded.

The *Leu*, or Fundamental Laws, are thoſe of which the Penal Code, upon its formation ſoon after the acceſſion of the preſent dynaſty, appears originally to have conſiſted, and which, being, at leaſt nominally, permanent,

nent, are reprinted in each ſucceſſive edition, without either alteration or amendment.

The *Lee*, or Supplementary Laws, are the modifications, extenſions, and reſtrictions of the Fundamental Laws, which, after undergoing a deliberate examination in the Supreme Councils, and receiving the ſanction of the Sovereign, are inſerted in the form of clauſes, at the end of each article or ſection of the Code, in order that they might, together with the Fundamental Laws, be equally known and obſerved They are generally, however, reviſed every fifth year, and ſubjected to ſuch alterations as the wiſdom of government determines to be expedient.

Under theſe two denominations, the whole body of Chineſe Penal Law is comprehended; but the number of documents which poſſeſs the force of laws without the name, muſt, under a government in which every authenticated expreſſion of the will of the Prince bears that character, neceſſarily be unlimited.

Each article of the Fundamental Laws is alſo accompanied by a familiar Expoſition, or rather Paraphraſe, which bears the name of the Emperor *YONG-TCHING*; and the whole of the text is further illuſtrated by extracts from the works of various commentators: Theſe appear to have been expreſsly written for the uſe and inſtruction of the magiſtrates, and accordingly form a body of legal reference, directly ſanctioned for that particular purpoſe by government.

Theſe extracts have not indeed been found to convey, on all occaſions, that ample and ſatisfactory information which was at firſt expected from them; but this will not appear very extraordinary, when it is conſidered, that the perſons whom they were deſigned to inſtruct, are excluſively natives, and, therefore, probably the leaſt in want of an explanation upon thoſe very points, which to a foreigner are neceſſarily the moſt perplexing.

Still

Still, however, the Tranflator has derived from a perufal of this part of the original work confiderable advantage; and when other fources of information failed to difpel the obfcurity of which the concifenefs of the text was fometimes productive, a reference to the expanded and explanatory form of expreffion, adopted in the paraphrafe of the Emperor *Yong-tching*, was often found to fupply every thing that was wanting to its complete elucidation.

Throughout the work, the Tranflator's firft object, and that which he has endeavoured to keep conftantly in view, has been to convey the full meaning of each article or paragraph fucceffively, in appropriate, and, at the fame time, intelligible language; in other words, to draw as juftly as poffible, the middle line between the unfaithfulnefs and and inaccuracy of a free, and the ungracefulnefs and almoft ungrammatical obfcurity of a clofe verfion.

He is very fenfible that his beft efforts cannot have wholly protected him from occafional deviations from the courfe which he has prefcribed to himfelf; but he trufts he fhall meet with the excufe, if not alfo with the approbation, of the reader, in entertaining in every doubtful cafe, a difpofition to prefer the latter of the oppofite alternatives. — He is, at the fame time, not unconfcious, that the prefervation of the ftyle and form of expreffion obferved in the original, is in itfelf, in this cafe, of little importance: that it is the nature and principles of the *laws*, not thofe of the language of the Chinefe people, which it is properly the object of his work to illuftrate. Under this impreffion, he has readily fubmitted to the neceffity, whenever it occurred, of altering the order of words, and the conftruction of fentences; he has feldom fcrupled to fupply the want of a fynonimous expreffion, by a definition; he has even ventured to embody in words thofe ideas which, though forming an integral part

part of the ſenſe of the text, were yet left, by a ſort of ellipſis, to be underſtood by implication and inference.

It is, laſtly, proper to notice, that in ſome few inſtances, the text has been found ſo obſcure, and its conſtruction ſo recondite, that no effort of attention was adequate completely to reconcile the apparent ſenſe of the words, when conſidered individually, with their collective meaning, ſuch as it was unanimouſly declared to be, by the moſt intelligent of the natives whom the Tranſlator had an opportunity of conſulting.

There is, certainly, ſomething in the figurative or poetic ſtyle, with which the Chineſe, on ſome occaſions, embelliſh their writings, that a foreigner can ſcarcely ever hope to fathom, by any ordinary means of analyſis or inveſtigation; but, fortunately, inſtances of this kind are ſo rare in the Penal Code, that they form only a very trifling exception to the general ſtyle of the work, which, on the contrary, is remarkable for its conciſeneſs and ſimplicity, and as familiar, as the ſubject and the uſe of technical phraſeology would permit. So peculiarly difficult, indeed, is the figurative and poetic ſtyle of certain compoſitions of the Chineſe, that one of the moſt diſtinguiſhed among the Miſſionaries, for his talents and knowledge of the language, declares in his preface to a tranſlation of an Imperial poem, which he entitles "Eloge de Mougden," that without a reference occaſionally to the Mantchoo Tartar tranſlation of that work, he never could have accompliſhed his undertaking.

In regard to terms, more or leſs peculiar to the Chineſe, ſuch as in a work of this nature would neceſſarily be of conſtant occurrence, the Tranſlator might eaſily have relieved himſelf from every reſponſibility, by retaining in each caſe the original Chineſe expreſſion; but, conſidering that the very ſounds of the language are ſtrange and unpleaſing to European ears, and, in fact, but very imperfectly capable of

being

being reprefented by any European alphabet, he has conceived it would on every account be moft defirable to reduce the untranflated words into as fmall a compafs as poffible, explaining the remaining few in notes in the margin; and remarking generally, with regard to the reft, that, as in the cafe of the words *Emperor*, *Tribunal*, and the like, they are approximations to the truth, whofe ambiguity, if any, the context is generally fully fufficient to remove.

The Tranflator may be allowed to remark, that the choice of his fubject was originally influenced by circumftances, in fome degree accidental. It firft occupied his attention in confequence of his having been perfonally a witnefs to many of the unneceffary provocations, groundlefs apprehenfions, and embarraffing difcuffions, of which, fince the firft commencement of our prefent important commercial and national intercourfe with the people of China, falfe or imperfect notions of the fpirit of their laws have been, but too often, the occafion: and although the tranflation of every part of the work did not promife, in this point of view, to be of equal utility, he always found it, at the leaft, a gratification to curiofity, and a not uninterefting employment of leifure hours: it is only, however, very recently, and in compliance with the perhaps too partial fuggeftions of thofe to whofe perufal the Tranflator has had the pleafure of fubmitting the manufcript, that he has allowed himfelf to believe it might prove not altogether unworthy of the attention of the Public at large.

He was fenfible that on this occafion it was his firft duty to affure himfelf of the fubftantial accuracy of his tranflation. But it was, at the fame time, his anxious wifh to render it, preparatory to its publication, as little exceptionable in other refpects, as a due regard to that primary object would admit. It therefore affords him a peculiar pleafure to be able in this place to acknowledge the valuable fuggeftions which, to this end, two of his friends in particular have kindly contributed;

both of them diſtinguiſhed as men of letters, the one with the addition of being pre-eminent in his profeſſion of the law, and the other in reſpect to his ſuperior knowledge of the Chineſe empire, and his ardent zeal to promote and extend its relations with Great Britain, for the mutual benefit of both countries.

In making this declaration, however, it is far from the Tranſlator's wiſh to avail himſelf of theſe reſpectable ſanctions for the protection from cenſure of a work, for which he muſt of neceſſity be ſolely reſponſible; nor can he pretend to have had, in this country, the advantage of that particular aſſiſtance, which an acquaintance with the language of the original could alone have placed his friends in a ſituation to afford him.

In order to give as much of that ſpecies of illuſtration, which an undertaking of this nature more particularly requires, an Appendix is ſubjoined, conſiſting, firſt, of tranſlations of ſome of the moſt intereſting of the Chineſe official documents in the Tranſlator's poſſeſſion, which happened to be either connected with or in any way applicable to the ſubject; ſecondly, of tranſlations of ſome of the moſt remarkable among the ſupplementary laws or clauſes; and laſtly, of occaſional remarks and notices upon particular paſſages, which occurred in the courſe of the work, but which could not have been conveniently inſerted in the margin.

Still, however, the Tranſlator is ſenſible, that, after every endeavour to render the following work as complete as poſſible, it muſt yet, in many points, be unavoidably defective; but he at the ſame time feels encouraged by the aſſurance, that his readers are too well acquainted with the nature of the undertaking, and the peculiar circumſtances connected with it, to entertain expectations founded upon a reference, either to the excellent treatiſes upon our own laws by Blackſtone and others, or even to the accounts which we poſſeſs of the laws of many foreign, but at the ſame time more eaſily acceſſible, countries. Being

alſo

alſo almoſt the firſt eſſay at tranſlation from a Chineſe original into the Engliſh language, he truſts that even in that point of view it will not be deemed undeſerving of indulgence.

His own wiſhes will be gratified in their full extent, if he can be conſidered to have ſucceeded in giving, through the medium of an authentic work, containing incidental notices upon the manners, cuſtoms, civil and religious habits, national characteriſtics, and moral principles of the Chineſe, a juſt idea of the ſpirit, and a ſufficiently extended ſpecimen of the ſubſtance, of the coercive and penal laws by which the government of that vaſt empire has ſo long been maintained and regulated.

TABLE
OF
CONTENTS.

PRELIMINARY MATTER.

FIRST

FIRST DIVISION, — *General Laws.*

BOOK I.

PRELIMINARY REGULATIONS.

XXII. In-

SECOND

SECOND DIVISION, — *Civil Laws.*

BOOK I.

SYSTEM OF GOVERNMENT.

BOOK II.

CONDUCT OF THE MAGISTRATES.

THIRD DIVISION, — *Fiscal Laws.*

BOOK I.

ENROLMENT OF THE PEOPLE.

BOOK II.

LANDS AND TENEMENTS.

BOOK III.

MARRIAGE.

CX.

BOOK IV.

PUBLIC PROPERTY.

BOOK V.

DUTIES AND CUSTOMS.

BOOK VI.

PRIVATE PROPERTY.

BOOK VII.

SALES AND MARKETS.

FOURTH DIVISION, — *Ritual Laws*.

BOOK I.

SACRED RITES.

BOOK II.

MISCELLANEOUS OBSERVANCES.

FIFTH DIVISION, — *Military Laws.*

BOOK I.

PROTECTION OF THE PALACE.

BOOK

BOOK II.

GOVERNMENT OF THE ARMY.

BOOK III.

PROTECTION OF THE FRONTIER.

BOOK IV.

MILITARY HORSES AND CATTLE.

BOOK V.

EXPRESSES AND PUBLIC POSTS.

CCXLVII.

SIXTH DIVISION, — *Criminal Laws.*

BOOK I.

ROBBERY AND THEFT.

BOOK II.

HOMICIDE.

BOOK III.

QUARRELLING AND FIGHTING.

BOOK IV.

ABUSIVE LANGUAGE.

BOOK V.

INDICTMENTS AND INFORMATIONS.

CCCXXXIX.

BOOK VI.

BRIBERY AND CORRUPTION.

BOOK VII.

FORGERIES AND FRAUDS.

BOOK VIII.

INCEST AND ADULTERY.

BOOK IX.

MISCELLANEOUS OFFENCES.

BOOK X.

ARRESTS AND ESCAPES.

BOOK XI.

IMPRISONMENT, JUDGMENT, AND EXECUTION.

CCCCV.

SEVENTH

SEVENTH DIVISION, — *Laws relative to Public Works.*

BOOK I.

PUBLIC BUILDINGS.

BOOK II.

PUBLIC WAYS.

APPENDIX.

X. Tranf-

XXIX. Tranſ-

嘉慶十年新鐫

遵照嘉慶六年奉
部頒行續纂并增修近年條例

大清律例重訂

輯註通纂

比引條例督
捕則例附後

工本浩繁每部發
價紋銀三兩六錢
翻刻必究

Mutlow sculp.

Fac-simile of the Title page of the latest edition of the

TA TSING LEU LEE

Published in the Year 1805, the 10th of the reigning Emperor Kia King.

see page lxiii. note.

Published March 9th 1810, by T. Cadell & W. Davies, Strand, London.

I.

TA TSING LEU LEE;

OR

THE LAWS AND STATUTES

OF

THE DYNASTY OF TSING,

A NEW EDITION,

PRINTED AND PUBLISHED IN THE FOURTH YEAR OF THE REIGN OF *KIA-KING*,

OF

THE ENTIRE CODE OF FUNDAMENTAL LAWS AND SUPPLEMENTARY STATUTES;

WHICH, AFTER HAVING BEEN REVISED AND COMPLETED, WAS, IN THE SIXTIETH YEAR OF THE REIGN OF *KIEN-LUNG*, PROMULGATED IN ITS PRESENT FORM, BY THE SUPREME COUNCIL OF STATE IN THE DEPARTMENT OF PUBLIC JUSTICE.

TO WHICH IS ADDED,

THE EXPLANATORY COMMENTARY ANNEXED TO THE FUNDAMENTAL LAWS, BY THE EMPEROR *YONG-TCHING*; AN EXTENSIVE COLLECTION OF ADJUDGED CASES AND A VARIETY OF USEFUL NOTES AND OBSERVATIONS DERIVED FROM THE MOST APPROVED SOURCES.

NOTE.—The above is an Abstract of the Title-Page to the Edition of the original Chinese Work, printed in the Year 1799, from which the Fundamental Laws, translated in the following Pages, have been extracted. — A still later Edition, exactly similar in respect to the Fundamental Laws, but containing a greater Number of Supplementary Statutes, and a different Selection of illustrative Notes, has likewise been occasionally consulted.

The Title-page of the later Edition may be translated as follows: "Recently engraved " in the 10th Year of *KIA-KING*, a new Edition of the Laws and Statutes of the great " Dynasty of *TSING*; comprising, agreeably to the universal Compendium promulgated " by the Supreme Court of Judicature on the 6th Year of *KIA-KING*, all the Additions " and Alterations which have been made of late Years in the supplementary Statutes; " also compendious Abstracts from the various Commentaries, and an Appendix, con- " sisting of two Books of additional supplementary Statutes. The whole carefully " revised and examined; and each Copy sold for three *leang* six *tsien* of silver."

II.

ORIGINAL PREFACE

TO

THE CHINESE PENAL CODE

BY

THE EMPEROR *SHUN CHEE*,

THE FIRST OF THE PRESENT DYNASTY.

WHEN we contemplate the progreſſive eſtabliſhment of our dominions in the Eaſt *, by our Royal Anceſtors and immediate Predeceſſors, we obſerve that the ſimplicity of the people originally required but few laws; and that, with the exception of crimes of extraordinary enormity, no puniſhments were inflicted beſides thoſe of the whip and the bamboo.

Since, however, the Divine Will has been graciouſly pleaſed to entruſt us with the adminiſtration of the Empire of China, a multitude of judicial proceedings in civil and criminal caſes, ariſing out of the various diſpoſitions and irregular paſſions of mankind in a great and populous nation, have ſucceſſively occupied our Royal attention. Hence we have ſuffered much inconvenience, from the neceſſity we have been almoſt conſtantly under of either aggravating or mitigating

* The princes of the family now on the throne of China, do not date their origin from any remote period. Their anceſtors were not eſtabliſhed at Mougden in Mantchoo or Eaſtern Tartary, before the year 1616; but they made a rapid progreſs from that period. In 1644, during the troubles and internal commotions which prevailed in China, under a declining dynaſty, they obtained poſſeſſion of the Chineſe capital, and in the courſe of a few years completed the conqueſt of the whole empire.

 the

the erroneous ſentences of the magiſtrates; who, previous to the re-eſtabliſhment of a fixed Code of Penal Laws, were not in poſſeſſion of any ſecure foundation, upon which they could build a juſt and equitable deciſion.

A numerous body of magiſtrates was, therefore, aſſembled at the capital, by our command, for the purpoſe of reviſing the Penal Code, formerly in force under the late dynaſty of *Ming* *, and of digeſting the ſame into a new Code, by the excluſion of ſuch parts as were exceptionable, and the introduction of others, which were likely to contribute to the attainment of juſtice, and to the general perfection of the work.

The reſult of their labours having been ſubmitted to our examination, we maturely weighed and conſidered the various matter it contained, and then inſtructed a ſelect number of our Great Officers of State, carefully to reviſe the whole, for the purpoſe of making ſuch alterations and emendations as might ſtill be found requiſite.

As ſoon as this object was accompliſhed, we iſſued our Royal authority for the impreſſion and publication of the work, under the Title of "*Ta tſing leu chee kiay foo lee*," or the General Laws of the Imperial Dynaſty of *Tſing*, collected and explained, and accompanied by ſupplementary clauſes.

Wherefore, officers and magiſtrates of the interior and exterior departments of our empire, be it your care diligently to obſerve the the ſame, and to forbear in future to give any deciſion, or to paſs any ſentence, according to your private ſentiments, or upon your unſupported authority.

Thus ſhall the magiſtrates and people look up with awe and ſubmiſſion to the juſtice of theſe inſtitutions, as they find themſelves reſpectively concerned in them: the tranſgreſſor will not fail to ſuffer

* The Dynaſty of *Ming* ſucceeded that of *Yuen*, or the Mongol Tartars, in the year 1568.

a ſtrict

a ſtrict expiation for his offences, and will be the inſtrument of deterring others from ſimilar miſconduct; and, finally, the government and the people will be equally ſecured for endleſs generations in the enjoyment of the happy effects of the great and noble virtues of our illuſtrious progenitors.

Dated the 5th Moon, of the third year, of *Shun-Chee*, A.D. 1647.

III.

PREFATORY EDICT

OF

THE EMPEROR *KAUNG-HEE*,

(OTHERWISE, BUT IMPROPERLY, *CAMHI*,)

THE SECOND OF THE PRESENT DYNASTY.

THE chief ends propoſed by the inſtitution of puniſhments in the empire, have been to guard againſt violence and injury, to repreſs inordinate deſires, and to ſecure the peace and tranquillity of an honeſt and unoffending community.

Laws have accordingly been enacted, numerous, as well as particular in their application, and ſubſequently varied and augmented at different times, as circumſtances were found to require, but without ever loſing ſight of thoſe principles of affection and benevolence, of which our Illuſtrious Predeceſſors, who laid the foundation of theſe inſtitutions, were invariably obſervant.

The people being, however, gradually ſeduced, by their irregular deſires, to diſregard the penalties to which an infringement of the laws expoſed them, to become the diſciples of violence and iniquity, and to oppreſs thoſe whom they found weak and defenceleſs, it became neceſſary to deviſe new regulations, and to ſtrengthen thoſe which already exiſted, by the denunciation of ſeverer puniſhments.

Neverthelеſs, offences againſt the laws are again frequent, and evil propenſities toward irregularities and crimes, do not appear to have been in any conſiderable degree repreſſed.

Thoſe crimes which are either committed againſt, or lead to a forfeiture of the lives of our ſubjects, have been the objects of our moſt ſerious conſideration, and their frequency is, to us, a ſource of much diſquietude.

It is, therefore, our pleaſure, that all the additional ſtatutes of a recent promulgation, whereby thoſe crimes which formerly were not puniſhed with death, have been rendered capital; or where the penalties of tranſgreſſion have been in any other manner altered or augmented, ſhall be taken into conſideration and reviſed by the miniſters of ſtate, the inſpectors general, and the preſidents of the ſix ſupreme tribunals, in order that theſe magiſtrates may be enabled to make a due report to us upon their fitneſs and efficacy.

Dated the 14th of the 9th moon of the 18th year of *Kaung-hee*, A.D. 1679.

IV. PRE-

IV.

PREFATORY EDICT

OF

THE EMPEROR *YONG-TCHING*,

THE THIRD OF THE PRESENT DYNASTY.

SINCE the period of our Acceſſion to the Imperial Throne of our Anceſtors, the criminals who, at different times, have been awaiting their ſentence in confinement, have not failed to ſhare our Royal compaſſion and conſideration. — The reports of all the caſes adjudged by the provincial magiſtrates, and requiring our ſanction to their deciſion, have been examined by us with the moſt ſcrupulous attention, leſt they ſhould contain any flaw or incongruity which might invalidate the reſults. — We have alſo conſidered that among our various inſtitutions, the Code of Penal Laws is the moſt varied and complicated in its conſtruction; and that, therefore, unleſs clear and invariable rules are pointed out, the magiſtrates muſt, in ſome inſtances, unavoidably take upon themſelves to aggravate or mitigate the puniſhment due to criminals, according to their own diſcretion; in which caſes, they muſt conſtantly be liable to commit great errors, and even flagrant injuſtice.

With the view of preventing as much as poſſible, all ſuch abuſes, we ſubmitted the Penal Code to the reviſion of the members of our Imperial college, and have ſince attentively conſidered their written obſervations thereon, annexing, at the ſame time, to each article, the mark of our approbation or diſſent. In conſideration, however, of the vaſt mportance of a work which is to guide and inſtruct the magiſtrates in all judicial proceedings,

proceedings, it is our pleaſure, that the nine principal officers of ſtate, reviſe, examine, and correct the reſults of all theſe operations, ſo as moſt effectually to fulfil our deſign of adapting the penalties of the laws in a juſt proportion to the crimes againſt which they are denounced.

Dated the 27th of the 5th moon, of the third year of *Yong-tching*, A.D. 1725.*

* In addition to theſe three Prefatory Edicts, two ſtate papers iſſued in the names of the late Emperor *Kien-lung*, and the reigning Emperor *Kia-King*, have been inſerted in the Appendix, No. I. and No. II. and although not directly connected with the ſubject of the Code, will, it is hoped, be found illuſtrative of many parts of it, and otherwiſe not uninteresting. The remaining articles of Preliminary Matter, which, in the original, precede the Table of Contents, have been omitted here, as not eſſential to the work, but their ſeveral titles will be found in the Appendix, No. III.

It has not been conceived neceſſary, or even deſirable, to introduce, in the courſe of theſe occaſional notes, any detailed references to the remarks of preceding writers. This has not, however, prevented the Tranſlator from ſpeaking generally, on one occaſion, (page 318.) of the valuable work of Mr. Barrow; or on another, (page 107,) of the intereſting tranſlation publiſhed by the Biſhop of Dromore; or, laſtly, from taking the preſent opportunity of noticing the ſhort, but excellent remarks on Chineſe Literature, which we owe to the learned and judicious author of the *Horæ Biblicæ*. And with reſpect to the works of the Miſſionaries, although the Tranſlator of the preſent work was aware that he ſhould not be juſtified in recommending an implicit reliance upon them, he has been happy to refer generally to the vaſt fund of curious and important information upon China, which, notwithſtanding this reſervation, the above claſs of writers muſt be admitted to have afforded. With regard to the work, which, as far as it extends, perhaps ſtands the higheſt in point of authority of any that has been written on the ſubject of China, the Tranſlator feels naturally a delicacy in ſaying any thing. — He has, however, the ſatisfaction to reflect, that the *Authentic Account of the Britiſh Embaſſy* does not, at this day, require any new arguments or teſtimony, to confirm it in its place in the public eſteem.

TABLE

V.

TABLE I.*

SCALE of Puniſhment Offences againſt Public and Private Property.

	Pecuniary Malverſation.	Theft.	Bribery for a lawful Object.	Bribery for an unlawful Object.	Theft of Public Property.	Embezzlement of Public Property.
	Amount in oz. of Silver†	Ditto.	Ditto.	Ditto.	Ditto.	Ditto.
20 Blows with the bamboo -	1 or leſs					
30 —— - - -	1 to 10					
40 —— - - -	20 —					
50 —— - - -	30 —					
60 —— - - -	40 —	1 or leſs	1 or leſs			
70 —— - - -	50 —	10 —	10 —	1 or leſs	1 or leſs	
80 —— - - -	60 —	20 —	20 —	1 to 5 oz.	1 to 5 oz	1 or leſs
90 —— - - -	70 —	30 —	30 —	10 —	10 —	1 to 2,5
100 —— - - -	80 —	40 —	40 —	15 —	15 —	5.
60 —— and 1 year's baniſhment	100 —	50 —	50 —	20 —	20 —	7.5
70 —— and 1½ —— ——	200 —	60 —	60 —	25 —	25 —	10.
80 —— and 2 —— ——	300 —	70 —	70 —	30 —	30 —	12.5
90 —— and 2½ —— ——	400 —	80 —	80 —	35 —	35 —	15.
100 —— and 3 —— ——	500 — and upwards	90 —	90 —	40 —	40 —	17.5
Diſt. *lee*						
100 —— and perpet. baniſh. 2000	—— —	100 —	100 —	45 —	45 —	20.
100 —— and —— —— 2500	—— —	110 —	110 —	50 —	50 —	25.
100 —— and —— —— 3000	—— —	120 —	120 —	55 —	55 —	30.
Death,—to be ſtrangled -	——	Upwards of 120 oz.	Upwards of 120 oz.	80 or 120 If an inferior Officer.	80 in extreme Caſes.	
Death,—to be beheaded - -	—— —	—— —	—— —	—— —	—— —	80 in extreme Caſes

* This Table is an abſtract of the principal articles of the laws ſpecially provided for the protection of public and private property. The ſubject is fully explained in the body of the code, (1ſt and 6th Book of the VIth Diviſion,) but the advantage of this Table conſiſts in its exhibiting the whole in a ſummary way, and upon a ſingle inſpection. Thus, it appears without reference, that whoever is guilty of any ſpecies of pecuniary malverſation, to the extent of 20 ounces of ſilver, ſhall, generally ſpeaking, be liable, at the leaſt, to a puniſhment of 40 blows: that whoever is guilty of a theft of private property, or of receiving a bribe for an object in itſelf lawful, to the ſame extent, is puniſhable with 80 blows: that whoever is guilty to the ſame extent of a theft of public property, or of receiving a bribe for an object in itſelf unlawful, is puniſhable with 60 blows, and baniſhment for the ſpace of one year: and, laſtly, that whoever is guilty of embezzling ſo much of the public property, will be puniſhable with 100 blows, and perpetual baniſhment to the diſtance of 2000 *lee*.

† The value of the *Leang*, or Chineſe ounce of ſilver, according to the eſtabliſhed rule of exchange at Canton, is 6s. 8d. or the third part of a pound ſterling.

VI. TABLE

VI.

TABLE II.*

SCALE of the Pecuniary Redemption of neceſſarily redeemable Puniſhments.	If well able to pay.		If not altogether deſtitute.		If aged, or under Age.		Females in certain Caſes.		Killing or wounding accidentally		Females in general.	
	oz.	dec.	oz.	dec.	oz.	dec.	oz.	dec.	oz.	dec.	Days confine^t.	Dec. of oz.
10 blows with the bamboo	—	2.5	—	3	—	7.5	—	1	—	—	20 and	105
20 —— - - - -	—	5	—	4.5	—	1.5	—	2	—	3.5.4	25 and	135
30 —— - - - -	—	7.5	—	6	—	2.2.5	—	3	—	3.3.2	30 and	165
40 —— - - - -	1	—	—	6.5	—	3	—	4	—	7.9	35 and	195
50 —— - - - -	1	2.4	—	9	—	3.7.5	—	5	—	8.8.7	40 and	225
60 —— - - - -	3	—	1	2	—	4.5	—	6	—	—	50 and	3
70 —— - - - -	3	5	1	3 5	—	5.2.5	—	7	—	—	55 and	3375
80 —— - - - -	4	—	1	5	—	6	—	8	1	4.1.9	60 and	375
90 —— - - - -	4	5	1	6.5	—	6.7.5	—	9	—	—		
100 —— - - - -	5	—	1	8	—	7.5	—	110	1	774		
1 year's Baniſhment -	7	5	3	6	1	5	1	7.5	3	548		
1½ —— —— -	10	—	5	4	1	8.7.5	1	1125	—	—		
2 —— —— -	12	5	7	2	2	2.5	1	15	5	322		
2½ —— —— -	15	—	9	—	2	6.2.5	1	1875	—	—		
3 —— —— -	17	5	10	8	3	—	1	2250	7	097		
4 —— —— -	20	—	14	4	4	—	—	—	—	—		
5 —— —— -	25	—	18	—	4	—	—	—	—	—		
Perpetual, —— —— diſt. 2000 lee.	—	—	—	—	—	—	1	30000	—	—		
——, —— —— 2500	—	—	—	—	—	—	1	3375	—	—		
——, —— —— 3000	—	—	—	—	—	—	1	375	10	645		
Death,—to be ſtrangled / Death,—to be beheaded	—	—	—	—	—	—	1	45	12	42		

* Upon the ſubject of this Table, ſee Note, page 24.

VII. TABLE

VII.

TABLE III.*

SCALE of pecuniary Redemption in fuch Cafes as are not legally excluded from the Benefit of general Acts of Grace and Pardon, and which, though not neceffarily redeemable, have, by an Edict of the 8th Year of the Emperor *Kien-lung*, been made redeemable upon Petition.

Rank of the Offender.	Sentence.	Pecuniary Commutation in ounces of filver.
An Officer above the fourth Rank -	Death by Strangulation or Decollation.	12000
——— of the fourth Rank - -		5000
——— of the fifth or fixth Rank		4000
——— of the feventh, or any inferior Rank, or a Doctor of Literature -		2500
A Graduate or Licenciate - -		2000
A private Individual - - -		1200
An Officer above the fourth Rank -	Perpetual Banifhment.	7200
——— of the fourth Rank - -		3000
——— of the fifth or fixth Rank		2400
——— of the feventh, or any inferior Rank, or a Doctor of Literature -		1500
A Graduate or Licenciate - -		1200
A private Individual - - -		720
An Officer above the fourth Rank -	Temporary Banifhment, or Blows with the Bamboo.	4800
——— of the fourth Rank - -		2000
——— of the fifth or fixth Rank		1600
——— of the feventh or any inferior Rank, or a Doctor of Literature -		1000
A graduate or Licenciate - -		800
A private Individual - - -		480

* This Table has, by miftake, been referred to in pages 19 and 24, as a part of the 5th article of the Appendix.

VIII.

TABLE IV.

DEGREES OF PUNISHMENT.

Degrees.	Nominally.	Reduced.	Inflicted with the Bamboo	In Breadth at its Extremities	Weight not to exceed.
1	10	4 Blows	*Che Tsun*† 5 5 in length	1½ *Tsun* by 1 *Tsun*.	1½ *Kin* ‡.
2	30	5 —			
3	20	10 —			
4	40	15 —			
5	50	20 —			
6	60	20 —		2 *Tsun* by 1½ *Tsun*.	2 *Kin*.
7	70	25 —			
8	80	30 —			
9	90	35 —			
10	100	40 —			
			Together with Banishment		and to the Distance of
11	60	20 —	For one year - - -		500 *lee*, or about 50 leagues
12	70	25 —	For one year and a half - -		500 — — —
13	80	30 —	For two years - - -		500 — — —
14	90	35 —	For two years and a half - -		500 — — —
15	100	40 —	For three years - - -		500 — — —
16	100	40 —	For life - - -		2000 — 200 —
17	100	40 —	For life - - -		2500 — 250 —
18	100	40 —	For life - - -		3000 — 300 —
19	Death, by Strangulation.				
20	Death, by Decollation.				

IX.

TABLE V.

SPECIFICATION of the ordinary Inſtruments of Puniſhment and Confinement.

THE BAMBOO.

A ſtraight poliſhed piece of bamboo, the branches cut away, and reduced to the length, breadth, and weight above deſcribed; and when uſed, to be held by the ſmaller end.

* This Table is explained in the firſt ſection of the Code, and in the Appendix, No. V.

† *Che* and *Tſun* are Chineſe meaſures of length, uſually denominated at Canton *Covids* and *puntos*. The *Che* (of which the *Tſun* is the tenth part), which is in ordinary uſe throughout the empire, exceeds the Engliſh foot by rather more than half an inch; but the *Che*, uſed at Canton for the meaſurement of goods in trade, is ſomewhat longer, being 14 inches and 625 decimals.

‡ The *Kin* exceeds the Engliſh pound weight by one-third.

THE *KIA*, OTHERWISE, BUT IMPROPERLY, CANGUE.

A ſquare frame of dry wood, three *Che* long, and 2 *Che* 9 *Tſun* broad; and weighing in ordinary caſes 25 *Kin*.

THE IRON CHAIN.

The greater and leſs criminals ſhall all be confined by an iron chain, 7 *Che* long, and weighing 5 *Kin*.

THE HAND-CUFFS.

The hand-cuffs ſhall be made of dry wood, and 1 *Che* 6 *Tſun* long, by 1 *Tſun* in thickneſs, and ſhall be uſed to confine capital offenders of the male ſex only.

THE FETTERS.

Iron fetters, weighing one *Kin*, ſhall be uſed to confine all ſuch offenders as are deſtined to baniſhment or capital puniſhment.

X.

TABLE VI.

DEGREES OF RELATIONSHIP, AND OF MOURNING.

THE mourning for the neareſt among relations in the firſt degree, ſhall be worn for three years, and ſhall be made of the coarſeſt hempen cloth, without being ſewn at the borders.

The mourning for other relations in the firſt degree ſhall be worn for three or five months, and be made of middling hempen cloth, ſewn at the borders.

The mourning for relations in the ſecond degree, ſhall be worn for nine months, and be made of coarſe linen-cloth.

The mourning for relations in the third degree, ſhall be worn for five months, and be made of middling coarſe linen-cloth.

The mourning for relations in the fourth degree, ſhall be worn for three months, and be made of middling fine linen-cloth.

The

The full mourning for three years, ſhall be worn

By a ſon, for his father or mother.

By a daughter, for her father or mother, when living under the parents' roof, although affianced to her intended huſband, or although once married, if afterwards divorced and ſent home.

By a ſon's wife, for her huſband's father or mother.

By a ſon and his wife, for his father's ſubſtituted firſt wife *; for the wife of his father ſubſtituted in the place of his mother, and for the wife of his father, who nurſed him.

By an inferior wife's ſon and his wife, for his natural mother, and for his father's firſt wife.

By an adopted ſon and his wife, for his adopted parents.

By a grandſon and his wife, for his paternal grand-parents.

By a wife, whether the firſt or inferior one, for her huſband †.

* That is to ſay, for the one among his father's wives, who upon the death of the firſt or principal wife, takes her place.

† See the Appendix, No. IV. It may be proper, in order to prevent any miſconception, to remark generally, in this place, that in whatever part of the tranſlation degrees of relationſhip or mourning are mentioned, it is always to be underſtood to be in reference to Chineſe, and not to European tables of alliance and conſanguinity.

THE

THE

PENAL LAWS

OF

CHINA.

FIRST DIVISION,

General Laws.

BOOK I.

PRELIMINARY REGULATIONS.

SECTION I. — *Deſcription of the Ordinary Puniſhments.*

THE lowest degree of puniſhment is a moderate correction inflicted with the leſſer bamboo, in order that the tranſgreſſor of the law may entertain a ſenſe of ſhame for his paſt, and receive a ſalutary admonition with reſpect to his future, conduct. Of this ſpecies of puniſhment there are five degrees:

The firſt	nominally a puniſhment of	10 blows,	of which only	4 blows	are to be inflicted.
The ſecond		20 blows,		5 blows	
The third		30 blows,		10 blows	
The fourth		40 blows,		15 blows	
The fifth		50 blows,		20 blows	

The ſecond degree, or diviſion of puniſhment, is inflicted with the larger bamboo, and is ſubdivided in the following manner:

The firſt	nominally a puniſhment of	60 blows,	of which only	20 blows	are to be inflicted.
The ſecond		70 blows,		25 blows	
The third		80 blows,		30 blows	
The fourth		90 blows,		35 blows	
The fifth		100 blows,		40 blows	

The third diviſion in the ſcale of puniſhments is, that of temporary baniſhment, to any diſtance not exceeding 500 *lee* *, with the view of affording an opportunity of repentance and amendment. Of this ſpecies of puniſhment there are alſo five gradations: namely,

Baniſhment for	1 year, and	60 blows	with the bamboo, reduced as above.
	1½ years, and	70 blows	
	2 years, and	80 blows	
	2½ years, and	90 blows	
	3 years, and	100 blows	

Perpetual baniſhment, the fourth degree of puniſhment in the order of ſeverity, is ſubdivided as follows; and is reſerved for ſuch of the more conſiderable offences whereupon the life of the criminal is ſpared by the mercifulneſs of the laws:

100 blows with the bamboo, and perpetual baniſhment to the diſtance of	2000 *lee.*
	2500 *lee.*
	3000 *lee.*

The fifth and ultimate puniſhment which the laws ordain, is death, either by ſtrangulation, or by decollation.

All criminals capitally convicted, except ſuch atrocious offenders as are expreſsly directed to be executed without delay, are retained in priſon for execution at a particular period in the autumn; the ſentence paſſed upon each individual being firſt duly reported to, and ratified by, the Emperor.

To this ſection of the fundamental laws a ſupplement is annexed, conſiſting of eighteen clauſes †.

* Ten *lee* are uſually eſtimated to be equal to three geographical miles, but the proportion varies a little in the different provinces of the empire.

† See Appendix, No. V.

SEC-

SECTION II. — *Offences of a treaſonable Nature.*

I. *Rebellion,* is an attempt to violate the divine order of things on earth; for as the fruits of the earth are produced in regular ſucceſſion under the influence of the preſiding Spirit, ſo is their diſtribution among the people regulated by the Sovereign, who is the ſacred ſucceſſor to the ſeat of his anceſtors: reſiſting and conſpiring againſt him is, therefore, an unſpeakable outrage, and a diſturbance of the peace of the univerſe.

II. *Diſloyalty,* is evinced by an attempt to deſtroy the imperial temples, tombs, or palaces; for as the imperial temples and tombs are intended to perpetuate the memory, and to receive the remains, of former Sovereigns, ſo the imperial palaces, being deſigned for the uſe of the reigning monarch, are equally ſacred and inviolable.

III. *Deſertion,* is a term which may be applied to the offence of undertaking to quit, or betray the intereſts of, the empire, in order to ſubmit or adhere to a foreign power, and may be conſidered as exemplified in the caſe of betraying a military poſt, or exciting the people to emigration.

IV. *Parricide,* is the denomination under which the murder of a father or mother, of an uncle, aunt, grandfather or grandmother, is comprehended, and is a crime of the deepeſt dye; for ſuch a violation of the ties of nature, which are conſtituted by the Divine Will, is in every caſe an evidence of the moſt unprincipled depravity.

V. *Maſſacre,* is held to be the murder of three or more perſons in one family, and comprehends other crimes ſanguinary and enormous in a ſimilar degree.

VI. *Sacrilege*, is committed by ſtealing from the temples any of the ſacred articles conſecrated to divine purpoſes, or by purloining any article in the immediate uſe of the Sovereign: ſimilar guilt is incurred by counterfeiting the imperial ſeal, by adminſtering to the Sovereign improper medicines, or, in general, by the commiſſion of any error or negligence, whereby the ſafety of his ſacred perſon may be endangered.

VII. *Impiety*, is diſcoverable in every inſtance of diſreſpect or negligence towards thoſe to whom we owe our being, and by whom we have been educated and protected.—It is likewiſe committed by thoſe who inform againſt, or inſult, ſuch near relations while living, or who refuſe to mourn for their loſs, and to ſhew reſpect for their memory, when dead.

VIII. *Diſcord*, in families, is the breach of the legal or natural ties which are founded on our connexions by blood or marriage; under this head may be claſſed the crimes of killing, wounding, or maltreating any of thoſe relations or connexions to whom, when deceaſed, the ceremony of mourning is legally due *.

IX. *Inſubordination*, is the riſing againſt, or murdering, a ſuperior magiſtrate by an inferior; or any inſurrection againſt the magiſtrates in general, by the people.

X. *Inceſt*, is the co-habitation, or promiſcuous intercourſe, of perſons related in any of the degrees within which marriage is prohibited †.

* The nature and extent of theſe connexions is in ſome degree ſhewn in the preliminary part of the code, and alſo occaſionally in ſome of the ſubſequent ſections, and in the Appendix.

† See the diviſion of the code, intitled, *Marriage*, and alſo the diviſion, intitled, *Inceſt and Adultery*.

The

The crimes here arranged and diſtributed under ten heads, being diſtinguiſhed from others by their enormity, are always puniſhed with the utmoſt rigour of the law; and, when the offence is capital, it is excepted from the benefit of any act of general pardon; being likewiſe, in each caſe, a direct violation of the ties by which ſociety is maintained, they are expreſsly enumerated in the introductory part of this code, that the people may learn to dread, and to avoid the ſame *.

No clauſe to this ſection.

SECTION III.—*The Privileged Claſſes.*

I. *The Privilege of Imperial Blood and Connections.*—Becauſe the members of the auguſt family of the Sovereign, who rules by the appointment of Heaven, are entitled to peculiar reverence in the adminiſtration of the laws with regard to them; therefore, this privilege ſhall extend to all the relations of His Imperial Majeſty, who are deſcended from the ſame anceſtors; to all the relations in the firſt, ſecond, third, and fourth degrees of His Imperial Majeſty's mother and grandmother; to all the relations of His Imperial Majeſty's conſort, the Empreſs, within the firſt, ſecond, and third degrees; and, laſtly, to all the relations of the conſort of the hereditary Prince, within the firſt and ſecond degrees only.

II. *The Privilege of long Service.*—This claſs comprehends all thoſe ancient ſervants of the crown, who are zealouſly attached and have been honourably diſtinguiſhed.—Such perſons are entitled to privilege, becauſe the Emperor has exalted them, and becauſe the length of their ſervices is a teſtimony of their unalterable fidelity.

III. *The Privilege of illuſtrious Actions.*—Thoſe are entitled to privilege under this claſs, who purſue the enemy to the diſtance of 10,000 lee, cut off the head of the general of the hoſtile army, tear

* See Appendix, No. VI.

down

down his ſtandard, and break his ſword; or who, having brought multitudes to ſurrender themſelves to the Imperial authority, reſtore peace and tranquillity to the age; and, laſtly, thoſe who by their talents and exertions ſhall extend the boundaries of the empire. Such deeds of valour ſhall be commemorated on tablets of ſtone.

IV. *The Privilege of extraordinary Wiſdom.*—Thoſe who are eminent for their wiſdom and virtue are entitled to privilege, becauſe by the advice of ſuch men the adminiſtration of government is brought to perfection. *Kia Yee* has ſaid, that the wiſe and good man may be afflicted with misfortunes, even unto death, without being ſubject to humiliation or diſgrace.

V. *The Privilege of great Abilities.*—Great abilities are rare; the actions of the able are ſuperior in value even to the words of the wiſe.—From thoſe who have the talent of commanding armies, and of conducting the different departments of the ſtate, the ſovereign ſelects the beſt and moſt efficacious miniſters of his power.

VI. *The Privilege of Zeal and Aſſiduity.*—This privilege is due to thoſe who, by night and by day, are zealouſly and aſſiduouſly engaged in the performance of their civil or military duties; and to thoſe who diſcharge any diſtant and arduous employment with diſtinguiſhed honour.

VII. *The Privilege of Nobility.*—This privilege is to be enjoyed by all thoſe who poſſeſs the firſt rank in the empire; all thoſe of the ſecond, who are at the ſame time employed in any official capacity whatever; and all thoſe of the third, whoſe office confers any civil or military command.

VIII. *The Privilege of Birth.*—The Emperor eſteems and protects thoſe who are diſtinguiſhed for their wiſdom and eminent ſervices, even to the ſecond and third generation *.

No clauſe.

* See Appendix, No. VII.

SECTION IV.—*Offences of Perſons entitled to Privilege.*

When any perſon entitled to privilege has committed an offence againſt the laws, a diſtinct ſpecification thereof ſhall be laid before the Emperor, and it ſhall not be lawful to try or examine ſuch perſon, until the receipt of His Majeſty's expreſs commands for that purpoſe— The Emperor's commands having been received, the trial and examination of the offender ſhall be inſtituted, and a report made of the whole of the proceedings, for the information and final deciſion of His Imperial Majeſty.

Neverthele ſs, if any privileged perſon commits an offence of a treaſonable nature, he ſhall not have the benefit of his privilege as provided by this law.

Five clauſes.

SECTION V.—*Relations of Perſons entitled to Privilege.*

When the father, mother, paternal grandfather or grandmother, wife, ſon, or grandſon of any perſon entitled to privilege, as belonging to one of the eight claſſes before mentioned, commits an offence againſt the laws, a diſtinct ſpecification thereof ſhall be laid before the Emperor, and it ſhall not be lawful to try or examine ſuch offender, until the Emperor's expreſs commands are received for that purpoſe.

The trial and examination having taken place, conformably to the Emperor's orders, a report of the whole of the proceedings ſhall be tranſmitted to the court, for the information and final deciſion of His Imperial Majeſty.

In the caſe of perſons privileged by their royal blood or illuſtrious ſervices, their paternal grandfathers and grandmothers, uncles, aunts, and

and coufins, as alfo their fons-in-law and nephews; and moreover the father, mother, or wife of an officer of government of the 4th or 5th rank, and the fons or grandfons, if inheriting their rank, fhall, in each cafe, although their offences fhall be inveftigated by the magiftrate of the diftrict, not be finally condemned to any fpecies of punifhment, except by a decree of His Imperial Majefty. — Neverthelefs, no diftinction fhall be made in favour of thofe perfons in cafes of treafon, rebellion, rapes, robberies, murders, or bribing for unlawful purpofes.

When any of the relations of privileged perfons, not being themfelves privileged, or their flaves, fervants, ftewards, tenants, and fuch like, avail themfelves of the authority and credit of their lords, mafters, or relations, to opprefs and injure the people, or to infult and refift the magiftrates, they fhall be punifhed one degree more feverely than in ordinary cafes of fimilar offences, but the privileged perfon fhall not be implicated in any judicial proceedings without a fpecial reference being had on the fubject to His Imperial Majefty.

When the tribunals of government undertake the inveftigation and trial of offenders fo connected with privileged perfons, if fuch perfons interpofe their influence and authority to interrupt the courfe of juftice, and prevent the offenders from anfwering the fummons of the magiftrate, the proper officer in the department in which fuch interpofition takes place, fhall lay a true and faithful report thereof before the Emperor, by whom alone the punifhment to be inflicted for fuch offence can be determined.

One claufe.

SEC-

SECTION VI. — *Offences committed by Officers of Government, how investigated.*

When any officer of government at court or in the provinces commits an offence againſt the laws in his public or private capacity, his ſuperior officer ſhall, in all caſes of importance, draw up a diſtinct ſpecification thereof for the information of the Emperor, and it ſhall not be lawful to proceed to try the offender without the expreſs ſanction of His Majeſty.

The trial and examination having taken place conformably to the Emperor's orders, His Majeſty ſhall be again adviſed by a due report of the reſult, after which a reſcript of one of the ſupreme * tribunals ſhall be ſufficient authority for paſſing and executing the ſentence which the laws require.

When any officer of government is injuriouſly treated by his ſuperior, he ſhall be at liberty to ſubmit a faithful ſtatement thereof in accuſation of ſuch ſuperior, to His Imperial Majeſty; but if he ſhould have been previouſly accuſed of any offence by his ſuperior, he ſhall not be permitted to recriminate in any manner, but muſt confine himſelf to the ſubject of the allegations preferred againſt him †.

Five Clauſes.

* The ſupreme tribunals or departments in which the general adminiſtration of the empire is conducted are ſix in number, and correſpond to the ſix principal diviſions of the code, to which the preſent is an introduction.

† A tranſlation of the official report of the trial of the prime miniſter and favourite of the late Emperor, of a viceroy of the province of Se-chuen, and of a governor of the city of Canton, are inſerted in the Appendix as examples of the mode of proceeding adopted in ſuch caſes; ſee Nos. VIII. IX. and X.

SECTION VII.—*Offences committed by Officers of Government in their public Capacity* *.

All civil and military officers of government, when convicted of any offence connected with the discharge of their public duty, and not of a perſonal nature, which offence in ordinary caſes is puniſhable by the infliction of corporal chaſtiſement, ſhall inſtead thereof be ſubjected to a fine or to degradation, according to the number of blows of the bamboo to which they are nominally liable.

Inſtead of nominally
- 10 blows, to forfeit one month's ſalary.
- 20 blows, to forfeit two months' ſalary.
- 30 blows, to forfeit three months' ſalary.
- 40 blows, to forfeit ſix months' ſalary.
- 50 blows, to forfeit nine months' ſalary.
- 60 blows, to forfeit one year's ſalary.
- 70 blows, to be degraded one degree of rank.
- 80 blows, to be degraded two degrees of rank.
- 90 blows, to be degraded three degrees of rank, but, as in the preceding caſe, to retain his ſituation.
- 100 blows, to be degraded four degrees, and to be removed from his ſituation.

Thoſe perſons who have official ſituations without being actually officers of rank in the government, ſhall not be exempt from corporal puniſhment, but may retain their employments †.

One clauſe.

SEC-

* The titles of this and the ſucceeding ſection would bear no other tranſlation than that which has been given to them, and it is therefore requiſite to add in explanation, that it appears from the notes in the original that the offences denominated *private*, in fact comprehend almoſt all caſes of direct criminality, whereas thoſe denominated *public*, are caſes of liability to puniſhment, ſolely from the official reſponſibility of the party implicated.

† Every officer of government from the firſt to the ninth rank, muſt be previouſly qualified by a literary or military degree, according to the nature of his profeſſion; but the clerks

SECTION VIII. — *Offences committed by Officers of Government, of a private and perſonal Nature* *.

All civil and military officers of government, when convicted of any offence unconnected with their public functions, or although connected therewith, yet of a private and perſonal nature, which offence in ordinary caſes expoſes the offender to corporal puniſhment, inſtead of the puniſhment awarded by the laws in general, ſhall be ſubjected to a fine, or to degradation, in proportion thereto in the following manner:

Inſtead of nominally
- 10 blows, to forfeit two months' ſalary.
- 20 blows, to forfeit three months' ſalary.
- 30 blows, to forfeit ſix months' ſalary.
- 40 blows, to forfeit nine months' ſalary.
- 50 blows, to forfeit one year's ſalary.
- 60 blows, to be degraded one degree.
- 70 blows, to be degraded two degrees.
- 80 blows, to be degraded three degrees.
- 90 blows, to be degraded four degrees, and in this, as well as in the three laſt caſes, to be removed from their ſituations.
- 100 blows, to be degraded entirely, and diſmiſſed from the ſervice of Government.

Thoſe perſons who have official ſituations below the rank of officers of government, ſhall not be exempt from corporal puniſhment, and if ſuch puniſhment amounts to 60 blows or upwards, they ſhall be diſmiſſed.

Two clauſes.

---

clerks and other inferior attendants in the employ of government are not conſidered to have any rank, or to be permanently diſtinguiſhed from the reſt of the community.

* The diſtinction between the offences treated of in this and in the preceding ſection has been already ſtated, and is alſo further illuſtrated in ſome of the ſubſequent ſections of the code, in which examples occur of each kind.

SECTION IX.—*Offenders who are not liable to Baniſhment.*

All the ſubjects of the empire, who are enrolled under the Tartarian banners *, when found guilty of committing any offences which render them liable by the laws in general to a corporal puniſhment, ſhall receive the whole number of blows ſpecified; but the chaſtiſement ſhall be inflicted with the whip inſtead of the bamboo: when guilty of offences puniſhable, in ordinary caſes, with baniſhment, they ſhall, inſtead thereof, be confined with the *cangue* or moveable pillory † for a number of days, proportioned to the length of the baniſhment in ordinary caſes, in the following manner:

Inſtead of baniſhment	for 1 year -	to wear the cangue for	20 days.
	for 1½ years -		25 days.
	for 2 years -		30 days.
	for 2½ years -		35 days.
	for 3 years -		40 days.
	for 4 years -		45 days.
Inſtead of perpetual baniſhment	diſtance 2000 lee		50 days.
	diſtance 2500 lee		55 days.
	diſtance 3000 lee		60 days.
Inſtead of the perpetual military baniſhment	to a remote ſtation		70 days.
	to a more remote ſtation		75 days.
	to a ſtill more remote ſtation		80 days.
	to the moſt remote ſtation		90 days.

* All the Tartars who have obtained ſettlements within the limits of China, ſince the acceſſion of the preſent dynaſty, are enrolled for military ſervice, and liable to be called upon to ſerve the Emperor under the banners to which they are ſeverally attached. The enrolment or mode of regiſtering the native Chineſe in their ſeveral diſtricts and provinces as preſcribed by their laws, is the ſubject of the firſt book of the third diviſion of this code.

† The inſtrument here mentioned (termed by the Chineſe *Kia*) is deſcribed in the preliminary part of the code.—Among the plates in the folio volume of the account of the embaſſy of the Earl of Macartney, there is one repreſenting an offender undergoing this ſpecies of puniſhment.

SEC-

SECTION X.—*Offenders of the Military Clafs**.

All perfons of the military clafs committing offences againft the laws, fhall undergo a corporal punifhment in the ordinary manner, and when condemned to the punifhment of temporary banifhment, fhall fuffer the fame during the term fpecified by the laws, but after the expiration thereof, fhall be fent back to their proper ftation and fervice. When condemned to perpetual banifhment, they fhall be detached and appointed to ferve at the military ftation which is neareft to the place of their deftined banifhment; but if condemned to the extraordinary military banifhment, the law fhall be executed in the ufual manner.

No claufe.

SECTION XI.—*Mitigation of Punifhment.*

There are various confiderations which fhall be admitted in mitigation of punifhment. When more perfons than one are engaged in the commiffion of an offence, the original contriver fhall be punifhed as the principal offender, and the reft one degree lefs feverely, being confidered only in the light of acceffaries. In the cafe of an offender furrendering himfelf to the officers of juftice upon hearing that an accufation is intended, fuch offender fhall be entitled to a mitigation of punifhment to the extent of two degrees. When an unjuft fentence of acquittal is pronounced defignedly, the law-officer or clerk of the court † in which fuch faulty fentence originates, provided he is able to recover the offender who had been unlawfully liberated, fhall, in confideration,

* This clafs comprehends thofe who are liable to ferve as well as thofe actually ferving in the army.

† The conftituent members of a court of juftice, or criminal tribunal, are more diftinctly ftated in a fubfequent part of the code, and are only noticed in this place in illuftration of the fubject of the fection.

of

of ſuch recovery be puniſhed leſs ſeverely by one degree; the deputy or executive officer of the court, if not intentionally concurring in the unjuſt ſentence, ſhall be puniſhed ſix degrees leſs than the expounder of the law or clerk of the court; one degree of mitigation being by virtue of his office, and the other five degrees becauſe he did not offend againſt the laws deſignedly *.

If the unjuſt ſentence was not wilful, the puniſhment thereof ſhall, in the caſe of the clerk of the court, be reduced three degrees; and if the unjuſt ſentence had not been executed, four degrees. In the caſe of the deputy of the court, there ſhall be another reduction, making, in the whole, five degrees. In the caſe of each of the aſſeſſors of the court, another reduction, making ſix degrees; and, laſtly, in the caſe of the preſiding officer, another, making, in the whole, ſeven degrees:—thus one caſe is exemplified in illuſtration of all others of complicated mitigation to be attended to in the infliction of puniſhment.

No clauſe.

Section XII.—*Officers of Government, when removed without being diſgraced.*

Such officers of government as, after the expiration of the appointed period of their reſpective functions †, are either removed to another office, or ceaſe to be employed, ſhall not loſe or forfeit any portion of the rank they held by virtue of any of their former offices.

* The law in theſe reſpects is explained at large in Section CCCCIX.

† The civil appointments in China are generally conferred for three years, at the end of which the appointments may be renewed, but the changes (in the higher departments eſpecially) are generally more rapid; ſo much ſo, that a new edition is found requiſite every three months of the Imperial Court Kalendar, which is a liſt of the civil and military appointments of the empire, filling ſix cloſely printed duodecimo volumes.

The

The ſame rule ſhall be obſerved upon their obtaining leave to retire on account of age, infirmity, or the death of relations; and alſo generally in the caſe of the removal or diſmiſſal of inferior officers of the minor departments or tribunals, unleſs the honorary rank of their families is, in conſequence of the circumſtances of the caſe, expreſsly taken away at the ſame time.

Likewiſe all perſons who have received honorary diſtinctions on account of the elevation and employment of their children or deſcendants, ſhall be held equal to them in rank.—Wives ſhall forfeit the rank derived from their huſbands, in the event of a divorce; but this circumſtance ſhall not deprive them of any rank derived from their children, with whom, notwithſtanding ſuch divorce between the parents, the original connection ſhall be held to ſubſiſt.

When any of the perſons aforeſaid commit offences againſt the laws, they ſhall be tried, examined, and puniſhed according to the ſame regulations as thoſe officers of government who are actually in employ.

One clauſe.

SECTION XIII.—*Offences committed by Officers of Government previous to their Elevation.*

All officers of government who are convicted of offences committed previouſly, but charged againſt them ſubſequently, to their elevation or coming into office, ſhall be permitted to redeem themſelves from puniſhment, provided the offence is of a public and not of a perſonal nature.

All officers of government who, after their promotion or removal, are convicted of any public offence, committed previous to ſuch promotion or removal, ſhall be fined or degraded according to the law concerning ſuch offences, when committed by officers of government, provided

provided that the offences would not in ordinary cafes have been punifhable more feverely than with 100 blows with the bamboo, but, otherwife, the offenders fhall be punifhed in fuch cafes according to the laws refpecting perfons in general: if the party, difcovered to have committed any offence of a public nature while in office, had, previoufly to fuch difcovery, been totally degraded and difmiffed from any poft under government, he fhall, in general, be excufed from any further punifhment for fuch implied malverfation; but if the offence concerns a falfe return of receipts of revenue, or a deficiency or concealment of any government property, the magiftrate, in whofe department it lies, fhall thoroughly and promptly inveftigate the affair, fo far as may be neceffary to afcertain the amount of property, whether in kind or value, which the offender is bound to replace or refund into the hands of government. If it is an offence of a private and perfonal nature, the laws fhall take their ordinary courfe.—With refpect to the clerks of all magiftrates, and of the feveral tribunals or departments of public affairs, committing offences of a public or a private nature, under any of the preceding circumftances, the laws fhall be executed in the ufual manner.

One Claufe.

Section XIV.—*Degraded Officers of Government liable to the fame Obligations as private Individuals.*

All civil and military officers of government who have been degraded and difmiffed for any offence of a private and perfonal nature, fhall likewife be deprived of the patent of rank granted to their families. In like manner, all the priefts of *Foe* or *Tao-fe* *, who fhall have been convicted and punifhed for any offence, fhall be deprived of their licence, and divefted of their facred character.

* See Section XLII.

All

All ſuch degraded perſons ſhall be replaced in the claſs of ſoldiers or citizens, from whence they were originally taken, and be liable to the cuſtomary demands of perſonal ſervice in either capacity *.

Two clauſes.

Section XV. — *Relations of Exiles.*

All the wives of baniſhed criminals ſhall follow them into exile: the parents, grand-parents, children, and grand-children of exiles, ſhall be at liberty to follow them or not, according to their own choice; and when they deſire it, a new ſettlement ſhall be given to them, at the place of baniſhment.—If the offenders die previous to the expiration of the term of baniſhment, their relations who had accompanied them, if deſirous of returning to their original place of ſettlement, ſhall be allowed to do ſo.

Neverthele∫s, the relations of perſons baniſhed in conſequence of being implicated in charges of treaſon, rebellion, poiſoning, magic, or murdering three or more perſons in one family, ſhall not be ſuffered to return to their original places of ſettlement, agreeably to the proviſions of this law.

Eighteen clauſes.

* It is not to be underſtood from this law, that there is in China any peculiar and indelible diſtinction of caſt, as in Hindoſtan, but merely that every individual ſhall be liable to demands of perſonal ſervice for public purpoſes, agreeably to the nature of his calling or profeſſion.—This is more fully ſtated in a ſubſequent diviſion of the code, intitled, "Enrolment of the People."

Section XVI. — *Extent of an Act of Grace or General Pardon* *.

From the benefit of any general act of grace or pardon thoſe offenders ſhall be excluded, who have been convicted of any of the ten treaſonable offences before mentioned; of murder; embezzlement of government ſtores; robbery or theft; wilful houſe-burning; unlawful grave-opening; bribery, whether the object be lawful or unlawful; forgery and fraud; inceſt, adultery, and the like; kidnapping; ſwindling; exciting to commit murder; deſignedly deviating from juſtice in the denunciation of puniſhment againſt offenders; conniving at, aſſiſting in, negociating, or conveying a bribe for the purpoſe of procuring a breach of the laws; and in general in all caſes where the laws have been tranſgreſſed by premeditation and deſign.

On the other hand, an act of grace ſhall relieve all thoſe from puniſhment, who have offended accidentally and inadvertently; ſuch as accidentally killing or wounding any individual; accidentally ſetting fire to houſes or other property; unintentionally or inadvertently waſting and occaſioning the loſs of government property, on the part of perſons having charge of it.

Secondly; An act of grace ſhall extend to all thoſe who are liable to puniſhment merely by implication, and in conſequence of the guilt of others.

Thirdly; An act of grace ſhall, further, relieve from puniſhment all thoſe, who are chargeable with public offences, not becauſe they have perſonally and deſignedly committed them, but becauſe ſuch offences either of commiſſion or omiſſion, had taken place within the limits of their juriſdiction or reſponſibility.

* An act of grace to the effect here ſtated, is uſually paſſed at the acceſſion of a new Emperor, and alſo in honour of ſome particular anniverſaries.

In

In all theſe caſes, an act of grace ſhall have the effect of an immediate and unconditional pardon *.

Particular acts of grace or pardon, in which the offenders are deſcribed by name, or in which the puniſhment of certain offences is mitigated only, are not ſubject to any of the limitations hereby provided.

Nine clauſes.

SECTION XVII. — *Effect of an Act of Grace on the Condition of Offenders in Exile.*

When any offender condemned to perpetual exile is overtaken on the journey by the official notice of a general act of grace or pardon, it cannot take effect with regard to him, if the period legally allowed for reaching the place of his deſtination had expired; as for inſtance, in the caſe of an individual ſentenced to be baniſhed to the diſtance of 3000 *lee*, he is ſuppoſed to travel at the rate of 50 *lee per* day, and therefore he muſt have received the act of grace before he had been ſixty days upon the journey, in order to be entitled to the benefit of it. — Nevertheleſs, if the prolongation of the time appears not to have been wilful, and the cauſe is duly certified by the proper magiſtrate, whether from the roads being impaſſable, from ſickneſs, robbers, or other caſualties, this objection in point of time ſhall be over-ruled.

If the offender, moreover, ſhould have made his eſcape previouſly to the receipt of the act of grace, he ſhall not afterwards be allowed the benefit of it, but if he dies before he is retaken, his family and relations

* The offences enumerated as pardonable by an act of grace, are alſo redeemable at other times by a fine, upon a petition being made to that effect. — This regulation is not included among the fundamental articles of the laws, but is inſerted in a note to the firſt ſection, under the authority of an act iſſued the eighth year of the late Emperor *Kien-lung*. — The particulars of this act, and of ſome of the more material clauſes to the firſt ſection, have been inſerted in the Appendix, No. V.

ſhall be allowed either to return to their original ſettlement, or to obtain a new eſtabliſhment at the deſtined place of baniſhment, according to their choice.

After the offender condemned to perpetual baniſhment reaches his deſtination, he ſhall no longer be capable of taking the benefit of any act of grace or general pardon, even although his offence may not have been ſuch as already ſtated to be generally unpardonable.

Thoſe who had only received ſentence of temporary baniſhment, may, on the contrary, always have the benefit of any general act of pardon; and by ſuch act, whenever it occurs, the execution of the remaining part of the ſentence of ſuch perſons ſhall be remitted.

Two clauſes.

SECTION XVIII. — *Indulgence to Offenders for the Sake of their Parents.*

When any offender under ſentence of death for an offence not excluded from the contingent benefit of an act of grace, ſhall have parents or grand-parents who are ſick, infirm, or aged above ſeventy years, and who have no other male child or grand-child above the age of ſixteen to ſupport them, beſide ſuch capitally convicted offender, this circumſtance, after having been inveſtigated and aſcertained by the magiſtrate of the diſtrict, ſhall be ſubmitted to the conſideration and deciſion of His Imperial Majeſty.

Any offender who, under ſimilar circumſtances, had been condemned to undergo temporary or perpetual baniſhment, ſhall, inſtead thereof, receive 100 blows, and redeem himſelf from further puniſhment, by the payment of the cuſtomary fine.

Sixteen clauſes.

SEC-

SECTION XIX. — *Offences of Aſtronomers* *.

All the members of the aſtronomical board † at Pekin, and other perſons recogniſed as aſtronomers, or obſervers of the heavenly bodies, when convicted of offences puniſhable with temporary or perpetual baniſhment, ſhall only ſuffer 100 blows, and redeem themſelves from further puniſhment by the payment of the cuſtomary fine; by which indulgence they are enabled to return to their profeſſion.

Nevertheleſs, this regulation ſhall not extend to any perſons who are under ſentence of baniſhment for treaſon or rebellion; for poiſoning, murdering, wounding, robbing, ſtealing, killing by magic, or for any ſuch offences as may ſubject the party to the puniſhment of being branded.

Two clauſes.

* This deſignation muſt of courſe be underſtood in a qualified ſenſe, adapted to the low ſtate of the ſcience at preſent in China, owing to the ignorance and ſuperſtition of its profeſſors, and the neglect or indifference of the government towards it. Still, however, this ſection of the laws, containing an exception expreſsly in favour of aſtronomers, and for ſecuring to the ſtate the benefit of their labours, is an honourable tribute to the excellence and utility of the ſcience, and a proof that its cultivation is ſtill conſidered in China an object of national importance.—It is alſo to be obſerved, that under the patronage of the enlightened Emperor *Kang-hee* the European miſſionaries at Pekin printed and publiſhed in the Chineſe character ſeveral uſeful works connected with this ſcience, ſome of which, particularly a beautiful edition of a table of logarithms, are at preſent in the library of the Royal Society.

† According to the Chineſe imperial kalendar, this board, uſually termed by the miſſionaries the Tribunal of Mathematics, conſiſts of ſeven members, among whom three are Europeans, and the reſt Tartars or Chineſe, including the preſident, who is always a prince of the blood. There are alſo other boards or departments ſubordinate to the principal one, conſiſting, according to the kalendar, of ſeventy-five perſons in the whole, all of whom are either Tartars or Chineſe; but although the names of only three of the miſſionaries appear on the official liſt, all thoſe who are retained in the ſervice of the Emperor at Pekin, are employed according to their capacities, and are decorated with the buttons denoting official rank.

SEC-

SECTION XX. — *Offences of Artificers, Muficians, and Women.*

All artificers and muficians * who are convicted of offences punifhable with temporary banifhment, fhall, in the firft inftance, fuffer the cuftomary number of blows with the bamboo; but inftead of being fubfequently fent into banifhment, they fhall be detained during the legal period of fuch banifhment at the tribunal † of the magiftrate of the diftrict, and employed for that time in the fervice of government.

This law fhall not be confidered to extend to fuch perfons as are fentenced to be branded, or to be banifhed, either for ftealing, or for any other more ferious offence.

Women convicted of offences punifhable with the bamboo, fhall be fuffered to retain a fingle upper garment, while the punifhment is inflicted, except in cafes of adultery, and the like, when they fhall be allowed the lower garment only.

Moreover, when the offences committed by women are fuch as are ufually punifhed alfo with temporary or perpetual banifhment, that part of the fentence fhall be always remitted upon payment of the

* Notwithftanding the fimplicity and unimproved ftate of the Chinefe mufic, it appears from the annals of the empire, that the art was anciently held in high eftimation, and even at prefent the mufical board is under the government of a prince of the blood, and is ranked with the other public offices at the capital.

With regard to artificers, it is probably confidered neceffary to fecure their fervices, by an exception in their favour, in order to carry on with lefs interruption the various public works, the laws relative to which form the concluding divifion of this Code.

† The word *tribunal* has been employed in various inftances, in which fome other term more generally received in our language, fuch as board, office, council, committee, department, &c. would at firft fight appear preferable, but the Chinefe term for a court of juftice being likewife applied to public offices in general, and the forms being fimilar in all cafes, notwithftanding the difference of the bufinefs tranfacted, the above expreffion has been chofen in this and moft inftances, not only as fanctioned by former writers on China, but as more generally applicable than any other.

cuftomary

cuſtomary fine; but the corporal puniſhment, to the extent of 100 blows, ſhall be inflicted.

Two clauſes.

SECTION XXI. — *Offences of Perſons already under Sentence of Puniſhment.*

When any perſon, after having been charged with an offence, commits another offence before the infliction of the puniſhment due to the former, the puniſhment of the greater offence ſhall always ſuperſede that of the leſſer.

But if the offender had been already ſent into baniſhment for the former offence, the puniſhment of the latter offence ſhall be inflicted according to the law in the uſual manner, except in the caſe of a ſecond ſentence of perpetual baniſhment, when the latter ſhall be commuted for a ſentence of extra-ſervice for four years.

In like manner, a ſecond ſentence of temporary baniſhment ſhall prolong the period of ſervice, but it ſhall never exceed four years on the whole.

When, after ſentence of baniſhment or of corporal puniſhment, a further offence puniſhable with blows of the bamboo is committed, a proportionate puniſhment ſhall be inflicted to the full extent directed by law, in the uſual manner.

Ten clauſes.

SECTION XXII. — *Indulgence to Offenders in Conſideration of their Age, Youth, or Infirmities.*

Any offender whoſe age is not more than fifteen nor leſs than ſeventy years, or who is diſabled by the loſs of an eye or a limb, ſhall be allowed to redeem himſelf from any puniſhment leſs than capital,

capital, by the payment of the eſtabliſhed fine *, except in the caſe of perſons condemned to baniſhment as acceſſaries to the crimes of treaſon, rebellion, murder of three or more perſons in one family, or homicide by magic or poiſoning, upon all of which offenders the laws ſhall be ſtrictly executed.

Any offender whoſe age is not more than ten nor leſs than eighty years, or who is totally diſabled by the loſs of both eyes or two limbs, ſhall, when the crime is capital, but not amounting to treaſon, be recommended to the particular conſideration and deciſion of His Imperial Majeſty.

In all caſes of robbery and wounding, which are not puniſhable capitally, when any perſons under the aforeſaid diſabilities are implicated therein, they ſhall always be liberated on paying the eſtabliſhed fine: in other caſes of a leſs ſerious nature, they ſhall not be held reſponſible in any manner whatever.

Offenders whoſe age is not more than ſeven nor leſs than ninety years, ſhall not ſuffer puniſhment in any caſe, except in that of treaſon or rebellion; but any perſon who ſhall be convicted of having inſtructed ſuch child or aged perſon in the commiſſion of any offence, ſhall ſuffer the ſame puniſhment as he would have been liable to, if he had actually committed the offence himſelf.

Eight clauſes.

* The amount of the fine is ſtated in the preliminary part of the code, but is ſo ſmall in each caſe as to be merely nominal, though the form is retained, probably in order to diſtinguiſh theſe caſes from others, in which the offender is entirely pardoned.—Several inſtances of diſtinctions of a ſimilar kind might eaſily be quoted from our own laws, and probably from thoſe of moſt other nations.

There are other caſes in which the fines are conſiderable in the amount, and levied under altogether different circumſtances.—They are deſcribed in the note to Section I. and XVI. and in the Appendix, No. V.

SEC-

SECTION XXIII. — *Plea of Age and Infirmities, how to be conſtrued.*

Whoever is aſcertained to be aged or infirm at the period of trial for any offence, ſhall be allowed the benefit of ſuch plea, although he may not have attained the full age, or laboured under the alleged infirmity at the time the offence was committed.

In any caſe of temporary baniſhment, the offender, on attaining the age, or becoming infirm as aforeſaid, ſhall, in like manner, become thereupon entitled to the privilege of redeeming himſelf from further puniſhment.—On the other hand, the privilege of youth may be pleaded when the age of the offender, at the time of committing the offence, did not exceed ſeven, ten, or fifteen years, whatever may be his age at the ſubſequent period of trial.

No clauſe.

SECTION XXIV. — *Reſtitution and Forfeiture of Goods.*

In any caſe of an illegal transfer of property, in which both parties are guilty, or when any perſon is convicted of poſſeſſing prohibited goods, ſuch goods or property ſhall be forfeited to the ſtate:—But when any article of property has been obtained from an individual by violence, injuſtice, extortion, or falſe pretences, it ſhall be reſtored to the owner.

In all caſes wherein the offender is liable to be puniſhed in his property as well as in his perſon, if a pardon arrives after the execution of corporal puniſhment, but before the confiſcation has taken place, or before the fine has been levied, the latter part of the ſentence ſhall be remitted.—If however the amount to be levied by fine or confiſcation, is actually received and appropriated before the notice of the general act of pardon arrives; or if the offence is connected with circumftances of a treafonable nature, the general act of pardon fhall, in that particular cafe, have no effect.

Moreover, in any cafe of an available pardon arriving before the execution of corporal punifhment, the property fequeftrated on account of government, if not fpecifically appropriated, fhall be reftored, and the family of the offender, who may have been likewife held bound to government, fhall be releafed from their refponfibility.

If the offence arifes from the unlawful poffeffion of any property, and the property, the reftitution of which is confequently claimed by government or by an individual, is ftill in exiftence, it fhall be duly transferred, and, when of a productive nature, with all its produce. If, however, the unlawful poffeffor had wafted it, and afterwards died, his heirs fhall not be compelled to make up the deficiency.

When the offence arifes from circumftances of a different defcription, the fine fhall be ftrictly levied, unlefs it be the wages of labour, in which cafe it fhall be remitted.

In eftimating the amount of the property and of the charges which are to be made good by the offender, the feveral articles fhall be rated at the price they bore at the time and place in which they were unlawfully acquired.

The wages of labour fhall be eftimated at 8 *fen* 5 *lee* and 5 *bao* *, for each man *per* day: the charges for the hire of horfes, cattle, carriages, boats, and fimilar articles, fhall be fixed at the current rate at the time and place in which fuch charges were incurred; provided always, that the total charge for the hire of any article, fhall not, in any cafe, exceed its full value.

* That is to fay, 0855 decimal parts of a *lean* or Chinefe ounce of filver, whofe eftimated value is 6*s*. 8*d*. fterling. According to this computation, the wages of labour will be reckoned at rather lefs than feven-pence *per* day; it is probable however, that this is not an invariable rule, but fubject to alteration at different periods according to circumftances.

The

The exact amount of the gold and ſilver * due to government, or to the individual owner, ſhall be made good agreeably to the original ſums, as ſtated in the information, whatever part of ſuch orignal ſum may have been diſpoſed of or waſted.

Eighteen clauſes.

Section XXV. — *Offenders ſurrendering voluntarily.*

Whoever, having committed an offence, ſurrenders himſelf voluntarily, and acknowledges his guilt to a magiſtrate, before it is otherwiſe diſcovered, ſhall be freely pardoned; but all claims upon his property, on the part of government or of individuals, ſhall nevertheleſs be duly liquidated.

Moreover, if an offender, after having been charged with any particular offence, ſhall confeſs himſelf guilty of another and a greater offence before the magiſtrate; or in general, if, in the courſe of the inveſtigation of the circumſtances of any one alleged offence, it ſhall be diſcovered, without the application of torture, that the accuſed is guilty of other offences, he ſhall ſtill only ſuffer puniſhment in proportion to the offence originally charged againſt him.

If the offender makes a timely confeſſion of his guilt as aforeſaid, through the intervention of another perſon, or if he is accuſed by, and through the ill-will of, his junior relations or dependants, he ſhall, in all caſes not expreſsly excepted, receive full pardon.

If the voluntary confeſſion of the offender is inaccurate and imperfect, he ſhall be liable to puniſhment for as much of the offence committed by him, as he had endeavoured to conceal; but in caſes of a capital nature, the puniſhment ſhall always, upon making any timely confeſſion whatever, be reduced one degree.

* The general currency in China is reſtricted to copper, but all accounts are kept in ounces, and the decimal parts of ounces, of ſilver.

If

If an offender does not confeſs his guilt until he is informed that a charge is prepared to be laid againſt him, or if he previouſly abſconds, or takes refuge out of the empire, his puniſhment ſhall not be entirely remitted, but mitigated two degrees.

In all caſes alſo of fugitives and deſerters returning to their original places of abode, the puniſhment to which they are liable by law ſhall be mitigated no more than two degrees.

The remiſſion of puniſhment, upon a timely and voluntary confeſſion of guilt, ſhall not be allowed in thoſe caſes of injury to the perſon or property which cannot be repaired by reſtitution or compenſation, or when the offence was known to the officers of juſtice while the offender was concealed, or in caſes of clandeſtinely paſſing public barriers.

If the robber, thief, or ſwindler, repenting of his conduct, reſtores the plunder to the perſons from whom he took it, or if the corrupt officer reſtores the amount of the bribe to the perſon from whom it was received, this reſtitution ſhall be deemed equal to a confeſſion at a legal tribunal, and in the ſame degree entitle the offender to pardon.

If, having notice of an information intended to be laid againſt him, the offender then goes to the owner of the property, and makes reſtitution, he ſhall only be entitled to a mitigation of the puniſhment to the extent of two degrees; but if a repentant thief or robber is fortunate enough to be the means of bringing to juſtice his accomplices, he ſhall receive full pardon, and moreover be entitled to the reward that may have been offered for the diſcovery of ſuch offenders. If, however, he ſhould ever commit a ſecond offence, the above privileges cannot be allowed in that or in any ſubſequent inſtance.

Eleven clauſes.

SEC

SECTION XXVI. — *Offenders charged with ſeveral Offences.*

When any perſon is convicted of two or more offences, all the offences ſhall be eſtimated together, and puniſhment inflicted conformably to the extent of the criminality of the principal charge: the puniſhment of all the reſt ſhall be conſidered as included in that of the firſt.—If the ſeveral offences are charged at different times, and the puniſhment of the firſt of the charges has been already inflicted, the latter charges ſhall not ſubject the offender to further puniſhment, unleſs of a more ſerious nature than the former, in which caſe the amount only of the difference between the legal puniſhments ſhall be inflicted.

In each ſeparate caſe, however, the law ſhall be fully executed ſo far as reſpects the reſtitution of property to individuals, or the forfeiture of it to government; and alſo with reſpect to the branding of the offender, and his degradation from office.

No clauſe.

SECTION XXVII. — *Proceedings in Caſes where all the Parties to an Offence have eſcaped.*

When all the parties to any offence have effected their eſcape from juſtice, if any individual amongſt them ſurrenders voluntarily, and alſo delivers into cuſtody one other more guilty than himſelf; or if, when the guilt is equal, the larger porportion of the party are delivered up by the ſmaller, thoſe who thus voluntarily ſurrender themſelves ſhall be pardoned, except in caſes of killing, of wounding, and of criminal intercourſe between the ſexes.—When ſeveral perſons are implicated in the guilt of one, who afterwards dies in priſon, the puniſhment of thoſe who are guilty by implication only, ſhall be thereupon reduced two degrees.

More-

Moreover, when any offender obtains a remiſſion or mitigation of his puniſhment, or permiſſion to redeem himſelf from the ſame by a fine, either in conſequence of a voluntary ſurrender and confeſſion, by a general act of grace, or by a ſpecial edict of the Emperor in his favour, in all ſuch caſes the ſeveral perſons who may have become liable to puniſhment by implication in his offence, ſhall be pardoned or favoured to the ſame extent.

No claue.

SECTION XXVIII. — *Offences of Members of Public Departments and Tribunals committed in their official Capacity.*

In all caſes of officers of government aſſociated in one department or tribunal, and committing offences againſt the laws as a public body, by falſe or erroneous deciſions, and inveſtigations, the clerk of the department or tribunal ſhall be puniſhed as the principal offender; the puniſhment of the ſeveral deputies, or executive officers, ſhall be leſs by one degree, that of the aſſeſſors leſs by another degree, and that of the preſiding magiſtrate leſs by a third degree *.

* In tranſlating the titles of the conſtituent officers of a Chineſe tribunal or public board, it was impoſſible to find terms that were not in ſome point of view exceptionable, but thoſe that have been choſen will ſhew, that the arrangement is analogous to that adopted in ſuch of our own colonial governments, as are adminiſtered by a preſident, members of council, ſecretaries, and clerks. What is the moſt remarkable in this reſpect in China, is that the loweſt officer incurs the greateſt ſhare of the reſponſibility; but this being confined to offences by implication only, it will not appear ſo extraordinary that, when the meaſures or the deciſions of a board or tribunal are found to be reprehenſible without any offence being directly imputable to a particular individual, that member of the tribunal ſhould be ſubjected to the largeſt ſhare of the puniſhment, by whoſe ſuggeſtion and inſtrumentality, the buſineſs had been conducted, and whoſe inferior ſtation might be ſuppoſed to have enabled him to gain a more accurate knowledge of the circumſtances upon which the juſtice or injuſtice of the deciſion depended, than was likely to have been in the power of his ſuperiors.

Although

Although there ſhould be a vacancy in, or a want of any of the intermediate ſtations, the reduction of the puniſhment ſhall always take effect to the ſame extent *.

If in the caſe of any deciſion of a tribunal contrary to the laws, only one member of the court was guilty of the deviation from juſtice, knowingly and intentionally, his particular offence being of a perſonal nature ſhall be puniſhed as ſuch; while the others, being only guilty of an erroneous judgment, ſhall be puniſhed more leniently, and according to the gradations preſcribed above.

If an inferior tribunal reports its erroneous judgment to a ſuperior, which ſuperior, neglecting to examine and diſcover the error, confirms the ſame, the members of the ſuperior tribunal ſhall be reſpectively liable to puniſhment leſs by two degrees than thoſe of the inferior tribunal.

On the other hand, when a ſuperior tribunal communicates its erroneous judgment to an inferior tribunal, if the members of the latter neglect to examine the ſame, and, having failed to diſcover the error, confirm it by their proceedings, they alſo ſhall be liable to puniſhment, though under a proportionate mitigation, in the caſe of each individual, to the extent of three degrees.

In all theſe caſes, the ſcale of the puniſhments incurred ſhall commence with the clerks of the reſpective courts.

No clauſe.

SECTION XXIX. — *Errors and Failures in public Proceedings.*

Upon any error or failure in the public proceedings of an officer of government, if he diſcovers and corrects, or remedies the ſame, he ſhall be pardoned. — Alſo, in the caſe of error or failure in the proceed-

* As for inſtance; the preſiding magiſtrates of theſe public boards or tribunals, in which from cuſtom or accident, there may not be any aſſeſſors or deputies, ſhall, in every caſe of imputed delinquency, be puniſhed three degrees leſs than the clerks, in the ſame manner as in thoſe boards or tribunals which are conſtituted in the regular way.

ings

ings of a public office or tribunal, if any one member difcovers fo as to correct or remedy the fame, all the members fhall obtain pardon. If however fuch error confifts in an aggravation of the fentence of the law, and is not difcovered until after the execution thereof, they cannot be entirely pardoned, but the punifhment fhall be mitigated three degrees.—If, on the other hand, the error confifts in pronouncing too lenient a fentence, the parties fhall be pardoned, although the error is not difcovered until after the execution of the fentence, provided they do themfelves difcover and rectify their error.

An extraordinary delay in iffuing public orders from any tribunal of juftice or other public department, renders all the members liable to punifhment; but if any one of them voluntarily interpofes, and prevents any further delay from taking place, all the magiftrates or officers of that tribunal or department fhall be pardoned; but the clerk fhall incur the full punifhment, except he had himfelf acknowledged the impropriety of the delay which had taken place, and interpofed to prevent its continuance; in which cafe, his punifhment fhall be reduced two degrees.

Five days fhall be allowed to difpatch bufinefs of fmall importance; ten days for bufinefs of ordinary importance; and twenty days for bufinefs of high importance.

No claufe.

SECTION XXX. — *Diftinction between Principals and Acceffaries.*

When feveral perfons are parties to one offence, the original contriver of it fhall be held to be the principal, and as fuch fuffer the punifhment required by the laws, in its full extent: the reft who followed, and alfo contributed to the perpetration thereof, fhall fuffer the punifhment next in degree, under the denomination of acceffaries.—When the parties to an offence are members of one family, the fenior and chief member of that family fhall alone be punifhable; but if he be upwards of eighty years of age, or totally difabled by his infirmities, the punifhment fhall fall upon the next in fucceffion.

When

When, however, the offence is a direct injury to the perſon or property of any indvidual, the ſeveral individuals ſhall, as in all ordinary caſes, be puniſhed as principals or acceſſaries in the manner previouſly ſtated.

When the relative ſituation of the parties engaged in the commiſſion of one offence, creates a difference in their liability to puniſhment, the principals ſhall ſuffer as principals in the offence committed by themſelves, but the acceſſaries ſhall be puniſhed as acceſſaries in the offence of which they would themſelves have been guilty, had they been in the place of the principal. As for inſtance: if a man engages a ſtranger to ſtrike his elder brother—the younger brother ſhall be puniſhed with ninety blows, and two years and a half baniſhment, for the offence of ſtriking his elder; but the ſtranger ſhall be only puniſhed with twenty blows, as in common caſes of an aſſault.—Alſo, if a younger relation introduces a ſtranger to ſteal to the amount of ten *leang* or ounces of ſilver of the family property, he ſhall only be puniſhed as waſting, or diſpoſing of without leave, the family property to that extent, whereas the ſtranger ſhall be puniſhed as in common caſes of theft.

When the law does not expreſsly declare, that the puniſhment ſhall be inflicted alike on all parties concerned, it is to be underſtood, that one only is to ſuffer as a principal, and the reſt as acceſſaries.—Nevertheleſs, in all caſes of attempting to enter any of the imperial palaces, or to paſs the public barriers clandeſtinely; avoiding the ſtated and lawful ſervices to government; committing adultery, and other offences of the ſame nature; the parties ſhall ſuffer puniſhment individually without any diſtinction between principals and acceſſaries, although the terms expreſsly including all parties equally, ſhould be omitted.

One clauſe.

SECTION XXXI. — *Proceedings relative to Offenders who have abſconded.*

When, of two perſons who have been parties to the perpetration of an offence, one has abſconded, and the other, who is in cuſtody, declares the former to have been the principal offender, and himſelf only an acceſſary, if there is no evidence to diſprove the aſſertion, he ſhall be puniſhed forthwith as an acceſſary. — If the offender who had abſconded is afterwards taken, and thereupon contends that, on the contrary, the other was the principal offender, the matter ſhall be diligently inveſtigated; and if the latter aſſertion is ſubſtantiated, the offender firſt ſeized ſhall ſuffer the remainder of the puniſhment due to him as a principal, and the reſt ſhall each ſuffer according to the law, as acceſſaries.

If, after an offence is known to have been perpetrated, it can be proved by ſufficient teſtimony, whether thoſe who, being known to be implicated therein and, having abſconded, are ſtill at large, were principals or acceſſaries, it ſhall not be deemed requiſite to confront all the offenders together, and they may therefore be tried and puniſhed, as they are ſucceſſively apprehended.

Four clauſes.

SECTION XXXII. — *Relations mutually aſſiſting and concealing each other*.*

All relations connected in the firſt and ſecond degree and living under the ſame roof, maternal grand-parents and their grandchildren, fathers and mothers-in-law, ſons and daughters-in-law, grandchildren's wives, huſbands' brothers and brothers' wives, when mu-

* Concerning the degrees of conſanguinity as diſtinguiſhed by the Chineſe, ſee the Table of Degrees of Mourning in the Preliminary Part of the Code, and alſo the Appendix thereto, No. IV.

tually

tually aſſiſting each other, and concealing the offences, one of another, and moreover, ſlaves and hired ſervants aſſiſting their maſters and concealing their offences, ſhall not, in any ſuch caſes, be puniſhable for ſo doing.

In like manner, though they ſhould inform their relations of the meaſures adopted for their apprehenſion, and enable them to conceal themſelves, and finally to effect their eſcape, they ſhall ſtill be held innocent.

When relations in the third and fourth degrees aſſiſt and protect each other from puniſhment in the manner here deſcribed, they ſhall for ſuch conduct be liable to puniſhment, but only in a proportion of three degrees leſs than would have been inflicted on ſtrangers under the ſame circumſtances.

The ſame offences committed by relations in ſtill more remote degrees of kindred, ſhall be puniſhed within one degree of the extent of the puniſhment inflicted in ordinary caſes. — Nevertheleſs, none of the proviſions of this law in mitigation or remiſſion of the puniſhment of harbouring, concealing, and aſſiſting relations, ſhall be pleaded, or have any effect, in caſes of high treaſon or rebellion.

One clauſe.

SECTION XXXIII. — *Puniſhment of Deſerters.*

When, in the frontier towns and other places of ſtrength, any of the ſoldiers are diſcovered to have formed a deſign to deſert and join the enemy, their commanding officer ſhall take them into cuſtody, and bring them for trial before his own immediate ſuperior, who, having ſtrictly inveſtigated the charges, and gone through the evidence, ſhall report the ſame to the viceroy and ſub-viceroy of the province: when the latter magiſtrates have finally aſcertained that there has been no partiality nor injuſtice in the caſe, they ſhall proceed, without further

delay,

delay, to carry the ſentence of the law into effect, and afterwards ſubmit the whole of the proceedings to His Imperial Majeſty.

When the army is in the field, and any of the ſoldiers openly attempt to deſert, if they can be ſeized immediately and put to death, it ſhall be lawful to do ſo, in conſideration of the urgency of the caſe; the proviſions of this law may therefore, under ſuch circumſtances, be ſo far diſpenſed with, but it is ſtill requiſite to report faithfully all ſuch tranſactions to the Emperor.

No clauſe.

SECTION XXXIV. — *Offences committed by Foreigners* *.

In general, all foreigners who come to ſubmit themſelves to the government of the empire, ſhall, when guilty of offences, be tried and ſentenced according to the eſtabliſhed laws.

The particular deciſions however of the tribunal *Lee-fan-Yuen* † ſhall be

* This ſection of the code has been expreſsly quoted by the provincial government of Canton, and applied to the caſe of foreigners reſiding there and at Macao for the purpoſes of trade. The laws of China have never, however, been attempted to be enforced againſt thoſe foreigners, except with conſiderable allowances in their favour, although, on the other hand, they are reſtricted and circumſcribed in ſuch a manner that a tranſgreſſion on their part of any ſpecific article of the laws, can ſcarcely occur; at leaſt not without, at the ſame time, implicating and involving in their guilt ſome of the natives, who thus, in moſt caſes, become the principal victims of offended juſtice.—The ſituation of Europeans in China is certainly by no means ſo ſatisfactory on the whole as might be deſired, or even as it may be reaſonably expected to become in the progreſs of time; unleſs ſome untoward circumſtance ſhould occur to check the gradual courſe of improvement; it muſt be admitted, however, that the extreme contrariety of manners, habits, and language, renders ſome ſuch arrangement, as that now ſubſiſting for the regulation of the intercourſe between the Europeans and the natives, abſolutely indiſpenſable, as well as conducive to the intereſts of both parties.—A tranſlation of ſome Chineſe official documents of a recent date, illuſtrative of the above remarks, is inſerted in the Appendix, No. XI.

† This tribunal might be styled the office or department for foreign affairs, but its chief concern is with the tributary and the ſubject ſtates of Tartary.

be guided according to regulations framed for the government of the Mongol tribes.

Three clauſes.

Section XXXV. — *Proceedings in Caſes where the Laws appear contradictory.*

When the law upon any particular caſe appears to differ from the general laws contained in this diviſion of the code, the magiſtrate ſhall always decide according to the former, in preference to the latter. — When the offence, of which an individual is convicted according to one law, is at the ſame time in itſelf an evidence of deſigns, which are, by another law, more ſeverely puniſhable than the act itſelf, ſentence upon ſuch an individual ſhall be pronounced and executed according to the latter inſtead of the former law. — If an offence is committed under aggravating circumſtances, of which the offender himſelf is ignorant at the time, he ſhall be ſentenced to ſuffer no more than the puniſhment due by law in ordinary caſes.

As for inſtance: if a nephew, being educated at a diſtance from his uncle, and not knowing his perſon, ſtrikes him in an affray, it ſhall be judged to be only an ordinary caſe of aſſault: — or if a thief ſteals any articles which are ſacred or imperial, without knowing them to be ſo, it ſhall be adjudged to be an ordinary inſtance of theft, and not ſacrilege. On the other hand, if the offence is committed under palliating circumſtances, which legally reduce the amount of the puniſhment, the offender ſhall, at all events, have the full advantage thereof; as for inſtance, when a father ſtrikes a perſon whom he ſuppoſes to be a ſtranger, but who was in fact his ſon.

No clauſe.

SEC-

SECTION XXXVI. — *Rules relative to the Increaſe and Diminution of Puniſhments.*

When the ſentence of the law is ſaid to be increaſed, it is implied, that the puniſhment ſhall be inflicted more ſeverely:—As for inſtance: a ſentence of forty blows increaſed one degree, becomes a ſentence of fifty blows: a ſentence of one hundred blows increaſed one degree, becomes a ſentence of ſixty blows and one year's baniſhment; the next degree is ſeventy blows, and one year and a half's baniſhment:—a ſentence of one hundred blows and three years baniſhment, when raiſed one degree, implies a ſentence of one hundred blows, and perpetual baniſhment to the diſtance of 2000 *lee*; and when raiſed another degree, a ſentence of one hundred blows, and perpetual baniſhment to the diſtance of 2500 *lee*.

When the ſentence of the law is ſaid to be diminiſhed, it is implied that the puniſhment is mitigated: As for inſtance—a ſentence of fifty blows diminiſhed one degree is a ſentence of forty blows:—one of ſixty blows and one year's baniſhment diminiſhed one degree, is one of one hundred blows: one of one hundred blows and three years baniſhment, diminiſhed one degree, is one of ninety blows and two years and a half's baniſhment.

In the reduction of puniſhments, the two modes of inflicting death, and three kinds of perpetual baniſhment, ſhall be eſtimated in each caſe as only a ſingle degree:—As for inſtance; if a ſentence of capital puniſhment by ſtrangling, or decollation, is mitigated one degree, the offender ſhall be baniſhed perpetually to the diſtance of 3000 *lee*; if two degrees, he ſhall be baniſhed for three years only.—In like manner, any ſentence of perpetual baniſhment, when reduced one degree, ſhall only ſubject the offender to baniſhment for three years.

When the puniſhment is increaſed a degree in a ſpecific caſe, the full extent required by law muſt be proved to warrant the ſame: as for inſtance; the increaſed puniſhment for bribery amounting to forty

leang

leang or ounces of ſilver, cannot be inflicted if the amount did not exceed thirty-nine ounces and ninety-nine decimal parts.

Moreover, whatever number of degrees the puniſhment is directed to be increaſed in certain caſes, it cannot be rendered capital by conſtruction, unleſs ſo eſpecially provided; and if it is provided that, in certain caſes, the offender ſhall be puniſhed capitally, either by ſtrangling or decollation, he muſt be executed in the manner ſtated, and not otherwiſe, under any circumſtances of aggravation of the offence.

Three clauſes.

SECTION XXXVII. — *Extent of the Privilege and Diſtinction of Imperial Rank.*

Whatever is ſtated in the laws concerning Imperial equipage, the Imperial preſence, and the like, ſhall be conſidered to extend not only to the Emperor, but alſo to the Empreſs Conſort, Empreſs Mother, and Empreſs Grandmother.—Alſo, all orders, inſtructions, and acts of any kind, termed Imperial, ſhall be underſtood to comprehend, beſide thoſe of the Emperor himſelf, thoſe of the Empreſs Mother and Empreſs Grandmother, and of the Imperial Prince appointed to the ſucceſſion *.

No clauſe.

SECTION XXXVIII. — *Relations in the firſt Degree.*

Whatever is declared in the laws to concern relations in the firſt degree, grand-parents or grand-children, ſhall likewiſe be underſtood to extend equally to great-grand-parents, and great-great-grand-parents, great

* The laſt diſtinction of rank can only have been ſtated hypothetically, as ſuch a nomination has never taken place under the preſent dynaſty, except upon the reſignation, or by the teſtamentary direction of the Emperor, publiſhed after his deceaſe. One of the charges againſt the late and favourite miniſter *Ho-chung-tong*, was that of his having divulged to the preſent Emperor, previous to his elevation, the ſecret of the preference intended to be ſhewn him by his imperial father.

great-grand-children, and great-great grand-children, except in cafes of conftructive crimes, when the law fhall be taken literally.

Alfo, the father's principal wife *, the father's wife fubftituted in the place of the principal wife after her death, the father's wife fubftituted in the place of the natural mother upon her death, and the adopted mother, fhall all hold equal rank with the natural mother, and be underftood to be referred to, in all laws in which the mother of the party concerned is only ftated generally, except in the cafe of fuch mother having been divorced, or in the cafe of her killing, or attempting to kill, fuch fon-in-law.

Alfo, except in cafes of conftructive offences, whatever the law ftates relative to the fons, fhall be applicable to the daughters alfo.

No claufe.

SECTION XXXIX. — *Participators in Offences* †.

Thofe, whom the law declares to be confidered as participators in an offence, fhall fuffer the punifhment incurred by it, without however including any circumftances of aggravation, which are perfonally applicable to the principal offender only; and in the cafe of capital offences, the participators in the offence fhall only receive one hundred blows, and fuffer perpetual banifhment to the diftance of 3000 *lee*: — they fhall moreover not be liable to be branded for their participation in any offence fo punifhable.

In cafes however of bribery and wilful connivance, all participators in the crime fhall participate in the punifhment, in its full extent,

* For an illuftration of the legal diftinction between the principal and inferior wives, fee the divifion of the code entitled *Marriage*.

† This, as well as fome other fections of the preliminary divifion of the code, are not fo much declaratory of the law, as explanatory of technical phrafeology, but being included among the fundamental articles, they could not, confiftently with the general plan be omitted.

efpecially

eſpecially when the offence amounts to an act of treaſon or rebellion:—for wilful connivance in the latter crimes, the laws have expreſsly provided a particular puniſhment.

When it is declared that an offence ſhall be conſidered as an act of bribery, or theft, puniſhment ſhall follow according to the laws relating thereto, except that the branding ſhall not be inflicted, and the capital part of the ſentence mitigated to perpetual baniſhment.—When, however, the caſe is referred directly to thoſe laws, they ſhall be executed againſt the offenders in their full extent.

SECTION XL. — *Reſponſible Superintendants.*

All officers of government are conſidered by law to be the reſponſible ſuperintendants of ſuch charges and departments of public affairs and public juſtice, as may be placed under their authority and controul.—All thoſe likewiſe, who have particular offices and charges in places and countries under the juriſdiction of others, and who have the particular government of treaſuries, granaries, and priſons, even thoſe who have only temporary and delegated authority therein, without being regularly eſtabliſhed in ſuch governments and appointments, ſhall, in every caſe, be conſidered the reſponſible ſuperintendants within the extent of their offices.

No clauſe.

SECTION XLI. — *Diviſion of Time.*

A day ſhall be conſidered to have elapſed when the hundred diviſions are completed—(at preſent, according to the Imperial Almanac, the day conſiſts of ninety-ſix diviſions) *.—A day's work or labour ſhall, however, be computed only from the riſing to the ſetting of the ſun.

* This obſervation is taken from a note in the original.

A legal

A legal year ſhall conſiſt of 360 days complete *, but a man's age ſhall be computed according to the number of years of the † cycle elapſed ſince his name and birth were recorded in the public ‡ regiſter.

When the law ſpeaks of ſeveral perſons, three at leaſt are to be underſtood; but when ſimply ſtating the circumſtance of an agreement or combination, any number not leſs than two may be implied.

No clauſe.

SECTION XLII. — *Laws relative to the Prieſthood.*

The *Tao-ſſe* and *Niu-quan* §, ſhall be ſubject in all caſes to the eſtabliſhed laws concerning the prieſthood of both orders, and both ſexes; the right and authority of the maſters and ſuperiors, and the duty of ſubmiſſion and ſubordination on the part of thoſe who are legally admitted

* The civil year in China ordinarily conſiſts of no more than 354 days, or twelve lunations, but an intercalary month is introduced as often as may be neceſſary to bring the commencement of every year to the ſecond new moon after each preceding winter ſolſtice.

† The moſt uſual date employed by the Chineſe, is the year of the reigning Emperor; but they have likewiſe, from a remote period of antiquity, computed time by cycles of 60 years, each year of ſuch period being diſtinguiſhed with a particular name, formed by a binary combination of ten initial, and twelve final, characters.

‡ As this mode of computation, which is generally in uſe among the Chineſe, is not fully explained in the text, it may be proper juſt to point out its peculiar inaccuracy, which conſiſts in its having always the effect of repreſenting the age of the individual greater than it is in reality.—Thus a child born the laſt day of the year, will, on the following day, be deſcribed as two years old, being conſidered to have lived in two of the years in the cycle.

§ The prieſts and prieſteſſes thus deſignated, and alſo thoſe of *Fo*, have uſually been deſcribed under the names of Bonzes and Bonzeſſes, which terms have probably been taken from the Japaneſe language, but the religion of the ſtate in China cannot properly be ſaid to have any prieſts whatever attached to its ſervice, the Emperor and his ordinary magiſtrates always officiating in the ſacred rites by law eſtabliſhed, as in the ritual diviſion of the code is particularly explained. The religious orders adverted to in this ſection are tolerated and regulated by government, but derive their ſupport entirely from their own funds, or from occaſional voluntary contributions.

mitted as apprentices or difciples, ſhall be the ſame as that eſtabliſhed between uncles and nephews in all ordinary caſes.

No clauſe.

Section XLIII. — *Execution of New Laws.*

All laws, characteriſed as, and intended to become, fundamental, ſhall, in general, take effect and be in full force from the day on which they are publiſhed, and every tranſaction ſhall be adjudged according to the moſt recent laws, although ſuch tranſaction ſhould have occurred previous to their promulgation. — Occaſional ſtatutes, which are modifications of the law, ſhall not however operate in thoſe caſes which were antecedent to their enactment; and when any period of days or years is aſſigned for the commencement of their operation, ſuch period ſhall be ſtrictly obſerved, except only in regard to ſtatutes providing a mitigation of the ordinary puniſhments, which ſhall be conſtrued to be immediately in force, in all caſes.

One clauſe.

Section XLIV. — *Determination of Caſes not provided for by any exiſting Law.*

From the impracticability of providing for every poſſible contingency, there may be caſes to which no laws or ſtatutes are preciſely applicable; ſuch caſes may then be determined, by an accurate compariſon with others which are already provided for, and which approach moſt nearly to thoſe under inveſtigation, in order to aſcertain afterwards to what extent an aggravation or mitigation of the puniſhment would be equitable.

A proviſional ſentence conformable thereto ſhall be laid before the ſuperior magiſtrates, and after receiving their approbation, be ſubmitted to the Emperor's final decifion.—Any erroneous judgment which may be pronounced in confequence of adopting a more fummary mode of proceeding, in cafes of a doubtful nature, fhall be punifhed as a wilful deviation from juftice.

One claufe.

SECTION XLV.—*Place of temporary and perpetual Banifhment.*

All perfons fentenced to undergo temporary banifhment, fhall be removed to the diftance of at leaft 500 *lee* from the place of their nativity, for the period fpecified in their fentence; which period fhall be computed to commence from their arrival at the place of banifhment, and from thence, at the moment the period expires, they fhall be at liberty to depart.

The place of perpetual banifhment fhall likewife be regulated according to the diftance prefcribed in the fentence pronounced on the offender, and a permanent fettlement fhall be allowed him on fuch coafts, iflands, or deferted and uncultivated diftricts, as circumftances may render moft eligible for the purpofe.—Thofe who are fentenced to the mitigated perpetual banifhment, fhall be fettled at the diftance of 1000 *lee* from the place of their nativity.—Temporary banifhment is of five kinds, but in no cafe fubjects the offender to be fent out of his native province.

Perpetual banifhment is of three kinds, and, conformably to the fentence, the offender fhall be banifhed to the nearer or more remote parts of the following provinces:

From	Pe-che-lee	to	Shen-fee
	Kiang-nan		Shen-fee
	Gan-wey		Shan-tung
	Shan-tung		Che-kiang
	Shan-fee		Shen-fee

From

From		to	
From	Ho-nan	to	Che-kiang
	Shen-fee		Shan-tung
	Kan-foo		Se-chuen
	Che-kiang		Shan-tung
	Kiang-fee		Quang-fee
	Hou-pe		Shan-tung
	Hou-nan		Se-chuen
	Fo-kien		Quang-tung
	Quang-tung		Fo-kien
	Quang-fee		Quang-tung
	Se-chuen		Quang-fee
	Quei-cheu		Se-chuen
	Yun-nan		Se-chuen.

Forty-feven claufes.

SECTION XLVI. — *Place of extraordinary or military Banifhment* *.

The feveral degrees of extraordinary or military banifhment, are, the ordinary or 2000 *lee*; the diftant or 2500 *lee*; the more diftant or 3000 *lee*, and the moft diftant or 4000 *lee*; and conformably to the fentence, the offenders fhall be perpetually banifhed in the manner hereafter provided; the fettlement of thofe banifhed from Pekin being determined by the tribunal for military affairs, and of thofe banifhed

* Befide the feveral degrees of banifhment defcribed in this and the preceding fection, a more fevere punifhment, of a fimilar defcription, has been introduced fince the original formation of the code by the prefent dynafty, and amounts to tranfportation to, and flavery for life at, *Elee*, a government ftation in a remote province of Tartary, annexed by the late Emperor *Kien-long*, to the dominions of China. This fpecies of punifhment is either inflicted as a mitigation of the fentence in certain capital cafes, or in aggravation of the punifhment of crimes, whofe frequency had increafed, as ftated in the Emperor *Kaung-hee's* introductory preface.—The numerous fupplementary claufes annexed to the preceding fection defcribe thefe regulations in detail.

from

from the provinces, by the different viceroys and ſub-viceroys; due information and notice ſhall alſo be given in the latter caſe to the ſaid tribunal, or ſupreme board for military affairs, upon each occaſion. The baniſhment ſhall, according to the ſentence, be adjudged to one or other of the following provinces *:

From Pe-che-lee to Shan-tung, or Shan-ſee, or Kiang-nan, or Hou-quang, or Shen-ſee, or Che-kiang, or Kiang-ſee, or Quang-tung.

From Kiang-nan to Hou-quang, or Shan-tung, or Che-kiang, or Shen-ſee, or Che-lee, or Shan-ſee, or Quang-tung.

From Shan-tung, to Teng-cheou-foo, or Che-lee, or Kiang-nan, or Shan-ſee, or Che-kiang, or Shen-ſee, or Quang-tung.

From Shan-ſee to Shan-tung, or Kiang-nan, or Shen-ſee, or Hou-quang, or Che-kiang, or Kiang-ſee, or Quang-tung.

From Ho-nan to Shan-tung, or Shen-ſee, or Hou-quang, or Che-lee, or Kian-nan, or Shen-ſee, or Che-kiang, or Quang-tung.

From Shen-ſee to Ning-hia-wey, or Ho-cheu-wey; or Che-lee, or Shan-ſee, or Sing-tu-ſee, or Shan-tung, or Hou-quang, or Kiang-nan, or Quang-tung.

From Che-kiang to Kiang-nan, or Shan-tung, or Hou-quang, or Che-lee, or Shan-ſee, or Shen-ſee, or Quang-tung.

From Kiang-ſee to Shan-tung, or Che-kiang, or Hou-quang, or Quang-tung, or Che-lee, or Shan-ſee, or Shen-ſee, or Se-chuen.

From Hou-quang to Nang-yang-foo, or Kiang-ſee, or Che-kiang, or Se-chuen, or Kiang-nan, or Shan-ſee, or Shen-ſee, or Che-lee, or Quang-tung.

* The enumeration which is here given of provinces and diſtricts in China, may ſeem very unimportant, but being printed in the original Chineſe work, as a part of the fundamental law, it has been retained in its place, in conformity to the general rule of ſelection which the tranſlator has preſcribed to himſelf, conceiving it to be (as already ſtated in another place) the leaſt liable to objection.

From

From Fo-kien to Che-kiang, or Kiang-ſee, or Kiang-nan, or Quang-tung, or Hou-quang, or Shan-tung, or Che-lee, or Se-chuen.

From Quang-tung to Chao-cheu-foo, or Hou-quang, or Shan-ſee, or Se-chuen, or Shan-tung.

From Quang-ſee to Kiang-ſee, or Hou-quang, or Se-chuen, or Shan-ſee, or Shen-ſee, or Che-kiang, or Quang-tung.

From Se-chuen to Yue-hee-wey, or Shen-ſee, or Hou-quang, or Kiang-ſee, or Shan-ſee, or Che-kiang, or Quang-tung.

From Que-cheu to Se-chuen, or Kiang-ſee, or Hou-quang, or Shen-ſee, or Kiang-nan, or Che-kiang, or Shan-ſee, or Quang-tung.

From Yun-nan to Quang-tung, or Hou-quang, or Shen-ſee, or Kiang-ſee.

Two clauſes.

END OF THE FIRST DIVISION.

SECOND DIVISION,

Civil Laws *.

BOOK I.

SYSTEM OF GOVERNMENT.

SECTION XLVII. — *Hereditary Succeſſion* †.

EVERY civil and military officer of government, whoſe rank and titles are hereditary, ſhall be ſucceeded in them by his eldeſt ſon born of his principal wife, or by ſuch eldeſt ſon's ſurviving legal repreſentative, choſen according to the general rule here provided.

If ſuch eldeſt ſon, and all thoſe who might legally have repreſented him are deceaſed, or incapacitated to ſucceed to the inheritance by incurable illneſs or miſconduct, the ſon next in age, or his ſurviving legal repreſentative choſen as aforeſaid, ſhall be called to the ſucceſſion.

When there are neither any ſons, nor any legal repreſentatives of ſuch ſons, by the principal wife, capable of ſucceeding, the ſeveral ſons of the other wives, and their legal repreſentatives, ſhall be entitled thereto according to ſeniority; upon failure of whom, the ſuc-

* Laws relating to the adminiſtration of the civil government.

† Although titles deſcendible to the heirs male are occaſionally conferred in China by the Emperor, as a reward for eminent ſervices, they are reſumable by the Crown at pleaſure, and the poſſeſſors of them enjoy few, if any, excluſive privileges.—None of the hereditary dignities which exiſted previous to the Tartar conqueſt in 1644, appear to have been recognized by the preſent government, except that attached to the family of Confucius, whoſe real or ſuppoſed deſcendants are at this day diſtinguiſhed with peculiar titles of honour, and maintained at the public expence.

ceſſion

ceſſion ſhall laſtly devolve upon the ſons of the younger brothers, taken in the order already mentioned. — Whoever enters upon the ſucceſſion to an hereditary dignity, in violation of the order preſcribed by this law, ſhall be puniſhed for ſuch offence with 100 blows and three years baniſhment.

When the claim of a ſon or grandſon to the ſucceſſion has been duly authenticated by the proper magiſtrate, it muſt be reported to the council of ſtate, through which channel it will be ſubmitted to the Emperor for ratification, and alſo for the authority to continue to the heir the emolument which may have been annexed to the dignity. —If the heir is a minor, he ſhall not be enrolled for public ſervice at Court, until he attains the age of eighteen years.

When the family title is extinct for want of lineal male heirs to ſucceed to the hereditary dignities; the widow of the laſt poſſeſſor ſhall receive the emoluments annexed thereto, during her life.

If a ſtranger's child is educated and brought up in a family of rank, in order, by deceiving the magiſtrates, to obtain the inheritance, ſuch ſuppoſititious heir ſhall receive 100 blows, and be ſent into remote baniſhment; the emoluments annexed to the rank ſhall alſo ceaſe from the time that ſuch fraudulent intention was diſcovered. — Whoever inſtructs and inſtigates others to commit this offence, ſhall ſuffer the ſame puniſhment.

Thoſe magiſtrates alſo, who connive at the fraud, and ratify the ſucceſſion, ſhall be equally puniſhed, as participating in the offence; but if really ignorant of the illegality of the tranſaction, they ſhall be excuſed.

If convicted at the ſame time of bribery, to ſuch an extent as, according to law, is more ſeverely puniſhable, the puniſhment of the greater offence ſhall, as in other caſes, ſuperſede that of the leſſer.

Fifteen clauſes.

SEC-

SECTION XLVIII. — *Great Officers of State not authorized to confer Appointments* *.

All the appointments and removals of officers, whether civil or military, ſhall depend ſolely upon the authority of the Emperor.—If any great officer of ſtate preſumes to confer any appointment upon his own authority, he ſhall ſuffer death by being beheaded, after remaining in priſon the uſual time.

It is likewiſe hereby prohibited to appoint or remove any relations of the great officers of ſtate, without an expreſs order from the Emperor for that purpoſe, and a breach of this regulation ſhall expoſe the offender to the ſame puniſhment as that of the preceding.

Any officer of government employed at court, and receiving the Emperor's perſonal commands to undertake the performance of any ſervice, or to reſign or change his employment, whether the object be near or remote, if he make any excuſe for not complying therewith, he ſhall receive 100 blows, and be rendered incapable of holding any office under government thenceforward †.

One clauſe.

* The viceroys and commanders-in-chief of provinces are conſtantly in the habit of filling up the various civil and military appointments under their reſpective juriſdictions, when they become vacant, but it is always done expreſsly by virtue of the authority conferred by the Emperor, and generally ſtated to be only *ad interim*, until His Majeſty's pleaſure is known.—The object of the law in this place appears to be to prevent any of the great officers of ſtate, or principal nobility, from encroaching upon the royal prerogative, by forming a petty court or principality, dependent on themſelves; an offence of this deſcription was the ſubject of one of the leading charges againſt *Ho-chung-tong*, the miniſter and favourite of the late Emperor, an account of whoſe trial and condemnation is given in the Appendix, No. VIII.

† The puniſhments to which officers of government are ſtated in any particular inſtance to be liable, muſt always be underſtood to be ſubject to the modifications provided by the VIth, VIIth, and VIIIth Sections, and alſo by the clauſes to the Firſt Section, inſerted in No. V. of the Appendix.

SECTION XLIX. — *Officers of Government not allowed to ſolicit hereditary Honours.*

When any officers of the civil department of government, who have not diſtinguiſhed themſelves by extraordinary and great ſervices to the ſtate, are recommended to the conſideration of the Emperor, as deſerving of the higheſt hereditary honours; ſuch officers, and thoſe who recommend them, ſhall ſuffer death, by being beheaded, after remaining the uſual period in priſon.

Nevertheleſs, thoſe who are recommended to ſuch honours in conſequence of their being the lineal deſcendants of diſtinguiſhed officers and magiſtrates, who by their valour and exertions had averted national calamities, protected the empire, and contributed to the eſtabliſhment of the Imperial Family, ſhall be free from any liability to the penalties of this law.

No clauſe.

SECTION L. — *Supernumerary Officers of Government.*

In every public office and tribunal, whether at court or in the provinces, the number of officers to be regularly employed in each, is permanently eſtabliſhed by law *, and whoever ſhall appoint, or cauſe to

* A detailed deſcription of the manner in which the ſeveral public offices and tribunals are conſtituted, and of their reſpective powers and functions, in carrying on the buſineſs of government, does not form a conſtituent part of the preſent work, although enough is ſtated on the ſubject, indirectly and incidentally, to afford, when conſidered together, a ſufficiently correct idea of the general ſyſtem.—To furniſh details of this kind, is one of the leading objects of another Chineſe work, entiled *Ta Tſing Hoey Tien*, or the Great general Code of the preſent Dynaſty, and which may be conſidered as the official account of the political conſtitution of China in its ſeveral branches, though it has been deſcribed in ſome of the works of the miſſionaries, rather improperly, as the legal code of the empire; and in terms, which excite more curioſity, than a tranſlation of the work, if it could be executed, would be likely

to be appointed any one ſupernumerary officer, ſhall be puniſhed with 100 blows, and one degree more ſeverely for every three ſupernumeraries ſo appointed, as far as 100 blows and three years baniſhment, beyond which degree the puniſhment ſhall not be increaſed, unleſs the party ſhall have been likewiſe convicted of bribery to ſuch an amount as may, by law, aggravate the puniſhment due to him.

Any perſon alſo, who employs, or cauſes to be employed, more than the eſtabliſhed number of the clerks, or of the civil and military attendants of a tribunal or public office, ſhall be puniſhed with 100 blows and two years baniſhment.

Any officer knowingly permitting one ſuch ſupernumerary to continue in the employ of government, ſhall be liable to the puniſhment of 20 blows, if the ſaid officer be a preſiding magiſtrate; to 30 blows, if a deputy; and to 40 blows, if a chief clerk of ſuch office or tribunal. — For every three ſupernumeraries thus ſuffered to remain in employ, the puniſhment ſhall be increaſed one degree, to any proportionate extent, not exceeding the limit of 100 blows.

The ſupernumerary ſhall not in theſe caſes be liable to any puniſhment. —If any perſons, who had formerly been officers or clerks in the ſervice of government, interfere in any manner in the adminiſtration of the public ſervice, by writing orders, and pretending to poſſeſs authority, or by any other means extort money from and oppreſs the people, they ſhall, at the leaſt, be puniſhed with 80 blows, and fined 20 *leang* or ounces of ſilver, which ſum ſhall be paid to the perſon informing againſt them; the corporal puniſhment ſhall, under any aggravating circumſtances,

likely to gratify. See the *Memoires ſur les Chinois*, vol. iv. page 220. and vol. viii. page 127. —Of this work, (*The Ta-Tsing Hoey Tieng*) in which a comparatively ſmall portion of curious matter is buried in a prodigious maſs of details of very inferior intereſt, the tranſlator is enabled to ſpeak from ſome degree of perſonal knowledge, having a copy in his poſſeſſion, conſiſting of 144 thin volumes, printed in the year 1764, the 29th of the reign of the late Emperor *Kien Lung*.

be

be as much more ſevere, as the laws in ſuch caſes provide.—Nevertheleſs, if the regular officers of government only hire the aforeſaid perſons occaſionally to aſſiſt when neceſſary in collecting the duties, or in completing the regiſters of the people, their employment ſhall not be conſidered as a breach of this law.

Four clauſes.

SECTION LI.—*Tranſmiſſion of Official Diſpatches.*

The official meſſengers who are employed in the ſeveral diſtricts of the empire under the juriſdiction of the cities of the firſt, ſecond, and third order*, for the tranſmiſſion of diſpatches relative to ordinary public buſineſs, or to the puniſhment of public tranſgreſſors, ſhall perform the ſervices upon which they are reſpectively employed, within the periods which, with a due regard to the diſtance, and other circumſtances, are in each caſe by law eſtabliſhed. For one day's delay beyond the legal period, they ſhall be liable to a puniſhment of 10 blows, which ſhall be increaſed one degree, until it amounts to 40 blows, for every additional day's delay.—If the governing magiſtrates in any of the

* The Chineſe empire is divided, in the firſt inſtance, into 18 provinces, which are governed either by a viceroy (*Tſong-too*), or a ſub-viceroy (*Foo-yuen*), or by two ſuch officers having a concurrent juriſdiction. Each province is ſubdivided into diſtricts under the government of the magiſtrates of the ſeveral cities of the firſt order, and theſe governments are again divided into ſmaller juriſdictions, whoſe magiſtrates are governors of cities of the ſecond or third in the empire.

According to one of the lateſt editions of the Chineſe Imperial Court Kalendar, there are 11 officers bearing the title of viceroy, 15 that of ſub-viceroy, 19 provincial treaſurers, 18 provincial judges, and 17 provincial examiners for degrees; alſo 184 governors of cities of the firſt order, 212 governors of cities of the ſecond, and 1305 of the third. Theſe numbers are nearly the ſame with thoſe ſtated in the authentic account of the Britiſh Embaſſy to China; but as the enumeration in the works of Du Halde and Groſier, differ from the above, and from each other, it was conſidered deſirable to give theſe particulars from an authority that might be conſidered as deciſive.

afore-

afore-mentioned diſtricts and diviſions of command, do not, when the adminiſtration of public affairs requires, ſend immediately the neceſſary orders and inſtructions to the officers ſubject to their authority, ſuch neglect ſhall be puniſhed with 100 blows.

The attention due to the repairing and inſpecting of roads and bridges; to accidents and affrays; to the ſeizing of criminals; confiſcation of property, and to any other ſuch ſpecific objects, being noticed and enforced elſewhere in this code, the neglect thereof is not to be puniſhed as a breach of this general article.

Two clauſes.

SECTION LII. — *Partiality in the Examination of Candidates for Degrees* *.

Whoever confers degrees of honour on perſons who are not worthy, or who are under any diſqualifications; and whoever, on the contrary, refuſes at the proper time to confer ſuch degrees upon thoſe who are entitled to them by their merit, as well as duly qualified, ſhall be puniſhed with 80 blows for a ſingle inſtance of ſuch offence, and one degree more ſeverely, as far as 100 blows, for every

* Theſe degrees have generally been conſidered as ſimilar to thoſe conferred upon ſtudents in European univerſities; but it is to be obſerved, that in China the examinations are not connected with any particular eſtabliſhments or ſyſtem of education, but conducted periodically by officers appointed by government, at each of the chief cities of the empire, and that they are, with few exceptions, open to all claſſes and deſcriptions whatſoever; the degrees alſo, inſtead of being merely literary, are, in fact, the ſole regular channel of introduction to official employment, and conſequently to rank and honours, in the empire.

With reſpect to the Tartars, theſe examinations are either wholly diſpenſed with, or very much relaxed in point of rigour, as well as conducted according to a different ſyſtem. The Chineſe are ſometimes enabled, by the means of their wealth, to obviate a part of the difficulties attending their progreſs by an authorized commutation, but there is no reaſon to believe, that the legal enquiry into the qualifications of the candidates can in any inſtance be altogether evaded.—Thoſe degrees which are partly obtained by purchaſe, although legal, are accounted leſs honourable. On this ſubject, ſee the Appendix, No. XII. containing a tranſlation of an Imperial Edict, extracted from the Pekin Gazette of the 23d of April 1800.

two

two additional inftances which may be proved upon investigation. If the individual fo improperly graduated is aware of his being ineligible, he fhall be punifhed as a participator in the offence, but otherwife fhall be held innocent.

If the prefiding examiner of the merits of the candidates defignedly makes a falfe report in any inftance, by elevating or depreffing their refpective claims, the punifhment of fuch examiner fhall be two degrees lefs than that of the officer who confers the degrees improperly*. If the report is erroneous, but not defignedly falfe, the punifhment fhall be lefs by three degrees, but liable in all cafes to be increafed whenever there is a conviction of bribery and corruption.

Seven claufes.

Section LIII. — *Relative to Officers of Government difmiffed for Mifconduct.*

When any officer of government has been tried for an offence, condemned to lofe his employment, and rendered incapable of fervice to the ftate, none of the members of any public office or tribunal fhall (regardlefs of fuch conviction) become refponfible for him, or take him again into employ.—Whoever employs fuch convicted perfon, in violation of this law, fhall be punifhed with 100 blows; the fame punifhment fhall likewife be inflicted on the party himfelf, and he fhall continue, as before, incapacitated to enter the public fervice.

When, however, an individual is difmiffed for inability, and not for corruption, or any other criminal practices, he may be employed whenever the officers into whofe department he is to be received, having examined him, pledge themfelves that he is duly qualified.

Nine claufes.

* It is evident from the gradations obferved in punifhing the mifconduct of thefe officers, that the department of the latter is of greater importance than the words feem to imply, but the text does not otherwife indicate the nature of their refpective functions.

Sec-

SECTION LIV. — *Officers of Government quitting their Stations without Leave.*

All civil and military officers, and their official attendants, whether at court or in the provinces, are prohibited from leaving their refpective ftations, except it be on account of ficknefs, or upon the public fervice, and fhall be punifhed with 40 blows for every breach of this law.—If they fhould abfent themfelves for the fake of avoiding the execution of any unpleafant or difficult part of their duty, fuch as the collection of taxes, or the feizure of criminals, they fhall be punifhed with 100 blows, as fugitives, and at the fame time difmiffed from their employments, as well as rendered for ever incapable of the public fervice. They fhall, moreover, be liable to any aggravation of the punifhment which may arife from the nature of the duty, the performance of which they had avoided.

As, for inftance: if a civil officer, appointed to fuperintend the fupplying of provifions to an army, fhould defert while the troops are in the field, the offence would be aggravated by the injury which might refult therefrom to the ftate, upon fuch a critical juncture.

If, in ordinary cafes, any officer or attendant of government is not on guard by day, or on watch by night, when it is his duty to be fo, he fhall be punifhed with 20 blows for fuch offence; but the punifhment fhall be increafed to 40 blows in every inftance of fimilar neglect, on the part of thofe who have the cuftody of granaries, treafuries, or prifons, or of any other places of fimilar importance.

It is only neceffary to carry this law into effect, when no injury nor lofs has enfued from the neglect above-mentioned, as in regard to the offence under fuch aggravated circumftances, particular punifhments are elfewhere provided.

Two claufes.

SECTION LV. — *Officers of Government to proceed to their Deſtinations without Delay.*

When a change has been determined to be made in the adminiſtration of any department of the public ſervice, the duty of the officer newly appointed, if at the court, ſhall commence from the delivery over of the charge; if in the provinces, from the receipt of the official order from the ſupreme council.—If, after ſuch period, the newly appointed officer ſhould, without aſſigning a ſufficient cauſe, unneceſſarily delay one day in proceeding to his ſtation, he ſhall incur a puniſhment of 10 blows; for every further delay of ten days, the puniſhment ſhall be increaſed one degree, until it amount to 80 blows; but in all ſuch caſes, the offender ſhall ſtill retain his new appointment.

Upon the arrival of a ſucceſſor, the officer in poſſeſſion ſhall, within the time, and in the manner preſcribed by law, make up and cloſe his ſeveral accounts relative to the collection of the revenue, and the execution of the laws againſt tranſgreſſors, that the ſaid accounts may be delivered over to the officer appointed to receive them: when the ſame is concluded, if the officer who had delivered up his charge remains on the ſpot, without aſſigning a ſufficient reaſon for ſo doing, more than ten days, he ſhall be puniſhed for ſuch delay two degrees leſs than is provided in caſes of officers not proceeding in due time to their new appointments.

If an officer of government is detained by winds or other obſtacles, is plundered by thieves, falls ſick, or loſes a parent, ſo as in any way to be prevented from proceeding to his deſtination, he ſhall make a due and circumſtantial report thereof to the proper magiſtrates, that it may be aſcertained by them whether the delay did not take place without ſufficient cauſe, or with ſome ſiniſter view; in either of which caſes ſuch miſconduct ſhall be puniſhed as the laws preſcribe.—If the magiſtrates receiving the report are guilty

of

of any improper partiality or collufion, they fhall be equally punifhable.

Five claufes.

SECTION LVI. — *Attendance of Officers of Government at Court.*

When an officer of government belonging to any of the interior departments, whatever may be his rank, does not prefent himfelf at court within due time; or, if belonging to a provincial government, he does not prefent himfelf at head-quarters; or laftly, when an officer of government, in either cafe, after having obtained a leave of abfence, does not return to his ftation as foon as his leave of abfence is expired, he muft give fufficient reafon for fuch omiffion, without which he will be punifhable with 10 blows for one day's delay; and one degree more feverely for every further delay of three days, until the fame amounts to 80 blows; but the tranfgreffion fhall not occafion the difmiffal or degradation of the party offending.

No claufe.

SECTION LVII. — *Irregular interference of Superiors with fubordinate Magiftrates.*

When any public meafure originates in a fuperior court or tribunal, it fhall be put upon record, and a period fixed for its execution:—A mandate fhall then be iffued, or a fpecial meffenger difpatched, to the inferior tribunals for their information and guidance.

If the officers of fuch inferior tribunals fhould afterwards be convicted of any error or delay in the execution of their duty, they fhall be punifhed according to the laws; but if the fuperior magiftrate unnecessarily interferes with, or fuperfedes, the determinations of an inferior tribunal, by fending for any of the clerks or members thereof, or by fending to them any of his own officers, by which interference or fuperfeffion the due courfe of juftice is impeded, the fuperior magiftrate fhall be punifhed with 40 blows, and the inferior magiftrate who confents to, and concurs therein, or permits the clerks to receive fuch irregular inftructions, fhall be liable to the fame punifhment.

Neverthelefs, in all ferious criminal or intricate revenue cafes, in which interference or confultation is requifite, it fhall be lawful to fummon the attendance of the members of the inferior tribunals; but they fhall be difmiffed immediately upon the termination of the inquiry.—If unneceffarily detained three days, the fuperior fhall be punifhed with 20 blows, and one degree more feverely, as far as 50 blows, for every additional three days detention *.

No claufe.

Section LVIII. — *Cabals and State Intrigues.*

Whoever, with malicious defign, provokes and excites by artful language any perfon, as yet innocent of a capital offence, to commit murder, fhall for fuch offence fuffer death, by being beheaded after the ufual period of confinement.

If any great officer of ftate is convicted of a crime, which according to the laws is deferving of death, and any of the inferior officers of govern-

* How far the inferior tribunals of juftice, and other departments of government, are connected with, and fubject to, the authority of their refpective fuperiors, will be beft underftood by a reference to particular inftances; and partly with this view, a tranflation of the official reports of fome remarkable legal proceedings have been introduced into the Appendix, each of which will be fpecifically referred to in its proper place.

As the inveftigation of all capital cafes muft pafs through every ftep, from the tribunal of the loweft magiftrate, to the throne of the Emperor; and as there is, generally fpeaking, a right of appeal through the fame channel in all cafes, whether civil or criminal, partiality and injuftice could, according to fuch a fyftem, fcarcely ever efcape detection and punifhment, if the interference and collufion above adverted to, did not, whenever it takes place, render the appeal hopelefs, and the repetition of the inveftigation nugatory.

ment,

ment, by artful repreſentations, endeavour to conceal his guilt and ſcreen him from puniſhment, in order to gain his good-will, they ſhall likewiſe ſuffer death, by being beheaded after the uſual period of confinement.

If any of the officers about the court cabal and combine together, in order to impede and obſtruct the meaſures of His Imperial Majeſty's government, all the parties to ſuch cabal, without diſtinguiſhing between principals and acceſſaries, ſhall be beheaded after the uſual period of confinement; their wives and children ſhall become ſlaves, and their fortunes ſhall be confiſcated *. — If the ſupreme court of judicature, or any other ſubordinate court of juſtice, ſhould refrain from carrying the laws into effect, in compliance with the wiſhes of any ſuperior magiſtrate, and ſhould unjuſtly aggravate or mitigate the puniſhment of offenders agreeably to the dictates of ſuch ſuperior, the offence ſhall be conſidered to come within the penalties of this law.

On the other hand, if the officers of any inferior court ſhould diſregard ſuch unlawful interpoſition, and, drawing up a faithful report thereof, as well as of any attempt that may have been made at ſubornation, lay the ſame perſonally before the Emperor, the puniſhment ſhall fall upon the ſuperior magiſtrate only, and the complainant ſhall not only be pardoned for any previous compliance with unjuſt commands, of which he might have been guilty, but rewarded with the whole of the confiſcated property of the offender.

If the complainant is an officer of government, he ſhall be raiſed in rank two degrees; if not an officer of government, he ſhall receive a ſuitable office or, if not deſirous of office, a further reward, inſtead thereof, ſhall be given to him of 2000 *leang* or ounces of ſilver.

No clauſe.

* See the Laws relative to Treaſonable Offences in general, in their proper place.

SEC-

SECTION LIX. — *Combination and Collufion between Provincial Officers and Officers of the Court.*

Any combination and collufion between the officers of the feveral tribunals of juftice throughout the empire, and the officers of the court in the immediate attendance on His Majefty, the object of which may be either, the betraying the fecrets of the State, unwarrantable pretenfions to offices of power and emolument, or joint addreffes to the Sovereign for private and unlawful purpofes, fhall fubject all the parties guilty of fuch an offence, to fuffer death, by being beheaded after the ufual period of confinement. — Their wives and children fhall be perpetually banifhed to the diftance of 2000 *lee*, and at the place of banifhment, be allowed to form new eftablifhments.

Neverthelefs, when the connexion and intercourfe between fuch parties fhall have arifen merely from their relationfhip to each other, and without any view to the unwarrantable objects above ftated, this law fhall not be put in force.

No claufe.

SECTION LX. — *Addreffes in favour of Great Officers of State.*

If an officer belonging to any of the departments of government, or any private individual, fhould addrefs the Emperor in praife of the virtues, abilities, or fuccefsful adminiftration, of any of His Majefty's confidential Minifters of State, it is to be confidered as an evidence of the exiftence of a treafonable combination fubverfive of government, and fhall therefore be inveftigated with the utmoft ftrictnefs and accuracy: the caufe and origin of thefe interefted praifes of perfons high in rank and office being traced, the offending party fhall fuffer death, by being beheaded,

beheaded, after remaining in prifon the ufual period.—His wives and children fhall become flaves, and his property fhall be confifcated.

If the confidential minifter or great officer of the crown, to whom the addrefs related, was privy to the defign, he fhall participate in the punifhment of the offence; but otherwife, fhall be excufed *.

One claufe.

* The feverity of the law in this, and in the fections immediately preceding, is probably grounded upon fome confiderations which are not explained in the text; but it is obvious, that the punifhments are not directed fo much at the acts themfelves, as at the treafonable motives they are fuppofed to indicate.

END OF THE FIRST BOOK OF THE SECOND DIVISION.

BOOK II.

CONDUCT OF THE MAGISTRATES.

SECTION LXI. — *Due Knowledge of the Laws.*

THE laws and ftatutes of the empire have been framed with deliberation, are fanctioned with appropriate penalties againft tranfgreffors, and are publifhed to the world * for perpetual obfervance.

All the officers and others in the employ of government ought to ftudy diligently, and make themfelves perfect in the knowledge of thefe laws, fo as to be able to explain clearly their meaning and intent, and to fuperintend and enfure their execution.

At the clofe of every year, the officers and other perfons employed by government, in every one of the exterior and interior departments, fhall undergo examination on this fubject before their refpective fuperiors, and if they are found in any refpect incompetent to explain the nature, or to comprehend the feveral objects, of the laws, they fhall forfeit one month's falary when holding official, and receive 40 blows when holding any of the inferior, fituations.

All thofe private individuals, whether hufbandmen, or artificers, or whatever elfe may be their calling or profeffion, who are found capable of explaining the nature, and comprehending the objects, of the laws, fhall receive pardon in all cafes of offences refulting purely from accident, or imputable to them only from the guilt of others, provided it be the firft offence, and not implicated with any act of treafon or rebellion.

* Literally, " to the Heaven-under," an expreffion fomething analogous to our epithet of fublunary, and here applied with Afiatic amplification to the Chinefe empire.

Whofoever

Whosoever, in the employ of government, fraudulently perverts or misconstrues, or presumptuously changes, abrogates or confounds the law upon any case, so as to produce disturbance and insurrection in the country, shall suffer death by being beheaded, after the usual period of imprisonment.

No clause.

Section LXII. — *Non-execution of an Imperial Edict.*

Whenever an Imperial Edict is issued on any subject, whoever wilfully omits the execution of any thing that is commanded therein, shall be punished with 100 blows. — In the case of the edict of the Imperial prince elect, the punishment shall be the same. — A failure in any such respect, from neglect or inadvertence, shall be punished three degrees less severely.

Moreover, any one who delays or postpones the execution of an Imperial edict for one day, shall be punished with 50 blows, and one degree more severely as far as 100 blows for each additional day of delay.

No clause.

Section LXIII. — *Destroying or discarding Edicts and Seals of Office.*

Whoever designedly discards or destroys an Imperial edict, or the official seal of any tribunal or department of state, shall suffer death, by being beheaded, after the usual period of confinement. — Whoever wilfully discards or destroys an edict issued by any individual officer, or by a tribunal of government, shall be punished with 100 blows, or as much more severely as the criminality of the motive may lawfully require; and if the edict destroyed or discarded concerned the affairs of war, or the supply of the army in the field with pro-

 visions,

viſions, the offence ſhall be puniſhed with death, and the offender ſtrangled, after the uſual period of confinement. — If the ſuperior officer of the offender is privy to the offence, and does not take cognizance of it, he ſhall be conſidered as equally guilty, and participate in the full extent of the puniſhment, excepting only a reduction of one degree in capital caſes. — When he is not aware of the offence having been committed, he ſhall be altogether excuſed. — Deſtroying, in any of the foregoing inſtances unintentionally, but through inadvertence, is puniſhable three degree leſs ſeverely than the wilful offence; and if it can be clearly ſhewn, that the diſcarding or deſtroying was the unavoidable conſequence of fire, water, or thieves, the puniſhment ſhall be remitted altogether.

Whoever loſes an imperial edict, or a ſeal of office, ſhall be puniſhed with 90 blows and two years and a half's baniſhment: if an edict of an officer of government, with 70 blows only; but in caſe ſuch edict concerns the affairs of war, or ſupplies for the army, the puniſhment ſhall be increaſed to 90 blows and two years and a half's baniſhment.

Immediately upon aſcertaining ſuch a loſs to have occurred, the payment of the ſalary of the offending party ſhall be ſuſpended; but if he is able to recover the official document that was loſt, within the ſpace of thirty days, he ſhall be pardoned; if not able to do ſo within ſuch period, the execution of his puniſhment ſhall not on any account be further delayed.

If an officer, having charge of government property, loſes his books and regiſters, whereby error or confuſion is introduced into the accounts of the revenue in ſtore, he ſhall be liable to ſuffer 80 blows, but allowed a ſufficient period to retrieve himſelf from ſuch puniſhment by the recovery of the documents that were miſſing.

The clerks of all public offices, upon the expiration of their reſpective terms of ſervice, ſhall deliver over to their ſucceſſors, all the books of official accounts, with a diſtinct record in each caſe of the actual balance,

and

and of the ſtate of the accounts in each department at the time when the transfer of the charge takes place, and any failure or neglect in theſe reſpects ſhall be puniſhed with 80 blows.—The deputy or executive officers of the ſeveral tribunals or public boards, ſhall be liable to ſimilar puniſhment, if they do not likewiſe aſcertain and verify the ſtate of each of the ſeveral accounts, whenever any ſuch transfers are effected.

Five clauſes.

SECTION LXIV. — *Errors and Informalities in public Documents.*

Whoever, in addreſſing the Emperor, irreverently, or inadvertently, makes uſe of His Imperial Majeſty's appellative, or that of any of his Imperial predeceſſors, ſhall, for ſuch offence, be puniſhed with 80 blows:—if the ſame is introduced improperly into any public document, not addreſſed as aforeſaid, the puniſhment ſhall be limited to 40 blows.—Whoever aſſumes for himſelf or others, any one of ſuch ſacred appellatives, thus employing it as the name of a private individual, ſhall be puniſhed with 100 blows:—Nevertheleſs, it ſhall not be conſidered as a violation of ſuch ſacred names, if in any caſe the ſound only is imitated *, or if only one of the characters of the name is employed †.—If any miſtake or error is committed in the ſtatements or ſuggeſtions contained in an addreſs to His Majeſty, the conſequence whereof may be injurious to the public ſervice; as, for inſtance, writing "inexcuſable" inſtead of "excuſable," writing "10 ſtone weight" inſtead of "1000 "ſtone weight ‡," the offender ſhall be puniſhed with 60 blows.

* The choice of ſounds in the Chineſe language is confined within ſuch narrow limits in compariſon to that of written words or characters, that any accidental agreement in the former reſpect, is not ſufficient to produce an equivoque, and therefore not deemed in theſe inſtances an act of diſreſpect to the Sovereign or His Imperial Family.

† Perſonal appellatives generally conſiſt of two words or characters, and family names of one only.

‡ The difference between the character expreſſing 10 and that expreſſing 1000 is not more than a ſingle ſtroke of the pencil.

 If

If a ſimilar error occurs in a report to any of the ſupreme courts, the puniſhment ſhall amount to 40 blows; and if in any official documents of an inferior deſcription, to 20 blows.—Nevertheleſs, ſuch errors as are of a trifling nature, and do not ſo materially alter the ſenſe of the record, as to impede the public ſervice, ſhall be excuſed, and therefore excepted from the operation of this law.

No clauſe.

SECTION LXV.—*Neglecting to make ſuch Reports to ſuperior Officers as are by Law required.*

When offences are committed by perſons entitled to privilege by law, if the officer of government, to whoſe department it belongs to take cogniſance thereof, does not report ſuch offences to the Emperor, or if he does not ſpecify the privilege to which the offending party is entitled, it ſhall be held to be a capital offence, but puniſhed only with five years baniſhment, as ordered in other capital offences of a miſcellaneous nature*.—When offences are committed by civil or military officers, the ſentence upon whom requires the Emperor's ratification before it can be legally executed, any omiſſion to lay the ſame before the Emperor ſhall be puniſhed with 100 blows, or as much more ſeverely as the circumſtances of the caſe may authorize by other laws ſpecifically applicable thereto.—The neglect to report to the Emperor any circumſtance of military affairs, concerning the revenue, legiſlation, ſelection of magiſtrates, puniſhments, public calamities, or any extraordinary circumſtances which by law it is requiſite to report to His Majeſty, ſhall be puniſhed with 80 blows.—Similar

* The cauſe of certain offences, which are puniſhed in each caſe with five years baniſhment, being denominated capital offences of a miſcellaneous nature, is not explained in the text, but it is probable that this form of expreſſion is retained for no other purpoſe, than that of preſerving a nominal uniformity, with a pre-eſtabliſhed ſyſtem in the adjuſtment of puniſhments, which in theſe inſtances is practically abandoned.

neglect

neglect to report to a ſuperior magiſtrate, what by law ought to be reported, ſhall be puniſhed with 40 blows.

Whoever, after having made a due report according to the laws, either to his immediate ſuperior in office, or to the Emperor, proceeds notwithſtanding to execute the laws upon the caſe, without waiting for the arrival of further inſtructions, ſhall be liable to the ſame puniſhment, (capital caſes excepted) that the law would have awarded had no report whatever been made.

When any tribunal or department of government addreſſes the Emperor upon affairs of ſtate, the members thereof ſhall report collectively their judgment on the caſe, agreeably to the laws applicable thereto, and, the ſtatement of the ſame being clearly drawn up, all thoſe who were parties to the deliberation thereon, ſhall affix their names.

If, in ſuch a report, the circumſtances of any important affair of ſtate are aggravated, palliated, or otherwiſe miſrepreſented, ſo as to miſlead His Majeſty, and fraudulently to obtain his royal orders conformably to ſuch falſe ſtatement, (although the deception ſhould not be diſcovered until an indefinite time after the orders were carried into effect), the authors thereof, whenever the truth is brought to light, ſhall be beheaded. — Upon any viſitation from the ſuperior magiſtrate, the officers of the inferior tribunal ſhall, previous to any joint deciſion upon official buſineſs, ſtate the circumſtances fully and in due order, together with the arguments for or againſt any propoſed arrangement, which, being duly regiſtered and authenticated by the ſignature of the parties, ſhall remain as an evidence of their proceedings, for reference upon any future inveſtigation.

If the inferior magiſtrate brings forward any improper propoſal, and by a falſe or inadequate explanation thereof, obtains, or pretends to have obtained, the conſent of his ſuperior, ſuch conduct ſhall be puniſhed according to the law againſt a falſe interpretation of the orders

orders of government, and as much more ſeverely as the circumſtances of the caſe may authorize.

Two clauſes.

SECTION LXVI. — *Officers on detached Service not reporting their Proceedings.*

Whoever, when detached upon any particular ſervice by an Imperial mandate, does not render an account of ſuch of his proceedings, upon the reſult of which other buſineſs may be depending, ſhall be puniſhed with 100 blows.

When detached on ſervice by a mandate of any tribunal or department of government, and failing to render an account of the proceedings undertaken in conſequence, the puniſhment ſhall likewiſe be 100 blows, provided military or other affairs of much importance are depending; if only ordinary affairs are depending, the puniſhment ſhall be limited to 70 blows.

If any perſon, acting under ſuch eſpecial authority, exceeds the limits of his commiſſion, and encroaches upon the province of others, he ſhall be puniſhed with 50 blows. — If the individual employed under an Imperial mandate, does not deliver up his powers or credentials within three days after his return, he ſhall be puniſhed with 60 blows, and one degree more ſeverely, as far as 100 blows, for every additional delay of two days, until ſuch token of his reſignation.

In like manner, when acting under any government commiſſion ſpecially iſſued by a public office, and not reſtoring or reſigning the ſame within the above period after his return, ſuch individual ſhall be puniſhed with 40 blows, and one degree more ſeverely as far as 80 blows, for each additional three days delay. —— In all caſes, if the offence puniſhable by this law, is connected with any aggravating circumſtances,

cumſtances, the puniſhment ſhall be increaſed to any extent that the laws applicable thereto may warrant.

No clauſe.

SECTION LXVII. — *Delay in expediting the Edicts of Government.*

When an edict or authentic act of any public office or tribunal is neglected to be expedited, the clerk of ſuch office or tribunal ſhall be puniſhed, for one day's delay, with 10 blows; and one degree more ſeverely, as far as 40 blows, for each three days further delay. — The deputies of the tribunal, being the immediate ſuperintendants of the clerks, ſhall be liable to puniſhment only leſs by one degree; but the ſuperior members thereof ſhall not be held reſponſible.

When any public board or tribunal receives a report upon official buſineſs from a ſubordinate department, the officers of the former ſhall proceed forthwith to examine into, and deliberate upon the propoſals therein ſubmitted to their deciſion, and having determined on the expedency of confirming, or rejecting the ſame, they ſhall iſſue their orders accordingly. — If, on the contrary, they reply equivocally and indiſtinctly, inſtead of giving any deciſion, ſo that the queſtions are repeatedly propoſed and remanded, and the public ſervice thereby materially injured and delayed, the officers of the ſuperior tribunal ſhall be puniſhed with 80 blows, for every ſuch attempt to avoid the reſponſibility which is attached to the performance of their public duty.

In like manner, if the officers of an inferior tribunal receive orders relative to a meaſure which is fit and practicable, and yet, inſtead of carrying it into effect, they, under pretence of doubts on the ſubject, refer it again to the conſideration of their ſuperiors, their puniſhment ſhall be the ſame as that provided in the caſe laſt ſtated.

Eight clauſes.

SEC-

SECTION LXVIII. — *Examination of official Records.*

The records of all ſuch public offices as have a ſpecific command, and a public ſeal, ſhall be regularly examined; and if the adjuſtment of one or two articles is found in any caſe to have been unneceſſarily retarded, the clerk of the office ſhall be puniſhable with 10 blows, if from three to five articles; with 20 blows, and one degree more ſeverely, as far as 40 blows, for each five additional articles unadjuſted.

The deputies of the tribunals of cities of the three ſeveral orders, and the ſuperintending officers over granaries, treaſuries, river police, and others, ſhall be puniſhable in ſuch caſes reſpectively leſs by one degree.

When any part of the records is found to be erroneous, or is kept back from examination; if in reſpect to one article only, the clerk of the office ſhall be puniſhed with 20 blows; if in reſpect to two or three articles, with 30 blows; and one degree more ſeverely, as far as 50 blows, for every three erroneous or ſuppreſſed articles, in addition to the number laſt mentioned.

The deputies of the tribunals of cities of the three ſeveral orders, and the ſuperintending officers of granaries, treaſuries, river-police, and others, ſhall be puniſhable, in each caſe, leſs by one degree. — Moreover, the preſiding officers or governors of ſuch cities, whenever it is found that from one to five articles are erroneous, or kept back from examination, ſhall forfeit one month's ſalary, and another month's ſalary, as far as three months, for each additional five articles ſo kept back or erroneous. — If ſuch incorrectneſs or ſuppreſſion of the articles of the records is practiſed from criminal motives, ſuch as, ſuppreſſion of the receipts of revenue, aggravation or palliation of offences, and the like, the puniſhment of ſuch miſconduct ſhall be proportionably increaſed according as the laws, applicable to ſuch caſes, direct.

Four clauſes.

SEC-

SECTION LXIX.—*Re-examination of outſtanding Articles of official Records.*

Thoſe officers in whoſe province it lies to re-examine the recorded tranſactions of the ſeveral tribunals and departments of government, ſhall inſpect all ſuch of the proceedings in the judicial and revenue departments as had been reported to have been found at the original examination unneceſſarily in arrear or erroneous. — Whatever, in the revenue department, is found, at the expiration of an interval of a quarter of a year, ſtill erroneous or defective, ſhall be charged againſt the magiſtrates of the ſeveral offices, and ſubject them to puniſhment according to the proportion which the erroneous and defective matter bears to the remainder of the proceedings—if one-tenth only, to 50 blows, and one degree more ſeverely, as far as 100 blows, for every further tenth part erroneous or defective.

If, in the judicial department, they find at the end of the quarter, any caſe unadjuſted or not corrected, which might and ought to have been adjuſted or corrected, the reſponſible magiſtrate ſhall be puniſhed with 40 blows, and the puniſhment ſhall be increaſed one degree for each additional month's delay, as far as 80 blows at the utmoſt, unleſs it happens to be a caſe of bribery, liable to ſeverer puniſhment, in which event the latter ſhall ſuperſede the former.

When any article is ſuppreſſed or kept back, for the purpoſe of avoiding the reſult of the re-examination, ſuch ſuppreſſion, if of one article only, ſhall be puniſhed with 40 blows, and one degree more ſeverely for each additional article ſo ſuppreſſed, as far as 80 blows at the utmoſt, except it be a caſe affecting the revenue, when the ſuppreſſion, in the caſe of one article only, ſhall be puniſhed with 80 blows, and one degree more ſeverely for each additional article ſuppreſſed, as far as 100 blows, or as much further as may be lawfully inflicted in conſequence of a corrupt or criminal deſign being ſubſtantiated againſt the offender. — If any officer of government, after the errors or omiſſions of which he had been guilty are diſcovered, ſhould fraudulently attempt to alter or interpolate the official records, the offence ſhall be puniſhed as any ordinary falſification of an official diſpatch.

All thoſe colleagues who aſſiſt in the commiſſion of this offence, and their ſuperiors who, having information of it, take no cogniſance thereof, ſhall participate in the puniſhment. If unacquainted with the circumſtances, or unconnected by office with the offending parties, they ſhall not be liable to puniſhment.

No clauſe.

Section LXX. — *Transfer or Exchange of official Duties prohibited.*

When it is the duty of an officer of government to inveſtigate or report upon any affair, whether in its progreſs from inferiors to ſuperiors, or from ſuperiors to inferiors *, if he employs any of his colleagues either to inveſtigate the matter, or to addreſs the Report of it, inſtead of doing both himſelf, he ſhall be puniſhed with 80 blows; and if it be a caſe of previous neglect or omiſſion, which it is thus attempted to repair by deputy, the puniſhment ſhall be increaſed one degree.—If, moreover, in any ſuch caſe, a deviation from juſtice either by aggravation or extenuation ſhould have been committed, the puniſhment ſhall be increaſed to any extent that the law, adapted to ſuch circumſtances, may authorize.

Three clauſes.

Section LXXI. — *Alteration of the Contents of an official Diſpatch.*

Whoever preſumes to alter an official diſpatch, by adding to, or taking from the ſenſe and words thereof, ſhall be puniſhed

* The regular courſe of proceedings in the ſeveral tribunals or courts of juſtice, is deſcribed in its proper place.

with

with 60 blows.—If ſuch alteration is effected with the view to accompliſh ſome unlawful purpoſe, not capitally puniſhable, the puniſhment incurred thereby ſhall, in conſequence of ſuch previous offence, be increaſed two degrees, but ſo as in no caſe to exceed 100 blows, and perpetual baniſhment to the diſtance of 3000 *lee.*—In any of the preceding caſes, if the unlawful object had not been attained, the puniſhment ſhall be leſs by one degree.

If the unlawful object be in itſelf a capital offence, the previous minor offence ſhall not cauſe any aggravation of the ſentence.—If the author of any official diſpatch alters it himſelf, with a view to any unlawful purpoſe, he ſhall only be ſubject to the puniſhment to which ſuch unlawful purpoſe renders him liable; except when ſuch alteration is made to ſcreen himſelf from the puniſhment of error or delay, for which offence he ſhall in ſuch caſe be liable to receive 40 blows at the leaſt.

If, in the courſe of tranſmitting, and re-iſſuing government orders upon judicial, revenue, military, or other important affairs, they are erroneouſly tranſcribed, or the emendations made in the originals omitted, the clerk of the office or tribunal guilty thereof ſhall be puniſhed with 30 blows, and the deputy of the tribunal ſhall be puniſhed one degree leſs for his neglect of reviſal.

If the alteration affects any orders for the employment of troops, or concerns the amount of ſupplies to be forwarded to the army, or to the frontier ſtations, the clerk and deputy who are reſponſible for the ſame, ſhall reſpectively receive 80 blows for ſuch neglect; but if it is a caſe of wilful miſconduct, and the alteration is made for any unlawful purpoſe, the puniſhment ſhall be rated according to the ſcale already exhibited in the caſe of altering an official diſpatch.—In general alſo, the non-execution of the unlawful purpoſe ſhall be conſidered ſo far to extenuate the offence, as to reduce the puniſhment one degree.—If, however, ſuch deviation, whether wilful or not, ſhould be the cauſe of the failure of any military operations, the perſon principally reſponſible ſhall be beheaded, after the uſual period of confinement. — The deputy, being conſidered as an acceſſary, ſhall, in ſuch caſe, receive 100 blows, and be baniſhed perpetually to the diſtance of 3000 *lee*. — When, however, any official diſpatch, or other document, is erroneouſly copied by mere accident, and does not concern the adminiſtration of military affairs, or of the judicial or revenue departments, but regards only the ordinary routine of buſineſs, the reſponſible parties ſhall not be held liable to puniſhment.

No clauſe.

SECTION LXXII. — *Uſe of the official or public Seal.*

In every department and tribunal of government, whether at court or in the provinces, the ſeal of office ſhall remain in the cuſtody of the preſiding magiſtrate or officer, and one of the magiſtrates or officers who are aſſeſſors, having ſtamped or affixed the impreſſion of the ſeal upon the records of their joint official proceedings, the members ſhall then individually ſubjoin their ſignatures. — When all the aſſeſſors are abſent from neceſſity, or engaged on other public ſervice, the deputy may be employed to authenticate the documents, by affixing the ſeal of office. — Otherwiſe a puniſhment of 100 blows ſhall follow any deviation from this law.

No clauſe.

SECTION LXXIII. — *Omitting to uſe, or imperfectly uſing, the official Seal.*

When a public document is iſſued under the official authority of any of the departments of government, with only a confuſed and imperfect impreſſion of the public ſeal, thoſe who are reſponſible for the ſealing fealing thereof, fhall be punifhed with 60 blows; and if they fhould, in any fimilar cafe, altogether omit to employ the public feal, the punifhment fhall amount to 80 blows.—If fuch unauthenticated or imperfectly authenticated document fhould in any manner concern the operations, or the fupply with ftores and provifions, of the troops in the field, the refponfible parties fhall be punifhed with 100 blows; laftly, if in confequence of fuch neglect, thofe to whom the public document is addreffed, doubt its authenticity, and hefitate to comply therewith, fo as to occafion the failure of any military operation then depending, the principal offender (being the clerk of the office where the neglect originated), fhall fuffer death by being beheaded at the ufual period; and the other officers implicated therein fhall fuffer 100 blows, and be banifhed perpetually to the diftance of 3000 *lee*.

Employing the feal of office in an inverted pofition fhall be confidered equivalent to the offence of impreffing it imperfectly, and fhall be punifhed accordingly.

Three claufes.

SECTION LXXIV. — *Employing the Sanction of the Seals of military Offices upon civil Affairs.*

All generals, commanders of troops, colonels of regiments, and other military officers, have their refpective feals; but, if inftead of referving the power and authority confided in them by thofe feals, to the authenticating of military orders, and the direction of the movements and diftribution of the cavalry and infantry under their authority, they prefume to give official anfwers to petitions, to grant paffes for goods, by which the revenue may be injured, or in any manner pretend to give inftructions on affairs exclufively under the civil jurifdiction, the clerks and deputies in the departments of fuch officers fhall ſhall receive 100 blows in each caſe, and be for ever excluded from the public ſervice.

The miſconduct of the preſiding officers ſhall be reported to the Emperor, and puniſhed agreeably to His Majeſty's deciſion.

One clauſe.

END OF THE SECOND DIVISION.

THIRD DIVISION.

Fiſcal Laws.

BOOK I.

ENROLMENT OF THE PEOPLE.

SECTION LXXV. — *Families and Individuals to be duly enrolled.*

WHEN a family has omitted to make any entry whatever in the public regiſter, the head or maſter thereof, if poſſeſſing any lands chargeable with contributions to the revenue, ſhall be puniſhed with 100 blows; but if he poſſeſs no ſuch property, with 80 blows only; and the family ſhall in the former caſe be regiſtered as accountable for future public ſervice, according to the amount of its taxable property, and in the latter, according to the number of male individuals of full age of which it conſiſts.

When any head or maſter of a family, has among his houſehold ſtrangers who conſtitute, in fact, a diſtinct family, but omits to make a correſponding entry in the public regiſter, or regiſters them as members of his own family, he ſhall be puniſhed with 100 blows, if any ſuch ſtranger poſſeſſes taxable property, and with 80 blows if he ſhould not poſſeſs any; and in all caſes, the regiſter ſhall be duly corrected, by the inſertion of a deſcription of ſuch ſtrangers as a diſtinct family.

If the perſon harboured without making any correſponding entry, or repreſented falſely as a member of the family, is not a ſtranger as in the laſt caſe, but a relation, poſſeſſing a ſeparate eſtabliſhment, the puniſhment of the head or maſter of the family ſo offending,

offending, ſhall be leſs than as aforeſaid by two degrees; the perſon harboured and concealed ſhall be liable to the ſame puniſhment, and be regiſtered ſeparately in the legal manner, as well as held accountable to the public ſervice conformably thereto.

Nevertheleſs, ſuch uncles, younger brothers, nephews, and ſons-in-law, who had never formed ſeparate eſtabliſhments, ſhall be exempted from the obligation of a ſeparate entry, preſcribed by this law.

If any perſon guilty of omitting to regiſter his family, is in the ſervice of government, and regiſtered as ſuch, the omiſſion ſhall be puniſhed only according to the number of individuals of full age omitted, as the record of any one perſon is equivalent to the record of the family.

If any head or maſter of a family omits to enter in the public regiſter any of the males belonging thereto, who have attained the full age of ſixteen, or if he falſely repreſents any individuals thereof to be under age, aged, infirm, or decrepid, ſo as to evade their liability to the public ſervice, he ſhall ſuffer the puniſhment of 60 blows, when the number of perſons does not exceed three, and be puniſhed one degree more ſeverely for every addition of three perſons to the number ſo omitted or falſely repreſented, as far as 100 blows at the utmoſt *.

Moreover, any head of a family omitting to make entry of from three to five males under the aforeſaid age, ſhall be puniſhed with 40 blows, and the puniſhment ſhall be increaſed one degree as far as 70 blows, for every additional five perſons under age, who may have been ſo omitted.

In all caſes the individuals found to have been omitted in the regiſter, ſhall be duly entered, and if of full age, made accountable to the public ſervice.

* In the Chineſe commentary annexed to the text in the original, it is ſtated that the firſt entry ſhall be made of children when they attain the age of four years, but the period of liability to public ſervice appears to be only between the ages of ſixteen and ſixty. Beſides the ordinary regiſters of the people, one of a more comprehenſive nature is occaſionally effected, compriſing perſons of both ſexes, and of all ages.

Neglecting

Neglecting to enter, or making a falfe entry of, a ftranger, fhall be punifhed in the fame manner and proportions; and the ftranger availing himfelf thereof fhall be liable to equal punifhment, as well as compelled to make entry and perform fervice, as a member of the family to which he really belongs *.

The head or refponfible inhabitant of the divifion, through whofe neglect and inadvertency, one or more families, as far as five, have evaded the infertion of their names in the public regifter, fhall be punifhed with 50 blows; and one degree more feverely, as far as 100 blows, for every additional five families fo omitted to be inferted.

In like manner, when the names of any individuals are omitted to be inferted in the regifters, the aforefaid refponfible inhabitant fhall be punifhed with 30 blows, when the number omitted does not exceed 10; and one degree more feverely for every additional 10 omitted, as far as 50 blows at the utmoft.

When the omiffion amounts to 10 families, the governor, deputy and clerk of the diftrict, fhall be liable to the punifhment of 40 blows, for their negligence in allowing the fame; and their punifhment fhall be greater by one degree as far as 80 blows for every additional 10 families fo allowed to be omitted.

When the omiffion amounts to 10 individuals, the faid magiftrates and clerks fhall be liable to 20 blows for their negligence in allowing the fame; and their punifhment fhall be greater by one degree for every additional 30 individuals omitted, as far as 40 blows at the utmoft.

When any of the preceding parties wilfully connive at fuch omiffion, they fhall be punifhed as feverely as the principal offenders; and if they are found guilty of receiving money, as the price of their connivance, they fhall fuffer any contingent aggravation of punifhment,

* In this cafe, the family of the ftranger is fuppofed to have been duly regiftered elfewhere, though the individual ftranger, being abfent from his family, had been omitted.

to which they may become liable from the amount thereof, according to the law againſt receiving a bribe for an unlawful purpoſe.

If, however, the officiating magiſtrates and clerks ſhall have three times ordered a reviſal of the cenſus of the people, and iſſued competent inſtructions and authority for ſuch inveſtigation to the head inhabitants of diſtricts, the ſaid head inhabitants ſhall alone be reſponſible for any ſubſequent omiſſion which may afterwards be diſcovered.

All caſes of wilful connivance are, at the ſame time, manifeſtly to be excepted.

Two clauſes.

SECTION LXXVI. — *Families and Individuals to be regiſtered according to their Profeſſions.*

All perſons whatſoever ſhall be regiſtered according to their accuſtomed profeſſions or vocations, whether civil or military, whether poſt-men *, artiſans, phyſicians, aſtrologers, labourers, muſicians, or of any other denomination whatever; wherever a military employment is repreſented as a civil one, or an artiſan endeavours to paſs himſelf as a mere labourer, or when any other device is employed to leſſen the individual's liability to the public ſervice, ſuch individual ſhall be puniſhed with 80 blows, and the magiſtrate who negligently conſents to ſuch omiſſion, irregularity, or confuſion in the entries on the public regiſter, ſhall be equally puniſhable.

Whoever falſely repreſents himſelf to belong to any military eſtabliſhment in garriſon, or in the field, and thereby evades all public ſervice whatever, ſhall receive 100 blows, and be ſent into the ulterior and perpetual military baniſhment.

Twenty-two clauſes.

* See the laſt Book of the Diviſion of Military Laws, entitled, "Expreſſes and Public "Poſts."

SEC-

SECTION LXXVII. — *Privately founding religious Houſes, and privately entering into the Order of Prieſthood**.

No religious houſes of the ſects of *Foe* and *Tao-ſe*, except thoſe which have been heretofore lawfully conſtituted and eſtabliſhed, ſhall be privately maintained, appropriated, or endowed, whether upon a new, or in addition to an old foundation, or in any other manner whatſoever.

Whoever offends againſt this law ſhall receive 100 blows; if a prieſt, he ſhall be diveſted of his ſacred character, and perpetually baniſhed beyond the frontier:—if a prieſteſs, ſhe ſhall become a ſlave to government; and in general all the real and perſonal property belonging to any ſuch illegal foundation ſhall be confiſcated.

Whoever ſubmits to the tonſure †, and joins a religious community as a prieſt or prieſteſs, without having previouſly obtained a government licence, ſhall be puniſhed with 80 blows, and be replaced in the claſs of ordinary citizens. When the offence is committed through the inſtigation of the head of the family, ſuch head of the family ſhall bear the puniſhment thereof. The members and governors of religious communities, who illegally admit ſuch perſons, ſhall alſo ſuffer the puniſhment decreed by this law ‡.

Six clauſes.

* See Section XLII. relative to the religious orders among the Chineſe.

† The prieſts of the ſect of *Foe* cloſely ſhave every part of the head; thoſe of the ſect of *Tao-ſe* wear their hair, but in a different manner from the natives in general.

‡ It is provided by the third clauſe to this ſection, that perſons deſirous of contributing to the foundation of a new temple, or other religious building, ſhall be allowed to apply for permiſſion to the viceroy of the province, in order that their deſires may be ſubmitted to the conſideration of His Imperial Majeſty.

Section LXXVIII. —*Rule of Succeſſion and Inheritance.*

Whoever appoints his heir and repreſentative unlawfully, ſhall be puniſhed with 80 blows *. — When the firſt wife has completed her fiftieth year, and has no children living, it is allowed to appoint the eldeſt ſon by the other wives to the inheritance; but if any other than the eldeſt of ſuch ſons is ſo appointed, it ſhall be deemed a breach of this law.

If a perſon, not having ſons himſelf, educates and adopts the ſon of a kinſman, having other ſons, but afterwards diſmiſſes ſuch adopted ſon, ſuch perſon ſhall be puniſhed with 100 blows, and the ſon ſhall be ſent back to, and ſupported, as before, by the adopting parents.

Neverthelefs, if the adopting parents ſhall have ſubſequently had other ſons, and the natural parents, having no other, are deſirous of receiving their ſon back again, they ſhall be at liberty ſo to do.

Whoever aſks for, and receives into his houſe as his adopted ſon, a perſon of a different family name, is guilty of confounding family diſtinctions, and ſhall therefore be puniſhed with 60 blows; the ſon ſo adopted ſhall, in ſuch caſes, always be returned to his family. — In like manner, whoever gives away his ſon to be adopted into a family of a different name, ſhall ſuffer the puniſhment decreed by this law, and receive ſuch ſon back again. Neverthelefs, it ſhall be lawful to adopt a foundling under three years of age, and to give the child the name of the family into which it is adopted; but ſuch adopted child ſhall not be entitled to the inheritance upon failure of the children by blood.

If the relative appointed to the inheritance, on failure of children, is not the eldeſt in ſucceſſion, it ſhall be deemed a breach of this law;

* See the rule of ſucceſſion to Hereditary Dignities in the ſecond diviſion to the code, and alſo the abſtract of the clauſes annexed to this law, in the Appendix, No. XII.

the

the relative ſo appointed ſhall be ſent back to his place in his own family, and the lawful heir appointed in his ſtead.

Whoever brings up in his family, as a ſlave, the male or female child of a freeman, ſhall be puniſhed with 100 blows, and the child ſhall regain its freedom.

Eight clauſes.

SECTION LXXIX. — *Regulations concerning ſtray Children.*

Whoever receives and detains the ſtrayed or loſt child of a free perſon, and, inſtead of preſenting to the magiſtrate, ſells ſuch child as a ſlave, ſhall be puniſhed with 100 blows, and three years baniſhment. Whoever ſells ſuch child for marriage or adoption into any family, ſhall be puniſhed with 90 blows and baniſhment for two years and a half. — Whoever ſo diſpoſes of a ſtrayed or loſt ſlave, ſhall ſuffer the puniſhment provided by this law, reduced one degree.

The perſon unlawfully ſold ſhall not in any of the above caſes be ſubjected to any puniſhment in conſequence, but returned to his family or right owner.

If any one receives and detains a fugitive child, and, inſtead of preſenting it to the magiſtrates, ſells ſuch child for a ſlave, he ſhall be puniſhed with 90 blows, and baniſhment for two years and a half. — Whoever ſells any ſuch fugitive child for marriage or adoption, ſhall ſuffer the puniſhment of 80 blows and two years baniſhment; in each of theſe caſes, the puniſhment ſhall be leſs by one degree, when the fugitive is found to be a ſlave.

All fugitives ſo diſpoſed of ſhall ſuffer puniſhment one degree leſs than that inflicted on the ſeller, except when the previous offence of the fugitive ſhall have been the greateſt, in which caſe the ſeverer of the two puniſhments to which he is liable, ſhall be inflicted.

Whoever,

Whoever, inſtead of ſelling, retains for his own uſe as a ſlave, wife, or child, any ſuch loſt, ſtrayed, or fugitive child, or ſlave, ſhall be equally liable to be puniſhed as above mentioned; but if only guilty of retaining the ſame for a ſhort time, the puniſhment ſhall not exceed 80 blows.

When the purchaſer, or the negociator of the purchaſe, is aware of the unlawfulneſs of the tranſaction, he ſhall ſuffer puniſhment one degree leſs than that inflicted on the ſeller, and the amount of the pecuniary conſideration ſhall be forfeited to government; but when he or they are found to have been unacquainted therewith, they ſhall not be liable to puniſhment, and the money ſhall be reſtored to the party from whom it had been received.

Whoever falſely claims a free perſon as his ſlave ſhall be puniſhed with 100 blows and three years baniſhment; if falſely claiming ſuch perſon as his wife or child, with 90 blows and baniſhment for two years and a half; if falſely claiming the ſlave of another perſon, with 100 blows only.

One clauſe.

SECTION LXXX.—*Impartiality in the Levy of Taxes and perſonal Services.*

In all diſtricts, where the taxes in money and in kind, and the extraordinary and miſcellaneous perſonal ſervices to be required from the people, are eſtimated and apportioned, due regard ſhall be had in each caſe to the extent of the family in point of numbers and to its ability to contribute, according to which the members thereof ſhall be rated in the ſuperior, middle, or inferior claſs, of inhabitants.

If the poorer inhabitants are compelled to perform the ſervices from which thoſe who are rich are excuſed, or any other ſuch unjuſt partiality

tiality is difcoverable in the conduct of the officers of government, it fhall be lawful for the injured poor to appeal and complain thereof to the tribunal of the immediate fuperiors of fuch officers, whence they may repeat the appeal to the feveral fuperior tribunals in fucceffion. — The officer and his official agents, who fhall be convicted of any fuch breach of this law, fhall, each of them, be punifhed with 100 blows, and the unjuft or partial arrangement fhall be annulled. The officers of any tribunal where fuch an appeal fhall have been refufed a hearing, fhall be punifhed with 80 blows; and if they fhall appear to have been bribed to make fuch refufal, they fhall be punifhed as many degrees beyond 80 blows, as the law againft bribery to commit an unlawful act, may warrant or require.

Five claufes.

SECTION LXXXI. — *Impartiality in the Allotment of perfonal Services.*

All perfons who, being engaged in providing perfonal fervices of labourers and artificers for government agreeably to the laws, do not duly provide, and impartially allot the fame, fhall be punifhed with 20 blows when there is a deviation in refpect to one individual; and one degree more feverely for every additional five individuals whom it may concern, as far as 60 blows at the utmoft.

If fuch perfons as are engaged to perform the required fervices delay, or fail in the execution of their engagements; or if the required fervices having been performed, they are ftill detained by the magiftrate beyond the lawful period, the offending party fhall be punifhed with 10 blows for one day, and one degree more feverely for every additional three days delay, as far as 50 blows at the utmoft.

No claufe.

SEC-

SECTION LXXXII. — *Evaſion of perſonal Service.*

All citizens who, not being obliged to labour for their own ſupport, place their unemployed ſons, grandſons, brothers, or nephews, in the ſuite of an officer of government, in order to evade the performances of the perſonal ſervices due by them to the ſtate, ſhall (being maſters of families) be puniſhed with 100 blows; the officer of government conniving at ſuch evaſion, ſhall be liable to the ſame puniſhment, or, in the event of his having received a bribe, to ſuch greater puniſhment as he might be liable to, for taking a bribe to ſuch an amount, for an unlawful purpoſe. — The perſon ſo placed in the ſuite of an officer of government, ſhall not ſuffer corporal puniſhment, but be ſent into the leſs remote military baniſhment.

When any of the ſuperior and diſtinguiſhed magiſtrates are guilty of ſuch connivance, they ſhall be tried according to this law, but the ſentence ſhall not be conſidered final until it has been ſubmitted to, and approved by, the Emperor.

No clauſe.

SECTION LXXXIII. — *Supernumerary Perſons exerciſing diſtrict Authority prohibited.*

In all diſtricts of the empire, 100 families ſhall form a diviſion, and ſhall conſult together, in order to provide a head and ten aſſeſſors, who are to attend ſucceſſively, in order to aſſiſt in the collection of the taxes, and duly to aſcertain the performance of all other public duties and ſervices.

If there are any other perſons who, falſely aſſuming authority under the characters of deputies, aſſiſtants, and the like, create diſturbances and haraſs the people, they ſhall be puniſhed with 100 blows and baniſhed.

The

The elders, who are to be appointed to theſe offices, ſhall be choſen among the moſt reſpectable perſons of maturer age who belong to the diſtrict, and no perſon ſhall be eligible to, or accept, the ſaid offices, who has ever held any civil or military employments, or who has ever been convicted of any crime.—Whoever accepts the ſame, in defiance of this law, ſhall be puniſhed with 60 blows, and diſmiſſed; the officer of government, who ſanctions ſuch undue appointment, ſhall be puniſhed with 40 blows, at the leaſt, and eventually ſuffer ſuch further puniſhment as he may be liable to, in conſequence of being guilty of receiving a bribe for an unlawful purpoſe.

One clauſe.

SECTION LXXXIV.—*Evaſion of perſonal Service by Concealment or Deſertion.*

All perſons and families, who ſhall remove to a neighbouring diſtrict or city, in order to conceal themſelves, and avoid rendering any perſonal ſervice, ſhall be puniſhed with 100 blows, ſent back to, and compelled to ſerve at, the place of their original ſettlement.

The head of the diſtrict, and the ſuperintending magiſtrates and clerks, if guilty of conniving at the departure of ſuch perſons; and all thoſe in the neighbouring diſtrict who may have harboured and concealed them, ſhall be held to be participators in the offence, and puniſhed accordingly.

Moreover, if the head man of the neighbouring diſtrict, knowing of the removal thereto of ſuch perſons, does not inform againſt and detain them; if the magiſtrate of the diſtrict to which they belong, does not iſſue letters of advice to the other magiſtrates, for the purpoſe of procuring their return; and laſtly, if, after the iſſue of ſuch letters, the magiſtrate of the diſtrict to which ſuch perſons have removed, declines to ſend them back, and protects them in defiance of the law, each of thoſe officers ſhall be puniſhed with 60 blows.

Any labourer, artificer, or other individual, who, during the period of his engagement to render perſonal ſervice to the ſtate, ſhall abſent himſelf for one day, ſhall be puniſhed with 10 blows, and one degree more ſeverely for every additional five days abſence, as far as 50 blows at the utmoſt.

The ſuperintending magiſtrate and his clerks, when they connive thereat, ſhall be conſidered as participators in the offence, and be alſo liable to any contingent aggravation of puniſhment which may ariſe from the law againſt bribery for an unlawful purpoſe.

If the offence ſhall not appear to have been committed through the connivance of the magiſtrate and clerks, they ſhall ſtill be liable to ſuffer the puniſhment of 20 blows, if five men eſcape; and to be puniſhed one degree more ſeverely, as far as 40 blows at the utmoſt, for every additional five men ſo offending: in the caſe of any number leſs than five, they ſhall be excuſed.

Three clauſes.

Section LXXXV. — *Selection of the Guards and Attendants of Priſons.*

The guards and attendants of priſons ſhall be ſelected from among the moſt truſt-worthy and experienced perſons in the employ of government; and any perſon who, after having been ſo ſelected, ſhall not attend, but name a ſubſtitute to perform his duty, ſhall be puniſhed with 40 blows for ſuch offence.

No clauſe.

SECTION LXXXVI. — *Perfonal Services of Labourers and Artificers required beyond the legal Extent, or for private Purpofes.*

All officers of government holding magifterial fituations, or fuperintending public works, who fhall compel perfons under their jurifdiction to ferve as labourers or artificers for any private purpofe, beyond the diftance of 100 *lee* from their houfes, or who fhall employ fuch perfons in their private concerns for a confiderable time at their own houfes, fhall be punifhable in the following manner: In the cafe of ordinary magiftrates fo offending, they fhall be punifhed with 40 blows, when one individual is unlawfully employed; and one degree more feverely, as far as 80 blows, for every additional five individuals concerned; in the cafe of fuperintendants of public works, the punifhment fhall in every inftance be more fevere by two degrees. Each individual employed as above, fhall receive a compenfation of 8 *fen* 5 *lee* 5 *hao per* day *. Temporary fervices, however, required on the occafion of mourning, or of a feftival, or under any other fuch accidental circumftances, fhall not be deemed an infringement of this law.

In general, not more than 50 perfons fhall be employed on any kind of fervice at one time, or any individual detained thereon beyond a period of three days; and whenever thefe limits are tranfgreffed, it fhall be always confidered and punifhed as a cafe of private fervice.

No claufe.

* ,0855 decimal parts of a *leang*, or ounce of filver, and equivalent to nearly feven pence fterling.

SEC-

SECTION LXXXVII. — *Individuals deſerting, or prematurely ſeparating from, their Families.*

Sons or grandſons who form to themſelves a ſeparate eſtabliſhment from their parents and grand-parents, and alſo make a diviſion of the family property, ſhall, provided ſuch parents and grand-parents perſonally proſecute, be puniſhed, on conviction, with 100 blows.

Alſo, the ſons of the ſame parents, who ſhall form to themſelves ſeparate eſtabliſhments, and divide their reſpective proportions of the inheritance, previous to the expiration of the lawful period of mourning, ſhall be puniſhed with 80 blows, provided they are convicted upon an information laid by an elder relation in the firſt degree, and provided that they had not been expreſsly directed to do ſo in the laſt will of their parent deceaſed.

One clauſe.

SECTION LXXXVIII. — *Younger and inferior Branches of a Family, diſpoſing of the Property without Leave.*

Any younger and inferior member of a family, living with the others under the ſame roof, who applies to his own uſe, or otherwiſe diſpoſes of, the joint family-property without permiſſion, ſhall be puniſhed with 20 blows, if the value amounts to 10 ounces of ſilver, and one degree more ſeverely as far as 100 blows, for every additional 10 ounces value.

An unjuſt or partial diviſion of the patrimony between the elder and younger branches of a family, upon their ſeparation, ſhall likewiſe be puniſhed agreeably to the tenor of this law *.

Two clauſes.

* On the ſubject of this and the preceding ſection, ſee the Appendix, No. XIII.

SEC-

SECTION LXXXIX. — *Care of the aged and infirm.*

All poor deſtitute widowers and widows, the fatherleſs and childleſs, the helpleſs and the infirm, ſhall receive ſufficient maintenance and protection from the magiſtrates of their native city or diſtrict, whenever they have neither relations nor connexions upon whom they can depend for ſupport. — Any magiſtrate refuſing ſuch maintenance and protection, ſhall be puniſhed with 60 blows.

Alſo, when any ſuch perſons are maintained and protected by government, the ſuperintending magiſtrate and his ſubordinates, if failing to afford them the legal allowance of food and raiment, ſhall be puniſhed in proportion to the amount of the deficiency, according to the law againſt an embezzlement of government ſtores *.

Six clauſes.

* Agreeably to the tenor of this law, there are at Pekin, and in other parts of China, certain eſtabliſhments for the ſupport and education of foundlings, and for the maintenance of the aged and deſtitute; but the ſacred regard which is habitually paid by the Chineſe to the claims of kindred, operates more effectually and extenſively in the relief of the poor, (except in the ſeaſons of ſcarcity and diſtreſs from accidental cauſes), than almoſt any legal proviſion could be expected to do in ſo vaſt and populous an empire.

END OF THE FIRST BOOK OF THE THIRD DIVISION.

BOOK II.

LANDS AND TENEMENTS.

SECTION XC. — *Fraudulent Evafion of the Land-Tax.*

WHOEVER fraudulently evades the payment of the land-tax, by fuppreffing or omitting the regifter of his land in the public books, fhall be punifhable in proportion to the amount of the chargeable land omitted, in the following manner:—When the unregiftered land amounts to one *meu* *, and does not exceed five *meu*, with 40 blows; and for every additional number of five *meu* fo fuppreffed, the punifhment fhall be increafed one degree, until it arrives at the limit of 100 blows. The unregiftered lands fhall be forfeited to the ftate, and the arrears of the land-tax (computed according to the period during which it had been unpaid, the extent of the land, and the rate at which it would have been lawfully chargeable), fhall be at the fame time difcharged in full.

When the land is entered in the regifter, but falfely reprefented, as unproductive when productive, lightly chargeable when heavily chargeable; or if the land is nominally made over in truft to another perfon, in order to exempt the real proprietor from perfonal fervice,

* A confiderable difficulty has been experienced in eftimating the exact extent of the divifion of land, called by the Chinefe *meu*, owing to the various modes of admeafurement practiced in China at different periods, and by different claffes of people; but from a comparifon of feveral accounts given in original Chinefe works, it appears certain that the legal meafure at prefent confifts of 240 fquare *Poo* or paces; that each *poo* is equal to fix *che*, and that a *che* exceeds the Englifh foot by rather more than half an inch.—According to this computation the *meu*, or Chinefe acre, may be roughly eftimated at a 1000 fquare yards of our meafure.

the

the punifhment, whether corporal or arifing out of the payment of the arrears of the tax, fhall be inflicted in the manner and according to the fcale above ftated; but inftead of a forfeiture of the lands, the regifter of them fhall fimply be corrected, and the affeffment and perfonal fervice of the real proprietor be eftablifhed agreeably thereto.

When the land is thus illegally made over in truft, the perfon who undertakes the truft fhall fuffer equal punifhment with the perfon who grants it.

If the head inhabitant of the diftrict is privy to any breach of the law, but does not take cognizance of it, he fhall be equally punifhable with the original tranfgreffors.

When any families or individuals return to the diftrict and calling to which they originally belonged, and there happens to be a deficiency of refident population, in proportion to the extent and productivenefs of the ancient allotments of lands therein, they fhall be allowed to contribute to the cultivation thereof, in proportion to their capacity; and upon a due reprefentation being laid before the magiftrates, an allotment of unoccupied lands fhall be made to them; and according to the entry thereof in the public regifters, they fhall thenceforwards be liable to the land-tax, and to perfonal fervice.

If any fuch individuals claim in their reprefentations an exceffive fhare of the unoccupied lands, fo that they are afterwards unable to cultivate what is granted to them, they fhall, when fuch excefs amounts to three *meu*, and does not exceed ten *meu*, be liable to a punifhment of 30 blows, and be punifhed one degree more feverely for every further excefs of ten *meu*, until the punifhment reaches the limit of 80 blows; the excefs fhall moreover be forfeited back to the ftate.

When applications of this nature are made to the magiftrate in any diftrict where the cultivating population is already fufficient or excef-five,

five, a part of the unoccupied lands in the nearest vicinity shall be allotted to the applicants, in proportion to their means of keeping up the cultivation.

Five clauses.

SECTION XCI. — *Personal Visitation of Lands suffering from any Calamity* *.

In all districts wherein the Lands have suffered from a temporary calamity, as from excessive rain, the overflowing of waters, excessive drought, unseasonable frosts, flights of locusts, and the like, the customary assessments shall be proportionally reduced, or remitted altogether; all representations on this subject the magistrates shall be obliged to receive; and if they fail to take cognizance thereof, both by reporting the same to the tribunals of their superiors, and by personally inspecting the injured lands; or if the magistrate of the superior tribunal does not dispatch an officer of government, under his immediate orders, to examine into and verify the facts reported to him by his inferiors; in all such cases, the omission shall be punished with 80 blows.

If the officer of government employed in the first visitation, or the officer employed in the re-examination, does not himself personally attend on the spot; or if although, he does personally attend, he afterwards, instead of making a faithful report, grounded on a diligent investigation, negligently trusts to the representations of the head inha-

* A remission of a part or of the whole of the regulated amount of the assessment of the land-tax; and, at the same time, a prompt distribution of a supply of grain from the public stores, are the means most usually employed by the government to alleviate the distress, which a deficient harvest, whenever it occurs, must, in an empire depending solely on its own productions for the subsistence of a population already for the most part redundant, necessarily occasion. In the Appendix, No. XIV., some account of one or two recent instances of this kind is inserted.

head inhabitant of the diſtrict, or his deputies, and thereupon deſcribes as productive what is ſterile, and as ſterile what is productive, or in any other manner extenuates or exaggerates the circumſtances of the caſe, ſuch a ſtatement muſt neceſſarily be founded upon fraud or colluſion, and, while it deceives the government, it muſt in an equal degree injure the people; the offender ſhall, therefore, be puniſhed with 100 blows, deprived of his office, and rendered incapable of afterwards holding any rank or office under government. The amount likewiſe of the taxes, which in conſequence of ſuch miſconduct had been either improperly levied, or cauſeleſsly remitted, ſhall be eſtimated, and conformably thereto a reference ſhall be made to the law concerning pecuniary malverſation in general, in order that, if the puniſhment authorized by the latter prove the greateſt, it may be inflicted in preference to that hereby provided.—The head inhabitant of the diſtrict, and his deputies, ſhall be liable to puniſhment in an equal degree, when participating in the foregoing offence, in the manner above ſtated; and if they are further convicted of bribery, they ſhall be liable to any aggravation of the puniſhment which may ariſe from a reference to the law againſt bribery for an unlawful purpoſe.

Nevertheleſs, if the incorrectneſs of the report of the inſpecting magiſtrate be merely imputable to an error, or to inadvertence in aſcertaining the limits, neither the officer of government, nor his clerks, nor the head inhabitant of the diſtrict, nor his deputies, ſhall be liable to puniſhment, when the error does not exceed ten *meu*; from ten to twenty *meu*, the puniſhment ſhall amount to 20 blows, and be encreaſed one degree for each additional extent of incorrectneſs of twenty *meu*, until it arrives at the limit of 80 blows; and this offence not being deemed of a private or perſonal nature, ſhall not ſubject the magiſtrates to a loſs of their rank or offices.

If, on any ſuch occaſion, an individual, or head of a family, repreſents his productive lands to be unproductive, and falſely pleads loſs by any temporary calamity, he ſhall be puniſhed with 40 blows when the miſrepreſentation exceeds one and is leſs than five *meu*; the puniſhment ſhall be encreaſed one degree for every additional five *meu* ſo falſely repreſented, until it arrives at the limit of 100 blows, and the full amount of the cuſtomary aſſeſſment upon ſuch lands ſhall be thenceforward ſtrictly levied.

Seventeen clauſes.

SECTION XCII. — *Lands of the Nobility and Officers of Government.*

All the lands and houſes compriſed in the eſtates of the nobility and officers of government, (except ſuch as by the expreſs direction and command of the Emperor, are exempted from taxation and perſonal ſervice,) ſhall be duly reported by the reſpective tenants or ſtewards to the magiſtrates of the diſtricts, and correctly entered on the public regiſters, that according to ſuch entries they may be aſſeſſed and held accountable for perſonal ſervices, as in all ordinary caſes.

The tenant or ſteward of the land ſhall be reſponſible for the execution of this law, and if he neglects to comply with it, he ſhall be puniſhed in proportion to the extent of the land omitted to be inſerted in the regiſter; that is to ſay, from one to three *meu* with ſixty blows, and one degree more ſeverely for every further omiſſion of three *meu* in the regiſter, provided the puniſhment does not in any caſe exceed 100 blows, and three years baniſhment. The lands ſhall moreover be forfeited to the ſtate, and the arrears of the tax diſcharged in full, agreeably to the extent, the time, and rate of legal aſſeſſment.

If the head inhabitants of the ſeveral diſtricts, or the magiſtrates thereof, upon a viſitation of ſuch lands, make falſe returns, in order to obtain favour with the proprietors; or if they connive at the omiſſions

in

in the regifters, of which the latter are guilty, they fhall equally participate in the punifhment. They fhall not, however, be punifhed under this law in any manner, for the offences of others, except when it is proved that they have thus actually connived at the fame.

No claufe.

SECTION XCIII. — *Fraudulent Sale of Lands and Tenements.*

Whoever fraudulently fells, exchanges, or profeffes himfelf proprietor of, the lands of other perfons; and whoever, by a fictitious agreement, without due pecuniary confideration, purchafes, or wrongfully takes poffeffion of, the lands or tenements of others, fhall be punifhed according to the extent of the land, or the number of the tenements in queftion; if not exceeding one *meu*, or one tenement, with 50 blows, and one degree more feverely for each addition of five to the number of *meu*, or three to the number of tenements, provided the punifhment do not in any cafe exceed 80 blows, and two years banifhment. — If, however, the lands or tenements in queftion are the property of government, the punifhment in each cafe fhall be proportionably greater by two degrees.

Whoever feizes by open violence the lands and tenements of government, or of individuals, (that is to fay, not only cultivated lands and inhabited houfes, but alfo burying-grounds, fifh-ponds, cane plantations, metal founderies, and the like,) fhall, without reference to the number or extent, receive 100 blows, and fuffer pepetual banifhment to the diftance of 3000 *lee*.

When any individual takes land, or the produce of land, under litigation or belonging to others, and upon the pretext of being the lawful proprietor thereof, prefents the fame to officers of government, or to other perfons having influence and authority, as a free gift or

 donation,

donation, the giver and receiver ſhall each be puniſhed with 100 blows, and three years baniſhment.

In general; all lands which, by fraud or force, have been unlawfully obtained, together with the produce thereof reaped during the unlawful poſſeſſion; ſecondly, the ſums for which any ſuch lands and produce may have been clandeſtinely ſold; thirdly, all the unreaped produce remaining on ſuch lands; and laſtly, the amount of all the other advantages whatſoever derived from ſuch lands, during the period of unlawful poſſeſſion, ſhall ſeverally become forfeitures, and be reſtored or repaid to whom they are due, whether to the ſtate, or to private individuals.

When this law is tranſgreſſed by any of the privileged officers of government, the circumſtances of the caſe ſhall be inveſtigated, and the nature of the puniſhment to be inflicted ſhall be determined as in ordinary caſes, but the latter ſhall not be carried into effect until the ſentence is ſubmitted to, and ratified by, His Imperial Majeſty.

Nine clauſes.

Section XCIV. — *Officers of Government reſtricted from purchaſing Lands within the Limits of their Juriſdiction.*

The officers and clerks officiating in any of the departments of government, which poſſeſs a territorial juriſdiction, ſhall not, during the exerciſe of their authority therein, purchaſe, or hold by purchaſe, any lands or tenements within the limits of ſuch juriſdiction; whoever is convicted of a breach of this law ſhall ſuffer 50 blows, and be removed from his office, but ſhall not be thereby rendered incapable of holding offices under government elſewhere; the lands and tenements ſo unlawfully held ſhall be forfeited to government.

Two clauſes.

SEC-

Section XCV. — *Law of Mortgages* *.

Whoever takes lands or tenements by way of mortgage, without entering into a regular contract, duly authenticated and assessed with the legal duty by the proper magistrate, shall receive 50 blows, and forfeit to government half the consideration money of the mortgage. —If the mortgager does not transfer to the mortgagee unreservedly the whole produce of the land upon which the taxes are charged and made payable to government, he shall be punished in proportion to the extent of the property, in the following manner: if from one to five *meu*, with 40 blows, and one degree more severely for each five additional *meu*, until the punishment amounts to 100 blows; the land so illegally mortgaged shall be forfeited to government.

If the proprietor of lands and tenements already mortgaged, attempts to raise money thereon by a second mortgage, the amount obtained upon such false pretences shall be ascertained, and the offender punished accordingly, as in the case of an ordinary theft to the same extent, except that he shall not be liable to be branded.

The pecuniary consideration received by the fraudulent mortgager shall be restored always to the mortgagee, unless such mortgagee is himself privy to the unlawfulness of the transaction, in which case it shall be forfeited to government.

The said mortgagee and the negotiator of the bargain, when either of them is acquainted with the unlawfulness of the transaction, shall

* The mode here described of lending money upon landed security, is a very ancient and frequent practice among the Chinese, and though certainly a species of mortgage, will be seen to be modified by some peculiar regulations. This subject has been already noticed by the missionaries in the *Memoires sur les Chinois*, vol. iv. p. 386. but as it is connected with the interesting and disputed question of the nature of the tenure of lands in China, an abstract of some of the more material clauses annexed to the law, have been inserted in further illustration of it, in the Appendix, No. XV.

moreover

moreover receive the ſame puniſhment as the mortgager. In all ſuch caſes, the firſt and lawful mortgagee ſhall remain in poſſeſſion.

If, after the period, ſpecified in the deed by which any lands or tenements are profeſſed to be mortgaged or pledged by the proprietor, is expired, the ſaid proprietor offers to redeem his property by the payment back of the original conſideration upon which he had parted with it, it ſhall not be allowed the mortgagee to refuſe to comply; any inſtance of ſuch refuſal ſhall ſubject him to the puniſhment of 40 blows, and to the forfeiture of all the produce of the land which he may have reaped after the expiration of ſuch period. Neverthelefs, this law ſhall only have effect when the proprietor is really able at the expiration of the preſcribed period to redeem his lands, and not otherwiſe.

Ten clauſes.

Section XCVI. — *Sowing and tilling Lands belonging to others.*

Whoever ploughs and ſows the lands of another clandeſtinely, that is to ſay, without giving notice to the proprietor, ſhall ſuffer puniſhment in proportion to the extent of the land illicitly cultivated; when not exceeding one *meu*, with 30 blows, and one degree more ſeverely in proportion to each additional five *meu*, as far as 80 blows. — If the land had not been previouſly under cultivation, the puniſhment ſhall be leſs in each caſe by one degree.

If the land of a ſtranger is cultivated by force, that is to ſay, in defiance of the proprietor, the puniſhment ſhall be one degree more ſevere in each caſe.

If the land is the property of government, the puniſhment of intruſive and unlawful culture ſhall be further aggravated two degrees; and in general, the profit derived from the cultivation of the land ſhall

ſhall be forfeited either to the individual proprietor, or to the ſtate, according to the circumſtances of the caſe.

One clauſe.

Section XCVII. — *Uncultivated and neglected Lands.*

In every diſtrict of the empire, when the lands which have been entered on the public regiſters as liable to the land-tax, and as ſubjecting the proprietors to the demands of perſonal ſervice, are, without any cauſe, ſuch as inundation, drought, or other calamity, neglected and omitted to be duly cultivated; as, for inſtance, if the eſtabliſhed mulberry, hemp, and other ſimilar plantations are not duly kept up, the head inhabitant of the diſtrict ſhall be held reſponſible, and puniſhed according to the relative extent of the uncultivated to that of the cultivated portion of the regiſtered lands in his diſtrict.—If the unclutivated portion is one-tenth of the whole, he ſhall be puniſhed with 20 blows, and one degree more ſeverely, as far as 80 blows, for each additional tenth uncultivated. The preſiding magiſtrate of the city of the third order, to which the diſtrict is ſubjected, ſhall likewiſe be puniſhable, but leſs ſeverely by two degrees in each caſe than the head inhabitant. The aſſeſſors of the chief magiſtrate ſhall ſuffer puniſhment as acceſſaries to his offence.

The individual proprietor alſo, who ſuffers his land to remain uncultivated, or who neglects his mulberry, hemp, or other plantations, ſhall be puniſhed according to the proportion which the neglected part bears to the whole of his regiſtered property,—if it amounts to one-fifth, with 20 blows, and one degree more ſeverely for every additional fifth left uncultivated.

His

His lands ſhall moreover be aſſeſſed with the land-tax in proportion to the amount of the produce they are judged capable of yielding, and the contribution ſhall be levied on the proprietor accordingly.

No clauſe.

SECTION XCVIII. — *Deſtroying or damaging the Harveſts and Articles connected therewith.*

Whoever purpoſely deſtroys, or abandons to deſtruction, any implements or utenſils of huſbandry, cuts down timber trees, or in general, damages the produce of the land, ſhall be puniſhed in proportion to the eſtimated amount of the damage, according to the law againſt theft to the ſame extent, except that he ſhall not be branded; — if the article or produce deſtroyed or damaged was the property of government, the puniſhment in ſuch caſe ſhall be encreaſed two degrees.

When the articles or produce of the earth belonging to government are loſt or deſtroyed by an inadvertence only, the puniſhment ſhall be three degrees leſs than in the caſe of a wilful offence to the ſame extent; but in all caſes, the extent of the damage ſhall be eſtimated, and the offender compelled to replace the amount to government, or to the individual proprietor, according to the circumſtances of the caſe. — When any private property is loſt or deſtroyed through inadvertence, corporal puniſhment ſhall not be inflicted on the offender, but he ſhall, as already ſtated, replace the amount of the damage or loſs ſuſtained by the injured party.

Whoever deſtroys the tomb-ſtones, or the emblematical figures cut in ſtone belonging to tombs, ſhall be puniſhed with 80 blows; whoever deſtroys the figures of domeſtic or drural eities ſhall be puniſhed with 90 blows; and generally, whoever deſtroys or damages the houſes,

houses, walls, or buildings of any kind belonging to others, shall be punished in proportion to the estimated expence of labour and materials necessary to replace the same, according to the law for the punishment of pecuniary injuries in general. — In all these cases, the damage shall be fully repaired by the offending party, whose punishment shall, moreover, be raised in each case two degrees, when the buildings damaged or destroyed had belonged to government. When, however, the buildings of government or individuals are damaged or destroyed inadvertently, the person who did the injury shall be liable to no other punishment beside the obligation to repair the damage, or re-place the value of the property he had destroyed.

One clause.

SECTION XCIX. — *Taking away, without Leave, the Fruit growing in Gardens, or Orchards.*

Whoever, without leave, takes away or eats the fruit growing in the grounds or gardens of another, shall be liable to punishment in proportion to the value thereof, according to the law concerning pecuniary injuries. — Destroying or damaging the fruit shall be punished according to the same scale; and if the fruit so eaten or destroyed is taken from grounds or gardens belonging to government which had been appropriated to the preparation of fermented or spirituous liquors, or of any articles of subsistence for the public service, the punishment shall be in each of such cases, two degrees more severe than it would have been otherwise.

If the person who has the charge of any such property of government, gives it away, or connives at its being taken away, he shall equally participate in the punishment of the receiver or consumer. If he appropriates the same to his own use, he shall suffer punishment in proportion to the amount, according to the law concerning the embezzlement of the property of government.

No clauſe.

SECTION C.—*Miſapplication of the Boats or Carriages of Government.*

If any perſon having the cuſtody of the property, or the ſuperintendance over any of the departments, of government, applies to his own private uſe and advantage, or lends out to others, the carriages, boats, warehouſes, mills, or other buildings or implements belonging to government; he, as well as the borrower of ſuch articles, ſhall ſuffer 50 blows; and if an officer of government, the offender ſhall moreover forfeit to the ſtate the eſtimated amount of the charge of the hire of the articles, to any extent not exceeding their value. The offenders ſhall likewiſe be liable to puniſhment in proportion to the amount of the aforeſaid charge, one degree more ſeverely than the law preſcribes in ordinary caſes of pecuniary injury, whenever ſuch puniſhment, being greater, ſuperſedes that hereby provided.

No clauſe.

END OF THE SECOND BOOK OF THE THIRD DIVISION.

BOOK III.

MARRIAGE *.

SECTION CI. — *Marriages how regulated.*

WHEN a marriage is intended to be contracted, it ſhall be, in the firſt inſtance, reciprocally explained to, and clearly underſtood by, the families intereſted, whether the parties who deſign to marry are or are not diſeaſed, infirm, aged, or under age; and whether they are the children of their parents by blood, or only by adoption; if either of the contracting families then object, the proceedings ſhall be carried no further; if they ſtill approve, they ſhall then in conjunction with the negociators of the marriage, if ſuch there be, draw up the marriage-articles, and determine the amount of the marriage-preſents.

If, after the woman is thus regularly affianced by the recognition of the marriage-articles, or by a perſonal interview and agreement between the families, the family of the intended bride ſhould repent having entered into the contract, and refuſe to execute it, the perſon amongſt them who had authority to give her away ſhall be puniſhed with 50 blows, and the marriage ſhall be completed agreeably to the original

* The peculiar cuſtoms and uſages which are adverted to in this book of the laws, will be found illuſtrated and exemplified in a pleaſing manner, together with an intereſting picture of domeſtic life in China, in an Engliſh tranſlation of a Chineſe novel, which was edited many years ago by the learned and ingenious Dr. Percy, Biſhop of Dromore, under the title of "*Hau-Kiou-Choaan*, or the Pleaſing Hiſtory." — The tranſlation of this little work, not having been edited by the tranſlator, and having, in part, been taken from a Portugueſe verſion, cannot be expected to be minutely accurate, though perhaps ſufficiently ſo for the purpoſe in view, and the tranſlator of the preſent work has had the ſatiſfaction of aſcertaining its authenticity, by a compariſon with the Chineſe original, of which he has a copy now in his poſſeſſion.

original contract. — Although the marriage-articles ſhould not have been drawn up in writing, the acceptance of the marriage-preſents ſhall be ſufficient evidence of the agreement between the parties.

If, after the female is affianced, but previous to the completion of the marriage, her family promiſes her in marriage to another, the perſon having authority to give her away ſhall be puniſhed with 70 blows; if ſuch promiſe is made after the firſt marriage is actually completed, (that is to ſay, the bride is perſonally preſented to and received by the bridegroom) the puniſhment ſhall be encreaſed to 80 blows.

If the perſon who accepts ſuch promiſe is, at the ſame time, aware of the exiſtence of a previous contract or marriage, he ſhall participate equally in the puniſhment, and whatever marriage-preſents he may have tranſmitted on the ſtrength of ſuch promiſe, ſhall be forfeited to government. — On the other hand, if ignorant thereof, he ſhall not be puniſhable, and the marriage-preſents made by him ſhall be reſtored. — The bride ſhall remain with the bridegroom to whom ſhe was firſt married or affianced, unleſs he declines, in which caſe he ſhall receive back the amount of his marriage-preſent, and the bride ſhall be transferred to the family of the bridegroom to whom ſhe was ſecondly affianced.

If the family of the intended bridegroom, after having agreed as aforeſaid, repents of the contract, and makes marriage-preſents to another woman, the ſame puniſhment ſhall be inflicted, as in the caſes already mentioned. The bridegroom ſhall be obliged to receive his originally intended bride; and the female, to whom he is ſecondly affianced, ſhall retain the marriage-preſents made to her, and be at the ſame time at liberty to marry another perſon.

If either of the contracted parties, previous to the completion of the marriage, are guilty of theft or adultery; that is to ſay, have been convicted of offences of ſuch a deſcription, the law for puniſhing a breach of the contract as aforeſaid ſhall not be enforced. If the family of the

the bride deceives the family of the bridegroom, ſo as to induce them to contract a marriage, by indicating and leading them to expect a different perſon from the one actually named and deſcribed in the contract, the giver away of the woman ſhall be puniſhed with 80 blows, and her family ſhall reſtore the marriage-preſents. If the family of the bridegroom is guilty of this offence, the puniſhment of the contractor ſhall be one degree more ſevere, and the marriage-preſents ſhall remain with the family of the bride. If ſuch marriage, thus contracted through miſrepreſentation, is not completed, the bride or bridegroom, whom the other party had been led to expect, ſhall complete the marriage, inſtead of the bride or bridegroom who had been deceitfully ſubſtituted; if the marriage under the aforeſaid falſe pretences, had nevertheleſs been completed, it ſhall be ſufficient that the parties be ſeparated.

Although the parties had been lawfully affianced to each other, and the marriage preſents delivered and accepted; yet if the bridegroom forcibly takes away his bride, previous to the period agreed upon, or if the bride is deſignedly retained and refuſed to the bridegroom, after ſuch period is arrived, the contractor of the marriage in the latter caſe, and the bridegroom in the former caſe, ſhall be puniſhed with 50 blows.

If, while a junior relation is at a diſtance from his family, and engaged either in trade, or in official employment under government, his grandfather, father, uncle, or ſenior couſin, binds him by a marriage-contract, and he, being ignorant thereof, happens to contract and complete a marriage with ſome other female during his abſence, ſuch marriage ſhall be held valid, and the contract made by his relations being therefore ſet aſide, the affianced female will be at liberty to contract another marriage. If however, ſuch abſent junior member of a family had only contracted a marriage, he ſhall relinquiſh it, and in preference fulfil that contract of marriage which had been made for him by his relations, the female to whom he had perſonally contracted himſelf, being alſo freed from her engagement to him. — A breach of

this

this law ſhall be puniſhed with 80 blows, and compliance with theſe regulations ſhall be duly enforced by the magiſtrate of the diſtrict.

Four clauſes.

Section CII. — *Lending Wives or Daughters on Hire.*

Whoever lends any one of his wives, to be hired as a temporary wife, ſhall be puniſhed with 80 blows,—whoever lends his daughter in like manner, ſhall be puniſhed with 60 blows; the wife or daughter in ſuch caſes, ſhall not be held reſponſible.

Whoever, falſely repreſenting any of his wives as his ſiſter, gives her away in marriage, ſhall receive 100 blows, and the wife conſenting thereto, ſhall be puniſhed with 80 blows.

Thoſe who knowingly receive in marriage the wives, or hire for a limited time the wives or daughters of others, ſhall participate equally in the aforeſaid puniſhment, and the parties thus unlawfully connected, ſhall be ſeparated; the daughter ſhall be returned to her parents, and the wife to the family to which ſhe originally belonged; the pecuniary conſideration in each caſe ſhall be forfeited to government. Thoſe who ignorantly receive ſuch perſons in marriage, contrary to the laws, ſhall be excuſed, and recover the amount of the marriage-preſents.

One clauſe.

Section CIII. — *Regard to Rank and Priority among Wives* *.

Whoever degrades his firſt or principal wife to the condition of an inferior wife or concubine, ſhall be puniſhed with 100 blows. Whoever

* The peculiar limitations under which polygamy is allowed in China require here ſome explanation, as it was impoſſible in tranſlating the text, to diſtinguiſh by any terms ſtrictly appropriate, the two modes of eſpouſal which are eſtabliſhed by the Chineſe laws, and which are equally diſtinct in point of form as in their legal conſequences.

The

ever, during the life-time of his firſt wife, raiſes an inferior wife to the rank and condition of a firſt wife, ſhall be puniſhed with 90 blows, and in both the caſes, each of the ſeveral wives ſhall be replaced in the rank to which ſhe was originally intitled upon her marriage.

Whoever, having a firſt wife living, enters into marriage with another female as a firſt wife, ſhall likewiſe be puniſhed with 90 blows; and the marriage being conſidered null and void, the parties ſhall be ſeparated, and the woman returned to her parents.

No clauſe.

Section CIV. — *Ejecting from Home a Son-in-law* *.

Whoever either ejects the huſband of his daughter whom he had received into his houſe as his ſon-in-law, or receives into his houſe another perſon, as the huſband of ſuch daughter, ſhall be puniſhed with 100 blows. The wife ſhall not be puniſhed unleſs ſhe had aſſiſted

---

The firſt or principal wife is uſually choſen for the huſband by his parents or ſenior relations, out of a family equal in point of rank and to other circumſtances to his own, and is eſpouſed with as much ſplendour and ceremony as the parties can afford; and the bride, when ſhe is received into the houſe of the bridegroom, acquires all the rights and privileges, which, under the degraded ſtate of the female ſex in Aſiatic nations, can be ſuppoſed to belong to a lawful wife.

A Chineſe may afterwards lawfully eſpouſe other wives, agreeably to his own choice, and with fewer ceremonies, as well as without any regard to equality in point of family and connexions: theſe wives are all ſubordinate to the firſt wife, but equal in rank among themſelves. In deſcribing this connexion, the term *inferior wife* has been preferred to that of hand-maid, or concubine, as there are always certain forms of eſpouſal, and as the children of ſuch wives have a contingent right to the inheritance.

* It is remarked in a note in the original Chineſe, that the bridegroom, who, inſtead of taking home his bride to his own houſe, lives with her at the houſe of her parents, by ſo doing, deviates from the eſtabliſhed forms of eſpouſal; but that having been once ſo received as a ſon-in-law, the law protects him in the right which he had acquired, of either remaining there with his wife, or taking her away with him to a ſeparate eſtabliſhment.

and

and concurred in the ejection of her hufband, in which cafe fhe fhall likewife fuffer 100 blows. The perfon, moreover, who is fecondly received as a fon-in-law, if privy to the illegality of the tranfaction, fhall participate equally in the punifhment, and forfeit to government the marriage-prefent, but otherwife, fhall be excufed from the punifhment and the forfeiture. When the firft marriage had been contracted, but not completed, the ejection of the intended fon-in-law fhall be punifhed lefs feverely by five degrees. — The woman fhall belong to her firft contracted hufband, and live with him feparately from her father and mother.

No claufe.

Section CV. — *Marriage during the legal Period of Mourning.*

If any man or woman enters into an equal marriage during the legal period of mourning for a deceafed parent, or any widow enters into a fecond and equal marriage within the legal period of mourning for her deceafed hufband, the offending party fhall be punifhed with 100 blows.

If it is not an equal match, that is to fay, if a man takes an inferior wife from a fubordinate rank, or a woman connects herfelf in marriage as one of the inferior wives of her hufband, the punifhment attending a breach of this law fhall be lefs by two degrees.

If a widow who, during the life of her hufband, had received honorary rank from the Emperor, ever marries again, fhe fhall fuffer punifhment as above defcribed, and moreover lofe her rank, as well as be feparated from her fecond hufband.

Whoever knowingly contracts marriage with a widow of rank, or with any widow during the legal period of mourning, fhall fuffer punifhment in each cafe proportionably lefs by five degrees, and the marriage-prefent fhall be forfeited to government; if ignorant of the illegality

illegality of his conduct, he ſhall be exempt from puniſhment, and recover the marriage-preſent, but ſtill be ſeparated from his wife, as in the caſes already ſtated.

Whoever marries on equal terms, during the period of legal mourning for a grand-father, grand-mother, uncle or aunt, elder brother or elder ſiſter, ſhall ſuffer 80 blows, but the marriage ſhall nevertheleſs be valid.

The marriage of, or with, inferior wives within ſuch period ſhall be excuſed.

Whoever within the period of mourning for a father, mother, father or mother-in-law, or for a huſband, completes an intended marriage to which the parties had been previouſly affianced, ſhall be puniſhed with 80 blows.

If a widow, after the expiration of mourning for her huſband, is really unwilling to enter into a ſecond marriage; and nevertheleſs, her parents, grand-parents, or the parents or grand-parents of her late huſband, force her to marry again, the party ſo compelling his daughter or grand-daughter to marry, ſhall be puniſhed with 80 blows. If the widow is ſo compelled by any other relation in the firſt degree, ſuch relation ſhall be puniſhed one degree more ſeverely;—if in a more remote degree, two degrees more ſeverely. Neither the widow nor her ſecond huſband ſhall in theſe caſes be puniſhable.—If the marriage is only contracted, but not completed, the widow ſhall remain in her firſt huſband's family, and be permitted to continue ſingle, and the marriage preſent ſhall be returned;—if the marriage has been completed, the widow ſhall live with her ſecond huſband, but the marriage-preſent ſhall be forfeited to government.

One clauſe.

SECTION CVI. — *Marriage during the Imprifonment of Parents.*

Whoever marries a wife or a hufband upon equal terms of efpoufal, having a father, mother, grand-father or grand-mother at the fame time under confinement in prifon for a capital offence, fhall be punifhed with 80 blows; — whoever at fuch time receives in marriage, or becomes by marriage, a fubordinate wife, fhall fuffer punifhment lefs by two degrees.

Neverthelefs, if any fuch perfon enters into the marriage ftate at fuch period, by the exprefs command of his or her parent or grand-parent in prifon, no punifhment fhall enfue, provided the ufual feaft and entertainment is omitted; otherwife a punifhment of 80 blows fhall ftill be inflicted.

No claufe.

SECTION CVII. — *Marriage between Perfons having the fame Family-Name.*

Whenever any perfons having the fame family-name intermarry, the parties and the contractor of the marriage fhall each receive 60 blows, and the marriage being null and void, the man and woman fhall be feparated, and the marriage-prefents forfeited to government *.

No claufe.

* The moft ufual term in the Chinefe language for defcribing "the people or nation," is *Pe-fing*, or "the hundred names." Although the names of families in China are at prefent fomewhat more numerous, they are very few in proportion to the immenfe population, and the reftrictions impofed by this law upon marriage muft therefore be often embarraffing and inconvenient, however little the choice and inclination of the parties themfelves, may under any circumftances, be confulted.

SEC-

SECTION CVIII. — *Marriage between Perſons related by Marriage.*

In general all marriages between perſons who through another marriage are already related to each other in any of the four degrees, and all marriages with ſiſters by the ſame mother, though by a different father, or with the daughters of a wife's former huſband, ſhall be conſidered as inceſtuous, and puniſhed according to the law againſt a criminal intercourſe with ſuch relations *.

A man ſhall not marry his father's or mother's ſiſter-in-law, his father's or mother's aunt's daughters, his ſon-in-law's or daughter-in-law's ſiſter, or his grandſon's wife's ſiſter, on pain of receiving 100 blows for ſuch offence.

Whoever marries his mother's brothers or mother's ſiſter's daughter, ſhall receive 80 blows, and in theſe as well as the foregoing caſes, the marriage ſhall be annulled, and the marriage-preſent forfeited.

Two clauſes.

SECTION CIX. — *Marriage with Relations by Blood, or with the Widows of ſuch Relations.*

Whoever marries a female relation beyond the fourth degree, or the widow of a male relation equally remote, ſhall be puniſhed with 100 blows. Whoever marries the widow of a relation in the fourth degree, or of a ſiſter's ſon, ſhall be puniſhed with 60 blows, and one year's baniſhment. — Whoever marries the widow of any nearer relation, ſhall be puniſhed according to the law againſt inceſtuous connexions with ſuch perſons. Neverthelefs, when the connexion had been broken by a divorce, or an intervening marriage with a ſtranger, the offence ſhall in general be only puniſhed with 80 blows.

* The book of the laws referred to in this and the following ſection is contained in the criminal diviſion of the code, and entitled, *Inceſt and Adultery.*

Whoever receives in marriage any of his father's or grandfather's former wives, or his father's ſiſters, ſhall, whether they had been divorced or re-married, in all caſes ſuffer death, by being beheaded. Whoever marries his brother's widow, ſhall be ſtrangled.

The foregoing caſes, in general apply to firſt wives only, and the puniſhment of marrying the inferior wives of ſuch relatives as aforeſaid, ſhall be leſs in each caſe by two degrees.

Whoever marries any female relation in the fourth, or any nearer degree, ſhall be puniſhed according to the law concerning inceſt, and all ſuch inceſtuous marriages ſhall be null and void.

Two clauſes.

SECTION CX. — *Marriage of Officers of Government into Families ſubject to their Juriſdiction.*

If any officer belonging to the government of a city of the firſt, ſecond, or third order, marries, while in office, the wife or daughter of any inhabitant of the country under his juriſdiction, he ſhall be puniſhed with 80 blows.

If any officer of government marries the wife or daughter of any perſon having an intereſt in the legal proceedings at the ſame time under his inveſtigation, he ſhall be puniſhed with 100 blows, and the member of the family of the bride, who gave her away, ſhall be equally puniſhable. The woman, whether previouſly married or not, ſhall be reſtored to her parents, and the marriage-preſent forfeited in every caſe to government.

If the officer of government accompliſhes the marriage by the force or influence of his authority, his puniſhment ſhall be increaſed two degrees, and the family of the female, being in ſuch a caſe exempt from reſponſibility, ſhe ſhall, if previouſly ſingle, be reſtored to her parents;

rents; and if previoufly married, to her former hufband; the marriage-prefent fhall not in either cafe be forfeited.

If any officer of government, inftead of marrying the female himfelf in any of the above cafes, gives her in marriage to his fon, grandfon, younger brother, nephew, or other perfon belonging to his houfehold, he fhall be liable to the fame punifhment as aforefaid, but neither the bride nor the bridegroom fhall fuffer for fuch offence.

When the marriage is a compenfation for fome unjuft decifion on a fubject under the magiftrate's inveftigation, the punifhment fhall be encreafed as far as the law, applicable to fuch a deviation from juftice, may authorize.

No claufe.

SECTION CXI. — *Marriage with abfconded Females.*

Whoever receives and marries a female criminal, who had abfconded from the fear of punifhment, fhall, whether fhe had been previoufly married or not, be punifhable to the full extent of the crime fuch female had committed, fetting afide only the aggravation of two degrees to which fhe is liable from her being a fugitive, and with a reduction of one degree, when the offence of the female is of a nature to be punifhable with death. The marriage fhall moreover be annulled, and the parties feparated, unlefs the female was previoufly fingle, and obtains the benefit of a fpecial or general pardon. When the perfon marrying a criminal fugitive had been ignorant of the circumftance of her being fuch, he fhall be excufed.

No claufe.

SECTION CXII. — *Forcible Marriage of a free Man's Wife or Daughter.*

Whoever, confiding in his power and influence, feizes by violence the wife or daughter of a free-man, and carries her away to make her one

one of his wives, ſhall ſuffer death, by being ſtrangled after the uſual period of confinement.

If the female was ſingle, ſhe ſhall be returned to her parents or relations; and, if previouſly married, to her lawful huſband.

Whoever, inſtead of marrying ſuch female himſelf, gives her in marriage to his ſon, grand-ſon, brother, nephew, or other perſon of his houſehold, ſhall be liable to the ſame puniſhment, and the parties ſhall be ſeparated, as in the former caſe; but the huſband, not being the contriver of the offence, ſhall not be puniſhable.

Four clauſes.

SECTION CXIII. — *Marriage with Female Muſicians and Comedians.*

If any officer or clerk of government, either in the civil or military department, marries, as his firſt or other wife, a female muſician or comedian, he ſhall be puniſhed with 60 blows, and the marriage being null and void, the female ſhall be ſent back to her parents and rendered incapable of returning to her profeſſion. The marriage-preſent ſhall be forfeited to government.

If the ſon or grand-ſon, being the heir of any officer of government having hereditary rank, commits this offence, he ſhall ſuffer the ſame puniſhment, and whenever he ſucceeds to the inheritance, his parental honours ſhall deſcend to him under a reduction of one degree.

No clauſe.

SECTION CXIV. — *Marriage of Prieſts of* Foe *or* Tao-ſſe *.

If any prieſt of *Foe* or *Tao-ſſe* takes a firſt or inferior wife, he ſhall be puniſhed with 80 blows, and expelled from the order to which he belonged. The member of the family of the female who gave her

* See Section XLII. and LXXVII. relative to theſe orders of prieſthood in China.

away

away in marriage ſhall be equally puniſhable; the marriage ſhall be null and void, the female ſent back to her family, and the marriage-preſent forfeited to government; all the other prieſts of the ſame eſtabliſhment who were privy to the offence, ſhall be ſubject to the ſame corporal puniſhment, but not to expulſion from their order; if ignorant of the offence having been committed, they ſhall not ſuffer puniſhment in any reſpect.

If a prieſt ſolicits a woman in marriage, under pretence of obtaining a wife for his relations or ſervants, and afterwards appropriates the female to himſelf, the offence ſhall be puniſhed according to the law prohibiting inceſtuous intercourſe and adultery.

No clauſe.

SECTION CXV. — *Marriage between Free perſons and Slaves.*

If any maſter of a family ſolicits and obtains in marriage for his ſlave, the daughter of a free-man, he ſhall be puniſhed with 80 blows; — the member of the family who gives away the female in marriage ſhall ſuffer the ſame puniſhment, if aware that the intended huſband is a ſlave, but not otherwiſe.

A ſlave ſoliciting and obtaining a daughter of a free-man in marriage, ſhall alſo be puniſhed in the ſame manner; and if the maſter of the ſlave conſents thereto, he ſhall ſuffer puniſhment leſs by two degrees; but, if he moreover receives ſuch free-woman into his family as a ſlave, he ſhall be puniſhed with 100 blows.

Likewiſe, whoever falſely repreſents a ſlave to be free, and thereby procures ſuch ſlave a free huſband or wife, ſhall ſuffer 90 blows. In all theſe caſes the marriage ſhall be null and void, and the parties replaced in the ranks they had reſpectively held in the community.

No clauſe.

SEC-

SECTION CXVI. — *Law of Divorce.*

If a hufband repudiates his firft wife, without her having broken the matrimonial connexion by the crime of adultery, or otherwife; and without her having furnifhed him with any of the feven juftifying caufes of divorce, he fhall in every fuch cafe be punifhed with 80 blows. Moreover, although one of the feven juftifying caufes of divorce fhould be chargeable upon the wife, namely, (1) barrennefs; (2) lafcivioufnefs; (3) difregard of her hufband's parents; (4) talkativenefs; (5) thievifh propenfities; (6) envious and fufpicious temper; and, laftly, (7) inveterate infirmity; yet, if any of the three reafons againft a divorce fhould exift, namely, (1) the wife's having mourned three years for her hufband's parents; (2) the family's having become rich after having been poor previous to, and at the time of, marriage; and, (3) the wife's having no parents living to receive her back again; in thefe cafes, none of the feven aforementioned caufes will juftify a divorce, and the hufband who puts away his wife upon fuch grounds, fhall fuffer punifhment two degrees lefs than that laft ftated, and be obliged to receive her again.

If the wife fhall have broken the matrimonial connexion by an act of adultery, or by any other act, which by law not only authorizes but requires that the parties fhould be feparated, the hufband fhall receive a punifhment of 80 blows, if he retains her.

When the hufband and wife do not agree, and both parties are defirous of feparation, the law limiting the right of divorce fhall not be enforced to prevent it.

If, upon the hufband's refufing to confent to a divorce, the wife quits her home and abfconds, fhe fhall be punifhed with 100 blows, and her hufband fhall be allowed to fell her in marriage; if, during fuch abfence from her home, fhe contracts marriage with another perfon, fhe fhall fuffer death, by being ftrangled, after the ufual period of confinement.

If,

If, previous to the expiration of a period of three years after a hufband had deferted and been no more heard of by his wife, fuch wife, without giving notice at a tribunal of government, fhould likewife quit her home and abfcond, fhe fhall be punifhed with 80 blows; and the punifhment fhall be increafed to 100 blows, if fhe fhould moreover prefume to contract another marriage within fuch period.

In all the foregoing cafes, the firft wife only is intended to be adverted to, but the laws in every inftance fhall be applied in cafes of the inferior wives, upon a reduction being made in the punifhment to the extent of two degrees for each offence.

To render the act of the wife a fecond marriage, there muft have been a perfon to give her away to the new hufband, and a delivery of marriage-prefents; otherwife, it is to be confidered fimply as a cafe of adultery.

If a female flave deferts from her mafter's houfe, fhe fhall be punifhed with 80 blows, or with 100 blows if fhe contracts a marriage during fuch abfence, and in both cafes fhe fhall be reftored to her mafter.

Whoever harbours a fugitive wife or flave, or marries them knowing them to be fugitives, fhall participate equally in their punifhment, except in capital cafes, when the punifhment fhall be reduced one degree. The marriage-prefent in all fuch cafes is forfeited to government. When, however, the perfon harbouring or marrying the fugitive is really ignorant of her criminality, he fhall not be fubject to any punifhment, and fhall be even entitled to demand the return of the marriage-prefent.

In the foregoing cafes, if the giver-away in marriage of a fugitive wife, in the abfence of her lawful hufband, is an elder relation in the firft degree of fuch female, the punifhment attending fuch unlawful marriage fhall be folely inflicted on the relation, and the female fhall fuffer, without aggravation, the punifhment to which fhe was liable as a fugitive.

If the giver-away in marriage of ſuch female was any more remote elder relation, the relation ſhall ſtill be puniſhed as in the laſt inſtance, but the female and the perſon marrying her, ſhall likewiſe be puniſhable, as acceſſaries to the aggravated offence. If, in ſuch caſes, the propoſal of the marriage is ſhewn to ariſe from the parties themſelves, they ſhall be puniſhed as principals, and the giver-away of the female as an acceſſary only; but the puniſhment of the latter, although in extreme caſes nominally capital, ſhall never exceed 100 blows and perpetual baniſhment to the diſtance of 3000 *lee.*

Two clauſes.

SECTION CXVII. — *Giving in Marriage unlawfully.*

In all marriages contracted contrary to law, if the giver-away of the bride, or the contractor of the marriage on the part of the huſband, is the paternal or maternal grand-father, grand-mother, father, mother, paternal uncle or aunt, or paternal elder male or female couſin, the puniſhment denounced by law ſhall be ſolely inflicted on ſuch relations, and the parties themſelves ſhall not be held reſponſible.

When the giver-away of the wife, or contractor of the marriage as aforeſaid, is a more remote relation of the party marrying, but is ſtill the chief agent in procuring the unlawful marriage, he or ſhe ſhall be puniſhed as a principal, but the huſband and wife ſhall likewiſe participate in the puniſhment of the offence, as acceſſaries.

If, on the contrary, the unlawful marriage contracted as above originated with the parties themſelves, they ſhall be puniſhed as principals in the offence, and thoſe who contracted the match for them, as acceſſaries only.

When, according to the application of theſe rules, the parties to a marriage are puniſhable as principals with death, the law ſhall be carried ſtrictly into effect; but, when the perſons who contracted an unlawful

lawful marriage in behalf of others, are nominally liable to capital punishment, it shall be mitigated one degree; those, however, who are punished as their accessaries, shall still suffer as accessaries to a capital offence.

Moreover, if the husband and wife, in consequence of having been previously terrified and threatened by their elder relations, had entered into an unlawful marriage, which they had not themselves devised or originated; or if the husband was not twenty years of age complete, and the wife had never previously quitted her parent's roof, the contractors on each side of the unlawful marriage shall, under such circumstances, be alone punishable and responsible.

When any unlawful marriage has been only contracted, but not completed, the punishment of the responsible parties shall always be less by five degrees.

The negotiator of any unlawful marriage, knowing it be unlawful, shall suffer punishment within one degree of that inflicted on the responsible party, but otherwise shall be excused.

In general, in every case in which it is directed that an unlawful marriage shall be annulled, the parties shall be placed in the same condition as that in which they were previous to the marriage; and although any general act of pardon should intervene, and occasion a remission of the punishment denounced by law against them as public offenders, such pardon shall be no bar to the divorce.

In general also, when the party giving the marriage-present is, at the same time, aware of the unlawfulness of the transaction, such present shall be forfeited to government; but otherwise it shall be restored to the giver.

Three clauses.

END OF THE THIRD BOOK OF THE THIRD DIVISION.

BOOK IV.

PUBLIC PROPERTY.

SECTION CXVIII. — *Regulations concerning Coinage* *.

ACCORDING to the regulations concerning coinage, there are founderies and mints where the metal is prepared and caſt, and alſo proper ſtore-houſes in which the coin is depoſited until required for the public ſervice. The quantity of metal coined in the former, and the periods of its iſſue from the latter, ſhall be ſtrictly conformable to the deliberate reſolutions thereon of the ſupreme court for affairs of revenue, in order that the ſucceſſive ſupplies of coin for the uſe of the people may correſpond with their wants, and be regulated according to the market-prices of gold, ſilver, grain, and other articles in general uſe and conſumption.

Whoever, having authority in any of theſe departments, retains and accumulates the coin, inſtead of diſtributing it at due ſeaſons, ſhall be puniſhed with 60 blows.

* It is well known to be the policy of the Chineſe government to have no other currency than a ſmall coin of baſe metal, chiefly copper, of which the legal value is one thouſandth part of a *leang*, or Chineſe ounce of ſilver; the actual exchange ſometimes riſes above, and ſometimes falls ſhort of this rate, in conſequence of the intrinſic value of the coinage of different dates varying according to the relative proportions as well as total quantities of the metals employed, while the value of ſilver is alſo neceſſarily ſubject to fluctuation, as that of any other marketable commodity.

On account of the inconvenience which would attend the payment of large ſums in a coin of ſo low a denomination, and as paper currency is at preſent altogether unknown in the empire, ingots of pure ſilver, of one and of ten Chineſe ounces weight, (uſually caſt in moulds, and diſtinguiſhed with a peculiar ſtamp,) are moſt generally employed on ſuch occaſions, eſpecially in all payments to government; but it is to be obſerved, that of late, the European trade has introduced the Spaniſh dollar into ſuch extenſive circulation in many of the provinces of China, that, excepting the officers of the government, it is very generally known and received among the natives, and even at a rate beyond its intrinſic value, in conſideration of the apparent ſecurity againſt fraud, which is afforded by the impreſſion.

In

In no private dwelling of any ſoldier or citizen ſhall any utenſils of copper, or chiefly of copper, be uſed, except mirrors, military arms, bells, and articles ſpecially conſecrated to religious purpoſes; but whatever quantity of copper any individual may have in exceſs, he ſhall be permitted to ſell to government at the rate of ſeven *fen*, (or hundreth parts of a *leang* or ounce of ſilver) for every *kin* weight of copper, or as much more or leſs as the ſtate of the market and circumſtances may authorize *.

Whoever buys or ſells copper clandeſtinely, or conceals the ſame in his houſe, inſtead of offering it for ſale to government, ſhall be puniſhed with 40 blows.

Three clauſes.

SECTION CXIX. — *Periods eſtabliſhed for collecting the Revenues in Kind.*

For the purpoſe of receiving the impoſt on the ſummer harveſt, conſiſting of wheat only, the granaries of government ſhall be opened on the 15th of the 5th moon, and the whole of the impoſt laid in by the cloſe of the 7th moon †.

For the purpoſe of receiving the impoſt on the autumnal harveſt, which is of grain in general, the granaries of government ſhall be re-opened on the firſt of the 10th moon, and the whole laid in by the end of the 12th moon.

This law ſhall not prevent the receipt of thoſe impoſts at an earlier period, provided an unuſually early harveſt ſhould admit of it, but if the ſummer impoſt is, at the end of the 8th moon, or the autumnal

* A Chineſe ounce of ſilver being eſtimated at *6s. 8d.* ſterling, the average value of copper will appear to be no more that $5\frac{6}{10}$ pence a *kin* weight, (exceeding the Engliſh pound by one-third,) but this (if it is not indeed merely ſtated at random) can only be conſidered as applicable to the period of the original promulgation of the code.

† Reſpecting the Chineſe mode of computing time, ſee the note to the XLI. Section.

impoſt

impoſt at the end of the 1ſt moon of the ſucceeding year, ſtill deficient, the magiſtrate of the diſtrict, the magiſtrate ſuperintending the collection of the revenue in grain, their reſpective clerks, the officiating head inhabitants of the diſtricts in which the collection has been deficient, and the landholders not duly contributing, ſhall all of them be ſeverally reſponſible, each in his proper degree, according to the proportion the deficiency bears in each particular caſe to the whole amount which was due, or which ought to have been collected or furniſhed. If one-tenth, the puniſhment ſhall amount to 60 blows, and the puniſhment ſhall be encreaſed one degree for every tenth deficient, as far as the limit of 100 blows.

If the magiſtrates, their clerks, or the head inhabitants, have been convicted of bribery, they ſhall be puniſhed as much more ſeverely as the law concerning bribery for unlawful purpoſes may authorize.

If the deficiency in the contribution is not made up within a twelvemonth after it was due, the land-holder and the head inhabitant ſhall reſpectively be puniſhed with 100 blows, and the magiſtrates and their reſpective clerks ſhall ſuffer puniſhment in the manner ordered and provided in the ſupplemental regulations.

Six clauſes.

SECTION CXX.—*Fairneſs and Impartiality in collecting the Revenues in Kind.*

The officers and attendants belonging to the granaries of government, when collecting the impoſts in grain, ſhall permit each of the contributors perſonally to attend and meaſure the proportions of grain for the delivery of which he is anſwerable; and all ſuch allowances ſhall be made ſuch contributors as are warranted by the particular regulations of the ſeveral provinces.

If

If the officer ſuperintending the grain department, or the collector under his controul, refuſes to receive fair meaſure from the contributing land-holder, and inſiſts on ſhaking the grain into as ſmall compaſs as poſſible, or piles the grain into a heap, inſtead of ſtriking it at the upper edge of the containing veſſel, he ſhall receive at the leaſt a puniſhment of 60 blows, and be liable to any increaſe in the puniſhment not exceeding 100 blows, which, according to the eſtimated value of the overplus, may reſult from the application to this caſe of the law for puniſhing pecuniary injuries in general.

Theſe laws, however, are only intended to be applied to the caſes in which the exceſs exacted from the contributors is duly appropriated to the uſe and ſervice of government. If the offender applies the exceſs ſo exacted to his own uſe and advantage, he will be liable to ſeverer puniſhment, as an embezzler of the property of government.

If the ſuperintending magiſtrate of the diſtrict is privy to the commiſſion of this offence, and does not take cognizance of it, he ſhall be equally puniſhable, but ſhall not otherwiſe be held reſponſible. The exceſs of grain which may have been exacted, ſhall be reſtored to the reſpective contributors.

Three clauſes.

SECTION CXXI. — *Concealing or waſting the Proportion of exciſeable Articles ſet apart for the Uſe of Government.*

In all caſes in which the land-holder or houſe-holder is allowed to deliver in himſelf the proportion of his goods ſettled at the examination of the exciſe-officer or collector, as in the inſtances of the ſilk-worm-feeder and the metal-worker; and, in general, when any individual is reſponſible for the delivery of any article whatever to government, if, after having received the official notice demanding the ſame, the contributor conceals, waſtes, or appropriates to his own uſe, any part of the amount of of the articles due by him to government, and attempts to deceive the magiſtrate by alleging that ſuch part had been loſt or deſtroyed by fire, water, or thieves, he ſhall be puniſhed in proportion to the eſtimated value of the amount remaining due by him, according to the law againſt theft in ordinary caſes; nevertheleſs, the puniſhment ſhall not in any caſe exceed 100 blows and perpetual baniſhment to the diſtance of 3000 *lee*, and the offender ſhall not be branded.

If the officers and clerks of the department are privy to the offence, they ſhall ſuffer equal puniſhment with the offending party, but otherwiſe ſhall not be held reſponſible. The offence, not being conſidered of a private and perſonal nature, ſhall not ſubject the magiſtrates to loſe their offices, unleſs they are at the ſame time convicted of bribery, which will render them liable to ſuch aggravation of the ſentence as may reſult from the law againſt bribery for an unlawful purpoſe.

Among others, the poorer land-holders and houſe-holders, who, when employed according to cuſtom in conveying or ſuperintending the conveyance of government property, avail themſelves of ſuch opportunities of committing any waſte or depredation, ſhall be puniſhable conformably to this law.

One clauſe.

Section CXXII. — *Vicarious Contributors to the Revenue.*

Whoever undertakes to deliver to government the amount of the impoſt due from another, ſhall ſuffer 60 blows, and ſhall ſtill, in behalf of the reſponſible proprietor, deliver into the granary of government the whole amount originally due, and half as much more, by way of forfeiture *.

* The object of the enactment of this law, appears to be to prevent any perſon from deriving an intermediate profit from the collection of the revenue, as ſuch profit muſt neceſſarily either reduce the receipts on account of government, or become an addition to the burthen ſuſtained by the contributor.

If

If the ſuperintending officer of government himſelf undertakes this vicarious mode of paying the legal contribution, his puniſhment ſhall (excluſive of the payment and forfeiture) be two degrees more ſevere than that of any other individual in a ſimilar caſe.

The penalties of this law ſhall not, however, extend to thoſe poorer land-holders or houſe-holders who, in conſequence of their reſpective ſhares of rice or wheat being individually leſs than the eſtimated ſhare of one family, unite together, and appoint one to contribute for the whole.

If the vicarious contributor is guilty of any deception, or does not contribute ſufficiently, he ſhall, moreover, be liable to puniſhment in the ſame manner as the ordinary contributors.

Two clauſes.

SECTION CXXIII. — *Premature Diſcharges, or Quittances for Taxes due to Government.*

The contribution to the revenue payable into the treaſuries in ſpecie, or to be depoſited in kind in the public granaries, muſt not fall ſhort of the amount determined by law; and if, previous to the full ſatiſfaction of the claims of government, the ſuperintendant of the department, in concurrence with the ſuperior officer commanding the diſtrict, grants a general acquittance to any inhabitant, all the officers of the ſeveral public boards thus concurring therein ſhall be puniſhed, each in proportion to the total amount deficient, according to the law regarding an embezzlement of government ſtores to the ſame extent.

When an officer of government is diſpatched to any quarter with ſpecial powers and inſtructions for the collection of duties and taxes, if, in conjunction with the magiſtrates of the revenue department, and of the diſtrict in general, he reports falſely or prematurely to his ſuperiors that all the claims of government are ſatisfied, he, and thoſe concurring with him, ſhall, in like manner, be liable to the penalties of this law.

If any of the offending parties ſhall have been bribed for this purpoſe, they ſhall be liable to any contingent aggravation of the puniſhment reſulting from the law againſt bribery for unlawful purpoſes.

If the officer intruſted with the collection of the revenue grants the partial receipts or quittances which are iſſuable from his department, without having obtained the articles in quality and quantity conformable to his inſtructions, he ſhall be liable to puniſhment as an embezzler of them, in proportion to the deficiency in quantity or value; and if the contributing inhabitant accepts any ſuch quittance when he is aware that he is not entitled to it, he alſo ſhall be liable to puniſhment, leſs by two degrees, but ſhall not be branded. Whatever ſum he may be found to have given to procure ſuch quittance, ſhall alſo be generally forfeited to government; this ſum ſhall, however, be returned to the giver, if he was not aware of the quittance having, in conſideration of it, been improperly granted to him, and in ſuch caſe he ſhall not in any reſpect be liable to puniſhment.

All thoſe officers who belonged to the ſame public boards with the offending parties, if privy to the offence, and neglecting to take cognizance of it, ſhall be conſidered as participators therein, and ſuffer equal puniſhment with the principals. Thoſe who neither knew of the offence indirectly, nor officiated when it was committed, ſhall only be puniſhable and reſponſible as guilty of neglect of examination.

Ten clauſes.

SEC-

SECTION CXXIV. — *Suppreſſion and Miſapplication of contingent Exceſs of Revenue.*

In all the tribunals, public boards, treaſuries, and magazines of government, the amount of the revenue received in ſilver, and in kind, beyond the ſum or value at which ſuch branch of the revenue was computed, ſhall be diſtinctly and faithfully reported, and the ſeveral ſums or quantities ſhall be placed accordingly to the credit of government on the records. If the ſuperintendant of the department privately tranſfers the exceedings of any one branch of the revenue, to ſome other branch, the receipt of which had been deficient, and thereby deceives the government by the falſe ſtatements which are thus introduced into his accounts, he ſhall be liable to puniſhment according to the law concerning the embezzlement of the property of government, in proportion to the amount ſo transferred; and he ſhall, moreover, be required to make good that deficiency in the other branch of the revenue, which he had, by ſuch transfer, endeavoured to conceal.

In all deliveries of precious metals or piece-goods * into the interior or private imperial treaſury, the accounts ſhould be cloſed on the day of delivery, but if they are not then completed, the unexamined parcels muſt not be removed, and the parties delivering in the ſame ſhall attend at the examination of the goods and cloſe of the accounts, on the day following.

Whatever exceſs may appear upon a computation of the articles, ſhall be diſtinctly reported to the ſupreme court of revenue for their deciſion reſpecting it, and if the ſuperintendant of the department, upon his own authority, preſumes to ſuffer any part of ſuch exceſs, after having been once received, to be removed again from the treaſury, he ſhall nominally be puniſhable capitally, but actually ſuffer only the alleviated ſentence of five years baniſhment.

* Silk, cotton or woollen ſtuffs, which are received and regiſtered by the roll or piece.

The officer on duty at the gate of the interior treaſury, by whoſe neglect or want of examination ſuch articles had been permitted to be carried away, ſhall ſuffer 100 blows. The articles carried away, whether conſiſting of precious metals, or piece-goods, ſhall moreover always be returned.

No clauſe.

SECTION CXXV. — *Privately lending or employing the Public Revenue.*

If any ſuperintending officer of government, having charge of a part of the produce of the revenue, whether in grain or the precious metals, borrows for his own uſe, or lends the ſame to others, although the acknowledgment and engagement in writing of the borrower ſhould have been duly obtained, ſuch ſuperintendant ſhall be puniſhed for every offence in proportion to the amount and value, according to the law concerning the embezzlement of the property of government.

If any other perſon borrows for his own uſe, or lends the produce of the revenues as aforeſaid, he ſhall be puniſhed in proportion to the amount and value, according to the law for puniſhing thefts committed upon the property of the ſtate.

The original article taken away ſhall in every caſe in which it may be practicable, be recovered in behalf of government.

If any perſon, moreover, exchanges any of his own goods with thoſe belonging to government, he ſhall, upon conviction, forfeit thoſe goods, and be further puniſhable in proportion to the amount of the goods of government withdrawn by ſuch exchange, according as by this law is already provided.

Six clauſes.

SEC-

Section CXXVI. — *Privately lending or employing Public Property.*

Any officer of government, who, having under his charge clothes, carpets, furniture, utenſils, porcelane, or other articles of a ſimilar deſcription, which are public or government property, employs, or lends the ſame to be employed for private purpoſes, ſhall, as well as alſo the borrower, be puniſhed with 50 blows; and if the articles are not replaced within ten days, their value ſhall be eſtimated, and the offending parties puniſhed in proportion thereto, according to the law concerning pecuniary injuries and malverſation in general, reducing the puniſhment in each caſe two degrees. The article borrowed muſt be moreover exactly replaced; and if loſt or damaged, the offending parties ſhall not only be reſponſible for the value thereof, but ſhall be likewiſe puniſhable according to the law applicable to the caſe of damaging or deſtroying the property of government; that is to ſay, if the damage was done by deſign, the puniſhment ſhall, proportionably to the amount, be two degrees more ſevere than in common caſes of theft; and in an encreaſing ratio, as far as 100 blows, and perpetual baniſhment to the diſtance of 3000 *lee*. — If the damage was the reſult of accident or inadvertence, the puniſhment ſhall in each caſe be three degrees leſs than when committed by deſign, and in no caſe ſhall it exceed 80 blows, and two years baniſhment.

No clauſe.

Section CXXVII. — *Receipt, Transfer, and Expenditure of the Revenue.*

In every public department and tribunal of the empire, the receipts and expenditures ſhall be particularly ſpecified, as well in the document preſerved to commemorate the tranſaction, as in the document iſſued to authorize the execution of it, upon which two documents laid

laid together, the impreſſion ſhall be affixed of the official ſeal, one half upon each document.

When the receipt and expenditure is not conformable to the tenor of theſe documents or vouchers, each alleged appropriation of the public property or funds, that is found to be unauthenticated, ſhall be diſallowed in the adjuſtment of the public accounts, and the ſuperintendant of the department ſhall be puniſhed in proportion to the deficiency, according to the law relative to embezzlement, the aſcending ratio of puniſhment being, however, limited to 100 blows and baniſhment to the diſtance of 3000 *lee*, and the offending party not liable in any caſe to be branded.

If the authority iſſued by any tribunal or department of ſtate for the expenditure of the public money, or public property, is not ſanctioned by half the impreſſion of the official ſeal, but is merely a written order to the ſame effect; or if, although the proper document is iſſued, no document of the ſame tenor, ſanctioned with the other half of the official ſeal, is retained; or again, if the ſuperintending officer of the treaſury or ſtore-houſe complies with a mere written order, without having any other authority legally authenticated in the manner above ſtated; or laſtly, if ſuch ſuperintending officer, after having received the neceſſary authority, makes the iſſue of money or goods required, without duly recording the ſame on the regiſters of his department; all ſuch caſes ſhall ſubject the offenders to the penalties of a tranſgreſſion of this law.

Nevertheleſs, when His Majeſty's troops are on their march, if the commanding officer makes the demand of proviſion and other neceſſaries in due form, ſuch demand ſhall be ſufficient to warrant the iſſue of the articles required at the different ſtations through which he paſſes; but the ſuperintending officer of the ſeveral departments ſhall not omit afterwards to make due report to their reſpective ſuperiors, of the amount and of the nature of the ſupplies they had afforded.

Any

Any ſuperintending officer, who refuſes to comply in ſuch a caſe with the demand made upon the ſtores under his control, ſhall be puniſhed with 60 blows for the offence.

Fourteen clauſes.

SECTION CXXVIII. — *Miſconduct of ſupernumerary Revenue Officers.*

If any one of the ſupernumerary attendants, who are hired occaſionally for the public ſervice, and employed in the treaſuries, ſtore-houſes, public offices, or manufactories, ſhould be guilty of appropriating to their private uſe, borrowing, or exchanging any part of the produce of the revenue, he ſhall incur the ordinary puniſhment of embezzlement; and, if the ſuperior who hired him was privy to the offence, and alſo a participator in the advantages ariſing from the unlawful tranſaction, he ſhall be equally puniſhable; but if he did not actually receive a ſhare of the profits ariſing from it, the puniſhment of the latter ſhall be proportionally leſs by one degree.

The officer who hired the ſupernumerary ſhall be liable to the ſame reduced puniſhment if, being privy to the offence, he takes no cognizance of it, or ſuppreſſes it, in his report to his ſuperiors. If ignorant of the offence having been committed, as well as without advantage from it, he ſhall not be puniſhed or held reſponſible.

One clauſe.

SECTION CXXIX. — *Fraudulent Appropriation of Public Property.*

If, in the diſtribution of the ſupplies for the army *, any of the officers, or official attendants belonging thereto, appropriate to themſelves any portion of what had been deſtined to the public ſervice, by

* Under this general term, the pay of the troops, as well as every other ſpecies of allotment to them, appears to be comprehended.

falſely

falſely aſſuming the names and authority of individual ſoldiers who have claims thereon, they ſhall be puniſhed in proportion to the amount, according to the law in caſes of theft in ordinary caſes.

If they appropriate to themſelves a portion of what had been deſtined to the public ſervice, by making a claim for the ſame in the aſſumed names, or in behalf of ſoldiers who, having deſerted, had ceaſed in fact to have any claims whatever, they ſhall be puniſhed in proportion to the amount, according to the ſeverer law, provided in caſes of ſtealing public property; laſtly, if any officer, perſonally entruſted with the diſtribution of ſtores to the troops, appropriates any part of the ſame to himſelf, he ſhall ſuffer puniſhment in proportion to the amount, according to the ſtill ſeverer law which is provided againſt the embezzlement of public property.

In none of theſe caſes, however, ſhall the offender be liable to be branded *.

No clauſe.

Section CXXX. — *Revenue Officers reciprocally anſwerable for each other.*

All the officers, clerks, collectors, inſpectors, receivers, and others attached to the revenue department, and having authority in the treaſuries and ſtore-houſes of government, ſhall poſſeſs a reciprocal controul and right of inſpection over each other's proceedings; and when any one individual is guilty of clandeſtinely applying to his own uſe, lending to others, or in any manner miſuſing the property of government, if thoſe who are privy to the removal of the public property from the treaſury or ſtore-houſe, conceal the offence, inſtead of informing againſt the offender, or otherwiſe wilfully connive at the tranſ-

* See the Appendix, No. XVI. for a notice of an offence of this deſcription, extracted from the Pekin Gazette of the 23d of April 1800.

action,

action, they shall participate equally in the punishment, except in capital cases, when they shall be entitled to a mitigation in the punishment of one degree.

Those who did not connive at the offence, but might have prevented it had they been vigilant and diligent in examination, shall suffer punishment proportionate to the offence, under a reduction of three degrees below that of the actual offender, and the reduced punishment shall not exceed in any instance 100 blows.

In cases however of the superior officers making false and unauthenticated records, and granting unauthenticated and premature releases, particular regulations have been provided, and the inferior collectors, inspectors, and others in the department of the revenue, shall not be responsible for any such offence, unless convicted of having been privy thereto.

No clause.

SECTION CXXXI. — *Responsibility of Revenue Officers in Cases of Theft.*

When any individual goes out of a public treasury or storehouse, to which he is not actually belonging, if the guards on duty neglect to search his person and examine him, they shall be punished with 20 blows each; and if, in consequence of such neglect, a thief succeeds in carrying away with him any of the property of government, the said guards shall suffer punishment within two degrees of the severity of that to which the thief himself is liable. If a theft is committed at night, in consequence of the want of vigilance of those on guard, they shall each suffer punishment within three degrees of that to which the thief is liable.

The superintending officers, inspectors, and others, not immediately on guard, shall, in cases of theft, suffer punishment within five degrees of that of the thief, for the want of vigilance which is imputable to them, but the puniſhment ſhall not, in any ſuch caſe of miſconduct by implication only, exceed 100 blows.

In any inſtance however of wilful connivance, the puniſhment of thoſe who connive ſhall be as ſevere as that of the thief, excepting only a reduction of one degree in capital caſes.

For acts of robbery and open violence, which the officers and others on duty really had not power to reſiſt, they ſhall incur no reſponſibility.

In caſes of implied neglect, the officers of government ſhall retain their places, the offence not being of a private and perſonal nature; but in all inſtances of connivance and wilful concurrence they ſhall be degraded and diſmiſſed.

Two clauſes.

Section CXXXII. — *Reſponſibility of Receivers and Diſtributors of Public Property.*

When any of the officers or inferior attendants in charge of, or employed in, the ſeveral public treaſuries and ſtore-houſes, have completed their reſpective periods of ſervice, they ſhall ſtill remain at their proper ſtations until their ſeveral accounts of receipt and expenditure have been audited by the ſuperior officer in the revenue department, whoſe duty it is perſonally to aſcertain that there is no incorrectneſs or deficiency; but after the audit has taken place, they ſhall be ſubject to no further detention.

The diſtribution of ſuch articles as are by law allotted in certain ſhares and proportions, ſhall be effected under the immediate direction and authority of the ſuperintending officers of the diſtrict and revenue department, and this duty ſhall not at any time be left to be performed by the officer of the treaſury or ſtore-houſe from whence the articles are to be iſſued, under the penalty of 100 blows for every ſuch offence.

When

When any public treafure, or other property, has been fealed with the feal of an officer of the revenue, it fhall not be lawful for any of the inferior officers or attendants of the department, to break open the fame, without previoufly requefting the officer who originally affixed the feal to be prefent; and whoever offends againft this regulation fhall fuffer 60 blows, and fhall be refponfible for the deficiency that may be imputable to his interference.

No claufe.

SECTION CXXXIII. — *Eftablifhed Regulations obferved in the Receipt and Iffue of Public Stores.*

If the officers having charge of the treafuries and ftore-houfes of government, and fuperintending the receipts and deliveries of public ftores, iffue frefh goods when they ought to have iffued fuch as had been laying on hand, or receive goods of an inferior quality, when they ought to have been of fuperior quality; or if the fuperintending officer purchafing or hiring goods for the public fervice, does not pay the ftipulated fum immediately, or ftipulates for more or lefs than the market price or rate of hire of the goods in each cafe, the amount of the excefs above, or of the deficiency below, what was fairly due, fhall be eftimated, and the offending party fhall be proportionably liable to punifhment according to the law applicable to the cafes of pecuniary malverfation in general; and he fhall moreover replace to government, or to the individual fufferer, whatever may have been improperly withheld.

The penalties of this law fhall extend to all thofe who, being entrufted with the payment and diftribution of falaries and wages, difcharge the fame in advance, inftead of waiting until they regularly become due.

If the fuperior officer is privy to the commiffion of any fuch offence on the part of his inferiors, and takes no cognizance of it, he fhall participate equally in the puniſhment, but ſhall not be in any manner reſponſible, unleſs acquainted with the fact.

Two clauſes.

Section CXXXIV. — *Vexatious Proceedings on the Occaſion of the Receipt or Iſſue of Public Stores.*

If the officers and clerks of government, entruſted with the ſuperintendance of the receipt and collection, or the iſſue and diſtribution, of the public property, inſtead of promptly collecting and promptly diſtributing it, in any manner vexatiouſly detain and maliciouſly obſtruct the claimants and contributors, they ſhall be liable to 50 blows for the delay of one day, and every addition of three days delay ſhall aggravate the puniſhment one degree, as far as 60 blows and one year's baniſhment.

The door-keepers who detain and impede perſons attending for the purpoſes aforeſaid, ſhall be puniſhed according to this rule, and in the ſame proportion.

If the officer on duty does not collect from the contributors, and diſtribute to thoſe entitled to receive, in the ſame order and ſucceſſion as that in which they attend his office or tribunal for the purpoſe, he ſhall ſuffer the puniſhment of 40 blows.

Three clauſes.

Section CXXXV. — *Purity of the Precious Metals payable to Government.*

Whoever has the charge of receiving and collecting the taxes due to government, or the proceeds of goods ſold on account of government, and payable in precious metals, ſhall be anſwerable for the delivery of the ſame in no other than perfectly pure bullion, whether gold or ſilver.

If

If the gold or silver delivered on these accounts into any of the public treasuries contains an admixture of alloy, the superintending officer, his clerks, and the assay-master, shall be respectively punishable with 40 blows, and shall be made jointly responsible for the deficiency in value of the bullion received.

If guilty of wilfully receiving alloyed silver or gold, with a corrupt view to private advantage, they shall further be liable to the punishment of an embezzlement of public property to the extent of the deficiency; when merely conniving at such fraud, they shall be punishable as in a common case of pecuniary malversation to the same amount.

No clause.

Section CXXXVI. — *Responsibility for the Damage or Loss of Public Stores.*

If those who have the charge of the public treasuries and storehouses, or of any collection and depôt of public property, do not place and arrange the stores according to the established rules, or omit to expose them to the sun and the air at proper times and seasons, by which omission and neglect the property entrusted to them is damaged or destroyed, the loss shall be estimated and the responsible parties punished in proportion to the amount according to the law concerning pecuniary malversation in general, and they shall be required moreover to make good to government the amount of the loss sustained.

Nevertheless, should sudden and unexpected rain penetrate the building, or fire be communicated to it from without, or thieves and robbers break in, so that from any of these causes damage or loss arises to the property under charge, if the superintending officer deputes a proper person to ascertain the nature and extent of the damage, and makes a clear and correct report thereof to his superiors, he shall be be pardoned, and excufed from his refponfibility to make good the deficiency.

On the other hand, if the fuperintending officer, having been guilty of any fraudulent difpofal, loan, or transfer of the public property, takes advantage of the fubfequent circumftance of an accidental lofs by fire, water, or thieves, to falfify the regifters of his office by attributing the whole lofs and deficiency to fuch accident, and then makes a report of the cafe conformably to fuch falfe record, in order to deceive his fuperiors and fcreen himfelf, he fhall be liable to punifhment in proportion to the amount of the total damage and deficiency, according to the law concerning embezzlement.

If thofe who are affociated with him in office are privy to, but take no notice of, fuch criminal proceeding, they fhall be equally punifhable, but otherwife fhall not be held refponfible.

One claufe.

SECTION CXXXVII. — *Regular Tranfmiffion of Public Stores from Inferior to Superior Jurifdictions.*

The taxes levied and collected in the feveral diftricts of the empire, the fupplies purchafed, and the feveral kinds of warlike ftores prepared and manufactured for the army, having been delivered into the charge of the feveral governments of cities of the fecond and third orders and having by them been tranfmitted in regular routine, and under the conduct of proper officers, to the governors of cities of the firft order to whofe jurifdiction they belong refpectively, if thofe governors do not immediately take the further tranfmiffion of the articles under their charge, and iffue the neceffary orders, as well as depute the proper perfons under their authority to fuperintend their conveyance and delivery to the treafurers of the refpective ſpective provinces, the preſident, deputy, and clerks of every government thus neglectful, ſhall ſuffer a puniſhment of 80 blows, but the offence ſhall not be deemed of a private or perſonal nature.

In like manner, if the provincial treaſurers do not immediately take charge of all the public property thus received, and adopt proper meaſures for effecting its conveyance to the ſupreme court for all affairs of revenue, the preſident, deputy, and clerks of the treaſurers' offices, ſhall be equally puniſhable as the other officers in the preceding inſtances *.

From the penalties of this law, exception is neceſſarily made in all ſuch caſes wherein a ſlower mode of tranſmiſſion than ordinary is eſpecially directed.

If thoſe officers with whom the tranſmiſſion of ſuch produce of the revenue towards its deſtination begins, or thoſe who afterwards ſuperintend and accompany the ſame, with the attendants who are employed in effecting the package, re-package, and transfer of the goods, do not place and diſpoſe them according to the eſtabliſhed regulations, in conſequence of which deviation or omiſſion a loſs or damage enſues, the extent of ſuch loſs or damage ſhall be eſtimated, and the offence puniſhed in proportion to the amount, according to the law concerning pecuniary malverſation or injury to property in general; the offending parties ſhall likewiſe make good the deficiency.

If, however, in a conveyance by water, accidents ſhould enſue from the winds and waves, upon ſudden and unexpected bad weather, or at any time fire ſhould be communicated from without, or thieves break in and ſteal, then, provided the ſuperintending officer, immediately after aſcertaining the circumſtance, makes a faithful report

* Theſe regulations obviouſly regard only the ſurplus revenue, or that which is not required for the ſervice of the provinces in which it is collected. The total amount of the revenue collected in the Chineſe empire has been ſtated at about 66,000,000l. and that of the ſurplus, remitted to Pekin, at about 12,000,000l. and theſe ſums are probably not far from the truth, though on ſuch a ſubject, the accuracy of the information which, in the preſent ſtate of our relations with China, is likely to be acceſſible to Europeans, muſt be in ſome degree queſtionable.

thereof,

thereof, and of the extent of the lofs or damage that has been fuftained, to his fuperior, and provided that the officer who fhall have been thereupon deputed by fuch fuperior to examine into the truth of the ftatement, confirms its accuracy and fidelity, the refponfible parties fhall become free, both from liability to punifhment, and from the charge of making good the deficiency; but fhould there prove to have been any deception or malverfation committed, then, whatever the caufe of lofs or damage may have been, the offending party fhall be liable to punifhment in proportion to the full amount, according to the law refpecting embezzlement.

If the officers with whom the tranfmiffion of the produce of the revenue begins, do not tranfmit the identical goods or articles received from the contributors, but purchafe other goods or articles to fubftitute in their room, the difference between the value of the articles tranfmitted and thofe withdrawn, fhall be eftimated, and the offence punifhed in proportion to fuch difference, according to the law concerning the embezzlement of public property.

Nineteen claufes.

Section CXXXVIII. — *Rule of Forfeiture and Reftitution.*

If any officer in pronouncing judgment in a cafe of property illegally holden, orders it to be reftored to the original proprietor, when it ought, conformably to the laws, to have been forfeited to the ftate, or directs a forfeiture of it to the ftate, when it ought by law to have been reftored to the proprietor, he fhall for fuch falfe judgment be punifhed in proportion to the amount of the property illegally awarded according to the provifions of the law againft pecuniary malverfation in general, but the punifhment fhall not in any of thefe cafes exceed the limit of 100 blows.

Two claufes.

SEC-

SECTION CXXXIX. — *Intermediate Charge of Public Property.*

In all cafes of public property which had been iffued from the treafuries and ftore-houfes of government to be delivered over, or paid away, to certain perfons, but not yet received by fuch perfons; and in all cafes of private property, which, being deftined to the fervice of government, has been received for that purpofe, but not actually depofited in the public treafuries or ftore-houfes, the goods fhall be confidered in the former cafe ftill to preferve, and in the latter cafe, already to have acquired, the character of public property.

Any fraudulent loan or mifapplication thereof fhall therefore fubject the holder of the goods, in proportion to the amount mifapplied, to the full punifhment provided by law in the cafe of directly embezzling any other kind of public property. — Upon the fame principle, the fraudulent application of fuch property, if imputable to perfons who have not the charge thereof, fhall be punifhed as an ordinary theft of public property.

One claufe.

SECTION CXL.—*Concealment or Denial, either of Property under Sentence of Forfeiture, or of Families under Sentence of Servitude.*

The enflaving of the families of offenders, and the forfeiture of their real and perfonal property, fhall not take place except in cafes of treafon, rebellion, or fome other of the ten treafonable offences, or where it is by law exprefsly ordered and provided; and if any officer of government paffes fuch fentence of forfeiture unauthorizedly and unjuftly, he fhall be punifhed as in the cafe of paffing a wilfully unjuft fentence of perpetual banifhment. — If the fentence was only pronounced, but not executed, the puniſhment ſhall be leſs by one degree.

If thoſe who are to give an account of the number of perſons in a family under lawful ſentence of perpetual ſervice, and alſo of the real and perſonal property of ſuch family which is by law forfeited to the ſtate, are guilty of any deception or concealment, they ſhall be puniſhed in the following manner:

In the firſt place, if they do not give a true and faithful account of the number of perſons in ſuch family, they ſhall be puniſhed in the ſame manner as is provided in an ordinary caſe of ſuppreſſing the number of perſons in the record of a family in the public regiſter.

In the ſecond place, if they do not give a true and faithful ſtatement of the forfeited lands of the ſaid family, they ſhall be puniſhed according to the law for puniſhing thoſe who falſely report the extent and value of their lands, to avoid duly contributing to the revenue. If they falſely report the amount of the houſes, cattle, and miſcellaneous articles under ſentence of forfeiture, they ſhall be further puniſhable in proportion to the value of the property ſuppreſſed and falſely reported, according to the law concerning pecuniary malverſation and injury to property in general; but the puniſhment ſhall not, in any of theſe caſes, exceed 100 blows.

All ſuch of the family, and ſuch portions of their poſſeſſions, as were attempted to be concealed in evaſion of the ſentence of the laws, ſhall be in the former caſe held accountable to the ſervice, and, in the latter caſe, forfeited to the uſe, of government, as previouſly provided and directed; but the puniſhment of miſrepreſentation ſhall be inflicted ſolely on the individual who made the falſe return.

If the head inhabitant of the diſtrict, from a partiality in favour of thoſe under condemnation, confirms the falſe report, and if the magiſtrate knowing it to be falſe connives at it, they ſhall be equally puniſhed punifhed with the individual with whom the falfehood originated, and the punifhment, inftead of being limited to 100 blows, fhall be regularly encreafed in proportion to the amount in queftion, according to the law above referred to.

If fuch officer or head inhabitant fhall have been bribed to connive on the occafion, he fhall be fubject to any contingent augmentation of punifhment, which may be found proportionate to the amount of the bribe, agreeably to the law againft receiving bribes for unlawful purpofes.

When, on the other hand, a falfe report is accepted as correct, not through wilful connivance, but through inadvertence and defect of examination, the punifhment fhall be three degrees lefs than that to which the falfe reporter is liable, and fhall not in any cafe exceed 50 blows.

Eight claufes.

END OF THE FOURTH BOOK OF THE THIRD DIVISION.

BOOK V.

DUTIES AND CUSTOMS.

SECTION CXLI.—*Duty on Salt**.

I. WHOEVER, not having a licence, engages in a clandeſtine traffic in ſalt, that is to ſay, poſſeſſes any quantity however ſmall of this article for ſale, ſhall be puniſhed with 100 blows, and baniſhed for three years.

If ſuch ſmuggler of ſalt is moreover provided with offenſive weapons, the puniſhment ſhall be aggravated one degree, ſo as to amount to perpetual baniſhment to the diſtance of 2000 *lee*.—If he falſely accuſes, and recriminates upon, innocent perſons, his puniſhment ſhall be encreaſed three degrees, whereby the place of his perpetual baniſhment will be removed to a diſtance of 3000 *lee*; if laſtly, he reſiſts the officers of juſtice employed to take him into cuſtody, he ſhall ſuffer death by being beheaded, after the uſual period of impriſonment.

Not only the article itſelf, but likewiſe the carriage or the veſſel by which it is conveyed, and the horſes or cattle by means of which it is drawn or tranſported, ſhall be forfeited to government.

* The ſalt trade in China, the duties upon which form a conſiderable branch of the revenue, is a regulated monopoly, carried on by a limited number of merchants, to whom licences are granted by the Crown, and whoſe proceedings are at the ſame time ſubjected to the inſpection and control of public officers eſpecially appointed to that ſervice, in each province.—The merchants who enjoy this monopoly, as well as thoſe who have the excluſive privilege of trading with foreigners, rank very high in point of opulence and reſpectability:—the chief ſalt merchant of Canton is at preſent conſidered to be the richeſt ſubject in the province, and the next to him in wealth is, probably, a merchant, now retired from buſineſs, but who till lately held the principal ſtation among thoſe engaged in the foreign trade, and who acquired nearly the whole of his extenſive fortune in the courſe of his tranſactions, and thoſe of his family, with the Engliſh Eaſt India Company.

The

The guide or conductor, the agent for the ſale, the harbourer of the ſmuggler, and the conſignee of the ſalt, ſhall be reſpectively puniſhed with 90 blows and two years and a half baniſhment, as acceſſaries.

Whoever carries, lets out beaſts of burthen to carry, or furniſhes any other means of conveying, this article without a licence, ſhall ſuffer the puniſhment of 80 blows and two years baniſhment.

If any perſon, although not bound by his office ſo to do, gives information of, and ſeizes any ſmuggled ſalt, he ſhall obtain the whole amount of the forfeiture as his reward. — In like manner, if one of a party of ſmugglers of ſalt ſurrenders himſelf, and gives information to government, he ſhall not only be pardoned, but rewarded with the whole amount of the forfeited article. — Even if a ſingle ſmuggler voluntarily ſurrenders himſelf, he ſhall be pardoned.

The magiſtrates, in taking cognizance of any caſe of ſmuggled ſalt which may be brought under their conſideration, ſhall confine their inveſtigation to the examination of the goods ſeized, and of the offences committed by the ſmugglers in cuſtody. — They ſhall not liſten to any charges the ſmugglers may allege againſt others, whether in recrimination upon their accuſers or otherwiſe. — Any magiſtrate who diſregards this reſtriction, ſhall be puniſhed as in an ordinary caſe of wilful deviation from juſtice, in determining the puniſhment of offences.

II. Whoever, being engaged and employed in a licenſed and eſtabliſhed ſalt-work, delivers out of the eſtabliſhment annually a greater quantity of ſalt than is permitted and ſpecified in the licence, or boils down ſalt brine clandeſtinely for private ſale, ſhall be proſecuted, and puniſhed in the ſame manner as the unlicenſed dealer; and all thoſe who, being privy to, connive at this unlawful tranſaction, or aſſiſt in the unlawful diſpoſal of the goods, ſhall be ſubject to an equal participation in the puniſhment by law provided.

III. When-

III. Whenever a married woman is guilty of any breach of the regulations of the ſalt-trade, if her huſband or ſons are at home, and privy to the offence, they ſhall ſuffer the puniſhment attending the breach of the law, inſtead of the woman; but if the huſband is abſent from home, and the ſons are of a tender age, the woman alone ſhall be puniſhed, and (according to the laws concerning females,) that part of the ſentence, which conſiſts of ſome degree of baniſhment, ſhall be commuted for the proportionate fine.

IV. Whoever purchaſes for uſe any ſalt that he knows to have been prepared without a licence and ſold clandeſtinely, ſhall be puniſhed with 100 blows; but if he ſo purchaſes the ſalt in order to ſell it again, he ſhall be puniſhed with 100 blows and three years baniſhment.

V. The ſuperintendants of the ſalt-duties, and the ſeveral officers of the civil and military departments, who may at any time be charged with the purſuit and ſeizure of clandeſtine and illicit traders, ſhall immediately deliver ſuch of the offenders as they may have ſeized, into the cuſtody of the ſuperior courts of the treaſurers of the provinces, not being themſelves empowered by the laws to examine into their offences; but if any of the ſuperior courts, in colluſion with the ſubordinate magiſtrates, ſuffer ſuch offenders to eſcape from trial and deſerved puniſhment, ſuch conduct ſhall render them (the members of ſuch courts) puniſhable in an equal degree with the original offenders; and if ſuch a colluſion is the conſequence of bribery, they ſhall experience any aggravation of the puniſhment which may reſult from the application to the caſe of the laws againſt bribery for unlawful purpoſes.

VI. The ſuperintendants of the ſalt-duties, and the ſeveral officers of the civil and military boards or tribunals, who may at any time be charged with the purſuit and ſeizure of clandeſtine and illicit traders, ſhall ſtation in convenient places within the limits of their juriſdictions, and

and eſpecially near ſalt-works eſtabliſhed according to law, a ſufficient number of revenue and police officers, to prevent and put a ſtop to all ſuch ſmuggling and clandeſtine proceedings, as are hereby prohibited. If any inſtances of ſmuggling take place notwithſtanding theſe regulations, the officer of the department, and thoſe deputed by him to ſuppreſs ſuch practices, ſhall upon the firſt occurrence of this nature be liable to be puniſhed with 40 blows; upon the ſecond, with 50 blows; and upon the third, with 60 blows; but this not being deemed an offence of a private and perſonal nature, the perſons guilty of it ſhall not be deprived of their offices and employments. On the other hand, if thoſe officers wilfully connive at any act of ſmuggling, or if any commanders of troops ſuffer their ſoldiers to carry on any ſuch illicit traffic, they ſhall ſuffer the ſame puniſhment as the ſmugglers, and be deemed, moreover, guilty of, and liable to, the conſequences of a private and perſonal offence, the puniſhment of which will again be ſubject to any further aggravation that may reſult according to law, upon a conviction of bribery. If the revenue officer employed upon this duty, ſuppreſſes the diſcovery of ſmuggled ſalt, and appropriates the amount to his own uſe, inſtead of delivering it up to his ſuperior officer's tribunal, he ſhall be puniſhed with 100 blows and three years baniſhment. If ſuch revenue officer falſely charges an innocent perſon with ſmuggling, his puniſhment ſhall be aggravated three degrees, and accordingly amount to a puniſhment of 100 blows and perpetual baniſhment to the diſtance of 3000 *lee*.

VII. Upon the removal of ſalt licenced by government, a regular permit ſhall be made out, expreſſing the quantities of ſalt in each bag, the allowance for tare, and the total amount of the ſalt intended to be removed; at each cuſtom-houſe on the route, the quantity of the article ſhall be aſcertained to be conformable to the permit, by weighing and examining ſome of the bags taken promiſcuouſly; if it is diſcovered that the quantity tranſported exceeds the amount ſtated in the permit,

permit, the offenders ſhall be puniſhed as in any ordinary caſe of unlicenſed trade in the ſame article. If the ſalt-merchant conveys the ſalt through an unuſual route, by which means the examination of the officers of government in the intervening ſtations is evaded, and their certificates conſequently found to be wanting upon the permit, ſuch merchant ſhall be puniſhed with 90 blows, and the goods ſent back to the ſtations where they had not but ought to have been examined, that the regular inſpection may take place; the merchant will be further contingently liable to an aggravation of his puniſhment if upon ſuch inſpection taking place, the ſalt in his poſſeſſion is found to exceed the amount ſpecified in the permit.

VIII. The ſalt merchants and traders ſhall always tranſport the licenced ſalt for ſale, in the exact quantities and proportions ſpecified in their reſpective permits or licences; if the ſalt is ſold in one place, while the permit is depoſited in another, and therefore cannot be produced on demand, they ſhall be liable to all the penalties of a clandeſtine ſale. If within ten days after having ſold off the whole of any quantity of ſalt for which a permit has been granted, the ſalt merchant does not deliver up ſuch permit to the proper officer of government in the diſtrict, he ſhall be liable to a puniſhment of 40 blows; and if he makes uſe of ſuch expired permit, to colour and legalize the ſale of any additional quantity of ſalt, he ſhall be held liable to the ſeveral pains and penalties denounced againſt the clandeſtine ſale of this article in ordinary caſes.

IX. In all caſes of the tranſportation of ſalt licenced by government, whether from the manufactory to the ſtore-houſe, or from one ſtore-houſe to another, if military weapons are carried for defence, or if any other veſſels than thoſe belonging to government are employed, it ſhall be deemed a clandeſtine trade, and puniſhed accordingly.

X. If any ſalt merchant, having ſubmitted the ſalt for which he held a licence to the inſpection of the officers of government, that it might be be aſcertained to be agreeable thereto, afterwards adulterates it with ſand or earthy matter, and in ſuch ſtate expoſes his goods for ſale, he ſhall be puniſhed with 80 blows.

XI. If any perſon takes the ſalt which the government licence expreſsly declared to be ſaleable only in a particular diſtrict or quarter of the country, and conveys it for ſale to any place not deſcribed in the licence, he ſhall be puniſhed with 100 blows; the perſon who knowingly purchaſes the article ſhall be puniſhed with 60 blows, but ſhall not be liable to ſuch penalty, if ignorant of the illegality of the tranſaction. The goods thus conveyed for ſale contrary to the terms of the licence, ſhall be forfeited to government.

Twenty-two clauſes.

Section CXLII. — *Superintendants of Salt Duties to receive no intermediate Profits.*

If any of the officers or clerks of the tribunals and departments, having the adminiſtration of the laws reſpecting ſalt, and the collection of the ſalt duties, take upon themſelves under aſſumed and fictitious names the payment of the duties intermediately, by purchaſing or otherwiſe procuring ſalt licences through the authority and influence of their ſeveral offices, and thus appropriate to themſelves thoſe profits which ought to have been enjoyed by private individuals of the community, they ſhall be puniſhed with 100 blows and three years baniſhment. Their property in ſalt, and the licences for vending it, ſhall both be forfeited upon conviction.

No clauſe.

Section CXLIII. — *Preſervation of the Salt Laws from Neglect.*

All the wholeſale merchants who purchaſe ſalt licences from government, ſhall perſonally receive their reſpective portions of the article

at

at the public works where it is prepared: if instead of so doing, they dispose of their licences to others at advanced prices, so that in the end, the salt regulations are evaded and counteracted, the seller and purchaser of the licence shall in each case be punished with 80 blows, and the negociator of the sale or of the transfer of the licence, shall suffer the punishment next in degree. The purchase-money received for the sale of the licence by the seller, and the salt obtained by the purchaser of the licence, conformably to the tenor thereof, shall equally be forfeited. The retail venders of salt, who receive and dispose of the article at the different markets on behalf of the wholesale dealer, are not however by any means to be considered as coming within the scope of this law, unless they should likewise engage in the trade as principals.

No clause.

SECTION CXLIV. — *Smuggling of Tea* *.

Whoever is guilty of a clandestine sale of tea, shall be liable to the same penalties as already provided in the case of a clandestine sale of salt. Whoever, having possession of a tea licence that had been acted upon, and noted accordingly by the officers of government to whom it had been presented for examination, avails himself of such expired and cancelled licence, to collect upon the authority thereof a fresh supply from the the tea plantations, shall be liable to all the penalties of smuggling tea in the ordinary manner.

Six clauses.

* The regulations comprised under this head relate solely to the home consumption. The laws framed for the government of the foreign trade, being for the most part of recent date, are not contained among the original institutions, and their application being also confined within narrow limits, they are not described at any length even in the supplementary part of the penal code.—Some official documents connected with the subject of foreign intercourse will be found in the Appendix, No. XI.

SEC-

SECTION CXLV. — *Smuggling of Allum.*

Whoever clandeſtinely manufactures allum and expoſes it to ſale, ſhall be ſubject to penalties ſimilar to thoſe already provided in the caſe of ſalt. In all places and ſituations which are found to yield a ſupply of this article, the amount, and the extent of the duty to be levied thereon, ſhall be aſcertained and determined upon fixed principles, and private individuals ſhall not be allowed to bring it to ſale without previouſly purchaſing licences for that purpoſe from government.

No clauſe.

SECTION CXLVI. — *Evaſion of Duties, or Smuggling in general**.

All merchants and dealers who defraud the revenue, by not duly contributing the amount of the rated and eſtabliſhed duties on their merchandize, ſhall be puniſhed with 50 blows, and forfeit half the value of the goods ſmuggled to government; three-tenths of ſuch forfeiture ſhall in general be given to the informer, but no ſuch reward ſhall be allowed when the ſmuggled goods are diſcovered and aſcertained, by the regular officer on duty.

Whoever conveys goods through a barrier or cuſtom-houſe ſtation, without taking out the regular permit, ſhall be liable to all the or-

* The rigour of the laws againſt ſmuggling has been latterly encreaſed by ſeveral ſtatutes and government edicts; and an inſtance occurred at Canton in the year 1801, in which a Chineſe merchant was condemned to pay a fine of one hundred times the legal duty, upon ſome goods that had been attempted to be ſmuggled from the ſhip for which (according to the cuſtom of the port) he had undertaken to become ſecurity.—It is to be obſerved, however, that this enormous fine was afterwards remitted, and that the ſentence to that effect was only paſſed by the officiating magiſtrate proviſionally, though recommended, at the ſame time, to the conſideration of the Emperor as an exception to the eſtabliſhed laws, which the peculiar circumſtances of the caſe, and the frequency of the offence had rendered expedient.

 dinary

dinary penalties of ſmuggling. The permit ſhall be drawn out conformably to the ſtatement made of the quantity and quality of the goods; agreeably to which likewiſe, the duties ſhall be levied.

Whoever, laſtly, purchaſes cattle without a ſtamped contract, ſhall be liable to puniſhment according to this law, and forfeit half the value to government.

Two clauſes.

SECTION CXLVII. — *Merchant Veſſels having falſe Manifeſts of their Cargoes.*

All large trading veſſels which navigate the ſeas, ſhall on their reaching their deſtined port, deliver in to the officers of the cuſtom-houſe, a full and true manifeſt of all the merchandize on board, that the duties payable thereon may be duly aſſeſſed. If the country merchant, or agent for the goods at the creek or reach where the veſſel remains, makes no report, or makes a falſe and defective report, he ſhall be puniſhed with 100 blows, and the whole amount of the goods not reported, or omitted in the report, ſhall be forfeited. The individual who receives on ſhore ſuch goods as had not been duly reported, ſhall be equally puniſhable.

The perſon who gives information of a breach of this law, ſhall receive a reward of 20 *leang* or ounces of ſilver.

No clauſe.

SECTION CXLVIII. — *Arrears of Duties and Cuſtoms to be paid within the Year in which they are due.*

The whole of the arrears of duties and cuſtoms for which any individual has rendered himſelf liable to government in the courſe of the year, either for ſalt or tea licences granted to him, or upon any other grounds whatſoever, ſhall be finally diſcharged before the end of ſuch year;

year; and if the demands of government are not liquidated by the time ſpecified, the defaulter of one-tenth of his dues ſhall be puniſhed with 40 blows, and the puniſhment ſhall be inflicted one degree more ſeverely for every additional tenth in reſpect to which any individual is deficient in his quota of contribution; the puniſhment ſhall not however exceed 80 blows at the utmoſt, but ſuch defaulter, beſides being puniſhed, ſhall continue to be held reſponſible for his arrears.

If the ſuperintendants of the ſalt and tea duties, the ſuperintending officers at the barrier cuſtom-houſes, and the collectors of every other deſcription of duties and cuſtoms, are not active and diligent in the performance of the buſineſs of their ſeveral departments, ſo that the produce of the revenue in conſequence of evaſion or the non-payment of arrears, is in any one year leſs by one-tenth than in the years immediately preceding, they ſhall be liable in every ſuch caſe to a puniſhment of 50 blows, and for every further defalcation of a tenth in the produce, there ſhall be an augmentation of one degree in the puniſhment, as far as the limit of 100 blows; the ſuperintending officers ſhall likewiſe be held anſwerable for the ultimate diſcharge of all ſuch arrears.

If the contributions due to the revenue are correctly made by the parties liable thereto, but fraudulently omitted to be entered in the regiſters of the revenue by the officers and clerks in that department, with the view of lending out to others, or applying to their private uſe and advantage, ſuch omitted portions of the revenue, the ſaid officers and clerks ſhall be liable to puniſhment in proportion to the amount ſo omitted, according the law in any ordinary caſe of the embezzlement of public ſtores.

Three clauſes.

END OF THE FIFTH BOOK OF THE THIRD DIVISION.

BOOK VI.

PRIVATE PROPERTY.

SECTION CXLIX. — *Ufury* *.

WHOEVER lends his money or other property of value, in order to derive a profit from fuch tranfaction, fhall be limited to the receipt of an intereft on the amount or value of the loan, at the rate of three *per cent. per* month; and, whatever the period of years or months may be, upon which intereft is due at the day of repayment, no more fhall be received or demanded, than the original fum lent, and the lawful intereft thereon, to any amount not exceeding the principal.

Whoever tranfgreffes this law, fhall be punifhable at the leaft with 40 blows, and as much more feverely as may be proportionate to the amount of the excefs of intereft according to the law concerning pecuniary malverfation in general; the punifhment fhall not however in any cafe exceed 100 blows.

Any fuperintending officer or clerk of a tribunal or department of government, lending money or other property of value to the people under the jurifdiction of fuch tribunal or department, in order to derive a profit and advantage from fuch loan, fhall be punifhed with 80 blows, although he fhould have taken no more than the lawful intereft; but if the intereft derived from the tranfaction is exceffive, he fhall be liable to fuch aggravation of his punifhment, as may render it proportionate to the amount of the excefs, conformably to the law againft receiving a bribe for a purpofe not in itfelf unlawful; that is

* See Appendix, No. XVII.

to

to say, if, the half sum of the several excesses of interest received from different persons, by an officer having a regular salary, amounts to 30 *leang* or ounces of silver, the punishment in each case shall be encreased to 90 blows. But in the case of an inferior officer, not having such regular salary, the encrease of punishment shall only take place, when the said half sum amounts to 40 ounces of silver.

In both cases, the punishment shall be subject to a further encrease of one degree for every addition of ten ounces value to the amount of the corrupt transaction, until it attains the extreme limit of 100 blows and perpetual banishment to the distance of 3000 *lee*. In both cases likewise, the excess of interest extorted from the borrower shall be refunded.

On the other hand, if the debtor does not fulfil his agreement with the creditor, both in respect to the repayment of the principal, and the payment of the lawful interest, he shall be liable to punishment according to the following scale.

If three months after the stipulated period, he falls short of the amount due to his creditor by five *leang* or upwards, he shall be liable to a punishment of 10 blows, and to an encrease of punishment at the rate of one degree for every additional month of delay, as far as 40 blows.

If three months after the stipulated period he falls short of the amount due to his creditor by fifty *leang* or upwards, he shall be liable to a punishment of 20 blows, and to an encrease of punishment at the rate of one degree for every additional month of delay, as far as 50 blows.

If, lastly, three months after the stipulated period, he falls short of the amount due to his creditor, by 100 *leang* or upwards, he shall be liable to a punishment of 30 blows, and to an encrease of punishment at the rate of one degree for every additional month of delay, as far

as

as the limit of 60 blows; and in this as well as in the preceding cases, the debtor shall continue responsible for the amount of the principal and interest lawfully due.

If a creditor whose debtor has failed to fulfil his agreement, instead of applying for redress at the tribunal of the magistrate of the district, relies on his own power and authority, and attempts to reimburse himself by seizing violently the cattle, furniture, or other property of such debtor, he shall be punished with 80 blows; the aforesaid punishment may however be redeemed by the payment of the established fine, provided the creditor is not found to have seized more in value than was actually due to him. On the other hand, if the estimated value of the property so unlawfully seized, exceeds the principal and interest due, the excess shall subject the offender to a punishment as much greater than 80 blows as may be found to be proportionate to the amount thereof, according to the law concerning pecuniary malversation in general; such excess in the amount or value of the seizure, shall moreover be returned to the debtor.

If a creditor accepts the wives or children of his debtor in pledge for payment, he shall be punished with 100 blows; and one degree more severely, if he is afterwards guilty of criminal intercourse with the same.

If the creditor seizes and carries off by force his debtors wives or children, he shall be punished two degrees more severely than in the case of receiving them in pledge by mutual agreement; and, lastly, if he is guilty of a criminal intercourse with the females so seized, he shall suffer death by being strangled, after the usual period of imprisonment.

All persons so unlawfully transferred, seized, or detained, shall be restored to their respective families, and the debt originally due in any such case, shall not afterwards be recoverable by the creditor.

Eight clauses.

SEC-

SECTION CL. — *Dilapidation of Property in Truſt.*

If an individual who is entruſted with the goods or live-ſtock of another waſtes or conſumes the ſame, without authority from the proprietor, he ſhall be puniſhed in proportion to the value, one degree leſs than is provided by the law concerning pecuniary malverſation in general, and the extreme extent of the puniſhment ſhall be limited to 90 blows, and baniſhment for two years and a half.

If ſuch truſtee ſhould moreover deceitfully allege the death of the cattle, or the loſs of the money or other property ſo intruſted to him, he ſhall be puniſhed in proportion to the amount or value, one degree leſs than is provided by law in caſes of theft, but ſhall not be branded, nor ſuffer more than 100 blows and three years baniſhment, however conſiderable the amount or value deficient.

In all ſuch caſes the truſtee ſhall be obliged to reſtore the property committed to his care, or its full amount and value, to the right owner.

Neverthelefs, if he can bring ſatisfactory evidence of the deſtruction or loſs of the goods by fire, water, or thieves, or of the ſickneſs and death of the live ſtock, he ſhall be thereby totally freed from puniſhment, as well as from pecuniary reſponſibility.

All incidental circumſtances of fraud, or fraudulent ſale of entruſted property, of which an offender againſt this law may be proved guilty, ſhall be moreover taken into conſideration in aggravation of his puniſhment, conformably to the laws ſpecially applicable in ſuch caſes.

One clauſe.

SECTION CLI. — *Loſt and forgotten Property.*

Whoever finds any loſt and forgotten goods ſhall, within five days time, deliver up the ſame to the magiſtrate of the diſtrict. If it is then aſcertained to have been public property, the entire amount ſhall be retained by government, but otherwiſe remain to be claimed and identified by the owner, to whom half ſhall be reſtored, and the remaining half allowed as a reward to the finder. If no perſon proves a claim to the property within thirty days, the finder ſhall then receive back and retain the whole.

If the finder of any loſt and forgotten goods, does not deliver up the ſame to a magiſtrate within the five days already ſtated, he ſhall be puniſhed in proportion to the amount or value, according to a ſcale grounded upon that eſtabliſhed by the law concerning pecuniary malverſation in general; that is to ſay, if it proves to be public property, he ſhall ſuffer the full extent of the puniſhment provided by that law, otherwiſe, a proportionate puniſhment leſs in each caſe by two degrees; half of the private property, the diſcovery of which had been unlawfully ſuppreſſed, ſhall be forfeited to government, and the other half reſtored to the owner, when an owner can be found; but if none, then the whole ſhall be retained by government.

If any perſon, by digging in private or public ground, diſcovers articles which had been buried and concealed in the earth, and to which no owner can be found, he ſhall be at liberty to retain the ſame for his own uſe, ſaving and excepting all ancient utenſils, bells, ſacred vaſes, ſeals of officers of government, and other ſuch extraordinary and uncommon articles as it is not befitting the people in general to poſſeſs; all which, within thirty days after the diſcovery, muſt be delivered up to government, on pain of receiving a puniſhment of 80 blows for omitting to do ſo, and ſtill continuing to be reſponſible for the ſurrender of the goods to government.

No clauſe.

END OF THE SIXTH BOOK OF THE THIRD DIVISION.

BOOK VII.

SALES AND MARKETS.

SECTION CLII.—*Licence of Commercial Agents.*

IN every city, public market, and village diſtrict, where there is a commercial agent ſtationed and authorized by government, and in every ſea-port and reach of a river, at which there are ſhip-agents, cuſtomarily ſtationed and authorized in the ſame manner, theſe agents ſhall be ſelected from ſuch of the inhabitants as are from their wealth enabled to ſuſtain the pecuniary reſponſibility attached to the ſituation; a regularly authenticated licence ſhall be granted to them by the officer of the diſtrict, and they ſhall be required to keep an official regiſter of the ſhips and merchants that ſucceſſively arrive, deſcribing their real names and references, and alſo the marks, numbers, quality and quantity of the goods imported or introduced into the market; which regiſter ſhall be ſubmitted to a monthly examination at the board or tribunal of the officer of the diſtrict, that he may act accordingly.

Whoever privately takes upon himſelf the buſineſs of ſuch agency without the licence of government, ſhall ſuffer a puniſhment of 60 blows, and forfeit to government the amount of his profits ariſing therefrom.

If the officers of government, or any of the eſtabliſhed agents, connive at ſuch illegal aſſumption of power, they ſhall be reſpectively puniſhed with 50 blows, and diſmiſſed from their employments.

Six clauſes.

SECTION CLIII. — *Valuation of Merchandize.*

The valuation and appraifement of goods and merchandize, fhall be effected by the commercial agents, after due confideration, and upon fair and equitable terms; any deviation on their part from fuch terms, either by enhancement or depreciation of value, fhall fubject the agent to a proportionate punifhment according to the law concerning pecuniary malverfation in general.

If the difference between his appreciation of the goods and their real value is converted by fuch agent to his own benefit and advantage, he fhall then be liable to the feverer punifhment provided by the law in cafes of theft, except that the part of the fentence which requires the offender to be branded, fhall, in thefe cafes, be remitted.

If the commercial agent eftimates the amount of a fine or forfeiture to which any offender is liable, more or lefs than is conformable to the juft execution of the laws, he fhall be liable to fuffer according to the fcale of punifhment, which officers of government are fubject to, by the law concerning a wilful deviation from juftice in pronouncing a judicial fentence.

If, laftly, the agent has been induced by a bribe to eftimate falfely the price of goods, or the amount of forfeitures, he fhall be liable to a punifhment as much more fevere than that already provided, as may be found to correfpond to the amount of the bribe, according to the law againft bribery for an unlawful purpofe, committed by officers who have not regular falaries.

One claufe.

SECTION CLIV. — *Monopolizers and unfair Traders.*

When the parties to the purchafe and fale of goods do not amicably agree refpecting the terms, if one of them monopolizing, or otherwife ufing uſing undue influence in the market, obliges the other to allow him an exorbitant profit; or if artful ſpeculators in trade, by entering into a private underſtanding with the commercial agent, and by employing other unwarrantable contrivances, raiſe the price of their own goods, although of low value, and depreſs the prices of thoſe of others, although of high value, in all ſuch caſes the offending parties ſhall be ſeverally puniſhed with 80 blows each for their miſconduct.

When a trader, obſerving the nature of the commercial buſineſs carrying on by his neighbour, contrives to ſuit or manage the diſpoſal or appreciation of his own goods in ſuch a manner, as to derange, and excite diſtruſt againſt, the proceedings of the other, and thereby draws unfairly a greater proportion of profit to himſelf than uſual, he ſhall be puniſhed with 40 blows.

The exorbitant profit derived from any one of the foregoing unlawful practices, ſhall, as far as it exceeds a fair proportion, be eſteemed a theft, and the offender puniſhed accordingly, whenever the amount renders the puniſhment provided by the law againſt theft more ſevere than that hereby eſtabliſhed and provided. The offender ſhall ſhall not however be branded as in the ordinary caſes of theft.

Eight clauſes.

Section CLV.—*Falſe Weights, Meaſures, and Scales.*

Whoever procures falſe meaſures, or falſe weights and ſcales, and makes uſe of them in the public market; and whoever adds to, or takes any thing away from, thoſe meaſures, weights and ſcales which have been iſſued and ſanctioned by government, ſhall be puniſhed with 60 blows. The ſame puniſhment ſhall likewiſe be inflicted on the artificer of ſuch articles.

If

If any meaſures, weights, or ſcales, not made according to the eſtabliſhed rules, are iſſued under the ſanction of government, the officer who iſſued, and the artificer who made them, ſhall alike be puniſhed with 70 blows. The inſpecting officers, if privy to, and conniving thereat, ſhall be equally puniſhable; but if only guilty of neglecting to examine and compare ſuch articles with the ſtandards eſtabliſhed and provided, their puniſhment ſhall be leſs by one degree.

If any meaſures, weights, or ſcales are made uſe of in the public market, which, however exactly conformable to ſtandard, have not been examined, compared and duly ſtamped by the officers or government, they ſhall be held to be unlawful, and the perſon employing them ſhall be accordingly puniſhable with 40 blows.

If the officers and others in the employ of government in the public treaſuries and ſtore-houſes, make any alteration in the meaſures, weights, and ſcales iſſued or ſanctioned by government, whereby more or leſs than the juſt amount of any article is received in contribution to the revenue, or iſſued upon the public ſervice, they ſhall be puniſhed with 100 blows at the leaſt, and as much more ſeverely, as the law reſpecting pecuniary malverſation may, proportionably to the amount of ſuch aforeſaid deviation, be found to authorize. — If however the conſequent exceſs of receipts, or amount of ſhort deliveries, has been converted by the offender to his own private uſe and advantage, his puniſhment ſhall be inflicted in proportion to the amount, according to the ſeverer ſcale eſtabliſhed by the law concerning the embezzlement of public property.

The artificer employed in effecting ſuch fraudulent alteration in the meaſures, weights or ſcales iſſued or ſanctioned by government, ſhall be puniſhed with 80 blows.

The ſuperintending officer having immediate juriſdiction over the department of the offender, ſhall be equally puniſhable, whenever

ever, being privy to, he takes no cognizance of ſuch tranſgreſſion; when it is imputable to his inattention and neglect only, his puniſhment ſhall be leſs than that of the original offender by three degrees, and in no caſe exceed 100 blows.

No clauſe.

SECTION CLVI. — *Manufactures not equal or conformable to Standard.*

If a private individual manufactures any article for ſale, which is not as ſtrong, durable, and genuine, as it is profeſſed to be, or if he prepares and ſells any ſilks or other ſtuffs of a thinner or ſlighter texture and quality, narrower, or ſhorter, than the eſtabliſhed or cuſtomary ſtandard, he ſhall be puniſhed with 50 blows.

One clauſe.

END OF THE THIRD DIVISION.

FOURTH DIVISION,

Ritual Laws.

BOOK I.

SACRED RITES.

Section CLVII. — *Adminiſtration of Sacred Rites.*

ALL the officers of government whoſe province it is to ſuperintend the grand Imperial ſacrifices and oblations to Heaven and Earth, and to the ſpirit preſiding over the productions of the earth and the generations of mankind *; and thoſe likewiſe who have the direction of the ſacred rites which are performed in the temple of the Imperial

* Whether theſe, and ſome other ſimilar terms employed by the Chineſe, are intended to imply the exiſtence of as many diſtinct objects of worſhip, or are in fact only deſcriptive of the different characters and attributes of one ſupreme Being, recognized and adored as ſuch, is a queſtion upon which even the miſſionaries, to whom the inveſtigation of the principles of the national or ſtate religion in China muſt have been an object of peculiar intereſt, were for a long time divided. The latter opinion was always ſtrenuouſly ſupported in the writings, and countenanced by the practice of the Jeſuits; but the former, though in a great meaſure incompatible with the pleaſing notions which have been entertained of the purity of this moſt ancient part of the Chineſe religious ſyſtem, appears at preſent to prevail, or at leaſt to be tacitly acknowledged in all the forms of inſtruction adopted in China by the teachers of Chriſtianity. The phraſes conſidered to be of queſtionable meaning are carefully excluded, and the Deity is addreſſed by the native converts under no other title than *Tien Chu* or " Maſter " of Heaven," a term or combination of words, previouſly unknown in the Chineſe language, but thus introduced by Europeans, in the idea that any other would be liable to abuſe or miſconception.

Family,

Family, ſhall prepare themſelves for every ſuch occaſion by abſtinence; they ſhall bind themſelves to the performance of ſuch abſtinence*, by ſolemn vows; and previous to making theſe vows, they ſhall announce the intended ſacrifices and oblations in the manner by law eſtabliſhed.

If they do not by ſuch preparatory declaration of the day appointed for the ſacred rite, give ſufficient notice to the tribunals and public boards the members of which are officially required to aſſiſt at the ceremony, they ſhall be puniſhed with 50 blows; and if, in conſequence of ſuch omiſſion, the ſolemn proceedings are in any reſpect irregularly or imperfectly conducted, the puniſhment ſhall be encreaſed to 100 blows.

When, after the regular notice has been duly given, any imperfection or irregularity occurs in the adminiſtration of the ſacred rites, all the individuals to whom ſuch imperfection or irregularity is attributable, ſhall be ſubject to the laſt mentioned puniſhment.

If any individual of the intended aſſemblage † of officers of government for the performance of ſacred rites, having had the Imperial command to prepare himſelf by abſtinence duly communicated to him, takes the oath of abſtinence, but afterwards violates it, either by mourning for the dead, viſiting the ſick, taking cognizance of capital offences, or partaking of public feaſts, he ſhall in all ſuch caſes forfeit one month's ſalary.

If the ſuperintendants of the rites are aware that any individual of the intended aſſemblage, has it incumbent on him to mourn for a relation within the four degrees, or was ever convicted of an offence

* The ſenſe in which the term abſtinence is employed is explained in a ſubſequent paragraph of this ſection.

† Literally "The one hundred officers of government," but meaning no more than a conſiderable aſſemblage of perſons, varying in number according to circumſtances.—In the ſame manner, when the expreſſion "ten thouſand" occurs in the Chineſe language, it does not generally imply any preciſe number, but merely a great or an indefinite multitude.

puniſhable

puniſhable with 50 or more blows of the bamboo, or with baniſhment, they ſhall not permit ſuch perſon to aſſiſt at the ceremony, on penalty of forfeiting themſelves the aforeſaid one month's ſalary.

The ſuperintendant of the rites, if ignorant of the cauſe of mourning, or former miſconduct, of a member of the aſſemblage, ſhall not be liable to the penalty; but it ſhall be levied on thoſe who, being ſubject to ſuch diſabilities, do not make known the ſame.

Moreover, all thoſe officers of government ſhall be liable to the ſame forfeiture, who, after having taken the oaths of abſtinence, do not paſs the night apart from their families, if on duty in the provinces, or at their official apartments, if on duty at court.

If the animals, precious ſtones, ſilks, grain, and other articles introduced in the grand ſacrifices and oblations, are not of the quality, and in the ſtate preſcribed by the ritual regulations *, the ſuperintendants ſhall be puniſhed with 50 blows; if an article of any kind is wanting, the puniſhment ſhall be encreaſed to 80 blows, and if any one of the altars is wholly unprovided, the puniſhment ſhall be further encreaſed to 100 blows.

If the officer of government having the charge of the animals reſerved for ſacrifice at grand ſolemnities, does not rear and feed them in the manner, and according to the practice by law eſtabliſhed, ſo that any one of them becomes lean, or is otherwiſe injured, he ſhall ſuffer 40 blows, and be liable to a puniſhment proportionally greater by one degree, as far as 80 blows, for every addition of one to the number of animals ſo circumſtanced. — When any one or more of theſe animals die in conſequence of ſuch neglect, the puniſhment ſhall be further encreaſed one degree.

* The code of ritual regulations which, in this diviſion of the Penal Laws, is frequently referred to, is, as might be expected from the national character and peculiar habits of the Chineſe, extremely voluminous; and the ſubject likewiſe occupies a very conſiderable portion of the great Chineſe work already noticed under the title of *Ta-tſing-hoey-tien*.

The ſame punishments and penalties ſhall likewiſe be inflicted in any caſes of a breach of the regulations eſtabliſhed reſpecting the intermediate and inferior ſacred and imperial rites, as far as the circumſtances correſpond.

Two clauſes.

SECTION CLVIII. — *Deſtroying Altars and Sacred Terraces.*

Whoever deſtroys or damages, whether intentionally or inadvertently, the altars, mounds, or terraces conſecrated to the ſacred and imperial rites, ſhall ſuffer 100 blows, and be perpetually baniſhed to diſtance of 2000 *lee*. — Whoever deſtroys, or occaſions any damage to, the gate or entrance to ſuch conſecrated ground, ſhall ſuffer puniſhment leſs by two degrees; that is to ſay, 90 blows and two years baniſhment.

Whoever diſcards, or deſtroys any articles, however trifling their value, which are conſecrated to the ſervice of ſacred and imperial rites, ſhall ſuffer 100 blows, and be baniſhed for three years; the puniſhment ſhall be leſs by three degrees in caſes of loſing or deſtroying ſuch articles inadvertently; that is to ſay, 70 blows and baniſhment for one year and a half.

When the value of ſuch articles is ſo conſiderable as to ſubject the offenders, conformably to the law againſt loſing or deſtroying the property of government, to ſeverer puniſhment than that hereby provided, ſuch ſeverer puniſhment ſhall be inflicted accordingly.

Two clauſes.

SECTION CLIX. — *Provincial Sacred Rites to be conformable to the Ritual Code.*

Within the limits of the juriſdiction of each city of the firſt, ſecond, and third order, the local genii, the genii of the hills, the rivers,

rivers, the winds, the clouds, and the lightnings, alſo the ancient holy Emperors, enlightened Kings, faithful miniſters, and illuſtrious ſages, ſhall all be ſeverally honoured and commemorated by the oblations and other holy rites which the ritual code preſcribes.

The ſuperintendants of the ſeveral diſtricts ſhall not fail to erect ſuitable monuments in honour and commemoration of theſe divine and holy perſonages, with tablets deſcribing their names and titles, and the days on which ſacrifices and oblations are appointed to be made to them *.

Theſe tablets ſhall be affixed in clean places near to running ſtreams; and if the ſacred rites which are thus publicly announced, are afterwards neglected when the day appointed arrives, the officers and others belonging to the board or tribunal reſponſible for the performance thereof, ſhall incur the puniſhment of 100 blows.

On the other hand, any officer of government who commemorates, or performs ſacred rites to the honour of, any ſpirit or holy perſonage, to whom neither honours nor oblations are decreed by the laws of the ritual code, ſhall be puniſhed with 80 blows.

No clauſe.

SECTION CLX. — *Care of the Tombs of diſtinguiſhed Perſonages.*

The ſepulchral monuments of ancient Emperors and princes, and alſo the tombs of ſaints, ſages, faithful miniſters, and other illuſtrious individuals, ſhall be carefully preſerved by the officers of the diſtrict in which they are ſituated; and no perſon ſhall preſume, on pain of receiving a puniſhment of 80 blows, to feed cattle, cut wood,

* Theſe monuments, commonly, but improperly, termed triumphal arches, are deſcribed in Mr. Barrow's Travels in China, p. 35., and a repreſentation of one of the moſt conſiderable of the kind, is given in one of the plates in the folio volume annexed to the account of the Britiſh Embaſſy.

or

or guide the plough in the places, where the remains of ſuch diſtinguiſhed perſonages are depoſited.

No clauſe.

Section CLXI. — *Diſhonouring Celeſtial Spirits, by unlicenſed Forms of Worſhip.*

If any private family performs the ceremony of the adoration of Heaven and of the North Star, burning incenſe for that purpoſe during the night, lighting the lamps of Heaven, and alſo ſeven lamps to the North Star, it ſhall be deemed a profanation of theſe ſacred rites, and derogatory to the Celeſtial Spirits; the parties concerned therein ſhall accordingly be puniſhed with 80 blows.

When the wives or daughters are guilty of theſe offences, the huſbands and fathers ſhall be held reſponſible.

If the prieſts of *Foe* and *Tao-ſſe*, after burning incenſe and preparing an oblation, imitate the ſacred Imperial rites, they alſo ſhall be puniſhed as aforeſaid, and moreover be expelled from the order of prieſthood.

If any officers of government, ſoldiers, or citizens, permit the females belonging to their families to go abroad to the temples of prieſts, in order to burn incenſe in token of worſhip, they ſhall be puniſhed with 40 blows; but when widows, or other women not under the guardianſhip of men, commit the ſame offence, the puniſhment ſhall fall on themſelves.

The ſuperior of the temple, and the porter at the gate, ſhall likewiſe be equally puniſhable for admitting them.

One clauſe.

Sec-

SECTION CLXII. — *Magicians, Leaders of Sects, and Teachers of false Doctrines.*

Magicians, who raife evil fpirits by means of magical books and dire imprecations, leaders of corrupt and impious fects, and members of all fuperftitious affociations in general, whether denominating themfelves *Mi-le-fo*, or *Pe-lien-kiao*, or in any other manner diftinguifhed, all of them offend againft the laws, by their wicked and diabolical doctrines and practices.

When fuch perfons, having in their poffeffion concealed images of their worfhip, burn incenfe in honour of them, and when they affemble their followers by night in order to inftruct them in their doctrines, and by pretended powers and notices, endeavour to inveigle and miflead the multitude, the principal in the commiffion of fuch offences fhall be ftrangled, after remaining in prifon the ufual period, and the acceffaries fhall feverally receive 100 blows, and be perpetually banifhed to the diftance of 3000 *lee*.

If at any time the people, whether foldiers or citizens, drefs and ornament their idols, and after accompanying them tumultuoufly with drums and gongs, perform oblations and other facred rites to their honour, the leader or inftigator of fuch meetings fhall be punifhed with 100 blows *.

If the head inhabitant of the diftrict, when privy to fuch unlawful meetings, does not give information to government, he fhall be punifhed with 40 blows.

The penalties of this law fhall not however be fo conftrued as to interrupt the regular and cuftomary meetings of the people, to in-

* As this prohibitory claufe defcribes nothing more than what is frequently and openly practifed in every part of the empire, the law in this refpect muft be either confidered as obfolete, or as an article retained for the purpofe of enabling the magiftrates to control and keep within bounds thefe popular fuperftitions, though it may have been found dangerous or unavailing to attempt to fupprefs them altogether.

voke

voke the terreſtial ſpirits in ſpring, and to return thanks to them in autumn *.

Eight clauſes.

* As the Catholic Chriſtians in China have been eſtimated at upwards of 200,000, and have been very frequently objects of the attention of the government, ſometimes encouraged, but much oftener ſeverely perſecuted, ſome ſpecific notice in this place of the Chriſtian ſect, might naturally have been expected: but, whether on account of its comparatively ſmall importance in the eyes of the Chineſe, or from ſome heſitation which may ſtill exiſt about pronouncing on its character a deciſive and irreverſible judgment, the ſubject is in this code entirely paſſed over in ſilence. — To make up in ſome degree for this defect of information on the intereſting queſtion of the preſent diſpoſition of the Chineſe government towards the Chriſtian religion (at leaſt in the form and under the appearance given to it by the Roman Catholic miſſionaries), a tranſlation has been inſerted in Appendix, No. XVIII. of two Imperial Edicts, which are expreſsly declaratory of the law on this ſubject, and were iſſued to the public as late as the year 1805.

END OF THE FIRST BOOK OF THE FOURTH DIVISION.

BOOK II.

MISCELLANEOUS OBSERVANCES.

SECTION CLXIII. — *Preparation of Medicines and Provifions for the Emperor.*

IF any phyfician inadvertently prepares and mixes the medicines deftined for the ufe of His Imperial Majefty, in any manner that is not fanctioned by eftablifhed practice, or does not accompany them with a proper defcription and directions, he fhall be punifhed with 100 blows. If the ingredients are not genuine and well chofen, as well as carefully compounded, the phyfician fhall be punifhed with 60 blows.

If the cook employed in preparing the Imperial repafts, introduces any prohibited ingredients into the difhes by inadvertence, he fhall be punifhed with 100 blows.

If any of the articles of liquid or folid food are not clean, he fhall be punifhed with 80 blows. If they are not genuine and properly felected, with 60 blows; and laftly, if the cook does not afcertain the quality of the difhes by tafting, he fhall be punifhed with 50 blows.

The fuperintending and difpenfing officers fhall in each cafe refpectively, be punifhed two degrees lefs feverely than the cook and the phyfician.

If either the fuperintending or difpenfing officer, or the cook, introduces into His Majefty's kitchen any unufual drug, or article of food,

food, he ſhall be puniſhed with 100 blows, and compelled to ſwallow the ſame.

If the ſuperintending or diſpenſing officers are aware of the cooks or others in the Imperial kitchen committing offences of this nature, and do not report the ſame to the Emperor, they ſhall participate equally in the puniſhment. When ſuch offences have been overlooked through the neglect of the officer on guard at the gates, or the officers about the Emperor's perſon, they alſo ſhall participate equally in the puniſhment; and in every caſe, the circumſtances immediately after they are diſcovered, ſhall be ſubmitted to His Majeſty's notice and deciſion.

One clauſe.

Section CLXIV. — *Charge of the Imperial Equipage and Furniture.*

Whoever, having charge of the Imperial equipage, or of any other articles deſtined for Imperial uſe, does not attend to their repair and preſervation in the manner preſcribed by the eſtabliſhed rules, ſhall be puniſhed with 60 blows: — Whoever having ſuch charge, preſents to the Emperor any articles for his Imperial uſe, in an improper manner, whether by omitting to preſent what is neceſſary, or by preſenting what ought not to be preſented, ſhall be puniſhed with 40 blows. — Whoever, having charge as aforeſaid, does not duly exerciſe and examine His Majeſty's horſes and carriages, ſo as to aſcertain that they are ſound, and fit for the ſervice of His Majeſty, ſhall be puniſhed with 80 blows.

Moreover, if any ſuch perſon ſhould appropriate to his own uſe, lend for the uſe of others, or wilfully diſcard or deſtroy, any part of His Imperial Majeſty's equipage, or any article whatſoever deſtined in like

like manner for the immediate uſe of His Majeſty, ſhall be puniſhed with 100 blows and three years baniſhment.

When any of the aforeſaid articles are loſt or deſtroyed, not wilfully, but inadvertently, either through idleneſs or neglect, the puniſhment ſhall be leſs by three degrees.

If His Imperial Majeſty's pleaſure boats and veſſels are not ſound and in good order, the artificer ſhall be puniſhed with 100 blows.

If the ſaid veſſels are not likewiſe in every other reſpect kept in good repair, or if they are not properly ſupplied with poles and planks, the puniſhment ſhall amount to 60 blows, and be inflicted on the perſon in charge, or on the artificer, according as the fault ſhall be found to be imputable to the one, or to the other.

The ſuperintending officer and diſpenſing officer of the department, ſhall each be liable to puniſhment proportionably leſs than that inflicted on the artificer or perſon in charge, by two degrees.

All offences puniſhable according to this law, ſhall however be made known immediately on diſcovery to His Majeſty, and the ſentence only executed ſo far as is conformable to His Imperial pleaſure.

No clauſe.

SECTION CLXV. — *Poſſeſſion and Concealment of prohibited Books and Inſtruments.*

Any private houſeholder or maſter of a family, who ſecretly keeps in his poſſeſſion celeſtial images, inſtruments for explaining and pourtraying the celeſtial bodies, aſtrological books, books for calculating good and bad fortune, or other books which are prohibited; or portraits and repreſentations of former Emperors and Kings, official ſeals cut in gold or in gems, or any other ſimilar articles which private individuals cannot lawfully uſe or poſſeſs, ſhall, if he does not

 voluntarily

voluntarily ſurrender up the ſame to government, be puniſhed with 100 blows, and be held anſwerable for the payment of a fine of 10 *leang* or ounces of ſilver, which ſum ſhall be beſtowed as a reward on the informer.

The aforeſaid articles ſhall in every caſe be forfeited to government.

No clauſe.

SECTION CLXVI. — *Tranſmiſſion of Imperial Preſents.*

When His Imperial Majeſty is pleaſed to make preſents of dreſſes or other articles to the officers of His Majeſty's government, if the officer deputed to execute His Majeſty's commands, does not perform in perſon the duty aſſigned to him, but on the contrary tranſmits the Imperial preſents to be delivered by other hands, he ſhall be puniſhed with 100 blows, and be rendered incapable of holding any employment in the public ſervice.

No clauſe.

SECTION CLXVII. — *Obſervance of Feſtivals and Days of Ceremony.*

Upon all ſolemn court feſtivals, and other occaſional public ſolemnities, appointed for the receipt with due honour of Imperial orders and communications, the officer having the ſuperintendance of this department ſhall give ſufficient previous notice, on pain of receiving a puniſhment of 40 blows, whenever he omits the ſame. — All thoſe, on the other hand, who after having received ſufficient notice, nevertheleſs perform their functions imperfectly or improperly upon ſuch occaſions, ſhall be liable to ſimilar puniſhment.

No clauſe.

SEC-

SECTION CLXVIII. — *Due Performance of appointed Ceremonies.*

If any of the officers of government who aſſiſt at the ſacred and Imperial rites, who attend the viſitation of the Imperial tombs, or who are preſent at the ſolemnity of a public audience given by the Emperor, miſtake, or in any manner deviate from, the eſtabliſhed ceremonial of the day, they ſhall forfeit one month's ſalary; and if thoſe who are appointed to preſide over the ceremonies overlook any ſuch miſtake or deviation, they ſhall be liable to the ſame penalty.

One clauſe.

SECTION CLXIX. — *Officers of Government to addreſs the Emperor in Succeſſion according to their Rank.*

When any of the officers of government in waiting, or in the train of His Imperial Majeſty, are ſpoken to, or queſtioned collectively, by His Majeſty; the firſt in rank ſhall come forward and ſpeak in reply firſt, and the others ſucceſſively according to their order of rank; if any one violates this order, by coming forward and ſpeaking, before or after his turn, he ſhall forfeit one month's ſalary.

No clauſe.

SECTION CLXX. — *Vexatiouſly detaining Officers of Government from the Imperial Preſence.*

If any officer of government, or other perſon who is entitled to the honour of being preſented to His Imperial Majeſty, is vexatiouſly detained and impeded upon unwarrantable pretexts by the ſuperintendant of the ceremonies, inſtead of being forthwith introduced by him

to

to the Imperial preſence, ſuch ſuperintendant ſhall, upon conviction of having ſo done by malicious deſign, be condemned to ſuffer death by being beheaded after confinement in priſon for the uſual period.

All the great officers of ſtate who are privy to this offence without making any enquiry into it, ſhall be puniſhed as equal participators in the guilt, but if ignorant thereof, ſhall be ſubject to no puniſhment or reſponſibility whatever.

No clauſe.

SECTION CLXXI. — *Addreſſes on Public Affairs.*

Whatever is erroneous in the general adminiſtration of public affairs, whatever is beneficial or injurious to the ſoldiers and people, and, in general, whatever tends to the acquiſition of a public benefit or the prevention of a public injury, ſhall be enquired into, and the reſult perſonally communicated to the Emperor, by the officers of the ſix ſupreme tribunals or departments of ſtate.

The cenſors *, the viceroys, and the deputy viceroys, ſhall likewiſe repreſent faithfully and unreſervedly whatever appears to them adviſeable to communicate on theſe ſubjects.

If any officer of government at court, or in the provinces, of high or low rank, is aware of any impropriety in the proceedings of the board or tribunal of which he is a member, he ſhall fully and diſtinctly ſtate to his ſuperior officer whatever may be requiſite and pro-

* The board or tribunal of the cenſorate has the power of inſpecting and animadverting upon the proceedings of all the other public boards and tribunals in the empire, and even on the acts of the ſovereign himſelf, whenever they are to be conceived to be cenſurable, but it may eaſily be imagined that in a government profeſſedly abſolute, the power aſcribed to the cenſors in the latter caſe, muſt be little more than a fiction of ſtate, inſtead of operating as a real and effective influence and control.

It muſt however be admitted that, from other circumſtances peculiar to the conſtitution and adminiſtration of the Chineſe government, ſome of which it is hoped this work may be found to elucidate, there are probably few regular and nominally abſolute monarchies, in which both the perſonal conduct and public meaſures of the ſovereign are neceſſarily ſo much under the united influence of laws, cuſtoms, and public opinion.

per

per to be ſubmitted on the ſubject to His Imperial Majeſty, to whom the ſame ſhall be faithfully reported in order to be decided upon according to his royal pleaſure. Thoſe who, although privy to, take no notice of, and connive at ſuch proceedings, during months and years, ſhall, if at court, be liable to an inveſtigation of their conduct in ſuch inſtances, by the cenſors; but by the viceroys and deputy viceroys, if their connivance ſhould have taken place in any of the provincial departments. When found guilty, they ſhall be puniſhed according to the law in ordinary inſtances of omitting to make due report upon public affairs to ſuperiors, or to His Imperial Majeſty.

In all repreſentations to the Emperor, the facts, and the reaſoning that is grounded upon them, muſt be ſtated ſimply and candidly; each article muſt be brought forward and explained ſeparately; and all empty phraſeology and unneceſſary repetition muſt be avoided.

If any officer of the ſtate, prompted by unprincipled ambition, addreſſes the Emperor in artful terms, and, upon colourable pretexts, ſolicits places and employments, he ſhall be puniſhed with 100 blows. If in ſuch addreſs he falſely criminates any officer or public board immediately entruſted or connected with the adminiſtration of civil or military affairs, and if he moreover borrows the ſanction of an official ſeal and envelope, in order to procure the addreſs to be received, both the lender and borrower of ſuch official ſeal and envelope, ſhall be beheaded.—The offence is however ranked among thoſe denominated miſcellaneous, and the puniſhment is reducible accordingly to baniſhment.

One clauſe.

SECTION CLXXII. — *Monuments raiſed by Officers of Government to commemorate their own Actions.*

If any officer of government during the period of his adminiſtration, preſumes to raiſe within the limits of his diſtrict, public monuments diſplaying difplaying infcriptions in honour of himfelf, when he had in fact performed no fervice to the ftate worthy of fuch commemoration, he fhall be punifhed with 100 blows.

If an officer fends any perfon to his fuperior to folicit his fanction to the elevation of honorary monuments as aforefaid, upon the pretext of fervices falfely alleged to have been performed by him, he fhall be punifhed with 80 blows, and the perfon who undertakes to convey the requeft under fuch circumftances fhall fuffer punifhment lefs by one degree. The monuments undeferveclly raifed, fhall be deftroyed, and the infcriptions effaced.

No claufe.

Section CLXXIII. — *Honorary Attendance on Superiors in Rank.*

When the fuperior officers of government, or other officers charged with a fpecial miffion by the Emperor, are proceeding through any part of the empire, if any of the officers or members of the feveral tribunals and departments of government in the diftricts through which they pafs, proceed beyond the walls of their refpective cities, either to meet them when approaching, or to accompany them when departing, they fhall be punifhed with 90 blows.

Whoever authorizes and allows fuch honorary attendance to be paid him, inftead of taking cognizance of it as an unlawful procedure, fhall be equally punifhable.

Six claufes. *

Sec-

* By the fourth claufe it is enacted that any foldier or citizen fhall be punifhable with 50 blows, who does not make way when he meets a civil or military officer of government on the public road, or who, if on horfeback, does not difmount on fuch an occafion.

In refpect to this law and others of the fame defcription it may be remarked, that however degrading and oppreffive they may appear in the eyes of a European, they are in China intimately connected with, and indeed no more than the natural confequence of the peculiar

SECTION CLXXIV. — *Official Meſſengers contemptuouſly treating the Officers of Diſtricts.*

When any officer or attendant of government is diſpatched upon a meſſage or miſſion relative to the public ſervice, if inſtead of conducting himſelf with civility and decorum, he contemptuouſly treats, either the military officers, who protect, or the civil officers, who govern the diſtrict, he ſhall be puniſhed with 60 blows. If inferior officers are guilty of ſuch miſconduct, they ſhall be puniſhed with either 70 or 80 blows, according to the nature of their ordinary employment in the public ſervice.

One clauſe.

SECTION CLXXV. — *Sumptuary Laws relative to Dreſs and Habitations.*

The houſes, apartments, carriages, dreſs, furniture, and other articles uſed by the officers of government, and by the people in general, ſhall be conformable to the eſtabliſhed rules and gradations. Accordingly any individual who poſſeſſes ſuch articles for uſe, contrary to theſe rules and gradations, ſhall, if an officer of government, be puniſhed with 100 blows, depoſed from his office, and rendered incapable of future ſervice; if a private individual is guilty of this offence, the maſter of the family in which the article is uſed, ſhall be puniſhed with 50 blows. In both caſes the offending party ſhall be required to alter and rectify the article in the manner the regulations preſcribe. The artificer ſhall alſo in both caſes be liable to 50 blows, unleſs he ſhould have ſurrendered himſelf voluntarily, in which caſe he ſhall be pardoned, but not in any caſe rewarded.

---

liar character and genius of the people.—In a country where forms and ceremonies are ſo cloſely interwoven with all the real buſineſs and purſuits of life, it is not felt to be either harſh or tyrannical, that they are thus enforced and regulated by the higheſt public authority.

If any perſon poſſeſſes for uſe, articles abſolutely prohibited, ſuch as ſilk ſtuffs repreſenting the Imperial Dragon (*Lung*), or the Imperial Phœnix (*Fung-whang*), he ſhall, whether an officer of government, or a private individual, be puniſhed with 100 blows and three years baniſhment; the officer of government thus offending ſhall moreover be depoſed and rendered incapable of future ſervice. The artificer ſhall be puniſhed with 100 blows, and the prohibited goods ſhall be forfeited to government. — Whoever gives information of the commiſſion of this offence, ſhall receive a reward of 50 *leang* or ounces of ſilver; even the manufacturer of the goods, if he gives information, ſhall not only be pardoned for his ſhare in the offence, but alſo receive the above reward *.

Sixteen clauſes.

SECTION CLXXVI. — *Dreſs and Conduct of the Prieſts.*

All perſons licenced to enter into religious orders as prieſts of *Foe* or *Tao-ſse*, ſhall nevertheleſs continue to viſit their parents, to ſacrifice and make oblations to their anceſtors, and to mourn for their recently deceaſed relations, in the ſame manner as is by law required from the people in general, on pain of receiving a puniſhment of 100 blows, and being obliged to renounce their religious orders.

All perſons in prieſt's orders ſhall wear ſtuffs and ſilks of a ſingle colour, and of a ſimple pattern; they ſhall abſtain from the uſe of damaſks,

* The law, which in this place enforces, what in other countries is uſually governed only by cuſtom or caprice, is, no doubt, frequently evaded by the private and domeſtic luxury of individuals; it is however certain that, generally ſpeaking, the pleaſure which the poſſeſſor of ſuperior wealth may be ſuppoſed to derive from the diſplay of it, a Chineſe, whatever his ſituation, is in great meaſure, if not wholly, precluded from enjoying.

At the ſame time there is nothing which leads to a belief that the law of extraordinary ſeverity mentioned in the deſcription of China compiled by the Abbé Groſier from the writings of the miſſionaries, for puniſhing with death thoſe who wear pearls, has any exiſtence either in theory or in practice.

damaſks, and flowered or variegated ſtuffs, on penalty of receiving a puniſhment of 50 blows, of being excluded from their order, and forfeiting all ſuch dreſſes to government.

Nevertheleſs the *Kia-ſha*, and other ceremonial veſtments excluſively worn by the prieſts ſhall not be conſidered to come within the ſcope of this regulation.

No clauſe.

SECTION CLXXVII. — *Neglect to obſerve and note the Celeſtial Appearances.*

Whatever concerns the ſcience of the celeſtial bodies, ſuch as the ſun, the moon, the five planets, the twenty-eight principal and other conſtellations; and alſo the obſervation of the celeſtial appearances, ſuch as eclipſes, meteors, comets, and the like, being the province of the officers of the aſtronomical board at Pekin, if they neglect duly to obſerve, and mark the times of the celeſtial appearances, in order to report them to His Imperial Majeſty, they ſhall be puniſhed with 60 blows for ſuch omiſſion.

One clauſe.

SECTION CLXXVIII. — *Conjurors and Fortune-tellers prohibited from propheſying Public Events.*

It ſhall not be allowed to conjurors and fortune-tellers to frequent the houſes of any civil or military officers of government whatever, under the pretence of propheſying to them impending national calamities or ſucceſſes, and they ſhall upon every ſuch offence ſuffer a puniſhment of 100 blows. This law ſhall not however be underſtood to prevent them from telling the fortunes and caſting the nativities of individuals by the ſtars in the uſual manner.

No clauſe.

SECTION CLXXIX. — *Evading the Duty, and concealing the occafion, of Mourning.*

If a fon on receiving information of the death of his father or mother, or a wife, receiving information of the death of her hufband, fuppreffes fuch intelligence, and omits to go into lawful mourning for the deceafed, fuch neglect fhall be punifhed with 60 blows, and and one year's banifhment. If a fon or wife enters into mourning in a lawful manner, but previous to the expiration of the term, difcards the mourning habit, and forgetful of the lofs fuftained, plays upon mufical inftruments and partakes of feftivities, the punifhment fhall amount for fuch offence to 80 blows.

Whoever on receiving information of the death of any other relation in the firft degree than the above-mentioned, fuppreffes the notice of it, and omits to mourn, fhall be punifhed with 80 blows; if previous to the expiration of the legal period of mourning for fuch relation, any perfon cafts away the mourning habit, and refumes his wonted amufements, he fhall be punifhed with 60 blows.

When any officer or other perfon in the employ of government, has received intelligence of the death of his father or mother, in confequence of which intelligence he is bound to retire from office during the period of mourning; if, in order to avoid fuch retirement, he falfely reprefents the deceafed to have been his grand-father, grand-mother, uncle, aunt, or coufin, he fhall fuffer the punifhment of 100 blows, be depofed from office, and rendered incapable of again entering into the public fervice.

On the other hand, if any officer of government falfely alleges the pretext of mourning, while his parents are ftill living, or after they are fo long dead that the period of mourning had expired, he fhall be liable to the fame punifhment as in the oppofite cafe laft mentioned.

If

If either of the foregoing mifreprefentations fhould be defigned to effect any criminal purpofe, the offender fhall be liable to any aggravation of the punifhment which may be conformable to the law, applicable to the cafe under fuch circumftances.

If, previous to the expiration of the lawful term of abfence in confequence of the lofs of a parent, any officer or other perfon in the employ of government, returns to, and refumes his office or command, he fhall be deprived thereof, and punifhed with 80 blows. If the fuperior officers of the fame department are aware that the return of the mourner is premature, and neverthelefs permit him to refume his functions, they fhall be equally punifhable; but if not aware of the fact, they fhall not be refponfible.

Thofe officers of government, who hold remote and important ftations and commands, fhall not be bound by the above regulations on the arrival of the intelligence of the death of their parents, as the line of conduct they are to purfue on fuch occafions will always be determined by exprefs orders from the Emperor.

Four claufes.

SECTION CLXXX. — *Officers of Government neglecting their Parents.*

If any perfon, in order to hold an office under government, abfents himfelf from a father, mother, paternal grandfather, or grandmother, who is either upwards of 80 years of age, or totally difabled by any infirmity, while fuch near relation has no other male offspring above fixteen years of age, to perform the duties of filial piety; or if, on the contrary, any perfon being in office, folicits permiffion to retire to his family, upon a falfely alleged pretext of the age or infirmity of any fuch near relation as aforefaid, the offender, in either of thefe oppofite cafes, fhall fuffer a punifhment of 80 blows.

Whoever

Whoever plays on muſical inſtruments, or partakes of feaſts at home or abroad, while her huſband, or his or her father, mother, paternal grandfather or grandmother, are in confinement upon a charge of a capital offence, ſhall alſo be liable to the aforeſaid puniſhment.

One clauſe.

SECTION CLXXXI. — *Regulations concerning Funerals.*

When a family has loſt any of its members by death, the ſurvivors muſt not fail to be obſervant of the eſtabliſhed rites and ceremonies, and to fix a proper time for the interment of the deceaſed; if, vainly ſeeking an auſpicious time and place, or upon any other pretext, any perſon detains the coffin of his relation unfeelingly expoſed in his houſe, and ſuffers it thus to remain for more than a twelvemonth unburied, he ſhall be puniſhed with 80 blows*.

Whoever, in compliance with the laſt wiſhes expreſſed by a ſenior relation, conſumes his corpſe with fire, or commits it to the waters, ſhall be puniſhed with 100 blows. In the caſe of a corpſe of a junior relation, the puniſhment ſhall be leſs by two degrees.

When however a relation happens to die in a diſtant country, and the children or grand-children are unable to bring the corpſe to be interred in the native diſtrict of the deceaſed, it ſhall in ſuch caſe be permitted to conſume it by fire.

The family of the deceaſed by whom the funeral obſequies are performed, ſhall lay out, and afterwards partake of, the funeral meats; but the male and female branches of the family ſhall by no means mix

* This law ſeems to have been required to check the abſurd conſequences of a ſuperſtitious notion univerſally prevalent among the Chineſe, of an intimate connexion always ſubſiſting between the advantageous or diſadvantageous mode and place of interment of perſons deceaſed, and the future good or bad fortune of their ſurviving relations.

indiſ-

indiſcriminately together, to eat meat and drink wine on ſuch occaſions; and if any maſter of a family permits this practice, he ſhall be puniſhed with 80 blows for ſuch miſconduct. Any prieſts who thus miſconduct themſelves, ſhall be puniſhed in the ſame manner, and moreover compelled to renounce their order.

Three clauſes.

SECTION CLXXXII. — *Regulations of Country Feſtivals.*

Among the inhabitants of villages and country diſtricts who aſſociate together, there is an eſtabliſhed rule of precedence and ſeniority at their ſolemn feaſts, and there are certain forms preſcribed; whoever diſregards either the one or the other, ſhall be puniſhed with 50 blows for his miſconduct.

Two clauſes.

END OF THE FOURTH DIVISION.

FIFTH DIVISION.

Military Laws.

BOOK I.

PROTECTION OF THE PALACE.

SECTION CLXXXIII. — *Unauthorizedly entering the Imperial Temple.*

ALL perſons paſſing unauthorizedly and without ſufficient cauſe, through the gate of the Imperial Temple, or of the inner encloſure of the Imperial burying-ground, ſhall be puniſhed with 100 blows. — Thoſe who paſs through the gate of the hall of Imperial ſacrifices, unauthorizedly and without ſufficient cauſe, ſhall in like manner be puniſhed with 90 blows. The offence of thoſe who come to, but do not paſs through, the gates aforeſaid, is puniſhable in each caſe leſs ſeverely by one degree. The officer on guard, who deſignedly permits ſuch offences to be committed, is generally puniſhable in an equal degree.

If, however, the offence ſhall have been committed by the neglect, but without the concurrence, of the officer on guard, his puniſhment ſhall be leſs in each caſe by three degrees.

No clauſe.

SECTION CLXXXIV. — *Unauthorizedly entering the Imperial Palace.*

All perſons unauthorizedly paſſing through any of the gates of the Imperial Citadel at Pekin, and entering therein, or into any of the Imperial gardens, ſhall receive 100 blows.

All perſons unauthorizedly entering any of the Imperial palaces, ſhall be puniſhed with 60 blows, and one year's baniſhment.

All perſons unauthorizedly entering any of the apartments in the actual occupation of the Emperor, or into his Imperial refectory, ſhall ſuffer death by being ſtrangled, after remaining in priſon the uſual period.

Thoſe who approach with an intent to paſs, but do not actually paſs, through the gates or entrances aforeſaid, ſhall be ſubject to a proportionate puniſhment, leſs in each caſe by one degree.

The apartments of the Empreſs, Empreſs-mother, and Empreſs-grand-mother, are protected by the laws in the ſame manner as thoſe of the Emperor.

All perſons who, not having been inſcribed in the proper regiſter, paſs or attempt to paſs through any of the gates or entrances aforeſaid, by means of aſſumed names, ſhall be puniſhed according to this law.

All perſons who, having ſtations and employments within the palace, either enter the ſame previous to the inſertion of their names in the proper regiſters, or remain after their duty ceaſed to require them, or do duty there out of their turn or order, ſhall in each caſe be puniſhed with 40 blows.

If any perſons, not having eſpecial duty to keep guard within the palace, bring in with them any of the ſoldiers, or come armed with ſharp weapons, they ſhall ſuffer death by being ſtrangled after the uſual period of confinement.

All

All perſons who under ſimilar circumſtances enter the Imperial citadel, ſhall be puniſhed with 100 blows, and baniſhed perpetually to the moſt remote frontier of the empire.

Thoſe officers and ſoldiers on guard at the ſeveral gates, who conſent or connive at the commiſſion of any of the aforeſaid offences, ſhall be held equally guilty with the party tranſgreſſing the law, except in capital caſes, when the puniſhment ſhall be reduced one degree. Officers and ſoldiers by whoſe neglect, but without whoſe concurrence, ſuch offences are committed, ſhall ſuffer the puniſhment provided by law, reduced three degrees; but they ſhall not in any caſe ſuffer more than 100 blows.

In reſpect to the laſt mentioned regulation, it is further provided that only thoſe ſoldiers whoſe day it was to be on duty ſhall be liable to puniſhment, and that their puniſhment ſhall be one degree leſs than that of their ſuperior officer, who in ſuch caſes is, in the contemplation of the law, the principal offender.

No clauſe.

SECTION CLXXXV. — *Imperial Guards failing to do their Duty.*

Every perſon who, after having been appointed to keep guard and to do duty at the gates of the Imperial citadel, or at the gates of any of the Imperial palaces, does not attend at his poſt when his turn arrives, ſhall be puniſhed with 40 blows.

All perſons who, in ſuch caſes, privately depute ſubſtitutes from among the other guards of the palace to ſupply their places, ſhall, as well as ſuch ſubſtitutes, be liable to the puniſhment of 60 blows.

If any ſuch ſubſtitute be a ſtranger, the puniſhment of both parties ſhall be encreaſed to 100 blows: in all caſes of officers on duty ſo offending, the puniſhment ſhall be one degree more ſevere.

 Perſons

Perſons quitting their poſts after having taken charge of them, ſhall be puniſhed under this law.

Perſons appointed to keep guard at any of the gates of the Imperial city, and offending in the manner already ſtated, ſhall ſuffer a puniſhment leſs in each caſe by one degree. Perſons appointed to keep guard at the gate of any other city, ſhall be liable to the puniſhments awarded by this law, reduced in each caſe two degrees.

The corporal or ſerjeant commanding the guard, if guilty of conſenting or conniving at the offence, ſhall be liable to the ſame puniſhments as the original offender.

If the offence is to be attributed to his neglect, but not to his connivance or concurrence, his puniſhment ſhall be reduced three degrees; when, however, the individual abſent had duly reported, and had alleged ſufficient cauſe for his intended abſence to his ſuperior officer, it ſhall be conſidered as a ſufficient juſtification and exempt all the parties from puniſhment.

No clauſe.

Section CLXXXVI.—*Imperial Retinue failing in their Attendance.*

If any of the perſons immediately attached to the ſuite or retinue of the Emperor do not attend at the time appointed, or if they quit their ſtations before the period of their ſervice had expired, they ſhall for the firſt day's abſence be liable to a puniſhment of 40 blows, and for every additional three days abſence, the puniſhment ſhall be encreaſed one degree, until it amounts to 100 blows.

If the offender is a civil or military officer, the puniſhment ſhall be encreaſed one degree, but not in any caſe exceed 60 blows and one year's baniſhment.

Any individual of the Emperor's retinue who deſerts his poſt, during any of the Imperial journies or provincial viſitations, ſhall be punifhed with 100 blows and perpetual banifhment to the moft remote frontier of the empire.

If the offender is a civil or military officer of government, he fhall fuffer death by being ftrangled, after the ufual period of confinement.

The corporal or ferjeant of the guard conniving at or confenting to fuch defertion, fhall be liable to the fame punifhment, except in capital cafes, when his punifhment fhall be reduced one degree.

If the defertion happened without his confent, and is only attributable to his neglect, his punifhment fhall be three degrees lefs than in the preceding cafe, and not in any inftance exceed 100 blows.

One claufe.

SECTION CLXXXVII.—*Trefpafs upon the Imperial Roads.*

No perfon fhall prefume to travel on the roads or to crofs the bridges which are exprefsly provided and referved for the ufe of the Emperor, except only fuch civil and military officers and other attendants, as immediately belong to His Majefty's retinue, and who are in confequence neceffarily permitted to proceed upon the fide-paths thereof.

All other perfons, whether civil or military officers, foldiers or people, who prefume to travel on the roads or to crofs the bridges aforefaid, fhall be punifhed with 80 blows.

In like manner, thofe who fhall prefume to proceed upon any of the particular paffages and pathways within the palace, which are exprefsly referved for the Emperor, fhall fuffer the punifhment of 100 blows; and the attendants on duty in the palace, who connive thereat, fhall be equally punifhable. But if the offence is merely attributable to their neglect, and not their confent or connivance, their punifhment fhall be reduced three degrees. When, in any of the foregoing cafes

cafes, the offence is only momentary, and not repeated, it fhall not be confidered requifite to carry this law into effect.

Two claufes.

SECTION CLXXXVIII. — *Rules concerning Labourers within the Palace.*

All labourers, meffengers, and other perfons, hired for any work or fervice within the palaces, treafuries, or other buildings, exclufively appropriated to His Imperial Majefty, fhall be provided with perfonal licences or paffports.

Any perfon attempting to introduce himfelf by means of a paffport or licence intended for another, and attempting to act as a fubftitute for fuch perfon, fhall, as well as the perfon transferring fuch licence or paffport, be liable to the punifhment of 100 blows.

The wages due to fuch perfon fhall alfo be forfeited to government.

No claufe.

SECTION CLXXXIX. — *Labourers in the Imperial Palace remaining there after the Conclufion of their Work.*

When labourers of any defcription are employed in the Imperial palaces, whether in the domeftic or ftate apartments, the officer of government who has the fuperintendance of their work, fhall give in an exact ftatement of the proper name and family name of each perfon to the officers on guard at the feveral gates, and alfo to the fuperior officers in waiting; when any fuch individual enters the palace for the firft time, his name and his perfon fhall be identified at the gate, and an exact notice taken of his figure and appearance.

In the courfe of the hour *Shin* (between three and five in the afternoon), the number of perfons, as well as the figure and appearance of each,

each, having been found to correſpond with the regiſter, they ſhall all depart through the identical gates by which they had been admitted.

If any of them wilfully remain within the palace, contrary to this regulation, they ſhall be liable to the puniſhment of death by being ſtrangled, after the uſual period of impriſonment.

Whenever it is found that the liſt of labourers departing from the palace is deficient in names or number, it ſhall be the duty of the ſuperintendants of the works, the officers and ſoldiers on guard, and thoſe attached to the ſeveral gates, immediately to make a diligent ſearch and enquiry, and alſo to give reſpectful intimation of the circumſtance to His Imperial Majeſty. All ſuch officers and others who are privy to and guilty of concealing the fact, ſhall be liable to the ſame puniſhment as the offender himſelf, except in the caſe of his being convicted capitally, when the puniſhment ſhall be reduced one degree.

When ſuch offence is committed without the knowledge and concurrence of the officers on duty, and is therefore to be attributed to their neglect only, the puniſhment with regard to them ſhall be reduced three degrees, and not in any caſe exceed 100 blows.

No clauſe.

SECTION CXC.—*Irregularity in paſſing through the Gates of the Imperial Palaces.*

If any perſons who, (having obtained leave of abſence, or having been appointed to quit the palace on duty,) ceaſe to have their names regiſtered at the ſeveral gates, nevertheleſs remain after their ſuppoſed departure; or if thoſe who have been tried on any charges, and in conſequence diſmiſſed altogether from the ſervice of the palace, unauthorizedly return thereto, they ſhall, whether their names had been ſtruck

ſtruck out or not from the regiſters, in each caſe be puniſhed with 100 blows.

When any of the guards of the palace are, in conſequence of charges exhibited againſt them, committed for examination and trial, if the commanding officer does not in the firſt inſtance take away the arms which had been allotted to ſuch perſons, he ſhall on his part be liable to the puniſhment laſt ſtated.

All thoſe who are regularly entered in the regiſters as having fixed ſtations within the palace, are, equally with other perſons, prohibited from paſſing to and fro after dark. If going in, they ſhall be puniſhed with 100 blows; if going out, with 80 blows. But if going in without having been regiſtered, the puniſhment ſhall be greater by two degrees: if moreover they are diſcovered with arms in their hands, they ſhall ſuffer death by being ſtrangled, after the uſual period of confinement.

No clauſe.

SECTION CXCI. — *Examination of the Certificates or Paſſports of Perſons having Employments in the Palace.*

When any perſon in the immediate ſervice of His Majeſty, or having any duty or ſuperintendance within the palace, quits the precincts thereof, his certificate or paſſport ſhall be required of him by the officer at the outer gate, whoſe duty it ſhall alſo be to retain the ſame, after having carefully identified the names, marks, and official ſtamps thereof; the officer ſhall likewiſe duly record whither the perſon quitting the palace is going, and upon what buſineſs. Every ſuch perſon ſhall moreover, previous to his departure, be perſonally examined by the officer on guard and his attendants, in order to aſcertain that he does not illicitly carry away any public or private property. Upon the return of the perſon to his employment within the palace, he ſhall again under-

go

go at the outer gate, previous to his certificate being returned to him, a ſimilar examination. There ſhall alſo be a monthly examination of the regiſters, to aſcertain how often each perſon has paſſed and repaſſed during each ſucceſſive interval.

If, in the courſe of examination, any perſon ſhould be found to carry about him drugs of a ſuſpicious nature, he ſhall be compelled to ſwallow the ſame.

If any perſon paſſing the gates preſumes to refuſe to ſubmit to the required examination, he ſhall be puniſhed with 100 blows and perpetual and remote baniſhment.

Any perſon who, without having His Majeſty's expreſs licence and authority ſo to do, carries arms and military weapons into the Imperial citadel, within which is the Imperial reſidence, ſhall be puniſhed with 100 blows, and ſent into perpetual and moſt remote baniſhment. If any perſon is detected carrying arms without authority as aforeſaid, into any of the Imperial palaces, he ſhall ſuffer death by being ſtrangled at the uſual period; and the officer of the gate, as well as the officer on guard, who neglected to examine and prevent the paſſage of ſuch perſon, ſhall be liable to the ſame puniſhment as the principal offender, excepting a reduction of one degree in capital caſes *.

No clauſe.

* Notwithſtanding the multiplicity and apparent rigour of the laws provided in this and other ſections of the code, for enſuring the ſafety of the perſon of the Sovereign, the preſent Emperor, in the year 1803, very narrowly eſcaped aſſaſſination within the precincts of his palace, from the hand of a ſingle, but deſperate intruder.—The official report of the circumſtances, which was publiſhed at the time, being illuſtrative of the law in this reſpect; and otherwiſe alſo, rather a curious and intereſting document, a tranſlation of it is inſerted in the Appendix, No. XIX.

SECTION CXCII. — *Shooting or throwing miſſile Weapons towards an Imperial Palace.*

All perſons who ſhall ſhoot arrows or bullets, or fling any bricks or ſtones, towards the Imperial temple, or towards any Imperial palace, whether a place of reſidence or appropriated to purpoſes of ſtate only, with any apparent poſſibility of hitting ſuch place or building, ſhall in each caſe ſuffer death by being ſtrangled at the uſual period: if towards the temple of Imperial ſacrifices, the offender ſhall be puniſhed with 100 blows and perpetual baniſhment to the diſtance of 3000 *lee.*

If any perſon within any of the buildings above-mentioned is wounded by ſuch means, the offender ſhall, in every ſuch caſe, be beheaded at the uſual period.

No clauſe.

SECTION CXCIII. — *Soldiers and Officers on Guard to be always armed.*

All perſons doing duty upon guard, by day or by night, ſhall conſtantly carry their arms about them, and are puniſhable with 40 blows upon any failure in this reſpect. If convicted of having been at any time abſent from their ſtation and duty, they ſhall be liable to 50 blows, and if paſſing the night elſewhere than at their appointed ſtation, the puniſhment ſhall amount to 60 blows; if the offender is an officer of government, the puniſhment ſhall in each caſe be more ſevere by one degree.

If the corporal or ſerjeant of the guard connives at, and concurs in, the commiſſion of the above offences on the part of the ſoldiers under his authority, he ſhall be liable to the ſame puniſhment; but if the offence takes place without his knowledge or concurrence, and is therefore attributable only to his neglect, his puniſhment ſhall be leſs by three degrees.

No clauſe.

SEC-

SECTION CXCIV. — *Convicted Perſons and their Relations not to be employed near the Imperial Preſence.*

In all caſes of perſons living within the juriſdiction of the Imperial city, being condemned to die by the ſentence of the law, their families, and all perſons whatſoever who reſided under the ſame roof with them, ſhall remove forthwith, and reſide in future under another juriſdiction.

All ſuch perſons as aforeſaid, all the other relations of perſons who have ſuffered under the laws, and alſo all perſons who have themſelves undergone any ſpecies of puniſhment by the ſentence of the law, ſhall be judged for ever incapable of holding any office near the perſon of His Imperial Majeſty, or of being entruſted with the duty of guarding any of the Imperial palaces, the Imperial citadel, or the gates of the city of Pekin.

Any perſon who ſhall abſurdly undertake any ſuch office, concealing the previous circumſtance by which he is diſabled from ſo doing, ſhall be beheaded at the uſual period.

Any officer of government who does not take proper care to aſcertain that the perſon whom he truſts or employs as above-mentioned is free from ſuch diſability, or who knowing him to be under ſuch diſability, accepts his ſervices in conſideration of a bribe, ſhall be liable to the ſame puniſhment, and accordingly be beheaded.

Neverthelеſs, if any relation of a criminal who has ſuffered capital puniſhment, or any perſon who has himſelf undergone any leſs puniſhment by the ſentence of the law, is, by an Imperial edict, expreſsly choſen to fill ſome one of the reſponſible ſituations abovementioned, and the ſuperior officer of the department lays before His Majeſty a due report of the former trial and puniſhment of ſuch perſon, or of his relations, as the caſe may be; this law in ſuch caſe ſhall not be put in force.

No clauſe.

SECTION CXCV. — *Intrufion into the Space allotted to the Imperial Retinue.*

During the Imperial journies and vifitations, all the foldiers and people fhall carefully make way for the approach of His Majefty, excepting only thofe forming his retinue, namely, the officers and foldiers on guard in fpecial attendance, and thofe immediately attached to his royal perfon. Any perfon who, notwithftanding, forcibly intrudes within the lines, fhall be condemned to fuffer death by being ftrangled; but the offence being ranked among the mifcellaneous, the punifhment may be mitigated to five years banifhment *.

When His Majefty travels in diftant places, and his retinue arrives at any place unexpectedly, it fhall be fufficient for thofe who are unable to retire in time, to proftrate themfelves humbly on the road fide, until the retinue has paffed them.

Any of the civil and military officers of government, who not belonging to the retinue, prefume to enter within the lines without being fummoned by His Majefty, or having other fufficient caufe, fhall be punifhed with 100 blows.

Any officer or foldier on guard belonging to the retinue, who defignedly permits any perfon to pafs the lines who is not entitled to do fo, fhall fuffer the fame punifhment as the original offender; but if the offence is committed merely through the neglect of fuch officer or foldier, the punifhment fhall in fuch cafe be lefs by three degrees.

Any perfon who is defirous of prefenting a complaint of injuftice, fhall be fuffered to proftrate himfelf for fuch purpofe on the road, but always outfide of the lines.

If any perfon fhould, neverthelefs, fuddenly force his way through the lines, in order to prefent a complaint, which afterwards proves

* See the note to Section LXV.

ground-

groundlefs, he fhall be condemned to fuffer death by being ftrangled, but the offence being ranked among thofe termed mifcellaneous, the punifhment may be mitigated to five years banifhment. When, however, the complaint proves juft, the intrufion within the lines fhall be pardoned.

If any of the foldiers, or people living in the neighbourhood through which the Emperor is paffing, do not confine their cattle, and fuch cattle through the neglect of the guards are fuffered to come within the lines, the guards fo in fault fhall receive 80 blows; and, if by a fimilar accident any cattle rufh into the Imperial citadel, the punifhment of the guards, for not preventing the fame, fhall amount to 100 blows. The punifhment of the perfons to whom the cattle belonged fhall be eftimated according to the feverer claufe of the law relative to offences againft propriety *.

Two claufes.

SECTION CXCVI. — *Paffing through Gates leading to an Imperial Palace.*

The fame laws fhall be enforced in refpect to perfons paffing the gates of the firft and fecond barriers leading to any palace, as in refpect to perfons paffing the gates of the Imperial citadel at Pekin, and the offence of entering through them unauthorizedly fhall be punifhed with 100 blows. The paffage through the inner gates ftyled *Ya-chang-men*, fhall be fubject to the fame reftrictions as the paffage through the gates of the palace, and any perfon entering through the fame unauthorizedly, fhall be punifhed with 60 blows, and one year's banifhment.

No claufe.

* See Section CCCLXXXVI.

Section CXCVII. — *Scaling the Walls of fortified Places.*

All perſons guilty of ſcaling the walls of the Imperial citadel in Pekin, ſhall ſuffer death, by being ſtrangled at the uſual period. In like manner, the offence of ſcaling the walls of the Imperial city of Pekin, ſhall be puniſhed with 100 blows and perpetual baniſhment to the diſtance of 3000 *lee*.

The offence of ſcaling the walls of any city of the firſt, ſecond, or third order, or of any fort, ſhall be puniſhed with 100 blows; and, laſtly, that of ſcaling the walls of any officer of government's official reſidence, with 80 blows; in each caſe, the attempt to ſcale, if unſucceſsful, ſhall ſubject the offender to the puniſhment above provided, reduced one degree.

If the perſon guilty of ſcaling any of the walls aforeſaid, is concerned at the ſame time in the commiſſion of any other offence, he ſhall be made to ſuffer for that one among his offences, which by law is the moſt ſeverely puniſhable.

One clauſe.

Section CXCVIII. — *Regulations concerning the Gates of Cities.*

Any perſon ſhutting at the proper period, but inadvertently neglecting to bolt, the gate of any city or fortified place, ſhall be puniſhed with 80 blows; and the puniſhment ſhall be encreaſed to 100 blows, if guilty of opening or ſhutting ſuch gates at an improper time. In reſpect to the gates of the Imperial city of Pekin, the puniſhment ſhall be one degree more ſevere than in other caſes; but in general, if the opening or ſhutting any of the gates above-mentioned at an irregular time, takes place in execution of the public ſervice, and upon a preſſing emergency, the puniſhment provided by this law ſhall not be inflicted.

flicted. Thofe perfons who, at the regular period of fhutting the gates of the Imperial citadel at Pekin, neglect to bolt them, fhall fuffer 100 blows, and be fent into perpetual and very remote banifhment: the perfon who opens or fhuts fuch gates at an irregular time, fhall be punifhed with death, by being ftrangled at the ufual period.

Neverthelefs, perfons bearing an Imperial order on any occafion, may open or fhut fuch gates at all times, without being liable to the penalties by this law provided.

No claufe.

END OF THE FIRST BOOK OF THE FIFTH DIVISION.

BOOK II.

GOVERNMENT OF THE ARMY *.

Section CXCIX. — *Unauthorizedly employing Military Force.*

WHEN any of the general officers or commanders in chief of the cavalry or infantry, ſtationed for the protection and defence of the cities, fortified towns, military poſts, and frontier encampments in the different parts of the empire, receive reports of ſymptoms of inſurrection and revolt having appeared within the limits of their reſpective commands, they ſhall immediately diſpatch proper perſons to aſcertain how far the reports are well founded, and how far the circumſtances are of ſuch a nature as to require the interference of military force.

If the reſult of the enquiry in any caſe, confirms the previous report, the commanding officer ſhall tranſmit a ſtatement of the particulars to his immediate ſuperior at the head quarters, that the ſame may be ſubmitted to the conſideration of His Imperial Majeſty, whoſe ſacred and royal orders on the ſubject ſhall, in ordinary caſes, be requiſite to ſanction the adoption of the meaſure of aſſembling and detaching an efficient body of troops for the ſuppreſſion of the inſurrection, and puniſhment of the inſurgents.

* As ſome account of the military operations of the Chineſe, as given in the reports of their own general officers, may contribute in a conſiderable degree to illuſtrate the abſtract which this book of the code contains of their martial laws, and be at the ſame time perhaps, a novelty not altogether unintereſting in itſelf, a tranſlation has been inſerted in the Appendix, No. XX. of a few extracts from the Pekin Gazette of the year 1800, relating to the proceedings of the Imperial army, on the occaſion of a formidable rebellion, which raged at that period, in two or three conſiderable provinces of the Chineſe empire.

If,

If, in a caſe of no actual emergency, any commander of the forces, without tranſmitting a previous ſtatement of the caſe to his ſuperior, or, having tranſmitted ſuch a ſtatement, without waiting for orders in reply, upon the ſtrength of his own authority, preſumes to iſſue inſtructions for the aſſembling of the infantry or cavalry within the limits of his command, ſuch commander, and the officers of the ſubordinate ſtations and garriſons, who furniſhed him with troops conformably to his requiſition, ſhall each be ſubject to receive 100 blows, and ſent into perpetual and remote military baniſhment.

On the other hand, if an enemy's force has already marched into any of the diſtricts of the empire in order to make an attack; if open revolt or mutiny breaks out in any of the cities, or other military ſtations; or if the condition and progreſs of the inſurgents is in any manner ſuch as to render it inexpedient to wait a return of the meſſenger with orders from the ſuperior officer, it ſhall in all ſuch caſes be lawful for the officer in command of the diſtrict, to take inſtant meaſures for the aſſembling the troops belonging to the ſeveral ſtations under his controul, and to employ them in any way that the exiſting circumſtances may render moſt conducive to the defeat and apprehenſion of the inſurgents. If the inſurrection ſhould have become ſo conſiderable in point of numbers and extent, as to render it expedient that the troops ſtationed in neighbouring diſtricts ſhould co-operate in the meaſures to be adopted againſt the inſurgents, it ſhall be lawful for the commander of the forces to demand the aid of ſuch troops, although beyond the limits of his ordinary command; but the ſeveral commanders of diſtricts, aſſiſting or requiring aſſiſtance, ſhall not fail in ſuch caſes, immediately to acquaint their ſuperiors with their reſpective proceedings, for the information of His Imperial Majeſty.

If, under ſuch circumſtances, the commanding officer of the diſtrict in a ſtate of inſurrection, and the commanding officer of the neighbouring diſtrict, whoſe aid is required, do not aſſemble and

 diſpoſe

difpofe of their forces as the cafe requires, or if they do not tranfmit information of their proceedings to their refpective fuperiors; or laftly, if the officers in the immediate command of the troops do not difpatch them according to the orders of their fuperior officers, the punifhment fhall be the fame as already ftated in the cafe of employing military force, without authority or neceffity.

The orders which any commanding officer of a diftrict may receive, to difpofe of and detach the forces under his controul, either from his fuperior military officer, or from the minifters of ftate, fhall not in ordinary cafes warrant their removal beyond the limits of the diftrict they are ftationed to protect, unlefs fuch orders are exprefsly ftated to be in obedience to the facred commands of the Emperor. In like manner the orders for the removal, promotion, degradation, or trial of any military officer on duty, fhall not be carried into effect, unlefs derived exprefsly from His Majefty's facred command; and whoever obeys any fuch orders, without the above fanction, fhall be punifhed in the fame manner as in the other cafes previoufly defcribed.

No claufe.

SECTION CC. — *Military Operations to be regularly reported.*

When any officer who commands a detachment or divifion of the forces on their march upon actual fervice, fubject to the orders of the general and commander in chief of the expedition, is directed to proceed againft any of the forts or other ftrong holds of the rebels, he fhall, immediately after having reduced the place, and accomplifhed the object of his deftination, difpatch a fwift meffenger with the intelligence to the commander in chief at head-quarters, and by him a correfponding communication fhall with equal expedition be made to the fupreme board for military affairs. The commander-in-chief fhall alfo draw

up

up another ſpecial report of the event, for the purpoſe of its being laid before His Imperial Majeſty.

If, on the other hand, the ſtrength and numbers of the rebels are found to be ſo conſiderable, that the force deſtined to proceed againſt them by the commander in chief is inadequate to the ſervice, the commanding officer of the detachment ſhall inſtantly tranſmit information of this ſtate of affairs to the ſaid commander in chief, that ſuch a reinforcement of infantry and cavalry may be ſent from head quarters, as may be neceſſary to enſure the defeat and apprehenſion of the rebels and inſurgents. If the commanding officer of the detachment omits to give ſuch information, the commander in chief ſhall determine and inflict ſuch puniſhment as may be warranted by the circumſtances of the caſe; but if a failure of the military operations of government in that quarter is the conſequence of ſuch omiſſion, the extent of the puniſhment ſhall be determined according to the law which is expreſsly applicable to ſuch a caſe, and elſewhere provided.

When any of the revolters and inſurgents voluntarily ſurrender themſelves to a detachment or diviſion of the forces, the commanding officer ſhall immediately deliver them over to the cuſtody of the commander in chief, that the latter may reſpectfully acquaint the Emperor with the circumſtance, and ſolicit a declaration of His Majeſty's pleaſure reſpecting their future diſpoſal.

If any ſuch commanding officer rapaciouſly plunders the property of thoſe who have voluntarily ſurrendered, and ſubſequently kills or wounds them; or if he oppreſſes them in ſuch a manner that they are driven to deſert, and either attempt or effect their eſcape, he ſhall be beheaded after remaining in priſon the cuſtomary period. If he does not kill or wound them, or drive them to the ſaid extremities by violence, the puniſhment ſhall be conformable to the law provided for caſes of defraudation only.

No clauſe.

SEC-

SECTION CCI. — *Expreſſes upon Military Affairs.*

Whenever any expreſſes, containing information and intelligence reſpecting military affairs, are received by the governors of the cities of the firſt and ſecond orders, from the diſtricts, ſtations, and governments, within the limits of their reſpective juriſdictions, the contents ſhall be reported in diſpatches entruſted to the care of ſpecial meſſengers, to the viceroy, ſub-viceroy, treaſurer, judge, and other heads of departments in the province, and ſubſequently alſo to the commander of the forces in the diſtrict, and to the commander in chief in the province.

The commanders of military ſtations ſhall addreſs their diſpatches upon military affairs only to the commander of the forces of the diſtrict, the commander in chief, the viceroy, and the ſub-viceroy.

When the intelligence arrives at the offices of the viceroy, ſub-viceroy, commander in chief, and other military officers of the firſt rank, they ſhall, on the one hand, tranſmit a particular ſtatement of the circumſtances to the ſupreme board for military affairs, and on the other, addreſs a reſpectful report of the caſe for the expreſs purpoſe of its being ſubmitted to the immediate conſideration of His Imperial Majeſty. If the aforeſaid ſuperior officers, after a joint deliberation on the ſubject, agree to ſuppreſs and conceal the intelligence, and, conformably to ſuch agreement, make no timely report to the Emperor, they ſhall be ſeverally puniſhed with 100 blows, deprived of their offices, and rendered incapable of the public ſervice. If the military operations then in progreſs are, in conſequence of ſuch concealment, erroneouſly or improperly conducted, the offenders ſhall ſuffer death, by being beheaded after the cuſtomary period of impriſonment.

No clauſe.

SEC-

SECTION CCII. — *Betraying the Secrets of the State.*

When any perfon is in poffeffion of important fecrets of ftate, fuch as the intended diftribution of the troops, and other meafures taken, and arrangements made by the Emperor, or by the commander in chief, for the attack and reduction by furprife of any foreign tribes, or for the defeat and feizure of revolters and infurgents; if fuch perfon betrays or in any manner divulges fuch ftate fecrets, fo that they come to the knowledge of the enemy, he fhall be beheaded after undergoing the cuftomary imprifonment.

In like manner, if any perfon betrays or divulges the contents of the reports of generals of the forces, addreffed to His Majefty from the frontiers, fo that the enemy comes to the knowledge thereof, he fhall be punifhed with 100 blows and banifhment for three years; but, if in this or the preceding cafe, the offending party fhall have been convicted of treafonable motives, he will be more feverely punifhable, as is elfewhere by law provided.

The firft divulger of the fecret fhall always fuffer the full punifhment of the law, as the principal offender, and each of thofe who afterwards fucceffively tranfmitted it, fhall fuffer the mitigated punifhment of acceffaries.

Whoever privately opens and reads any fealed government or official difpatch whatever, fhall be punifhed at the leaft with 60 blows; but if it relates to any important military affairs, he fhall be punifhed with 100 blows and three years banifhment, as a divulger of ftate fecrets.

If any of the officers of government holding employments and places immediately about His Majefty's perfon, divulge an important fecret of the court, they alfo fhall fuffer death for the offence, by being beheaded after the ufual period of imprifonment; and even if they divulge any fecrets upon ordinary affairs, they fhall be punifhed with

with 100 blows, deprived of their places, and rendered incapable of the public ſervice *.

Three clauſes.

SECTION CCIII.—*Application for, and Tranſmiſſion of Military Supplies.*

Whenever there is any deficiency of grain, ſpecie, or military ſtores at any of the frontier ſtations, the commanding officer of the poſt ſhall ſend a meſſenger to give notice thereof to the treaſurer of the province, and ſhall at the ſame time addreſs official letters to the viceroy, ſub-viceroy, and chief military officers of the province, requeſting their ſanction to the iſſue of a further ſupply. The chief authorities in the province ſhall make known the application for ſupplies, deſcribing their nature and amount, to the ſupreme board in that department at Pekin, and through that channel information ſhall, laſtly, be conveyed to the Emperor, conformable to whoſe orders, the ſupplies ſhall be iſſued and diſtributed.

If any unneceſſary delay retards the progreſs of the application for, and iſſue of, the ſupplies in the different ſtages; if the Emperor is not informed of the application as ſoon as it is received; or if the officer ſtationed at the frontier does not duly and regularly make the application as often as is neceſſary, the individual failing to perform his duty, ſhall be puniſhed with 100 blows, deprived of his ſituation, and rendered incapable of the public ſervice.

If through the miſconduct thus puniſhable, ſo great a deficiency in point of ſupplies is experienced at the period of a ſubſequent conflict with an enemy, that the military operations of government are in that inſtance rendered unſucceſsful, the delinquents ſhall ſuffer death, by being beheaded after the uſual period of confinement.

No clauſe.

* The firſt clauſe to this ſection denounces the puniſhment of perpetual baniſhment againſt thoſe who betray the ſecrets of ſtate, by clandeſtinely viſiting and plotting with the members of foreign embaſſies.

SEC-

SECTION CCIV. — *Errors and Failures in Military Operations.*

When the troops of government are on the point of taking the field upon any public ſervice, if the ſupplies of arms, ammunition, ſtores, and requiſite proviſions of all kinds are not found to have been completed within the period previouſly determined, the officer of government who occaſioned the delay, whether by a tardy tranſmiſſion of the proper orders or a tardy execution of them, ſhall be puniſhed with 100 blows.

If any ſuch delay or neglect ſhall occaſion a deficiency in the aforeſaid articles when the troops are near to, and on the point of engaging the enemy; if the commanding officers of the troops who have received orders to co-operate on ſuch occaſions, loſe time and wait the iſſue of events, inſtead of aſſembling their forces on the day, and at the place appointed; or laſtly, if thoſe who are entruſted with the orders or diſpatches for aſſembling the troops, as aforeſaid, do not execute their commiſſions in due time; any error or failure in the military operations that may ariſe from ſuch cauſes ſhall ſubject the offending parties to the puniſhment of death, by being beheaded after the cuſtomary period of confinement.

No clauſe.

SECTION CCV. — *Military Officers and Troops not taking the Field according to their Inſtructions.*

When a certain number of military officers, together with the troops under their command, have been ſelected for the performance of any particular military ſervice; as ſoon as the ſeaſon approaches for the commencement of their operations, a day ſhall be fixed for their marching from their quarters, and after that period arrives any delay of a ſingle day ſhall ſubject the offending party to a puniſhment of of 70 blows; and the punifhment fhall encreafe at the rate of one degree for every further delay of three days, of which any individual is guilty.

If any one fhall defignedly wound or maim himfelf, or pretend ficknefs or infirmity, in order to evade his duty on fuch an occafion, the punifhment fhall be one degree more fevere, and be encreafed according to the number of the days of the delay, until it attain the limit of 100 blows. The offender fhall ftill be compelled to join the army in the field, unlefs he has maimed himfelf in fuch a manner as to be unfit for fervice, in which cafe, his diftrict fhall be obliged to find a fubftitute.

After the troops have entered the deftined field of their operations, whoever under any pretext abfents himfelf a day beyond the period fixed for repairing to his ftation, fhall be punifhed with 100 blows; and whoever abfents himfelf for three days, under the like circumftances, fhall, although no ill confequence to the military operations fhould arife therefrom, fuffer death, by being beheaded after the ufual confinement, and be executed under the immediate direction of the commander in chief; but if the offender is capable of redeeming his credit, by zealous exertions in the line of his duty, the commander in chief fhall poffefs the difcretionary power of remitting his punifhment, and of deciding relative to his future difpofal.

One claufe.

SECTION CCVI. — *Soldiers ferving by Subftitutes.*

When any individual of the military profeffion, inftead of perfonally joining the army when fummoned, fends a fubftitute whom he has hired to affume his name, and ferve for him, the fubftitute fhall be punifhed with 80 blows, and the individual who hired him, with 100 blows; and the latter fhall be compelled to take a ftation in the ranks inftead of the former.

Any

Any ſoldier of a garriſon who hires a temporary ſubſtitute to perſonate and ſerve for him in his abſence, ſhall, as well as ſuch ſubſtitute, be liable to puniſhment within two degrees of the ſeverity of that provided in the former caſe.

Nevertheleſs, if the ſon, grandſon, nephew, younger brother, or other relation, living on the farm, or eſtabliſhment of the perſon liable to ſerve, voluntarily offers himſelf without any pecuniary conſideration, he ſhall be allowed to ſupply the place of the other, provided the individual declining ſervice is really neceſſitated to do ſo, by age or infirmities.

The individual offering to ſerve ſhall addreſs a ſtatement of the caſe to the commanding officer, who, having verified and duly inveſtigated the ſame, ſhall grant the other his diſcharge. If the perſons of the medical profeſſion who are held in requiſition to attend and prepare medicines for the army, evade their duty by hiring itinerant quacks and ignorant perſons, to perſonate them and ſerve in their ſtead, the ſubſtitute and the individual hiring him, ſhall each ſuffer the puniſhment of 80 blows; and whatever pecuniary conſideration the former may have received from the latter, he ſhall forfeit to government.

One clauſe.

Section CCVII. — *Officers on the Field of Battle unfaithful to their Truſt.*

If any general or other commanding officer entruſted with the charge of a city, fortreſs, or other military ſtation, when it is attacked or inveſted by rebels or inſurgents, ſuddenly deſerts and flies from his poſt, inſtead of effectually maintaining and defending it; or if ſuch general or commanding officer, having neglected the previous adoption of proper meaſures of defence and ſecurity, ſuffers the enemy to come upon him unawares, and take poſſeſſion of ſuch city, fortreſs,

or

or military ſtation, he ſhall in either caſe ſuffer death, by being beheaded, after the cuſtomary period of confinement. If, when the army is in the neighbourhood of the lines of the rebels or inſurgents, the ſcouts and advanced guards ſtationed on the heights, do not take care to give timely notice of the enemy's motions; and if, in conſequence of their neglect, the fortreſſes are taken, or the forces of government worſted by an unexpected attack, the ſcouts or guards ſhall, for ſuch miſconduct, be alſo liable to the puniſhment of death, by being beheaded after the uſual period of confinement.

If the neglect of proper precautions on the part of the general, or of due communication of intelligence, on the part of the ſcouts or advanced guards, is not attended with the loſs of any fortreſs, or with any other conſequences directly injurious to the forces of government, but ſtill enables the inſurgents to advance beyond their former limits, and to ravage the country and plunder the inhabitants, the individual whoſe offence occaſioned ſuch misfortunes, ſhall be puniſhed with 100 blows, and ſent into perpetual and remote military baniſhment.

If, when the forces of government are drawn out to engage the enemy in a pitched battle, or to inveſt or aſſault the enemy's fortreſſes, any of the officers or ſoldiers ſet the example of giving way and retreating, they ſhall ſuffer death by being beheaded, after the uſual period of confinement.

Three clauſes.

SECTION CCVIII. — *Connivance at the Depredations of the Soldiers.*

Any commanding officer of troops in the field, or at a frontier ſtation, who privately authorizes or inſtructs his ſoldiers to proceed beyond the limits of the territories under ſubjection, in order to ſeize and plunder the inhabitants, ſhall be puniſhed with 100 blows, deprived of his office, and ſent into the leſs remote military baniſhment.

If

If the ſuperior authorities in the provinces authorize ſuch conduct on the part of the military officers, they ſhall ſuffer puniſhment leſs by one degree; and if the civil officers in the ſtation concur therein, they ſhall ſuffer puniſhment leſs by two degrees.

Thoſe only who authorize the pillage ſhall be puniſhable, and therefore the ſoldiers, when warranted by the permiſſion of their ſuperiors, ſhall not be held reſponſible.

If, on the other hand, any of the ſoldiers go beyond the boundaries, and pillage the country, without any authority or licenſe to that effect from their ſuperior officers, the ringleaders ſhall be puniſhed with 100 blows, and the reſt ſeverally with 90 blows; if in the courſe of ſuch unwarrantable proceedings, they ſhould wound any of the inhabitants, their ringleader ſhall be beheaded, after the uſual confinement, and the reſt puniſhed ſeverally with 100 blows, and ſent (as alſo the offenders in the former caſe) into remote military baniſhment. If, on theſe occaſions, the immediate ſuperior of the ſoldiers guilty of this offence, is chargeable with a neglect of proper diſcipline, he ſhall be puniſhed with 60 blows, but retain his office.

Nevertheleſs, when any of the inſurgents eſcape beyond the frontiers, this law ſhall not be conſtrued ſo as to prevent the officers of garriſons in frontier ſtations from detaching parties of troops acroſs the boundaries, to purſue and reduce ſuch fugitive inſurgents into ſubjection.

If at any time the troops are guilty of pillage within the boundaries of the empire, or of countries reduced to ſubjection, they ſhall, without any diſtinction between principals and acceſſaries, ſuffer death by being beheaded, after the cuſtomary confinement.

If the immediate ſuperiors of the ſoldiers guilty of this offence are chargeable on ſuch occaſions with a neglect of proper diſcipline, they ſhall be puniſhed with 80 blows, but retain their offices.

If the commanding and other officers of the troops are privy to their designs of pillaging the country and inhabitants, within or without the boundaries of the empire, and yet connive at, and permit such unwarrantable proceedings, they shall be liable to the same punishment as the soldiers, excepting only the customary reduction of one degree in capital cases.

Two clauses.

SECTION CCIX. — *Exercise and Discipline of the Troops.*

If the commanding officer of any military post or station, either upon the frontiers or elsewhere within the empire, does not preserve military law and discipline; if he does not constantly employ his troops in military exercises; if he does not keep the walls and fortifications in a state of repair; or lastly, if he does not provide an adequate supply, in proper condition, of clothes, armour, arms, and ammunition; he shall in every such case be punished with 80 blows, when it is the first offence, and with 100 blows, when it is the second offence.

If through a relaxation from the due severity of precautionary discipline, or an ill-judged exercise of military authority in dispensing rewards and punishments, the troops at length mutiny and desert to the enemy, all the officers who held commands over such troops, shall be punished respectively with 100 blows, their families degraded, and themselves dismissed into remote and perpetual military banishment.

If in consequence of the desertion or mutiny of the troops, any officer shall fly from his post, he shall suffer death by being beheaded, after the usual period of confinement.

One clause.

SEC-

SECTION CCX. — *Exciting and causing Rebellion by oppressive Conduct.*

If any officer of government, whose situation gives him power and controul over the people, not only does not conciliate them by proper indulgence, but exercises his authority in a manner so inconsistent with the established laws and approved usages of the empire, that the sentiments of the once loyal subjects being changed by his oppressive conduct, they assemble tumultuously and openly rebel, and drive him at length from the capital city and seat of his government; such officer shall suffer death, after the usual period of confinement. If the rebellion does not extend so far as to occasion the loss of the government station, subject to the authority of such officer, the case shall be considered similar to that of a criminal neglect of discipline leading to mutiny, which is treated of in the preceding section; but the final decision upon the extent of the punishment due to the offender, shall remain with His Imperial Majesty.

Two clauses.

SECTION CCXI. — *Clandestine Sale of Horses taken in Battle.*

Whenever the troops of government take and secure any of the horses belonging to the enemy, the full number of the animals captured shall be reported to the superior officer on the spot; if any soldier sells such horses to private individuals, receiving goods or money in return, he shall be punished with 100 blows; if any officer of government is guilty of a similar offence, he shall receive the same punishment, and moreover be deprived of his office and command.

The purchaser shall also be punished with 40 blows; the horses, and the amount of the purchase-money, shall be forfeited to government.

When

When the purchaser is an officer or soldier of government, he shall not himself be punishable, but the amount of the money paid by him to the seller shall be forfeited; the horses shall likewise be forfeited when the purchaser is an officer having rank over, or a soldier of the same division with, the seller, as he is in such case supposed to have had an opportunity of knowing the illegality of the transaction.

One clause.

Section CCXII. — *Clandestine Sale of Military Arms and Accoutrements.*

If any soldier sells to a private individual the clothes, armour, swords, spears, flags, standards, or any of the other necessary military accoutrements delivered to his charge on the account of government, and actually receives a valuable consideration in exchange for the same, he shall be punished with 100 blows, and sent into remote and perpetual military banishment. If any military officer of government is guilty of a similar offence, he shall suffer the same number of blows, be degraded, and sent into the less remote military banishment.

The purchaser of the military accoutrements shall in these cases be punished with 40 blows, although it should be an article, not in itself prohibited; but if prohibited, he shall, in such case, be liable to greater punishment, according to the law against private individuals retaining possession of such articles; that is to say, according to circumstances, from 80 blows as far as 100 blows, and perpetual banishment to the distance 3000 *lee*.

The military accoutrements, as well as the purchase-money, shall in general be forfeited; but when the purchaser is an officer or soldier of government, such purchaser shall be liable to no punishment, and the

the forfeiture ſhall then be limited to the amount of the purchaſe-money received by the ſeller.

No clauſe.

SECTION CCXIII. — *Deſtroying and caſting away Military Arms and Accoutrements.*

If, after the accompliſhment and termination of any military ſervice or expedition, the commanding officer does not, within the period of ten days, reſtore to the proper officer of government all the additional arms and accoutrements that had been entruſted to his charge for the public ſervice, ſuch defaulter ſhall be puniſhed with 60 blows; the puniſhment ſhall be encreaſed as far as 100 blows, at the rate of one degree for each additional period of ten days, during which he retains poſſeſſion of ſuch articles.

If, after the concluſion of any ſuch military ſervice or expedition, the commanding officer wilfully caſts away or deſtroys any one article belonging and neceſſary to the military equipment, he ſhall be puniſhed with 80 blows, and one degree more ſeverely for every additional article caſt away or deſtroyed, until the number exceeds 20, when he ſhall be liable to ſuffer death after the uſual period of confinement.

If, any ſuch officer ſhall unintentionally loſe, or inadvertently deſtroy, one or more of the articles aforeſaid, the puniſhment ſhall be proportionately leſs by three degrees, than that inflicted for the wilful offence; and if in any of the preceding caſes the offender is a private ſoldier, inſtead of being an officer, the puniſhment ſhall be further reduced proportionably, one degree.

The amount and value of the articles loſt or deſtroyed ſhall be carefully aſcertained in each caſe, that the offender may be required to make good the loſs ſuſtained by government.

When,

When, however, any ſuch military ſtores or accoutrements had been loſt or deſtroyed in actual ſervice or in battle, no puniſhment ſhall be inflicted, nor any compenſation for the loſs required.

Two clauſes.

SECTION CCXIV. — *Poſſeſſion of prohibited Arms and Accoutrements.*

If any private individual ſecretly retains in his poſſeſſion, armour for man or horſe, ſhields, tubes for firing large cannon, Imperial flags and ſtandards, or any other ſimilar articles excluſively of military uſe, he ſhall be puniſhed with 80 blows, though he ſhould poſſeſs only one article, and one degree more ſeverely for every additional article of the kind, in his poſſeſſion. If he is likewiſe the maker or manufacturer of the articles, his puniſhment ſhall be proportionately more ſevere in each caſe, by one degree, as far as 100 blows, and perpetual baniſhment to the diſtance of 3000 *lee.*

If the articles are not completed ſo as to be fit for immediate uſe, neither the poſſeſſor nor manufacturer ſhall be liable to puniſhment, but they ſhall deliver up all ſuch unfiniſhed articles to government.

This prohibition does not compriſe bows and arrows, ſlings, ſpears, or knives, or any of the inſtruments uſed in fiſhing or agriculture.

Seven clauſes.

SECTION CCXV. — *Relaxation of, and Abſence from, Military Duties.*

If any colonel or inferior officer of a regiment, or any ſerjeant of a particular troop, ſuffers or licenſes the ſoldiers under his command to proceed under the pretext of buying or ſelling, to a diſtance of more than 100 *lee* from their ſtation, or clandeſtinely to cultivate lands; or if if any officer or ſerjeant as aforeſaid, ſhall require ſuch ſoldiers to perform private ſervices, which interfere with, and occaſion a neglect of, his military duties and exerciſes, ſuch officer or ſerjeant ſhall be puniſhed in proportion to the number of ſoldiers ſo miſemployed; that is to ſay, with 80 blows, if one man; and one degree more ſeverely for each addition of three to the number miſemployed, until the puniſhment amounts to 100 blows; in which caſe the offender ſhall be deprived of his office and command. If a bribe is given and received, in conſideration of ſuch a breach of diſcipline, the puniſhment ſhall be ſubject to ſuch augmentation as may be warranted by the law applicable to all caſes of bribery for unlawful purpoſes. The ſoldier who avails himſelf of any criminal relaxation of diſcipline, or conſents to employ himſelf inconſiſtently with his military duty, ſhall be puniſhed with 80 blows.

If any officer or ſerjeant diſpatches a ſoldier beyond the frontiers, and in conſequence thereof ſuch ſoldier loſes his life, or is taken and detained by rebels or enemies, the officer or ſerjeant ſhall be puniſhed with 100 blows, degraded, and ſent into perpetual and remote military baniſhment.

If the number of ſoldiers ſo loſt to the ſervice amounts to three or more, the officer or ſerjeant ſhall ſuffer death by being ſtrangled, after the cuſtomary confinement.

If the commanding officer of the ſtation or encampment, or the ſerjeants in his attendance, knowingly ſuppreſs and aſſiſt in the concealment of ſuch circumſtances, by concurring with the officer or ſerjeant in fault, in a fictitious ſtatement to government of the natural death or deſertion of the individuals who had in fact been loſt to the ſervice in the manner aforeſaid, they ſhall, except as to forfeiture of life, be equally puniſhable with the original offenders.

In general, when the colonel, inferior officer, or ſerjeant of a regiment, authorizes or occaſions a dereliction and neglect of military duties and exercifes among the troops; if the commanding officer of the ftation or encampment avowedly confents to, or privately connives thereat, inftead of taking cognizance of every fuch offence againft military difcipline; or if, when the commanding officer is guilty of authorizing or occafioning a dereliction of duty, the colonel, inferior officer, or ferjeant of the troops, being acquainted therewith, does not complain of, and inform againft him, the party directing, and the party conniving, fhall be equally punifhed, in the manner already provided.

If, from the neglect to maintain authority by proper feverity and ftrictnefs of difcipline, the foldiers become licentious and tranfgrefs the law, in any of the aforefaid refpects, although without exprefs inftruction or permiffion fo to do; or if any fuch mifconduct is permitted through inattention and want of inveftigation, although not defignedly concealed or connived at, the extent of the punifhment fhall be apportioned in the following manner: The ferjeant fhall be punifhable with 40 blows, when a fingle individual under his command tranfgreffes; the centurion with the fame, when five tranfgrefs; the colonel or commander of 1000 men with the fame, when 10 tranfgrefs; and laftly, the commanding officer of the encampment or ftation fhall be liable to be punifhed as above, when 50 tranfgrefs. 50 blows fhall be the punifhment of the ferjeant when two tranfgrefs, of the centurion when 10 tranfgrefs, of the colonel when 20 tranfgrefs, and of the commander in chief, when 100 tranfgrefs.

The officers in fuch cafes fhall not forfeit their commands, nor fuffer the punifhment here ftated, unlefs the full number of the foldiers under their refpective commands are proved to have been tranfgreffors.

If any military officer fhould employ a foldier in private domeftic fervice, although without exempting or removing him from the difcharge of his public duty, or from the performance of his military exercifes,

exercifes, he fhall ftill be punifhed with 40 blows, and the amount of his punifhment fhall be progreffively encreafed as far as 80 blows, at the rate of one degree for every five men fo illegally employed. He fhall, moreover, forfeit the amount of the wages of fuch men, efti-mated at the rate of 8 *fen* 5 *lee* 5 *hao* (about feven-pence fterling) *per* man *per* day.

Neverthelefs, the officer borrowing the fervices of his men only upon occafional mournings and rejoicings, fhall be excepted from the penalties of this law.

One claufe.

SECTION CCXVI. — *Princes and hereditary Nobility employing the Troops of Government.*

The princes and hereditary nobility fhall not be permitted to call for the affiftance of the officers or troops of government, or to dif-patch them on any particular fervice, unlefs exprefsly authorized fo to do, by an edict iffued by the Emperor.

The firft and the fecond offence of this kind fhall, however, be par-doned; but the third fhall be taken into cognifance by the magiftrates, and reported for the decifion of His Majefty.

If any military officers of government comply with fuch unlawful demands, or, when unengaged in actual fervice, ferve and do honorary duty at the gate or palace of any prince or hereditary nobleman, they fhall be all equally punifhed with 100 blows, degraded, and fent into remote and perpetual military banifhment. Private foldiers committing this offence fhall be punifhed in the fame manner.

No claufe.

 SEC-

Section CCXVII. — *Desertion from Military Service.*

If any officer or soldier selected for, and actually employed in, any military expedition or detached public service, deserts his post and station, whether in order to return to his home or to go elsewhere, he shall for the first offence be punished with 100 blows, and compelled to proceed to his original destination; for the second offence, he shall be punished with death, by being strangled, after the usual period of confinement.

Any person who is privy to the crime of desertion, and who harbours the deserter, shall, whether it is the first or second offence, be punished with 100 blows, and subjected to military banishment.

If either the head-inhabitant of the district of which the deserter is a native, or the head-inhabitant of the district in which he has concealed himself, is acquainted with the fact, but omits to give any information thereof to government, he shall be punished with 100 blows.

If, after the conclusion of any service in which the troops were engaged, any individual amongst them presumes to quit the ranks, and to return home before the rest of the army, he shall be punished five degrees less severely than in the last instance; that is to say, with 50 blows; but if, to avoid such punishment, he at such time deserts altogether, he shall be liable to suffer the punishment of 80 blows.

If any of the troops stationed at the Imperial city of Pekin are guilty of desertion, they shall be punished with 90 blows for the first offence; the troops employed to garrison any of the other cities or fortified stations in the empire, shall be punished with 80 blows for the first offence; for the second offence the troops of any garrison, whether of the Imperial city or of any other fortification, shall be punished with 100 blows, and sent into perpetual and remote military banishment. For the third offence they shall, in each of the above cases, suffer death, by being strangled, after the usual period of confinement.

In

In general, all perſons harbouring or concealing deſerters, knowing them to be ſuch, ſhall be puniſhable in an equal degree, as partners in their guilt, excepting only the caſes of remote baniſhment and capital puniſhment, upon all of which the harbourer of the criminal ſhall ſuffer only the puniſhment of the leſs remote military baniſhment.

If the head-inhabitant of the diſtrict in which the deſerter is harboured is privy to the fact, but does not give information of it to government, he ſhall ſuffer puniſhment in proportion to that to which the harbourer of the deſerter is liable, but leſs in each caſe by two degrees.

If the ſerjeant of any troop knowingly ſuffers his men to deſert, his puniſhment ſhall be the ſame as theirs, except that it ſhall in no caſe exceed 100 blows, degradation, and the leſs remote military baniſhment.

During an interval, beginning on the day upon which any individual deſerts from the army, and ending when an hundred days are expired, ſuch deſerter ſhall be freely pardoned, if he voluntarily ſurrenders himſelf to government; but after that period a voluntary ſurrender will only entitle him to a reduction in his puniſhment of two degrees. A voluntary ſurrender may be made at any military ſtation, and the officer of the ſtation ſhall have full power to accept the ſame, as well as altogether to remit, or partially to reduce the puniſhment of the deſerter in conſideration thereof, according to the circumſtances of the caſe. Any ſoldier who deſerts his own troop or battalion in order to enter into another ſhall equally be liable, according to the nature of the caſe, to all the ſeveral penalties of deſertion.

Six clauſes.

SEC-

SECTION CCXVIII.—*Favour to be ſhewn to the Relations of Officers and Soldiers deceaſed.*

When any officers or ſoldiers are killed in battle, or die of ſickneſs, their ſurviving relations ſhall be provided by government with preſent ſubſiſtence, and with the means of returning to their reſpective homes and families.

If the officers of any diſtrict, through which they have occaſion to paſs, detain them unneceſſarily a ſingle day, ſuch officers ſhall be puniſhed with 20 blows; and one degree more ſeverely, until the puniſhment amounts to 50 blows, for every additional three days delay.

One clauſe.

SECTION CCXIX.—*Regulations of the Nocturnal Police.*

All perſons in the Imperial city of Pekin are ſtrictly prohibited from ſtirring abroad during the night, and whoever tranſgreſſes this law after the third bell of the firſt watch has ſounded, (twelve minutes paſt nine in the afternoon), or before the third bell of the fifth watch has been ſtruck (twelve minutes paſt five in the morning), ſhall be puniſhed with 30 blows; whoever tranſgreſſes this law during the ſecond, third, and fourth watches (from ten P. M. to four A. M.), ſhall ſuffer the ſeverer puniſhment of 50 blows. In all other cities and fortifications of the empire, the ſame prohibitions ſhall be enforced, but the puniſhment attending a tranſgreſſion of this article of the laws ſhall be leſs in each caſe by one degree.

From theſe reſtrictions, however, exception ſhall be always made in favour of perſons ſtirring abroad at night upon public buſineſs, or upon private affairs of an urgent nature, ſuch as ſudden illneſs, women taken in labour, deaths, burials, and other ſimilar emergencies.

On

On the other hand, if the patroles maliciouſly arreſt and detain any perſons before the ſtriking of the evening bell, or after the ſtriking of the morning bell *, falſely charging them with having violated the rules of the watch, they ſhall themſelves undergo the puniſhment of the offence imputed to the perſon unjuſtly detained.

If any perſon who had really violated the rules, nevertheleſs refuſes to ſurrender, and ſucceeds in making his eſcape from the patrole, he ſhall be puniſhed with 100 blows. If in the ſcuffle, he ſtrikes the patrole, ſo as to wound him in any degree, he ſhall ſuffer death, by being ſtrangled, after the cuſtomary impriſonment; if he kills the patrole, he ſhall ſuffer death by being beheaded.

If at any time a ſcuffle of the ſame kind takes place between the patrole and any perſon whom he had ſeized and attempted to detain, contrary to the laws; in ſuch caſe, the perſon ſeized and attempted to be detained, ſhall not be liable to ſuffer for any of the conſequences of his reſiſtance, otherwiſe than he would have done in an ordinary caſe of a ſcuffle or affray between equals.

One clauſe.

* It may be proper to explain, that it is not intended to be underſtood that a bell, according to the ſtrict interpretation of the term, is employed in China to announce the ſucceſſive periods of time; but merely that ſome article is uſed for the purpoſe, which, when ſtruck, is capable of returning a ſufficiently audible ſound.

END OF THE SECOND BOOK OF THE FIFTH DIVISION.

BOOK III.

PROTECTION OF THE FRONTIER.

Section CCXX. — *Croſſing a Barrier without a Licenſe.*

WHOEVER, without being provided with a regular licenſe or paſſport, proceeds either by land or water-carriage, clandeſtinely through any barrier ſtation, ſhall be puniſhed with 80 blows; whoever, in order to avoid examination at the barrier, paſſes it by any other than the cuſtomary road, channel, or ford, ſhall be puniſhed with 90 blows.

Whoever in a ſimilar manner paſſes, without ſubmitting himſelf to examination, any of the barriers or poſts of government at the frontiers, ſhall be puniſhed with 100 blows, and baniſhed for three years.

If ſuch individual proceeds afterwards ſo far as to have communication with the foreign nations beyond the boundaries, he ſhall ſuffer death by being ſtrangled, after the cuſtomary period of confinement.

The examining officer of the ſtation, when aware of the intentions of ſuch offender and guilty of conſenting thereto, ſhall be equally puniſhable, except that in capital caſes the ſentence of death ſhall be commuted for that of baniſhment.

The reſponſible officers of government, to whoſe want of vigilance and examination a breach of this law is at any time attributable, ſhall, in each caſe, ſuffer a puniſhment proportionably leſs by three degrees than the original offender, and in no caſe exceeding 100 blows.

The

The military attendants who were on guard on the day upon which the laws were thus tranſgreſſed, ſhall, proportionably to the nature of the offence, be puniſhed one degree leſs in each caſe, than their ſuperior officers.

Whoever fraudulently obtains leave to proceed through a barrier ſtation, by preſenting a licenſe intended for another perſon, ſhall be puniſhed with 80 blows.

When the ſervants or inmate relations of any family commit this offence, the maſter of ſuch family ſhall be held reſponſible, and puniſhed accordingly. The examining officer of the ſtation, if privy to the fraud, ſhall be equally puniſhed as an abettor of the offence, but if not privy thereto, he ſhall not be held in any manner reſponſible.

Whoever clandeſtinely, or under cover of a licenſe granted for other purpoſes, leads or drives his horſes or aſſes through any barrier ſtation, ſhall be puniſhed with 60 blows. If any perſon leading or driving ſuch animals, avoids the barrier altogether, by bringing them to the oppoſite ſide by an unuſual route, the puniſhment ſhall be encreaſed to 70 blows.

Nine clauſes.

SECTION CCXXI. — *Granting or obtaining Paſſports and Licenſes, under falſe Pretences.*

Whoever grants a paſſport to thoſe to whom it ought not to be granted, ſuch as exiles, and reſidents expreſsly ſettled by the laws; whoever applies for a paſſport under a feigned name, or pretending to be of the military, when belonging to the civil profeſſion and *vicè verſâ*; and laſtly, whoever, having legally obtained a paſſport, delivers it over to a perſon for whom it was not intended, ſhall in every caſe be puniſhed with 80 blows. If the officers of a government ſtation through which any perſon, having a paſſport, takes his route, preſume to renew the paſſport after it had legally expired; or if any civil or military board or tribunal, in compliance with the deſires of an officer of government or other perſon of authority and influence, grant general letters of protection from examination inwards or outwards in favour of the goods of any perſon, the individual officer or the members of the tribunal, as the caſe may be, ſhall be puniſhed with 100 blows.

Nevertheleſs, this law ſhall not be conſtrued as a prohibition to renew the cuſtomary annual paſſports of any officer, clerk, or artificer of government, if applied for in proper time, at the office where it was granted originally. Any officers of government who attend to unwarranted and illegal applications for paſſports, and who, knowing them to be ſo, yet grant the paſſports requeſted, ſhall be liable to puniſhment in an equal degree with the perſons applying for the ſame; but if the officer is not aware of the fraud intended, or if, as ſoon as aware thereof, he refuſes to comply with the application, he ſhall not be liable to puniſhment.

Alſo, if any of the inferior officers and examiners exceed the limits of their authority, by granting ſuch paſſports, they ſhall be puniſhed in the ſame manner as in the laſt caſe of granting paſſports, when unlawfully applied for.

If any member of a public board or tribunal, authorized to grant paſſports or licenſes, iſſues the ſame to any perſon, without correctly filling up in each document, the date, deſcription, and other neceſſary remarks, and alſo making a record thereof in his office, he ſhall be puniſhed at the leaſt with 100 blows and three years baniſhment; and as much more ſeverely as the law may aſſign, in the event of his having been influenced by bribery or any other corrupt motive.

No clauſe.

SEC-

SECTION CCXXII. — *Vexatious Treatment of Travellers at the Barriers.*

On the arrival of any veſſels in the inland navigation at a barrier ſtation, the proper officers ſhall immediately examine them, and prepare the paſſports or clearances conformably to their cargoes and other circumſtances, in order that they may with the leaſt poſſible delay be free to proceed on their route: if, on the contrary, the ſaid officers unneceſſarily detain the veſſels and paſſengers one day, they ſhall be puniſhed with 20 blows, and one degree more ſeverely as far as 50 blows, for every additional day of detention. When any money is extorted, the puniſhment ſhall be increaſed according to the law applicable to ſuch caſe.

If any officer of government or other perſon, confiding in the ſtrength of his influence and authority, when paſſing a barrier ſtation, refuſes to ſubmit to the cuſtomary examination and verification of his paſſport, he ſhall be puniſhed with 100 blows.

When there is any riſk from winds or waves, the boatmen belonging to paſſage-boats ſhall not attempt to croſs the ferries on pain of receiving puniſhment to the extent of 40 blows; but if they ſhould have attempted to croſs the water in deſpite of winds and waves, the officers of the cuſtoms ſhall not ſtop them in the middle of the current for the purpoſe of urging the demand for toll-money, on pain of receiving 80 blows. If in ſo doing they ſhall occaſion the death or bodily injury of any perſon, they ſhall be liable to the ſame puniſhment as in caſes of killing and wounding by deſign. If no demand of toll-money ſhall have been made as aforeſaid, the death or injury any perſon may ſuſtain by the deſtruction of the boat, ſhall be deemed accidental.

No clauſe.

SECTION CCXXIII. — *Aſſiſting and favouring the Eſcape of the Wives and Daughters of Deſerters.*

If any military officer or ſoldier upon guard in the Imperial city of Pekin, ſhall in any manner aſſiſt the wives and daughters of deſerters in effecting their eſcape beyond the walls of the ſaid Imperial city, they ſhall be ſentenced to ſuffer death by being ſtrangled, but the puniſhment ſhall be reduced to baniſhment as in the caſe of other offences termed miſcellaneous. If any private individual is guilty of ſuch an offence, he ſhall be puniſhed with 100 blows.

If the military officers or ſoldiers of any ordinary city, garriſoned ſtation, or plantation *, ſhall aſſiſt and favour the eſcape of the wives and daughters of deſerters from ſuch ſtations, they ſhall be ſeverally puniſhed with 100 blows and three years baniſhment; private individuals committing the like offence, ſhall ſuffer 80 blows.

When the offending party has been convicted of receiving a bribe to tranſgreſs the law, he ſhall be liable to ſuch aggravation of his puniſhment, as may be conformable to the law againſt bribery for unlawful purpoſes. If the deſerter himſelf had either implored or purchaſed the aſſiſtance of any perſon to effect the releaſe of his wives or daughters, he ſhall be liable to that aggravation of the puniſhment due to him as a deſerter, which may be the conſequence of his being held an equal participator in the offence puniſhable by the preſent regulation.

If the officer on guard at the gate of the city or fortification, knowing the circumſtances of the caſe, connives at, and permits the paſſage of ſuch perſons, he ſhall ſuffer puniſhment as an equal participator in the offence of forwarding their eſcape. When nothing more than a neglect of due examination is imputable to ſuch officer, the puniſhment ſhall be proportionably leſs by three degrees, and in no caſe exceed 100 blows.

* This refers to the new colonies eſtabliſhed in different parts of Chineſe Tartary.

The

The punifhment of the private foldiers of the guard fhall, in each cafe, be one degree lefs than that of their commanding officer. Whoever affifts the efcape beyond the city walls, of the wives and daughters of perfons not coming under the defcription of deferters, but otherwife held to be criminals, either by their own act or by implication, fhall be punifhed with 80 blows, or as much more feverely as the corrupt and culpable motive of affording fuch affiftance may, conformable to any other exifting law or ftatute, be found to deferve.

No claufe.

SECTION CCXXIV. — *Examination and Detection of fufpected Perfons.*

If, in any of the chief barrier ftations along the frontiers, or in any of the paffes or other places of importance in the interior, there are plotters, feeking to carry out to ftrangers beyond the boundaries, the internal productions and inventions; or any fpies, fecretly introducing themfelves from without, in order to give intelligence concerning the affairs of the empire; when perfons of this defcription are difcovered and brought before the tribunals of government, they fhall be ftrictly examined, and as foon as they fhall have been convicted, either of introducing themfelves or others into the empire, or of having plotted the means of removing themfelves or others out of the empire, they fhall all, without any diftinction between principals and acceffaries, be condemned to fuffer death by being beheaded, after the ufual period of confinement.

If any of the examining officers of government at the different barrier ftations through which fuch criminals fhall have travelled, knowing their guilt, purpofely conceal their arrival, and connive at their departure, they fhall be held equally guilty, and fuffer in the

fame

ſame manner, except that capital puniſhments ſhall be commuted for baniſhment. If no greater crime than want of vigilance and due examination is imputable to ſuch officers, their puniſhment ſhall be limited to 100 blows, and that of the ſoldiers who were on guard on the day on which the criminals paſſed, to 90 blows *.

Eleven clauſes.

SECTION CCXXV.—*Illicit Exportation of Merchandize.*

Whoever clandeſtinely exports to ſea, or conveys for ſale beyond the boundaries of the empire on the land-ſide, horſes, cattle, iron-work capable of being wrought into military weapons, copper coin, ſilks, gauzes, or ſattins, ſhall be puniſhed with 100 blows: whoever with ſuch unlawful deſign carries for hire, or places upon any beaſt of burthen, or upon any vehicle, any of the aforeſaid articles, ſhall ſuffer the puniſhment next below that inflicted by law upon the exporter.

The goods clandeſtinely exported ſhall be forfeited, together with the carriages or veſſels employed for their conveyance.—Three-tenths of the amount of the goods ſhall be given as a reward to the perſon informing againſt the offending party. Whoever exports by ſea or land any military arms or accoutrements ſhall ſuffer death by being ſtrangled after the uſual period of confinement. If ſuch exportation leads to the diſcloſure of any ſtate affairs, the offender ſhall be beheaded.

* By the 11th clauſe to this ſection, it is provided with the view of more effectually preventing improper communications with foreigners by ſea, that none of the ſmall iſlands along the coaſt which are at any diſtance from the main land, ſhall be built upon or in any manner inhabited.—The abſolute want of a competent naval force has however diſabled the Chineſe government from giving any effect to ſuch a regulation, and theſe iſlands are at preſent the conſtant or chief reſort, not only of fiſhermen, but alſo of the numerous pirates, by whom the unprotected coaſts of China are infeſted.

If

If the governing or examining officers at the port or ftation are themfelves parties in the clandeftine exportation of fuch goods, or if they knowingly and purpofely fuffer fuch illicit exportation to take place, they fhall fuffer the fame punifhment as the exporter, excepting only, that in capital cafes, the punifhment fhall be reduced to perpetual banifhment.

If only a defect of vigilance and want of due examination is imputable to the governing and examining officers, their punifhment fhall be proportionably lefs than that of the exporter by three degrees, and never exceed 100 blows. The foldiers whofe turn it was to be on guard at the time the clandeftine exportation of the goods took place, fhall likewife fuffer punifhment, but proportionably lefs than their fuperiors by one degree, being at the fame time, however, fubject, in cafes of bribery, to be punifhed as much more feverely as the laws applicable thereto require *.

Thirty-feven claufes.

SECTION CCXXVI. — *Employment of Bowmen upon private Services* †.

Whoever employs upon a private fervice any foldier of the corps of bow-men, fhall be punifhed with 40 blows, and one degree more feverely as far as 80 blows, for every three foldiers in addition to the

* In the feveral claufes annexed to this fection of the laws, (a tranflation of one or two of the moft remarkable of which is inferted in the Appendix, No. XXI.) various prohibitory and reftrictive regulations are introduced againft foreign intercourfe generally, but thofe which particularly concern Europeans, are chiefly comprized in the occafional edicts of the emperors and of the provincial magiftrates, a tranflation of fome of which will be found in the Appendix, No. XI.

† It is explained in the commentary annexed to the original Chinefe, that this law particularly relates to thofe foldiers, who are detached from the military department, to that of the revenue or of the police.—The term bow-men certainly does not convey the precife idea, and the bow and arrow are, in fact, the military weapons moft generally in ufe among the Chinefe.

number

number ſo illegally employed. The offender againſt this law ſhall likewiſe forfeit to government the eſtimated amount of the wages of the bow-men, at the rate of 8 *fen*, 5 *lee*, 5 *bao*, (about ſeven pence ſterling) *per* man *per* day. The officer who grants the ſervice of ſuch men to any perſon, ſhall be ſubject to the ſame puniſhment as thoſe who employ them.

No clauſe.

END OF THE THIRD BOOK OF THE FIFTH DIVISION.

BOOK IV.

MILITARY HORSES AND CATTLE.

SECTION CCXXVII. — *Reſponſibility of the Charge of Government Cattle.*

EVERY officer in charge of the rearing and feeding of the horſes, horned cattle, camels, mules, aſſes, and ſheep belonging to government, ſhall be reſponſible for an hundred head of animals, (that is to ſay, the following puniſhments are provided on a ſuppoſition of the number in charge being preciſely one hundred, and therefore the following numbers ſhall vary and be more or leſs, in proportion as the total is more or leſs than one hundred ;) and a ſtrict and faithful report ſhall be made to government of the death, loſs, or partial injury which occurs to any of them, that the neglect and miſmanagement which, unleſs the contrary is proved, is in conſequence imputable to the rearers and feeders, may be puniſhed as hereafter provided.

Moreover, under whatever circumſtances the animals die, the ſkin, the hair of the tail, and the bullock's tendons and horns, ſhall be duly delivered to the charge of the proper officer of government ; the rearer and feeder, and all his aſſiſtants, ſhall ſeverally be puniſhed with 30 blows, when one horſe, bullock, or camel dies ; and one degree more ſeverely for every three that die in addition to the number, until the puniſhment amounts to 100 blows ; beyond which it ſhall encreaſe at the rate of one degree for each addition of 10 to the number of deaths, until the puniſhment amounts to 100 blows and three years baniſhment. The death of ſheep ſhall ſubject the rearers and feeders

 to

to puniſhment proportionably leſs ſevere than in the caſe of horſes by three degrees; and the death of mules and aſſes to a puniſhment leſs than in the caſe of horſes, by two degrees.

When any of the aforeſaid animals are brought forth dead, or die of old age, if they are thereupon duly ſubmitted to the official inſpection of the proper officers, the rearers and feeders ſhall be excuſed from puniſhment.

When any of the animals are loſt, the rearers and feeders ſhall make up the full number or value; when any are maimed or injured ſo as to be unfit for uſe, the puniſhment of the reſponſible perſons ſhall be proportionably leſs than in the caſe of the death of the animals by one degree, but they ſhall continue to be reſponſible for the full original number; the dead or maimed cattle ſhall be ſold towards replacing the ſame with living and perfect animals.

One clauſe.

SECTION CCXXVIII. — *Breeding of Horſes.*

The reſponſibility attending the charge and ſuperintendance of breeding mares ſhall be eſtimated according to the produce of the ſeveral droves, conſiſting of 100 in a drove. Every year the breeder in charge of the animals ſhall be anſwerable for the production of one hundred foals from every three droves. If three droves yield no more in the year than 84 foals, the breeder ſhall be puniſhed with 50 blows; if leſs than 74 foals, with 60 blows.

The ſuperintending officer, being in ſuch caſe held guilty of neglecting to attend and inſpect this department, ſhall ſuffer puniſhment proportionably leſs than the breeder by three degrees. The officers of the tribunal at court, ſuperintending this department, ſhall be alſo liable to puniſhment in theſe caſes further reduced proportionably two degrees.

One clauſe.

SEC-

SECTION CCXXIX. — *Examination of Animals to be purchafed by Contract.*

In the examination and felection of horfes, cattle, camels, mules, and affes to be purchafed by contract for the ufe of government, if the officers do not report and eftimate every animal truly and juftly, they fhall, in the cafe of one animal falfely defcribed, be punifhed with 40 blows, and one degree more feverely as far as 100 blows, for every addition of three to the number of animals defcribed falfely.

In the cafe of the examination and felection of fheep, the punifhment fhall be proportionably lefs by three degrees.

Every exceffive appreciation being injurious to government, and every inadequate appreciation being equally a hardfhip on individuals, the offenders fhall be punifhable in proportion to the amount of the deviation in either way, as much more feverely as the law concerning pecuniary injuries and malverfation is found to authorize.

In like manner alfo, if the difference between the true and the fictitious value of the animal, had been appropriated to the private advantage of the offender, the punifhment fhall be increafed as far as the law concerning the embezzlement of ftores, to the fame amount and value, would have warranted.

One claufe.

SECTION CCXXX. — *Exercife of the Veterinary Art.*

If the horfes, horned cattle, camels, mules, or affes belonging to government are lean or difeafed, in confequence of not having been managed and treated according to the approved and eftablifhed practice, the farrier or veterinary furgeon fhall be punifhed with 30 blows; and if any one animal dies in confequence of fuch improper treatment, the punishment shall be increased to 40 blows, and progressively one degree more, for every three additional deaths, until the punishment reaches the limit of 100 blows. With regard to sheep, the punishment of mismanagement shall be proportionately less in each case by three degrees.

No clause.

SECTION CCXXXI. — *Improper Usage and Neglect of Cattle.*

When the horses, horned cattle, camels, mules, or asses belonging to government are harnessed to draw vehicles, or otherwise employed on service, if the attendant places the harness improperly, so as to injure the back and neck of any of the animals by the yoke, and to produce a wound three *Tsun* * in circumference, he shall be punished with 20 blows; and if the wound is five or more *Tsun* in circumference, the punishment shall be encreased to 50 blows.

If any of the aforesaid animals become lean from being ill-fed, the feeder, the superintendant, and his deputies, shall, whenever the proportion of lean cattle under the charge of each of them respectively, amounts to ten in an hundred, be severally punishable with 20 blows. The punishment shall be progressively encreased as far as 100 blows, in the proportion of one degree for every additional tenth of lean animals. In respect to the care of sheep, the punishment in each similar case shall be proportionately less by three degrees.

The superior officers of the department shall be liable to similar punishment, according as one or more tenths of the superintendants of cattle under their authority are convicted of the above delinquency. The members of the supreme board for this department at court, shall

* The *Che*, of which the *Tsun* is a tenth, is equivalent to about twelve inches and a half of British measure.

be

be puniſhable, in the proportion of three degrees leſs than the laſt mentioned ſuperior officers.

One clauſe.

SECTION CCXXXII. — *Neglecting to break in, and Exerciſe the Horſes of Government.*

If any officer who has the charge and ſuperintendency of the horſes of government, ſuffers them to be rode by ſtrangers, or does not attend to their being duly broke in and exerciſed, he ſhall, when the law is infringed in reſpect to one horſe only, be puniſhed with 20 blows, and one degree more ſeverely for every addition of four horſes, to the number of thoſe inſufficiently attended, until the puniſhment attains the limit of 80 blows.

No clauſe.

SECTION CCXXXIII. — *Killing Horſes, Horned Cattle, and other Animals.*

Whoever clandeſtinely, that is to ſay, without the permiſſion of government, kills his own horſes or horned cattle, ſhall be puniſhed with 100 blows: if his camels, mules, or aſſes, with 50 blows; and the horns and ſkins of the animals killed ſhall in each caſe be forfeited to government.

If the animals are killed by inadvertence, or die of diſeaſe, the owners ſhall not be held reſponſible.

Whoever deſignedly kills another man's horſes or cattle, ſhall be puniſhed with 70 blows, and baniſhed for one year and a half; if he kills another man's camels, mules or aſſes, he ſhall be puniſhed with 100 blows. In either caſe, the puniſhment ſhall be ſubject to

increaſe

increafe in proportion to the value of the animals killed, according to the fcale provided by the law againft theft in ordinary cafes.

The fame punifhment fhall be inflicted for killing animals belonging to government, except that the contingent increafe fhall be rated, not according to the law concerning ordinary theft, but according to the law concerning the theft of government property.

In the one cafe, the value of the animal killed fhall be made good to the owner, in the other cafe, to government: the offenders fhall not in either cafe be branded.

Any perfon who wounds any of the aforefaid animals, or kills any fwine or fheep, fhall, without making any diftinction between public and private property, be punifhed, in the former cafe in proportion to the confequent diminution of the value of the wounded animals; and in the latter, in proportion to the full value of the animals killed, according to the fcale provided by law againft theft in ordinary cafes.— The lofs in every cafe fhall be made good to the injured party, whether a private individual or government.

If there is no affignable diminution in the value of the animals wounded, the offender fhall ftill be punifhed with 30 blows. If any one fhould, by inadvertence, kill or wound any fuch animals, he fhall not be liable to punifhment, but fhall be obliged to make good the amount of the lofs fuftained by the proprietor of the animals.

The punifhment of the acceffaries to the offence of defignedly killing or wounding any of the animals belonging to private individuals, fhall be one degree lefs than that of the principal offenders; but in the cafe of killing or wounding the animals of government, the punifhment fhall be the fame.

If any perfon defignedly kills the horfes, horned cattle, camels, mules or affes belonging to any of his relations within the four degrees, he fhall fuffer the reduced punifhment provided in the cafe of an individual clan-

clandeſtinely killing thoſe belonging to himſelf; he ſhall however be further required in theſe caſes, to make good the loſs to the owner.

Whoever kills the ſheep or ſwine belonging to his relations within the aforeſaid degrees, ſhall be puniſhed in proportion to eſtimated value of the animals ſlaughtered, according to the ſcale provided by the law concerning pecuniary injuries in general, but the puniſhment ſhall in no caſe exceed 80 blows. Deſignedly wounding, or inadvertently killing, animals belonging to relations, ſhall not be puniſhed, but ſhall be ſubject to the obligation of making good the loſs to the proprietors.

If any animals, whether they are government or private property, are ſuffered to feed upon ſuch of the ſtores of private individuals or of government, as are likely from their nature, to occaſion death or bodily injury to ſuch animals, thoſe who permit or are the cauſe thereof, ſhall be puniſhed proportionately leſs by three degrees than in the caſe of deſignedly killing or injuring ſuch animals; they ſhall moreover make good the loſs to the owners; on the other hand, the owners of the cattle ſhall make good to the owners of the ſtores, the value of the amount conſumed.

If the proprietor of private cattle, or the feeder of government cattle, deſignedly ſuffers the animals to feed upon private or government ſtores, he ſhall be puniſhed with 30 blows; and as much more ſeverely as may be adequate to the value of the amount of the ſtores conſumed, according to the law concerning pecuniary injuries in general.

The puniſhment ſhall be leſs by two degrees in each caſe, when the proprietor or feeder of the cattle has ſuffered ſuch treſpaſs to be committed, through inadvertence only, but he ſhall be equally liable to make good the loſs to the injured party.

The loſs ſhall not however in ſuch caſe be made good, when the treſpaſſing animal is public property.

In

In all cafes of animals or their offspring, attempting or endeavouring to ftrike with their horns, or to kick or bite, the perfon who, being fo attacked, immediately kills or wounds the attacking animal, fhall, whether it be public or private property, neither be liable to corporal punifhment, nor even to any pecuniary refponfibility.

Four claufes.

SECTION CCXXXIV. — *Vicious and dangerous Animals.*

When horfes, horned cattle, or dogs are vicioufly inclined, either to kick or bite, or horned cattle to ftrike with their horns; if the owner does not fet a mark on them, and tie them up in the cuftomary manner, or if he does not kill his dogs when they become mad, he fhall be punifhed with 40 blows. If, in confequence of fuch neglect, any perfon is killed or wounded, the owner of the animal fhall be obliged to redeem himfelf from the punifhment of man-flaughter, or man-wounding, by the payment of the legal fine.

If any owner of fuch animals defignedly loofens them, or encourages them to attack, fo as to kill or wound any perfon, he fhall be punifhable proportionately lefs feverely by one degree than in the cafe of killing or wounding fuch perfon in an affray.

Neverthelefs, if a farrier or veterinary furgeon, hired to cure the difeafe of any animal, approaches without properly fecuring it, or if an indifferent perfon carelefsly ftrikes any animal, and is killed or wounded by it in return, the owner fhall not be refponfible.

Whoever, laftly, defignedly fuffers his dogs to kill or wound the animals of other perfons, fhall be punifhed with 40 blows, and compelled to make good the amount of the lofs, to the injured party.

No claufe.

SEC-

SECTION CCXXXV.—*Concealment of the Increafe of Animals belonging to Government.*

The rearers and feeders of the horfes, mules, and affes of government fhall report to the proper officer, every time that each animal produces a foal, within ten days after the birth. If, on the contrary, they fuffer the period to elapfe, and afterwards endeavour to conceal the produce, they fhall be punifhed in proportion to the value of it, according to the fcale provided by law in cafes of theft, but the punifhment fhall in no inftance exceed 100 blows, and perpetual banifhment to the diftance of 3000 *lee*; if they are further guilty of fraudulently felling or exchanging fuch produce, they fhall be punifhed in proportion to the amount of the lofs fuftained by government, according to the fcale eftablifhed in the different cafes of embezzlement, and which, when the goods embezzled equal or exceed 40 *leang* or ounces of filver in value, fubjects the offender, nominally to the punifhment of death by being beheaded, though in effect only to five years banifhment, in confideration of the offence coming within the clafs of thofe termed mifcellaneous.

If the fuperior officers, and the members of the chief board for this department at court, are privy to fuch fraudulent proceedings, and take no cognizance of them, they fhall participate equally in the punifhment; but otherwife, they fhall not be held refponfible. The purchafers or receivers in exchange of the produce, if privy to the fraud, fhall be punifhed in the fame manner as purchafers of ftolen goods in ordinary cafes, and forfeit their purchafes to government.

Two claufes.

SECTION CCXXXVI. — *Privately lending the Animals belonging to Government.*

If any governor, ſuperintending officer, or clerk in any department, privately takes to his own uſe, or lends out to others, the horſes, horned cattle, camels, mules, or aſſes belonging to government, whether many or few, for a ſhorter or longer period; the lender and the perſon to whom the animals are lent, ſhall, at the leaſt, be ſeverally puniſhable with 50 blows. The period during which ſuch animals are thus fraudulently employed ſhall at the ſame time be aſcertained, that the amount of hire due to government may be calculated, and required from the offenders. Moreover, if the puniſhment proportionate thereto, according to a ſcale, raiſed one degree above that preſcribed in ordinary caſes of pecuniary injuries, exceeds 50 blows, the puniſhment ſhall be encreaſed accordingly.

The hire, however, of any animal, ſhall never be calculated ſo as to exceed its full value. If the animals die while thus employed contrary to law, the offenders ſhall be puniſhed as in the caſe of a theft of goods of the ſame intrinſic value.

No clauſe.

SECTION CCXXXVII. — *Public Meſſengers uſing the Horſes of Government without Authority.*

If any public meſſenger or other perſon ſo employed, makes a demand for the uſe of the horſes of government at the different ſtations through which he paſſes, without being warranted to do ſo, or when he ought to have employed the ordinary poſt-horſes, he ſhall be puniſhed

puniſhed with 60 blows; if demanding the uſe of the aſſes or mules of government, with 50 blows.

The officers or clerks of government who delivered the horſes, aſſes, or mules, thus unwarrantably demanded, ſhall, in general, be liable to puniſhment leſs than as aforeſaid by one degree; but the puniſhment in theſe caſes ſhall never extend beyond thoſe who were immediately parties to the illegal tranſaction.

No clauſe.

END OF THE FOURTH BOOK OF THE FIFTH DIVISION.

BOOK V.

EXPRESSES AND PUBLIC POSTS*.

SECTION CCXXXVIII. — *Conveyance of Government Orders and Dispatches.*

THE military post-soldiers charged with the transmission of government orders and dispatches, must proceed on their route at the rate of 300 *lee* in a day and a night: If through dilatoriness they exceed the time to the extent of three quarters of an hour, (an hour and a half European computation) they shall be punished with 20 blows; and the punishment shall increase by a progressive ratio of one degree for each additional delay of three-quarters of an hour, until it amounts to 50 blows.

Immediately that the dispatches of government arrive at any military post or station, the post-master shall not fail to forward them, whether many or few, under the charge of the soldiers who are placed under his jurisdiction for that purpose.

* The government-post in China, which is the subject of the several sections of this book of the Penal Code, though not professedly open to the people in general, is an establishment of considerable utility and importance, and carried to a degree of perfection, which in an empire so extensive, as well as so ill adapted, from the inequalities and intersections of the surface of the country, to an expeditious mode of internal communication, could scarcely have been expected.

Although the distance from Pekin to Canton by land exceeds 1200 English miles, government dispatches have been known to arrive in twelve days, and within a period of thirty days, answers and instructions have frequently been received by the magistrates from the court, even upon affairs of no extraordinary importance.

If

If, inftead thereof, the poft-mafter waits for fubfequent difpatches, in order to forward them all at one time, he fhall be punifhed with 20 blows.

If the military poft-foldiers rub or tear the cover of a government difpatch entrufted to them, but not fo as to break the feal thereof, they fhall be punifhed with 20 blows, and the punifhment fhall increafe progreffively, in the ratio of one degree for every three additional covers fo injured, until it amounts to 60 blows.

If the wrapper or cover is entirely deftroyed, but the inner feal of the difpatch not broken, the punifhment fhall be fixed at 40 blows at the leaft, and encreafed progreffively as far as 80 blows, at the rate of two degrees for every additional wrapper or cover fo deftroyed.

If any one difpatch is fuppreffed or deftroyed altogether, or the inner feal of it removed or broken, the punifhment fhall amount to 60 blows, and be encreafed progreffively as far as 100 blows for every additional difpatch fo fuppreffed, deftroyed, or broken open.

In the latter cafe, if the difpatches were fecret, or concerned military operations, the punifhment fhall not be lefs than 100 blows, however fmall may have been the number of the difpatches deftroyed or broken open; and the punifhment fhall be as much more fevere than 100 blows, as may be warranted by any other article of the laws, which the offender had tranfgreffed in the courfe of the fame tranfaction.

If the poft-mafters do not report the mifconduct of the military poft-foldiers, they fhall be liable to equal punifhment; and if, having duly reported the fame to the fuperior officers of government, thofe officers decline to take cognizance thereof, their punifhment fhall be proportionably lefs than the aforefaid, only by two degrees.

The poft-mafter-general of each diftrict fhall diligently infpect and fuperintend the proceedings of all the poft-mafters and poft-foldiers in his

his department; and the viſiting officer and clerks ſhall perſonally viſit and inſpect all the ſtations once a month.

If the number of leſſer offences, ſuch as rubbing and tearing the wrappers of diſpatches, or dilatorineſs in forwarding them, which are overlooked or connived at by theſe officers, exceeds ten, the poſt-maſter-general of the diſtrict ſhall be puniſhed with 40 blows, the clerks of the tribunal of the viſiting officer with 30 blows, and the viſiting officer himſelf with 20 blows.

When any greater offence, ſuch as the ſuppreſſing, deſtroying, or breaking open of a diſpatch, is overlooked and connived at, the poſt-maſter-general of the diſtrict ſhall be equally puniſhable with the poſt-ſoldier; the viſiting officer's clerks one degree leſs; the viſiting officer two degrees leſs; and the governors of cities of the firſt and ſecond orders, when officiating as ſuperior viſiting officers, three degrees leſs.

Six clauſes.

SECTION CCXXXIX. — *Intercepting Addreſſes to Government.*

When an officer of any greater or leſſer provincial board or tribunal has diſpatched, in the lawful manner, an addreſs of information or complaint to His Imperial Majeſty, if his ſuperior officer intercepts the progreſs of ſuch diſpatch, by ſending a meſſenger to any of the military ſtations through which it was to have been forwarded to court, with orders to detain and ſuppreſs it, the poſt-maſter and poſt-ſoldiers at the ſtations to which ſuch orders were addreſſed, ſhall immediately wait on the governor of the diſtrict to report the circumſtance, by whom information thereof ſhall be tranſmitted to the ſuperior officer of the province, and by him again, to the ſupreme board at Pekin, the officers whereof ſhall, laſtly, enter into a ſtrict inveſtigation of the circumſtances of the tranſaction, and lay before the Emperor the final reſult;

refult; if the charge is fubftantiated, the offender fhall receive fentence of death, to be inflicted by beheading, after the ufual period of confinement.

If the poft-mafter and poft-foldiers comply with fuch unlawful requifition, and conceal the fact when aware of its unlawfulnefs, they fhall each of them be punifhed with 100 blows; the governor of the diftrict fhall be liable to fimilar punifhment, if, after the poft-mafter or poft-foldiers duly report the circumftance, he declines to take cognizance of it.

In like manner, if any fuperior officer intercepts the progrefs of any true and lawful difpatch addreffed by his inferior to any of the fupreme departments of ftate at Pekin, punifhment fhall be inflicted on the feveral parties proportionably lefs by two degrees.

Although this law is exprefsly defigned to prevent fuperior officers from intercepting the complaints which may be brought forward againft them by their inferiors, it fhall equally apply to the cafe of inferiors attempting to intercept the tranfmiffion of the charges exhibited againft them by their fuperiors.

No claufe.

SECTION CCXL. — *Poft-Houfes to be kept in Repair.*

When any military ftation through which exprefs pofts are forwarded, falls into a decayed and ruinous ftate, if it is not put into good repair, and all the requifite appurtenances provided and completed; or when the eftablifhment of poft-foldiers falls fhort of the full complement, if the vacancies are not filled up; or if weak and aged perfons are employed on fuch a fervice, the poft-mafter-general of the diftrict fhall be punifhed in each of the feveral cafes with 50 blows, and the prefident and other members of the vifiting and infpecting board or tribunal, fhall each be punifhed with 40 blows.

One claufe.

SEC-

SECTION CCXLI. — *Poſt-Soldiers to be employed on no other Service.*

The officers and attendants of the ſeveral boards or tribunals of government, when travelling upon the public ſervice, are not permitted, even on ſuch occaſions, to employ the poſt-ſoldiers of the ſtations through which they paſs, either in tranſporting from place to place the property of government, or their own private baggage and travelling furniture.

For every offence againſt this law, they ſhall be liable to a puniſhment of 40 blows, and forfeit to government the amount of the wages of ſuch ſoldiers at the rate of 8 *fen*, 5 *lee*, 5 *hao*, (about ſeven-pence ſterling) *per* man *per* day.

No clauſe.

SECTION CCXLII. — *Expreſs-Meſſengers delaying upon the Road.*

Any light-horſeman diſpatched upon ordinary buſineſs ſhall perform his duty within the time appointed by law conformably to the diſtance and other circumſtances; if he exceeds the ſame by one day, he ſhall be puniſhed with 20 blows, and his puniſhment ſhall be increaſed one degree, as far as 60 blows, for every addition of three days dilatorineſs. If the diſpatch concerns military affairs of importance, the puniſhment ſhall be proportionably greater in ſuch caſe by three degrees.

If ſuch delay occaſions the failure and miſcarriage of the military operations then in progreſs, the meſſengers ſhall ſuffer death, by being beheaded after due impriſonment. If the ſeveral poſt-horſe-officers upon the road, or any of them, reſerve the beſt horſes, or upon any pretence refuſe to grant them to the uſe of the expreſs-meſſenger, and thereby occaſion the delay which has been ſtated to be puniſhable by this law; the circumſtances of the caſe ſhall be accurately inveſtigated,

and

and if their guilt is ſubſtantiated, the meſſenger ſhall be releaſed from his reſponſibility, and the puniſhment to which he would have been liable, ſhall be inflicted upon them only.

When an inundation or other unavoidable obſtruction upon the road, ſhall have impeded the progreſs of the expreſs-meſſenger, and occaſion the legal period to be exceeded, all the reſponſible parties ſhall be excuſed.

If a light-horſe expreſs-meſſenger, charged with a government diſpatch, miſtakes the direction of it, and, having in conſequen e conveyed it differently from its deſtination, does not afterwards rectify his error within the legal period of the proper delivery of the diſpatch, the puniſhment, in ordinary caſes, ſhall be proportionably leſs by two degrees than that in the caſe of an intentional delay; but in extraordinary caſes affecting military operations of importance, the puniſhment of delay ſhall be the ſame, whether imputable to error or to deſign, but be inflicted ſolely on the party that occaſioned it, whether the meſſenger himſelf or the poſt-horſe officer on the road. On the other hand, if the delay ariſes from the expreſs-meſſenger having been miſguided by an improper and erroneous direction upon the cover of the diſpatch, the puniſhment ſhall fall upon the perſon who wrote the direction inſtead of either of the former.

Three clauſes.

Section CCXLIII. — *Expreſs-Meſſengers exceeding the Allowance of Horſes and Equipage fixed by Government.*

If any meſſenger or officer of government, diſpatched upon expreſs ſervice with authority to make uſe of the poſt-horſes and expreſs-boats of government, employs one horſe or one boat more than the proper number, he ſhall be puniſhed with 80 blows; and for every additional horſe or boat ſo employed, there ſhall be a proportionate incr aſe of one degree in the punifhment. If fuch officer or meffenger employs horfes, when it was lawful only to employ affes; or if he infifts upon having the ufe of the beft horfes, when it was only lawful for him to have employed the middling or inferior fort, he fhall be punifhed with 70 blows.

If, in difputing the matter with the poft-horfe officer upon the ftation, the meffenger ftrikes or wounds him, the punifhment fhall be encreafed proportionately in fuch cafe one degree; but if the blow or wound is attended with ferious bodily injury, the punifhment fhall be rated according to the rule applicable to affrays in ordinary cafes.

If the poft-horfe officer fubmits to, and complies with, the unlawful demand, he fhall participate in the punifhment attending the tranfgreffion of this law, at the rate of one degree lefs in each cafe, than that on the exprefs-meffenger.

The above punifhment fhall be inflicted on, and confined to, the poft-horfe officer, when fuch officer gives middling or inferior horfes to thofe meffengers who are warranted in claiming the beft; except he fhould happen not to have any of the beft horfes at his command, which circumftance fhall excufe him, as well alfo as the other party, from punifhment.

If the exprefs-meffengers quit the direct road, and thereby avoid the poft-houfes, or when paffing the poft-houfes, if they do not exchange their horfes for frefh ones, or their boats for a new fet of boats, they fhall be punifhed with 60 blows; and if by fuch deviation or omiffion they ride any of the government poft-horfes fo as to occafion their death by over-fatigue, the punifhment fhall be more fevere by one degree, and they fhall forfeit to government a fum equal to the value of the horfes.

If the meffengers of government difpatched upon bufinefs of no extraordinary urgency, though without having been guilty of the deviation or omiffion here defcribed, ride their horfes to death, they fhall forfeit to government a fum equal to the value of the horfes, but not be liable in confequence to further punifhment.

When

When, however, the meſſengers are diſpatched upon urgent military affairs, or the next ſtations happen to be unprovided with the boats or horſes required for their accommodation, neither the deviation, omiſſion, or exceſſive riding, ſhall expoſe them to any pecuniary forfeiture, or corporal puniſhment, provided the juſtifying circumſtances are properly ſubſtantiated.

Four clauſes.

SECTION CCXLIV. — *Expreſs-Meſſengers exceeding the fixed Allowance of Money and Proviſions.*

If any officers or meſſengers travelling expreſs upon public ſervice, demand a larger ſupply of money or proviſions on the road, than the laws authorize, they ſhall be puniſhed in proportion to the amount or value of the exceſs, according to the ſcale provided by the law againſt receiving bribes for purpoſes not in themſelves unlawful.

The officer of government who grants ſuch exceſſive ſupplies, ſhall participate in the puniſhment due to this offence, at the rate of one degree leſs in each caſe, than the receiver.

If the officer or meſſenger travelling expreſs, extorts by violence ſuch exceſſive ſupplies, he ſhall be puniſhed in proportion to the amount of the exceſs, according the ſeverer ſcale provided by the law againſt bribery for unlawful purpoſes: but the officer from whom they are obtained, ſhall, in ſuch caſes, be excuſed.

One clauſe *.

* In this clauſe it is declared, that whereas all foreign embaſſies travelling through the empire, are duly ſupplied by government with every thing they require upon the road, the ſhop-keepers who clandeſtinely ſell to, or buy from, ſuch foreigners any article whatever, ſhall forfeit to government whatever they may have received for the ſame in exchange, and ſhall moreover be condemned to wear for the ſpace of one month the *Cangue* or moveable pillory.

SECTION CCXLV. — *Express-Post to be reserved for important Dispatches.*

All the Emperor's orders relative to the disposition and employment of the military forces; all urgent communications of important military intelligence from the court to the frontier stations; and all addresses upon urgent military affairs from the several public boards and tribunals in the empire, to the Emperor, shall be forwarded by messengers riding express; whoever designedly omits to send dispatches of this nature to the post-houses, with instructions that they may be forwarded express, shall be punished with 100 blows; but if the omission occasions the failure and miscarriage of the military operations to which those dispatches relate, the individual so offending shall suffer death, by being beheaded, after undergoing the customary confinement.

All addresses announcing to the Emperor desirable public events, soliciting aid to provinces suffering from dearth or scarcity, or reporting extraordinary occurrences and calamities, shall likewise be forwarded express, as well as in general, all communications respecting the supplies required by the army, and other affairs of similar importance. — Whoever designedly omits to forward such dispatches in that manner, shall be punished with 80 blows, and be further responsible, as in the preceding case, for the contingent consequences of such omission.

On the other hand, those who designedly transmit to the express-post-houses, those government dispatches which, having relation to ordinary affairs only, were not intended to be forwarded by that mode, shall be punished with 40 blows.

No clause.

SEC-

SECTION CCXLVI. — *Dilatorineſs in Tranſmiſſions and Removals connected with the Public Service.*

In all caſes of the public ſervice requiring that the property of government in goods or cattle, or that priſoners or exiles, ſhould be removed from one ſtation to another, they are to be committed to the care of a particular perſon in the employ of government, who ſhall be reſponſible for the performance of this ſervice within the period appointed by law; if through any dilatorineſs he exceeds ſuch period by a ſingle day, he ſhall be puniſhed with 20 blows, and be liable to a puniſhment progreſſively increaſed as far as 50 blows, at the rate of one degree for every three days further delay: any ſimilar delay in forwarding the proviſions and ſupplies of the army, when in the field, ſhall be puniſhed two degrees more ſeverely in each caſe, and the ſcale of puniſhment ſhall be carried on as far as 100 blows.

If, in conſequence of ſuch delay, the deficiency of the requiſite ſupplies at the moment of engaging the enemy is ſo great, as to fruſtrate, and occaſion the miſcarriage, of the military operations depending thereon, the offender ſhall ſuffer death by being beheaded, after the uſual confinement.

If the individual entruſted in ordinary caſes with ſuch charge, exceeds the period allowed for performing the ſervice allotted to him, not intentionally, but from having miſunderſtood the written orders on the ſubject, and in conſequence loſes time by proceeding in a direction contrary to his real deſtination, his puniſhment ſhall be proportionally leſs, in each caſe, by two degrees; but if the charge concerns any military operations, the delay ſhall be attended with the ſame puniſhment, whether it be the reſult of inadvertence or of deſign.

If the miſtake aroſe from the orders on the ſubject having been erroneouſly written, the puniſhment ſhall fall upon the writer thereof,

thereof, inftead of being inflicted upon the perfon fuperintending the removal of perfons or goods, on account of government.

Two claufes.

SECTION CCXLVII. — *Occupation of the principal Apartments in Poft-Houfes.*

If any meffengers or ordinary officers difpatched upon public fervice, prefume to occupy, or in any refpect to avail themfelves of the accommodation of the principal and moft honourable apartments in the poft-houfes, they fhall be punifhed with 50 blows; fuch principal apartments, including the chief hall of reception, being referved for the particular ufe and benefit of regular officers of government and other fuperior guefts.

No claufe.

SECTION CCXLVIII. — *Tranfmiffion of private Property by Government Poft-Horfes.*

If any of the officers or meffengers, difpatched upon the public fervice, and therefore entitled to employ on the occafion the poft-horfes of government, carry with them, befides clothes and neceffary accoutrements, any other articles of baggage weighing ten *kin* * or more, they fhall be punifhed with 60 blows; the punifhment fhall alfo be progreffively encreafed as far as 100 blows, for every additional 10 *kin* of weight.

When the mules or affes, inftead of the horfes of government are thus over-loaded, the punifhment fhall, in each cafe, be proportionably lefs by one degree.

* The *kin* is generally eftimated at one-third more than the Britifh pound.

The

The amount or value of the excefs in weight of the property conveyed, fhall be forfeited to government: If the animals thus overloaded are killed, the punifhment of the offender fhall be encreafed as far as the law provided againft fuch contingency authorizes.

One claufe.

SECTION CCXLIX. — *Officers and others compelling the Inhabitants of their diftrict to carry their Palanquins* *.

If any officers or clerks of a tribunal or other department of government, or any other officers or meffengers, employ the inhabitants of the diftrict to carry their palanquins, except as hereafter provided, they fhall be punifhed with 60 blows, and the fuperintending officer of the diftrict who connives at, or authorizes the fame, fhall fuffer punifhment lefs by one degree, as a participator in the offence.

If any private individuals, relying on their influence and riches, employ the labourers or cultivators of the foil to carry their palanquins, without paying the wages due for the labour, they fhall be punifhed in the fame manner. In every cafe they fhall be obliged to make good the amount of the wages, at the rate of 8 *fen*, 5 *lee*, 3 *hao*, (about feven-pence fterling) *per* man *per* day.

* The Chinefe fedan or palanquin is figured and defcribed in the authentic account of the Britifh Embaffy. The fedan with two bearers, is the ordinary mode of conveyance by land, for almoft every defcription of unprivileged perfons. The fedan with four bearers is exclufively employed by officers of the government, and not allowed even to certain claffes of perfons who enjoy all the other honorary marks of diftinction belonging to that rank. — Some of the great officers of ftate have the further privilege of being carried, upon particular occafions of ceremony, by eight bearers; but to His Imperial Majefty alone, is referved the honour of being carried by fixteen.

Whenever

Whenever the inhabitants have been regularly hired, and the wages of their labour duly paid, this law ſhall not take effect.

Two clauſes.

SECTION CCL.—*Families of deceaſed Officers to be removed at the Public Expence.*

When any of the civil or military officers of the empire fall ſick and die while in employ at their reſpective ſtations, their families, if not in poſſeſſion of the means of returning to their native homes, ſhall be removed thither at the public expence; the officers of the ſeveral diſtricts through which they have occaſion to paſs, ſhall appoint the eſcorting officers, provide a ſufficient number of carriages, boats, porters, and horſes for their conveyance, and iſſue rations of proviſions from the public ſtores, in proportion to the number of individuals in each family; the quantities required being previouſly aſcertained by perſonal inveſtigation.

Any officer of a diſtrict, who neglects to provide for ſuch families, and to ſuperintend their progreſs homeward in the manner here directed, ſhall be puniſhed with 60 blows.

One clauſe.

SECTION CCLI.—*Hiring Subſtitutes, and entruſting to them an allotted perſonal Service.*

If any perſon, being charged with the conveyance of government property, whether goods or cattle, or with the removal of priſoners and exiles, inſtead of perſonally performing ſuch ſervice, hires a ſubſtitute to perform his duty in his ſtead, he ſhall be puniſhed with 60 blows; and if, in conſequence of ſuch ſubſtitution, any of the property

perty of government is injured or loſt, or any of the priſoners eſcape, he ſhall ſuffer puniſhment as much more ſevere as the law, particularly provided for puniſhing the neglect of perſons in charge under ſuch circumſtances, may be found to preſcribe.

Whoever undertakes for hire or otherwiſe, to officiate as the ſubſtitute of another in any of theſe reſpects, ſhall participate in the puniſhment of the offence, at the rate of one degree leſs in each caſe, than the perſon whoſe office he undertakes to perform.

Whenever two or more perſons are jointly entruſted with the performance of any ſuch ſervice as above deſcribed, if they mutually replace, and agree alternately to connive at the abſence of each other, they ſhall be puniſhed with 40 blows; and in caſe any bribes ſhould have been given and received, as much more ſeverely as the law provided againſt bribery for purpoſes not in themſelves unlawful, may be found to preſcribe.

When any ill conſequences enſue, ſuch as the injury or loſs of the property, or the eſcape of the priſoners entruſted to their charge, they ſhall be condemned to ſuffer a puniſhment as much more ſevere as may be conformable to the law particularly applicable under ſuch circumſtances; and in general, in all caſes of perſons jointly entruſted with any affair or duty, the party abſenting himſelf, and the party undertaking the vacant charge, ſhall be equally puniſhable, inſtead of the puniſhment of the acceſſary being mitigated, as uſual in other inſtances. The parties however ſhall not be liable to the aggravation of puniſhment, ariſing from fraud or connivance, except as far as they are individually and perſonally privy to, or concerned therein.

One clauſe.

SECTION CCLII. — *Conveyance of private Property at the Charge of Government.*

All thofe who, being engaged in the public fervice, have authority to employ, when travelling, the horfes, cattle, camels, mules, or affes belonging to government, but who do not come under the defcription of travellers licenfed to proceed by the exprefs poft, fhall, in fuch cafes, be reftricted from loading the animals with more than 10 *kin* weight of baggage, befide the clothes and cuftomary accoutrements about their perfons; if they exceed this allowance by five *kin* weight, they fhall be punifhed with 10 blows, and the punifhment fhall be progreffively encreafed one degree for every addition of ten *kin* weight, until it amounts to 60 blows.

All perfons authorized in the fame manner to employ in travelling, the carriages or boats which belong to government, fhall, in fuch cafes, confine themfelves to thirty *kin* weight of baggage; and if they exceed that limit by ten *kin* weight, they fhall be punifhed with 10 blows, and the punifhment fhall be progreffively increafed one degree for every addition of 20 *kin* weight, until it amounts to 70 blows.— For this offence, the mafters, and not the fervants, fhall be refponfible.

When the excefs of weight arifes from the amount of goods undertaken to be conveyed for another perfon, the proprietor configning his property to be fo conveyed, fhall participate equally in the punifhment denounced againft this offence; and in every cafe the goods thus illicitly conveyed fhall be forfeited to government.

The fuperintending officer of the diftrict fhall alfo participate in the fame degree in the punifhment, when he is privy to the commiffion of the offence, but not otherwife.

When, however, whole families are to be conveyed from place to place at the expence of government, as in the cafe of the return of the

the relations of deceaſed ſoldiers, and of civil and military officers, the amount and weight of their baggage ſhall not be ſubject to any of the ordinary limitations hereby impoſed.

Three clauſes.

Section CCLIII. — *Privately lending the Poſt-Horſes of Government.*

Any poſt-horſe officer who employs for his private uſe, or lends out to others, the poſt-horſes of government, and alſo, whoever borrows the ſame, ſhall, for each offence, be puniſhed with 80 blows, and one degree leſs in the caſe of aſſes ſo employed.

The eſtimated ſum due for the daily hire of ſuch animals ſhall likewiſe become a forfeiture to government, and the puniſhment ſhall be ſubject to any contingent increaſe, which the ſcale provided by the law againſt pecuniary injuries, proportionably aggravated two degrees, may be found to preſcribe.

No clauſe.

END OF THE FIFTH DIVISION.

SIXTH DIVISION,

Criminal Laws.

BOOK I.

ROBBERY AND THEFT.

Section CCLIV. — *High Treaſon.*

HIGH treaſon, is either treaſon againſt the ſtate, by an attempt to ſubvert the eſtabliſhed government; or treaſon againſt the Sovereign, by an attempt to deſtroy the palace in which he reſides, the temple in which his family is worſhipped *, or the tombs in which the remains of his anceſtors are depoſited.

All perſons convicted of having been principals or acceſſaries to the actual or deſigned commiſſion of this heinous crime, ſhall ſuffer death by a ſlow and painful execution †.

All

* That is to ſay, the temple in which certain ceremonies and oblations are performed periodically in honour of the Imperial family.

† This mode of execution is not noticed among the ordinary puniſhments, but is particularly deſcribed in one of the notes ſubjoined to the original text. It has been termed in the works of the miſſionaries, " cutting into ten thouſand pieces," and appears to amount, at the leaſt, to a licence to the executioner to aggravate and prolong the ſufferings of the criminal undergoing the ſentence of the law, by any ſpecies of cruelty he may think proper to inflict. It is however underſtood to be the ordinary exertion of the Emperor's prerogative

All the male relations in the firſt degree, at or above the age of ſixteen, of perſons convicted as aforeſaid; namely, the father, grandfather, ſons, grandſons, paternal uncles, and their ſons reſpectively, ſhall, without any regard to the place of reſidence, or to the natural or acquired infirmities of particular individuals, be indiſcriminately beheaded.

All the other male relations at or above the age of ſixteen, however diſtant their relationſhip, and whether by blood or by marriage, ſhall likewiſe ſuffer death, by being beheaded, if they were living under the ſame roof with the treaſonable offender, at the time the offence was committed.

The male relations in the firſt degree, under the age of ſixteen, and the female relations in the firſt degree, of all ages, ſhall be diſtributed as ſlaves to the great officers of ſtate.

The property of every deſcription belonging to treaſonable offenders, ſhall be confiſcated for the uſe and ſervice of government.

The female relations of ſuch criminals, who ſhall have been previouſly married into other families, and alſo thoſe females who, although affianced to ſuch criminals, or to the ſons or grandſons of ſuch criminals, ſhall not have been taken home and married, ſhall always be excepted from the penalties of this law.

All perſons who, when privy to the commiſſion of, or to the intent to commit the crime of high treaſon, wilfully conceal and connive at the ſame, ſhall be beheaded.

Any perſon who ſhall apprehend, and deliver into the cuſtody of a magiſtrate, an offender againſt this law, ſhall be employed forthwith

---

rogative of mercy, to commute this terrible ſentence for the milder one of death, by ſimply ſevering the head from the body; but there are certainly ſome inſtances in which, with a view to public example, or from other cauſes, this law has been rigorouſly executed.

under

under government, according to his qualifications; or if already an officer in the employ of government, he ſhall be ſuitably promoted; and in every caſe he ſhall be rewarded with the poſſeſſion of the whole of the confiſcated property of the offender *.

Any perſon who ſhall give the information which may be requiſite towards enabling the magiſtrates to bring ſuch offenders to juſtice, ſhall be rewarded with the whole of the property, which may conſequently be confiſcated; but not entitled as in the preceding inſtance, either to employment or promotion in the ſervice of government.

If any perſon who is privy to the intention to commit, or to the actual commiſſion of the aforeſaid crime of high treaſon, is guilty of neglecting to communicate to the magiſtrate of the diſtrict the information he poſſeſſes, he ſhall, although not expreſsly chargeable with any acts of connivance and concealment, be puniſhed with 100 blows, and baniſhed perpetually to the diſtance of 3000 *lee*.

If the relations of perſons intending to commit the aforeſaid crime ſhall, previous to the commiſſion of any overt act, deliver them up to the officers of juſtice, thoſe who are ſo delivered up, and their ſeveral relations, ſhall all of them, be entirely pardoned.

If the relations of perſons actually guilty of any acts of high treaſon, voluntarily ſurrender them into the cuſtody of the magiſtrates, ſuch relations, and all other perſons guilty by implication only, ſhall

* As this appropriation of the confiſcated property of the offender, is an exception to the general rule noticed in a preceding paragraph, it is probably by no means the ordinary reward of the police officer on ſuch occaſions, but only of the perſon who volunteers his ſervices, and who being the proſecutor and public accuſer, thereby expoſes himſelf to all the penalties of a falſe accuſation, whenever the charges are not ſubſtantiated. — When the crime is public and notorious, or committed by perſons high in rank or office, of whom the ſovereign himſelf is generally the only avowed accuſer, thoſe who are inſtrumental in bringing the criminal to juſtice, merely in the courſe of their official duty, are not, it is conceived, intended to be benefited in the event of his conviction, any more than they would be liable to ſuffer, on the event of his acquittal. — For the puniſhment to which in different caſes falſe accuſers are liable, ſee Section CCCXXXVI.

be

be pardoned; but with regard to the principal offenders, the laws muſt be ſtrictly executed.

Four clauſes *.

SECTION CCLV. — *Rebellion and Renunciation of Allegiance.*

All perſons renouncing their country and allegiance, or deviſing the means thereof, ſhall be beheaded; and in the puniſhment of this offence, no diſtinction ſhall be made between principals and acceſſaries.

The property of all ſuch criminals ſhall be confiſcated, and their wives and children diſtributed as ſlaves to the great officers of ſtate.— Thoſe females however, with whom a marriage had not been completed, though adjuſted by contract, ſhall not ſuffer under this law; from the penalties of this law, exception ſhall alſo be made in favour of all ſuch of the daughters of criminals as ſhall have been married into other families.— The parents, grand-parents, brothers, and grand-children of ſuch criminals, whether habitually living with them under the ſame roof or not, ſhall be perpetually baniſhed to the diſtance of 2000 *lee*.

All thoſe who purpoſely conceal and connive at the perpetration of this crime, ſhall be ſtrangled.

Thoſe who inform againſt, and bring to juſtice, criminals of this deſcription, ſhall be rewarded with the whole of their property.

Thoſe who are privy to the perpetration of this crime, and yet omit to give any notice or information thereof to the magiſtrates, ſhall be puniſhed with 100 blows, and baniſhed perpetually to the diſtance of 3000 *lee*.

If the crime is contrived, but not executed, the principal ſhall be ſtrangled, and all the acceſſaries ſhall, each of them, be puniſhed

* A tranſlation of the ſupplemental clauſes annexed to this law, is inſerted in the Appendix, No. XXII.

with

with 100 blows, and perpetual baniſhment to the diſtance of 3000 *lee*.

If thoſe who are privy to ſuch ineffective contrivance, do not give due information and notice thereof to the magiſtrates, they ſhall be puniſhed with 100 blows, and baniſhed for three years.

All perſons who refuſe to ſurrender themſelves to the magiſtrates when required, and ſeek concealment in mountains and deſert places in order to evade, either the performance of their duty, or the puniſhment due to their crimes, ſhall be held guilty of an intent to rebel, and ſhall therefore ſuffer puniſhment in the manner by this law provided. If ſuch perſons have recourſe to violence, and defend themſelves when purſued, by force of arms, they ſhall be held guilty of an overt act of rebellion, and puniſhed accordingly.

Eight clauſes *.

SECTION CCLVI.—*Sorcery and Magic.*

All perſons convicted of writing and editing books of ſorcery and magic, or of employing ſpells and incantations, in order to agitate and influence the minds of the people, ſhall be beheaded, after remaining in priſon the uſual period. If the influence of ſuch acts ſhall not have extended beyond a few perſons, the criminal ſhall be baniſhed perpetually to the diſtance of 3000 *lee*; and generally, the puniſhment ſhall be proportionate to the nature of the caſe, and therefore more or leſs ſevere according to circumſtances.

All perſons who are guilty of retaining in their poſſeſſion, and concealing from the magiſtrates, any books of the above deſcription, ſhall be puniſhed with 100 blows, and baniſhed for three years.

Four clauſes †.

* A tranſlation of the clauſes annexed to this law is inſerted in the Appendix, No. XXIII.

† A tranſlation of theſe clauſes is inſerted in the Appendix, No. XXIV.

Section CCLVII. — *Sacrilege.*

All perſons guilty of ſtealing the conſecrated oblations offered up by the Emperor to the ſpirits of Heaven and Earth, or any of the ſacred utenſils, cloths, meat-offerings, and precious ſtones uſed on ſuch occaſions, ſhall, whether principals or acceſſaries to the offence, whether previouſly entruſted or not with the charge of the ſaid articles, in all caſes, be beheaded.

The offence of ſtealing articles prepared and deſigned for conſecration, but not actually conſecrated or offered up as aforeſaid, and alſo that of ſtealing ſuch conſecrated articles and oblations, after they had ceaſed to be applied to ſacred uſes, ſhall be puniſhed with 100 blows and baniſhment for three years.

When the amount of the articles ſacrilegiouſly ſtolen is conſiderable, they ſhall be valued, and the puniſhment inflicted on the offender ſhall, at the leaſt, exceed that awarded in ordinary caſes of theft by one degree.

The offenders in theſe caſes ſhall be likewiſed branded in the arm, in the manner deſcribed in Section CCLXIV.

No clauſe.

Section CCLVIII. — *Stealing Edicts and Ordinances of Government.*

All perſons guilty of having been principals or acceſſaries to the crime of ſtealing an Imperial edict, after it has received the impreſſion of the great Imperial ſeal, ſhall be beheaded.

The crime of ſtealing the authenticated edict of any governing magiſtrate or tribunal, or an edict of the Emperor, not yet authenticated by the impreſſion of the Imperial ſeal, ſhall be puniſhed with 100 blows; the criminal ſhall be moreover branded in the arm. —
When

When any corrupt motive is aſſignable, the theft ſhall be puniſhed according to the moſt ſevere among the different laws applicable to the caſe. If the edicts ſtolen, concerned the collection of ſupplies for the army, or were connected with any military operations, the principals and acceſſaries ſhall be ſtrangled.

No clauſe.

SECTION CCLIX. — *Stealing Seals and Stamps of Office.*

All perſons guilty of having been principals or acceſſaries to the crime of ſtealing the official ſeal of any magiſtrate or tribunal, or any ſeal or ſtamp whatever iſſued by the Emperor, ſhall be beheaded.

The crime of ſtealing the official ſeals or ſtamps, of perſons employed by the magiſtrates, or employed in public offices by the authority of the magiſtrates, ſhall be puniſhed with 100 blows; the criminal ſhall be moreover branded in the arm.

No clauſe.

SECTION CCLX. — *Stealing from an Imperial Palace.*

All perſons found guilty of having been principals or acceſſaries to the crime of ſtealing any articles from the Imperial palace, or from the private Imperial treaſury, ſhall receive ſentence of death by decollation, but this is one of the offences in which capital puniſhment is commutable for five years baniſhment.

One clauſe.

SECTION CCLXI. — *Stealing the Keys of the Gate of a Fort or City.*

All perſons found guilty of having been principals or acceſſaries to the crime of ſtealing the key of the gate of the Imperial city, ſhall be

 ſentenced

ſentenced to ſuffer 100 blows, and perpetual baniſhment to the diſtance of 3000 *lee*, but this offence ſhall be ranked among thoſe in which the puniſhment of perpetual, is commutable for that of temporary, baniſhment.

The crime of ſtealing the key of the gate of any other city, or of any town, fortreſs or barrier ſtation, ſhall be puniſhed with 100 blows, and baniſhment for three years; that of ſtealing the key of a granary, treaſury, or other government building or public office, ſhall be puniſhed with 100 blows, and the thief ſhall be branded in the arm.

All perſons who, having the charge of the key of a gate of a city or fortreſs, are convicted of having loſt ſuch key, or of having, on any pretext, ſuffered the ſame to be out of their poſſeſſion, ſhall be puniſhed with 90 blows, and baniſhed for two years and a half.

One clauſe.

Section CCLXII. — *Stealing military Weapons and Accoutrements.*

All perſons found guilty of ſtealing any of the ordinary military weapons and accoutrements, ſuch as the common military dreſs, ſwords, and bows and arrows, ſhall be puniſhed in proportion to the amount and value of the articles ſtolen, according to the law applicable to theft in ordinary caſes; but thoſe who ſteal any of the weapons and accoutrements which are excluſively military, and which it is therefore unlawful for the people in general to poſſeſs, ſuch as coats of mail, breaſt-plates, and fire-arms, ſhall, at the leaſt, be puniſhed as ſeverely as is provided by the law prohibiting the poſſeſſion of ſuch articles.

When ſoldiers in actual ſervice are guilty of ſtealing arms and accoutrements of any kind from each other, they ſhall be puniſhed according to the law againſt theft in ordinary caſes, except that when the

the articles ſtolen are voluntarily ſurrendered to government, the puniſhment ſhall be leſs in each caſe, than it would have been otherwiſe, by two degrees.

One clauſe.

SECTION CCLXIII. — *Stealing Timber from a Burying-Ground.*

All the principals and acceſſaries to the offence of ſtealing, (that is to ſay, privately cutting down and removing,) any of the trees growing within the boundaries of the Imperial cemetery or burying-ground, ſhall be puniſhed, at the leaſt, with 100 blows and three years baniſhment.

The principal in the offence of ſtealing any of the trees growing in a private burying-ground, ſhall be puniſhed, at the leaſt, with 80 blows, and each of the acceſſaries thereto, with 70 blows.

If the value of the timber cut down and carried away is conſiderable, it ſhall be eſtimated, and the puniſhment increaſed in proportion to the reſult, to ſuch an extent, as in every caſe to exceed by one degree that which would have been legally inflicted for an ordinary theft to the ſame amount and value.

*Five clauſes *.*

SECTION CCLXIV. — *Embezzlement of Public Property.*

When any of the perſons who are lawfully entruſted with the public property depoſited in the treaſuries and ſtore-houſes of government, are found guilty of having been concerned as principals or acceſſaries in the offence of embezzling any part thereof, they ſhall be puniſhed according to the following ſcale, in proportion to the total amount embezzled at one time, without paying any regard to the number and ex-

* A tranſlation of theſe clauſes is inſerted in the Appendix, No. XXV.

tent

tent of the ſhares, into which the embezzled property may have been divided.

The offenders ſhall moreover be branded or marked in the arm between the wriſt and the elbow, with the three following, words *tao quan* {*leang*, / *vo*, / *yn*,} ſtealer of government {Grain, / Stores, / Silver,} according as the caſe may be, each character being diſtinctly marked, and of the dimenſion of one *Tſun* and a half in the ſquare.

Value leſs than	1 *leang* (ounce) of ſilver	80	blows with the bamboo.
Value exceeding	1	90	blows with the bamboo.
Value exceeding	5	100	blows with the bamboo.
Value exceeding	7½	60	blows and baniſhment for 1 year.
Value exceeding	10	70	blows and baniſhment for 1½ years.
Value exceeding	12½	80	blows and baniſhment for 2 years.
Value exceeding	15	90	blows and baniſhment for 2½ years.
Value exceeding	17½	100	blows and baniſhment for 3 years.
Value exceeding	20	100	blows and perpetual baniſhment, diſtance 2000 *lee*.
Value exceeding	25	100	blows and perpetual baniſhment, diſtance 2500 *lee*.
Value exceeding	30	100	blows and perpetual baniſhment, diſtance 3000 *lee*.
Value exceeding	40		Death, by being beheaded *.

Ten clauſes †.

* In a note in the original Chineſe it is ſtated, that in caſes nominally puniſhable with perpetual baniſhment by this law, the offenders ſhall be baniſhed for four years only; and that, in thoſe nominally puniſhable capitally, the offenders ſhall, inſtead thereof, be baniſhed for five years, unleſs the value of the property embezzled exceeds 100 ounces, and falls ſhort of 1000 ounces, when the baniſhment of the offender ſhall be perpetual.—If the value exceeds the latter ſum, it is again declared, that the offender ſhall be beheaded.

† For a tranſlation of the clauſes to this law, ſee the Appendix, No. XXVI.

SEC-

Section CCLXV. — *Theft of Public Property.*

All perſons found guilty of ſtealing, or attempting to ſteal, the property of government, depoſited in the public treaſuries and ſtore-houſes, ſhall be puniſhed for their offences in the following manner:—

The principals in an attempt to ſteal, ſhall be puniſhed with 60 blows, and each of the acceſſaries to ſuch an attempt, with 50 blows.

If the theft is accompliſhed, the offenders, as in the preceding article, relative to the embezzlement of the ſame ſpecies of property, ſhall be puniſhed in proportion to the total amount ſtolen at one time, and likewiſe branded in the arm, in the manner there deſcribed, but the ſcale of puniſhment ſhall be leſs ſevere, and as follows:—

Value leſs than	1 *leang* (ounce) of ſilver	70	blows with the bamboo.	
Value exceeding	1	80	blows with the bamboo.	
	10	90	blows with the bamboo.	
	15	100	blows with the bamboo.	
	20	60	blows and baniſhment for	1 year.
	25	70	blows and baniſhment for	1½ years.
	30	80	blows and baniſhment for	2 years.
	35	90	blows and baniſhment for	2½ years.
	40	100	blows and baniſhment for	3 years.
	45	100	blows and perpetual baniſhment to diſtance of	2000 *lee.*
	50	100	blows and perpetual baniſhment to diſtance of	2500 *lee.*
	55	100	blows and perpetual baniſhment to diſtance of	3000 *lee.*
	80	Death, by being ſtrangled*.		

Two clauſes†.

* When the amount ſtolen does not exceed 100 ounces, it is provided, as in the preceding ſection, that the puniſhments of death and perpetual baniſhment ſhall be commuted for baniſhment, in the former caſe for five years, and in the latter for four years.

† For a tranſlation of the clauſes annexed to this law, ſee the Appendix, No. XXVII.

SECTION CCLXVI. — *Robbery — Highway Robbery* *.

All perſons found guilty of having been jointly concerned as principals or as acceſſaries, in an attempt to ſeize the property of another by force, that is to ſay, to commit a robbery, ſhall be puniſhed with 100 blows and perpetual baniſhment to the diſtance of 3000 *lee*; when a robbery is actually effected, all the individuals concerned in the commiſſion thereof, ſhall be beheaded, whether participators or not in the booty, and however ſmall may be the total amount of the plunder.

If the contriver of the robbery does not actually contribute to the perpetration thereof, nor afterwards participate in the booty obtained, he ſhall not ſuffer death, but receive 100 blows, and be ſent into perpetual baniſhment at the diſtance of 3000 *lee*. All other perſons who, although belonging to the gang or aſſociation, neither actively contribute to the perpetration of the robbery, nor afterwards partake of the booty, ſhall be ſeverally diſmiſſed, after undergoing the puniſhment of 100 blows.

Whenever ſtupifying drugs, or other means, are previouſly employed in order to deprive the perſon intended to be plundered, of the uſe of his ſenſes, and ſuch perſon is thereby incapacitated from making any reſiſtance, this proceeding ſhall be conſidered as equivalent to an act of open violence, and although, in other reſpects, merely a theft, ſhall always be puniſhed as a robbery.

If thieves, when caught in the act of ſtealing, refuſe to ſurrender, and continue their reſiſtance ſo long as to kill or wound any perſon, they ſhall be beheaded.

If, upon the occaſion of a theft being committed, females are alſo violated, the theft ſhall be puniſhed as a robbery, but thoſe of the

* See Section CCLXVIII.

party,

party, who were guilty as acceſſaries to the theft only, ſhall not participate in the conſequent aggravation of the puniſhment of their companions.

A thief who, when purſued, caſts away the ſtolen goods, but afterwards defends himſelf by force, and refuſes to ſurrender, ſhall be puniſhed, according to the law in ordinary caſes of criminals not ſurrendering, with 70 blows at the leaſt; but a thief who upon ſuch an occaſion wounds any perſon, ſhall be ſtrangled; and a thief who upon ſuch an occaſion, kills any perſon, ſhall be beheaded.

Thirty-four clauſes *.

SECTION CCLXVII. — *Reſcue from Priſon.*

All perſons concerned as principals or acceſſaries in the offence of forcibly reſcuing, or attempting to reſcue any lawful priſoner, ſhall ſuffer death by being beheaded, after confinement during the uſual period.

All perſons, relations as well as others, who are guilty of clandeſtinely releaſing any priſoner, ſhall be puniſhed with the ſame degree of ſeverity as that to which the priſoner himſelf is liable, excepting the cuſtomary reduction of one degree in capital caſes.

All thoſe who are guilty of having made the attempt, though unſucceſsfully, privately to releaſe a priſoner, ſhall ſuffer puniſhment proportionately leſs than that to which the priſoner is liable, by two degrees. If thoſe who make the attempt, are guilty of wounding any perſon, the principal offender amongſt them ſhall ſuffer death by being ſtrangled, after confinement during the uſual period; when guilty of killing any perſon, the principal among them ſhall ſuffer death by

* For a tranſlation of ſome of the moſt material clauſes annexed to this law, ſee the Appendix, No. XXVIII.

being beheaded. In general, in all the cafes of attempting to releafe a prifoner clandeftinely, the punifhment of the acceffary fhall be lefs than that of the principal by one degree.

In all cafes of perfons affembling in the public highways *, to oppofe by force a fervant of government, appointed by the magiftrates to perform any official duty, fuch as the collection of the revenue, or the purfuit and feizure of offenders, the principal fhall fuffer the punifhment of 100 blows and perpetual banifhment to the diftance of 3000 *lee*. If upon fuch an occafion the individual thus employed in the fervice of government is wounded, the principal offender fhall fuffer death by being ftrangled, after being confined during the ufual period.

If, in this latter cafe, the number of perfons riotoufly affembled amounts to ten or more, or if, whatever the number of perfons affembled, the individual employed in the fervice of government is killed in the courfe of the affray, the principal among the offenders fhall be beheaded, and as many of the others as are found guilty of having ftruck a mortal blow, fhall be ftrangled. All the other acceffaries, in this and in the preceding cafes, fhall fuffer a punifhment one degree lefs fevere than that inflicted upon their refpective principals.

When the mafter of a family affembles his houfehold, in order to oppofe the officers of government, he alone fhall be punifhable and refponfible, unlefs his followers are guilty of ftriking fo as more or lefs to wound, in which cafe they fhall be punifhed as independent perfons in ordinary cafes.

Three claufes.

* It is ftated in a note in the original, that the act of affembling in the public highways, is the particular circumftance of aggravation which diftinguifhes this offence from that of refifting, and refufing to admit the vifits of the officers of juftice and the revenue, in ordinary cafes, which, under the head of Fifcal Laws, has been already noticed.

SEC-

SECTION CCLXVIII. — *Robbing in open Day**.

All perfons found guilty of taking unlawful poffeffion of the property of others, in open day and by forcible means, fhall, however fmall the amount of the property fo taken, be punifhed with 100 blows and banifhment for three years.

If the value of the property in queftion is confiderable, it fhall be eftimated, and the punifhment of the offending parties fo far increafed, as to render it two degrees more fevere than it would have legally been, in a cafe of privately ftealing to a fimilar amount; but it fhall not in any cafe become capital, unlefs there are other aggravating circumftances.

When the individual plundered is likewife wounded, the principal offender fhall fuffer death, by being beheaded, after remaining during the ufual period in confinement.

The acceffaries to that fpecies of robbery which is in the contemplation of the law in this fection, fhall in all cafes be punifhed one degree lefs feverely than the principal offenders; and all the individuals concerned therein, principals as well as acceffaries, fhall be

* There is a perceptible difference in the meaning of the Chinefe expreffion at the head of this fection, and that at the head of fection CCLXVI., and which requires perhaps fome further explanation. It is ftated in a note in the original Chinefe, that although open violence is implied in the one inftance, as well as in the other, yet the former fection of the law is to be underftood to apply more particularly to thofe cafes, in which a number of perfons had, for the exprefs purpofe of committing a robbery, affembled together, and provided themfelves with offenfive weapons, all which circumftances of aggravation are in this latter fection fuppofed to be wanting; it is however added, that the magiftrates are not intended to be bound by this precife interpretation, but allowed to exercife a difcretionary power, in adopting the more or lefs fevere law, according as the circumftances of each particular cafe are, upon a general view, more or lefs atrocious.

The expreffion *open day* is alfo explained to imply nothing more than that the offence in queftion, is perpetrated openly, and without fear of obfervation.

branded

branded in the lower part of the left arm, with the words *Tſiang to* ſignifying robber.

All perſons who take an opportunity to plunder in a caſe of fire or ſhipwreck; or who, in the latter caſe, contribute in any manner to the deſtruction of the veſſel, ſhall be puniſhed according to this law.

Thoſe who, in the caſe of an affray, or upon the occaſion of their being authorized and employed by government in the purſuit and apprehenſion of offenders, take an opportunity of ſtealing, ſhall be puniſhed as in ordinary caſes of theft, unleſs they are guilty of uſing force, in which caſe the puniſhment ſhall be proportionately increaſed two degrees, but the parties ſhall not be branded for the offence, nor liable, under any circumſtances, except thoſe of killing or wounding the individual plundered, to ſuffer capital puniſhment.

Twenty-four clauſes.

Section CCLXIX. — *Stealing in general.*

All perſons found guilty of an attempt to ſteal, ſhall be puniſhed with 50 blows.

When a theft is actually committed, that is to ſay, poſſeſſion obtained of the property intended to be ſtolen, all the parties concerned, whether ſharers or not in the plunder, ſhall be puniſhed in proportion to the amount of the largeſt ſum ſtolen from any one individual, according to the ſubjoined ſcale: The principal offender in each caſe ſhall ſuffer the full puniſhment therein ſtated, and the reſt ſhall be puniſhed one degree leſs ſeverely as acceſſaries. It is likewiſe always to be underſtood, that the puniſhment ſhall be eſtimated, not according to the ſhare of the plunder which any one of the offenders may receive or obtain individually, but, as above ſtated, according to the total amount of the ſum which they had been jointly concerned in ſtealing from any one individual: for example, if ten perſons jointly ſtole to the amount of of 40 ounces of ſilver in value, they would, although their reſpective ſhares would not exceed four ounces in value, be liable to ſuffer the full puniſhment of ſtealing forty ounces of ſilver, ſuch being the value of the total amount ſtolen.

For the firſt offence, the individuals convicted of being concerned in a theft, ſhall be branded in the lower part of the left arm with the words *Tſie tao*, ſignifying thief; for the ſecond offence they ſhall be branded again with the ſame words, in the lower part of the right arm; for the third offence, or for having defaced the ſaid marks, they ſhall ſuffer death by being ſtrangled, after remaining the uſual period in confinement.

Value not exceeding	1 ounce of ſilver		60	blows with the bamboo.	
	10 ounces	-	70		
	20	- -	80		
	30	- -	90		
	40	- -	100		
	50	- -	60	blows and baniſhment for	1 year.
	60	- -	70		1½ year.
	70	- -	80		2 years.
	80	- -	90		2½ years.
	90	- -	100		3 years.
	100	- -	100	blows and perpetual baniſhment to diſtance of	2000 *lee*.
	110	- -	100		2500 *lee*.
	120	- -	100		3000 *lee*.
Value exceeding	120	- -		Death, by being ſtrangled, after the uſual confinement *.	

Thirty clauſes.

Section CCLXX. — *Stealing Horſes and other domeſticated Animals.*

All perſons found guilty of ſtealing the horſes, horned cattle, aſſes, mules, ſheep, fowls, dogs, geeſe, and ducks of private individuals,

* Although that part of the law in this place which ſtates, that a theft ſhall in certain caſes be puniſhed with death, does not appear to have been expreſsly repealed, there is every reaſon to believe that it is never enforced.

ſhall

ſhall ſuffer, conformably to a valuation of the animals ſtolen, the ordinary puniſhment of theft.

When the animals ſtolen are the property of government, the puniſhment of the offending party ſhall be the ſame as in other caſes of a theft of government-property to the ſame extent in value.

If any perſon ſteals a horſe or a cow, and afterwards kills the animal, he ſhall be puniſhed, at the leaſt, with 100 blows and three years baniſhment; if the animal ſtolen and killed is an aſs or a mule, the puniſhment ſhall not be leſs than 70 blows and baniſhment for a year and a half. In both caſes, when the value of the animals ſtolen and killed is conſiderable, they ſhall be eſtimated, and the puniſhment of the thief ſo far increaſed beyond that already provided, as to render it one degree more ſevere than that of an ordinary theft to the ſame extent in value.

Fourteen clauſes.

SECTION CCLXXI.—*Stealing Corn and other Produce in the open Field.*

All perſons found guilty of ſtealing any kind of grain, fruit, or vegetables growing in the open fields, and not cuſtomarily guarded by any perſon, or by any contrivance, ſhall be puniſhed according to the amount in value of the produce ſtolen, as in ordinary caſes of theft, except that the offenders ſhall not be branded *.

All perſons unauthorizedly taking away ſtones, timber, or bruſhwood, which although found in uncultivated places, had been cut or otherwiſe prepared for uſe, ſhall be puniſhed in the ſame manner as is above provided.

Twenty clauſes.

* When the fields in which a theft is committed are known to be uſually watched and guarded by the proprietor, the offence is more ſeverely puniſhable, according to a law in a preceding ſection, againſt "robbing in open day."

SEC-

SECTION CCLXXII. — *Stealing from Relations and Connections.*

All perfons found guilty of ftealing from a relation by blood, or by marriage, in the firft degree, fhall fuffer a punifhment five degrees lefs fevere than that which is legally inflicted in ordinary cafes of theft to the fame extent *.

In like manner, all perfons guilty of ftealing from relations, in the fecond degree, fhall fuffer a punifhment four degrees lefs fevere than that legally inflicted in ordinary cafes: — In the cafe of ftealing from relations in the third degree, the punifhment of the offenders fhall be three degrees lefs than in ordinary cafes: — In the cafe of ftealing from relations in the fourth degree, the punifhment fhall be two degrees lefs than in ordinary cafes: — and, laftly, the punifhment of ftealing from any relation, in a more remote degree than the aforefaid, fhall be but one degree lefs than in ordinary cafes.

In general the punifhment of the acceffaries fhall be one degree lefs fevere than that of the principals in each cafe; but regard is always to be had, at the fame time, to the relationfhip which fuch acceffary bears, and not merely to that which the principal offender bears, to the perfon upon whom the theft is committed.

Perfons ftealing from their relations fhall not, as other thieves, be fubject to be branded for their offences.

In cafes alfo of robbery among relations, that is to fay, a violent as well as unlawful feizure of the property of a relation; when an elder relation is the offending party, a reduction in the punifhment fhall be allowed, fimilar to that already provided in cafes of theft; but if the

* The mitigation of punifhment provided by this law, in confideration of circumftances, which at firft view appear to aggravate the guilt of the offender, is in fact eafily reconciled with the general fpirit of the code; as according to the Chinefe patriarchal fyftem, a theft is not in this cafe a violation of an exclufive right, but only of the *qualified* intereft, which each individual has in his fhare of the family property.

offending

offending party is a junior relation, the puniſhment ſhall be the ſame as is inflicted in the ordinary caſes of the commiſſion of the ſame offence.

If the robbery is accompanied by the additional crime of killing or wounding the relation who is plundered, the offender ſhall ſuffer for the aſſault, or for the robbery, according as the one or other offence proves, under all the circumſtances of the caſe, the moſt ſeverely puniſhable.

If the junior of two relations reſiding together under the ſame roof, introduces a ſtranger to ſteal the property of his elder relation, he ſhall ſuffer a puniſhment two degrees more ſevere than that provided by law, for uſing and conſuming, without permiſſion, an equal amount of the joint family property, in ordinary caſes *; but the puniſhment of a relation in this caſe, ſhall never be ſo far increaſed, as to exceed 100 blows. — The ſtranger thus introduced to ſteal, ſhall be puniſhed one degree leſs ſeverely than in ordinary caſes of ſtealing, and not be branded.

If hired ſervants or ſlaves ſteal from their maſters, or from each other, the puniſhment ſhall be one degree leſs ſevere than in ordinary caſes of theft, and the thief ſhall not be branded †.

Five clauſes.

SECTION CCLXXIII. — *Extorting Property by Threats.*

All perſons who are guilty of extorting from any individual his property, by the uſe of threatening language, ſhall be puniſhed one

* See Section LXXXVIII., under the head of Fiſcal Laws.

† Notwithſtanding the tenor of the laſt paragraph of this article, it is provided in one of the ſupplementary clauſes, that the puniſhment of ſlaves guilty of theft, ſhall be, at the leaſt, equal to that of thieves in general, and one degree more ſevere, when the offence is committed by them, in combination with ſtrangers.

degree

degree more ſeverely than in ordinary caſes of theft to the ſame amount, but ſhall not be branded.

A junior relation extorting the property of his ſenior by threats, ſhall be puniſhed in the ſame degree, as if there had been no relationſhip whatever between the parties; but a ſenior relation guilty of extorting by threats, the property of his junior, ſhall have the full advantage of the mitigation of puniſhment which the law allows in ordinary caſes of pecuniary differences between relations.

Eight clauſes.

Section CCLXXIV. — *Obtaining Property under falſe Pretences.*

All perſons obtaining public or private property, by any fraudulent means, or upon falſe pretences, ſhall be puniſhed with the ſame degree of ſeverity, as if guilty of ſtealing, to an equal amount, and under ſimilar circumſtances in other reſpects, but ſhall not be branded.

In all caſes of a ſenior relation defrauding his junior, or a junior his ſenior, the puniſhment ſhall be as much leſs than in ordinary caſes of fraud, as under circumſtances of relationſhip, in inſtances of theft and other offences of a ſimilar nature, has been already ſtated and provided.

When two or more perſons are jointly intruſted with the cuſtody of government or public property; if one of them fraudulently and upon falſe pretences, obtains from the reſt, any part thereof for his own uſe, he ſhall be puniſhed in the ſame manner as if he had been an embezzler to a ſimilar amount of the public property under his own individual cuſtody.

When the offence amounts to an attempt only, the puniſhment ſhall in each of the ſeveral caſes, be leſs than is above provided, by two degrees.

In general, whenever any ſpecies of property is fraudulently obtained, whether by aſſerting falſely a claim to it, by deceiving the owner by a fabricated ſtory, or by prevailing on the owner to truſt the property on any pretence out of his poſſeſſion, it ſhall be deemed an offence againſt this law, and puniſhed accordingly.

Six clauſes.

SECTION CCLXXV.—*Kidnapping, or the unlawful Seizure and Sale of free Perſons.*

All perſons who are guilty of entrapping by means of ſtratagems, or of enticing away under falſe pretences, a free perſon, and of afterwards offering for ſale as a ſlave ſuch free perſon, ſhall, whether conſidered as principals or as acceſſaries, and whether ſucceſsful or not, in effecting ſuch intended ſale, be ſeverally puniſhed with 100 blows, and baniſhed perpetually to the diſtance of 3000 *lee*.

All thoſe who are guilty of entrapping, or enticing away any perſons in the manner aforeſaid, in order to ſell them as principal or inferior wives, or for adoption, as children or grand-children, ſhall, if conſidered as principals, be puniſhed with 100 blows, and three years baniſhment.

When the perſon who is attempted to be entrapped or enticed away, reſiſts, and is wounded, the offender againſt this law ſhall ſuffer death, by being ſtrangled, after the uſual period of confinement.

When ſuch perſon, in conſequence of having reſiſted, is killed, the offender ſhall ſuffer death, by being beheaded, after the uſual confinement.

In all of the preceding caſes, except the firſt, the puniſhment of the acceſſaries ſhall be leſs ſevere than that of their reſpective principals, by one degree.

The

The perſons kidnapped, or attempted to be kidnapped, ſhall not in any of the aforeſaid caſes be liable to any puniſhment, but ſhall be reſtored without delay to their reſpective families.

All ſuch perſons alſo, as receive the children of free parents, upon the faith of a promiſe to educate and adopt them as their own, and nevertheleſs ſell them afterwards to others, ſhall be puniſhable according to this law, except in thoſe caſes in which it can be proved that a pecuniary conſideration was given and received in the firſt inſtance.

When the perſons enticed away, had not been deceived by any falſe pretences, but had yielded themſelves up voluntarily, thoſe who, under ſuch circumſtances, ſell them as ſlaves, ſhall be puniſhed with 100 blows, and three years baniſhment. Thoſe who, under the ſame circumſtances, ſell ſuch perſons, as principal or inferior wives, or for adoption, as children or grand-children, ſhall be puniſhed with 90 blows, and baniſhed for two years and a half.

The perſons who thus voluntarily ſubmit themſelves to be ſold, ſhall be puniſhed likewiſe; and their puniſhment ſhall be but one degree leſs ſevere than that of thoſe who ſell them.

When the ſale of a perſon willing to be ſold, is propoſed, but not completed, the puniſhment of the ſeveral parties to the offence, ſhall be reſpectively leſs ſevere than in the caſe of an actual ſale, by one degree.

When the perſons kidnapped or enticed away are under ten years of age, they ſhall not be deemed capable of conſenting thereto, and therefore held innocent of any participation in the offence of the kidnappers, who, under ſuch circumſtances, ſhall always ſuffer puniſhment according to the ſeverer law.

The offence of entrapping and carrying off for ſale, or perſuading to come away voluntarily for the ſame purpoſe, the lawful ſlave of any perſon, ſhall be puniſhed one degree leſs ſeverely than that of kidnapping a free perſon under ſimilar circumſtances.

 Any

Any perſon who ſells his children or grand-children againſt their conſent, ſhall be puniſhed with 80 blows *.

Any perſon who in like manner ſells his younger brother or ſiſter, his nephew or niece, his own inferior wife, or the principal wife of his ſon, or his grandſon, ſhall be puniſhed with 80 blows, and two years baniſhment: — the puniſhment inflicted for the ſale of the inferior wife of a ſon or grandſon, ſhall be leſs ſevere than that laſt mentioned by two degrees. Whoever, laſtly, ſells his junior firſt couſin, junior ſecond couſin, or his grand-nephew, in the manner aforeſaid, ſhall be puniſhed with 90 blows, and baniſhed for two years and a half.

When, in any of the preceding caſes, the ſale had been effected with the free conſent of the party ſold, the puniſhment of the ſeller ſhall be leſs ſevere by one degree. In general alſo, when an unlawful ſale is only proved to have been propoſed, the puniſhment ſhall always be one degree leſs ſevere, than it would have been in the caſe of ſuch ſale having actually taken place.

The children, or junior relations, although conſenting to be thus unlawfully ſold, ſhall not in any caſe be liable to puniſhment for ſuch conſent, in conſideration of the obedience which is always due from them to their ſenior relations, and they ſhall therefore ſimply be reſtored, upon conviction, to their families.

Any perſon who is guilty of ſelling his firſt wife, or any relation of his in a more remote degree than thoſe already ſpecified, ſhall ſuffer

* Although it would appear from this reſtriction, that the power of a parent over his child, according to this code, is much leſs extenſive than that allowed by the laws of the ancient Romans, yet as the adoption of children, and the purchaſe of inferior wives or concubines, is a tranſaction of conſtant occurrence, and one in which the real parents lawfully may, and uſually do, receive a pecuniary conſideration, it can ſcarcely be denied that the ſale of children in China, is practically allowed. — The crime of infanticide, the exiſtence of which has been ſo often alleged as a ſtain upon the national character of the Chineſe, as well as upon their laws and government, will be noticed in another place. See Section CCCXIX.

the

the unabated punifhment of feizing and felling free perfons in ordinary cafes.

If the harbourers, and purchafers of the perfons kidnapped, are aware of the unlawfulnefs of the tranfaction, they fhall fuffer equal punifhment with the kidnappers, excepting only the ufual reduction of one degree in the punifhment of participators in offences, in capital cafes.

The perfon who becomes a party to the tranfaction, by making himfelf anfwerable that the fale fhall be completed, fhall, (if aware of its unlawfulnefs, and not otherwife) be punifhed one degree lefs feverely than the principal offender. — When the purchafer is thus a participator in the offence committed, the pecuniary confideration given to the feller fhall be forfeited to government, but otherwife fhall be reftored to the purchafer, in confequence of the fale being null and void *.

Fourteen claufes.

SECTION CCLXXVI. — *Difturbing Graves.*

All perfons guilty of digging in, and breaking up another man's burying-ground, until at length one of the coffins which had been depofited therein, is laid bare and becomes vifible, fhall be punifhed with 100 blows, and perpetual banifhment to the diftance of 3000 *lee.*

Any perfon who, after having been guilty as aforefaid, proceeds to open the coffin, and uncover the corpfe laid therein, fhall be punifhed

* From the length of this fection, and alfo from fome of the obfervations contained in the official report of the charges againft the governor of Canton (fee Appendix, No. X.) it is certainly to be inferred, that the abufes here adverted to, are not unfrequent. It is to be obferved, indeed, that the flavery which is recognized and tolerated by the laws of China, is a mild fpecies of fervitude, and perhaps not very degrading in a country, in which no condition of life appears to admit of any confiderable degree of perfonal liberty and independence.

nifhed with death, by being ftrangled, after undergoing the ufual confinement *.

Thofe who are guilty of digging in, and breaking up a burying-ground, but do not proceed fo far as to expofe any of the coffins, fhall be punifhed with 100 blows, and three years banifhment.

Thofe who on fuch occafions practice incantations, in order to call up the fpirit from the grave, fhall be confidered as acceffaries, and accordingly punifhed one degree lefs feverely than the principals.

The offence of ftealing a coffin from an old grave or burying-place, which had fallen in, or was broken down, as well as that of ftealing a coffin from above ground, fhall be punifhed only with 90 blows, and banifhment for two years and a half.

Breaking open an unburied coffin, and expofing the body to fight, is nominally a capital offence, but the punifhment fhall be limited to five years banifhment.

The offence of ftealing bricks, ftones, or other articles, from a burying-ground, fhall be punifhed according to the value of the articles ftolen, as in ordinary cafes of theft, but the offenders fhall not be branded.

A junior relation within the degrees of mourning, breaking up the grave of his elder relation, fhall be punifhed as in the ordinary cafes of the offence above ftated: but if he opens the coffin to fee the body, he fhall be beheaded, after remaining in prifon the ufual period. If he cafts away the corpfe, and fells the ground, he fhall be punifhed in the fame manner. — The purchafer of the ground and the negociator of the fale, if privy to the breach of the laws, fhall be punifhed each with 80 blows. The land fhall be reftored to the family, and the pur-

* This very long article, in fome of the provifions of which there is an apparent inconfiftency, is evidently connected with certain fuperftitious notions and practices of the Chinefe, and probably may alfo have been requifite to protect even the dead, from the vengeance and from the rapacity of the living.

chafe-chaſe-money ſhall be forfeited, but all ſuch of the relations as were not privy to the tranſaction ſhall be held to be exempt from reſponſibility.

An elder relation in the fourth degree, breaking up the grave and opening the coffin of his junior, ſhall be puniſhed with 100 blows, and three years baniſhment. In the caſe of any nearer elder relation, the puniſhment ſhall be leſs ſevere by one degree. — A father breaking up the grave, and opening the coffin, of his ſon, or a grand-father that of his grand-ſon, ſhall be puniſhed with 80 blows. — Nevertheleſs, if, in any of the preceding caſes, the grave be broken open upon a ſufficient cauſe, and the coffin removed with all due rites and ceremonies, the parties ſhall not be puniſhable. — Deſtroying, mutilating, or throwing into the water the unencloſed and unburied corpſe of a ſtranger, is an offence puniſhable with 100 blows, and perpetual baniſhment to the diſtance of 3000 *lee*.

The offence of deſtroying, mutilating, or caſting away, the unburied corpſe of an elder relation, ſhall be puniſhed with death, by being beheaded, after the uſual period of confinement.

The puniſhment in the two laſt mentioned caſes ſhall be reduced one degree, if the injury done to the corpſe amounts only to the loſs of the hair, or if the corpſe, after being caſt away, is found again.

If the offence is committed by an elder, inſtead of a junior relation, the puniſhment ſhall be one degree leſs ſevere, than in ordinary caſes.

If a father deſtroys or caſts away the corpſe of his ſon, or a grandfather that of his grandſon, he ſhall be puniſhed with 80 blows.

But if a ſon deſtroys or caſts away the corpſe of his father or mother, a grandſon that of his grandfather or grandmother; a ſlave or hired ſervant that of his maſter, they ſhall in each caſe, whether the corpſe ſo caſt away is afterwards recovered or not, be beheaded after the uſual period of confinement.

If

If any perſon in digging the earth ſhould diſcover an unclaimed body, and not immediately bury it, he ſhall be puniſhed with 80 blows.

If any perſon having lighted a fire on the grave of a ſtranger to drive away foxes by the ſmoke, ſuffers the fire to communicate, ſo as in any manner to burn the coffin depoſited underneath, he ſhall be puniſhed with 80 blows, and two years baniſhment; but if the body is likewiſe conſumed, the puniſhment ſhall be increaſed to 100 blows, and three years baniſhment;—if the party offending is a junior relation, the puniſhment ſhall be increaſed one degree; if a ſenior, abated one degree.

If a ſon, lighting a fire on the grave of his father or of his mother, for the aforeſaid purpoſe; a grandſon, on the grave of his grandfather or grandmother, a ſlave or hired ſervant, on that of his maſter, thereby burns the coffin, they ſhall, in each caſe, be puniſhed with 100 blows, and three years baniſhment. If the body is burned likewiſe, they ſhall be ſtrangled, after remaining in confinement during the uſual period.

Any perſon who levels the burying-place of a ſtranger, in order to convert the ground to the purpoſes of agriculture, ſhall, although none of the coffins ſhall have been diſturbed, be puniſhed with 100 blows, and obliged to replace every thing in its former condition.

Any perſon who privately buries a corpſe in another man's ground, ſhall be puniſhed with 80 blows, and alſo be obliged to remove ſuch corpſe within a limited period.

Whenever an unclaimed corpſe is found in any diſtrict or village, if the head or preſiding inhabitant thereof, inſtead of reporting the ſame, in order that the corpſe may be examined by the proper magiſtrate, of his own accord removes or buries it, he ſhall be puniſhed with 80 blows; if the body is in conſequence loſt, he ſhall be puniſhed with 100 blows.

If

If the body is deſtroyed or caſt into the water, the principal in the commiſſion of ſuch an offence ſhall be puniſhed with 60 blows, and one year's baniſhment. If the perſon who contrives, likewiſe carries the deſign into effect, he ſhall be baniſhed perpetually. If the body is caſt away, but not loſt; or is injured, but entire, the puniſhment ſhall be reduced one degree.

Stealing the clothes belonging to a dead body, ſhall be puniſhed according to their value, as an ordinary caſe of theft, but the offender ſhall not be branded.

Thirteen clauſes.

SECTION CCLXXVII. — *Unauthorizedly entering a Dwelling-houſe by Night.*

All perſons who unauthorizedly, and without lawful cauſe, enter the dwelling-houſe of a ſtranger by night, ſhall be puniſhable, at the leaſt, with 80 blows. — If the maſter of the houſe at the moment of any ſuch perſon entering, kills him, he ſhall not be puniſhed for doing ſo; but if after having ſeized ſuch perſon, he then kills or wounds him without neceſſity, he ſhall be puniſhed but two degrees leſs ſeverely than is provided by law in caſes of killing or wounding in an affray; the puniſhment ſhall not however in any caſe exceed 100 blows, and three years baniſhment.

One clauſe.

SECTION CCLXXVIII. — *Harbouring Thieves and Robbers.*

Whenever any perſons who are harbourers of robbers; that is to ſay, maſters and proprietors of the cuſtomary habitations and retreating places of robbers, are diſcovered and found guilty of having likewiſe in

 any

any inſtance contrived a robbery, and of having afterwards participated in the booty thereof, they ſhall, although they had not perſonally aſſiſted in the perpetration of the crime, be beheaded as principals.

It has already been provided by a preceding article of the laws, that all thoſe who perſonally aſſiſt in the perpetration of a robbery, ſhall, without making any diſtinction between principals and acceſſaries, be indiſcriminately beheaded. When, however, the contriver of a robbery, and harbourer of robbers, neither gives any aſſiſtance in effecting the robbery nor participates in the plunder after it is obtained, he ſhall be puniſhed only with 100 blows, and perpetual baniſhment to the diſtance of 3000 *lee*.

If the harbourer of the robbers, though not a contriver of the robbery, is privy to the deſign, and either accompanies the robbers without participating in the booty, or participates in the booty without accompanying the robbers, he ſhall be beheaded, without any diſtinction being made between the caſes of principals and thoſe of acceſſaries.

If, in the laſt caſe, the harbourer of robbers neither accompanies them, nor participates in their plunder, he ſhall be puniſhed with 100 blows only.

All harbourers of thieves, who contrive a theft, and afterwards receive a ſhare of the booty, ſhall be puniſhed as principals in ſuch theft, although they had not been perſonally engaged therein. If the plan is contrived at the moment previous to execution, the leader only ſhall be eſteemed a principal, and the harbourer of the thief an acceſſary; he ſhall likewiſe be deemed no more than an acceſſary, if he aſſiſts in obtaining without partaking of, or partakes of without aſſiſting in obtaining, the plunder. If the harbourer of the thief neither aſſiſts in obtaining, nor partakes of the plunder when obtained, his puniſhment ſhall be limited 40 blows.

If a number of individuals, meeting without any previous deliberation or contrivance, commit a theft or a robbery, the propoſer and leader

leader ſhall, in the caſe of a theft be eſteemed the principal, and the reſt only acceſſaries; but in the caſe of a robbery, no diſtinction ſhall be made, and accordingly, all the offenders puniſhed alike.

All perſons participating in property known to have been obtained by robbery or theft, or in any ſum received as the purchaſe-money of a free perſon unlawfully ſold, ſhall, at the leaſt, be puniſhed as acceſſaries to a theft to the ſame amount, but ſhall not be branded.

The offence of purchaſing goods knowing them to have been ſtolen, ſhall be puniſhed as an ordinary caſe of pecuniary malverſation or unlawful acquiſition of property.

Any perſon who, knowing any article of property to have been ſtolen, nevertheleſs conſents to take charge of it, ſhall be puniſhed one degree leſs ſeverely than an unlawful purchaſer. When, however, ſuch purchaſer and ſuch conſignee of ſtolen property, in any caſe are ignorant of its having been unlawfully acquired, they ſhall not be eſteemed guilty, or anywiſe puniſhable, merely in conſequence of their being implicated in a charge againſt others.

Seventeen clauſes.

SECTION CCLXXIX. — *Rules by which the Acceſſaries to a Theft, and the Acceſſaries to a Robbery are diſtinguiſhed.*

In all caſes of perſons concurring in a deſign to commit a robbery, if any of them do not afterwards actively engage therein, or only ſo far, as to commit a theft; and if the original contriver of the plan, although a partaker of the booty, is one of theſe, he ſhall be puniſhed only as a principal in a theft. Thoſe who, though they aſſiſted therein, neither contrived the criminal enterpriſe, nor participated in the plunder, ſhall (except the leader, who ſhall ſtill be deemed a principal) be eſteemed acceſſaries; as alſo thoſe who merely contrived the criminal enterpriſe, without either partaking of, or aſſiſting in obtaining, the plunder.

All the others, who merely concurred in the firſt deſign, without having been the contrivers of it, aſſiſting to carry it into execution, or profiting by it afterwards upon a diviſion of the plunder, ſhall be puniſhed with 50 blows each.

In caſes of perſons concurring in a deſign to commit a theft, if any of them in purſuance thereof, commit a robbery inſtead of a theft, the contriver of the original plan, although a partaker of the plunder, ſhall, if not an agent in obtaining it, be puniſhed only as a principal in a theft, ſimilar in amount to the robbery; and the other partakers, not being agents or contrivers, ſhall be puniſhed as acceſſaries thereto. But all thoſe who were actively engaged in the robbery, ſhall be puniſhed as principals in ſuch robbery, whether or not contrivers thereof, and whether participators or not in the booty.

No clauſe.

Section CCLXXX. — *What conſtitutes a Theft or Robbery, and what an Attempt only.*

In general an open and violent taking, conſtitutes a robbery, and a private and concealed taking, a theft; but the attempt is to be diſtinguiſhed from the accompliſhment of the criminal purpoſe, differently in different caſes, in the following manner: — In caſes of ſtrings of copper-money, utenſils, and other eaſily moveable articles of that deſcription, poſſeſſion muſt not only be obtained, but they muſt have been removed out of the place or apartment in which they were found, otherwiſe a theft or robbery of ſuch articles is only to be conſidered as having been attempted. In the caſe of pearls or precious ſtones, and other ſmall and valuable articles,

articles, it is ſufficient that they are found on the perſon of the offender. On the contrary, in the caſe of large heavy articles of wood or ſtone, which the unaſſiſted ſtrength of man is not adequate to remove to any diſtance, they muſt not only have been diſplaced, but actually lifted upon the cart, or on the animal, provided for their removal.

In reſpect to horſes, aſſes, mules, and cows, they muſt have been taken out of the ſtable; and alſo in reſpect to dogs, hawks, and animals of the like kind, there muſt have been ſome evidence of exertion on the part of the offender to make himſelf maſter of them, and of their having been, in conſequence of ſuch exertion, actually in his poſſeſſion; thus, if one horſe is ſtolen, and the reſt follow, the thief is not reſponſible for more than the theft of one horſe; but if he ſteals a mare, and the foal follows, his offence is to be deemed a theft of both the mare and the foal.

Theſe obſervations are applicable to all the preceding caſes in this book. In general, when there are circumſtances to trace, and witneſſes to give evidence of the overt act, but not of any actual poſſeſſion of the goods, the offence ſhall always be puniſhed as an attempt only. When actual poſſeſſion is proved, the theft or robbery ſhall then be conſidered to have been completely carried into effect, and puniſhed accordingly.

No clauſe.

SECTION CCLXXXI. — *Defacing or deſtroying the Marks with which Thieves had been branded.*

All convicted thieves are in ordinary caſes branded with appropriate characters, as a warning to others, and a reproach to themſelves, the impreſſion

impreſſion of which it is equally neceſſary to preſerve undefaced, whether the offenders are permitted to return to their diſtricts immediately after receiving a corporal puniſhment, condemned to undergo temporary baniſhment, or exiled perpetually. Therefore, when guilty of defacing the characters, ſo as to render them illegible, they ſhall be puniſhed with 60 blows, and the characters ſhall be branded anew.

Fifteen clauſes.

END OF THE FIRST BOOK OF THE SIXTH DIVISION.

BOOK II.

HOMICIDE.

SECTION CCLXXXII. — *Preconcerted Homicide; Murder* *.

IN every caſe of perſons preconcerting the crime of homicide, whether with or without a deſign, againſt the life of a particular individual, the original contriver ſhall ſuffer death, by being beheaded, after the uſual period of confinement. All the acceſſaries to the contrivance, who likewiſe contribute to the perpetration of the preconcerted homicide or murder, ſhall ſuffer death, by being ſtrangled, after being confined until the uſual period.

The other acceſſaries not actually contributing to the perpetration of the murder, ſhall be puniſhed with 100 blows, and perpetual baniſhment to the diſtance of 3000 *lee*. In theſe caſes, ſentence is not to be pronounced finally, until the deceaſe of the perſon mortally wounded.

When the wounds inflicted in conſequence of a previous deſign to commit murder, do not prove mortal, the original contriver of the deed ſhall be ſtrangled, after remaining in confinement the uſual period. The acceſſaries contributing to the perpetration, ſhall be puniſhed with 100 blows, and perpetual baniſhment to the diſtance of 3000 *lee*. The other acceſſaries ſhall be puniſhed with 100 blows, and three years baniſhment.

* The diſtinguiſhing character of the crime which is the ſubject of this ſection, appears to be *previous contrivance*. In reſpect to the crime of *killing*, *with an intent to kill*, noticed in Section CCXC, every idea of combination is there excluded, and the deſign is ſuppoſed to have originated at the moment, or nearly ſo, of its execution.

When

When a homicide has been preconcerted as aforefaid, but no blow ftruck, the original contriver fhall be punifhed with 100 blows and three years banifhment: — the acceffaries to fuch contrivance fhall be each punifhed with 100 blows.

The original contriver fhall fuffer punifhment as a principal, though not otherwife contributing in any manner to carry the defign into effect; but the acceffaries to the contrivance who are not guilty of any fubfequent overt act, fhall fuffer punifhment lefs by one degree than thofe of the acceffaries, who acted in fome refpects upon the contrivance, although they did not perfonally contribute to the perpetration of the deed.

Thofe who commit murder for the fake of plunder fhall, as in the cafe of a robbery, all of them be beheaded, without any diftinction whatever between principals and acceffaries.

Eight claufes *.

Section CCLXXXIII. — *Murder of an Officer of Government.*

When an ordinary officer of government is guilty of defigning to kill an officer invefted with peculiar or extraordinary powers by the Emperor; when a private inhabitant of a diftrict is guilty of defigning to kill the governor or fupreme officer of the fame; when a private foldier is guilty of defigning to kill his commanding officer; and, laftly, when an official attendant of a public office or tribunal, is guilty of defigning to kill an officer of the fifth, or any fuperior rank: — in all thefe cafes, if the individual entertaining fuch criminal defign and contrivance, is the original contriver, he fhall, though a blow had not been ftruck in execution thereof, be punifhed with 100 blows, and banifhment to the diftance of 2000 *lee*. If a blow is ftruck, fo as more or lefs to wound, the principal offender fhall be ftrangled; if

* A tranflation of thefe claufes is contained in the Appendix, No. XXIX.

the

the murder is actually perpetrated, all the parties thereto ſhall be beheaded. In the other caſes the puniſhment of acceſſaries ſhall be one degree leſs ſevere than that of their reſpective principals. All perſons not holding offices or rank under government, when capitally convicted under this law, ſhall be executed immediately; but the execution of officers of government ſhall not take place till after the uſual period of confinement.

Acceſſaries to the contrivance, who are not guilty of any ſubſequent overt act; attendants of tribunals and public offices, guilty of deſigning to kill an officer of government of the ſixth or any inferior rank; and, laſtly, private inhabitants or ſoldiers, guilty of deſigning to kill any officers to whoſe juriſdiction they are not ſubject, ſhall only be puniſhed as in ordinary caſes *.

No clauſe.

Section CCLXXXIV. — *Parricide.*

Any perſon convicted of a deſign to kill his or her father or mother, grand-father or grand-mother, whether by the father's or mother's ſide; and any woman convicted of a deſign to kill her huſband, huſband's father or mother, grand-father or grand-mother, ſhall, whether a blow is, or is not ſtruck in conſequence, ſuffer death by being beheaded. In puniſhing this criminal deſign, no diſtinction ſhall be made between principals and acceſſaries, except as far as regards their reſpective relationſhips to the perſon againſt whoſe life the deſign is entertained. If the murder is committed, all the parties concerned therein, and related to the deceaſed as above-mentioned, ſhall ſuffer

* That is to ſay, in caſes of a deſign to kill a ſtranger and an equal, under circumſtances which are not legally conſidered either to palliate or to aggravate the guilt of ſuch deſign.—The meaning however of an expreſſion which occurs ſo frequently, muſt already have been apparent to the reader from the context.

death

death by a ſlow and painful execution. If the criminal ſhould die in priſon, an execution ſimilar in mode ſhall take place on his body. The acceſſaries more diſtantly related, ſhall be puniſhed according to the law particularly applicable to the caſes of perſons ſo related; and thoſe acceſſaries who are not related at all, ſhall be puniſhed as ſimilar offenders would be in ordinary caſes.

The principal in a deſign to kill any other ſenior relation within the four degrees of connexion and conſanguinity, ſhall, if no blow is ſtruck, be puniſhed with 100 blows, and perpetual baniſhment to the diſtance of 2000 *lee*. The acceſſaries to a deſign to kill a perſon ſo related to them, ſhall be puniſhed with 100 blows, and three years baniſhment. If a blow is ſtruck ſo as to wound, the principal ſhall be ſtrangled, and the reſt puniſhed in the degree and proportion provided in ordinary caſes. If the intended murder is actually committed, all ſuch of the principals and acceſſaries, as are related as above deſcribed, to the deceaſed, ſhall be beheaded.

The puniſhment of entertaining a deſign to kill a junior relation within any of the aforeſaid degrees of connexion or conſanguinity, ſhall be two degrees leſs ſevere than that elſewhere provided in the caſe of killing with an intent to kill, ſuch junior relation. The puniſhment of wounding with an intent to kill, ſuch junior relation, ſhall be leſs ſevere than that of killing, by one degree; when the murder is actually perpetrated, the puniſhment ſhall be the ſame as that already ſtated to have been elſewhere provided *.

Any ſlave or hired ſervant deſigning to murder, or murdering his or her maſter, or any relation of his or her maſter, living under the ſame roof, ſhall be liable to the ſame puniſhment as has been provided in the caſe of a ſon or grandſon being guilty of ſuch a criminal act or deſign.

Five clauſes.

* See Section CCCXVII. in the following book, entitled, "Quarrelling and Fighting."

SEC-

Section CCLXXXV.—*Killing an Adulterer.*

When a principal or inferior wife is diſcovered by her huſband in the act of adultery, if ſuch huſband at the very time that he diſcovers, kills the adulterer, or adultereſs, or both, he ſhall not be puniſhable. If in ſuch a caſe, he does not kill the adultereſs, ſhe ſhall be puniſhed according to the law applicable thereto, and afterwards ſold in marriage. The money paid for her, ſhall be a forfeiture to government.

If there had not been an actual commiſſion of adultery, but only ſuch an intercourſe as implied a deſign to commit that crime; or if the adulterer and adultereſs had ſurrendered themſelves to the huſband; or if, laſtly, they had removed from the apartment where the adultery had been committed, the huſband who kills either of the guilty parties under any ſuch circumſtances, ſhall not be juſtified or protected by this law.

If the guilty wife ſhall contrive with the adulterer to procure the death of her huſband, ſhe ſhall ſuffer death by a ſlow and painful execution, and the adulterer ſhall be beheaded.—If the adulterer kills the huſband, without the knowledge or connivance of the wife, ſhe ſhall ſuffer death by being ſtrangled.

Twenty-five clauſes.

Section CCLXXXVI.—*Widows killing their deceaſed Huſband's Relations.*

If any widow, whether married or not to a ſecond huſband, is guilty of killing her deceaſed huſband's father, mother, grand-father or grand-mother, ſhe ſhall ſuffer the ſame puniſhment as if guilty of killing the ſaid relations, while ſuch huſband was ſtill living;

 the

the caſe of widows who had been divorced from their former huſbands, is the only one in which this law ſhall not take effect.

A ſervant or ſlave killing the perſon who had been, but was no longer his maſter, ſhall only be puniſhed as in ordinary caſes of murder, except in the inſtance of a ſlave who had been manumitted by his maſter; where, the party being bound by ſuch an obligation, ſhall be liable to the aggravated puniſhment, which is applicable to the caſe of ſlaves killing their maſters, and is elſewhere provided.

No clauſe.

SECTION CCLXXXVII. — *Murder of three or more Perſons in one Family.*

Any perſon who is guilty of killing, by previous contrivance, intentionally but without premeditation, or in the courſe of a robbery or houſe burning three or more perſons, whereof none were guilty of capital offences, and all of whom were relations in the firſt degree, or inmates of one family; and alſo any perſon who is guilty of mangling and dividing the limbs, and thus in a cruel and revengeful manner killing any individual, ſhall, when convicted of being a principal offender, ſuffer death by a ſlow and painful execution. The property of ſuch principal offender ſhall be forfeited to the uſe of the ſuffering family, and his wives and children ſhall be baniſhed perpetually to the diſtance of 2000 *lee*. Acceſſaries, contributing to the perpetration of the crime, ſhall be beheaded. The other acceſſaries ſhall be puniſhed as acceſſaries in ordinary caſes of murder. Where the original deſign had been to kill one perſon only, but from any ſubſequent cauſe three or more are killed, the original contriver, if not contributing to the execution, ſhall be beheaded; and the individual who firſt propoſed upon the ſpot, the killing of three or more perſons, ſhall be executed as the principal, agreeably to this law.

Twelve clauſes.

SEC-

SECTION CCLXXXVIII. — *Murder, with an Intent to mangle and divide the Body of the deceaſed, for Magical Purpoſes.*

The principal in the crime of murdering, or of attempting to murder any perſon, with a deſign afterwards to mangle the body and divide the limbs of the deceaſed, for magical purpoſes, ſhall ſuffer death by a ſlow and painful execution. His wives, ſons, and all the other inmates of his houſe, although innocent of the crime, ſhall be perpetually baniſhed to the diſtance of 2000 *lee*. — The acceſſaries contributing to the perpetration of this crime ſhall be beheaded, and the other acceſſaries who neither contributed thereto, nor were inmates of the houſe in which the principal offender reſided, ſhall be puniſhed as acceſſaries in ordinary caſes of murder *.

If the crime had been contrived, but no perſons killed or wounded in order to carry it into effect, the principal offender ſhall be beheaded; and his wives and ſons baniſhed perpetually to the diſtance of 2000 *lee*. The acceſſaries contributing to any overt act, ſhall be puniſhed with 100 blows, and perpetual baniſhment to the diſtance of 3000 *lee*. The other acceſſaries ſhall ſuffer the laſt mentioned puniſhment reduced one degree.

The head inhabitant of the village or diſtrict, when privy to the commiſſion of, or the deſign to commit this crime, and not giving information thereof, ſhall be puniſhed with 100 blows; but if really ignorant thereof, he ſhall not be liable to any puniſhment. All perſons giving information by which ſuch offenders are brought to juſtice, ſhall receive from government a reward of twenty ounces of ſilver.

One clauſe.

* As this law is only followed by one ſupplementary clauſe or ſtatute, it is probable, that the attention of the government has not been frequently drawn to ſuperſtitious and ſanguinary practices of the above deſcription; but the caſe does not appear to be altogether an imaginary one, as two perſons are recorded in a note in the original, to have been capitally convicted under this law, in the 14th year of *Kien-lung*.

SEC-

SECTION CCLXXXIX. — *Rearing venomous Animals, and preparing Poiſons.*

All perſons rearing venomous animals, or preparing drugs of a poiſonous nature, for the purpoſe of applying the ſame to the deſtruction of man, or inſtructing others ſo to do, ſhall be beheaded, although no perſon is actually killed by means of ſuch drugs or animals. The property of the perſon guilty of this crime, ſhall be forfeited to government, and his wives and children, as well as the other inmates of his houſe, although innocent of the crime, ſhall be perpetually baniſhed to the diſtance of 2000 *lee* *.

The relations and inmates of any family in which an individual has been poiſoned by ſuch drugs or animals, ſhall not be liable to be ſent into baniſhment, unleſs privy to the circumſtances which led to his death.

The head inhabitant of the village or diſtrict, when privy to, and failing to give information of this crime, ſhall ſuffer a puniſhment of 100 blows; but if really ignorant thereof, he ſhall be excuſed. Perſons giving the requiſite information ſhall receive from government a reward of 20 ounces of ſilver.

All perſons guilty of uſing magical writings and imprecations with a view to endeavour to occaſion the death of any perſon therewith, ſhall ſuffer the puniſhment of contriving a murder in ordinary caſes. If any perſon is killed by means of ſuch proceedings, the offending parties ſhall be puniſhed as in the caſe of a contrived murder, actually carried into effect. All perſons uſing ſuch magical writings and imprecations, in order to produce diſeaſe and infirmity in any individual, ſhall ſuffer a puniſhment leſs by two degrees than that above provided; except

* It is probably ſuppoſed that the relations of the criminal, although innocent of the particular crimes imputed to him, muſt have been familiarized to, and acquainted with his art, and that therefore they ought to be baniſhed, as dangerous members of ſociety.

in

in the caſe of a child againſt his parent, a grand-child againſt his grand-father or grand-mother, or a ſlave or hired ſervant againſt his maſter, each of whom for ſuch an offence ſhall be beheaded.

In general, all perſons guilty of poiſoning with drugs, ſhall be beheaded. If in any caſe the poiſon ſhall have been adminiſtered without proving mortal, the offender ſhall be ſtrangled.

All perſons guilty of purchaſing a poiſonous drug for the purpoſe of killing, ſhall be puniſhed with 100 blows, and three years baniſhment. Perſons ſelling ſuch drugs, knowing the object, ſhall ſuffer the ſame puniſhment as the purchaſers; except in capital caſes, where the puniſhment ſhall be reduced one degree. When the ſeller is really ignorant of the criminal object of the purchaſer, he ſhall not be puniſhable.

One clauſe.

SECTION CCXC. — *Killing with an Intent to kill, and killing in an Affray.*

All perſons guilty of killing in an affray; that is to ſay, ſtriking in a quarrel or affray ſo as to kill, though without any expreſs or implied deſign to kill, ſhall, whether the blow was ſtruck with the hand or the foot, with a metal weapon, or with any inſtrument of any kind, ſuffer death, by being ſtrangled, after the uſual period of confinement.

All perſons guilty of killing with an intent to kill, ſhall ſuffer death by being beheaded, after being confined until the uſual period.

When ſeveral perſons contrive an affray, in the courſe of which an individual is killed, the perſon who inflicts the ſevereſt blow or wound, ſhall be ſtrangled, after the uſual period of confinement. The original contriver of the affray, whether he engages in it or not, ſhall be puniſhed at the leaſt, with 100 blows, and perpetual baniſhment to the diſtance

diſtance of 3000 *lee*. The reſt of the party concerned ſhall be puniſhed with 100 blows each.

Twelve clauſes.

SECTION CCXCI. — *Depriving of Food or Raiment.*

In every caſe of the offence of applying any ſubſtance capable of occaſioning an injury to the noſe, ears, or other natural outlets of the body of any perſon; and alſo in every caſe of depriving any perſon of his neceſſary food and raiment, ſo as in any inſtance to produce an aſſignable injury, the offending party ſhall be puniſhed with 80 blows.

Not only thoſe who ſtrip others of their clothing in winter, and thoſe who deprive of their food or drink the hungry and the thirſty, but alſo thoſe who privately take away the ladder from a man who has aſcended a height, or the bridle from a man on horſe-back, ſhall be liable under this law to puniſhment for the conſequences of ſuch conduct. Whenever any of the natural faculties are permanently injured, the offender ſhall be puniſhed with 100 blows, and three years baniſhment. If the injury amounts to abſolute imbecillity and irremediable infirmity *, the offender ſhall be puniſhed with 100 blows, and perpetual baniſhment to the diſtance of 3000 *lee*: moreover, half his property ſhall be forfeited for the ſupport and indemnification of the ſufferer. If the wound or injury ſuſtained proves mortal, the offender ſhall ſuffer death, by being ſtrangled, after remaining in confinement during the uſual period.

Whoever is guilty of wilfully occaſioning a ſnake, or other venomous animal to bite any perſon, ſhall be puniſhed according to the

* The degree of injury which is in this place intended to be implied, could not be expreſſed in terms having as preciſe a meaning as thoſe contained in the original, but in the firſt article of the next book, entitled, " Quarrelling and Fighting," an explanation is given in the text.

extent

extent of the injury ſuſtained, as in the caſe of wounding in an affray.

If the bite proves mortal, the offender ſhall be beheaded, after remaining in confinement during the uſual period.

No clauſe.

SECTION CCXCII. — *Killing or wounding in Play, by Error, or purely by Accident.*

All perſons playing with the fiſt, with a ſtick, or with any weapon, or other means whatſoever, in ſuch a manner as obviouſly to be liable by ſo doing to kill, and thus killing or wounding ſome individual, ſhall ſuffer the puniſhment provided by the law in any ordinary caſe of killing or wounding in an affray; likewiſe any perſon who, being engaged in an affray, by miſtake kills or wounds a by-ſtander, ſhall be puniſhed in the ſame manner; that is to ſay, the perſon killing another in the manner above ſtated, ſhall ſuffer death by being ſtrangled. If guilty of wounding only, he ſhall be puniſhed more or leſs ſeverely, according to the nature of the wounds inflicted.

Deliberately contriving, or ſimply entertaining an intention, to kill one particular perſon, but by miſtake killing another, ſhall be puniſhable in the ſame degree as any ordinary caſe of intended homicide, and ſuch offender ſhall accordingly be beheaded, after remaining in confinement the uſual period.

If any perſon, knowing that a place reſorted to in order to ford a river, is deep and full of mud, deceitfully repreſents it to be ſhallow and good ground; or, knowing that the planks of a bridge or ferry-boat are rotten, and therefore not truſt-worthy, deceitfully repreſents the ſame to be good and ſecure, ſuch perſon ſhall in either caſe be chargeable with the conſequences, according to this law; —when, therefore, any individual is induced on the ſtrength of ſuch wilfully falſe information to croſs the water, and is drowned, or in any manner injured by making ſuch attempt, the offending party ſhall be deemed guilty of playing with the means by which he was aware an individual might be killed, and in conſequence ſhall ſuffer the puniſhment provided by the law in the caſes of killing or wounding in an affray.

All perſons who kill or wound others purely by accident, ſhall be permitted to redeem themſelves from the puniſhment of killing or wounding in an affray, by the payment in each caſe of a fine to the family of the perſon deceaſed or wounded.

By a caſe of pure accident, is underſtood a caſe of which no ſufficient previous warning could have been given, either directly, by the perceptions of ſight and hearing, or indirectly, by the inferences drawn by judgment and reflection; as for inſtance, when lawfully purſuing and ſhooting wild animals, when for ſome purpoſe throwing a brick or a tile, and in either caſe unexpectedly killing any perſon; when after aſcending high places, ſlipping and falling down, ſo as to chance to hurt a comrade or by-ſtander; when ſailing in a ſhip or other veſſel, and driven involuntarily by the winds; when riding on a horſe or in a carriage, being unable, upon the animal or animals taking fright, to ſtop or to govern them; or laſtly, when ſeveral perſons jointly attempt to raiſe a great weight, the ſtrength of one of them failing, ſo that the weight falls on, and kills or injures his fellow-labourers: — in all theſe caſes there could have been no previous thought or intention of doing an injury, and therefore the law permits ſuch perſons to redeem themſelves from the puniſhment provided for killing or wounding in an affray, by a fine * to be paid to the family of the deceaſed or wounded perſon, which fine will in the former inſtance be applicable to the purpoſe of defraying the expence

* The fine is determined by the ſecond clauſe annexed to this law, at twelve ounces of ſilver and forty-two decimals, or about *4l.* *2s.* *10d.* ſterling.

attending

attending the burial, and in the latter, to that of procuring medicines and medical aſſiſtance *.

Thirteen clauſes.

SECTION CCXCIII. — *A Huſband killing his culpable Wife.*

If a wife ſtrikes and abuſes her huſband's father or mother, grand-father or grand-mother, and the huſband, inſtead of accuſing her before a magiſtrate, kills her in conſequence of ſuch offence, he ſhall be puniſhed with 100 blows.

If a wife, having been ſtruck and abuſed by her huſband, in conſequence thereof kills herſelf, the huſband ſhall not be reſponſible. When a wife, after her huſband's father and mother, grand-father and grand-mother are dead, is guilty of diſreſpect to their memory only, or is charged with ſome other fault not worthy of death according to the laws, if thereupon the huſband kills her, he ſhall ſuffer the puniſhment of death, by being ſtrangled, after the uſual period of confinement.

Two clauſes.

* From this ſection of the laws it clearly appears, that although a peculiar degree of ſtrictneſs may exiſt in China in enforcing the puniſhment of homicide in general, the commonly received notion of the rigour of the law being ſuch, that no allowance is made even in caſes purely accidental, is totally without foundation.

Upon a late occaſion, when one of our ſeamen at Canton was held reſponſible for the murder of a native Chineſe, under circumſtances indeed, of a peculiar nature, and by which for a time the Britiſh intereſts in China were very ſeriouſly involved, and all commercial intercourſe between the two nations ſuſpended, he was ultimately acquitted agreeably to the proviſions of the law contained in this ſection: — had it not been known at the time that ſuch a law exiſted, and had not the Chineſe government been almoſt neceſſitated as it were, by the firm, but temperate and judicious meaſures adopted on the occaſion by the Eaſt India Company's repreſentatives, to apply it to that particular inſtance, the forms of Chineſe juſtice could not have been ſubmitted to, without riſking unwarrantably the ſacrifice of the life of a Britiſh ſubject. See a tranſlation of the Chineſe official report of the affair in the Appendix, No. XI.

Section CCXCIV. — *Killing a Son, Grandſon, or Slave, and attributing the Crime to an innocent Perſon.*

Whoever is guilty of killing his ſon, his grandſon, or his ſlave, and attributing the crime to another perſon, ſhall be puniſhed with 70 blows, and one and a half year's baniſhment.

Any perſon attributing, previous to burial, the death of his father, mother, grand-father or grand-mother; and any ſlave in like manner, attributing the death of his maſter to a perſon innocent thereof, ſhall, if aware of the falſehood of the imputation, be puniſhed with 100 blows, and three years baniſhment.

Any perſon in like manner falſely attributing to an innocent perſon the death of any other of his relations in the firſt degree, ſhall be puniſhed with 80 blows, and three years baniſhment.

If the caſe concerns a more diſtant relation, the puniſhment ſhall be reduced at the rate of one degree for each degree of remoteneſs in the relationſhip.

Any perſon in like manner falſely attributing the death of his junior relation, or of any indifferent perſon, ſhall be puniſhed with 80 blows.

If, in any of the preceding caſes, an accuſation ſhould actually have been laid before a magiſtrate, the offence ſhall be puniſhed according to the law againſt falſe and malicious accuſations.

If by falſely attributing the crime of murder as aforeſaid, any money or property is fraudulently extorted from the party accuſed, the offence ſhall be puniſhable as a theft, proportionably to the amount. If, in like manner, any money or property is extorted by actual violence, the offence ſhall be puniſhed as a robbery in open day, but in neither caſe ſhall the offender be branded. The puniſhment inflicted

ſhall

ſhall moreover be always the ſevereſt applicable to the caſe, whether that of falſely attributing murder, or that of a theft or robbery.

Five clauſes.

SECTION CCXCV. — *Wounding mortally or otherwiſe, by ſhooting Arrows and ſimilar Weapons.*

All perſons who cauſeleſsly ſhoot with a bow, either arrows or any other weapons, or throw bricks or ſtones, towards walled towns, places of trade, or any other places or buildings whatſoever which are the reſidence and habitation of man, ſhall be puniſhed with 40 blows for every ſuch offence, although no perſon ſhall have been ſtruck or wounded thereby. — If any perſon is ſtruck or wounded, the puniſhment ſhall be reduced one degree below that provided by the law in the caſe of ſtriking or wounding in a ſimilar degree in an affray; but no part of the property of the offender ſhall, as there provided, be forfeited to the uſe of the ſufferer.

If any perſon is killed by ſuch aforeſaid act, the offender ſhall be puniſhed with 100 blows, and perpetual baniſhment to the diſtance of 3000 *lee*.

Although, according to the general principle on which the laws are framed, the puniſhment ought be aggravated when the perſon killed is a relation of the offender, yet as the offender in the preſent caſe is not ſuppoſed to foreſee the particular conſequences of his offence, the relationſhip between the parties ſhall be diſregarded. In all theſe caſes however, ten ounces of ſilver ſhall be paid to the relations of the deceaſed to defray the expences of burial *.

No clauſe.

SEC-

* See a tranſlation of the report of a trial of an offender convicted agreeably to this law, in the Appendix, No. XXX., and alſo another in Mr. Barrow's Travels in China, p. 370.

SECTION CCXCVI.—*Wounding mortally, or otherwife, by means of Horfes and Carriages.*

Whoever caufelefsly drives carriages, or rides horfes with extraordinary fpeed, through ftreets, markets, military ftations, or any other places of refort, and by fo doing happens to wound any perfon, fhall fuffer the punifhment provided by the law in the cafe of wounding in a fimilar degree in an affray, reduced one degree.—If any perfon is killed, the offender fhall be punifhed with 100 blows, and banifhed to the diftance of 3000 *lee*.

Thofe who caufelefsly ride or drive as aforefaid in the open country, where people do not commonly refort, although they fhould happen, by fo doing, to wound any perfon, fhall not be punifhable, unlefs the wound proves mortal, in which cafe they fhall fuffer 100 blows, and under all circumftances pay ten ounces of filver to the family of the deceafed.

When any perfon proceeding with great fpeed upon urgent public bufinefs, either on horfeback or in a carriage, happens by fo doing to kill or wound any one, the cafe fhall be deemed purely accidental, and the punifhment redeemable accordingly, by the payment of a fine to the relations of the deceafed.

One claufe.

---

p. 370.—Although fince the publication of that work, fome points may have been placed, by the difcovery of new facts, in a light fomewhat different, fo as perhaps to warrant in thofe refpects an opinion rather lefs difadvantageous of the Chinefe character, the general view which has been taken by Mr. Barrow, of the prefent ftate of the people and government of China, is fo unqueftionably juft and excellent, his defcriptions fo happy, and the information interfperfed throughout fo various and interefting, that inftead of quoting particular paffages occafionally in illuftration of the prefent work, the tranflator conceives that he fhall contribute ultimately more to the fatisfaction of the reader, by taking this opportunity of making one general reference to that valuable publication.

SEC-

SECTION CCXCVII. — *Practitioners of Medicine killing or injuring their Patients.*

When unſkilful practitioners of medicine or ſurgery * adminiſter drugs, or perform operations with the puncturing needle, contrary to the eſtabliſhed rules and practice, and thereby kill the patient, the magiſtrates ſhall call in other practitioners to examine the nature of the medicine, or of the wound, as the caſe may be, which proved mortal; and if it ſhall appear upon the whole to have been ſimply an error, without any deſign to injure the patient, the practitioner of medicine ſhall be allowed to redeem himſelf from the puniſhment of homicide, as in caſes purely accidental, but ſhall be obliged to quit his profeſſion for ever.

If it ſhall appear that a medical practitioner intentionally deviates from the eſtabliſhed rules and practice, and while pretending to remove the diſeaſe of his patient, aggravates the complaint, in order to extort more money for its cure, the money ſo extorted ſhall be conſidered to have been ſtolen, and puniſhment inflicted accordingly, in proportion to the amount.

If the patient dies, the medical practitioner who is convicted of deſignedly employing improper medicines, or otherwiſe contriving to in-

* Strictly ſpeaking, the art of Surgery is unknown in China, and the term is here employed merely to point out the diſtinction which the Chineſe make in the medical profeſſion, between external and internal operations.

It is a fact worthy of notice in this place, though not immediately connected with the objects of the preſent work, that notwithſtanding the peculiar prejudices of the Chineſe on the ſubject of medicine, and their general averſion to every ſpecies of innovation, more eſpecially to that which is derived from the ſuggeſtions of foreigners, the benefits of Dr. Jenner's invaluable diſcovery of the vaccine inoculation, are at preſent enjoyed in a conſiderable degree by the natives of the ſouthern coaſt of the Chineſe empire, through the ſkilful and indefatigable exertions of Mr. Pearſon, the principal ſurgeon of the Eaſt India Company's factory at Canton.—See that gentleman's intereſting communication on the ſubject, in the Medical Journal for November 1808.

jure his patient, ſhall ſuffer death by being beheaded, after the uſual period of confinement.

No clauſe.

SECTION CCXCVIII.—*Killing or wounding by means of Traps or Springes.*

All perſons, huntſmen by profeſſion, digging pit-falls, and laying traps or ſpringes in mountainous or deſert places, where wild animals are ſuppoſed to haunt, but omitting at the ſame time to give warning thereof, by diſtinguiſhing each of ſuch places by a flag-ſtaff, and a ſmall cord ſtretched acroſs, at the height of a man's eye from the ground, ſhall be puniſhed with 40 blows, although no miſchief to any one ſhould enſue.

If any perſon is hurt or wounded for want of ſuch warning, the puniſhment of the reſponſible perſon ſhall be only two degrees leſs than that provided by law in the caſe of wounding in a ſimilar degree in an affray.

If any perſon is killed, the offender ſhall be puniſhed with 100 blows, and three years baniſhment, and ſhall moreover pay ten ounces of ſilver to the family of the deceaſed, to defray the expences of burial.

If ſuch pit-falls are dug, and traps or ſpringes placed, without the above preſcribed warnings, in places cultivated and inhabited by man, the offending parties ſhall be puniſhed according to the law againſt ſhooting with bows and arrows or other weapons, againſt places ſo cultivated and inhabited.

No clauſe.

SECTION CCXCIX. — *Occaſioning the Death of an Individual by violent and fearful Threats.*

Any perſon who, with a view to accompliſh ſome object, ſuch as a marriage-contract, the transfer of property, payment of debts, and the like, alarms another to ſuch a degree by violent threats, that he kills himſelf in deſpair, ſhall, whenever reaſonable grounds can be ſhewn to have exiſted for ſuch extreme apprehenſions on the part of the deceaſed, be puniſhed with 100 blows.

Any officer of government who ſhall be guilty of ſuch conduct, when not acting in execution of his public duty, ſhall be liable to the ſame puniſhment; and in every caſe the offender ſhall pay ten ounces of ſilver to the family of the deceaſed to defray the expences of burial.

If any perſon ſhall thus alarm with violent threats an elder relation in the firſt degree, ſo that ſuch relation kills himſelf in conſequence thereof, the junior ſo offending, ſhall ſuffer death, by being ſtrangled, after the uſual period of confinement.

Every ſimilar offence againſt an elder relation in any of the more remote degrees, ſhall be ſubject to the puniſhment laſt mentioned, under a reduction of one degree for each degree of additional remoteneſs, in the relationſhip.

All perſons guilty of alarming to death with violent threats, as above mentioned, in order to accompliſh any object criminal and unlawful in itſelf, ſuch as theft or adultery, ſhall, whether ſuch criminal and unlawful object is, or is not attained, be puniſhed with death, by being beheaded, after the uſual period of confinement.

Eighteen clauſes.

SECTION CCC.—*Compromiſing and concealing the Crime of killing an elder Relation.*

If, in the event of the murder of a grandfather, grandmother, father, mother, huſband, or maſter of a family; the grandſon, ſon, wife, ſlave, or hired ſervant, as the caſe may be, agrees to a compromiſe with the murderer, and conceals the crime, the party ſo offending ſhall be puniſhed with 100 blows, and baniſhed for three years.

In the event of the murder of any other elder relation in the firſt degree, being compromiſed and concealed by the junior relation, ſuch junior relation ſhall be puniſhed with 80 blows, and two years baniſhment; and in caſe of any relationſhip between the parties in a more remote degree, the puniſhment of the junior ſhall be reduced at the rate of one degree for each degree of additional remoteneſs.

An elder relation compromiſing and concealing the murder of a junior, ſhall, in general, be puniſhed one degree leſs ſeverely than ſuch junior relation would have been, had the caſe been reverſed.

Any perſon, laſtly, who is guilty of compromiſing and concealing the murder of his ſon, grandſon, wife, ſlave, or hired ſervant, ſhall be liable to the puniſhment of 80 blows. When any bribe is received in conſideration of ſuch compromiſe and concealment, the receiver ſhall be held guilty of a theft to the ſame amount, and the puniſhment ſhall be either that provided by law in the caſe of ſuch a theft, or that already ſtated conformably to the circumſtances of the compromiſe, whichever proves to be the moſt ſevere. The amount of the bribe ſhall be forfeited to government.

Compromiſing and concealing the murder of a ſtranger ſhall ſubject the offending party to the puniſhment of 60 blows; and when the offence is committed in conſideration of a bribe, the puniſhment ſhall

be

be ſubject to ſuch aggravation, as may be conformable to the law againſt receiving bribes for unlawful purpoſes.

One clauſe.

SECTION CCCI. — *Neglecting to give Information of, or to interfere and prevent a violent Injury which is known to be intended.*

When any perſon is aware that his comrade has contrived the means of inflicting a violent injury, and is deſirous of executing ſuch unlawful purpoſe, if he does not endeavour to prevent the deſign from being carried into effect, ſo as to preſerve harmleſs the object of it; or, when unable ſo to do, if he does not, at leaſt, after the crime is committed, give information thereof to a magiſtrate, he ſhall be puniſhed for the omiſſion with 100 blows.

No clauſe.

END OF THE SECOND BOOK OF THE SIXTH DIVISION.

BOOK III.

QUARRELLING AND FIGHTING.

SECTION CCCII. — *Quarrelling and Fighting between Equals in ordinary Cafes.*

IN all ordinary cafes of quarrelling and fighting, every perfon who ftrikes another with his hand or foot, but not fo as to produce any affignable hurt or wound, fhall be punifhed with 20 blows.

If a blow is ftruck with the hand or foot, and produces a hurt or wound; or is ftruck with a cudgel, or any other fimilar weapon, but produces no affignable hurt or wound, the punifhment, in either cafe, fhall amount to 30 blows. — If, in the latter cafe, any hurt or wound is occafioned by the blow, the punifhment fhall be increafed to 40 blows. — Whenever the part of the body ftruck, fwells or inflames, the injury received fhall be deemed a hurt or wound; in general alfo, when any blow is ftruck, otherwife than fimply by the hand or foot as aforefaid, that circumftance fhall always occafion an aggravation of one degree in punifhment. — A foldier ftriking with the back of his fword, fhall alfo be liable to the aggravated punifhment.

The offence of tearing away more than an inch (*Tfun*) of hair, fhall be punifhed with 50 blows. — If a blow has been ftruck in fuch a manner as to occafion blood to flow from the eyes or ears, or to be difcharged from the ftomach in confequence of fome internal injury, the offender fhall be punifhed with 80 blows. — In the cafe however of blood flowing only from the noftrils, or immediately from the part of the body where the blow was received, merely in confequence of the fkin ſkin upon ſuch part having been broken, the puniſhment ſhall not be more ſevere than in the caſe of an ordinary hurt or wound above mentioned.

The offence of throwing filth and ordure on the head or face, ſhall alſo be puniſhable with 80 blows. — Breaking a tooth, a toe, a finger, or any bone in the body; wounding an eye, without totally deſtroying the ſight; materially injuring and disfiguring the ears or noſe; ſcalding with hot water; burning with fire; wounding with copper or iron needles; or filling up the mouth and noſe with filth or ordure, ſhall in each caſe ſubject the offender to a puniſhment of 100 blows.

Breaking two teeth, two fingers, two toes, or tearing away all the hair of the head, ſhall in each caſe ſubject the offender to a puniſhment of 60 blows and one year's baniſhment.

Breaking a rib; wounding both eyes; ſtriking a woman ninety days gone with child, ſo as to occaſion miſcarriage or abortion; or wounding in any caſe with the edge of a ſharp inſtrument, ſhall ſubject the offender to a puniſhment of 80 blows, and two years baniſhment.

Breaking a leg or an arm, or the back-bone, or deſtroying one eye, is conſidered by the law to be an infliction of a permanent and irremediable injury, and ſhall ſubject the offender to the puniſhment of 100 blows and three years baniſhment.

Breaking both legs, both arms, or a leg and an arm; deſtroying both eyes; or doing any other injury which produces entire diſability and incurable infirmity; cutting out the tongue ſo as to deprive the ſufferer of the faculty of ſpeech; or violently injuring a perſon of either ſex, ſo as to incapacitate ſuch perſon from becoming a parent, ſhall ſubject the offender, in each caſe, to the puniſhment of 100 blows, and perpetual baniſhment to the diſtance of 3000 *lee*; half the property of the offender ſhall alſo, in ſuch caſes, be forfeited to the ſupport of the perſon injured.

In

In the caſe of a woman being violently injured, but not to the extent of rendering her incapable of becoming a mother, this law ſhall ſtill be put in force, except in as much as reſpects the forfeiture of half the property of the offender. When there are more offenders than one, and they agree together to attack jointly, they ſhall be puniſhed according to the ſeverity of the blows reſpectively inflicted by them, except in the caſe of the original contriver, who, whether he joined in the attack or affray or not, ſhall always ſuffer, at the leaſt, a puniſhment but one degree leſs ſevere than that which is inflicted on him who ſtruck the ſevereſt blow. — In the caſe of an ordinary affray, no other perſons ſhall be liable to ſuffer puniſhment in conſequence of their being implicated therein, beſide the original contriver, and ſuch of the parties as may be convicted of actually ſtriking a blow: but if any perſon is killed in the courſe of an affray, all the perſons who were privy to and in any manner concerned in the ſame, ſhall, at the leaſt, be liable to a puniſhment of 100 blows each.

If ſeveral perſons jointly attack another, and in courſe of the affray, mortally wound him, the perſon who ſtruck the laſt and ſevereſt blow, ſhall be eſteemed the principal in the homicide: in thoſe caſes of promiſcuous fighting, in which it is impoſſible to aſcertain who ſtruck the firſt blow, and who the laſt, who ſtruck the lighteſt, and who the heavieſt, the original contriver ſhall in general be eſteemed the principal; and when there is no evidence of previous contrivance, the reſponſibility, as principal offender, ſhall attach to the perſon who firſt engaged in the affray, or commenced the quarrel.

In the caſe of a combat between two perſons; and in the caſe of ſeveral perſons engaging in an affray, and promiſcuouſly ſtriking and fighting each other, they ſhall be puniſhed reſpectively, according to the blows duly aſcertained, and proved by the examination of the effects, to have been received by their antagoniſts, except that the puniſhment of the perſon or perſons who only return the blows received, and have the right and juſtice of the diſpute on his or their ſide, ſhall be reduced

reduced two degrees in conſideration of ſuch favourable circumſtances: but this reduction ſhall not take place in the inſtance of ſtriking an elder brother or ſiſter, or an uncle; or when inflicting, in any caſe, a mortal blow.

As for inſtance; let *Kia* * and *Yee*, be ſuppoſed to quarrel and fight, and that *Kia* deprives *Yee* of an eye, and *Yee* deprives *Kia* of a tooth; now the injury ſuſtained by *Yee* is the heavieſt, and ſubjects *Kia* to the puniſhment of 100 blows and three years baniſhment, whilſt the leſſer injury ſuſtained by *Kia* ſubjects *Yee* to a puniſhment of 100 blows only: — nevertheleſs, if it appears that *Kia* only returned the attack, and had the right on his ſide, his puniſhment ſhall be reduced two degrees, and accordingly amount to 80 blows and two years baniſhment: — on the contrary, if *Yee* only returned the attack, and had the right in the diſpute, his puniſhment ſhall be reduced two degrees, and amount to 80 blows only; the puniſhment to which the antagoniſt is ſubjected remaining in either caſe the ſame as before: when the puniſhment originally included a forfeiture of half the property of the offender, that penalty ſhall not in any caſe, be reduced.

Eight clauſes.

SECTION CCCIII. — *Periods of Reſponſibility for the Conſequences of a Wound.*

When any perſon is wounded, the magiſtrates ſhall diſtinctly examine, and take evidence reſpecting the wound, in order to aſcertain the nature thereof, and the manner in which it was inflicted; which having done, they ſhall according to the circumſtances determine the period during which the offender is to be held reſponſible for the conſequences,

* *Kia* and *Yee* are names uſed merely by way of exemplification, in the ſame manner as with us ſometimes, the letters of the alphabet, or the fictitious names introduced into the proceedings of our civil courts of juſtice.

fequences, that is to fay, ftrictly bound both to provide medicinal affiftance for the wounded perfon for fuch time, and alfo to anfwer for the contingency of his death, either on account of fuch wound, or from any external caufe operating thereon, previous to the expiration of the period.

If the wounded perfon fhould die after the expiration of the period; or even within the period, provided he had recovered from the wound, and is clearly proved to have died from fome other caufe, the offender fhall not be held guilty of a capital offence, but be punifhed according to the apparent nature of the wound inflicted, as ftated in the preceding fection.

If, on the contrary, the wounded perfon not only furvives the period affigned, but by the aid of medicine entirely recovers within the fame, the punifhment of the offender for inflicting fuch wound fhall be reduced two degrees.

Neverthelefs, if any permanent injury, difability, or bodily infirmity remains, after a recovery from the immediate effect of the wound, the law fhall be executed on the offender in its full extent.

When a wound has been inflicted with the hand or foot, or with any article which is not an ordinary weapon of offence, and the injury fuftained is apparently not confiderable, a period of twenty days refponfibility fhall only be required.

When a wound has been inflicted with a fharp inftrument, with fire, or with fcalding water, the period of refponfibility fhall be extended to thirty days.

When any bones are broken or diflocated, or the body or limbs violently injured; and when, in any cafe, the fufferer happens to be a woman with child, the period fhall be extended to fifty days, in whatever manner the blow may have been inflicted *.

Seven claufes.

* According to one of the fupplemental claufes annexed to this law, an intermediate period of forty days is eftablifhed for cafes of gun-fhot wounds; the judicious application of

SECTION CCCIV. —*Quarrelling and Fighting within the Imperial Palace.*

All perſons who are guilty of diſputing and quarrelling within the precincts of the Imperial Palace, ſhall be puniſhed with 50 blows.

If they proceed ſo far as to ſtrike one another, or if the ſound of the voices of the diſputants reaches to the apartments of His Majeſty, the puniſhment ſhall be increaſed to 100 blows.

If, as aforeſaid, within the precincts of the palace, a cutting wound is inflicted, the puniſhment of the offenders ſhall be two degrees more ſevere than in ordinary caſes. If the offence is committed in the preſence chamber, or in any of the Imperial halls of audience, the puniſhment ſhall be further aggravated one degree, but limited in all caſes ſhort of homicide, to 100 blows and perpetual baniſhment to the diſtance of 3000 *lee*. As in every quarrel and diſpute under theſe circumſtances, both parties are conſidered culpable, if the injury occaſioned by the wound received by one of the offending parties is incurable, or amounts to complete diſability, the ſufferer muſt ſtill redeem himſelf from his ſhare in the puniſhment ordained by this law, by the payment of the ordinary fine, and ſhall not receive that portion of the property of the other offender, which is always granted in ordinary caſes of perſons ſuſtaining a ſimilar injury.

One clauſe.

---

of this particular law, it is worthy of notice, once very materially contributed to extricate the Eaſt India Company's repreſentatives in China, from very ſerious difficulties, and from the diſtreſſing alternative, of either ignominiouſly ſacrificing the life of a Britiſh ſubject, or totally abandoning the important commercial intereſts under their management.

SECTION CCCV. — *Striking or wounding an Individual of the Imperial Blood.*

Any perſon who ſtrikes an individual of the Imperial Blood, although not one within any of the four degrees of relationſhip to the Emperor, ſhall be puniſhed with 60 blows, and one year's baniſhment; ſlightly wounding ſuch perſon, ſhall be puniſhable with 80 blows and two years baniſhment; inflicting a cutting wound, ſhall be puniſhed two degrees more ſeverely than in ordinary caſes between equals, provided the puniſhment do not in any ſuch caſe exceed 100 blows, and three years baniſhment.

If the individual of Imperial blood is related to the ſovereign in the fourth degree, the puniſhment ſhall be aggravated one degree; and if more nearly related, the puniſhment ſhall be aggravated an additional degree for each degree of approximation in relationſhip, but in no caſe exceed 100 blows and perpetual baniſhment to the diſtance of 3000 *lee*, except the conſequent injury amounts to total diſability and incurable infirmity; when, in all ſuch inſtances of injuries ſuſtained by perſons of Imperial blood, the offenders ſhall ſuffer death, by being ſtrangled, after the uſual period of impriſonment.

When in any of the preceding caſes death enſues, the offenders ſhall be beheaded, after the uſual confinement.

Two clauſes.

SECTION CCCVI. — *Striking ordinary and extraordinary Officers of Government.*

Any ordinary officer of government ſtriking an officer of government inveſted with extraordinary powers by the Emperor; any private inhabitant of a diſtrict, ſtriking the governor or chief officer of the ſame; any private ſoldier ſtriking his commanding officer; and, laſtly, any

any official attendant of a tribunal ſtriking a preſiding officer who is at the ſame time, of the fifth, or of any rank ſuperior thereto, ſhall in every ſuch caſe be puniſhed with 100 blows, and three years baniſhment. If the blow produces a ſlight wound or bruiſe, the puniſhment ſhall be increaſed to 100 blows, and perpetual baniſhment to the diſtance of 2000 *lee*.

If the blow produces a ſevere cutting wound, the offender ſhall ſuffer death, by being ſtrangled, after the uſual period of confinement.

Any official attendant of a tribunal, (that is to ſay, a perſon having a civil or military office or command below the regular officers of government,) ſtriking a preſiding officer or magiſtrate below the fifth rank, ſhall be puniſhed according to the nature of the blow, in the proportion above ſtated, but with a reduction of three degrees in each caſe. — If the officer or magiſtrate who is ſtruck, is only an aſſeſſor of the tribunal, the puniſhment ſhall be further reduced one degree, and it ſhall be again reduced another degree, if he is the loweſt officer of ſuch tribunal. — Nevertheleſs, no reduction ſhall take effect ſo as to render the puniſhment leſs, than one degree more ſevere than in ordinary caſes.

In all the preceding caſes, when the injury ſuſtained produces entire diſability and incurable infirmity, the offender ſhall ſuffer death, by being ſtrangled; and when it occaſions the death of the ſufferer, the offender ſhall be beheaded, after having in either caſe remained in priſon until the uſual period of execution.

Officers of government not yet raiſed to any of the regular ranks, perſons having official employments immediately under the civil or military officers of government, ſoldiers, and private individuals, when ſtriking any civil or military officer of the third, or any rank ſuperior thereto, but to whoſe juriſdiction or command they were not ſubject, ſhall, in each caſe, be liable to a puniſhment of 80 blows, and two years baniſhment.

If guilty of wounding ſo as to bruiſe, the puniſhment ſhall be increaſed to 100 blows, and three years baniſhment. — If guilty of cutting and wounding, the puniſhment ſhall be further increaſed to 100 blows, and perpetual baniſhment to the diſtance of 2000 *lee*.

If the officer ſtruck or wounded as above, is of the fourth or fifth, inſtead of the third, or any ſuperior rank, the puniſhment ſhall, according to the caſe, be proportionably reduced two degrees; but neither in this, nor in the preceding caſes, nor in the caſe of the perſons above mentioned ſtriking or wounding an officer of government below the fifth rank, ſhall any reduction in the puniſhment operate ſo as to render it leſs, than two degrees more ſevere than in ordinary caſes.

Official meſſengers on duty, ſtriking or wounding the officer of government to whom they are diſpatched, ſhall be puniſhed as above ſtated, conformably to this law.

When the offender and the ſufferer belong to different diſtricts ſubject to diſtinct juriſdictions, the cognizance and trial of the offence ſhall always take place in the diſtrict of the latter.

Four clauſes.

SECTION CCCVII. — *Subordinate Officers of Government ſtriking Perſons who are their Superiors both in Rank and Juriſdiction.*

If in any court, tribunal, or public office of government, the deputies thereof, or the magiſtrates holding ſubordinate courts, tribunals, or public offices, ſtrike or wound the preſident of ſuch ſuperior court or tribunal, the puniſhment ſhall be leſs by two degrees, than that already provided in the caſe of the official attendant thereof committing a ſimilar offence. — If the aſſeſſors of ſuch tribunals and public offices ſtrike or wound the preſidents thereof, their puniſhment ſhall be fixed according

according to a further reduction of two degrees below that of the deputies or subordinates aforesaid, under similar circumstances.

Nevertheless no reduction shall take place so as to render the punishment less than one degree above that which is provided by the law in ordinary cases between equals.

In each of the preceding cases, if total disability and incurable infirmity are occasioned by the blows inflicted, the offender shall suffer death, by being strangled, after the usual period of confinement. — If death ensues, the offender shall be beheaded at the usual period.

No clause.

Section CCCVIII. — *Co-ordinate or independent Officers of Government striking each other.*

Any assessor or deputy of a court, tribunal or government station, who strikes an officer of government, holding the presidency of a subordinate court, tribunal, or government station, shall, without regard to the respective rank of the parties, be punished as in ordinary cases, between equals. — Likewise officers of government belonging to distinct and independent tribunals, if of the same rank, shall, when striking each other, be punished as in ordinary cases.

No clause.

Section CCCIX. — *Officers of Government striking their Superiors in Rank, but not in Jurisdiction.*

Any officer of government below the regular ranks, or of the ninth, eighth, seventh, or sixth rank, striking an officer of government of the third, second, or first rank, who is not at the same time his commanding officer, shall be punished with 60 blows, and one year's banishment.

If

If a blow inflicted as aforesaid produces a cutting wound; if any one of the aforesaid officers of government strikes an officer of the fifth or fourth rank, who is not his commander; or if under similar circumstances an officer of the fifth or fourth rank, strikes an officer of the second or first rank, the punishment shall, in each case, be two degrees more severe than in ordinary cases: — but this aggravation of the punishment shall not extend to cases of wounds occasioning the entire disability or death of the injured party.

No clause.

SECTION CCCX. — *Resisting and striking any Person employed officially by Government on Public Service.*

All persons resisting and striking those who, under the authority of any public office or officer of government, are employed in collecting duties, or enforcing any legal and public services, shall be punished at the least with 80 blows: — all persons so resisting, and striking severe blows, causing a discharge of blood from the stomach, and the like, shall suffer a punishment two degrees more severe than that which would have been inflicted according to law in ordinary cases between equals: — but the punishment shall not, in any case, exceed 100 blows, and perpetual banishment to the distance of 3000 *lee*; unless the blows which are inflicted occasion, what the law considers a total disability and incurable infirmity, in which event, the offenders shall suffer death by being strangled, after the usual period of confinement:— if death ensues, they shall be beheaded.

These are the punishments to be inflicted in the different cases of resistance to lawful authority, employed in the collection of duties, or in the enforcement of any other services of a public nature: but if any such offender had been antecedently guilty of neglect or wilful delay, in discharging the former, or performing the latter, he shall be punished according

according to the law provided againſt thoſe who, after having been ſubjected to a criminal proſecution for their offences, reſiſt, and defend themſelves againſt the officers of juſtice.

No clauſe.

SECTION CCCXI. — *Diſciples and Apprentices ſtriking their Maſters.*

A knowledge of letters, of huſbandry, of arts and manufactures, and of commerce, cannot be acquired without regular diſcipline, and ſufficient apprenticeſhip, and gratitude is therefore due to thoſe from whom the neceſſary inſtruction has been received.

A diſciple of the literary claſs, is held to be bound in gratitude from the very commencement of his apprenticeſhip; but the diſciples of huſbandry or agriculture, of arts and manufactures, and of commerce, are only held to be thus bound, after having concluded their apprenticeſhips, and ſeverally entered into the profeſſions, the knowledge of which they had thereby acquired. They ſhall, accordingly, be liable to a puniſhment two degrees more ſevere than in ordinary caſes between equals, whenever they are guilty of ſtriking, in the latter three caſes, the perſons who have been, or in the firſt caſe, the perſons who either are, or have been, their maſters and inſtructors.

Neverthleſs, the puniſhment ſhall not be, in any caſe, capital, unleſs death enſues from the blows inflicted, and then the offender ſhall ſuffer the puniſhment of death, by being beheaded, after the uſual period of confinement.

Two clauſes.

SECTION CCCXII. — *Unlawful and forcible Impriſonment.*

All perſons who have quarrels and diſputes, ought to forbear from ſeeking redreſs otherwiſe than by complaining to the proper officer

officer of government, and ſubmitting the juſtice of their cauſe to his deciſion: — all thoſe on the contrary, who, relying on their ſtrength and power, ſeize, and carry away their opponents, and attempt in private houſes to confine and torture them, ſhall, even if no aſſignable injury be actually inflicted, be puniſhed with 80 blows. — If any ſevere or internal injury is done to the individual ſo ſeized, the offender ſhall be puniſhed according to the nature of the wounds inflicted, two degrees more ſeverely than in ordinary caſes. — If death enſues, the offender ſhall be ſtrangled at the uſual period.

If any perſon hires another thus to maltreat his opponent, the perſon ſo hired ſhall be deemed an acceſſary, and ſuffer puniſhment leſs than that of his principal by only one degree.

If more than one perſon is hired, the chief agent among them ſhall be the only one to be puniſhed as an acceſſary under this law.

Four clauſes.

Section CCCXIII. — *Slaves and free Perſons aſſaulting and ſtriking each other.*

A ſlave ſtriking a free man ſhall, proportionably to the conſequences, be puniſhed one degree more ſeverely than is by law provided in ſimilar caſes between equals. — If the blow produces entire diſability and incurable infirmity, the offender ſhall be ſtrangled. — If death enſues, the offender ſhall be beheaded.

A freeman ſtriking a ſlave, ſhall, in like manner, be puniſhed leſs ſeverely by one degree than in the ordinary caſes of the ſame offence; but in the caſe of the death of a ſlave, in conſequence of the injury received, and in the caſe of a ſlave having been killed deſignedly, the offender ſhall be ſtrangled. — Slaves ſtriking, wounding, or killing one

one another, ſhall be puniſhed as already provided in ordinary caſes between equals.

In caſes of ſtealing, and other ſimilar offences, between free perſons and ſlaves, the law of diminution and aggravation of puniſhment ſhall not take effect.

Striking the ſlave of a relation in the third or fourth degree, but without producing a cutting wound, ſhall not be puniſhable. — If the blow produces any greater injury, ſhort of occaſioning death, the puniſhment ſhall be two degrees leſs ſevere than in ordinary caſes. — Striking the ſlave of a relation in the ſecond degree, ſhall be puniſhed three degrees leſs ſeverely than in ordinary caſes. — If, in either caſe, the blow occaſions death, the offender ſhall be puniſhed with 100 blows, and three years baniſhment: — if the blow proves mortal, and has likewiſe been ſtruck with an intention to kill, the offender ſhall ſuffer death, by being ſtrangled. In the caſe of killing accidentally, no puniſhment ſhall be required.

Striking the hired ſervant of a relation in the third or fourth degree, but without producing a cutting wound, ſhall not be puniſhable. If the blow produces any greater injury ſhort of occaſioning death, the puniſhment ſhall be one degree leſs ſevere than in ordinary caſes: the puniſhment of ſtriking the hired ſervant of a relation in the ſecond degree, ſhall be two degrees leſs than in ordinary caſes. — Killing by ſuch blows, or intentionally killing, ſhall, in either of the caſes laſt ſtated, ſubject the offender to the puniſhment of death, by being ſtrangled, at the uſual period.

Accidentally killing ſuch hired ſervant, ſhall not render the perſon convicted thereof, liable to any fine or puniſhment.

The offence of aſſaulting and ſtriking the hired ſervant of a ſtranger, ſhall ſubject the party guilty thereof, to the ſame puniſhment as is provided and inflicted in ordinary caſes.

One clauſe.

SECTION CCCXIV. — *Slaves ſtriking their Maſters.*

All ſlaves who are guilty of deſignedly ſtriking their maſters, ſhall, without making any diſtinction between principals and acceſſaries, be beheaded.

All ſlaves deſignedly killing, or deſignedly ſtriking ſo as to kill their maſters, ſhall ſuffer death by a ſlow and painful execution.

If accidentally killing their maſters, they ſhall ſuffer death, by being ſtrangled at the uſual period.

If accidentally wounding, they ſhall ſuffer 100 blows, and perpetual baniſhment to the diſtance of 3000 *lee*; not being allowed, as under ſimilar circumſtances in ordinary caſes, to redeem themſelves from ſuch puniſhment by a fine *.

Slaves who are guilty of ſtriking their maſter's relations in the firſt degree, or their maſter's maternal grandfather or grandmother, ſhall be ſtrangled at the uſual period. If more than one are concerned, the principal ſhall be ſtrangled, and the reſt ſuffer the puniſhment next in degree. — All ſlaves who ſtrike ſo as to wound ſuch perſons, ſhall, without diſtinction between principals and acceſſaries, be beheaded at the uſual period.

If accidentally killing, the puniſhment ſhall be two degrees leſs ſevere than in the caſe of intentionally ſtriking ſuch perſons. — If accidentally wounding, the puniſhment ſhall be another degree leſs ſevere than in the caſe of intentionally ſtriking. — All ſlaves who are concerned in the crime of deſignedly killing ſuch perſons, ſhall ſuffer death by a ſlow and painful execution.

* This part of the law, denouncing puniſhment even in caſes which are admitted to have been purely accidental, is in ſome degree modified in the ſupplemental clauſes.

A ſlave

A ſlave who is guilty of ſtriking, or ſtriking and ſlightly wounding his maſter's relation in the fourth degree, ſhall be puniſhed with 60 blows, and one year's baniſhment: if guilty of ſtriking his maſter's relation in the third degree, he ſhall be puniſhed with 70 blows, and baniſhment for a year and a half: if guilty of ſtriking his maſter's relation in the ſecond degree, the puniſhment ſhall be 80 blows, and two years baniſhment.

If a ſlave is guilty of ſtriking any of his maſter's relations in the fourth degree, ſo as to produce a ſevere cutting wound, the puniſhment ſhall be one degree more ſevere than it would have been if he had ſo wounded a free perſon in ordinary caſes: in the caſe of a maſter's relation in the third degree, two degrees more ſevere; and in the caſe of a maſter's relation in the ſecond degree, three degrees more ſevere.—If by theſe augmentations, the puniſhment, in any caſe, becomes capital, the offender ſhall be ſtrangled at the uſual period; but if the wound occaſions death, then, whether there was originally a deſign to kill or not, all the ſlaves concerned ſhall be beheaded.

If a hired ſervant ſtrikes his maſter, his maſter's relations in the firſt degree, or his maſter's maternal grandfather or grandmother, he ſhall be puniſhed with 100 blows, and three years baniſhment.—If he ſtrikes in ſuch a manner as to wound, he ſhall be puniſhed with 100 blows, and perpetual baniſhment to the diſtance of 3000 *lee*.—If he ſtrikes ſo as to produce a cutting wound, he ſhall be ſtrangled at the uſual period: if he ſtrikes ſo as to occaſion death, he ſhall, in the caſe of his maſter being the perſon ſtruck, be beheaded immediately on conviction; in the other caſes, at the uſual period. If he deſignedly kills any of the aforeſaid perſons, he ſhall ſuffer death by a ſlow and painful execution.—If the killing or wounding is purely accidental, the puniſhment ſhall be two degrees leſs than that eſtabliſhed by the laws, in proportion to the conſequences of blows, in ordinary caſes.

A hired ſervant who is guilty of ſtriking, or ſtriking and ſlightly wounding his maſter's relations in the fourth degree, ſhall be puniſhed with 80 blows; if guilty of ſtriking his maſter's relations in the third degree, with 90 blows; if guilty of ſtriking thoſe in the ſecond degree, with 100 blows.—If ſtriking and wounding ſo as to produce an internal injury, ſpitting of blood, and the like, the puniſhment of ſo ſtriking his maſter's relations in the third or fourth degree, ſhall be one degree more ſevere than that provided by law in ordinary caſes; and if guilty of ſo ſtriking his maſter's relations in the ſecond degree, the puniſhment ſhall be two degrees more ſevere than in ordinary caſes; but ſhall not exceed 100 blows and perpetual baniſhment, unleſs death enſues; in which event, all the parties to the offence ſhall be beheaded at the uſual period.

If, in the caſe of a ſlave having been guilty of theft, adultery, or any other ſimilar crime, his maſter, or ſome one of his neareſt relations in the firſt degree, or his maſter's maternal grandfather or grandmother, inſtead of complaining to a magiſtrate, privately beats to death ſuch ſlave, the perſon who ſo offends ſhall be puniſhed with 100 blows.

If any ſuch perſon as aforeſaid, beats to death, or intentionally kills a ſlave belonging to his family, who had not been guilty of any crime, the perſon ſo offending ſhall be puniſhed with 60 blows, and one year's baniſhment; and the wife or huſband, as well as the children of ſuch deceaſed ſlave, ſhall be thereupon entitled to their freedom. The maſter, or relations of the maſter of a guilty ſlave, may however chaſtiſe ſuch ſlave in any degree ſhort of occaſioning his death, without being liable to any puniſhment.

When a maſter, or ſome one of his relations as aforeſaid, ſtrikes a hired ſervant, the perſon ſo ſtriking the ſervant ſhall not, whether ſuch fuch fervant merited or not his chaftifement, be punifhable, unlefs the blow produces a cutting wound; in which event alfo, the punifhment fhall be three degrees lefs than in ordinary cafes. If death enfues, the offender fhall be punifhed with 100 blows, and three years banifhment.

If defignedly killing fuch hired fervant, the offender fhall fuffer death, by being ftrangled at the ufual period. — Neverthelefs, if a mafter, or his aforefaid relations, in order to correct a difobedient flave or hired fervant, fhould chaftife him in a lawful manner on the back of the thighs, or on the pofteriors, and fuch flave or hired fervant happens to die; or if he is killed in any other manner accidentally, neither the mafter nor his aforefaid relations, fhall be liable to any punifhment in confequence thereof *.

Seventeen claufes.

Section CCCXV. — *Wives ftriking their Hufbands.*

If a principal or firft wife is guilty of ftriking her hufband, fhe fhall be liable to the punifhment of 100 blows; and the hufband, if defirous thereof, may obtain a divorce by making application for the fame to the magiftrate of the diftrict. If any fuch wife ftrikes fo as to wound her hufband, fhe fhall be punifhable three degrees more feverely than in the cafe of ftriking in the fame manner an equal in ordinary cafes. — If the blow occafions, what is in the contemplation of the law, entire difability and permanent infirmity, the wife fhall be

* A tranflation of the official ftatement of a cafe of a mafter convicted of the crime of killing his fervant, extracted from a printed collection of Chinefe law reports, is inferted in the Appendix, No. XXXI., and may contribute fomething to the illuftration both of this particular fection, and of the manner in which the laws in general are carried into effect in criminal cafes.

ftrangled

ſtrangled immediately after conviction.—If death enſues, the wife ſhall be beheaded immediately after conviction.

If any ſuch wife deſignedly kills her huſband by blows, poiſon, or other means, ſhe ſhall ſuffer death by a ſlow and painful execution.

If any inferior wife ſtrikes her huſband, or her huſband's firſt wife, the puniſhment ſhall, in each caſe, be one degree more ſevere than that of the firſt wife ſtriking her huſband.

If the augmentation renders the puniſhment capital, the offender ſhall be ſtrangled; in the latter caſe, at the uſual period; but in the former, immediately after conviction.—In the more atrocious caſes, the puniſhment of the inferior wife ſhall correſpond, and be equal in all reſpects to that of the firſt.

A huſband ſhall not be puniſhed for ſtriking his firſt wife, unleſs the blow produces a cutting wound; in which caſe, complaint having been made by the wife to a magiſtrate, puniſhment ſhall be awarded two degrees leſs than in ordinary caſes between equals; but it ſhall be duly aſcertained, before puniſhment is actually inflicted, whether the parties are deſirous or not of a divorce; becauſe, in the latter caſe, the huſband ſhall be allowed to redeem himſelf from puniſhment by a fine.

If the blows, whether ſtruck with a previous intention to kill or not, ſhould prove mortal, the huſband ſhall ſuffer death, by being ſtrangled at the uſual period.

A huſband who ſtrikes and wounds any of his inferior wives, ſhall be puniſhed one degree leſs ſeverely, than in the caſe of a huſband ſtriking his firſt wife; if the blows ſtruck by the huſband as aforeſaid prove mortal, he ſhall be puniſhed with 100 blows, and three years baniſhment.

A firſt wife who is guilty of ſtriking any of the inferior wives of her huſband, ſhall be puniſhed in the ſame manner as is already provided

vided in the caſe of a huſband ſtrking his firſt wife. — Accidentally killing in theſe caſes ſhall not entail any fine or puniſhment.

The offence of ſtriking a firſt wife's father or mother ſhall be puniſhed with 60 blows, and one year's baniſhment; the offence of ſtriking ſo as to wound ſuch perſons in any manner, ſhall be puniſhed two degrees more ſeverely than an equal offence in ordinary caſes; when the injury amounts to total diſability and permanent infirmity, the offender ſhall be ſtrangled: if death enſues from the blows ſtruck, either with or without a previous intention to kill, the offender ſhall be beheaded at the uſual period.

Four clauſes.

SECTION CCCXVI. — *Striking a Relation not within any of the four Degrees.*

In all caſes of aſſaulting and ſtriking, which occur between relations of the ſame name, but not within the degrees for which mourning is enjoined, a diſtinction ſhall be made between the junior and the ſenior; and the blow ſtruck by a junior ſhall accordingly be puniſhed one degree more, and that ſtruck by a ſenior one degree leſs ſeverely, than an equal offence would have been in ordinary caſes between equals: — Provided, nevertheleſs, that ſuch aggravation do not render any offence capital that previouſly was not ſo. When the act of the offender is already by law a capital offence, it ſhall be puniſhed as provided in ordinary caſes.

No clauſe.

SEC-

SECTION CCCXVII. — *Striking a Relation in the ſecond, third, or fourth Degree.*

A junior relation ſtriking his ſenior in the fourth degree, who is alſo equi-diſtant from the parent ſtock, ſhall be puniſhed with 100 blows: — if in the third degree, with 60 blows, and one year's baniſhment; and if in the ſecond degree, with 70 blows, and baniſhment for a year and a half. — If the relation ſtruck is not only elder but nearer to the parent-ſtock, the puniſhment ſhall be ſtill ſeverer by one degree. — In caſes of ſtriking ſo as to wound, the puniſhment ſhall be generally one degree more ſevere than in ordinary caſes, but limited to 100 blows, and perpetual baniſhment, except when the wound produces permanent diſability and infirmity, in which event the offender ſhall be ſtrangled.

When death enſues, the offender ſhall be beheaded. If the deceaſed is an elder relation in the ſecond degree, this ſentence ſhall be executed immediately after conviction; but otherwiſe, not until the uſual period.

A ſenior relation in the ſecond, third, or fourth degree, ſhall not be liable to puniſhment for ſtriking his junior, unleſs the blow ſhould produce a cutting wound; and in ſevere caſes, the puniſhment of a ſenior relation in the fourth degree, ſhall be reduced one degree; if in the third degree, two degrees; and if in the ſecond degree, three degrees below that provided in ordinary caſes of a ſimilar offence between equals. — If the wound occaſions death, the offender, in all the above caſes, ſhall, whether killing with or without a previous deſign to kill, ſuffer death by being ſtrangled. — Nevertheleſs, a perſon who ſtrikes either his junior firſt couſin, his junior firſt couſin's children, or his grand-nephew or grand-niece by the brother's ſide, ſo as to occaſion death

death, but without any direct intention to kill, ſhall only be puniſhed with 100 blows, and perpetual baniſhment to the diſtance of 3000 *lee*; if at the ſame time guilty of deſigning to kill, the offender ſhall, in every ſuch caſe, be ſtrangled *.

Seven clauſes.

Section CCCXVIII. — *Striking a Relation in the firſt Degree.*

Any perſon who is guilty of ſtriking his elder brother or ſiſter, ſhall be puniſhed, at the leaſt, with 90 blows and baniſhment for two years and a half; but if guilty of ſtriking ſo as to wound, with 100 blows and three years baniſhment; if guilty of ſtriking ſo as to cauſe a cutting wound, with 100 blows and perpetual baniſhment to the diſtance of 3000 *lee*. The offence of ſtriking and in any manner wounding with a ſharp-bladed inſtrument ſuch aforeſaid relations, breaking a bone, or blinding an eye, ſhall be puniſhed (the offender being the principal, in this as well as in the preceding caſes,) with death, by being ſtrangled. If the blow inflicted proves mortal, the principal, and all the acceſſaries related as aforeſaid to the deceaſed, ſhall be beheaded. — If a nephew ſtrikes his paternal uncle or aunt, or a grandſon his maternal grandfather or grandmother, the puniſh-

* As almoſt every imaginable degree and ſpecies of affinity by blood, or connexion by marriage, is diſtinguiſhed in the Chineſe language by a ſpecific and appropriate term, it would have been impoſſible, in many caſes, to convey in the tranſlation the preciſe idea, without burthening the text with very tedious and unimportant definitions. It is hoped, however, that the general terms employed, will be deemed by the European reader ſufficiently explanatory. — The nice and apparently trifling refinements which extend this book of the laws to an immoderate length, it might alſo, in many inſtances, be more ſatisfactory to have been juſtified in omitting, but theſe details, however unintereſting in themſelves, are characteriſtic of the general ſyſtem of the code, and could not have been retrenched without partially abridging the text, and thus deſtroying the unity as well as impairing the authenticity of the tranſlation.

ment ſhall, according to the conſequences, be one degree more ſevere than in the caſe of ſtriking an elder brother or ſiſter. — If any perſon accidentally kills or wounds ſuch of his relations, the puniſhment ſhall be two degrees leſs than that of killing or wounding an elder brother or ſiſter, as already provided, and ſhall not be redeemable, as in other caſes of accident, by a fine. — All the principals and acceſſaries to the crime of intentionally killing any perſon related as laſt mentioned, provided each of them is individually ſo related to the deceaſed, ſhall ſuffer death by a ſlow and painful execution. — Nevertheleſs, if the principal and contriver of the murder is a ſtranger, the acceſſaries thereto, related as above ſtated, ſhall only be puniſhed as acceſſaries in ordinary caſes. — The offence of wounding ſo as to kill a younger brother or ſiſter, a brother's ſon or daughter, a grandſon or grand-daughter by a daughter, ſhall, in each caſe, be puniſhed with 100 blows and three years baniſhment.

The offence of intentionally killing ſuch junior relations ſhall ſubject the offender to a puniſhment of 100 blows and perpetual baniſhment to the diſtance of 2000 *lee*: killing by accident, or wounding in any manner without killing ſuch junior relations, ſhall not be attended with any puniſhment *.

Fourteen clauſes.

Section CCCXIX. — *Striking a Father or Mother, paternal Grandfather or Grandmother.*

Any perſon who is guilty of ſtriking his father, mother, paternal grandfather or grandmother; and any wife who is guilty of ſtriking

* Notwithſtanding this general exemption from puniſhment, it is provided by the ſixth clauſe, that a ſenior relation ſtriking his junior maliciouſly, and ſo as to occaſion entirely diſability and incurable infirmity, ſhall be puniſhed but one degree leſs ſeverely than already provided in the caſe of mortally wounding.

her

her huſband's father, mother, paternal grandfather or grandmother, ſhall ſuffer death by being beheaded. — Any perſon who is guilty of killing ſuch a near relation, ſhall ſuffer death by a ſlow and painful execution.

Any perſon who kills ſo near a relation, purely by accident, ſhall ſtill be puniſhed with 100 blows and perpetual baniſhment to the diſtance of 3000 *lee*. In the caſe of wounding purely by accident, the perſon convicted thereof, ſhall be puniſhed with 100 blows and three years baniſhment: in theſe caſes, moreover, the parties ſhall not be permitted to redeem themſelves from puniſhment by the payment of a fine, as uſual in the ordinary caſes of accident.

If a father, mother, paternal grandfather or grandmother, chaſtiſes a diſobedient child or grandchild in a ſevere and uncuſtomary manner, ſo that he or ſhe dies, the party ſo offending ſhall be puniſhed with 100 blows. — When any of the aforeſaid relations are guilty of killing ſuch diſobedient child or grandchild deſignedly, the puniſhment ſhall be extended to 60 blows and one year's baniſhment *.

In the caſe of a mother-in-law or adopted mother ſo offending, the puniſhment ſhall be increaſed one degree beyond that provided in the pre-

* It is manifeſt from this article, that parents are not in any caſe abſolutely entruſted with a power over the lives of their children, and that accordingly the crime of infanticide, however prevalent it may be ſuppoſed to be in China, is not in fact either directly ſanctioned by the government, or agreeable to the general ſpirit of the laws and inſtitutions of the empire. This practice, ſo revolting to the feelings of humanity, muſt certainly be acknowledged to exiſt in China, and even to be in ſome degree tolerated, but there are conſiderable reaſons for ſuppoſing that the extent has been often over-rated; and at all events it does not ſeem allowable to lay any very great ſtreſs upon the exiſtence of ſuch a practice, as a proof of the cruelty or inſenſibility of the Chineſe character. — Even the dreadful crime of a parent deſtroying its offspring, is extenuated by the wretched and deſperate ſituation to which the labouring poor in China, to whom the practice of infanticide is admitted to be in general confined, muſt, by the univerſal and almoſt compulſory cuſtom of early marriages, often be reduced, of having large and increaſing families, while, owing to the already exceſſive population of the country, they have not the moſt diſtant proſpect of being able to maintain them.

ceding caſe; but if the connexion had been previouſly diſſolved by a divorce between the parents, or otherwiſe, the crime of killing, either with or without a previous deſign to kill, ſhall be puniſhed with death, by being ſtrangled.—If a father, mother, paternal grandfather or grandmother chaſtiſes a ſon's or grandſon's wife, or an adopted child or grandchild, in a ſevere and uncuſtomary manner, ſo as to produce a permanent injury, they ſhall ſuffer the puniſhment of 80 blows.

If the chaſtiſement produces total diſability and irremediable infirmity, the puniſhment ſhall be increaſed to 90 blows, and in every ſuch caſe, the adopted child and own child's wife ſhall be ſent back to the family whence they were taken.

In the caſe of the wife, the marriage preſent ſhall be refunded, and ten *leang* or ounces of ſilver added to it by the offending party, towards the ſupport of the ſufferer; in that of the child, the two families ſhall raiſe jointly the ſum requiſite for that purpoſe.—If the blows given as aforeſaid prove mortal, the offenders ſhall be puniſhed with 100 blows and three years baniſhment: if the blows which proved mortal were ſtruck with an intention to kill, the puniſhment ſhall be further increaſed to 100 blows and perpetual baniſhment to the diſtance of 2000 *lee*.

If, in any of theſe caſes, the ſon's or grandſon's wife was not the firſt or principal wife, the puniſhment ſhall be proportionably leſs in each caſe by two degrees, and the family ſhall not be compelled in any ſuch inſtance, to concur in providing for the ſupport of the wife, after ſhe is reſtored to her family.

If a ſon or grandſon abuſes and ſtrikes his father, mother, paternal grandfather or grandmother, or a wife her huſband's father, mother, paternal grandfather or grandmother; and ſuch father, mother, grandfather or grandmother, in conſequence, ſtrikes or beats to death ſuch child or grandchild; or if ſuch child or grandchild being diſobedient, his or her relations as aforeſaid chaſtiſe him or her in a lawful and cuſtomary manner,

manner, and under ſuch chaſtiſement he or ſhe accidentally and unexpectedly dies; or laſtly, if by mere chance or accident any perſon is killed by any of his or her aforeſaid near relations, the party convicted of homicide under ſuch circumſtances, ſhall not be liable to any puniſhment.

Nine clauſes.

SECTION CCCXX. — *Wives ſtriking their Huſband's Relations.*

A principal or other wife ſtriking any of her huſband's relations in the firſt, ſecond, third, or fourth degree, ſhall be puniſhed in the ſame manner as the huſband would have been, had he been guilty of ſtriking ſuch perſons, except that, unleſs the blows occaſion death, the puniſhment of the wife ſhall not exceed 100 blows and perpetual baniſhment. — If the blows occaſion death, the wife ſhall, in the caſe of a ſenior relation, be beheaded at the uſual period, and in the caſe of a junior relation, ſtrangled at the uſual period. — In the caſe of a principal wife, ſtriking ſo as to kill her huſband's brother's children, the puniſhment ſhall amount to 100 blows and perpetual baniſhment to the diſtance of 3000 *lee*; but in the caſe of killing ſuch perſons deſignedly, the puniſhment ſhall be that of death, by being ſtrangled. — Any other wife than the principal, ſtriking her huſband's junior relations, ſhall (in exception to the foregoing rule) be puniſhed as ſeverely as is provided by the laws in ordinary caſes between equals.

A ſenior relation in any of the four degrees, ſtriking his junior relation's principal wife, ſhall be puniſhed one degree leſs ſeverely than in ordinary caſes between equals. — If ſtriking any of the inferior wives, the puniſhment ſhall be further reduced one degree.

Neverthеleſs, if death enſues, whether or not in conſequence of a previous intention to kill, and whether the deceaſed had been or not a principal wife, the offender ſhall be ſtrangled.

If

If a younger brother or ſiſter ſtrikes an elder brother's principal wife, the puniſhment ſhall be one degree more ſevere than in ordinary caſes between equals.

If an elder brother or ſiſter ſtrikes a younger brother's wife; if an elder brother's principal wife ſtrikes her huſband's younger brother or ſiſter, or younger brother's wife, the puniſhment ſhall, in each caſe, be one degree leſs ſevere than in ordinary caſes; and when the wife who is ſtruck is not the principal one, the puniſhment ſhall be further reduced one degree.

A man guilty of ſtriking the huſband of any of his ſiſters, or any of his principal wife's brothers, and a principal wife guilty of ſtriking the huſband of any of her huſband's ſiſters, ſhall only be puniſhed as in ordinary caſes. — Nevertheleſs, within the limits of offences not capital, the puniſhment in the caſe of an inferior wife offending ſhall be one degree more ſevere than in that of the principal one, that is to ſay, one degree more ſevere than in ordinary caſes between equals — If an inferior wife ſtrikes any of her huſband's other inferior wives' children, the puniſhment ſhall be two degrees leſs ſevere than in ordinary caſes between equals; but if any ſuch inferior wife ſtrikes any of her huſband's principal wife's children, the puniſhment ſhall be the ſame as in ordinary caſes between equals.

If a principal wife's child ſtrikes his or her father's inferior wife, the puniſhment ſhall be one degree more ſevere than in ordinary caſes. — If a child of one of the inferior wive's ſhould ſtrike any other of the inferior wives, except its own mother, the puniſhment ſhall be further increaſed two degrees; theſe ſeveral augmentations ſhall not however have effect ſo as to render any puniſhment capital, that would not have been ſo in ordinary caſes. — When death enſues, the puniſhment of ſuch offenders ſhall be inflicted in the degree and manner provided in the caſe of ſimilar offences committed between equals in ordinary caſes.

Two clauſes.

SEC-

Section CCCXXI. — *Striking a Wife's Children by her former Hufband.*

When any perfon ftrikes his wife's children by a former hufband, he fhall, if living with fuch children under the fame roof, be punifhed two degrees, but if living feparately, one degree only, lefs feverely than in ordinary cafes between equals.

Whenever in fuch cafes, the blows ftruck prove mortal, the offenders fhall fuffer death, by being ftrangled at the ufual period.

Any perfon ftriking his or her ftep-father, fhall be punifhed with 60 blows, and one year's banifhment.

In all aggravated cafes, the punifhment fhall be one degree more fevere if the parties live feparately, and two degrees more fevere than in ordinary cafes, if they live under the fame roof: but thefe augmentations fhall not, in any cafe, render the punifhment capital: — when death enfues, the offenders fhall be beheaded, whether the deceafed was ftruck with or without a previous intention of killing.

When the parties neither lived under the fame roof at the time, nor had ever lived fo previoufly, this law fhall not take effect; and all reciprocal offences between them fhall be punifhed as in ordinary cafes between equals.

No claufe.

Section CCCXXII. — *Widows ftriking the Parents of their deceafea Hufbands.*

Any principal or inferior wife ftriking her hufband's father or mother, paternal grandfather or grandmother, after the death of fuch hufband, and even after having entered into a fecond marriage, fhall (except in the cafe of her having been divorced from fuch former hufband)

hufband) be liable to the fame punifhment for each offence, as if fuch former hufband had been ftill living. — In like manner, any perfon ftriking his or her deceafed fon's widows, except as aforefaid, in the cafe of a divorce having taken place, fhall, even after fuch wife had entered into a fecond marriage, only be liable to the punifhment provided in the cafe of ftriking fuch a relation during the fon's lifetime.

When however a divorce has taken place, the connexion between the parties and their relations is thereby totally diffolved, and all reciprocal injuries between them are accordingly punifhable in the fame manner as between equals in ordinary cafes.

When a mafter ftrikes his former flave, or a flave his former mafter, the parties fhall be punifhed as in ordinary cafes between flaves and freemen, the connexion which had previoufly exifted having been broken by the fale and purchafe. — But if a mafter manumits or releafes his flave, the original right and obligation not having been transferred to another, and the original connexion being ftill in fome fenfe unbroken, the provifions contained in this law fhall not take effect, and punifhment fhall therefore be awarded in all fuch cafes in the fame manner as if no manumiffion had taken place.

No claufe.

SECTION CCCXXIII. — *Striking in Defence of a Parent.*

Whoever, upon perceiving a father, mother, paternal grandfather or grandmother, to be ftruck by any perfon, immediately interpofes in defence of fuch near relation, and ftrikes the aggreffor, fhall, unlefs ftriking fuch a blow as to produce a cutting wound, be entirely juftified and free from refponfibility; and even if the wound inflicted by the individual who interpofes under fuch circumftances is fevere, he fhall be punifhed

punifhed lefs feverely by three degrees than in ordinary cafes; excepting only thofe inftances in which the blows ftruck prove mortal, when the punifhment fhall be the fame as in ordinary cafes. To entitle, however, any perfon to the benefit of this law, it muft always be ftrictly proved that the blows were inflicted on the impulfe of the moment, and actually in defence of fuch aforefaid relation.

If a fon or grandfon, upon the event of a father or mother, a paternal grandfather or grandmother having been murdered, inftead of complaining to the magiftrate, takes revenge by killing the murderer, he fhall be punifhed with 60 blows; fuch fon or grandfon fhall be however entirely juftified, if he kills the murderer upon the impulfe of the moment, and at the inftant that the murder is committed. — At the fame time, this law is not by any means to be pleaded in juftification of a fon or grandfon, who enters jointly into a quarrel or affray with his parents or grandparents; and accordingly the offenders in all fuch inftances fhall be punifhed either as principals, or as acceffaries, as the cafe may be, in the fame manner as they would have been in ordinary cafes: — And altho' it fhall be lawful to defend any of the aforefaid near relations, not only againft ftrangers, but alfo againft other relations lefs nearly connected, it fhall not be allowed to ftrike any of the latter relations in return, and all fons or grandfons who are guilty thereof fhall be punifhed in the ordinary manner according to the law in fuch cafes provided.

When any perfon kills the murderer of any of his other relations, inftead of lawfully complaining to a magiftrate, he fhall, if it appears upon the trial, that he was really actuated by no other motive befide that of revenging the death of fuch relation, only be punifhed with 100 blows.

Three claufes.

END OF THE THIRD BOOK OF THE SIXTH DIVISION.

BOOK IV.

ABUSIVE LANGUAGE *.

Section CCCXXIV. — *Abufive Language between Equals.*

IN ordinary cafes, all perfons guilty of employing abufive language fhall be liable to a punifhment of 10 blows; and perfons abufing each other, fhall be punifhable with 10 blows refpectively.

No claufe.

Section CCCXXV. — *Abufive language to an Officer of Government.*

When any civil or military officer of a diftrict addreffes abufive language to a magiftrate invefted with efpecial powers by the Emperor; when any private individual addreffes abufive language to the governor, or other fuperior officer having authority in his diftrict; when any private foldier addreffes abufive language to an officer having a command directly or indirectly over him; and laftly, when any perfon having a civil or military employment in any public office, or under any civil or military officer of government, addreffes abufive language to an officer of government having authority over him, and being of the fifth or any fuperior rank; the offender in each of thefe cafes fhall be punifhed with 100 blows.

* It is obferved in the Chinefe commentary that "opprobrious and infulting language "having naturally a tendency to produce quarrels and affrays, this book of the laws "is exprefsly provided for its prevention and punifhment." It is not however to be fuppofed that laws of this nature are often, or very ftrictly enforced.

Any

Any perſon who, having a civil or military employment as in the caſe laſt mentioned, abuſes an officer having immediate authority over him, but yet only of the ſixth or of any ſtill lower rank, ſhall be liable to a puniſhment of 70 blows only. — If the inferior officer of government who had been abuſed, was only the aſſeſſor or deputy of the tribunal or public office to which the perſon abuſing him belonged, the puniſhment ſhall be further reduced to 60 blows: and in this, as well as in all the preceding caſes, in order to convict the offender, it is neceſſary that the abuſive language ſhall have been actually heard by the perſon to whom it was addreſſed.

Two clauſes.

SECTION CCCXXVI. — *Abuſive Language between Officers of the ſame Tribunal.*

If, in any government tribunal or public office, abuſive language is addreſſed to the preſiding member, by the deputy thereof, or by the preſiding member of any government tribunal or public office which is ſubordinate, the puniſhment ſhall, in each caſe, amount to 80 blows, provided the preſiding member who is abuſed is of the fifth or any ſtill higher rank; otherwiſe the puniſhment ſhall be 50 blows only. — If the abuſive language is addreſſed by the aſſeſſor of any tribunal or public office to the preſiding member thereof, the puniſhment ſhall, agreeably to the diſtinction made in the preceding caſes, amount to 60 or to 30 blows, according as ſuch preſident is or is not of the fifth or any ſuperior order of rank in the ſtate.

In no caſe ſhall the offender be convicted, unleſs the abuſive language had been actually heard by the perſon to whom it was addreſſed.

No clauſe.

SECTION CCCXXVII. — *Abuſive Language from a Slave to his Maſter.*

A ſlave guilty of addreſſing abuſive language to his maſter ſhall ſuffer death, by being ſtrangled at the uſual period.

If guilty of addreſſing abuſive language to his maſter's relations in the firſt degree, or to his maſter's maternal grandfather or grandmother, he ſhall be puniſhed with 80 blows, and two years baniſhment: — If addreſſing abuſive language to his maſter's relations in the ſecond degree, the puniſhment ſhall be 80 blows; if in the third degree, 70 blows; if in the fourth degree, 60 blows.

A hired ſervant addreſſing abuſive language to his maſter, ſhall be puniſhed with 80 blows, and two years baniſhment; if to his maſter's relations in the firſt degree, or maternal grandfather or grandmother, his puniſhment ſhall amount to 100 blows; if to his maſter's relations in the ſecond degree, to 60 blows: if to the relations in the third degree, to 50 blows; and if to the relations in the fourth degree, to 40 blows. — In theſe caſes, as well as others, the abuſive language muſt have been heard by the perſon to whom it was addreſſed, and ſuch perſon muſt always be the complainant.

No clauſe.

SECTION CCCXXVIII. — *Abuſive Language to an elder Relation.*

Any perſon who is guilty of addreſſing abuſive language to an elder relation in the fourth degree, equi-diſtant from the parent ſtock, ſhall be puniſhed with 50 blows: if to a relation in the third degree, under ſimilar circumſtances, with 60 blows: and if to a relation as aforeſaid, in the ſecond degree, with 70 blows; but when ſuch relation is alſo one or more generations nearer to the parent ſtock, the puniſhment ſhall be more ſevere, in each caſe, than above provided, by one degree.

Whoever

Whoever addreſſes abuſive language to his elder brother or ſiſter, ſhall be puniſhed with 100 blows: whoever abuſes his paternal uncle or aunt, or his maternal grandfather or grandmother, ſhall be puniſhed one degree more ſeverely than in the caſe laſt mentioned: — but, as it has been ſtated in the preceding articles, the law can only be enforced when the perſon to whom the abuſive language was addreſſed, actually heard it, and is himſelf the complainant.

No clauſe.

SECTION CCCXXIX. — *Abuſive Language to a Parent, Paternal Grandfather or Grandmother.*

A child or grandchild who is guilty of addreſſing abuſive language to his or her father or mother, paternal grandfather or grandmother; a wife who is guilty of addreſſing abuſive language to her huſband's father or mother, paternal grandfather or grandmother, ſhall in every caſe ſuffer death, by being ſtrangled; provided always however, that the perſons abuſed, themſelves complain thereof to the magiſtrates, and had themſelves heard the abuſive language which had been addreſſed to them.

One clauſe.

SECTION CCCXXX. — *Abuſive Language from a Wife to her Huſband's Relations.*

A principal or inferior wife who is guilty of addreſſing abuſive language to any of her huſband's relations within the four degrees, ſhall be liable to the ſame puniſhment as her huſband would have been for uſing towards ſuch perſons the ſame language. — An inferior wife abuſing her huſband or huſband's principal wife, ſhall be puniſhed with 80 blows. — A huſband abuſing his wife's father or mother, ſhall be be liable to a punifhment of 60 blows; but in all cafes fuch abufive language muft, as already obferved, have been heard and complained of by the parties to whom it was addreffed.

There is no claufe refpecting abufive language addreffed by a principal wife to her hufband, as the interpofition of the laws can fcarcely be fuppofed to be neceffary; yet if fuch a cafe fhould occur, the magiftrates may lawfully award a punifhment of 50 blows, according to the law refpecting offences againft propriety.

No claufe.

SECTION CCCXXXI. — *Abufive Language addreffed by a Widow to her deceafed Hufband's Parents.*

If any principal or inferior wife is guilty of addreffing abufive language to her hufband's father or mother, paternal grandfather or grandmother, after the death of fuch hufband, and even after having entered into a fecond marriage, fhe fhall (except in the cafe of her having been divorced from fuch former hufband,) be liable to the fame punifhment for each offence, as if fuch hufband were ftill living.

A flave addreffing abufive language to his former mafter, fhall only be punifhed as in ordinary cafes, the connexion between the parties having been broken by the transfer to another mafter; but a flave addreffing abufive language to the mafter who had manumitted or releafed him, fhall be liable to the fame punifhment as he would have been if he had continued in fuch mafter's fervice.

No claufe.

END OF THE FOURTH BOOK OF THE SIXTH DIVISION.

BOOK V.

INDICTMENTS AND INFORMATIONS.

Section CCCXXXII. — *Irregularity in preſenting Informations.*

ALL the ſubjects of the empire, whether ſoldiers or citizens, who have complaints and informations to lay before the officers of government, ſhall addreſs themſelves in the firſt inſtance, to the loweſt tribunal of juſtice within the diſtrict to which they belong, from which the cognizance of the affair may be transferred to the ſuperior tribunals in regular gradation *. — Any individual who, inſtead of addreſſing himſelf to the proper magiſtrate within his diſtrict, proceeds at once to lay his complaint and information before a ſuperior tribunal, ſhall be puniſhed with 50 blows, although his complaint ſhould be juſt, and his information correct.

It is however lawful to appeal to a ſuperior magiſtrate, when the inferior officer of juſtice refuſes to receive the information and complaint, or decides thereon unjuſtly; but not otherwiſe.

Whoever, in order to preſent an information, detains an officer of juſtice in his public progreſs; and whoever, for the ſame purpoſe, ſummons any officer of juſtice to his tribunal by beat of drum, ſhall be puniſhed with 100 blows, if his information be falſe and complaint groundleſs; and if he ſhould be likewiſe guilty of the crime of a falſe and malicious accuſation againſt any perſon, he ſhall be puniſhed as

* For an exemplification of the ordinary routine of judicial proceedings in the more ſerious criminal caſes, ſee the official report of the inveſtigation of charges againſt an Engliſh ſeaman, in the Appendix, No. XI.

much

much more ſeverely as the law applicable to ſuch caſes of criminality may authorize.

Nevertheleſs, if his cauſe is found to be a juſt one, the irregularity of his proceedings ſhall be pardoned *.

Twenty clauſes.

SECTION CCCXXXIII. — *Anonymous Informations.*

Any perſon who addreſſes and preſents an information and complaint to an officer of government, containing direct criminal charges againſt a particular individual, without having inſerted therein his (the informant's) proper name and family name, ſhall, although the charges ſhould prove true, be puniſhed with death, by being ſtrangled at the uſual period.

Whenever any ſuch anonymous information or complaint is diſcovered, it ſhall be immediately burned or otherwiſe deſtroyed; and if the perſon who accidentally finds ſuch a document, inſtead of ſo doing, preſents it to a magiſtrate or ſome other officer of government, he ſhall be puniſhed with 80 blows.

Any officer of government who, nevertheleſs, takes upon himſelf to act upon any ſuch anonymous information and complaint, ſhall be puniſhable with 100 blows; and no perſon, whether accuſed juſtly or not, ſhall be liable to be in any caſe convicted or puniſhed on the ground of anonymous charges.

* It appears from this and other articles of the code, that an appeal from the lower to the higher tribunals is allowed both in civil as well as criminal cauſes, not, as has been ſuppoſed, in criminal cauſes only; indeed there are no traces of any ſuch diſtinction, as that of civil and criminal, in the juriſprudence of the Chineſe; but it is probable, that as thoſe cauſes which might be denominated *civil*, are, from the ordinary tenure of property and other circumſtances, of comparatively ſmall importance in China, they are not neceſſarily referred to the deciſion of the higher courts, and therefore, generally ſpeaking, decided by the officers of the diſtricts in which ſuch diſputes originate.

Every

Every officer of government who has unlawfully acted as aforesaid, shall likewise be obliged to make a compensation of ten ounces of silver to each of the persons whom, on account of anonymous charges, he may have summoned to his tribunal.

According to this law, all those also shall be punished who, under assumed or forged names, pretend to give information to the officers of government of any undiscovered crimes or other secret and hidden transactions; or who, availing themselves of blank stamped papers belonging to others, fill them up with accusations, and prevail upon or bribe the soldiers or other attendants of tribunals, to deliver them to the sitting magistrates.

This law shall not however extend to those who may have prepared, or be in possession of, such anonymous informations, unless they shall likewise have been instrumental in their presentation to the officers of government; nor shall this law extend to those anonymous informations, which, although actually presented, merely contain general censure and abuse, without precise charges of crimes against particular individuals.

Three clauses.

SECTION CCCXXXIV. — *Neglecting or declining to receive Informations.*

When an information concerning a charge of high treason or rebellion is regularly presented to an officer of government, if he does not immediately receive and act thereon, that is to say, take measures for seizing the culprits, and preventing the progress of such disorders, he shall be liable to a punishment of 100 blows and three years banishment, although no evil consequences should ensue from his neglect: but if through his inattention, considerable numbers are suffered to

 assemble

aſſemble tumultuouſly, attacking fortified ſtations, ravaging the country, and diſtreſſing the inhabitants, ſuch officer of government ſhall ſuffer death, by being beheaded at the uſual period.

In like manner, any officer of government who declines to receive, and to act upon an information containing a charge of parricide, or of ſome other enormous crime of a private nature, ſhall be puniſhed with 100 blows.

If the rejected information contained a charge of robbery, murder, or of any like offences, the officer of government ſhall be puniſhed with 80 blows.

If the offence charged in the rejected information, was a breach of the laws againſt quarrelling and fighting, or of thoſe concerning marriage and landed property, or concerning any other laws of the ſame claſs, the puniſhment of the officer of government for not receiving the ſame, ſhall be two degrees only leſs than that to which the accuſed perſon would have been liable, except that it ſhall not, in any of theſe caſes, exceed 80 blows. — If ſuch officer of government had been bribed by the accuſed party, he ſhall be puniſhed proportionably to the amount of the bribe, according to the law againſt receiving a bribe for an unlawful purpoſe, whenever the puniſhment is greater than that provided by the law above ſtated.

When the accuſer and the accuſed party belong to different diſtricts and juriſdictions, the magiſtrates having authority over the latter, ſhall take cognizance of, and pronounce judgment upon the charges made in the diſtrict of the former, and if he ſhould endeavour to excuſe himſelf from ſuch duty, he ſhall be puniſhed according to this law.

When any cauſe comes before the tribunal of the viceroy, ſub-viceroy, or ordinary or extraordinary judge in any province, which cauſe had either not been reported at all, or if reported, not finally judged and determined by the magiſtrate to whoſe juriſdiction it belonged, it ſhall be duly regiſtered, and an entry made of the particulars thereof, by by the viceroy or other ſuperior officer having cognizance thereof, in order that a certain limited period may be fixed for its final determination by the proper magiſtrate; and if, when ſuch magiſtrate commits any miſtake, or is guilty of any culpable delay, the viceroy and other ſuperior officers connive thereat, inſtead of rectifying or accelerating the deciſion, as the caſe may require, they ſhall be liable to the ſame puniſhment as the inferior magiſtrates.

If, in any caſe of an official report, or of a criminal information having been laid before the proper officer or magiſtrate, ſuch magiſtrate refuſes to receive the ſame and act thereon, or if, after having received, he acts upon it unjuſtly and illegally, the officers and magiſtrates of ſuperior tribunals are bound to take cognizance thereof in regular gradation and ſucceſſion, and if the ſaid ſuperior officers excuſe themſelves from receiving and acting upon ſuch appeals from inferior juriſdictions, or transfer the cognizance of them to a deputy, or ſend them back unexamined to the magiſtrates from whoſe tribunals the appeals had been made, they ſhall, in each caſe, be puniſhable under this law.

In general, every magiſtrate and tribunal ſhall, conformably to the extent of their powers and juriſdiction, not only receive and undertake to inveſtigate, but alſo bring to a final iſſue and adjudication, each of the ſeveral criminal cauſes and queſtions on official buſineſs that lawfully come before them; and whenever they, on the contrary, depute or inſtruct other magiſtrates to continue any ſuch inveſtigations in their place and ſtead, the magiſtrates and members of tribunals ſo offending ſhall be liable to puniſhment, in the ſame manner as above provided.

Nine clauſes.

SECTION CCCXXXV. — *Informations which muſt be transferred to the Cognizance of others.*

Whenever any information is laid before a magiſtrate, who is related by blood or by marriage to the accuſer or to the accuſed, who was educated by, or had ever ſerved under either party, or who, laſtly, had been habitually the enemy or public adverſary of either; in all ſuch caſes the magiſtrate muſt decline to act thereon, and ſhall therefore transfer it forthwith to another juriſdiction.

Any magiſtrate who takes cognizance of a cauſe under ſuch circumſtances, ſhall be liable to a puniſhment of 40 blows, although he ſhould have pronounced a juſt and impartial ſentence: — otherwiſe, he will be liable to the ſeverer puniſhment attending an intentional deviation from juſtice.

No clauſe.

SECTION CCCXXXVI. — *Falſe and malicious Informations**.

Whoever lays before a magiſtrate a falſe and malicious information, in which ſome perſon is expreſsly charged with a crime puniſhable with any number of blows, not exceeding 50, ſhall ſuffer a puniſhment two degrees more ſevere than that which the accuſed would have merited had the accuſation been true. — If the crime falſely alleged was puniſhable

* The following long article, by which the reſponſibility of each individual for the truth of the charges he may bring forward publicly before a magiſtrate, is, in every imaginable caſe, preciſely determined, ſeems in great meaſure to correſpond in its object with the laws in force in European countries, againſt (what is denominated by us) wilful and corrupt perjury.

The Chineſe do not indeed ſpecifically puniſh the breach of an oath, becauſe although frequently introduced into the private inveſtigation and adjuſtment of diſputes, oaths are never required, or even admitted, in judicial proceedings.

with

with more than 50 blows, or with temporary or perpetual baniſhment, the puniſhment of the accuſer ſhall be three degrees more ſevere than that to which the accuſed is rendered liable; but ſhall not, in theſe, or in any of the preceding caſes, be ſo increaſed as to become capital.

When the accuſed perſon, having been condemned upon ſuch falſe accuſation as aforeſaid, ſhall have proceeded to the place to which he had been ſentenced to be either temporarily or perpetually baniſhed; although he ſhould have been afterwards ſpeedily recalled on a diſcovery of his innocence, an eſtimate ſhall be made and verified before the magiſtrate, of the expences he may have incurred by his journey, that the falſe accuſer may be compelled to reimburſe him to the full amount; and the falſe accuſer ſhall likewiſe be obliged to redeem, or re-purchaſe for him, any lands or tenements which he may have ſold or mortgaged to defray ſuch expences. — Moreover, if ſuch unmerited baniſhment ſhould occaſion the death of any of the relations of the innocent perſon, who may have followed him to his deſtination, the falſe accuſer ſhall ſuffer death, by being ſtrangled; and beſides the reimburſement aforeſaid, half his remaining property ſhall be forfeited to the uſe of the innocent perſon. — When any perſon is falſely accuſed of a capital offence, and upon ſuch accuſation has been condemned and executed, the falſe accuſer ſhall be either ſtrangled or beheaded, according to the manner in which the innocent perſon had been executed, and half his property ſhall be forfeited as in the preceding inſtance.

If the execution of the ſentence of death againſt the innocent perſon had been prevented by a timely diſcovery of the falſehood of the accuſation, the falſe accuſer ſhall be puniſhed with 100 blows and perpetual baniſhment to the diſtance of 3000 *lee*, and moreover ſubjected to extra-ſervice during three years.

If the falſe accuſer is proved to be really ſo poor as to be unable to reimburſe the innocent perſon to the amount of his expences, his puniſhment

punishment shall not be aggravated on account of such incapacity. — If the innocent person should in his complaint or appeal to the magistrates, attempt to aggravate the guilt of the false accuser, by falsely alleging the death of a relation, or upon some other pretext, he shall, in his turn, be liable to the punishment of a false accuser, and the offence of the former shall be punished only according to its real extent.

When any person accuses another of more offences than one, if the lesser charge proves false, and the greater true; or among charges of equal criminality, if one only proves true, and the rest false, the accuser shall, in both cases, be excused from the penalties and punishment of a false and malicious information.

When, on the other hand, any person accuses another of two or more offences, whereof the lesser only proves true; and when in the case of a single offence having been charged by one person against another, the statement thereof is found to exceed the truth; upon either supposition, if, the punishment of the falsely alleged, or falsely aggravated offence, had been actually inflicted in consequence of such false accusation, the difference (estimated according to the established mode of computation hereafter exemplified,) between the falsely alleged and the actually committed offence, or between the falsely alleged greater, and the truly alleged lesser offence, shall be inflicted on the false accuser:— but if punishment, conformably to the nature of the falsely alleged, or falsely aggravated offence, shall not have actually been inflicted, having been prevented by a timely discovery of the falsehood of the accusation, the false accuser shall be permitted to redeem, according to an established scale *, the whole of the punishment which would have been due to him in the former case, provided it does not exceed

* See the introductory table. — The fines, it will be perceived, are little more than nominal.

100 blows; but if it ſhould exceed 100 blows, the 100 blows ſhall be inflicted, and he ſhall be only permitted to redeem the exceſs.

TABLE of Reference in Caſes of falſe and malicious Informations.

Degree.	Actual Puniſhment. Blows.	Baniſhment.	Eſtimated Equivalent. Blows.
1.	10	none - -	10
2.	20	none - -	20
3.	30	none - -	30
4.	40	none - -	40
5.	50	none - -	50
6.	60	none - -	60
7.	70	none - -	70
8.	80	none - -	80
9.	90	none - -	90
10.	100	none - -	100
11.	60	for one year - -	120
12.	70	for one year and a half -	140
13.	80	for two years - -	160
14.	90	for two years and a half -	180
15.	100	for three years. - -	200
16.	100	for life, diſtance 2000 *lee* -	220 } or 240
17.	100	for life, diſtance 2500 *lee* -	240 } or 240
18.	100	for life, diſtance 3000 *lee* -	260 } or 240

Baniſhment for life ſhall be eſtimated at 240 blows, when compared with any of the inferior degrees of puniſhment.

The uſe of the foregoing table may be illuſtrated by the following examples:

1. When the alleged and real offence are both puniſhable with the bamboo; as for inſtance, alleging a blow producing a bruiſe, and puniſhable with 40 blows, when abuſive language, which is puniſhable with 10 blows, had been the only offence committed.— The difference in this caſe is 30 blows, and ſhall be inflicted on the accuſer, if the accuſed had actually undergone the aggravated puniſhment, but otherwiſe may be redeemed.

2. When

2. When the alleged offence is puniſhable with temporary baniſhment, and the real offence, with the bamboo only; as for inſtance, alleging a blow occaſioning a fracture of a limb, or violent injury to the body, which offence is puniſhable with 100 blows and three years baniſhment, when in fact, only a bruiſe had been inflicted, which latter offence is puniſhable with 40 blows; the former puniſhment is in this caſe equivalent, according to the preceding table, to 200 blows, and the difference will therefore be 160 blows, equivalent (according to the ſame table) to 80 blows and two years baniſhment.

If in any ſuch inſtance, the accuſed has been condemned to ſuffer, and had actually proceeded to undergo the aggravated puniſhment, the accuſer ſhall be puniſhed with 80 blows and two years baniſhment; otherwiſe he ſhall ſuffer 100 blows, and redeem the remaining 60 by the payment of a fine.

3. When the alleged offence is puniſhable with perpetual baniſhment, and the real offence with the bamboo only; as for inſtance, alleging a blow ſtruck ſo as to break both thigh bones, which is puniſhable with 100 blows and perpetual baniſhment to the diſtance of 3000 *lee*, when only a bruiſe had been inflicted, which is puniſhable with 40 blows: now the latter puniſhment being generally eſtimated at 240 blows, the difference will be 200 blows, which, again is eſtimated to be equivalent to 100 blows and three years baniſhment; accordingly, if the accuſed had been condemned to ſuffer, and had actually proceeded to undergo the aggravated puniſhment, the accuſer ſhall be puniſhed with 100 blows and three years baniſhment; but otherwiſe he ſhall only ſuffer the 100 blows, and be permitted to redeem himſelf from the remaining puniſhment of baniſhment.

4. When the alleged and real offence are both puniſhable with temporary baniſhment; as for inſtance, alleging a theft to the amount to ninety ounces of ſilver, which offence is puniſhable with 100 blows and three years baniſhment, when it is afterwards proved that no more than fifty

fifty ounces had been ſtolen, which latter offence is puniſhable only with 60 blows and one year's baniſhment: ſince by the preceding table the former offence is equivalent to 200 and the latter to 120 blows, the difference will be 80 blows, and ſhall be accordingly inflicted on the accuſer if the accuſed had undergone the heavier puniſhment, but otherwiſe, be redeemable by the eſtabliſhed fine.

5. When the alleged offence is puniſhable with perpetual and the real offence with temporary baniſhment; as for inſtance, alleging the offence of ſacrilegiouſly digging up another man's burying ground, ſo as to lay a coffin bare, which offence is puniſhable with 100 blows and perpetual baniſhment to the diſtance of 3000 *lee*, when it afterwards appears on examination, that the ſacrilegious digging, not having been carried to the extent of laying bare any coffin, was puniſhable only with 100 blows and three years baniſhment; the former puniſhment being eſtimated at 240 and the latter at 200 blows, the difference will be 40 blows, and as ſuch ſhall be inflicted on the accuſer if the heavier puniſhment had been actually executed upon the accuſed, but otherwiſe, be redeemable by the ordinary fine.

6. Laſtly, when the alleged and real offence are both puniſhable with perpetual baniſhment, but to a greater diſtance in the former caſe than in the latter; as for inſtance, alleging a theft of one hundred and twenty ounces of ſilver, which is puniſhable with 100 blows and perpetual baniſhment to the diſtance of 3000 *lee*, when in fact, no more than one hundred ounces had been ſtolen, and the theft therefore puniſhable only with 100 blows and perpetual baniſhment to the diſtance of 2000 *lee*. In this caſe, by referring to the eſtimated equivalents of the ſeveral degrees of perpetual baniſhment in the table, as compared with each other, it will be found that the difference amounts to 40 blows; and therefore puniſhment to that extent ſhall be inflicted upon the accuſer,

if

if the accuſed had actually undergone the aggravated puniſhment; but otherwiſe ſhall be redeemable as in the preceding caſes.

In every caſe, when an offence has been committed which is not capital, the perſon falſely alleging another offence which is capital, or falſely aggravating the offence committed, ſo as to make it appear capital, ſhall, in the event of the accuſed perſon having been condemned and executed, ſuffer death in the ſame manner; in the event of execution not having been the conſequence of ſuch falſe information, the falſe accuſers ſhall be puniſhed with 100 blows and perpetual baniſhment to the diſtance of 3000 *lee*; but not be liable to the extra ſervice ſtated in a ſimilar caſe previouſly deſcribed.

Moreover, no aggravated or exaggerated ſtatement of an offence, on the part of the informant, ſhall be conſidered or puniſhed as ſuch, however much the offence may have been falſely alleged to be greater than it afterwards proves to be on examination, provided ſuch exaggeration does not, according to the exiſting laws, expoſe the offender to a ſeverer puniſhment: as for inſtance; alleging the acceptance of a bribe to the extent of two hundred ounces, when one hundred and thirty ounces was the real amount of the bribe; now, becauſe the receipt of a bribe to any extent beyond one hundred and twenty ounces is equally puniſhable with death by being ſtrangled at the uſual period, the additional charge againſt the offender of ſeventy ounces, does not in this caſe tend to aggravate his puniſhment. — If the different charges are not made againſt one and the ſame, but againſt different perſons, the truth of the charges againſt one or more perſons ſhall not be deemed any palliation of the offence of falſely accuſing other perſons, and all ſuch falſe accuſations ſhall be therefore regarded and puniſhed as diſtinct caſes.

When any of the magiſtrates ſuperintending the public tribunals are guilty of preferring falſe accuſations, or any public officers having high judicial and miniſterial powers, addreſs falſe accuſations of each other

other to the Emperor, they ſhall be puniſhed according to this law; and, in the latter caſe, the leaſt puniſhment incurred, will be that provided by law in ordinary caſes of a falſe ſtatement being wilfully made in an addreſs to his Imperial Majeſty.

If the relations of a priſoner, who had brought himſelf into that ſituation by his own miſconduct, and who had therefore in fact ſuffered no injuſtice, groundleſsly appeal and complain to the tribunals of government againſt his confinement and condemnation, they ſhall ſuffer a puniſhment three degrees leſs than that incurred by the priſoner, ſuch reduced puniſhment being at the ſame time limited to the extent of 100 blows.

If any ſuch juſtly condemned perſon, after having undergone the ſentence of the law, whether of corporal puniſhment with the bamboo, or the ſame, together with the addition of ſubſequent baniſhment, ſhould himſelf groundleſsly complain of his having ſuffered injuſtice, and attempt to frame and exhibit before the public tribunals, charges of culpability againſt the magiſtrates and clerks who had tried and condemned him, his puniſhment ſhall be three degrees more ſevere than that of the crime which he falſely alleges againſt ſuch magiſtrates and clerks; but nevertheleſs ſhall not exceed 100 blows, and perpetual baniſhment to the diſtance of 3000 *lee*.

If a perſon, juſtly condemned as aforeſaid, brings forward a falſe accuſation previous to the complete execution of his ſentence of baniſhment, his puniſhment ſhall be further regulated according to the law provided for the caſes of offences committed by exiles during the period of their baniſhment.

Twenty-three clauſes.

SECTION CCCXXXVII. — *Informations againſt Relations.*

A ſon accuſing his father or mother; a grandſon his paternal grandfather or grandmother; a principal or inferior wife, her huſband, or

 her

her husband's father or mother, paternal grandfather or grandmother, shall, in each case, be punished with 100 blows and three years banishment, even if the accusation prove true: the individuals so accused by their relations, if they voluntarily surrender and plead guilty, shall in each case also, be entitled to pardon.

In any of the above instances, if the charge should prove either in part or wholly false, the accuser shall suffer death by being strangled.

A junior relation accusing an elder relation in the first degree; a grandson accusing his maternal grandfather or grandmother, or an inferior wife accusing her husband's first wife, shall in each case suffer 100 blows, although the accusation should prove true.—In like manner, justly accusing an elder relation in the second degree, shall subject the accuser to be punished with 90 blows; an elder relation in the third degree, with 80 blows; and in the fourth degree, with 70 blows.

In the first of these cases, if the accused surrenders voluntarily, he or she shall be pardoned; in the other cases, the punishment shall be three degrees less than if the parties had been accused under the same circumstances by strangers.—In all these cases, if the accusation should prove to be false, the punishment of the junior relation accusing, shall be three degrees greater than when falsely accusing strangers in ordinary cases, except that such augmentation shall not in any case have the effect of rendering the punishment capital:—in cases of falsely accusing an elder relation beyond the fourth degree, the punishment shall exceed that provided in ordinary cases, by two degrees.

From the provisions of this law, an exception shall be made in favour of all those who justly accuse their relations of treason, rebellion, concealment of criminals, and the suppression or compromise of any of the greater offences against the state; and also in the case of the step-mother, mother in law, or natural mother killing the accuser's father; or the accuser's adopted mother killing his natural mother; or lastly in cases of the

the accuſer having been himſelf robbed or maltreated by a relation. — In all the caſes herein excepted, it ſhall be lawful to complain to the magiſtrates.

When juſtly accuſing a junior relation in the firſt or ſecond degree, or a ſon in law, if the accuſed voluntarily ſurrenders and confeſſes his offence, he ſhall be pardoned.

In the caſe of a relation in the third or fourth degree, the puniſhment of the accuſed under the ſame circumſtances, ſhall be reduced three degrees.

Falſely accuſing a junior relation in the firſt degree, ſhall be puniſhed three degrees leſs ſeverely than in ordinary caſes: in the ſecond degree, two degrees leſs; and in the third or fourth degree, one degree leſs:— a huſband falſely accuſing his principal wife, or a principal wife falſely accuſing any of the inferior wives of her huſband, ſhall be only liable to the ordinary puniſhment reduced three degrees. — The ſlaves of any family accuſing, whether truly or falſely, the maſter thereof, or any of his relations within the four degrees, ſhall be liable to the ſame puniſhment as the ſons or grandſons in ſuch family would have been, for accuſing truly or falſely their elder relations within the ſame degrees of affinity.

When accuſing ſuch perſons truly and juſtly, the puniſhment of hired ſervants ſhall be one degree leſs than that of ſlaves; but if falſely and unjuſtly, the ſame.

When ſlaves or hired ſervants are accuſed by their maſters, or their maſters relations, they ſhall not be entitled to pardon, as junior relations are ſtated to be in the preceding caſes, although voluntarily ſurrendering themſelves and acknowledging their offences.

A parent falſely accuſing his child; a paternal or maternal grandfather or grandmother their grandchild, or grandſon's principal or inferior wife; a huſband his inferior wife, or a maſter his ſlave or hired ſervant, ſhall not, in any caſe, be puniſhable. — Although the mutual accuſations of fathers and

and mothers in law on the one hand, and of ſons in law on the other, are generally to be judged according to the proviſions of this law; yet, when the connexion between the parties ſhall have been diſſolved by long ſeparation, by a divorce between the huſband and wife, or by the death of one of them; or laſtly, by any offence in direct violation of the connexion originally ſubſiſting between the parties, the laws ſhall be adminiſtered as in ordinary caſes between ſtrangers.

Three clauſes.

SECTION CCCXXXVIII. — *Diſobedience to Parents.*

All children and grand-children who are diſobedient to the inſtructions and commands of their fathers, mothers, paternal grandfathers and grandmothers, or who do not adequately provide for their ſupport and ſuſtenance, ſhall be puniſhable with 100 blows.

This law ſhall nevertheleſs only be underſtood to apply to caſes of wilful diſobedience of lawful inſtructions and commands, and to caſes of wilful neglect of maintenance, on the part of ſuch children or grand-children as have the means thereof; and it ſhall be moreover neceſſary in each caſe, that the near relation ſo diſobeyed or neglected, ſhould perſonally complain of, and inform againſt the offender.

Three clauſes.

SECTION CCCXXXIX. — *Informations preſented by Criminals under Confinement.*

Criminals, while in confinement, ſhall not be allowed to preſent or proſecute informations againſt any perſon or upon any affair whatſoever, except only when the object is to make complaint of ill treatment againſt the officers or inferior perſons belonging to the priſons; or to confeſs and give information upon other offences committed by themſelves, beſides befides thofe for which they are confined; or laftly, to give evidence againft and accufe the partners of their guilt, in which cafes their informations fhall be received and acted upon in due courfe of law, as under ordinary circumftances.

Perfons upwards of eighty or under ten years of age, perfons totally and incurably infirm, and females, in all cafes, are incapacitated from prefenting and profecuting any informations, excepting only fuch as concern the crimes of high treafon and rebellion, or the impiety of their children or grand children, or fuch as concern defigned murders, robberies, thefts, wounds, frauds, and the like, againft themfelves or perfons living with them under the fame roof. — On any other fubjects the informations of fuch perfons muft be rejected, becaufe in all ordinary cafes they are entitled to redeem themfelves from punifhment by a fine, and therefore not deterred from making falfe accufations by the apprehenfion of the confequences to which, under the fame circumftances, other perfons would become liable.

All magiftrates, therefore, who receive and act upon fuch unlawful informations, fhall be punifhed with 50 blows for their mifconduct.

One claufe.

SECTION CCCXL. — *Exciting and promoting Litigation.*

In all cafes of exciting and difpofing others to inform and profecute, the perfon who draws up the information for the profecutor, and by any aggravation or extenuation deviates from the truth, fhall be liable to the fame punifhment as the falfe accufer; except in a capital cafe, when his punifhment fhall be reduced one degree. — In the cafe of hiring any perfon to prefent and profecute a falfe accufation, the perfon hired fhall be liable to the fame punifhment as the

the falſe accuſer, under the ſame mitigation in capital caſes, as in the preceding inſtance.

If the perſon who is hired had received a reward in money, ſuch reward ſhall be conſidered as a bribe for an unlawful purpoſe, and the puniſhment which is legally proportionate to ſuch offence ſhall be inflicted, whenever it proves on compariſon more ſevere than that by this law provided.

Neverthelefs, if any one meets with a ſimple and uninformed perſon, who is unable to ſtate the injuries and injuſtice which he has ſuffered; and conſequently adviſes and inſtructs ſuch perſon rightly and truly how to act upon the occaſion, and moreover, without extenuating or aggravating the particulars, draws up an information for him in the legal and cuſtomary manner, the giver of ſuch aſſiſtance ſhall not, under theſe circumſtances, be in any manner puniſhable.

An adulterer who is guilty of adviſing and inſtructing the adultreſs to accuſe her legitimate ſon of a neglect of his filial duty, ſhall be puniſhed as a contriver of murder.

Ten clauſes.

SECTION CCCXLI. — *Informations on Subjects affecting Civil as well as Military Affairs.*

In caſes of homicide charged againſt perſons enrolled in the military claſs, the commanding officer of the perſons charged therewith ſhall aſſiſt and be preſent, when the civil magiſtrate of the diſtrict inveſtigates and decides upon the caſe, of which he only has competent authority to take cogniſance. — In all caſes of adultery, robbery, frauds, aſſaults, breach of laws concerning marriage, landed property, or pecuniary contracts, and of any other the like offences, committed by or againſt individuals in the military claſs; if any of the people are implicated or concerned,

the

the military commanding officer and the civil magiſtrate ſhall have a concurrent juriſdiction; if not, the military officer in command ſhall examine and decide the caſe between the parties, at his own tribunal.—Whenever, in any of the preceding caſes, the officers of a military tribunal interpoſe an undue influence and authority in order to impede the regular progreſs of judicial proceedings, and to protect the criminals belonging to their particular juriſdiction from merited puniſhment, the deputies adminiſtering in, and the inferior officers belonging to ſuch tribunal, ſhall each be liable, at the leaſt, to a puniſhment of 50 blows.

This law ſhall alſo extend to all military officers who exceed their powers by receiving and acting upon informations belonging of right to the civil juriſdiction.

Seven clauſes.

Section CCCXLII.—*Informations and Proſecutions on the Part of Officers of Government.*

All officers of government of every deſcription, including thoſe having official ſituations without rank, when intereſted in any private cauſes reſpecting marriage, pecuniary contracts, debts, or the diviſion of landed property, ſhall, inſtead of proſecuting or defending their ſuits perſonally, appoint a ſervant or other perſon belonging to their family to perform that ſervice; and at the ſame time refrain from interpoſing their influence and authority by any official communication on the ſubject with the magiſtrates who have the cognizance of the affair.

40 Blows ſhall be the puniſhment of any breach of this law.

No clauſe.

SECTION CCCXLIII. — *Falſe Accuſation of Offences puniſhable with extraordinary Baniſhment.*

All perſons falſely accuſing others of offences puniſhable with any kind of extraordinary perpetual baniſhment, ſhall ſuffer baniſhment of the ſame kind and in the ſame degree: all officers of government pronouncing an unjuſt ſentence of extraordinary perpetual baniſhment, ſhall be liable to the ſame puniſhment as provided in caſes of an unjuſt ſentence of ordinary perpetual baniſhment.

In the caſe of a falſe accuſation of an offence puniſhable with the remote or extraordinary temporary baniſhment, it ſhall be eſtimated as two years baniſhment, and the puniſhment of the falſe accuſer increaſed thereon, either three degrees or otherwiſe, according to the circumſtances.

No clauſe.

END OF THE FIFTH BOOK OF THE SIXTH DIVISION.

BOOK VI.

BRIBERY AND CORRUPTION *.

SECTION CCCXLIV. — *Accepting a Bribe.*

ALL civil and military officers, and alfo all perfons who have employments without rank under government, fhall, when convicted of accepting a bribe for a lawful or for an unlawful purpofe, be punifhed in proportion to the amount thereof, as ftated in the fubjoined table; and moreover be deprived of their rank and offices, if having any; and if not, of their actual employments whatever they may be. — Thofe who are not in the receipt of any falary, or of a falary not amounting to one ftone of rice † *per* month in value, fhall be punifhed lefs feverely, in every cafe, by one degree.

* How far the various and feemingly appropriate provifions contained in this book of the code, againft bribery in almoft every fhape which it can be fuppofed to affume, are reconcileable with the fyftematic corruption which, under the lefs odious name of prefents, muft be acknowledged to be but too prevalent in the various departments of the adminiftration of public affairs and public juftice in China, it is not eafy to determine. — That flagrant acts, at leaft, of bribery do not always efcape unpunifhed, appears from a note in the original Chinefe, inferted in this place, and containing an abridgement of the official report of the trial of a governor of a city in the province of Pekin; who, in the 33d year of the Emperor *Kien-lung*, appears to have accepted a bribe of 7000 ounces of filver, which had been offered him as an inducement to ftop certain proceedings in a cafe of diforderly conduct and contempt of court; but afterwards to have returned the money, on finding himfelf unable to accomplifh the object for which it was given: — yet, at the clofe of a detailed inveftigation of the cafe, it is ftated that he was finally fentenced to fuffer death for his original acceptance of the bribe, by being ftrangled at the ufual feafon.

† Suppofed to be 120 *kin* or 160 pounds Britifh weight.

Thoſe who negociate, and through whoſe hands the bribe paſſes, if they are perſons of the former claſs, ſhall be puniſhed one degree leſs, and if of the latter claſs, two degrees leſs than the receiver; but, to which ever claſs they belong, they ſhall not be liable in any caſe to a greater puniſhment than 100 blows and two years baniſhment; if participating themſelves in the bribe, they ſhall either ſuffer the puniſhment incurred by receiving a bribe themſelves, or the puniſhment of negociating one for another, according as the one or the other is found, by a computation of the amount in each caſe, and a regard to the circumſtances, to be the moſt ſevere.

When the object for which the bribe is received is unlawful, all the ſums received by the offender from different perſons, but charged againſt him at the ſame time, and in the ſame information, ſhall be added together and eſtimated as one bribe; and if, after puniſhment is inflicted, another inſtance of bribery is diſcovered, that offence, whether greater or leſs than the former, ſhall likewiſe entail a puniſhment proportionate to its amount.

When, on the contrary, the object for which the bribe is received is in itſelf lawful, though unlawfully ſought after, all the ſums received, and charged in the ſame information, ſhall be added together as in the former caſe, but only half the aggregate ſhall be referred to the ſcale of puniſhments in the annexed table, for bribes for purpoſes which in themſelves are lawful.

TABLE of Reference in cafes of regular Officers of Government being guilty of receiving Bribes.

When the Object is in itfelf lawful.

Amount received. Value in Ounces of Silver.	*Punifhment.* Blows.	Banifhment.
1 or lefs	60	none.
1 to 12	70	none.
20	80	none.
30	90	none.
40	100	none
50	60	for one year.
60	70	for one year and half.
70	80	for two years.
80	90	for two years and a half.
90	100	for three years.
100	100	for life, diftance 2000 *lee*.
110	100	for life, diftance 2500 *lee*.
120	100	for life, diftance 3000 *lee*.
Upwards of 120	Death, by being ftrangled at the ufual period.	

When the Object is unlawful.

Amount received. Value in Ounces of Silver.	*Punifhment.* Blows.	Banifhment.
1 or lefs	70	none.
1 to 10	80	none.
10	90	none.
15	100	none.
20	60	for one year.
25	70	for one year and a half.
30	80	for two years.
35	90	for two years and a half.
40	100	for three years.
45	100	for life, diftance 2000 *lee*.
50	100	for life, diftance 2500 *lee*.
55	100	for life, diftance 3000 *lee*.
80 and upwards.	Death, by being ftrangled at the ufual period.	

Perfons

Perſons who are not in the receipt of what is conſidered a regular ſalary from government, ſhall, when guilty of accepting a bribe for an unlawful object, be ſubject only to the puniſhment proportionally reduced one degree, below that already ſtated; but ſhall be puniſhed with death, by being ſtrangled at the uſual period, when the amount of the bribe which they are found guilty of having accepted, exceeds in any degree 120 ounces.

In the caſe of a bribe being accepted to a ſimilar extent, for a lawful object, the puniſhment of perſons guilty thereof under thoſe circumſtances, ſhall never exceed 100 blows, and perpetual baniſhment to the diſtance of 3000 *lee*.

Fourteen clauſes.

SECTION CCCXLV. — *Pecuniary Malverſation.*

When any officers of government, or other perſons, whatever may be their denomination, are guilty of receiving, appropriating, or expending any ſum or ſums unwarrantably, if the offence does not come under the deſcription of a bribe to do any ſpecific act, lawful or unlawful, the different ſums received, appropriated, or expended unwarrantably, and charged againſt an offender at any one time, ſhall be added together, and half of the aggregate ſhall be the eſtimated amount of the unwarrantable tranſaction; according to which the offender ſhall receive puniſhment, as ſtated in the following table; but if the amount was not in any manner applied by the offender to his own benefit and advantage, he ſhall not loſe his rank or employments. — The perſon who preſented any ſum which was thus unwarrantably received and diſpoſed of, ſhall be puniſhed five degrees leſs than the receiver.

TABLE

TABLE of Reference.

Amount in Ounces of Silver.			Punishment. Blows.	Banishment.
less than 1	-	-	20	none.
1 to 10	-	-	30	none.
20	-	-	40	none.
30	-	-	50	none.
40	-	-	60	none.
50	-	-	70	none.
60	-	-	80	none.
70	-	-	90	none.
80	-	-	100	none.
100	-	-	60	for one year.
200	-	-	70	for a year and a half.
300	-	-	80	for two years.
400	-	-	90	for two years and a half.
500	and upwards		100	for three years.

The provisions of this law are designed to comprehend every species of pecuniary over-charge, in cases of blows, theft, and the like injuries; presents of all kinds, made to civil and military officers upon taking charge of their governments, eatables only excepted; exaction of more than the just and due proportion of revenue, or (in an unfavourable season) of more than the people are fairly able to contribute; unnecessary and extravagant expenditure of public money, and of the labour of the people, although not conducive to the advantage or emolument of the offender. — If, in any case, the giver or receiver is implicated in any other manner by the transaction, his punishment shall always be measured and inflicted in conformity to the law, applicable to the greater and more severely punishable offence of which he may be found guilty.

No clause.

SEC-

SECTION CCCXLVI. — *Receiving Money corruptly by way of Reward.*

All officers of government, and others having official employments, who, although not bribed in the firſt inſtance, afterwards receive ſums by way of reward for any tranſaction in their official capacity, ſhall, if there had been any thing unlawful in ſuch tranſaction, be puniſhed in the ſame manner as in a caſe of bribery to do an unlawful act; but if the tranſaction had been in itſelf lawful, then the receipt of a reward for it ſhall be puniſhed, as the receipt of a bribe to the ſame amount for the ſubſequent performance of any act in itſelf lawful.

The ſame diſtinction ſhall be made as heretofore, between perſons with and without regular ſalaries, and they ſhall, in both caſes, loſe their rank and employments; but the honorary diſtinctions which had been allowed by the Emperor ſhall not be taken away from their families.

The puniſhment of officers of government having high judicial and miniſterial ſituations, ſhall be two degrees more ſevere than that of ordinary officers, in this, as well as in the other caſes.

No clauſe.

SECTION CCCXLVII. — *Contracting for, and agreeing to accept a Bribe.*

All officers of government, and other perſons having official employments, contracting for, or agreeing to accept a bribe to do any lawful or unlawful act, but not having actually received the ſame, ſhall, upon competent evidence being had of the agreement, and the amount ſtipulated for, be puniſhed according to the law provided againſt receiving a bribe for a lawful or an unlawful act, rejecting the capital caſes, and further reducing the puniſhment in each caſe one degree: the conſequence thereof will be, that the puniſhment of this offence

offence will not, in any cafe, exceed 100 blows and three years banifhment.

Neverthelefs, if the unlawful act be in itfelf an offence fubject by any other law to a more fevere punifhment than that incurred by the mere ftipulation for the bribe, the former punifhment fhall be inflicted inftead of the latter.

One claufe.

SECTION CCCXLVIII.—*Offering a Bribe.*

If an individual of any defcription whatever, having an affair to fubmit to the decifion of an officer of government, endeavours, by the offer of a bribe, to prevail on him to deviate from the law, he fhall be punifhed in proportion to the amount, according to the law concerning pecuniary malverfation in general; but if the attempt to procure the commiffion of fuch unlawful act, whether with a view to obtain an advantage, or to avoid an evil, is by law more feverely punifhable than the offer of a bribe, the punifhment fhall be eftimated according to the former offence, inftead of the latter.—Neverthelefs, if the officers of government, and others, having official fituations, vexatioufly and violently extort money as a bribe, which, in the firft inftance, had not been offered to them, the perfons complying and giving what was required fhall not be punifhed.

In all cafes, the amount of the bribe offered or received fhall be forfeited to government.

One claufe.

SECTION CCCXLIX. — *Extortion of Loans, and unfair Sales.*

When any ſuperintending officers of government, or any other perſons in official ſituations, avail themſelves of the influence of their authority, or any private individuals, of their perſonal ſtrength and reſources, and by means thereof extort loans of the goods or money of the inhabitants of their diſtricts, they ſhall be puniſhed proportionately to the eſtimated value of the goods or money borrowed, according to the law againſt bribery to do an act which is in itſelf lawful; but when actual force and violence is uſed, the offenders ſhall be puniſhed proportionately to the amount, according to the law againſt bribery for unlawful purpoſes. — In each caſe, the puniſhment of perſons without ſalaries ſhall be leſs by one degree. — The articles borrowed ſhall be reſtored without reſerve or delay, to the owners.

When perſons in authority as aforeſaid, lend their own money or goods to the inhabitants of their diſtricts upon exorbitant intereſt, or buy or ſell goods upon an unfair valuation, the unlawful advantage accruing from ſuch tranſactions, whether by exceſs of intereſt, or buying at a lower rate, and ſelling at an higher rate, than the market allows, ſhall be eſtimated, and the offender puniſhed as in the caſes of bribery for a lawful object; but if the influence exerted amounted to compulſion, the puniſhment ſhall be rated as in caſes of bribery for unlawful objects.

The articles lent or ſold by the offenders ſhall be forfeited to government, and the articles borrowed or bought by them ſhall be reſtored to the owners.

If perſons in authority do not, when purchaſing articles from the inhabitants of their diſtrict, immediately pay the price thereof; or if they borrow from them, clothes, table or houſe furniture, and the like, without returning the ſame within one month, they ſhall ſuffer puniſh-punifhment proportionately to the amount, according to the law concerning pecuniary malverfation; that is to fay, corrupt tranfactions without direct bribery; and in all cafes the goods delivered fhall be immediately reftored to the owners. — The fame perfons, when convicted of privately borrowing from the people, their horfes, horned cattle, camels, mules, affes, carriages, boats, mills, houfes or barns, and the like, fhall be liable to the punifhment of the law againft pecuniary malverfation, according to the eftimated amount of the hire of fuch articles during the time that they were retained; which eftimate fhall, however, in no cafe, exceed the actual value of the articles.

The aforefaid perfons, when guilty of accepting at any time, from the inhabitants of their diftrict, prefents confifting of the produce or manufacture thereof, fhall be punifhed, at the leaft, with 40 blows, and the giver fhall fuffer punifhment lefs than the receiver only by one degree. — If fuch prefents are made and accepted with a view to any future and fpecific official tranfaction on the part of the receiver, whether a lawful or an unlawful one, punifhment fhall be inflicted as in the ordinary cafes of bribery for fimilar purpofes, already ftated.

Neverthelefs, all prefents of eatables to fuch perfons, when upon any official progrefs, and prefents of all kinds, when made to them by their relations, on particular occafions, fhall be excepted from the prohibitions and penalties of this law. — All perfons, laftly, who when detached or fent upon government fervice, as meffengers, or otherwife, on fuch occafions extort loans, buy or fell unfairly, or receive prefents, fhall be liable to the fame punifhments as are above provided in the cafes of fuperintending officers, or others having official fituations under government.

 When

When abdicated or fuperfeded officers of government are guilty of extorting loans, receiving bribes, and the like, from the inhabitants of the diftricts formerly under their jurifdiction, they fhall fuffer a punifhment lefs fevere by three degrees than that which they would, under fimilar circumftances, have incurred, had they been ftill in office.

Eight claufes.

SECTION CCCL. — *Extortion and other Corrupt Practices of Perfons in the Families of Officers of Government.*

All perfons belonging to the family of an officer of government, or of any individual having official employment under government, whether brothers, fons, nephews, flaves, or fervants, fhall, when guilty of extorting loans, receiving prefents, unfairly trading, or otherwife unlawfully acting towards the inhabitants of the diftrict or ftation in which their relation or mafter has a jurifdiction, fuffer punifhment lefs by two degrees than the mafter of the family would have incurred under fimilar circumftances; but in the cafe of receiving a bribe for any fpecific object, they fhall be punifhed as the cafe may be, without any reduction, according to the different rules eftablifhed in ordinary cafes of bribery for lawful, and bribery for unlawful purpofes.

The mafter of the family, if privy to the offence committed by the perfon belonging thereto, fhall be punifhed in an equal degree; but if ignorant thereof, fhall be excufed.

One claufe.

SECTION CCCLI. — *Extortion and other Corrupt practices of Great Officers of State.*

All fuch officers of government as are invefted with judicial or minifterial fituations, rendering them fuperior in rank and jurifdiction

tion to the governors of the cities of the firſt order, ſhall, when guilty of any corrupt tranſactions with the inhabitants of the country ſubject to their authority or influence, whether by receiving bribes or preſents, extorting loans, buying or ſelling unfairly, or committing any other ſimilar offences, be puniſhed two degrees more ſeverely than any inferior officers of government would have been under ſimilar circumſtances; except that ſuch augmentation of puniſhment ſhall not take place in capital caſes, or render any puniſhment capital that would not have been ſo otherwiſe.

No clauſe.

SECTION CCCLII. — *Levying extraordinary Contributions on the Plea of public Service.*

If any civil magiſtrate of a diſtrict, levies perſonally, or through the intervention of perſons in his employ, extraordinary contributions from the people, on the plea of public ſervice, without any expreſs orders or authority from a ſuperior officer for that purpoſe; or if any military officer attempts in any caſe to levy ſimilar contributions on the people, upon the plea of paying the troops, he ſhall, in each caſe, ſuffer at the leaſt, the puniſhment of 60 blows, although the contributions exacted ſhould not have been applied to any corrupt or private purpoſe; and if the ſum levied is conſiderable, it ſhall be eſtimated, and puniſhment inflicted in proportion to the amount according to the law againſt pecuniary malverſation in general:— But if the ſums contributed are converted by the receiver or collector to his own uſe, puniſhment ſhall be inflicted conformably to the law againſt bribery for unlawful purpoſes.

If, on the other hand, any ſuch contributions are raiſed without expreſsly alleging the falſe plea of public ſervice; then, although the amount

amount ſhould be appropriated by the offender to his own uſe, the puniſhment ſhall only be rated according to the law againſt bribery for purpoſes in themſelves lawful.

In theſe caſes it ſhall not be conſidered as making any difference in the nature of the offence, whether the offender applies the ſum contributed to his own uſe, or diſtributes the ſame in preſents to others.

Two clauſes.

SECTION CCCLIII. — *Suppreſſing the Diſcovery of Stolen Goods.*

When the police officers who are, by the authority of the ſuperior magiſtrates, engaged in the purſuit and apprehenſion of criminals, recover any ſtolen or plundered effects, if they do not deliver up the ſame forthwith to government, they ſhall be puniſhed with 80 blows; and if they appropriate the articles or ſums of money ſo obtained, to their own uſe, they ſhall be further liable to the puniſhment of bribery for lawful objects, in proportion to the amount.

Upon eſtimating the guilt of the thief or robber, the plunder previouſly ſurrendered to government, ſhall be added to whatever had been ſubſequently recovered, but unlawfully retained by the officers of government; and if in conſequence of ſuch retention, an inſufficient puniſhment had been inflicted on the offender, the remainder ſhall be executed afterwards.

In the caſe of ordinary ſoldiers and thief-takers offending againſt this law, the puniſhment, ſhall not, in any inſtance, exceed 80 blows.

One clauſe.

SEC-

SECTION CCCLIV. — *Receiving Presents from the Higher Hereditary Nobility* *.

All military officers of government, whether stationed at court or in the provinces, are prohibited from receiving presents of gold, silver, silk-stuffs, clothes, wages, or board-wages, from individuals in any of the three principal ranks of hereditary nobility; upon any breach of this law they shall be deprived of their rank and employments, suffer the punishment of 100 blows, and be sent into the more remote perpetual banishment; for the second offence they shall suffer death.

The nobleman making the present shall be excused for the first and second offence; but upon the third offence, he shall be accused in due form, and the nature and degree of his punishment referred to the decision of the Emperor. — Nevertheless, when a nobleman of the rank above mentioned is invested by His Majesty with special powers to administer any department of the public service, and with a view to promote the execution thereof, makes presents, or allows wages to the civil or military authorities belonging to such department, neither the giver nor the receiver shall be liable to any punishment in consequence thereof.

No clause.

* The hereditary nobles alluded to, are, for the most part, Tartar chieftains, who altho' reduced to vassalage, may be supposed to be desirous of acquiring, by the means here described, a certain degree of power and influence in the state, independent of the crown, and therefore dangerous to the Imperial prerogative.

END OF THE SIXTH BOOK OF THE SIXTH DIVISION.

BOOK VII.

FORGERIES AND FRAUDS.

SECTION CCCLV. — *Falsification of an Imperial Edict.*

ALL the principals and acceſſaries to the crime of falſifying an Imperial edict; that is to ſay, pretending any document to be an Imperial edict which is not one, or adding to, or ſubſtracting from a real one, ſhall, in the event of ſuch falſified document having been actually publiſhed and ſent forth, be beheaded at the uſual period; but if the ſame is only found prepared and ready for publication, the principal offender ſhall be ſtrangled at the uſual period, and the acceſſaries puniſhed leſs ſeverely by one degree. In either caſe the crime ſhall always be imputed to the framer or contriver, and not to the mere tranſcriber.

All perſons who are guilty of an error or omiſſion in engroſſing an Imperial edict, ſhall be puniſhed with 100 blows, and the acceſſaries thereto with 90 blows.

All perſons guilty of the falſification of an edict of any one of the ſix ſupreme boards or councils of ſtate, of the board of cenſors, of any of the commanders in chief of the Imperial armies, of the viceroys, ſub-viceroys, or generals of provinces, or of the governors of any important frontier towns, whether by the forgery of the requiſite marks and ſignatures, by the privately affixing of the official ſeal to a falſe document or to a blank paper, or by any other contrivance adequate to the ſaid criminal purpoſe, ſhall, if ſuch falſe document

ſhould

ſhould have been actually ſent forth and publiſhed as a real one, be ſtrangled at the uſual period, without any diſtinction being made between the principals and the acceſſaries; but if the falſified document was only prepared for publication, the puniſhment of the principal offender ſhall be one degree leſs, and that of the acceſſaries, two degrees leſs, than it would have been, had the ſaid document been actually publiſhed.

The principal in the offence of falſifying an edict of any of the other important but ſubordinate public boards, ſuch as the ſubordinate board of cenſors, that of the judges, and of the treaſurers of provinces, and thoſe of the governors of cities of the firſt, ſecond, and third rank, ſhall be puniſhed with 100 blows, and perpetual baniſhment to the diſtance of 3000 *lee*.

The principal offender in the falſification of the edict of any ſtill lower public officer or public board, ſhall be puniſhed with 100 blows and three years baniſhment; the acceſſaries thereto, one degree leſs, and there ſhall be a further reduction of one degree in both caſes, if the falſe document was only prepared for publication, inſtead of being actually publiſhed.

In every caſe, if the falſification of an official document is contrived and executed with any unlawful and corrupt motive, ſuch as is puniſhable by law more ſeverely than the mere crime of falſification, the puniſhment ſo incurred ſhall be inflicted in preference to that by this law provided.

If the officer of government to whom any of the aforeſaid pretended edicts are addreſſed, receives and acts upon the ſame, knowing them to be forged, he ſhall ſuffer the ſame puniſhment as the falſifier, with the exception only of one degree in capital caſes: but if ignorant of the forgery, ſuch officer ſhall be excuſed.

Three clauſes.

SECTION CCCLVI. — *Falsification of Verbal Orders.*

All persons who are guilty of delivering falsely any verbal orders of his Imperial Majesty, shall, if principals in the offence, be beheaded at the usual period; and if accessaries thereto, shall be punished with 100 blows and perpetual banishment to the distance of 3000 *lee*.

In like manner, those who are guilty of falsely delivering any verbal orders of the Empress or of the hereditary prince, shall, if principals in the offence, be strangled at the usual period, and if accessaries, punished with 100 blows and perpetual banishment to the distance of 3000 *lee*.

All persons who, under the influence of a corrupt motive, falsely deliver the verbal orders of an officer of a public board or tribunal of government of the first or second rank, shall, if such orders had been issued upon the public service, in behalf of the public board, and for the information and guidance of the officers of subordinate jurisdictions, be punished with 100 blows and three years banishment. — In the case of falsely delivering, likewise under the influence of a corrupt motive, the verbal orders of any officer of a tribunal of the third or fourth rank under the same circumstances, the punishment shall amount to 100 blows; and if of any officer of an inferior tribunal, to 80 blows; in each of these cases, the punishment of the accessaries shall be proportionably less by one degree.

If the offender had been bribed in any case to falsify the verbal orders entrusted to him to communicate, the amount of the bribe received shall be ascertained, and the offender made liable to the punishment of bribery with a lawful, or bribery with an unlawful object, according as the falsification of the orders had been designed to effect a lawful or an unlawful purpose.

In

In all cafes, the moft fevere of the two or more punifhments to which, from the application of different laws, the offender may be liable, fhall be inflicted, and by including, fuperfede the others.

The punifhments provided by this law, fhall only be underftood to affect the original falfe-deliverer or falfifier of the orders, and not be applied to any of the cafes of fubfequent falfe deliveries of the orders, through intermediate and innocent perfons.

If the officer of government to whom any falfified verbal orders are officially addreffed, receives and acts upon the fame, knowing them to be falfe, he fhall be liable to the fame punifhment as the perfon uttering the falfehood, with the ufual exception only of a reduction of one degree in capital cafes:— But if really ignorant of the falfehood thereof, he fhall be excufed. — If any of the officers of tribunals engaged in the trial of offenders, or in the collection of the revenue, after having received the Imperial commands to defift from the fame in any particular inftance, neverthelefs continue fuch proceedings on pretence of acting as before under the Imperial authority, they fhall conformably to the principle of this law, be beheaded at the ufual period.

No claufe.

SECTION CCCLVII. — *Falfely and Deceitfully addreffing the Sovereign.*

If any individual makes a falfe and deceitful communication to the fovereign, either verbally or in writing, either in an ordinary addrefs concerning the affairs of a particular department, or in an extraordinary one concerning public affairs in general, fuch individual fhall be punifhed with 100 blows and three years banifhment:—if in fuch addrefs fecrets of ſtate, ſuch as treaſon or rebellion, are alleged in caſes where they do not exiſt, the puniſhment ſhall be more ſevere by one degree.

If any one, when engaged in a criminal inveſtigation, or other judicial proceedings in obedience to the Imperial commands, makes a falſe and deceitful report thereof, he ſhall be puniſhed with 80 blows and two years baniſhment, or as much more ſeverely as he may appear to deſerve, according to the law againſt an intentional deviation from juſtice, in pronouncing a judicial ſentence.

No clauſe.

Section CCCLVIII.—*Counterfeiting any Official Seal or the Imperial Almanac.*

Whoever counterfeits the official ſeal of any officer or tribunal of government, the Imperial almanac, or the ſtamps which are uſed to authenticate the land or water permits which it is uſual to iſſue for the conveyance of tea or ſalt through the empire, ſhall, if a principal in the crime of engraving ſuch counterfeits, be beheaded at the uſual period; and if an acceſſary, puniſhed with 100 blows and perpetual baniſhment to the diſtance of 3000 *lee*.

Whoever ſeizes and delivers up ſuch an offender to the officers of juſtice, ſhall be rewarded by government with fifty ounces of ſilver.

Whoever counterfeits cuſtom-houſe ſtamps, or the official ſeals of perſons not having the rank of regular officers of government, ſhall be puniſhed with 100 blows and three years baniſhment; and any perſon who ſeizes and delivers up ſuch an offender, ſhall be rewarded with thirty ounces of ſilver.

All the acceſſaries to their offences, as well as alſo all thoſe who make uſe of ſuch ſeals or ſtamps knowing them to be counterfeit, ſhall ſuffer the puniſhment next in degree.

If

If the counterfeiting of any ſeal is attempted, but not completed or perfected, the puniſhment for ſuch an attempt ſhall in each caſe, be further reduced one degree. — All officers of government likewiſe, who knowingly acquieſce in and connive at ſuch counterfeiting, or employment of counterfeits, ſhall ſuffer the ſame puniſhment as the original offenders, but the acquieſcence of thoſe who were ignorant of the fraud ſhall always be excuſed.

As the ancient characters, and all other marks whatever, which are uſed in, and which diſtinguiſh official ſeals and ſtamps, may be imitated upon divers materials beſides the metals of which the genuine ſeals or ſtamps are compoſed, it ſhall be ſufficient that the counterfeit reſemble the original with apparent exactneſs, and that the legend thereon be the ſame; but if it be only a groſs imitation, and the characters are not identically the ſame, it ſhall be conſidered as an attempt only, and the offender puniſhed accordingly: — if no ſtamp at all is employed, but the characters and marks are merely drawn upon the paper, ſo as to reſemble the impreſſion of a ſeal, the offence ſhall not be conſidered to come within the meaning and intent of this law.

Four clauſes.

SECTION CCCLIX. — *Counterfeiting the current Coin of the Realm.*

All perſons who privately caſt copper coin, that is to ſay, all the maſters of private manufactories of copper coin, and the workmen employed therein, ſhall ſuffer death by being ſtrangled, at the uſual period: — Whoever is an acceſſary to this offence, and whoever purchaſes for uſe ſuch copper coin, knowing it to be counterfeited, ſhall ſuffer the puniſhment of the principal offenders, reduced one degree. — Whoever ſeizes and delivers up any ſuch aforeſaid coiner, ſhall be rewarded with fifty ounces of ſilver by government. — If the reſponſible inhabitant of the village or diſtrict, in which ſuch unlawful manufacture and coinage is carried on, is acquainted therewith, and does not give information to government, he ſhall be puniſhed with 100 blows; but if ignorant thereof, he ſhall be excuſed.

All thoſe alſo who take an opportunity of clipping or filing down the current coin of the realm when it paſſes through their hands, in order to make a profit thereby, ſhall in like manner be puniſhed with 100 blows.—Thoſe moreover who contrive mixtures of copper, iron, quickſilver, and the like, in order to imitate and counterfeit gold or ſilver, ſhall be puniſhed with 100 blows, and three years baniſhment: all acceſſaries to the offence, and thoſe who purchaſe ſuch imitations of gold or ſilver, in order to paſs the ſame in trade, knowing them not to be genuine, ſhall ſuffer the puniſhment of the contrivers thereof, reduced one degree.

Thoſe however who merely ſell gold or ſilver below the ſtandard weight or color, ſhall not, in conſequence, be held liable to any of the penalties of this law.

Five clauſes.

Section CCCLX.—*Impoſtors pretending to be Officers of Government.*

Whoever contrives a falſe deed or inſtrument of inveſtiture, and therewith repreſents himſelf to be an officer of government; and whoever, having contrived ſuch falſe deed, or obtained the genuine one of any officer deceaſed, pretends to inveſt any perſon therewith, ſhall ſuffer death, by being beheaded at the uſual period.

The individual who accepts of ſuch a deed of inveſtiture, knowing it not to be genuine, ſhall be puniſhed with 100 blows, and perpetual baniſhment to the diſtance of 3000 *lee*; but if ignorant of the forgery, he ſhall be excuſed.

If any private individual, although not pretending to any ſuch inveſtiture as aforeſaid, yet aſſumes the character of an officer of government,

ment in order to accompliſh a particular purpoſe, or if he falſely pretends to have the authority of any officer or tribunal of government to arreſt ſome perſon; or, laſtly, if he aſſumes the family name, and proper name, of any perſon actually in office, in order to accompliſh a particular purpoſe under ſuch aſſumed character, he ſhall in each caſe be liable to 100 blows, and three years baniſhment.

Whoever impoſes himſelf on others as the ſon, grandſon, brother, nephew, ſervant, or authorized agent of any perſon in office, in order to carry any particular point with the inhabitants under the juriſdiction of ſuch officer, by the influence of an aſſumed character, ſhall receive 100 blows, and the acceſſaries to the deception, 90 blows.

If the perſon guilty as aforeſaid, ſhould obtain or extort any money or goods from different individuals by means of his aſſumed character, the largeſt of the ſums ſo received from any one perſon ſhall be eſtimated, and referred to the table of puniſhments proportionate to any amount of a theft in ordinary caſes; the puniſhment which reſults conformably to the table (the branding excepted) ſhall be inflicted, inſtead of that already ſtated, whenever it proves, by compariſon, the moſt ſevere. — All officers of government, who connive at, and concur in ſuch impoſtures, ſhall be puniſhed as impoſtors themſelves (capital caſes only excepted), but if ignorant thereof, ſhall be excuſed.

Eight clauſes.

SECTION CCCLXI. — *Impoſtors pretending to be Great Officers of State.*

If any perſon falſely impoſes himſelf on the officers of government and the other inhabitants of any of the provinces, as a great officer of ſtate diſpatched from court with extraordinary powers, or as a member of one of the ſix ſupreme tribunals or councils of ſtate, of the tribunal of cenſors, or of any of the other principal boards

or

or tribunals at Pekin; and upon the ſtrength of ſuch falſely aſſumed authority, inveſtigates the provincial affairs, deceives the provincial government, and influences in a dangerous manner the minds of the people, he ſhall be beheaded at the uſual period, even although he ſhould not have actually provided himſelf with any forged inſtrument of inveſtiture.

Thoſe who concur in, and connive at ſuch deception, and form a part of the ſuite of the impoſtor, and alſo thoſe officers of government who receive and countenance the impoſtor, knowing him to be ſuch, ſhall in each caſe be puniſhed with 100 blows, and perpetual baniſhment to the diſtance of 3000 *lee*: — But if the latter perſons have really been deceived themſelves, they ſhall be excuſed.

If any perſon, even without producing any forged or pretended powers, falſely aſſerts himſelf to be an officer of government diſpatched from court on public ſervice, and upon that plea, employs the poſt-horſes and other travelling equipage provided at different ſtations by the authority and for the uſe of government, he ſhall in ſuch caſe be puniſhed with 100 blows, and perpetual baniſhment to the diſtance of 3000 *lee*: — All acceſſaries to the offence ſhall ſuffer the puniſhment next in degree. — Thoſe officers of the public poſts, who, although aware of the impoſition, nevertheleſs provide what is demanded, ſhall ſuffer the ſame puniſhment; and although ignorant thereof, ſhall ſtill ſuffer 50 blows as a puniſhment for their neglecting to make a proper inveſtigation and inquiry. — When, however, the impoſtor produces apparently authentic powers, they ſhall be excuſed.

Two clauſes.

SEC.

SECTION CCCLXII. — *Officers of State, and others belonging to the Court, interfering without Authority.*

If any one of the officers of government attached to the court, and employed near the perfon of the fovereign, proceeds privately to inveftigate ftate affairs in any part of the empire, pretending to have efpecial authority for that purpofe; and thereby in a dangerous manner influences and agitates the minds of the people, he fhall be beheaded at the ufual period.

No claufe.

SECTION CCCLXIII. — *Pretending to difcover Prognoftics.*

Whoever falfely afferts that he has difcovered prognoftics in the Heavens, fhall be punifhed with 60 blows and one year's banifhment; but whenever there are really any omens of a calamity, if the officers of the aftronomical board fail to give a true and faithful notice thereof, they fhall fuffer a punifhment two degrees more fevere than that laft mentioned.

No claufe.

SECTION CCCLXIV. — *Pretending Sicknefs or Death.*

If any regular officer of government, any perfon employed by government in an inferior ftation, or any private individual, falfely alleges ficknefs or infirmity, as an excufe for not performing the more difficult parts of his duty, fuch as the collection of the revenue, and the purfuit and feizure of criminals, he fhall be punifhed with 40 blows; and if the cafe is important, with 80 blows. — If any officer of government, or other perfon, who has been guilty of any offences

 againft

againſt the laws, in the interim previous to the examination, wounds, or otherwiſe diſables himſelf, in order to become entitled to an exemption from the queſtion by torture, he ſhall be puniſhed with 100 blows for ſuch conduct; and if he further feigns death, in order to avoid diſmiſſion and diſgrace, he ſhall be puniſhable with 100 blows and three years baniſhment.

In either caſe, if the offence, the inveſtigation of which the offender endeavours to avoid, is more ſeverely puniſhable; ſuch puniſhment ſhall take place inſtead of that hereby ordained and provided.

If any officer of government, or other perſon, without having in view to evade any duty, or any impending inveſtigation into his conduct, but merely in order to alarm and implicate others, wounds and diſables himſelf, or procures himſelf to be wounded and diſabled in the manner aforeſaid, he ſhall be puniſhed with 80 blows; and in every caſe of a perſon being hired or employed to inflict ſuch wound, and thereby occaſioning diſability, ſuch perſon ſhall ſuffer the ſame puniſhment.—If death enſues from ſuch wounding, the perſon ſo hired or employed, ſhall ſuffer puniſhment one degree leſs ſeverely than in caſes of killing in an affray.

If any officer of government having authority to interfere in ſuch caſes, inſtead of ſo doing, adviſedly connives at the deceptions practiced by the officer or other perſon who is ſubordinate to him; either by ſuffering ſuch perſon to retire upon a falſe plea of indiſpoſition, to evade the queſtion by torture on the plea of his purpoſely acquired diſability and infirmity, or to withdraw himſelf altogether from further examination and puniſhment, by feigning death; the officer ſo conniving, ſhall be equally puniſhed with the perſon whoſe offence is connived at; but if really ignorant in any particular inſtance of the falſehood of the pretence, his acquieſcence ſhall be excuſed.

Two clauſes.

SEC-

SECTION CCCLXV. — *Seducing Perſons to trangreſs the Laws.*

All deſcriptions of perſons who, having with fallacious words or arts ſeduced and inſtructed any individual to tranſgreſs the laws, or who, having prevailed on any individual to combine with them for any unlawful and criminal purpoſe, afterwards become informers, and ſeize, or direct others to ſeize and inform againſt, ſuch offending individual, whether doing ſo with a view to injure the party ſo ſeduced and miſled, or merely with a view to the profit or reward expected to accrue from his apprehenſion, ſhall be held equally guilty, and liable to the ſame puniſhment as the offender, in all caſes except thoſe of capital offences; in which the uſual reduction ſhall be allowed of one degree.

Four clauſes.

END OF THE SEVENTH BOOK OF THE SIXTH DIVISION.

BOOK VIII.

INCEST AND ADULTERY.

SECTION CCCLXVI. — *Criminal Intercourſe in general.*

CRIMINAL intercourſe by mutual conſent with an unmarried woman, ſhall be puniſhed with 70 blows; if with a married woman, the puniſhment ſhall be 80 blows.

Deliberate intrigue with a married or unmarried woman ſhall be puniſhed with 100 blows.

Violation of a married or unmarried woman; that is to ſay, a rape, ſhall be puniſhed with death by ſtrangulation.

An aſſault with an intent to commit a rape, ſhall be puniſhed with 100 blows, and perpetual baniſhment to the diſtance of 3000 *lee*. — In theſe caſes however, the conviction of the offenders muſt be founded on deciſive evidence of force having really been employed.

Criminal intercource with a female under twelve years of age, ſhall be puniſhed as a rape in all caſes.

In caſes of criminal intercourſe by previous agreement, or by any intrigue, the man and woman ſhall be eſteemed equally guilty; and if any male or female child be the fruit of ſuch connexion, it ſhall be ſupported at the expence of the father; the mother ſhall either be ſold in marriage or remain with her huſband, according to his choice; but if the huſband is guilty of ſelling his wife in marriage to the adulterer, the parties to ſuch an illicit agreement ſhall be reſpectively puniſhed with 80 blows; the woman ſhall be ſent back to her family, and the price paid for her, forfeited to government. — The woman upon whom a rape is committed ſhall not be liable to any puniſhment.

Perſons

Perſons aiding and aſſiſting, or conniving at the meeting of the parties guilty of a criminal intercourſe as aforeſaid, ſhall ſuffer the puniſhment next in degree, as uſual in the caſe of acceſſaries.

Perſons diſcovering a criminal intercourſe, and afterwards ſubmitting to a compromiſe, by which the ſame is concealed, ſhall ſuffer the puniſhment due to the offenders, reduced two degrees.

A perſon charged with a criminal connexion, ſhall not be convicted unleſs poſitively proved to have been on the ſpot, where the fact was ſtated to have taken place.

When, however, a woman is found with child, ſhe ſhall be liable to the penalties of this law, though the father ſhould not be diſcoverable.

Twelve clauſes *.

SECTION CCCLXVII. — *Conniving at, or conſenting to a Criminal Intercourſe.*

In all caſes of a huſband conſenting to, or conniving at, the adultery of the principal or any other of his wives, the huſband, the adulterer, and the adultreſs, ſhall each be puniſhed with 90 blows.

Any individual compelling his principal or inferior wife, or any female educated under his roof as an adopted daughter, to engage in a criminal intercourſe, ſhall be puniſhed with 100 blows, and the adulterer or fornicator ſhall be puniſhed with 80 blows; but the woman ſhall be conſidered innocent, and ſent back to her parents or family.

Any perſon who conſents to, or connives at the compulſion of his wives or adopted daughters in the manner aforeſaid, or who compels his

* The clauſes annexed to this law contain an application of it, which, though neceſſary to be ſtated, is very properly perhaps, reſerved for the ſupplement. — For a tranſlation of three of theſe clauſes ſee the Appendix, No. XXXII.

his own daughters, or the wives of his ſons or grandſons, to engage in a criminal intercourſe, ſhall be puniſhed as above ſtated.

Any perſon who parts with his wife and transfers her to another for a pecuniary conſideration, ſhall, as well as alſo the purchaſer, and the wife, if conſenting to the transfer, undergo the puniſhment of 100 blows, and the wife ſhall be ſent back to her family. — The money paid for the tranſaction ſhall be forfeited to government.

If the wife and the perſon propoſing the purchaſe, ſhall have combined together to oblige the huſband to conſent to a ſeparation from her, and no corrupt motive be imputable to him in the tranſaction, he ſhall not be puniſhed; but the wife, and the perſon whom ſhe propoſes to herſelf as a huſband, ſhall be reſpectively condemned to ſuffer 60 blows, and one year's baniſhment: the baniſhment, in the caſe of the woman, ſhall be commuted for a fine, and ſhe ſhall either remain in her firſt condition, or be ſold in marriage, at the choice of the firſt huſband.

If the caſe relates to any other wife except the firſt, the puniſhment of the parties ſhall be reduced in every inſtance one degree.

Perſons aiding, aſſiſting, or negotiating in the buſineſs, ſhall be puniſhed one degree leſs ſeverely than the principals.

When the huſband diſcovers the wife to have committed adultery, and ſells her in marriage to the adulterer, he ſhall be puniſhed with 100 blows; the other parties, as already ſtated.

No clauſe.

SECTION CCCLXVIII. — *Inceſt; or Criminal Intercourſe between Relations.*

A criminal intercourſe between relations more remote than the fourth degree, or with the wives of ſuch remote relations, ſhall be puniſhed with 100 blows: — if a rape is committed, the offender ſhall be beheaded.

A crimi-

A criminal intercourſe with relations in the fourth degree; with a wife's former huſband's daughters, or with ſiſters by the ſame mother, but by different fathers, ſhall be puniſhed with 100 blows and three year's baniſhment.

When in ſuch caſes a rape is committed, the offenders ſhall be beheaded.

A criminal intercourſe with a grandmother's ſiſters, couſins by the father's ſide, the wives of brothers or the wives of nephews, ſhall be puniſhed with death by being ſtrangled immediately upon conviction. — If a rape is committed, the party offending ſhall be beheaded.

A criminal intercourſe with a father's or grandfather's inferior wife, with a father's ſiſters, or father's brother's wives, or the wife of a ſon or grandſon, ſhall be puniſhed with death, by being beheaded immediately upon conviction.

In general in the caſes of inferior wives, the puniſhment ſhall be reduced one degree, unleſs otherwiſe provided.

Nine clauſes.

SECTION CCCLXIX. — *Accuſing an Elder Relation of Adultery.*

When a wife falſely accuſes her father-in-law or her elder brother-in-law, of having obliged her to conſent to an inceſtuous intercourſe, ſhe ſhall ſuffer death by being beheaded.

No clauſe.

SECTION CCCLXX. — *Criminal Intercourſe between Slaves or Servants, and their Maſter's Wives.*

All ſlaves or hired ſervants who have been guilty of a criminal intercourſe with their maſter's wives or daughters, ſhall be beheaded imme-

immediately after conviction: when guilty of a criminal intercourſe with their maſter's female relations in the firſt degree, or with the wives of the male relations of their maſters in the ſame degree, they ſhall be ſtrangled after remaining in priſon the uſual period. In the above caſes, the puniſhment of the woman, if conſenting, ſhall be leſs, only by one degree. When guilty of a criminal intercourſe with their maſter's more diſtant female relations, or with the wives of his more diſtant male relations, they ſhall be puniſhed with 100 blows, and perpetual baniſhment to the diſtance of 2000 *lee*.

If guilty of committing a rape upon the latter perſons, they ſhall be beheaded after remaining in priſon the uſual period: except in the caſes of rape, the puniſhment of a criminal intercourſe with any of the inferior wives, ſhall, generally ſpeaking, be leſs than in the caſe of principal wives by one degree.

Three clauſes.

Section CCCLXXI. — *Criminal Intercourſe between Officers of Government and Females under their Juriſdiction.*

In all caſes of civil or military officers of government and of their official clerks and attendants, being guilty of a criminal intercourſe with any the wives or daughters of the inhabitants of the country under their juriſdiction, the puniſhment ſhall be two degrees more ſevere than in ordinary caſes between equals; — they ſhall alſo be deprived of their offices and employments, and moreover rendered incapable of returning afterwards to the public ſervice.

The woman, if conſenting, ſhall be puniſhed for ſuch conſent, only as in ordinary caſes.

If ſuch officers, or any of the perſons ſerving under them, are guilty of having a criminal intercourſe with a female convict who is under confinement in priſon, they ſhall be puniſhed with 100 blows and three

three years baniſhment: the female convict ſhall not ſuffer any aggravation of the puniſhment to which ſhe had previouſly been liable: when in ſuch caſes violence is offered, the offending party ſhall be ſtrangled.

Two clauſes.

SECTION CCCLXXII.—*Criminal Intercourſe during the Period of Mourning.*

All perſons who, during the period allotted to mourning for a parent or huſband; or who, being attached to either of the acknowledged ſacred orders, in the characters of prieſts or prieſteſſes, are guilty of any ſpecies of criminal intercourſe, ſhall ſuffer puniſhment two degrees more ſeverely than in ordinary caſes between equals; the other party to any ſuch criminal intercourſe ſhall be puniſhed only in the uſual degree.

Two clauſes.

SECTION CCCLXXIII.—*Criminal Intercourſe between Free Perſons and Slaves.*

A ſlave who is in any caſe guilty of a criminal intercourſe with the wife or daughter of a freeman, ſhall be puniſhed, at the leaſt, one degree more ſeverely than a freeman would have been under the ſame circumſtances.

On the contrary, the puniſhment of a freeman for having criminal intercourſe with a female ſlave, ſhall be one degree leſs than in ordinary caſes.

When both parties are ſlaves, the criminal intercourſe ſhall be puniſhed in the ſame manner as in the caſe of free perſons.

No clauſe.

Section CCCLXXIV. — *Officers of Government frequenting the company of Proſtitutes and Actreſſes.*

Civil or military officers of government, and the ſons of thoſe who poſſeſs hereditary rank, when found guilty of frequenting the company of proſtitutes and actreſſes, ſhall be puniſhed with 60 blows.

All perſons who are guilty of negotiating ſuch criminal meetings and intercourſe, ſhall ſuffer the puniſhment next in degree.

One clauſe.

Section CCCLXXV. — *Strolling Players.*

All ſtrolling players who are guilty of purchaſing the ſons or daughters of free perſons, in order to educate them as actors or actreſſes; or who are guilty of marrying or adopting as children ſuch free perſons, ſhall, in each caſe, be puniſhed with 100 blows.

All perſons who knowingly ſell free perſons to ſuch ſtrolling players, and all females born of free parents, who voluntarily intermarry with them, ſhall be puniſhable in the manner aforeſaid.

The perſon who negotiates the tranſaction, ſhall in each caſe ſuffer the puniſhmemt next in degree; the money paid, ſhall always be forfeited to government, and the females ſhall be ſent back to their parents or families.

Three clauſes.

END OF THE EIGHTH BOOK OF THE SIXTH DIVISION.

BOOK IX.

MISCELLANEOUS OFFENCES.

SECTION CCCLXXVI.—*Deſtroying Public Monuments.*

ANY perſon who is guilty of defacing or deſtroying any of the public monuments and buildings, which have been erected in honour and commemoration of particular individuals and events; and any perſon who defaces or deſtroys the inſcribed tablets upon, or within the ſame, ſhall be puniſhed with 100 blows and perpetual baniſhment to the diſtance of 3000 *lee*; the offender in theſe caſes ſhall be moreover compelled to repair the damage.

One clauſe.

SECTION CCCLXXVII.—*Care of Soldiers, and of Labourers for the Public, when Sick.*

In all civil and military juriſdictions, where there are private ſoldiers attached to the government ſtations, or labourers employed in the public works; whenever ſuch perſons are ſuffering under any diſeaſe or infirmity, the officer in command ſhall duly communicate the circumſtance to the officer whoſe province it is to furniſh medicines and medical aid to the ſick; if he fails to make ſuch communication, or in the event of ſuch communication having been made, if the proper officer does not provide ſufficient medical aſſiſtance, the individual neglecting his duty ſhall be liable to the puniſhment of 40 blows; and this puniſhment ſhall be increaſed to 80 blows, whenever the ſick perſon dies in conſequence of ſuch neglect.

No clauſe.

Section CCCLXXVIII. — *Gaming* *.

All perſons convicted of gaming, that is to ſay, of playing at any game of chance for money or for goods, ſhall be puniſhed with 80 blows; and the money or goods ſtaked, ſhall be forfeited to government.

All thoſe likewiſe, who keep gaming-houſes, ſhall ſuffer the ſame puniſhment, although not actually joining in the game; and the houſe appropriated to gaming, whether it is at the ſame time, the ordinary habitation of the proprietor, or one expreſsly purchaſed by him for the ſaid unlawful purpoſe, ſhall be forfeited to government. — A conviction however ſhall not take place under this law, by implication, but only upon direct evidence againſt the accuſed parties.

All officers of government offending againſt this law, ſhall be puniſhed one degree more ſeverely than other perſons; nevertheleſs, a few friends playing together, for articles of food or drink, ſhall not, in any caſe, be puniſhed under this law.

Eighteen clauſes.

Section CCCLXXIX. — *Eunuchs.*

No private individual, nor any officer of government, excepting only the princes of the Imperial family, ſhall preſume to educate caſtrated children, in order to their being employed as eunuchs in their domeſtic eſtabliſhments; every breach of this law ſhall be puniſhed

* There is probably no vice to which the Chineſe are more generally addicted than that of gaming, but it is, generally ſpeaking, the vice of the lower claſſes: a certain degree of diſcredit is attached to every game which depends either partly or wholly on chance, and between the ſharper and the honourable player the line does not ſeem to be very diſtinctly drawn; perſons therefore in official ſituations, or who value themſelves upon their reputation, are ſeldom known to engage in play, even within limits and under circumſtances, which might be conſidered to render it perfectly innocent and allowable.

niſhed with 100 blows, and perpetual baniſhment to the diſtance of 3000 *lee*: and the caſtrated children ſhall be ſent back to the families whence they were taken, or to which they belonged *.

Four clauſes.

SECTION CCCLXXX. — *Making illegal Propoſals.*

Any regular officer of government, any perſon having an official employment under government, and any private individual, whatever his deſcription may be, who is guilty of ſuggeſting and recommending to perſons in authority an illegal act, whether with a view to his own advantage, or to that of any other perſon, ſhall be puniſhed, at the leaſt, with 50 blows. — The officer or perſon in the employ of government, who aſſents to ſuch ſuggeſtion and recommendation, ſhall be liable alſo, at the leaſt, to the ſame puniſhment; if the illegal act ſhall have been carried into effect conformably thereto, his puniſhment ſhall be increaſed to 100 blows; and if the act of injuſtice thereby ſuffered or committed, is puniſhable by the law againſt an unjuſt deciſion more ſeverely than by 100 blows, he ſhall be puniſhed accordingly.

When the illegal act is ſuggeſted and recommended, not upon directly perſonal conſiderations, but in favour of a relation, or ſome other third perſon, the propoſer ſhall, if the nature of the tranſaction renders the officer of government, or other perſon, who complies there-

* The number of eunuchs employed within the precincts of the Imperial palace has ever been conſiderable; and, from the acceſs they muſt neceſſarily have at all times to the ſovereign, in the capacity of his domeſtic ſervants, it is not improbable, that they may ſtill continue to exert ſome degree of undue influence: it does not however appear that they are ever likely to enjoy under a Tartar dynaſty, that excluſive and dangerous confidence, which, while the government was in the hands of native princes, was ſometimes repoſed in them.

with,

with, liable to a feverer punifhment than that of 50 blows already provided, be punifhed in every fuch cafe, according to the rate of three degrees lefs feverely than fuch officer or perfon in authority: the former is not fuppofed, in this cafe, to exercife any pofitive influence or controul, and therefore the latter, through the refponfibility of his fituation, is held to be guilty to a greater extent. In general, however, the punifhment of the propofer fhall be one degree more fevere than that provided according to the reduced rate laft mentioned, whenever the illegal act propofed regards his immediate intereft.

If any officer of government makes, and ftrongly urges fuch illegal propofition to a perfon who is by his office or fituation fubordinate to him, the punifhment of the former fhall be increafed beyond that in other cafes provided, as far as 100 blows; and fhall be fubject to further aggravation agreeably to the law concerning an intentional deviation from juftice; but in capital cafes there fhall, neverthelefs, be a reduction in favour of the propofer of one degree. — If there fhould have been any act of bribery involved in the tranfaction, the punifhment arifing therefrom, in proportion to the amount, according to the law concerning bribery for unlawful purpofes, fhall, if the moft fevere, be inflicted in preference to any other which by this article of the laws has been provided.

In every cafe of recommendatory propofitions, their illegality muft entirely depend upon an implied defire and defign of deviating from the laws.

If an act of bribery is proved, though committed without any fuch defire and defign, the offenders will be punifhable according to the law relative to the offer and acceptance of bribes, for purpofes not in themfelves unlawful. — If neither any pecuniary or valuable confideration had been given and received, nor the object of the propofition in itfelf illegal, the tranfaction muft then neceffarily be confidered as innocent.

If

If any officer, or other perſon employed by government, diſregarding the urgency and influence of his ſuperior, refuſes to aſſent to his illegal propoſition, and inſtead of carrying his wiſhes into effect, informs againſt him at a ſtill higher tribunal; ſuch perſon, if an officer of government, ſhall be raiſed a degree of rank, or if not yet a regular officer, ſhall be raiſed one degree, as ſoon as he becomes one.

One clauſe.

Section CCCLXXXI. — *Compromiſing Offences, and withdrawing them from the Cogniſance of the Magiſtrates.*

If any perſon agrees privately to overlook, and thus compromiſes, any offence againſt public juſtice, ſo that in the end it is illegally withdrawn from the cogniſance of the magiſtrates, he ſhall be puniſhed only two degrees leſs ſeverely than the perſon whoſe offence was compromiſed; the puniſhment of ſuch a compromiſe ſhall not however, in any ordinary caſe, exceed 50 blows.

The act of compromiſing an offence in caſes of life and death, ſuch as that of homicide; and in caſes injurious to public morals, ſuch as that of adultery, is puniſhable by other laws, and therefore the laſt mentioned limits are not in ſuch caſes to be regarded.

No clauſe.

Section CCCLXXXII. — *Accidental Houſe-burning.*

Any perſon who accidentally ſets fire to his own houſe, ſhall, at the leaſt, be puniſhable with 40 blows; and if ſuch fire ſhould chance to communicate to any other buildings, public or private, the puniſhment ſhall be increaſed to 50 blows. — If ſuch fire ſhould occaſion the death

death of any perſon, the puniſhment of 100 blows ſhall be inflicted: — In each caſe, the individual who was the cauſe of the accident, whether the maſter of the houſe, or not, ſhall be the only perſon reſponſible. — If the fire ſhould extend to any of the Imperial temples, or to the gates of the Imperial palace, the individual who was the occaſion of ſuch accident, ſhall ſuffer death, by being ſtrangled at the uſual period. — If it ſhould extend to any of the monuments conſecrated to the ſpirit of the earth, the puniſhment ſhall be leſs by one degree.

Any perſon who accidentally ſets fire to the monumental or other buildings within the precincts of the Imperial cemetery, ſhall be puniſhed with 80 blows and two years baniſhment; and if the conflagration extends to the burning of any of the trees within the ſame, the puniſhment ſhall be increaſed to 100 blows, and perpetual baniſhment to the diſtance of 2000 *lee*.

If any perſon ſhould accidentally ſet fire to a government reſidence, treaſury, or ſtore-houſe, ſuch perſon ſhall be puniſhed with 80 blows, and two years baniſhment; if the ſuperintendant thereof takes the opportunity of fraudulently appropriating to himſelf any of the property of government, his offence ſhall be puniſhed, as an act of embezzlement in ordinary caſes.

If any of the public buildings aforeſaid take fire from without, the perſon having the cuſtody thereof, ſhall be liable to a puniſhment three degrees leſs ſevere than that provided in the caſe of a ſimilar accident originating from within.

All perſons lighting fires within government treaſuries or ſtore-houſes, ſhall be puniſhed with 80 blows, although no miſchief ſhould enſue.

Thoſe alſo, who are entruſted with the care and ſuperintendance of palaces, treaſuries, or ſtore-houſes, or who have the cuſtody of criminals,

nals, ſhall, from the moment that a fire is found to have accidentally commenced from within or without, attend diligently at their reſpective poſts, and ſhall be puniſhed with 100 blows whenever guilty of deſerting the ſame upon ſuch occaſions.

Two clauſes.

SECTION CCCLXXXIII. — *Wilful and malicious Houſe-burning.*

Any perſon who wilfully ſets fire to his own houſe, ſhall be puniſhed with 100 blows; and if the fire ſo kindled ſhould communicate, in conſequence, to any other building, or to any property ſtored up for uſe, public or private, the puniſhment ſhall be increaſed to 100 blows and three years baniſhment. — If the perſon guilty of ſuch wilful and malicious burning, ſhould take the opportunity of purloining any goods or property, he ſhall be beheaded at the uſual period; and if ſuch burning ſhould be the cauſe of the death or ſevere wounding of any perſon, the offender ſhall be puniſhed, at the leaſt, according to the utmoſt ſeverity of the law concerning intentionally killing or wounding.

All the acceſſaries, as well as principals, to the crime of wilfully and maliciouſly ſetting on fire any reſidence, either of an officer of government, or of any private individual, their own only excepted, or to the crime of, in the ſame manner ſetting fire to any government or private building, treaſury, or ſtore-houſe, in which public or private property of any kind is ſtored and depoſited, ſhall be puniſhed with death, by being beheaded at the uſual period.

To convict ſuch offenders, it is neceſſary that they ſhould have been taken or diſcovered on the ſpot where the fire took place, and that the fact of their having been wilful incendiaries, be proved by the direct teſtimony of competent witneſſes.

The crime of wilfully and maliciouſly ſetting fire to empty and uninhabited buildings, or to grain and other property of the like kind, which is ſtacked and ſtored up in fields and open places, ſhall be puniſhed one degree leſs ſeverely than the crime laſt mentioned.

All the property of the offenders ſhall, in ſuch caſes, be ſequeſtrated, and charged with the reparation of the loſs or damage ſuſtained, whether by private individuals or by government; and when ſuch property does not prove ſufficient, it ſhall be divided into ſhares proportionate to the reſpective loſſes of the individual proprietors and of government.

Slaves and hired ſervants offending againſt this law, ſhall be puniſhed in the ſame manner as other individuals.

Two clauſes.

SECTION CCCLXXXIV. — *Theatrical Repreſentations.*

All muſicians and ſtage-players ſhall be precluded from repreſenting in any of their performances, Emperors, Empreſſes, famous princes, miniſters, and generals of former ages; and ſhall be puniſhed with 100 blows for every breach of this law. — All officers of government and private individuals likewiſe, who receive ſuch comedians into their houſes, and employ them to perform ſuch prohibited entertainments, ſhall ſuffer the ſame puniſhment.

Neverthele ſs, by this law it is not intended to prohibit the exhibition upon the ſtage of fictitious characters of juſt and upright men, of chaſte wives, and pious and obedient children, all which may tend to diſpoſe the minds of the ſpectators to the practice of virtue *.

Two clauſes.

* As the repreſentations here deſcribed as prohibited, are in fact in China the favourite and moſt uſual theatric exhibitions, this article of the laws muſt either be conſidered to have become obſolete, or to be enforced only ſo far as may be neceſſary to confine ſuch exhibitions within the limits approved by government, and which may not be always the ſame, at different times, and under different circumſtances.

SEC-

SECTION CCCLXXXV. — *Transgression of Standing Rules and Orders.*

Whoever is guilty of a transgression of any standing rules and orders, shall, although such transgression is not specifically punishable by any existing law, be punished with 50 blows.

No clause.

SECTION CCCLXXXVI. — *Improper Conduct not specifically punishable* *.

Whoever is guilty of improper conduct, and such as is contrary to the spirit of the laws, though not a breach of any specific article, shall be punished, at the least, with 40 blows; and when the impropriety is of a serious nature, with 80 blows.

No clause.

* This article has been sometimes referred to under the title of offences against propriety.

END OF THE NINTH BOOK OF THE SIXTH DIVISION.

BOOK X.

ARRESTS AND ESCAPES.

SECTION CCCLXXXVII. — *Duty of Police Officers.*

ALL perfons who, after having entered into the fervice of government as conftables, bailiffs, thief-takers, or in any capacity of that defcription, at any time allege pretexts for excufing themfelves from the duty of purfuing and feizing offenders; or do not actually purfue and feize thofe offenders, with the place of whofe retreat they are acquainted, fhall, in each cafe, be liable to the punifhment next in degree to that which is due to the offender, or to the moft guilty of the offenders, if there fhould be more than one, whom their neglect had occafioned to remain at large.

Neverthelefs, a period of thirty days fhall be allowed from the iffue of the orders of the magiftrate; during which, if more than one half of the offenders directed to be feized and brought to juftice, fhould be overtaken, or even any lefs proportion of them, provided fuch proportion includes the moft guilty, the original neglect and mifconduct of the refponfible police officers fhall be pardoned. — And this indulgence fhall extend to all the officers employed, although only one of them fhould have the merit of bringing the offender to juftice.

If, moreover, within the aforefaid interval, the offender or offenders fhould die, or furrender themfelves voluntarily, the failure of the police officers fhall likewife, in either cafe, be excufed. — And, in general, when any proportion whatever of the total number of the offenders fhall have died, or furrendered within the prefcribed period, the refponfibility of the officers of the police, fhall be meafured only accord-

ing

ing to the number and criminality of thofe of the furviving offenders who are ftill at large.

In the cafe of fimilar neglect on the part of other perfons in the fervice of government, who may on particular occafions have been detached and employed in the purfuit of criminals, out of the regular line of their duty, the punifhment fhall be proportionably lefs by one degree, than that which the eftablifhed police officers would have incurred under the fame circumftances. Whenever it further appears, that the remiffnefs of thofe employed in the purfuit of criminals has been the effect of bribery, the perfon guilty of receiving bribes, fhall not have the benefit of the pardon held out to the reft on the condition of the feizure of the principal criminals within a limited period, and they fhall therefore fuffer punifhment to the full extent, to which the criminals at large are liable, capital cafes only excepted; or inftead thereof, the punifhment of accepting bribes for unlawful purpofes, according as the former or the latter is found in any particular cafe to be the moft fevere.

Ten claufes.

SECTION CCCLXXXVIII. — *Criminals refifting the Police Officers.*

Whenever a criminal, at any time after a difcovery has been made of his guilt, that is to fay, at any time after charges againft him have been legally prefented to, and received by an officer of government, takes flight, or without having taken flight, refifts and defends himfelf againft the police officers employed in the purfuit of him, his punifhment fhall be two degrees more fevere than that to which his original offence had rendered him liable, previous to this circumftance of aggravation; this aggravation of punifhment fhall not, however, take place in capital cafes, or render thofe cafes capital, which

which would not have been ſo otherwiſe. If, in any of the preceding caſes, an offender ſhould ſtrike the police officers ſo as to inflict a cutting wound, he ſhall be ſtrangled at the uſual period; and if he ſhould kill any of them, beheaded.

All the acceſſaries in theſe caſes ſhall ſuffer the puniſhment of the principal, reduced one degree.

If the criminal who reſiſts, is armed with any weapons of defence, and the police officers kill him, in endeavouring to ſecure his perſon; or if the criminal eſcapes from their cuſtody, or from priſon, and is killed upon a renewal of the purſuit; or if, laſtly, the criminal when driven to the laſt extremity, deſtroys himſelf; in ſuch caſes, the police officers ſhall in no wiſe be anſwerable for his death.

On the other hand, if a police officer at any time kills or ſeverely wounds a criminal, who is not capitally puniſhable, and who had ſurrendered without reſiſtance, either immediately, or as ſoon as overtaken; ſuch police officer ſhall be puniſhed according to the law againſt killing or wounding in an affray.—In the caſe of killing a criminal whoſe offence was capital, the puniſhment of the police officer ſhall not exceed 100 blows, unleſs it ſhould appear that the homicide was the reſult of a previous contrivance and deſign.

Nine clauſes.

Section CCCLXXXIX.—*Priſoners eſcaping, or riſing againſt their Keepers.*

Whenever an offender in confinement quits his cell, and having contrived to releaſe himſelf from his fetters and hand-cuffs *, eſcapes from priſon, he ſhall ſuffer a puniſhment two degrees more ſevere than that to which he had expoſed himſelf by his original offence; and if he takes the opportunity of releaſing at the ſame time, any of the

* A particular deſcription of theſe is given in the introductory part of the code.

other

other offenders, who were with him in confinement, he ſhall be liable to the puniſhment of the moſt guilty of thoſe whoſe eſcape he had ſo aſſiſted; provided, nevertheleſs, that in no caſe the puniſhment be increaſed beyond 100 blows, and perpetual baniſhment to the diſtance of 3000 *lee*, unleſs the offender contriving the means of eſcape as aforeſaid, had been previouſly liable to capital puniſhment, in which caſe the ſentence ſhall be executed without alteration.

If one or more offenders in confinement riſe againſt their keepers, and thus forcibly effect their eſcape, they ſhall all ſuffer death, by being beheaded, whatever might have been originally the nature or degree of their offences.

It is hereby provided, at the ſame time, that thoſe of the priſoners who had really no knowledge of, nor concern in the inſurrection, ſhall not, in any reſpect, be made to participate in the puniſhment of the guilty.

Ten clauſes.

SECTION CCCXC.—*Returning or eſcaping from a Place of Baniſhment.*

All offenders, who, after having been condemned to, and arriving at the place of their baniſhment, whether ordinary or extraordinary, temporary or perpetual, deſert the ſame, and endeavour to effect their eſcape, ſhall, for the firſt day's abſence, be puniſhed with 50 blows, and for every additional three days abſence, one degree more ſeverely, as far as 100 blows; and as ſoon as retaken, ſhall be remanded to the place of their baniſhment; and if they had been ſentenced thereto only for a limited period, ſuch period ſhall recommence from their return after their laſt attempt to eſcape, inſtead of being computed from the original date of their condemnation.

An offender, alſo, who deſerts and attempts to effect his eſcape at any time after the declaration of his ſentence, but previous to his

his arrival at the place of his deſtination, ſhall be equally liable to the penalties of this law.

In the former caſe, the ſuperintendant at the place of baniſhment, and in the latter, the conductor of the offenders thither, ſhall be held reſponſible; and in any caſe of neglect by which one offender eſcapes, they ſhall be puniſhed with 60 blows; and one degree more ſeverely as far as 100 blows, for every additional individual who ſo eſcapes from their cuſtody.

One hundred days ſhall however be allowed for their retrieving themſelves from the conſequences of ſuch neglect, by retaking the offenders and producing them at the ſtations appointed for their baniſhment.

In theſe caſes, the puniſhment of the inſpecting or conducting officer, ſhall be leſs by three degrees than that of the ſuperintending or conducting ſoldier or conſtable.

The miſconduct of all the reſponſible parties ſhall however be pardoned, whenever, within the one hundred days above mentioned, the offenders die, ſurrender voluntarily, or are in any way whatever retaken.

On the other hand; if, in any inſtance, the offenders are deſignedly ſuffered to eſcape, the perſons guilty thereof, whether officers of government, or ſubordinate attendants of the police, ſhall undergo the identical puniſhment to which the releaſed offenders had been condemned. — If ſuch wilful breach of duty is the effect of bribery, the puniſhment ſhall be computed in proportion to the amount of the bribe, according to the law againſt receiving a bribe for an unlawful purpoſe, and inflicted inſtead of the former, whenever it proves the moſt ſevere.

Twenty-three clauſes.

SEC-

SECTION CCCXCI. — *Delaying the Execution of a Sentence of Baniſhment.*

Whenever a ſentence of baniſhment, ordinary or extraordinary, temporary or perpetual, has been regularly pronounced againſt any offender, the officer of government at whoſe tribunal the offender had been tried, ſhall, within the ſpace of ten days, deliver over ſuch offender, fettered and handcuffed in the lawful manner, to a competent guard, with full inſtructions, and properly authenticated powers, to conduct him to the place of his deſtination.

The cauſeleſs detention of an offender under ſentence of baniſhment three days beyond the period ſtated, ſhall be puniſhed with 20 blows; and puniſhment ſhall be increaſed as far as 60 blows, at the rate of one degree for every additional three days of cauſeleſs detention: — In all ſuch caſes of imputed neglect, the chief clerk of the court ſhall be deemed the principal offender *.

If an offender avails himſelf of the opportunity afforded by ſuch cauſeleſs detention, to make his eſcape, the ſalary of the preſiding magiſtrate ſhall be ſuſpended until he is retaken, and the clerk of the court ſhall be baniſhed during the ſame period.

The penalties of this law ſhall likewiſe take effect in the caſe of every cauſeleſs detention of offenders proceeding into baniſhment, attributable to thoſe officers of government and others, in whoſe cuſtody and under whoſe ſuperintendance they happen to be, at any ſubſequent period, previous to their arrival at their deſtination.

When offenders under ſentence of baniſhment are proceeding, in the uſual way, to their deſtination, if the inſpecting officers do not effectually provide for their ſafe cuſtody, by fetters and handcuffs, and in the lawful manner; ſo that they are able to releaſe themſelves from

* Relative to the clerks of tribunals, ſee note, page 30.

ſuch fetters or handcuffs, or in any other manner to effect their eſcape, they ſhall be liable to the ſame puniſhments as thoſe already provided in the caſe of ſuch eſcapes being attributable to the careleſſneſs of the conductors.

In every inſtance of a bribe having been received for any ſuch unlawful purpoſe, the law upon the caſe ſhall be conſulted, and always preferred, whenever it is found to aggravate the puniſhment.

Three clauſes.

Section CCCXCII. — *Jailors and others ſuffering their Priſoners to eſcape.*

Whenever any offenders eſcape from priſon through the neglect of the jailors, the jailor who was principally reſponſible in the caſe, ſhall be puniſhed only two degrees leſs ſeverely, than the moſt guilty of the eſcaped offenders.

If any ſuch offenders forcibly effect their eſcape by riſing againſt their keepers or jailors, the puniſhment of the jailors ſhall admit of a further reduction of two degrees; and in either caſe, a period of one hundred days ſhall be allowed, within which, if they, or any other perſons, retake the offenders, or if the offenders either die or ſurrender voluntarily, the previous neglect of the jailors ſhall be pardoned.

In the preceding caſes, the puniſhment of the principally reſponſible individual of the directing board or tribunal of the priſon, being the clerk thereof, ſhall, under a reduction of three degrees, be proportionate to that of the jailors.

If the inſpecting officer of the priſon had gone through the due and accuſtomed examination of the priſoners, each individually, and had perſonally aſcertained them to have been fettered and handcuffed in the legal manner, and if he had finally given the neceſſary inſtruc-

tions

tions to the ſuperintending magiſtrate and jailors reſpecting their ſafe cuſtody, he ſhall not be reſponſible for their ſubſequent eſcape; but if he had omitted ſuch viſitation of the priſoners at the proper period, he ſhall, in the event of their eſcaping, ſuffer puniſhment, equally with the ſuperintending magiſtrate of the priſon.

When, in any caſe ſimilar to the preceding, the priſoners had been wilfully and adviſedly permitted to eſcape, the individual convicted thereof, whether a magiſtrate or a jailor, ſhall be puniſhable in an equal degree with the moſt guilty of the offenders ſo releaſed and ſuffered to eſcape, capital caſes only excepted, and not be allowed the benefit of a period of one hundred days, to redeem himſelf from puniſhment; nevertheleſs, when an offender has ſo eſcaped previous to condemnation, and, within the aforementioned period, is by any means retaken, dies, or ſurrenders himſelf, ſuch circumſtance ſhall have the effect of mitigating the puniſhment of the magiſtrate or jailor who had deſignedly permitted him to eſcape, one degree.

In any caſe of a bribe having been received as a conſideration for ſuch connivance, the law againſt bribery for an unlawful purpoſe, ſhall be referred to, and acted upon whenever it is found to aggravate the puniſhment.

Whenever thieves and robbers break into a priſon from without, and, overpowering the keepers, carry off any of the priſoners by open violence, the penalties to which jailors and others are ſubjected by this law in all ordinary caſes of priſoners effecting their eſcape, ſhall not take effect, and the reſponſible parties ſhall be accordingly excuſed.

The laws determining the reſponſibility of jailors and others in caſes of offenders eſcaping from priſon, ſhall moreover have the ſame force and application, in all ſimilar caſes of offenders eſcaping from their conductors, between the priſons and the tribunals of juſtice.

Fourteen clauſes.

Section CCCXCIII. — *Privately aſſiſting and concealing Criminals.*

If any perſon who knows that an information has been laid againſt an offender before a magiſtrate, and that orders are iſſued in conſequence to purſue and apprehend him, receives notwithſtanding ſuch offender into his houſe, and there conceals him, inſtead of delivering him up to juſtice, or, knowing the premiſes, aſſiſts ſuch offender to make his eſcape, by ſupplying him with clothes and proviſions, or by indicating to him a place of retreat; ſuch perſon ſhall, in all caſes, except thoſe of a relationſhip exiſting between the parties, ſuffer a puniſhment only leſs by one degree, than that incurred by the offender thus aſſiſted, harboured, or concealed.

It is however provided, that the perſon harbouring an offender, ſhall be puniſhable only in proportion to ſuch of the offender's criminal acts, as he muſt have been aware of at the time, and not in proportion to others, of which he may have been alſo guilty, and which may be alleged againſt him in the courſe of the trial. — In caſes of perſons harbouring known offenders previous to the iſſue of the warrant for their commitment, this law cannot take effect; but the perſon guilty of ſuch an act may be puniſhed according to the law applicable to caſes of improper conduct not ſpecifically puniſhable *.

All thoſe likewiſe, who ſucceſſively entertain and accommodate offenders in their flight, ſhall be liable to the penalties of this law, whenever they ſhall appear to have been acquainted with the premiſes aforeſaid, but otherwiſe ſhall be excuſed.

All perſons moreover, who, upon being informed of the meaſures taken by government for purſuing and overtaking a criminal, divulge and publiſh the ſame, ſo as defeat the object thereof, and enable the criminal to eſcape, ſhall be puniſhable in proportion to the guilt

* See Section CCCLXXXVI. among the miſcellaneous offences.

of

of ſuch criminal, under a reduction of one degree in each caſe, except that it ſhall ſtill be in their power, by overtaking and perſonally delivering the criminal up to juſtice, previous to the final determination of his caſe, to obtain entire pardon; but if the criminal dies, ſurrenders, or is taken by any other means, within the ſame period, they ſhall only obtain a mitigation in their puniſhment of one degree.

One clauſe.

SECTION CCCXCIV. — *Periods allowed for the Purſuit of Thieves and Robbers.*

In ordinary caſes of robbery, if the ſoldiers and attendants of the police, employed on the public ſervice in the diſtrict in which the offence is committed, do not ſeize and bring to juſtice the robbers within one month, computed from the day on which the information was laid before the magiſtrates, ſuch attendants and ſoldiers ſhall be puniſhed with 20 blows; if unſucceſsful at the end of two months, with 30 blows; at the end of three months, with 40 blows; and in the laſt caſe, the ſuperintending magiſtrate ſhall likewiſe forfeit two months' ſalary.

If, in a caſe of theft, the police officers fail to ſeize and bring to juſtice the thieves, within the period of one month, they ſhall receive a puniſhment of 10 blows, if unſucceſsful at the end of two months, a puniſhment of 20 blows; and at the end of three months, a puniſhment of 30 blows; and in the latter caſe, the ſuperintending magiſtrate ſhall likewiſe be puniſhed for the failure, by a forfeiture of one month's ſalary. When more than one robber or thief are charged in the information, it ſhall be ſufficient that half the number are ſeized and brought to juſtice within the preſcribed period, to exempt the

the reſponſible parties from the puniſhments and penalties aforeſaid:— They ſhall, moreover, be exempt therefrom, when the plaintiff or party aggrieved, had neglected to lay his information before the magiſtrate within twenty days from the date of the commiſſion of the offence.

In reſpect to the proviſions of this law, thieves who have likewiſe committed murder, ſhall be conſidered in the ſame light as robbers.

Thirty clauſes.

END OF THE TENTH BOOK OF THE SIXTH DIVISION.

BOOK XI.

IMPRISONMENT, JUDGMENT, AND EXECUTION *.

SECTION CCCXCV. — *Securing the Perfons of Prifoners.*

IF in any cafe of imprifoned offenders, the fuperintending magiftrate does not ftrictly confine thofe, who, according to the laws, ought to be ftrictly confined, fuch as all ordinary prifoners charged with offences punifhable with banifhment or death, and not privileged in confideration of their rank, tender youth, extreme age, or bodily infirmities; or if the fuperintending magiftrate does not confine with fetters and handcuffs, thofe who, by law, ought to be fo confined; or having fo confined, afterwards releafes

* Although clofe imprifonment is not awarded by the Chinefe laws, as the ordinary punifhment of any fpecific offence, and is confidered in this book of the code, only as far as it is applicable and neceffary to the fafe cuftody of accufed perfons, between the period of their arreft and that of their conviction or acquittal; or that of condemned perfons between the period of their conviction and that of their execution: yet, in fome inftances, chiefly thofe of European miffionaries, capitally convicted during occafional perfecutions, a fentence of death has been, through the Imperial clemency, commuted for that of imprifonment during a limited period. The moft recent inftance of this kind is that of an Italian prieft of the name of Joakim, who has been releafed from the prifons of Canton, within the prefent year (1809), after undergoing three years clofe confinement, to which he had been fentenced, in confequence of having been unfortunately difcovered and apprehended, when on his way to join his brethren in the interior. — It does not appear that he has fuffered any very ferious hardfhips; but the report and edict, of which tranflations are given in the Appendix, No. X., clearly prove, that in the adminiftration of the prifons in China, very enormous abufes have at times been committed. — At the fame time, it is but juft to obferve, that it is not improbable there may be fome exaggeration in the fub-viceroy's report of thofe abufes, which he would naturally picture in ftrong colours, as an accufer, and alfo as one to whom the merit was due of the difcovery.

releaſes them, his puniſhment ſhall be proportionate to the guilt of the offenders in queſtion, in the following manner:

In the caſe of an offender puniſhable with the bamboo only, the magiſtrate ſhall be liable to ſuffer 30 blows; with temporary baniſhment, 40 blows; with perpetual baniſhment, 50 blows; and if with death, 60 blows. — In the caſe of confining a criminal with fetters, who ought according to the laws to have been handcuffed, or *vicê verſâ*, the puniſhment of the ſuperintending magiſtrate ſhall, having regard to the circumſtances already ſtated, be proportionably leſs by one degree.

If the governing magiſtrate of the priſon, his official attendants, or the jailors, releaſe any of the priſoners from their fetters and handcuffs, or permit them ſo to releaſe themſelves, they ſhall be equally liable to the penalties of this law, as the ſuperintending magiſtrate would have been under ſimilar circumſtances.

Again, if the inſpecting magiſtrate of the priſon is privy to ſuch a neglect of the laws, and does not notice the ſame to the ſuperior juriſdiction, he ſhall be liable to the ſame puniſhment as thoſe actually guilty of the neglect; but if unacquainted therewith, he ſhall not be reſponſible.

On the other hand, if any unneceſſary ſeverity is practiſed by the magiſtrates or officers aforeſaid, by confining with particular ſtrictneſs, or confining with fetters and handcuffs, any of the priſoners, without being legally required or authorized ſo to do, ſuch miſconduct ſhall be puniſhed in every inſtance with 60 blows.

Whenever any of the aforeſaid offences are found to have been the reſult of bribery, the legal puniſhment, proportionate to the amount thereof, according to the law againſt bribery for an unlawful object, ſhall be aſcertained, and if it proves to be more ſevere than that provided by this law, it ſhall be inflicted in preference.

Seven clauſes.

SEC-

Section CCCXCVI. — *Imprifonment of, and Procedure againft, unaccufed and unimplicated Perfons.*

All officers of government, and their official attendants, who, inftigated by private malice or revenge, defignedly commit to prifon an unaccufed and unimplicated individual, fhall be punifhed with 80 blows; and if fuch falfe imprifonment fhould directly or indirectly occafion the death of fuch individual, they fhall fuffer death, by being ftrangled at the ufual period.

The infpectors and governors of prifons, their official attendants, and the jailors, when privy to, and not giving information againft, fuch illegal proceedings, fhall be liable to the fame punifhments, except in capital cafes, when a mitigation of one degree fhall take place; but when unapprized of the illegality of the procedure, they fhall not be liable to any punifhment whatever.

When, in the examination of offences connected with the public fervice, any individuals are brought before the magiftrates merely to give evidence; if fuch individuals, without being chargeable with any participation in the unlawful tranfactions under inveftigation, are inadvertently committed to prifon, inftead of being fimply held refponfible for their re-appearance, the fuperintending magiftrate fhall be fubjected to the punifhment of 80 blows, in every cafe of fuch perfons dying, either directly or indirectly, in confequence of fuch irregular imprifonment.

But in all cafes of imprifoning in the lawful manner perfons who are actually charged with, or implicated in, any criminal tranfactions, the magiftrates fhall be entirely free from any refponfibility for the confequences.

Moreover, all officers of government, and their official attendants, who, inftigated by private malice or revenge, defignedly examine with judicial ſeverities, any unaccuſed and unimplicated perſon, ſhall, although they ſhould not by ſo doing actually wound ſuch perſon, be puniſhed with 80 blows; if guilty of inflicting, by ſuch procedure, any cutting or ſevere wound, they ſhall be puniſhed according to the law againſt cutting and wounding in an affray in ordinary caſes; laſtly, if death enſues, the ſuperintending magiſtrate ſhall be beheaded.

The aſſeſſors, and other officers of juſtice concerned in the tranſaction, ſhall, if aware of the illegality of their act, ſuffer puniſhment according to the ſame rule, except in capital caſes, upon which they ſhall be allowed a reduction of one degree in the puniſhment. — When, however, they are really unconſcious of the illegality of the tranſaction, and the blows with the bamboo, or the queſtion by torture, although illegal, under the circumſtances of the caſe, are adminiſtered by the official attendants in the cuſtomary manner, the ſaid officers ſhall be reſpectively exempted from any participation in the puniſhment of the preſiding magiſtrate.

Laſtly, if in the courſe of proceedings connected with the public ſervice, any of thoſe perſons, whom, although not perſonally implicated in an illegal tranſaction, it may have been requiſite to examine, obſtinately perſiſt, after the charges have been clearly proved by evidence and corroborating circumſtances, in denying or endeavouring to ſuppreſs the truth, in order to protect the guilty, it ſhall be lawful for the magiſtrates to adminiſter the queſtion according to the ſeverities allowed by the laws applicable to extreme caſes, and they ſhall not be puniſhable, even if the perſon ſo examined, and ſubjected to torture, ſhould accidentally and unexpectedly die under the ſame.

Six clauſes.

SEC-

SECTION CCCXCVII.—*Delay in executing the Sentence of the Law.*

When any perſon in cuſtody has been brought to trial, and the judicial proceedings inſtituted upon all charges legally exhibited againſt him, either in the peculiar juriſdiction of the courts of judicature at Pekin, or in any of thoſe of the provincial tribunals of the ſeveral viceroys and ſub-viceroys, are finally cloſed, upon its having ſatisfactorily appeared upon the trial, that nothing had been falſely alleged, or inſufficiently inveſtigated; then, provided it be a caſe in which the ſentence, conformable to the laws, may be pronounced and executed without reference to the ſupreme authority, ſuch ſentence ſhall, within the ſpace of three days, be pronounced and executed, as far as regards any corporal puniſhment to which the culprit may be liable.—And when the remainder of the ſentence conſiſts of temporary or perpetual baniſhment, the culprit ſhall, within the ſpace of ten days, be diſpatched towards the place of his deſtination. For a delay of three days beyond the period allowed by this law, the officers of the tribunal in which the affair had been inveſtigated, ſhall be puniſhed with 30 blows, and the puniſhment ſhall be increaſed as far as 60 blows, at the rate of one degree for every additional three days delay.—If in conſequence of any unlawful delay of juſtice, an offender happens to die, either previous to the infliction of corporal puniſhment, previous to his departure conformably to his ſentence of baniſhment, or previous to the execution of his ſentence in any other reſpect, the officers of the tribunal ſhall, in the caſe of capital offenders, be puniſhed with 60 blows; in a caſe of a ſentence of perpetual baniſhment, with 80 blows; in a caſe of a ſentence of temporary baniſhment, with 100 blows; and in a caſe of merely corporal puniſhment with the bamboo, with 60 blows, and one year's baniſhment.

Four clauſes.

 SEC-

SECTION CCCXCVIII. — *Ill treatment of Prisoners.*

All jailors, and others having the care and custody of prisoners, when guilty of striking, wounding, or otherwise ill treating them, shall be punished in proportion to the injury done, according to the law against striking or wounding in ordinary cases of an affray. In all cases also, of the jailors or others suppressing any part of the government allowance of clothes and provisions, the deficiency shall be estimated, and the offence punished as an embezzlement of government stores to the same amount and value: and if any prisoner dies in consequence of such default in his allowance, the jailor or other attendant guilty thereof, shall suffer death by being strangled at the usual period.

If the inspecting and superintending magistrates of the prison, upon being made acquainted with the misconduct of the jailors, take no cognizance thereof, they shall, excepting the usual reduction of one degree in capital cases, equally participate in their punishment; and even when ignorant thereof, they shall still be liable to punishment according to the law respecting offences by implication *.

Twelve clauses.

SECTION CCCXCIX. — *Allowing Prisoners Sharp Instruments.*

All jailors and other attendants of prisons, who shall be found to have provided any of the prisoners with sharp weapons of metal, or with any other articles by means of which they might possibly kill or release themselves, shall be punished with 100 blows.

If any prisoners should, by such means so provided, effect their escape, or wound themselves or others, the punishment of the persons

* See Section CCCLXXXVI.

providing

providing the ſaid inſtruments or articles, ſhall be increaſed to 60 blows and one year's baniſhment. — If any of the priſoners ſhould kill themſelves therewith, the puniſhment of the perſons guilty as aforeſaid, ſhall be further increaſed to 80 blows and two years baniſhment; and laſtly, if in conſequence of having obtained ſuch inſtruments, they riſe againſt their keepers and effect their eſcape by force, or commit murder, the jailor or attendant who had provided the inſtruments, ſhall ſuffer death by being ſtrangled at the uſual period.

If, however, in any of the preceding caſes of a criminal making his eſcape in conſequence of being thus provided with the means thereof, the criminal ſhould, before the judicial proceedings upon the caſe are finally cloſed, die, ſurrender himſelf, or by any means be retaken, the perſon puniſhable under this law, ſhall be allowed a reduction in his puniſhment of one degree.

In the caſe of ſuch prohibited articles being ſupplied to a priſoner by a ſtranger, by a ſon to his parent, or by a ſlave or hired ſervant to his maſter, when in ſuch a ſituation, the puniſhment ſhall be one degree leſs than that of the jailor would have been under the ſame circumſtances.

Whenever the inſpecting and ſuperintending officers, and their clerks or aſſiſtants, are privy to, and yet take no cognizance of this offence, they ſhall be liable to the ſame puniſhment as the jailors and other immediate attendants of the priſon, according to the circumſtances, excepting only the uſual reduction of one degree in capital caſes.

If bribes had been received by the offending parties to ſuch an extent as would, conformably to the law againſt bribery for an unlawful purpoſe, aggravate the puniſhment, the puniſhment ſhall be aggravated accordingly.

If the jailors and other reſponſible perſons, although not actually chargeable with having ſupplied the means by which miſchief might be effected, are not duly vigilant and attentive in guarding againſt accidents,

accidents, and it happens in confequence that any of the prifoners fucceed in an attempt to deftroy themfelves, the jailors fhall be punifhable with 60 blows, the fuperintending officers and attendants with 50 blows, and the infpecting officers and their attendants with 40 blows.

No claufe.

SECTION CCCC. — *Encouraging and exciting Prifoners to make groundlefs Appeals.*

All officers, official attendants and jailors, belonging to prifons, who inftruct or encourage prifoners to appeal againft their fentence under frivolous pretexts, after their juft and lawful condemnation; or who affift them in communicating with others out of prifon for the fame purpofe, fhall, according to the nature of the defigned diminution of the prifoner's offence, or of the extent of the offence which wholly or in part is by implication imputed to the informer, be punifhed conformably to the law againft a fimilar intentional deviation from juftice in awarding judgment.

The punifhment of a ftranger, or of a relation of the prifoner, when offending in the fame manner, fhall be lefs than that inflicted upon the officers of the prifon when guilty, by one degree. — Moreover, the officers and attendants of prifons who fuffer, or connive at improper communications of this defcription between the prifoners and ftrangers, fhall, although fuch communications fhould not have the effect of increafing or diminifhing the punifhment of any perfon, be punifhed, at the leaft, with 50 blows; and, as in all the preceding cafes, when any of the parties have been bribed, the legal punifhment of fuch bribery fhall be inflicted in preference to any other, if it proves, on comparifon, to be more fevere than the punifhment otherwife provided.

Three claufes.

SEC-

SECTION CCCCI.—*Supply of Food and Clothes to Prisoners.*

Whenever the individuals committed to prison, have no families or relations by whom they may be supplied with necessaries, the superior authorities shall be addressed for leave to supply them with clothes and provisions, and, whenever they are sick, with medicines and medical assistance; leave shall also be asked in favor of those who are not charged with capital crimes, that they may, when sick, be released from their fetters and handcuffs; and in favor of those who are only liable to a punishment of 50 blows or less, that they may, when sick, be let out of prison, upon sufficient security being given for their return; and lastly, in favor of those who are dangerously sick or incurably infirm, that their families may have free access to them.

Although it is not left at the option of the officers and attendants of the prisons to grant any of these indulgences, yet, if they do not solicit them in behalf of the prisoners when lawfully allowable, they shall suffer a punishment of 50 blows for such neglect; and if in the meanwhile any capitally punishable offender dies for want of such indulgence, the above neglect shall be punished with 60 blows; if any offender punishable with perpetual banishment dies, with 80 blows; if an offender punishable with temporary banishment dies, with 100 blows; and lastly, if any offender punishable with the bamboo only, dies for want of any of the said indulgences, the neglect of the officers of the prison shall be punished with 60 blows and one year's banishment.

If the inspecting officer of the prison is privy to the neglect of the others, and yet takes no cognizance thereof, he shall be liable to the same punishment.

When the officers of the prisons have duly solicited any such indulgences conformably to the laws, if the superior officer delays one day in complying with their lawful requests, he shall be punished with 10 blows and

and for every additional day of delay, one degree more ſeverely, until the puniſhment amounts to 40 blows.

If, in conſequence of ſuch remiſſneſs or delay on the part of the ſuperior officer, the priſoner dies; then, in the event of his having been a capital offender, ſuch ſuperior officer ſhall be puniſhed with 60 blows; if he had been puniſhable with perpetual baniſhment, with 80 blows; if he had been puniſhable with temporary baniſhment, with 100 blows; and if with the bamboo only, with 60 blows, and baniſhment for the ſpace of one year.

Nine clauſes.

SECTION CCCCII. — *Indulgence in conſideration of the Rank and former Services of Priſoners.*

All offenders in confinement, who had held the fifth or any ſuperior rank among the officers of government, or who had at any time diſtinguiſhed themſelves by their public ſervices, ſhall be allowed a free communication with their relations and connections while in priſon, and ſuch relations and connections ſhall likewiſe be freely permitted to accompany them, when undergoing a ſentence of temporary or perpetual baniſhment. — If any ſuch favourably conſidered offender falls ſick and dies, either in priſon, on his journey to, or after his arrival at the place of his baniſhment, the officer of government in whoſe juriſdiction ſuch event takes place, ſhall immediately diſpatch a meſſenger with information of the circumſtances to the relations of the deceaſed, that they may in due form apply to the ſovereign for leave to recover his body. — Every officer of government ſhall be liable to a puniſhment of 60 blows, who under ſuch circumſtances fails to comply with the proviſions of this law.

No clauſe.

SEC-

SECTION CCCCIII. — *Prifoners committing Suicide.*

In all cafes of capitally convicted offenders, who, after having confeffed their guilt, fhall have been induced, under apprehenfions of the confequent execution of their fentence, to inftruct and employ their relations or near friends to kill them, or to hire fome third perfon to kill them; the relation or friend hiring a third perfon, and the individual who ftrikes the blow, whether a relation, a friend, or hired ftranger, fhall fuffer the ordinary punifhment of killing in an affray, reduced two degrees: — but if the capitally convicted offender had confeffed his guilt without having made fuch a requeft to his relations and friends, or had made the requeft without having confeffed his guilt; in either cafe, the relation or friend hiring a perfon to kill, and the perfon killing, fhall be punifhed according to the law in ordinary cafes of killing and wounding in an affray, without any reduction.

In regard to either of the preceding cafes however, it is provided, that if the party killing the prifoner or hiring another to do fo, be the fon or grandfon, flave or hired fervant, of fuch prifoner, he fhall invariably be beheaded at the ufual period, for fo great an offence againft piety or fubordination.

No claufe.

SECTION CCCCIV. — *Torture not to be ufed in the judicial Examination of Children or of the Aged.*

It fhall not, in any tribunal of government, be permitted to put the queftion by torture to thofe who belong to any of the eight privileged claffes, in confideration of the refpect due to their character; to thofe who have attained their feventieth year, in confideration of their advanced age; to thofe who have not exceeded their fifteenth year, out of indulgence to their tender youth; and laftly, to thofe who labour under any permanent difeafe or infirmity, out of commiferation for their fituation and fufferings. — In all fuch cafes, the offences of the parties accufed fhall be determined on the evidence of facts and witneffes alone; and all officers of government who difregard the reftrictions of this law, fhall be punifhed either according to the law againft a defigned, or the law againft a carelefs aggravation of the punifhment of an offender, according as the faid mifconduct on the part of the magiftrate is attributable to defign, or to inattention.

Moreover, in all cafes in which the circumftances or connexion between the parties, produce a legal incapacity, or in the cafe of individuals arrived at eighty, or under ten years of age, or entirely and permanently infirm, it fhall not be permitted even to require or to receive their teftimony; every breach of this law in any tribunal of government, fhall be punifhed accordingly with 50 blows, and the clerk of the court efteemed, as in all other cafes of mifconduct in a joint and official capacity, the principal offender.

No claufe.

SECTION CCCCV. — *Confronting Offenders with their Affociates.*

All officers of government in whofe tribunals the trial and inveftigation of the charges againft any offenders has commenced, fhall ftop their proceedings whenever any of the affociates or accomplices of fuch offenders are afcertained to be in the cuftody of any other officers of government, in order that they may be confronted one with another; for which purpofe the officer of government engaged in the inquiry, fhall claim from the officers having any of the faid accomplices in cuftody, their delivery and tranfmiffion to his tribunal, by official letters to that effect, although their refpective jurifdictions fhould be be altogether independent of, and unconnected with each other; ſuch official requeſts ſhall in general be complied with before the expiration of three days; beyond that period a delay of one day ſhall be puniſhed with 20 blows, and there ſhall, for every additional day of delay, be an augmentation of one degree in the puniſhment, as far as 60 blows in the whole. — On all ſuch occaſions, the officer of government making the application ineffectually, ſhall accuſe the other of delay, before the ſuperior authorities to which he is ſubjected, in order that the offence of which he is guilty may be inveſtigated, as well as his compliance with the ſaid application enforced, according as the laws direct.

If the trial and inveſtigation of the charges againſt ſuch accomplices or implicated perſons had actually commenced in the juriſdiction to which they belonged, previous to their being officially demanded on the ground of the neceſſity of confronting them with the other offenders at the ſame time under examination elſewhere, it ſhall be obſerved as a conſtant rule, that the priſoner charged with the leſſer offence, be removed to the tribunal in which the priſoners charged with greater offences are under examination; but if the offences are ſimilar in degree, then the few ſhall be transferred to the tribunal having within its juriſdiction the greater number; and if the numbers are likewiſe equal, then the priſoners laſt accuſed ſhall be removed to the juriſdiction in which the firſt accuſation was made.

It is however provided, that if the diſtance between the aforeſaid independent juriſdictions exceed 300 *lee*, (in which caſe it may be inexpedient to remove the priſoners on account of the riſk of eſcape) each charge ſhall be examined and determined ſeparately.

Every neglect of the proviſions of this law, ſhall be puniſhed with 50 blows; nevertheleſs, when the greater offenders have been actually transferred to the juriſdiction in which the leſſer had been appre-

apprehended, or the many to the few, the firſt accuſed to the laſt accuſed, the officer of government receiving them ſhall not decline to undertake the trial at his tribunal, under the pretext of being under an obligation to refer them back again, according to this law, to their proper juriſdiction; he ſhall, however, give due information of the irregularity, to the ſuperior authorities over the officer who had been the occaſion thereof, that by ſuch ſuperior authorities the ſaid irregularity may be inveſtigated and puniſhed.

If, in any of theſe caſes, the magiſtrate, after the arrival of the priſoners at his tribunal, delays for one day to take cognizance of their offences, he ſhall ſuffer a puniſhment of 20 blows; and the puniſhment ſhall be augmented as far as 60 blows, at the rate of one degree for every additional day of delay.

Eleven clauſes.

Section CCCCVI. — *Examination of Offenders to correſpond with the Charges againſt them.*

Every trial and examination of a priſoner brought before a tribunal of government, ſhall, generally ſpeaking, be ſtrictly confined to the ſubject of the information laid againſt him; if, on the contrary, any preſiding magiſtrate urges an inquiry upon matters irrelevant thereto, in order in one way or other to fix guilt upon a priſoner, he ſhall be liable to puniſhment conformably to the law concerning magiſtrates deſignedly over-rating the guilt, and aggravating the puniſhment of offenders under examination: — The aſſeſſors of the tribunal, when they do not perſonally inveſtigate in this unlawful manner, ſhall not be anſwerable.

At the ſame time, it ſhall not be underſtood that this law forbids the examination of any criminal acts and circumſtances of which a diſcovery may have neceſſarily taken place, either in the courſe of ſecuring the

the perſon of an offender, or in the regular proceſs of the inquiry into the charges for which he had been brought to trial.

One clauſe.

SECTION CCCCVII. — *Proſecutors not to be detained after a Trial is concluded.*

In all caſes of trials and inveſtigations of charges which have been duly laid before the tribunals of government, as ſoon as the facts alleged are fully ſubſtantiated, and confeſſed by the criminals themſelves, the accuſers and informants ſhall ceaſe to be ſubject to detention or to examination; the preſiding magiſtrate ſhall therefore diſmiſs them forthwith, and abſolve them from all further reſponſibility. — If he ſhould, on the contrary, deſignedly prolong the detention of ſuch perſons, for three days, he ſhall be liable to a puniſhment of 20 blows; and puniſhment, in theſe caſes, ſhall be further increaſed, at the rate of one degree, as far as 40 blows, for every additional three days of detention.

Two clauſes.

SECTION CCCCVIII. — *Offenders recriminating upon innocent Perſons.*

All offenders who, while in durance, or under examination, maliciouſly charge with crimes any innocent perſons, ſhall be liable to puniſhment to the ſame extent as falſe accuſers in ordinary caſes, and ſuch puniſhment ſhall be inflicted inſtead of that to which the offenders thus recriminating were liable on account of their original offences, in the event of the former being more ſevere than the latter.

Neverthele<ſ>s, if an offender, without entertaining a previous intention of recrimination upon any innocent perſon, ſhould be required and

and compelled ſo to do, by the unlawful application of torture, the preſiding magiſtrate ſhall be reſponſible for the ſame, according to the law concerning an intentional and unjuſt aggravation of the guilt of perſons accuſed, as in ordinary caſes.

In like manner, if a revenue officer engaged in the recovery of the amount of duties payable by a defaulter, at the ſame time urges and compels him to accuſe an innocent perſon of a ſimilar default, the amount of the exceſſive contribution to the revenue, which may be in conſequence extorted, ſhall be aſcertained, and reſtored to the injured party, while the magiſtrate ſhall be puniſhable according to the law relative to pecuniary malverſation in ordinary caſes.

If, moreover, in any of theſe caſes, the magiſtrate detains the perſon, whom he had occaſioned to be, or known to have been, falſely criminated by an offender, he ſhall be liable to the puniſhment of 20 blows, when ſuch detention is continued for three days; and the puniſhment ſhall be increaſed as far as 60 blows, at the rate of one degree, for every additional three days of detention.

If, in the courſe of the trial and inveſtigation of any offence, the witneſſes and by-ſtanders, in conſequence of being under the influence of private partiality, or of other improper motives, do not, when examined, give true evidence of the facts, or deſignedly and falſely criminate any perſon, ſuch falſe and prevaricating witneſſes ſhall be puniſhed two degrees leſs ſeverely than is legally proportionate to the amount of the deviation from juſtice in the ſubſequent ſentence of the offender; but if, in the caſe of the trial and inveſtigation of the offences of foreigners, the official interpreters are found to be actuated by private motives, and therefore to interpret falſely, ſuch interpreters ſhall ſuffer puniſhment to the full extent of the conſequent deviation from juſtice.

No clauſe.

SEC-

Section CCCCIX. — *Pronouncing and executing an unjuſt Sentence**.

Whenever, by the authority of a tribunal of juſtice, conſiſting of regular officers of government, and of official clerks, an unjuſt ſentence is wilfully and deſignedly pronounced and executed, whether by the acquittal and diſmiſſal of a priſoner, who ought to have been condemned to the full extent of the charges againſt him; or by the condemnation and puniſhment (whether capitally, or otherwiſe,) of a priſoner, conformably to the full extent of the charges againſt him, who ought, on the contrary, to have been acquitted and diſmiſſed; in every ſuch caſe, the member of the court who ſtands firſt in point of reſponſibility, ſhall ſuffer puniſhment equal in degree with that which was, when it ought not to have been, or was not, when it ought to have been, inflicted.

If the ſentence pronounced and executed by the authority of any tribunal, is not wholly unjuſt and groundleſs; but yet, in point of ſeverity, either falls ſhort of, or exceeds to a certain extent, that ſentence which the laws applicable to the circumſtances of the caſe would have juſtified, the amount of the deviation from a juſt and lawful ſentence ſhall be computed by eſtimating each ſix months of temporary baniſhment at 20 blows, and every augmentation of 1000 *lee* in the diſtance of perpetual baniſhment, as equivalent to one half year's temporary baniſhment; the amount thus computed, if it does not exceed 100 blows of the bamboo, ſhall be inflicted therewith on the officer of the court principally reſponſible; but if exceeding the ſame, ſhall be divided into two equal portions, one of which ſhall be

* This ſection of the laws is of very extenſive application, as is apparent from the frequent references made to it; theſe references will eaſily be diſtinguiſhed when they occur, though the context has not always admitted of the preciſe terms of the title being adhered to.

inflicted

inflicted corporally, and the other exchanged for baniſhment, according to the preceding computation.

Nevertheleſs, when any ſentence of capital puniſhment, which is in any reſpect unjuſt, is wilfully and knowingly pronounced and executed, there ſhall be no deduction whatever in conſideration of the priſoner being in ſome degree guilty, and the officer of the court principally reſponſible ſhall be puniſhed with death, in the ſame manner as the unjuſtly condemned and executed priſoner. — Whenever the unjuſt ſentence had not been pronounced wilfully, but through error, there ſhall be a reduction in each caſe, of three degrees in the puniſhment, if the injuſtice conſiſted in an aggravation; and of five degrees, if it conſiſted in a mitigation of the ſentence.

In general, the clerk of the court ſhall be puniſhed as the individual principally reſponſible; the executive or deputy officer ſhall ſuffer the puniſhment reduced one degree; the aſſeſſor or aſſeſſors of the court, reduced two degrees; and the preſiding officer, judge, or magiſtrate, the ſame reduced three degrees.

If the unjuſt condemnation had only been pronounced, but not executed, or if the unjuſt acquittal had been pronounced, but the priſoner either not diſmiſſed, or recovered after having been diſmiſſed; or, laſtly, if the natural death of the priſoner had prevented the execution of the unjuſt ſentence of condemnation, or had prevented the ſubſequent pronouncing and executing of one that was lawful; in all ſuch caſes, the puniſhment incurred by a falſe judgment ſhall be reduced one degree.

The ſyſtem of puniſhment in all imaginable caſes of falſe judgment, will more diſtinctly appear, by a reference to the ſeveral examples in the following table.

An unjuſt ſentence of capital puniſhment, if not executed, ſhall be deemed equivalent to an unjuſt ſentence of perpetual baniſhment already

ready executed; but every unjuſt ſentence of capital puniſhment which has been executed, ſhall be puniſhed with death.

Six clauſes.

TABLE of EXEMPLIFICATION.

	Grounds of Eſtimate of Injuſtice.				Sentence having been executed.								Sentence pronounced but not executed.							
	The Sentence having been unjuſt, wilfully, or by Deſign.																			
	The Sentence which ought to have been pronounced and executed.		The Sentence which actually was pronounced.		Puniſhment of the Clerk of the Court.		Puniſhment of the Deputy or Executive officers of the Court.		Puniſhment of the Aſſeſſors.		Puniſhment of the preſiding Magiſtrate.		Puniſhment of the Clerk of the Court.		Puniſhment of the Deputy or Executive Magiſtrate.		Puniſhment of the Aſſeſſors.		Puniſhment of the preſiding Magiſtrate.	
	Blows of the Bamboo.	Baniſhment, temporary or perpetual.	Blows of the Bamboo.	Baniſhment, temporary or perpetual.	Blows.	Baniſhment.	Blows.	Baniſhment.	Blows.	Baniſhment.	Blows.	Baniſhment.	Blows.	Baniſhment.	Blows.	Baniſhment.	Blows.	Baniſhment.	Blows.	Baniſhment.
						yrs.		years		yrs.		yr.		yrs.		yrs.		yr.		
Aggravated.	10	—	80	2 years	70	2	60	1½	50	1	90	—	60	1½	50	1	90	—	80	—
	80	—	60	1 year	40	—	30	—	20	—	10	—	20	—	10	—	—	—	—	—
	80	—	100	2500 *lee*	60	2	60	1	100	—	80	—	60	1	100	—	80	—	60	—
	60	1 year	90	2½ years	60	—	40	—	20	—	—	—	40	—	20	—	—	—	—	—
	70	1½ years	100	2000 *lee*	60	½	60	—	40	—	20	—	60	—	40	—	20	—	—	—
	100	2000 *lee*	100	3000 *lee*	—	1	—	—	—	—	—	—	—	—	—	—	—	—	—	—
Mitigated.	60	1 year	50	—	70	—	50	—	40	—	30	—	50	—	40	—	30	—	20	—
	90	2½ years	100	—	80	—	60	—	40	—	20	—	60	—	40	—	20	—	10	—
	100	3 years	70	1½ years	60	—	40	—	20	—	—	—	40	—	20	—	—	—	—	—
	100	2000 *lee*	40	—	80	2½	80	2	70	1½	60	1	80	2	70	1½	60	1	100	—
	100	3000 *lee*	80	2 years.	40	1½	40	—	20	—	—	—	40	—	—	—	—	—	—	—
	The Sentence having been unjuſt through Error.																			
Aggravated.	10	—	80	2 years	90	—	80	—	70	—	60	—	80	—	70	—	60	—	50	—
	80	—	60	1 year	—	—	—	—	—	—	—	—	—	—	—	—	—	—	—	—
	80	—	100	2500 *lee*	80	—	60	—	40	—	20	—	60	—	40	—	20	—	10	—
	60	1 year	90	2½ years	—	—	—	—	—	—	—	—	—	—	—	—	—	—	—	—
	70	1½ years	100	2000 *lee*	20	—	—	—	—	—	—	—	—	—	—	—	—	—	—	—
	100	2000 *lee*	100	3000 *lee*	—	—	—	—	—	—	—	—	—	—	—	—	—	—	—	—
Mitigated.	60	1 year	50	—	10	—	—	—	—	—	—	—	—	—	—	—	—	—	—	—
	90	2½ years	100	—	—	—	—	—	—	—	—	—	—	—	—	—	—	—	—	—
	100	3 years	70	1½ years	—	—	—	—	—	—	—	—	—	—	—	—	—	—	—	—
	100	2000 *lee*	40	—	80	—	60	—	50	—	40	—	60	—	50	—	40	—	30	—
	100	3000 *lee*	80	2 years	—	—	—	—	—	—	—	—	—	—	—	—	—	—	—	—

Section CCCCX. — *Reverſal of a falſe Judgment.*

Whenever the tribunals of juſtice in the provinces, or in the capital, have occaſion to take cognizance of a caſe of falſe judgment, an accurate and faithful report of the circumſtances thereof, and of the extent of the injuſtice alleged, ſhall be laid before the Emperor, in order that a ſpecial commiſſion may be granted for trying the ſame. — When the falſehood of the accuſation if falſe, and the injuſtice of the ſentence if unjuſt, are ſatisfactorily proved, the inveſtigating magiſtrate ſhall, in the firſt inſtance, rectify the ſentence with regard to the accuſed and ſentenced perſon, and then proceed to decide upon the guilt incurred, and the puniſhment conſequently merited, either by the accuſer, or by the magiſtrate, according as the unjuſt ſentence had, or had not been conformable to the accuſation.

On the contrary, when any tribunal of juſtice groundleſsly reverſes a former judgment, and charges it, in a report to the Emperor, with injuſtice; the principal offender, among the members of ſuch tribunal, ſhall be liable, at the leaſt, to a puniſhment of 100 blows, and three years baniſhment; but if the conſequent falſe condemnation of the accuſer, or of the judging magiſtrate, be more ſeverely puniſhable, the puniſhment ſhall be eſtimated and inflicted according to the laws againſt ſuch a deviation from juſtice.

If the juſtly accuſed and condemned offender ſhall have been a party to ſuch undue reverſal of judgment, he ſhall be liable to the ſame puniſhment, as far as it may tend to aggravate that to which he was liable in the firſt inſtance; but if ignorant and unconcerned therein, he ſhall only ſuffer puniſhment conformably to the nature of his original offence.

Nine clauſes.

SECTION CCCCXI. — *Execution of Judgment.*

The trial and inveſtigation of the offences of all priſoners in cuſtody, ſhall be effected with clearneſs and preciſion, by the authorities to which they are reſpectively ſubject; thoſe who are in a lawful manner convicted of offences puniſhable with baniſhment, temporary or perpetual, ordinary or extraordinary, ſhall be ſeverally ordered to their deſtination, each conformably to his ſentence, by the governor of the city or juriſdiction in which they were condemned. But in all caſes of a capital nature, the trial and inveſtigation of the alleged offence, ſhall be renewed, if at Pekin, by the courts of judicature; and if in the provinces, by the reſpective viceroys and ſub-viceroys thereof; in order that it may be aſcertained with more than ordinary care and deliberation, that no error nor injuſtice had been committed; when the ſentence is thus confirmed, a final report of the circumſtances and of the judgment pronounced, ſhall be tranſmitted for the information of His Imperial Majeſty.

If the Imperial orders on the ſubject contain a warrant for the execution of the offender conformably to his ſentence, an officer ſhall be ſpecially appointed to carry the ſame into effect, and ſhall be liable to a puniſhment of 60 blows for any wilful delay on his part therein.

If, during the proceſs of the final inveſtigation, the offender retracts his confeſſion, and appeals againſt his ſentence, or his relations complain of the injuſtice thereof, in his name, the ſuperior authorities are bound to take cognizance of ſuch appeal; and if the complaint and appeal be found well grounded, they ſhall not fail to reverſe ſuch unjuſt ſentence, and they ſhall likewiſe proceed criminally againſt the judges of the tribunal, in which it had been pronounced.

If the ſuperior authorities refuſe or neglect to inquire into, and to take cognizance of ſuch lawful appeal and complaint of injuſtice, when duly brought forward to their notice, they ſhall be liable to puniſhment conformably to the law againſt an erroneouſly or wilfully unjuſt ſentence, according as their guilt is found to be, upon an inveſtigation of the circumſtances, imputable to error or to deſign.

Fifty clauſes.

SECTION CCCCXII. — *Examination of the Body in Caſes of Homicide.*

Whenever an inqueſt is to be held on the body of any perſon deceaſed, in order to aſcertain the nature of the wounds and of the injuries ſuſtained by the ſame; if the magiſtrate in whoſe department it lies to perform ſuch duty, does not proceed to examine the body immediately on the receipt of his inſtructions, in conſequence of which omiſſion, a change takes place in the corpſe before it is viſited; if, inſtead of attending the examination perſonally, he deputes any of the civil or military attendants of his tribunal, and thereby expoſes himſelf to be deceived by a falſe report; if he allows the previous and ſubſequent examiners privately to compare, in order to agree in their reports; or laſtly, if he does not examine carefully and minutely, or repreſents one thing inſtead of another, the ſlight for the ſevere, and the ſevere for the ſlight, ſo that his ſtatement of the wounds and injuries being incorrect, the cauſe of death, and the other circumſtances of the caſe cannot be diſtinctly traced and aſcertained; in all ſuch caſes the magiſtrate preſiding ſhall ſuffer a puniſhment of 60 blows, his deputy, a puniſhment of 70 blows, and the officiating clerk, a puniſhment of 80 blows: — The attendants likewiſe, who perform the manual part of the operation, ſhall be puniſhed with 80 blows, if implicated in the offence.

When, in conſequence of the inſufficient or inaccurate examination of the body of any perſon deceaſed, the crime of the perſon accuſed of homicide

micide ſhall have been aggravated or palliated unjuſtly, the parties to the examination ſhall be puniſhable according to the law againſt either a wilful or an erroneous deviation from juſtice, as the caſe may be.— If any of the parties have been bribed to make ſuch defective examination and conſequently falſe report, they ſhall be liable to the puniſhment of bribery for an unlawful purpoſe, as far as ſuch puniſhment exceeds that to which they were previouſly liable by this law, or by the law againſt an intentional or erroneous deviation from juſtice.

Eighteen clauſes.

SECTION CCCCXIII.—*Infliction of Puniſhment in an illegal Manner.*

If, in any tribunal of juſtice, puniſhment is inflicted illegally, by the employment of the larger bamboo inſtead of the leſſer, or otherwiſe, ſuch a deviation from the law ſhall be puniſhed with 40 blows; and if the puniſhment ſo illegally inflicted occaſions death, the deviation ſhall be puniſhed with 100 blows, and ten ounces of ſilver ſhall be forfeited to the family of the deceaſed, to defray the expences of burial.

In each caſe, the puniſhment of the attendant who inflicts the blows, ſhall be leſs by one degree.

If the attendant of the tribunal appointed to inflict the blows, contrives to ſtrike in ſuch a manner as not to touch the ſkin *, the number of ſuch ineffectual blows ſhall be aſcertained, and inflicted effectually, either on the attendant himſelf, or on the perſon under whoſe orders he acted, according as, by an inveſtigation of the circumſtances of the caſe, the contrivance is found to be imputable to the one or to the other.

* A deception of this kind is ſaid to be frequently practiſed in favour of ſuch offenders as are able to purchaſe it; the attendant in ſuch caſes contrives that the effect of each blow ſhould be intercepted by the extreme end of the bamboo hitting the ground.

In

In all cafes in which a bribe has been accepted as an inducement to aggravate or mitigate the punifhment in the manner above defcribed, the parties to the deviation from the laws fhall fuffer the punifhment of bribery for an unlawful purpofe, whenever it exceeds that to which they were otherwife liable.

If a fuperintending officer of government on the occafion of any breach of civil or military duty, directs his official attendants to inflict chaftifement on a more vulnerable part, than is warranted by the law; or if he inflicts himfelf, or directs others to inflict, punifhment in a violent and unlawful manner, either with the large bamboo, with the hand, with the foot, or with any metal weapon, fo as to produce a cutting wound, the individual who inflicts, or caufes to be inflicted, fuch unlawful and unwarrantable chaftifement, fhall be punifhed for the confequences, only two degrees lefs feverely than is provided by law in ordinary cafes of fimilar injuries being inflicted in affrays between equals.

If, in fuch cafes, death enfues, the punifhment fhall be increafed to 100 blows, and three years banifhment, and ten ounces of filver fhall be, moreover, forfeited to the relations of the deceafed, to defray the expences of burial.

The punifhment of the perfon who inflicts, in obedience to orders, fuch irregular and unlawful chaftifement, fhall, in each cafe, be lefs fevere than that of his fuperior, by one degree.

Neverthelefs, when it fo happens, that immediately after the infliction of punifhment, on the upper part of the back of the thighs, and in a lawful manner, the culprit commits fuicide, or dies in any manner in confequence of the punifhment he had undergone, no perfon fhall be held refponfible for the fame.

One claufe.

SEC-

SECTION CCCCXIV. — *Proceedings againſt Offences committed by Superior Magiſtrates.*

Whenever the preſiding officer of any provincial tribunal commits an offence againſt the laws, at the place of his official reſidence, or any extraordinary officer furniſhed with the commands of the Emperor, at the place of his official deſtination, the ſubordinate officers of government ſhall not in either caſe tranſgreſs the limits of their authority, by inquiring into the offence, but merely report the ſame to ſuch of the ſuperior authorities as have a juriſdiction over the offender. — In the caſe however of a charge of a capital offence, it ſhall be lawful for the ſubordinate magiſtrate to take the offender into ſafe cuſtody proviſionally, until inſtructions for further proceedings are received in reply from the ſuperior authorities; and in the mean while, the ſeals of office, and the keys of the priſons, treaſuries or ſtore-houſes under his juriſdiction, ſhall all be delivered over to the next in command.

This law ſhall apply to the caſe of any ſuperior officer, although he ſhould not happen to be the preſiding officer of his tribunal; and in general, the ſubordinate officer who in any inſtance neglects the proviſions of this law, ſhall be puniſhed at the leaſt with 40 blows.

No clauſe.

SECTION CCCCXV. — *Laws, Statutes, and Precedents, which are to be obſerved in paſſing Sentence.*

In all tribunals of juſtice, ſentence ſhall be pronounced againſt offenders according to all the exiſting laws, ſtatutes, and precedents applicable to the caſe, conſidered together, the omiſſion of which, in any reſpect, ſhall be puniſhed at the leaſt with 30 blows; when, however,

however, any article of the law is found to comprife and relate to other circumftances befides thofe which have occurred in the cafe under confideration, fo much only of the law fhall be acted upon, as is really applicable.

Thofe determinations of the punifhment of offences, which have been announced by the fpecial edicts of his Imperial Majefty, and carried into effect as conformable to the exigency of the cafe in particular inftances, without being declared to be defigned as a rule for future guidance, fhall never be confidered or received as precedents; and whoever wilfully or erroneoufly fo receives and confiders them, fhall be liable to the punifhment provided by law againft a wilful or erroneous act of injuftice.

Four claufes.

SECTION CCCCXVI. — *Prifoners upon Trial at liberty either to plead Guilty, or to proteft againft their Sentence.*

After a prifoner has been tried and convicted of any offence punifhable with temporary or perpetual banifhment, or with death, he fhall, in the laft place, be brought before the magiftrate together with his neareft relations and family, and informed of the offence whereof he ftands convicted, and of the fentence intended to be pronounced upon him in confequence; their acknowledgment of its juftice, or proteft againft its injuftice, as the cafe may be, fhall then be taken down in writing: and, in every cafe of their refufing to admit the juftice of the fentence, their proteft fhall be made the ground of another and more particular inveftigation.

The magiftrate who, in a cafe of banifhment, refufes to receive fuch a proteft, fhall be punifhed with 40 blows, and in a capital cafe with 60 blows. — In all cafes however, in which the relations of the prifoner ſoner are at any diſtance beyond 300 *lee*, it ſhall be ſufficient to ſummon the priſoner ſingly, and to proceed as aforeſaid, according to his individual proteſt or individual avowal.

No clauſe.

SECTION CCCCXVII. — *Miſapplication or Diſregard of an Act of Grace and Pardon.*

Whenever any tribunal of government, on the occaſion of an act of grace and pardon, pronounces a ſentence of puniſhment in a caſe in which, conformably to ſuch act, it ſhould have been remitted; or a ſentence of puniſhment in its full extent, inſtead of the mitigated one; or laſtly, mitigates the puniſhment in a caſe not entitled to the benefit of the act, the determination and execution in each caſe ſhall, as far as is practicable, be rectified: if the deviation ariſes from error, it ſhall be pardonable by the exiſting act of grace, but if intentional, the officers of the tribunal ſhall not have the benefit of ſuch act of grace, although the general remiſſion of puniſhment ſhould even extend to all other offences of the ſame deſcription, namely, a wilful deviation from juſtice.

Five clauſes.

SECTION CCCCXVIII. — *Offending deſignedly in the Expectation of Impunity through an Act of Grace and Pardon.*

All thoſe who, having previous knowledge and information of an act of grace and pardon, deſignedly tranſgreſs the laws, in the expectation of being able to eſcape with impunity, ſhall not only be excluded from the benefit of ſuch act of grace and pardon, but ſhall moreover ſuffer puniſhment one degree more ſeverely than in ordinary caſes.

On the other hand, any magiſtrate who is adviſed or informed of the intended iſſue of an act of grace and pardon, and nevertheleſs directs the execution of puniſhment upon thoſe offenders who are, in ſuch caſes, pardonable, ſhall be liable to puniſhment according to the law againſt an unjuſt aggravation in pronouncing ſentence.

No clauſe.

SECTION CCCCXIX. — *Services to be performed by temporarily baniſhed Offenders.*

All thoſe temporarily baniſhed offenders, who, when deſtined to perform ſervice in the iron or ſalt works of government, do not perform the ſame; and thoſe who, having obtained leave of abſence on account of ſickneſs, do not, after their recovery, work an additional number of days, correſponding to the number of thoſe during which they were abſent, ſhall, in each caſe, be puniſhed (as alſo the police officer having authority over them, who ſuffers ſuch neglect) with 20 blows for the firſt three days, and one degree more ſeverely, as far as 100 blows, for every additional three days, in which they are deficient in the performance of their duty. — If the conſtable or officer having authority over a baniſhed criminal, permits him to hire a ſubſtitute, and upon that pretext to return, previous to the expiration of the period declared in his ſentence, from his baniſhment, ſuch conſtable or officer ſhall ſerve in his ſtead, during the time that remains to be completed; and if guilty of bribery, ſhall ſuffer aggravated puniſhment, according to the law againſt bribery for an unlawful purpoſe.

The criminal returning from baniſhment, ſhall be puniſhed and ſent back, according to the law upon the caſe already provided.

No clauſe.

SEC-

SECTION CCCCXX. — *Puniſhment of Female Offenders.*

Female offenders ſhall not be committed to priſon except in capital caſes, or caſes of adultery.

In all other caſes, they ſhall, if married, remain in the charge and cuſtody of their huſbands, and if ſingle, in that of their relations, or next neighbours, who ſhall, upon every ſuch occaſion, be held reſponſible for their appearance at the tribunal of juſtice, when required.

All magiſtrates committing women to priſon contrary to the proviſions of this law, ſhall ſuffer the puniſhment of 40 blows.

If any female who is condemned to corporal puniſhment, or to the queſtion by torture, is diſcovered to be with child, ſhe ſhall be ſent back to the cuſtody of the reſponſible perſons aforeſaid, and not be ſubjected to puniſhment or to the queſtion by torture, until 100 days complete are elapſed from the period of her delivery.

If, by a neglect of this law, the infliction of torture or of puniſhment ſhould deſtroy the child in the womb, the officers of the tribunal reſponſible for ſuch neglect, ſhall ſuffer puniſhment within three degrees of the ſeverity of that which is incurred by law for inflicting ſuch an injury in ordinary caſes. — If the woman with child ſhould die in conſequence of the infliction of torture, or of puniſhment of any kind, under ſuch circumſtances, the puniſhment of the officers of juſtice ſhall be increaſed to 100 blows and three years baniſhment; the puniſhment of the officers of juſtice ſhall however be leſs ſevere than the aforeſaid by one degree, when death is occaſioned by the infliction of puniſhment or torture, not previous, as in the caſes above ſtated, but within the hundred days after parturition.

When any woman who is condemned to be executed for a capital offence, proves to be with child, ſhe ſhall be attended in priſon by a midwife, and be reprieved from the execution of the ſentence of the law, until 100 days are expired from the period of her being delivered.

The officers of juſtice who execute any criminal ſo circumſtanced, previous to her delivery, ſhall be puniſhed with 80 blows; if within the ſaid period of one hundred days after her delivery, with 70 blows; and if, after the expiration of ſuch period, they delay any longer to execute the criminal, they ſhall be puniſhable with 60 blows.

In all the caſes here deſcribed, the officers of juſtice are ſuppoſed to offend wilfully: — when merely offending through an error of judgment, the puniſhment ſhall, in every inſtance, be proportionably leſs ſevere by three degrees.

Six clauſes.

SECTION CCCCXXI. — *Execution of Criminals without waiting for the Emperor's Ratification.*

All magiſtrates who authoriſe the execution of any capitally convicted offender, without waiting for the Imperial reſcript, containing the ratification of the ſentence grounded upon their final report of the caſe, ſhall be puniſhed, at the leaſt, with 80 blows.

After the warrant of execution is received, a further delay ſhall be allowed, of three days, during which if the criminal is executed, or after which, if he is not immediately executed, the reſponſible officer of government ſhall be liable to the puniſhment of 60 blows. — Nevertheleſs, in the caſe of robbers, and thoſe who are ſentenced to be executed for any of the ten treaſonable offences, a breach of this law ſhall only be puniſhed with 40 blows.

Three clauſes.

SEC-

SECTION CCCCXXII. — *Execution of a Sentence by a falſe Conſtruction of the Laws.*

If, after a ſentence is pronounced againſt an offender in a tribunal of juſtice, he is permitted to redeem himſelf from baniſhment or corporal puniſhment, in a caſe that is not by law redeemable; or if he is baniſhed or corporally puniſhed, in a caſe that is redeemable, the puniſhment of ſuch falſe conſtruction of the laws, ſhall be only one degree leſs ſevere than that of an entirely unjuſt and groundleſs ſentence, under ſimilar circumſtances.

If an offender who, conformably to the laws, ought to be ſtrangled, is beheaded; or beheaded, when he ought to have been ſtrangled; ſuch deviation, if wilful, ſhall be puniſhed with 60 blows; if committed by miſtake, with 30 blows.

Moreover, the offence of mangling or disfiguring the body of a capitally executed criminal, in any manner not preſcribed by law, ſhall be puniſhed with 50 blows.

If a magiſtrate, charged with the execution of the laws againſt the relations and dependants of traitors and rebels, in any inſtance diſmiſſes thoſe, whom he ought to have retained in a ſtate of perpetual ſervitude to government, or retains, with that deſign, thoſe whom he ought to have diſmiſſed; he ſhall be liable to the ſame puniſhment as thoſe magiſtrates who are guilty of improperly condemning, or improperly omitting to condemn, perſons accuſed of offences puniſhable with perpetual baniſhment.

The diſtinction between the offence by deſign and by miſtake ſhall be attended to in this, as in other ſimilar caſes.

No clauſe.

SEC-

SECTION CCCCXXIII. — *Clerks of Tribunals altering the Statements of Informers.*

In all tribunals of government in which crimes are inveſtigated, and puniſhments inflicted, the proceedings of the magiſtrates muſt neceſſarily depend upon the nature of the depoſitions made by the parties concerned. — If therefore, in any ſuch tribunal, the clerks thereof tranſcribe falſely, add any thing to, or take away any thing from, ſuch documents and writings, ſo as to miſlead the magiſtrates by a concealment or perverſion of the truth, ſuch clerks ſhall, conformably to the extent of the falſe judgment awarded in conſequence, ſuffer the puniſhment provided by law in ordinary caſes of injuſtice to ſuch an extent.

When a priſoner upon trial is really ignorant of letters, it ſhall he allowable to employ ſome indifferent and unintereſted perſon to write down his depoſition; but the clerks of the court ſhall not preſume, even in ſuch a caſe, to undertake to write a depoſition in behalf of any perſon under examination, on pain of being puniſhed as in a caſe of diſobedience *, although a falſe judgment ſhould not be the conſequence of their interference.

One clauſe.

* According to the law in Section CCCLXXXV.

END OF THE SIXTH DIVISION.

SEVENTH DIVISION,

Laws relative to Public Works.

BOOK I.

PUBLIC BUILDINGS

SECTION CCCCXXIV.—*Ordering Public Works without ſufficient Authority.*

ALL civil and military officers of tribunals, within the limits of whoſe reſpective juriſdictions public works are occaſionally requiſite, ſhall, in every inſtance, according to the nature of their offices, and the circumſtances of each particular caſe, either give information thereof to their ſuperiors, or await the report of their inferiors; and if, inſtead of ſo doing, they proceed immediately to employ labourers and others, on ſuch ſervice, the wages of the perſons ſo employed ſhall be eſtimated at 8 *fen* 5 *lee* 5 *bao per* man *per* day *, and according to the amount of a ſum, produced by computing their number, and the number of days they were employed, the reſponſible officer of government ſhall be liable to puniſhment, conformably to the ſcale provided by law in ordinary caſes of pecuniary malverſation.

Moreover, when labourers and others are employed otherwiſe than in the legal manner, and at the legal period, then, although the

* Not quite ſeven-pence ſterling.

proper

proper information ſhould have been given, or the cuſtomary report awaited, the reſponſible officer of government ſhall be liable to puniſhment, according to an eſtimate made upon the ſame principles as in the preceding caſe.

Neverthleſs, when any of the walls of cities or other fortifications, or of any incloſures in public buildings, happen to fall down, and when any of the public granaries, treaſuries, offices or reſidences, are injured and damaged, the officer in charge thereof, who thereupon immediately appoints proper ſuperintendants, and employs proper labourers, in order to reſtore or repair the ſame, ſhall be ſubject to none of the penalties of this law.

If any officer of government, when ſoliciting aid from his ſuperior to enable him to carry into effect any public works, does not truly ſtate the extent of the labour and quantity of the materials required, he ſhall be puniſhed with 50 blows; and, if in conſequence, any materials are injured or waſted, or any labour unneceſſarily expended, the value of the former, and amount of the hire of the latter, ſhall be eſtimated, and theſe ſums taken together ſhall be held to be the amount of the pecuniary malverſation attributable to the reſponſible magiſtrate, conformably to which he ſhall be puniſhed, agreeably to the law reſpecting that offence, the puniſhment not exceeding however in its utmoſt extent, the limit of 100 blows, and three years baniſhment.

Six clauſes.

Section CCCCXXV. — *Unneceſſary and unſerviceable Works.*

If any of the officers of government, or other perſons who have the immediate ſuperintendance of any public works, employ ſtone or timber, or burn bricks or tiles, ſo as to occaſion an unneceſſary waſte of materials and of labour, or employ the ſame in ſuch a manner as to be unſerviceable, the amount and value of ſuch miſemployed labour and materials ſhall be eſtimated, and the reſponſible perſon puniſhed in proportion

proportion thereto, according to the law againſt pecuniary malverſation in general; the puniſhment in no caſe exceeding 100 blows, and three years baniſhment.

If, through ſuch aforeſaid miſmanagement, or want of due diligence and precaution, houſes or walls fall down, or any other accident happens, by which ſome perſon is killed, the ſuperintendant of the work, or other perſon who is reſponſible by virtue of his office, ſhall pay a fine to the relations of the deceaſed, in the ſame manner as in ordinary caſes of accidental homicide.

No clauſe.

SECTION CCCCXXVI. — *Public Works and Manufactures to be conformable to Rule and Cuſtom.*

If a perſon ſerving in, and belonging to, any department of the public ſervice, performs, or cauſes to be performed, any public work or manufacture, contrary to the eſtabliſhed rule aud cuſtom, he ſhall be puniſhed, at the leaſt, with 40 blows; and in the caſe of any ſueh deviation being made in the manufacture of military weapons, ſilks, ſtuffs, and the like valuable articles, the puniſhment ſhall be increaſed to 50 blows: if the deviation is ſo conſiderable, as to render the manufactured articles totally unſerviceable, or to render it neceſſary to employ additional labour and expence in adapting them for uſe, the ſaid labour and expence attending the repair, or re-placing of the articles, ſhall be eſtimated, and the reſponſible perſon puniſhed in proportion to the amount, according to the law reſpecting pecuniary malverſation in ordinary caſes.

If ſuch improperly prepared or manufactured articles, had been deſtined for the immediate uſe of His Majeſty, the puniſhment ſhall, in each caſe, be more ſevere by two degrees, and extend accordingly in

 extreme

extreme cafes, as far as the limit of perpetual banifhment, to the diftance of 2500 *lee*.

The perfon immediately concerned in the manufacture, fhall, in general, be efteemed the principal offender; the punifhment of the fuperintending officer of the eftablifhment fhall be lefs by one degree; and that of the officer fuperintending the fupplies, by two degrees; and the refponfible perfons fhall, moreover, always reimburfe government to the extent of the additional expence occafioned by their mifconduct.

One claufe.

SECTION CCCCXXVII. — *Mifapplication of Public Stores.*

If, in any government manufactory, or upon the occafion of any work being conducted or undertaken at the public charge, the principal or managing workman obtains upon falfe pretences more than the neceffary quantity of raw materials, in order to apply the fame, or the produce thereof, to his own private ufe or emolument, the quantity and value of the public ftores thus fraudulently applied, fhall be eftimated, and the offender punifhed in proportion thereto, according to the law applicable to the embezzlement of ftores belonging to government, in ordinary cafes.

The officer fuperintending the manufacture, or (if there fhould be no fuperintendant) the officer in whofe immediate department it lies, fhall, if convicted of knowing, and agreeing to connive at the perpetration, of fuch fraud, be liable to the fame punifhment as the aforefaid offender, except only in capital cafes, when he fhall be allowed the ufual mitigation of one degree.

If the fraud is perpetrated without the knowledge or concurrence, and therefore attributable merely to the neglect of fuch officer, his punifh-

punifhment fhall be three degrees lefs fevere than that of the principal offender, and not in any cafe exceed 100 blows.

Nine claufes.

SECTION CCCCXXVIII. — *Mifapplication of the Public Looms.*

If any officer, or other perfon in the employ of government, who poffeffes authority or jurifdiction over any government manufactory, unduly avails himfelf of fuch authority, by fending raw materials of his own, to be manufactured into filks and ftuffs in the public looms, for his own private ufe, he fhall be punifhed with 60 blows, and the filks or ftuffs fo manufactured fhall be forfeited to government: the workman who is concerned therein, fhall be punifhed with 50 blows; the fuperintending officer of the manufactory, if acquainted with the tranfaction, and failing to give information thereof, fhall fuffer the fame punifhent as the officer of government principally offending: but if chargeable with neglect only, not having been actually privy to the tranfaction, his punifhment fhall be lefs fevere by three degrees.

No claufe.

SECTION CCCCXXIX. — *Working Silks or Stuffs according to prohibited Patterns.*

Any private individual who fhall be convicted of manufacturing for fale, filks, fatins, gauzes, or other fimilar ftuffs, according to the prohibited pattern of the *lung* (dragon), or the *fung whang* (phœnix), fhall be punifhed with 100 blows, and the goods fo manufactured, fhall be forfeited to government.

Any individual who is guilty of purchafing, and actually wearing fuch prohibited ftuffs, fhall be punifhed with 100 blows, and three

3 O 2 years

years baniſhment; but if guilty of purchaſing only, with 30 blows.—The working weaver, and the embroiderer of ſuch ſtuffs, ſhall be condemned as equal participators of the offence of the maſter of the houſe or manufactory, by whoſe order they were prepared.

No clauſe.

SECTION CCCCXXX.—*Irregularity in the Supplies of Raw Materials, and in the Iſſue of manufactured Goods.*

A determinate quantity of ſilks and ſtuffs, and of military weapons, ſhall be annually manufactured and prepared for the public ſervice, in each ſubdiviſion of the department of public works; and if any of the workmen fail to provide in due ſeaſon their aſſigned proportion, they ſhall be liable, at the leaſt, to a puniſhment of 20 blows; and the puniſhment ſhall be increaſed as far as 50 blows, at the rate of one degree for every additional tenth deficient: the puniſhment of the ſuperintending officer of the work, ſhall be one degree leſs ſevere, and that of the officer ſuperintending the ſupplies, two degrees leſs ſevere, than that of the workman.

On the other hand, if the raw materials are not delivered to the workmen in ſufficient quantities, and at proper times, the ſuperintending officer of the manufactory ſhall ſuffer a puniſhment of 40 blows, and the ſuperintendants of ſupplies a puniſhment 30 blows; the workmen ſhall, in ſuch caſes, be excuſed.

No clauſe.

SECTION CCCCXXXI.—*Due Preſervation and Repair of Public Buildings.*

When any of the government reſidences, granaries, treaſuries, manufactories, or other buildings, are in a defective or ruinous condition,

dition, the officer having charge thereof, ſhall immediately report the ſame to his ſuperior, and ſtate the nature of the repairs that are required; and he ſhall be liable to a puniſhment of 40 blows, whenever he neglects to do ſo: if, in conſequence of ſuch neglect, any public property ſhould happen to be injured or deſtroyed, he ſhall, beſides the aforeſaid puniſhment to which he is liable, be obliged to make good the ſame to government.

On the other hand, if, a regular notice having been given to the ſuperior officer, the latter neglects to authorize the neceſſary repairs, he alone will be liable, both to the puniſhment, and to the obligation of making good the amount of the contingent damages.

One clauſe.

SECTION CCCCXXXII. — *Officers of Government not reſiding in the Habitations allotted to them.*

If any of the governors of cities of the firſt, ſecond, or third order, or of any other provincial ſub-diviſions, inſtead of inhabiting the public buildings expreſsly allotted to their uſe, hire, and reſide in private houſes belonging to the inhabitants of the diſtricts under their authority, they ſhall, for every ſuch offence, be puniſhable with 80 blows.

Likewiſe, if an officer, or other perſon employed in the public ſervice, is convicted of concealing any furniture, utenſils, or other articles belonging to government, and of finally withdrawing them altogether from the public ſervice; or in any way loſing or deſtroying, without in due time replacing them, he ſhall be puniſhed according to the law which is applicable in ordinary caſes of loſing or deſtroying public ſtores,

ſtores, and is already provided; namely, if wilfully deſtroying ſuch articles, the officer ſhall be puniſhed two degrees more ſeverely than in the caſe of a common theft, except that the branding ſhall be omitted; and if loſing, three degrees leſs ſeverely than when wilfully deſtroying to the ſame amount.

One clauſe.

END OF THE FIRST BOOK OF THE SEVENTH DIVISION.

BOOK II.

PUBLIC WAYS.

Section CCCCXXXIII. — *Damaging Embankments of Rivers.*

ANY perſon who damages or breaks down by ſtealth, any of the embankments of great rivers, which are maintained at the expence, and by the authority of government, ſhall be puniſhed with 100 blows; and any perſon who damages or breaks down the embankments of fiſh-ponds, or of ſmall rivers, ſuch as are maintained by private individuals at their own expence, ſhall be puniſhed with 80 blows, although no miſchief ſhould enſue in either caſe; but if the waters overflow in conſequence, and ſuch an inundation takes place, as is injurious to, or deſtructive of the houſes, goods, or cultivated lands in the neighbourhood, the amount of the damage ſhall be eſtimated, and the offender puniſhed in proportion thereto, according to the law concerning pecuniary malverſation.

If the effects of the inundation ſhould extend ſo far as to do bodily injury to, or occaſion the death of any perſon, the offender ſhall be puniſhed one degree leſs ſeverely than in the caſe of killing or wounding in an affray.

If any perſon, from vengeful or intereſted motives, ſhould openly and daringly damage or break down any of the embankments, maintained as aforeſaid by government, he ſhall be puniſhed with 100 blows, and three years baniſhment; and puniſhed two degrees leſs ſeverely, in the caſe of damaging under ſimilar circumſtances the embankments maintained by private individuals.

If,

If, in either of theſe caſes, the waters overflow and are deſtructive as aforeſaid; the perſon who openly and daringly offends, ſhall be puniſhed in proportion to the eſtimated amount of the damage ſuſtained, according to the law in the caſe of a common theft to the ſame extent; except that he ſhall not be branded in the manner there provided.

Laſtly; if the deſtruction enſuing from the offence openly and daringly committed, extends to the loſs of any lives or the bodily injury of any perſon, the offender ſhall be puniſhed according to the law againſt killing or wounding deſignedly.

Four clauſes.

SECTION CCCCXXXIV. — *Neglecting duly to Repair and Maintain Embankments.*

When the embankments of great rivers are not duly repaired and maintained, or repaired unſeaſonably, the ſuperintending officer in that department ſhall be puniſhed with 50 blows; if any lands, goods, or other articles of property of any kind, are damaged by an inundation in conſeqnence of ſuch neglect and miſconduct, the puniſhment ſhall be increaſed to 60 blows; and if any perſons are killed or injured, to 80 blows. — In the caſe of private embankments, the reſponſible perſons neglecting to repair them at the proper ſeaſons, ſhall be liable to a puniſhment of 30 blows; and if any damage enſues, in conſequence of ſuch neglect, to a puniſhment of 50 blows.

Nevertheleſs, in reſpect to thoſe ſudden and impetuous inundations, which are produced by heavy rains, or other ſimilar cauſes, and which ſometimes waſh away, and break down irreſiſtibly, all ordinary embankments; as it is not in the power of man always to foreſee

and

and guard againſt ſuch accidents, the parties uſually held reſponſible, ſhall not be liable in ſuch caſes to any puniſhment.

Three clauſes.

SECTION CCCCXXXV. — *Encroaching upon Public Highways.*

Any perſon who encroaches upon the ſpace allotted to public ſtreets, ſquares, high-ways, or paſſages of any kind; that is to ſay, who appropriates a part of any ſuch ſpace to his own uſe, by cultivating it, or building on it, ſhall be puniſhed with 60 blows, and obliged to level and reſtore the ground to its original ſtate.

Any perſon who opens a paſſage through the wall of his houſe, to carry off filth or ordure into the ſtreets or high-ways, ſhall be puniſhed with 40 blows; but in the caſe of a paſſage being opened to carry off water only, no penalty or puniſhment ſhall be inflicted.

No clauſe.

SECTION CCCCXXXVI. — *Repair of Roads and Bridges.*

The repair and preſervation of all bridges, whether permanent or formed for temporary uſe, of boats only; and alſo of all roads and high-ways, ſhall come under the cognizance and juriſdiction of the governors of the cities of the different orders, their aſſeſſors, and deputies; and there ſhall be a ſpecial examination of the ſame, during the interval between the harveſts of each year, in order to aſcertain that the bridges are maintained in a firm and complete condition, and that the roads are ſolid and even: when the regular communication by any of the ſaid eſtabliſhed roads and bridges is interrupted, for want of due attention to the neceſſary repairs, the reſponſible magiſtrate ſhall ſuffer a puniſhment of 30 blows for his neglect:

alſo in places of cuſtomary communication, where bridges ought to be built, or ferry-boats ſtationed for the accommodation of the inhabitants, a failure to do ſo in either caſe, ſhall be puniſhed with 40 blows *.

No clauſe.

* The original work, it is proper to notice, concludes with two ſupplemental books, containing fifty-ſeven articles each, relating, however, almoſt wholly to the Tartar ſubjects of the empire; theſe books therefore, upon the ſame principle that has been acted upon in reſpect to the other ſupplemental parts of the work, has been omitted in the preſent tranſlation.

END OF THE PENAL CODE.

APPENDIX.

APPENDIX.

No. I.

[Referred to from the Tranſlation of the Third prefatory Edict.]

Tranſlation of the Teſtamentary Edict of KIEN-LUNG *Emperor of China* *.

ON the ſeventh day of the ſecond moon of the fourth year of KIA KING †, is recorded the teſtamentary edict of His late Majeſty, by the grace and appointment of Heaven, THE MOST HIGH EMPEROR, in theſe words.

We ‡ have remarked that all thoſe ſovereign princes on whom the decrees of Heaven have conferred a long and uninterrupted enjoyment of proſperity, have been diſtinguiſhed by their exemplary conduct, and by an innate integrity of diſpoſition, which bears a reſemblance to the excellence of the Divine perfection. Virtues like theſe attending them through life, failed not to ſecure a laſting and abundant felicity. With this perſuaſion, it has been moſt conſtantly our endeavour to guard againſt every ſuch want of application or want of energy on our part, as might counteract the execution of the gracious deſigns of Heaven.

We were at the ſame time fully ſenſible how arduous it is to poize with an unerring hand an overflowing fulneſs, how arduous, to preſerve entire the harmony and integrity of a vaſt empire; nor were we unconſcious that to perſevere from the

* The hiſtory of this Emperor is too well known to need any comment. He ſucceeded his father *Yong-tching*, in 1736, reſigned the throne after a reign of ſixty years, to his ſon *Kia King*, the preſent Emperor, and died the ſeventh of February, 1799, aged eighty-ſeven years four months and thirteen days; — according, however, to the Chineſe mode of computing, he was in the eighty-ninth year of his age.

† Twelfth of March 1799.

‡ The plural is here introduced, not ſolely in conformity to European uſage, but alſo as the neareſt approximation to the pronoun excluſively appropriated in the Chineſe language to ſovereignty. The phraſe " *I the Emperor*" might perhaps be more ſtrictly correct, but its adoption would have been in many places very inconvenient.

begin-

beginning to the end, with unabated attention, is an undertaking ftill more difficult of performance.

Chiefly we are indebted to the all-powerful protection of Heaven, and to the fublime inftructions which have been left by our anceftors for the guidance of their pofterity; we have likewife gratefully to acknowledge the rare affection fhewn towards us in our early youth by our Imperial grandfather, as well as the wife and provident felection of minifters which was made by our Imperial father, from whom alfo we received the facred fceptre of this realm.

From the very commencement of our reign we noted the progrefs of each day with careful folicitude; we beheld an era of profound tranquillity and glorious profperity; but we never dared to give way to exultation or to indulge in the full enjoyment of thefe advantages: we rather engaged our attention in the contemplation of the grand duties of a prince; namely, on the one hand, a reverent obfervance of the laws of Heaven, together with a due veneration for the memory of his forefathers; and on the other, a diligent and benevolent adminiftration of his people. Thefe maxims are, indeed, eafily acquired and retained in remembrance; but their execution is not therefore the lefs arduous or perplexing. During the long courfe of years, however, which has elapfed fince our acceffion, we certainly have ftrictly adhered to the obfervance of the duties of our ftation, and have forborne to relax in our attention, from the earlieft dawn to the clofe of day, to any of our various avocations.

In the practice of devotion, we have fedulоufly obferved the appointed facrifices and occafional oblations to the Divinity, and have always perfonally affifted at each ceremonial, in order to teftify the purity of our heart and the unfeigned piety by which we were actuated, even at a time when our extreme age had a claim to fome degree of relaxation and indulgence.

Four times in the courfe of our reign we perfonally undertook a journey to our city of Mougden, in order to pay our humble adorations at the tombs of our Imperial anceftors.

When the adminiftration of this empire was committed to our charge, we indeed beheld before us a tafk of ferious difficulty, but we were rendered thereby, only more earneft and folicitous in avoiding all deviation from the ftrict line of conduct we had prefcribed to ourfelves. All parts of our various and widely extended domains fhared equally our attention, and frequently during the darknefs of the night, as well as at the middle hour of the day, we have attended, unconfcious of fatigue, in the councils of our minifters, for the purpofe of communicating our decifions on their reports, and of iffuing new ordinances for the public weal, that thus no day might be permitted to pafs away, without having been duly filled and employed.

The

The abundance or ſcarcity of rain, the favourable or deficient harveſts, and the other caſualties which influence the proſperity of our various provinces, are objects in which we have been always moſt deeply intereſted. Six times, therefore, we have viſited our provinces of *Kiang-nan* and *Kiang-ſee*, with the view of directing the embankment of the rivers, and the conſtruction of dykes and cauſeways to repel the encroachments of the ſea.

Regarding the people alſo as our children, and as looking up to us their father for ſupport and protection, we have taken occaſion five times to grant a univerſal remiſſion of all the taxes that are uſually received in ſpecie; and thrice have granted a ſimilar remiſſion of all ſuch duties as are payable in kind. On other occaſions, likewiſe, we granted a remiſſion of taxes to the inhabitants of particular provinces, eſpecially when afflicted by an inundation, drought, or other partial calamity; and, in ſuch caſes, we frequently ſuperadded a bountiful diſtribution of millions to the poor, in order to alleviate their diſtreſſes; being perſuaded, that in thus providing for the happineſs and proſperity of our ſubjects, we accompliſhed the moſt important duty of an upright adminiſtration.

Through the protecting influence of Heaven, and the wiſe counſels left us by our anceſtors, we have ſucceeded in eſtabliſhing peace and tranquillity throughout our dominions. The bordering countries, we have placed in a ſtate of cultivation and improvement; we have eſtabliſhed order and reſtored tranquillity throughout the ſtates of *Eli* *, *Whee-poo* †, and the greater and leſſer *Kin-tchuen* ‡. The tribe of *Mien-tien* ‖ has ſubmitted to our authority; the King of Cochin-china had acknowledged himſelf our vaſſal; and we have laſtly dictated a peace to the nation of *Ko-ur-ke* §.

Even thoſe nations who viſit this country by navigating their ſhips acroſs the ocean, have bowed down before our throne, and brought preſents for our acceptance.

With reſpect to the inhabitants of the interior of the empire, who have excited commotions and diſorders among themſelves, we may ſhortly expect that this evil will be eradicated, and that the tranquillity of the provinces will be re-eſtabliſhed.

The reports, however, of the advantages obtained by our generals over theſe internal enemies, clearly indicate that the employment of troops againſt them was unavoidable.

* The Eleuth Tartars.

† Little Boucharia.

‡ Countries inhabited by tribes of Tartars, immediately bordering on the province of *Se-chuen*.

‖ This people inhabit the countries immediately bordering on the province of *Yun-nan*.

§ Probably Napaul.

Thus,

Thus, during the long and eventful period of our reign, the weighty affairs of government have been the objects of our constant regard; and, deeply impressed with the critical importance of the charge, we never ventured to pronounce the objects of government to have been so completely attained, or the peace of the empire so immutably established, as to admit of our relaxing our efforts or indulging in repose.

Ultimately, however, we recalled to our recollection the mental prayer which we had addressed to the Supreme Being on our accession to the Imperial dignity, and in which we had made a solemn intimation of our intention to resign to our son and successor the sovereignty of the realm, if the Divine Will should grant to our reign a sixty years continuance; forasmuch as we were unwilling to exceed in any case, the duration of our Imperial grandfather's government *.

Our years had indeed already amounted to twenty five, when we thus provided for the event of a sexagenary reign, as if we were gifted with a prescience to enable us to anticipate so protracted a period; it is under the guardian auspices of our Imperial progenitors that this inestimable favor of a reign so glorious, and so happily prolonged, has been extended to us.

While surrounded with numerous relations, and witnessing at once five generations of our family and descendants, we finally observed the progressive revolution of a cycle to be accomplished since the empire had been committed to our hands; and when we then reflected on our original wishes and designs, the contemplation of the corresponding event impressed us with the warmest sensations of joy and gratitude.

Accordingly, on the first day of the year *Ping-shin* † we transferred to our son, the present Emperor, the seals of the sovereign authority, reserving to ourself the title of MOST HIGH EMPEROR, as a distinctive appellation, thus accomplishing in the end, what in our solemn invocation to Heaven we had originally proposed.

We did not, indeed, conceive this arrangement with a view to obtain a respite from fatigue, or to indulge ourself in repose, by terminating the labours of an active and eventful reign with that ease and tranquillity, which our numerous and declining years seemed to warrant and require; we were rather influenced in our resolution of resigning the more immediate duties of government, by the consideration of our being enabled thenceforward to be more immediately occupied in aiding and instructing our successor in the guidance of public affairs, as long as our strength and ability remained unexhausted.

* The Emperor *Kaung-hee* reigned sixty one years.

† The eighth of February 1796.

To

To retire from the cares of government, merely with a view to our perſonal eaſe and convenience, would, indeed, be an ungrateful requital for the favor and protection of Heaven and of our anceſtors; an act repugnant to our feelings, which we could neither wiſh nor dare to commit.

Upwards of three years have ſince paſſed away, during which we have diligently devoted our attention to the inſtruction, and direction of the government of our ſucceſſor.

We have witneſſed of late the operations of an active campaign againſt the rebels of *Se-chuen*, and have obſerved, with ſatisfaction, the numerous advantages and repeated victories which have been obtained by the diligent exertions of our Imperial troops; we are even in the immediate expectation of the ſurrender of all the rebellious leaders, and anticipate the day on which hoſtilities will ceaſe, and univerſal tranquillity be re-eſtabliſhed in theſe dominions.

Being arrived therefore at an era ſo juſtly to be deemed auſpicious, and ſo peculiarly diſtinguiſhed by the happineſs and welfare of our people, we might certainly venture at length to relax from our uſual ſolicitude; but to a mind accuſtomed to look forward to the ſeaſon of difficulty, in order to meet its approach with eaſe and promptitude, it is impoſſible to unbend altogether from care.

As upon the year *Keng-ſhin* *, which is the next following to the preſent, would occur the ninetieth anniverſary of our age, laſt year, the Emperor, our ſon, in concert with the princes and great officers of ſtate, was deſirous of determining upon the celebration of that event by a congratulatory feſtival, and earneſtly requeſted our conſent to the carrying the ſame into effect; to which we, ſhortly after, in conſideration of the meritorious motives which actuated them in their proceedings, replied by an edict expreſſive of our approbation and concurrence.

Viewing, indeed, the advanced age of upwards of fourſcore years, which we had then attained in the full enjoyment of every proſperity, the Emperor, our ſon, and the inhabitants of our vaſt domains, were naturally filled with joy and exultation: no event could certainly have been more ardently deſired by our ſon and the great officers of the empire, than an opportunity of celebrating ſuch an anniverſary.

The grandeur, however, and profuſion attendant on a general rejoicing were by no means the objects of our deſire; we were ſatisfied with the contemplation of the maxim of antiquity, which enumerates a life prolonged to an advanced age amongſt the five inſtances of human felicity: for although among our ancient monarchs, ſome have likewiſe attained a very advanced period of life,

* The year 1800.

according to the teſtimony of the annals of the empire, yet it may be obſerved, that within the full period of an hundred years, the longevity to which they had aſpired has in every inſtance received its termination.

We have already attained the eighty-ninth year of our age; therefore but a few ſhort years are wanting to complete the utmoſt period of longevity: it then only further behoves us reverently to employ the remaining days of our life, and patiently to await the hour which is to conclude it. For ſhall we not doom the portion of life allotted to us ſufficient, nor ever ceaſe to indulge hopes, however immoderate, of prolonging our exiſtence!

A ſtrong conſtitution and temperament of body have happily preſerved us from indiſpoſition until this winter, when, in the courſe of the twelfth moon of the laſt year, we were ſuddenly attacked by a diſorder proceeding from cold, and though we were apparently reſtored to health by the aid of medicine, we perceived that the diſeaſe had left our ſtrength of body materially impaired, and, ſhortly after we had received the congratulations of our miniſters in the hall of audience in the palace of *Kan-tſing-kung* on the firſt day of the new year, our appetite wholly failed us; we are now alſo ſenſible that our faculties of ſight and hearing are declining apace.

The Emperor, our ſon, has indeed been piouſly engaged in procuring medical aſſiſtance, and aſſiduouſly attentive in ſeeking the means moſt likely to conduce to our recovery, but we feel that at our advanced period of life, medicine can prove of very little avail, and therefore make this preparation previous to the laſt mortal paroxyſm of diſeaſe. After a long ſucceſſion of years we are about to cloſe a reign ſuſtained with caution and aſſiduity, and invariably favoured by the diſtinguiſhed protection of Heaven and of our anceſtors. We are now about to reſign for ever the adminiſtration of this empire; but ſhall leave it in the hands of the Emperor, our ſon, whoſe eminent abilities and pious diſpoſition are in every reſpect conformable to our wiſhes, and will, doubtleſs, enſure to him a felicity like ours in his future undertakings; an idea which furniſhes us with the moſt grateful conſolation.

To all the nobility and magiſtrates, from the higheſt to the loweſt rank, in the exterior as well as interior departments of the empire, we eſpecially recommend, diligently to execute their reſpective employments, and to preſerve their hearts free from all taint and corruption, that they may worthily and effectually ſerve the Emperor and promote the objects of his government, and finally, that their conduct may enſure to the millions of people ſubjected to his authority, univeral proſperity and peace.

We ſhall then depart hence, and aſſociate in Heaven with the ſouls of our glorious anceſtors, without leaving a wiſh that is not ſatisfied, or a deſire that is not fulfilled.

With

With respect to the solemnization of mourning, we direct, that it may be observed for twenty-seven days, in the first instance, and in all other respects conformably with the sacred institutions of the empire; we have lastly, and especially to enjoin our posterity, that the respect and oblations due to the spirits of Heaven and Earth, to our ancestors, and to their sacred monuments, be ever diligently and faithfully observed.

This our last will and pleasure, we hereby publish and declare, that it may be generally known and respected.

No. II.

[Referred to from the Translation of the Third prefatory Edict.]

Translation of the Edict extraordinary of the present Emperor of China, by which the Death of His Father, the Emperor KIEN-LUNG, *was first officially made public* *.

HIS Majesty the Emperor, by the grace and appointment of Heaven, issues this Edict extraordinary.

With feeble virtues, and inspired with awe by a sense of our own insufficiency, we have held the vast inheritance of these dominions, since it pleased our Imperial Father, THE MOST HIGH EMPEROR, on the first day of the year *Ping-shin*, (the 8th of February 1796,) to transfer the seals of the empire to our charge.

We applied with unremitting diligence and attention to the discharge of the high duty then imposed on us, that we might not frustrate the gracious designs that were executed in our favour, though our firmest reliance was placed in the protection of Heaven and of our illustrious ancestors.

Our Imperial Father, however, continued to enjoy his wonted health, accompanied by such vigour of mind as well as of body, as enabled him to continue to direct us in the administration of the empire. We daily attended his royal presence, listened to the instructions he was graciously pleased to communicate, and submitted the various affairs of government to his consideration. In the annual visitation which His Majesty was pleased to make through different parts of

* The Edict forms a kind of supplement to the preceding; and though in itself less important, may not be found altogether uninteresting.

the empire, the people were exhilarated by his presence, and thronged from all quarters to behold his august person.

After making our accustomed enquiries concerning his health, and assisting at his Imperial repast, we had always the satisfaction to observe, that time had not materially affected the hale constitution of body, and animated spirits of our Imperial Father; a view that penetrated the utmost recesses of our heart with the most delightful consolation.

Last year, having respectfully considered, that on the approaching year *Keng-shin* (A. D. 1800) the glorious anniversary would occur of the 90th year of the age of THE MOST HIGH EMPEROR, we summoned an extraordinary council of the princes and great officers of state, in order jointly to solicit His Majesty's consent to a due celebration of that event; this he was graciously pleased soon after to grant to our desire, and we were ready to call Heaven and Earth to witness the lively satisfaction and gaiety of heart which we experienced in anticipation of that event.

Viewing with veneration the exalted age of our Imperial Parent, and the unparalleled felicity by which, as it were a birth-right, he has been attended from his infancy, until the latter days in which he is surrounded by relatives of five generations, every one would doubtlessly concur in expressing by words and actions their congratulations on a subject so justly entitled to their praise, as his prosperous reign and inestimable virtues.

We have ourselves addressed the most fervent prayers to Heaven still to prolong his days, and to crown them as heretofore with uninterrupted felicity: indeed, we complied with the sacred precept only, where it saith, "Thou shalt "rejoice;" yet were unwilling to observe it, when it proceeds to say, "and "thou shalt tremble also."

Freedom from indisposition and peaceful repose, however, continued to bless the declining years of our Imperial Father; the peculiar protection of Heaven preserved his happy constitution from the approaches of infirmity during a long succession of years, like the transition of a single day, until this winter, when, in the last moon of the year just concluded, he met with an indisposition arising from cold, and occasioned by a sudden exposure to wind.

Medical aid seemingly restored his health; but his wonted strength was evidently impaired by the attack, though he still continued to impart to us his gracious advice and instruction, as he had done previous to his indisposition.

The various *Mon-gou*, and other tributary princes, as well as the ambassadors of foreign states, still continued therefore, as last year, to anticipate their introduction to his Imperial presence, for the purpose of receiving the gracious communications, which he might be pleased to make to them upon the occasion; nor were they unpre-

unprepared, on their part, to celebrate with due honours His Majesty's almost centenary age.

On the first day of the new year we waited on his august person, in company with the princes of the blood and great officers of state of civil and military rank, in order to offer our humble congratulations upon that festive day, after which we flattered ourselves that the entire re-establishment of his health would be accomplished in the progress of the ensuing spring.

But our expectations were deceived; on the 8th hour of the morning of the 3d day of the first moon, (February 7, 1799,) our Imperial Father suddenly departed from among his ministers and people. The Imperial Spirit ascended to the regions above.

We may strike the earth with our feet, lift our voices to Heaven, rend our hearts, and shed tears of blood, but we can never repay the vast debt of gratitude we owe; it is all of no avail.

Respectfully reviewing the period of sixty years during which our Imperial Father swayed the sceptre of these dominions, we see that the people were constantly animated by his virtues and benevolence, as the earth is gladdened by refreshing showers. The very vitals and inmost recesses of their hearts were conscious of the benign influence of his government.

All creatures that breathe the air, and possess blood in their veins, must acknowledge the ties of kindred, and surely will mourn the loss now sustained, like that of a father or of a mother, of whom they had recently been bereft.

As for ourself, to whom by his gracious goodness the Imperial succession had previously been granted, the grief by which we are penetrated upon this awful event, is more cutting than sharp instruments.

But what avail our words and lamentations; we rather ought to meditate on the weighty and important charge which our Imperial Father has assigned us, and endeavour to practise the virtuous maxims and institutions, as well as to seek to fulfil the wishes and designs, of our illustrious predecessor.

These are the duties, which, however weak and inadequate, we are now called on to discharge, and anxiously as we may now wish for the gracious aid and instruction of our Imperial Father, we know that that resource has irrecoverably failed us, and in this hour of affliction and distress, we have yet more especial reason to apprehend ourselves unequal to the burthen.

It is therefore upon the upright and faithful conduct of the various officers and magistrates in the interior and exterior departments of our dominions that we must chiefly rely; we do indeed confide in their utmost exertions for the support of our government, and the dignity of our person, and expect that they will thereby testify the sense with which they are impressed of the gracious benefits conferred on them by our Imperial Father. The commanders in chief, and other officers serving in our armies, should also recollect with gratitude, the important and signal favours conferred by the Sovereign who appointed them to their respective stations and commands; they should likewise recal to their minds the wise instructions and advice by which he aided and directed their proceedings; and thus, renewing in themselves a spirit of energy and activity, finally clear the country from all enemies whatever of the public peace.

They will thereby afford a grateful consolation to the sacred spirit which is ascended, and which, though now become a blessed inhabitant of Heaven, will not be unconscious of their exertions.

With regard to the due observance of the rites and ceremonies of mourning upon this occasion, we appoint their highnesses *Chun-ying* prince of *Jui-ching*, *Yun-sing* prince of *Ching-ching*, and *Yung-sun* prince of *Yee-kiun*; the ministers of state, *Ho-quen* and *Vang-kie*; the presidents of tribunals, *Foo-kaung-gan*, *Te-ming*, *King-quee*, *Tung-tcho*, and *Ping-yung-sing*, to form a council for administering the same in the public department; we likewise appoint the great officer of state *Wun-pu-ching-chu*, to superintend the ceremonial thereof in the private department; and we especially direct, that they do carefully examine the ancient regulations, and after diligently consulting and deliberating upon each question, regularly inform us of the result.

This edict and notification extraordinary we now publish for general information and obedience. *Khin-tse.*

No. III.

[Referred to from the Translation of the Third Prefatory Edict.]

NOTE.

THE following are titles of articles of preliminary matter which are prefixed to the original work, but which it has not been deemed necessary to introduce into the translation.

Second prefatory edict of the Emperor YONG-TCHING, dated the 9th day of the 9th moon of the 3d year of his reign, A. D. 1725.

Prefatory edict of the Emperor KIEN-LUNG, dated the 5th year of his reign, A. D. 1740.

First rescript of the supreme court for the execution of public justice, (*Hing-Poo*), dated the 21st day of the 12th moon of the 52d year of KIEN-LUNG, A.D. 1788.

Second

Second refcript of the fame fupreme court, dated the 2d day of the 2d moon of the 55th year of KIEN-LUNG, A. D. 1790.

Third refcript of the fame, dated the 18th of the 3d moon of the 60th year of KIEN-LUNG, A. D. 1795.

Preface of the compilers of the prefent edition of the Penal Code, bearing date the 4th year of KIA-KING, A. D. 1799.

Lift of the names of the compilers, and others, fixteen in all, who were employed in editing the work.

Preface of the fuperintendant of the prefs.

General defcription of the work, of its fubdivifions, and of its arrangement.

No. IV.

[Referred to from the Introductory Table of Degrees of Mourning.]

NOTE.

IN addition to the detail which has been tranflated of the cafes in which full mourning is ordered to be worn, it may be fufficient to notice briefly, that the text then proceeds to particularize the twenty-four relationfhips in the firft degree, in which mourning is only required to be worn from three to five months; the fourteen relationfhips which are comprifed in the fecond degree; the twenty-one relationfhips which are comprifed in the third degree; and the forty-two which are comprifed in the fourth or remoteft degree.

In the original text, there are likewife tables fubjoined of confanguinity under various circumftances, and one table in particular, which defcribes thofe who are confidered by the laws to be ftep-fathers and ftep-mothers, in the following manner:

Step-Fathers
1. Mother's fecond hufband, if alfo an adopted father.
2. Mother's fecond hufband, if not an adopted father.
3. Deceafed father's fecond wife's fecond hufband.

Step-Mothers
1. Father's principal wife.
2. Father's wife, fubftituted in the place of the principal wife, deceafed.
3. Father's wife, by whom nurfed or fuckled.
4. Father's wife, who was fubftituted in the place of the natural mother.
5. Father's other wives, excepting the one who is the natural mother.
6. Father's repudiated wife, if alfo the natural mother.
7. Father's re-married widow, if alfo the natural mother.
8. Adopted mother.

The

The father's principal wife has diſtinct rank and privileges and is, in ſome reſpects, the legally adopted mother of all the children; but each child is alſo bound by law in a particular manner, to its natural mother, except under certain circumſtances, as in the ſixth and ſeventh caſes above deſcribed.

No. V.

[Referred to from Section I. Page 2.]

NOTE.

THE number of ſupplementary clauſes annexed to each ſection in the original, is regularly noticed, and will enable the ſtudent of the Chineſe language, if deſirous of inveſtigating the ſubject of any particular ſection more cloſely, to judge how far a reference to the original text is likely to afford him ſatisfaction.

The following is a tranſlation of the moſt material among the clauſes ſubjoined to the firſt ſection.

TRANSLATION.

Inſtruments of torture of the following dimenſions, may be uſed upon an inveſtigation of a charge of robbery or homicide:

The inſtrument for compreſſing the ancle-bones, ſhall conſiſt of a middle-piece, 3 *Che* 4 *Tſun* * long, and two ſide-pieces, 3 *Che* each in length; the upper end of each piece ſhall be circular, and 1 *Tſun* 8 decimals in diameter; the lower ends ſhall be cut ſquare, and, 2 *Tſun* in thickneſs: — At a diſtance of 6 *Tſun* from the lower ends, four hollows, or ſockets, ſhall be excavated, 1 *Tſun* 6 decimals in diameter, and 7 decimals of a *Tſun* in depth each: one, on each ſide the middle-piece, and one in each of the other pieces, to correſpond.—The lower ends being fixed and immoveable, and the ancles of the criminal under examination being lodged between the ſockets, a painful compreſſion is effected by forcibly drawing together the upper ends.

The inſtrument of torture for compreſſing the fingers, ſhall conſiſt of 5 ſmall round ſticks, 7 *Tſun* in length, and $\frac{45}{100}$ of a *Tſun* in diameter each: the application of this inſtrument is nearly ſimilar to that of the former.

In thoſe caſes wherein the uſe of torture is allowed, the offender, whenever he contumaciouſly refuſes to confeſs the truth, ſhall forthwith be put to the queſtion by torture;

* The *Che* exceeds the Britiſh meaſure of a foot by about half an inch; the *Tſun* is its decimal part.

torture; and it ſhall be lawful to repeat the operation a ſecond time, if the criminal ſtill refuſes to make a confeſſion. — On the other hand, any magiſtrate who wantonly or arbitrarily applies the queſtion by torture, ſhall be tried for ſuch offence, in the tribunal of his immediate ſuperior; and the latter ſhall make due enquiry into the circumſtances, on pain of being himſelf accuſed before the ſupreme court of judicature at Pekin, if guilty of wilful concealment or connivance.

Ordinary priſoners are to be confined with the ſmall chain: the *Cangue*, or moveable pillory is never to be uſed, except expreſsly directed by the laws; nor to exceed 25 *Kin* * in weight, unleſs otherwiſe ſpecially determined and expreſſed.

When a ſentence of baniſhment is paſſed againſt the relations, or others, implicated in the guilt of an offender, the corporal puniſhment, which is uſually inflicted in different degrees, proportionate to the duration of the baniſhment, ſhall be underſtood to be altogether remitted.

From the 25th of the 4th moon, to the laſt day of the 6th moon of each year, (in conſideration of the heat at that ſeaſon), the puniſhment of the leſſer bamboo ſhall be remitted altogether; and that of the greater bamboo ſhall be reduced one degree, and further mitigated, by inflicting only eight for every ten blows to which the offender is condemned †. — This indulgence ſhall not, however, be extended to any other offenders beſide thoſe who are actually to be diſcharged within the period above-mentioned. — During the ſame interval, a particular degree of relaxation ſhall alſo be allowed to priſoners in general; and offenders ſentenced to wear the *Cangue* ſhall be permitted to lay it aſide, provided they can find ſecurities for their ſubſequently fulfilling the law, by reſuming it at the expiration of the ſaid period.

Offenders convicted of thieving, robbing, wounding, or aſſaulting, ſhall be excluded from the benefit of the laſt-mentioned regulation.

No capital execution ſhall take place during the period of the firſt or ſixth moons of any year; and in the event of any conviction of a crime in a court of juſtice during the ſaid intervals, for which the law directs immediate execution, the criminal ſhall, nevertheleſs, be reſpited until the firſt day of the moon next following.

The mitigation of the law concerning the infliction of corporal puniſhment during the ſummer months, ſhall take effect without any particular reference to the Emperor.

* The *Kin* exceeds the Britiſh pound by one-third.

† This reduction is over and above that already ſpecified in the text of the fundamental law.

The inſtruments for extorting confeſſion ſhall be given into the charge of the magiſtrates of diſtricts; but ſhall in the firſt inſtance, be examined and approved by the governors of the cities to whoſe juriſdiction they belong; ſecondly, by the chief judge of the province; and laſtly, by the viceroy or ſub-viceroy. — Any magiſtrate uſing illegal or unexamined inſtruments of torture, will be liable to be accuſed thereof before the ſupreme court.

No. VI.

[Referred to from Section II. Page 5.]

NOTE.

THE title of this ſection might be, perhaps, more literally tranſlated, "*The* "*Ten Wickedneſſes,*" or "*The Ten Abominations;*" but the choice of terms is not very material, as the text fully explains the nature of the offences ranked under this claſs; as well as the reaſons for introducing a deſcription of them in this place, though a declaration of the puniſhments incurred by ſuch tranſgreſſions, is reſerved for another part of the code. — In order to give, if poſſible, the full force of the expreſſions employed, this article has been tranſlated with more freedom than thoſe which are merely declaratory of puniſhment, or leſs deſcriptive of the character of the offence. — Theſe obſervations will equally apply to the ſubject of the next ſection, and the manner in which it has been tranſlated.

No. VII.

[Referred to from Section III. Page 6.]

NOTE.

THE nature and extent of the privileges enjoyed by theſe claſſes are deſcribed in the two following ſections. — Excepting the firſt and ſeventh claſſes, it can be ſcarcely ſuppoſed, that this claſſification has any exiſtence in practice; and, in fact, the firſt and ſeventh claſſes muſt, generally ſpeaking, comprehend all thoſe who have any claim to be ranked among the others.

Excluſive of the limited privilege of birth here noticed, there are a few hereditary dignities occaſionally conferred by the Emperor, which deſcend to to the children in the manner defcribed in the firft fection of the next divifion of the code.

No. VIII.

[Referred to from Section VI. Page 9.]

NOTE.

A Short ftatement of the charges againft the minifter of China *Ho-chung-tong*, or more properly *Ho-quen*, and the final adjudication of his fentence, has already appeared in England; but the celebrity of his fate may render acceptable an entire verfion, as well as juftify the introduction in this place of a few obferva-tions regarding the hiftory of that extraordinary man.

Although he had long poffeffed eminent power in the ftate, it does not appear that the peculiar character and hiftory of this minifter had been known in Europe previous to the period of the Britifh embaffy.

The powerful influence which he difplayed on that occafion foon dif-covered, that to his talents and authority the difpofal of public affairs in China was principally confided; and the difinclination which he was found to have en-tertained to the Britifh interefts, is conceived to have had a principal fhare in counteracting the views of that expedition.

It is obferved in the authentic account of that embaffy, that *Ho-chung-tong*, " who enjoyed almoft exclufively the confidence of the Emperor, was faid to be " a Tartar of obfcure birth, raifed from an inferior ftation about twenty years " before, when, while he was on guard at one of the palace gates, the Em-" peror paffing through it, was ftruck merely with the comelinefs of his counte-" nance; but afterwards finding him to be a man of talents and education, he " quickly elevated him to dignity; and he might be faid to poffefs, in fact, under " the Emperor, the whole power of the empire."

It is fubjoined, that " His Imperial Majefty was not, however, blindly guided " by his advice, and once on conceiving that he had attempted to impofe on his " mafter by a falfehood, he was difgraced as fuddenly as he had formerly been " raifed, and he was reduced to his original low ftation for about a fortnight; " when a fortunate accident having proved to the Sovereign, that there was no " real ground for his diffatisfaction, he reftored his late fervant to his wonted " favour, and to a power bounded only by his own."

It would thus ſeem, that the vigour and wiſdom of the Emperor KIEN-LUNG was, until that time, ſufficient to reſtrain within due bounds of ſubordination the ambitious ſpirit and enterprizing genius of the favourite; but it is the general opinion in China, that he took advantage of the ſtate of dotage, into which the aged Emperor latterly declined. — This circumſtance is, indeed, ſtrongly implied to have been the caſe, though not directly expreſſed, out of reſpect to the memory of KIEN-LUNG, in the articles of accuſation which the preſent Emperor brought forward againſt *Ho-chung-tong*, almoſt immediately after His Imperial Parent's demiſe.

Some of the charges may appear frivolous, and others the mere ſuggeſtion of perſonal enmity; but the preſumptive and corroborating evidence ariſing from the immenſe and almoſt incalculable treaſures which he was found, upon an examination of his property, to have amaſſed, afford a ſufficiently convincing proof of his guilt and corruption. According to a ſtatement that was received as authentic at Canton at the time of the confiſcation of his effects, it appears, that beſides lands, houſes, and other immoveable property to an amazing amount, not leſs than 80 millions of Chineſe ounces of ſilver, or about 23,330,000*l.* ſterling value in bullion or gems, was found in his treaſury. This ſum, though immenſe, is not incredible; when the vaſt extent of the empire is conſidered, over the various departments of which, he had certainly for many years a very unuſual, and indeed almoſt an unbounded influence.

A diſcloſure of the real character of the favourite was, however, it ſeems, for a conſiderable time prevented by the exertion and diſplay of ſome eſtimable as well as ſplendid talents, for which he was remarkable. It is obſerved in the account of the Britiſh Embaſſy, that " the manners of *Ho-chung-tong* were not leſs pleaſing " than his underſtanding was penetrating and acute. He ſeemed, indeed, to " poſſeſs the qualities of a conſummate ſtateſman. He was called to office and " authority, no doubt, by the mere favour of the Sovereign, as muſt be the caſe " in moſt monarchies; but he was confirmed and maintained in it by the " approving voice of ſuch perſons of rank and eminence as have influence in the " determinations of the moſt abſolute governments. In thoſe governments in " Aſia, the prince is not afraid, as is the caſe in Europe, to debaſe his dignity " by alliances with his ſubjects; and the number of children of Aſiatic monarchs " by different wives and concubines, occaſion ſo many matrimonal connections " with the crown, that the influence ariſing from them is counteracted by com- " petition. A tie, however, of this ſort, added to power already acquired, in- " creaſes and ſecures it. A daughter of the Emperor is married to a ſon of " *Ho-chung-tong*. This circumſtance was thought ſufficient to alarm ſome of the " Imperial Family, and other loyal ſubjects of the empire, as if they were fear- " ful of the heights to which the ambition of that favourite might aſpire."

The

The ſon, who was thus honoured, is likewiſe included in the ſentence of condemnation; but, on account of the connection he had formed with the Imperial Family, he experienced no more than a trifling diminution of rank, and a removal from public affairs, while the other relations of the miniſter appear to have been proſecuted and diſgraced with an almoſt undiſtinguiſhing ſeverity, according to the long eſtabliſhed maxim of the Chineſe laws, which eſteems a degree of criminality to be inherent in all who are in any reſpect connected or allied with perſons guilty of heinous offences.

It was, however, at the ſame time preſcribed to the ſon to confine himſelf to the ſociety of his family, that he might have no opportunity of reviving any of the dangerous pretenſions of his father, or of executing any ſchemes of revenge for the fate to which he had been condemned.

Apprehenſions were alſo previouſly entertained, that the views of *Ho-chung-tong*, might lead him to attempt an open revolt, or at leaſt to endeavour to eſcape from a court, in which, after the death of the late Emperor, he ceaſed to have any protection, except what his connections and perſonal reſources might afford him. It was probably with the view of defeating ſuch deſigns, that the new Emperor appointed him to the honourable office of one of the chief ſuperintendants of the mourning on the occaſion of his father's deceaſe; as it thus became eaſy to arreſt his perſon, while engaged in the diſcharge of a duty which confined him to the palace, and precluded him from taking any meaſures for his ſafety, or conſulting with and aſſembling his adherents.

The promptitude and vigour with which the Emperor, almoſt at the moment of his acceſſion to independent power, ſtruck at the root of a dangerous combination of intereſts which he had good reaſon to ſuppoſe ſecretly menaced his crown and dignity; and the immediate condemnation to death of this formidable ſtate culprit, together with the puniſhment or humiliation of all his connections and adherents, while they were yet diſconcerted in their projects by the ſudden event of the late Emperor's deceaſe, are certainly ſome proofs of that political courage and ſagacity which are requiſite in the character of a monarch of great and powerful empire.

1. *Tranſlation of an Imperial Edict, containing the Articles of Impeachment exhibited againſt* Ho-chung-tong *(otherwiſe* Ho-quen*) Miniſter of China, by the Emperor* KIA-KING, *in the 4th Year of his Reign.*

ON the 25th day of the 1ſt moon of the 4th year of KIA-KING, the ſupreme council for military affairs tranſmitted, by an extraordinary courier, His Imperial Majeſty's decree of the 11th day of the 1ſt moon, which is as follows:

Extraordinary

Extraordinary marks of the royal favour of our moſt auguſt, and now departed Father, were granted to *Ho-quen*, by elevating him through ſucceſſive degrees, from an attendant at the palace to the ſupreme rank of a Miniſter of the empire, and beſtowing on him an important command in the Imperial army, the advantages of which he continued to enjoy for many years by an exertion of royal munificence, far beyond his deſerts, as well as unexampled among the nobility of the court.

Since we received the important truſt of the government of this empire, and particularly ſince we have been plunged into affliction by the awful event of the deceaſe of our Imperial Father, we have repeatedly meditated on the paſſage of the *Lun-yu*, which recommends the virtue of a three-years forbearance from change when ſucceeding to an inheritance. But, with regard to our Imperial Father, whoſe profound obſervance of the laws of Heaven, and pious veneration for his anceſtors were ſo conſpicuous; who reigned over his people with no leſs vigilance than affection, and whoſe ſincerity of heart and rectitude of government, all countries whether within or without the limits of his dominions, both knew and gratefully acknowledged; the decrees of ſuch a prince ſhould be obſerved for ten thouſand years, and ever regulate the adminiſtration of his ſucceſſors, inſtead of being extended only to a triennial duration.

Deeply impreſſed with theſe ſentiments, we are moſt unwilling to diſplace any of the choſen ſervants of the ſtate whom our Imperial Father had employed or honoured with his confidence; and wherein they might be found guilty, every palliation and excuſe would be admitted, in order to enable us to diſpenſe with the rigorous execution of juſtice.

Theſe, we declare before the light of Heaven, are our ſincere ſentiments and deſire. But the crimes for which *Ho-quen* now ſtands impeached in ſeveral diſtinct charges by the united voice of the principal magiſtrates and nobles of the ſtate, are of ſuch magnitude and importance as appear to exclude even the poſſibility of extenuation.

As ſoon, accordingly, as we had performed the immediate duties which were impoſed on us by the demiſe of our Imperial Father, we iſſued orders that *Ho-quen* ſhould be diveſted of all his dignities and employments, and committed to trial on the following charges, or articles of impeachment:

1ſt, When our Royal Father, on the 3d day of the 9th moon of the 60th year of his reign, elected ourſelf to be his heir and ſucceſſor, *Ho-quen* waited on us, on the 2d of the moon previous to the diſcloſure of the Imperial edict, and preſented us with the inſignia of the rank newly conferred on us, thereby betraying an important ſecret of the ſtate that had been confided to him, in the expectation that ſuch conduct would be meritorious in our eſtimation.

2d, On receiving the ſummons of our Imperial Father, on the 1ſt moon of the preceding year, to attend at the palace of *Yuen-ming-yuen*, he ventured to ride in

on

on horseback through the left gate, and by the great hall of *Ching-ta-quang-ming* as far as the bottom of the mount called *Sheu-ſhan*, regardleſs to a degree beyond example, of a Father and a Sovereign.

3d, When formerly ſuffering from a lameneſs in his feet, he went into the interior of the palace in a palanquin, and paſſed and repaſſed through the gate of *Shin-vu-men* in a wheel chair before the gazing eyes of the multitude, and without the ſmalleſt fear or heſitation.

4th, The young females that were educated for the ſervice of the palace, he took from thence, and appropriated to himſelf as concubines, without any ſenſation of ſhame or regard to decorum.

5th, During the latter campaigns againſt the rebels in the provinces of *Se-chuen* and *Hou-quang*, when our Imperial Father waited with anxious expectation for intelligence from the army, ſo as to be bereft of ſleep and appetite, *Ho-quen* received himſelf, the various reports that arrived from the troops ſtationed in different quarters of the empire, and detained them according to his pleaſure, with a view to deceive his ſovereign by miſrepreſentation and concealment; in conſequence whereof the military operations of the campaign were for a conſiderable time incomplete and ineffectual.

6th, Having been appointed, by a decree of our Imperial Father, to the Preſidency of the ſupreme board for civil affairs, and alſo to that of the ſupreme court of judicature; and afterwards, on account of ſome experience acquired in ſuperintending the diſburſements of the army, having been directed by another Imperial decree to officiate as ſecretary to the ſupreme board of revenue; he immediately united in his own perſon the power and authority which were reſpectively annexed to theſe ſeveral high offices.

7th, Laſt winter, when the venerable perſon of our Imperial Father laboured under infirmity, his ſignature and hand-writing were in ſome places confuſed and not eaſily diſtinguiſhable; whereupon *Ho-quen* had the audacity to declare, that they had "*better be thrown aſide*;" and then iſſued orders of his own ſuggeſtion.

8th, In the laſt moon of the preceding year, *Kieu-ko* reported, that in the diſtricts of *Sin-Wha* and *Quei-Te*, a party of above a thouſand of the rebels had collected, and forcibly carried away a herd of cattle belonging to the *Da-lai-la-ma's* merchants, as well as mortally wounded two perſons, and that they ſtill continued to ravage the diſtrict of *Ching-hay*. *Ho-quen* however rejected and diſmiſſed the report, and, concealing the whole tranſaction, took no meaſures in conſequence.

9th, On the late event of our Imperial Father's deceaſe, we iſſued our orders, declaring that the attendance of ſuch of the princes and chieftains of the *Mongou* tribes as had not had the ſmall-pox would be diſpenſed with; but *Ho-quen*, in oppoſition to our commands, ſignified to them to attend indiſcriminately, whether having

having or not having had that diſeaſe; regardleſs of the intention of our government to ſhew to foreign tribes our kindneſs and conſideration. The motives of his conduct herein it would indeed be difficult to inveſtigate.

10th, The miniſter of ſtate *Su-lin-go*, was entirely deaf, and worn out by age and infirmity; yet, becauſe he was connected by marrriage with *Ho-lin*, the younger brother of *Ho-quen*, his incapacity to diſcharge the duties of his ſituation was artfully concealed from the Emperor's knowledge.

11th, The officers *Ou-ſung-lan*, *Ly-han*, and *Ly-quang-yun*, having received their education at the houſe of *Ho-quen*, have been ſince promoted to the moſt reſpectable offices in the ſtate.

12th, Many of the principal officers whoſe names have been regiſtered in the different civil and military departments have been, in inſtances too numerous to be particularized in this place, removed and diſmiſſed according to his pleaſure, and by his ſole authority.

13th, In the late confiſcation of the property of *Ho-quen*, many apartments were found to be built in a moſt coſtly manner of the Imperial wood *Nan-moo*, and ſeveral ornamented terraces and ſeparate incloſures were obſerved to have been conſtructed in the ſtyle and reſemblance of the Imperial palace of *Ning-ſheu-kung*: the gardens were likewiſe laid out in a ſtyle little differing from that of *Yuen-ming-yuen* and *Fung-tao-yao-tay*; but with what view or deſign we cannot imagine.

14th, Among his treaſures of pearls and precious ſtones, upwards of two hundred ſtrings or bracelets of the former were diſcovered, many times exceeding in value thoſe in our Imperial poſſeſſion. One among the pearls belonging to *Ho-quen* was of an enormous ſize, and exceeded even that which adorns the Imperial crown. There were likewiſe found various buttons diſtinguiſhing princely rank, carved out of precious ſtones, ſuch as his ſituation by no means entitled him to wear. Many ſcore of theſe gems were diſcovered, beſides pieces of the ſame kind in the rough ſtate, to an incalculable amount, and in an endleſs variety, unknown even among the Imperial treaſures.

15th, An eſtimate of the property in gold and ſilver which has been confiſcated is not yet completed; but the ſum is already found to exceed many millions of ounces of ſilver.

16th, The avarice by which he appears to have been actuated, and the corruption by which his wealth has been amaſſed, cannot be equalled in the hiſtory of preceding ages.

Theſe articles of accuſation have been thoroughly inveſtigated and proved by a council of princes and miniſters of ſtate, aſſembled for the purpoſe; and have alſo been acknowledged without reſerve in his own verbal confeſſion.

Ho-quen,

Ho-quen, thus deeply criminal, blind to every virtuous ſentiment, and unmindful of his Sovereign Maſter, perverted and injured the civil and military government of this empire, uſurped the higheſt authority for unwarrantable purpoſes, and perfidiouſly omitted, or ſet aſide, the execution of the laws, while his inſatiable and inordinate avarice ceaſed not to enrich his family, by ſapping the vigour of the ſtate.

Yet theſe crimes are ſmall, in compariſon with the baſe ingratitude with which he requited the gracious bounty of our Imperial Father, who, in his royal wiſdom would moſt certainly have withheld his favour and protection, had any one in the Imperial court poſſeſſed ability or inclination to preſent a timely accuſation of this miniſter's offences.

Not one, however, of the officers of the empire, either of thoſe attached to the court or of thoſe employed in provincial departments, ventured to charge him with his crimes; ſome forbearing out of reſpect to the venerable age of our deceaſed father, and diſinclination to give diſquiet to his royal breaſt; others from the apprehenſion of this miniſter's extraordinary influence and power, which we ourſelf have indeed witneſſed, and have known through its effects.

Now, at length, the crimes alleged againſt *Ho-quen* are brought to light; more eſpecially thoſe offences which concerned our Imperial Father. They are, indeed, more numerous than the hairs on his head, and a hundred tongues would be unable to find an excuſe for them.

Suppoſing that we were to decline the puniſhment of theſe offences, how ſhould we afterwards appear before the Holy Spirit that is in heaven, and reconcile ſuch an omiſſion to the purity of our conſcience.

Be it therefore known by theſe preſents to the officers and magiſtrates of our dominions, that we have reſolved to refer the further trial and inveſtigation of the above charges, to a council of the princes, nobles, and miniſters of ſtate, to be held at our court of Pekin; excluſive of which, we iſſue our general orders to the viceroys of the ſeveral provinces of the empire, to take ſingly into conſideration the charges brought againſt the miniſter *Ho-quen*, and to record their real ſentiments concerning the puniſhment ſuch offences, or any other offences of which he may have been guilty, demand; and then report the ſame to us, with the utmoſt expedition.

Khin-Tſe *.

* It has been omitted to notice, that a termination with theſe words, which may be literally tranſlated, "*Reſpect this,*" is, in China, one of the peculiar diſtinctions of an Imperial Edict.

2. *Translation of an Imperial Edict, containing the Sentence of* Ho-quen, *Minister of China, and of the other Persons who were connected with him, or implicated in the Charges against him.*

The supreme council extraordinary, consisting of the ministers, great officers of state in the civil and military departments, the presidents of the Imperial college and tribunal of censors, and others, having finally determined upon the articles of accusation exhibited against *Ho-quen*, and *Foo-chang-gan*, have now submitted to our consideration, that the said *Ho-quen* do receive sentence of a slow and painful death, according to the law against the crime of high treason; and that the said *Foo-chang-gan*, do receive sentence of decollation, according to the law against the crime of abetting, and being accessary thereto; and that therefore the sentence on the one, and on the other, be duly and immediately carried into execution, according to the said laws.

The unprincipled violence and daring usurpation, which are so manifest throughout the various criminal acts whereof *Ho-quen*, stands convicted, indeed debar him from the slightest claim to any mitigation of the rigour of lawful punishment.

On a reviewal of the grounds of the capital condemnation of *Gao-pay*, by our Imperial ancestor KAUNG-HEE; that on *Nien-keng-yao*, under the authority of our Imperial grandfather YONG-TCHING; and lastly, that of *Na-tching*, by the orders of our Imperial Father, lately deceased; we find that the rank of these criminals corresponded with that of *Ho-quen*, but that his guilt has far surpassed theirs, by its heinous enormity. Proceeding in the investigation, we observe that the royal indulgence was extended to *Gao-pay* and *Nien-keng-yao*, by the permission which was granted to each to become his own executioner; but that *Na-tching* was immediately executed in the presence of the army, as his guilt had, in a peculiar manner, been detrimental to the military operations of the state. In the present instance, however, the wilful delays interposed to the operations of the army; the desire of impeding their success, by criminally intercepting the public reports, and communicating no more than was agreeable to himself; and lastly, the failure to provide the necessary supplies, so as to render the said operations for a long time incomplete and ineffectual, all of which appear in the articles of accusation exhibited against *Ho-quen*, involve a far greater degree of criminality, than any breach of duty in a military capacity ever could amount to.

If we should, therefore, by any consideration, be induced to remit the sentence of a slow and painful death, according to the law against high treason, his

his offences would, at least, demand a sentence equal in severity with that passed on *Na-tching*, in the precedent before us; from which it would indeed be absolutely impossible for us to depart, by allowing of any kind of alleviation, were the execution of the criminal not necessarily to take place within the limits of a three years general mourning.

Even at this moment, when the awful event of our Imperial Father's decease is still recent, the crimes of *Ho-quen* are still such as to justify and require an immediate and exemplary execution.

There are, nevertheless, some considerations upon which we are inclined to pause. For although the guilt of *Ho-quen* bears so great a similarity in its consequences with that of *Na-tching*, yet as the former did not hold a command in the army, a certain distinction undoubtedly exists in the nature of their respective offences, moreover, although in this realm, laws have been framed, and a power established, to which subjects of royal blood and elevated rank are undoubtedly amenable for their offences; and although *Ho-quen*, whose hardness of heart and blindness to every virtuous sentiment are disgraceful to human nature, is a delinquent whom, as far as respects himself, we cannot redeem, and whom the present decree of council has condemned to undergo the unabated rigour of the law; yet, moved by the consideration that he once held the post of highest honour and dignity in the service of this empire, we resolve, in spite of the unpardonable guilt which he has incurrred, to spare him the disgrace of a public execution.

Ho-quen is hereby permitted, through our royal favour, to become his own executioner; but, be it known, that it is our regard for the honour and dignity of the administration of this empire, and not any personal consideration for *Ho-quen*, that has influenced this our present determination.

Foo-chang-gan was likewise highly favoured by our Imperial Father, and second only to *Ho-quen*, of whom he was the constant associate, and with every article of whose delinquency he must have been intimately acquainted.

If he had, during the many private audiences to which he was admitted, laid before his Sovereign a true and faithful report of the criminal conduct of the minister, our Imperial Father would immediately have sanctioned the execution of the laws against *Ho-quen* according to their utmost rigour, and certainly not have protected him, or have transferred the imputation of guilt to *Foo-chang-gan*, under the plea of his having borne false testimony.

If it is urged, that out of respect to the venerable age of our Imperial Father, it was feared to excite his sacred anger, the excuse, though in some degree admissible, is weak and unworthy of that genuine attachment and fidelity which is becoming in a minister; but from the time that we were appointed to the Imperial inheritance, and put in possession of the seals of the empire, *Foo-chang-gan* has been a conſtant reſident in the palace; what obſtacle did then exiſt againſt his requeſting a private audience with us during the hours of his abſence from *Ho-quen*, or addreſſing to us a ſecret memorial, and ſetting forth his crimes?

Had *Foo-chang-gan* in any manner anticipated our preſent deciſion, by drawing up the ſlighteſt ſtatement impeaching the conduct of *Ho-quen*, we ſhould not now have deemed him implicated in the guilt of that miniſter, nor even have deprived him of any of the honours or dignities which he has acquired.

From the commencement, however, to the laſt moment, not a word of this tendency has ever fallen from him; upon which we cannot but infer an intention of abetting and concealing the ſame, an act in itſelf of ſo criminal a nature, that a hundred tongues would be unable to pronounce an excuſe for it.

In the preſent confiſcation and examination of his houſes and other property, moveable as well as immoveable, many things have been diſcovered therein which were extremely unſuitable to his rank and ſtation; and which he could not have acquired and collected without having evinced himſelf at various times both avaricious and corrupt.

It is highly juſt and reaſonable, therefore, that the ſentence conformable to law, which the miniſters of ſtate and other members of the council have awarded, ſhould be executed againſt him.

In conſideration, however, that the board of cenſors has not exhibited any ſpecific charges of guilt againſt *Foo-chang-gan*; and that in the confiſcation and examination of his effects, they did not appear to amount to above a fiftieth or a hundredth part of thoſe found in the poſſeſſion of the miniſter *Ho-quen*, whoſe ſentence we have mitigated to a private and ſelf-execution; we reſolve likewiſe to extend our royal favour to *Foo-chang-gan*, by poſtponing the execution of his ſentence to the uſual ſeaſon for capital puniſhments in the enſuing autumn; and we therefore direct that he ſhall remain in confinement until that period.

We likewiſe direct, that at the hour of the execution of *Ho-quen*, *Foo-chang-gan* ſhall be conveyed to his cell, in order to witneſs the fate of that miniſter; and be re-conducted after the event to confinement at his own priſon.

With regard to *Ho-lin*, brother of *Ho-quen* *, no merit can juſtly be aſcribed to his proceedings; for although upon the trial of *Foo-kaung-gan* (brother of *Foo-chang-gan*), he was principally inſtrumental in bringing forward the impeachment, it is evident that *Ho-lin* did not accuſe him from a deſire of obtaining impartial juſtice, but merely as an inſtrument in the hands of *Ho-quen*, and with a view to procure the deſtruction of *Foo-kaung-gan*. In the preſent confiſcation of the property of *Ho-quen*, ſeveral buildings have been diſcovered of the wood *Nan-moo*, and alſo other illicit articles; when this is compared with the circumſtance of ſecreting

* *Ho-lin* was not living at the period of this trial, as appears by the ſequel.

prohibited

prohibited timber, alleged in charge againſt *Foo-kaung-gan*, it is evident which ought to be deemed a heinous, and which a venial offence.

With regard alſo to the campaign of *Foo-kaung-gan* in the province of *Hou-nan*, againſt the *Miao-fee* rebels, he was to that degree thwarted and impeded in his operations by the conduct of *Ho-lin*, who was in office at court, that the expedition proved ultimately unſucceſsful, and he himſelf fell in the field of battle. From this view it appears, that, upon the charge relating to the campaign againſt the *Miao-fee*, *Ho-lin*, inſtead of deſerving any credit, is himſelf involved in the delinquency it was intended by him to impute to others.

According, therefore, to the deciſion of the council, the hereditary title of *Kung* given to *Ho-lin* ſhall be annulled. With regard, alſo, to the inſcription of his name in the ſacred temple, an honour to which few can aſpire; what can entitle *Ho-lin* thus to rank with thoſe virtuous miniſters to whom we owe the eſtabliſhment of our empire? Conformably then to the deciſion of council, the inſcription of his name ſhall be eraſed from the monuments of the ſacred temple; and, in like manner, the altar which his ſurviving family have erected to his memory ſhall not be permitted to remain in exiſtence.

Fung-ſhin-yn-te (ſon of *Ho-quen*) has acquired by marriage a princely rank, and the princeſs his wife ever enjoyed the parental affection of our Imperial Father, and was peculiarly the object of his royal kindneſs. By utterly degrading *Fung-Shin-yn-te* from his rank and dignity, his family would be reduced to a level with the loweſt populace; an extreme diſgrace, which is inconſiſtent with the favour and compaſſion we are, on the above account, inclined to teſtify towards him.

According, however, to the deciſion of the council, we annul the hereditary title of *Kung*, which *Ho-quen* had obtained for his ſervices in the overthrow of the rebel *Vang-ſan-quay*, ſo as not to be inheritable by his poſterity; but to his rank as *Tſe* of the empire, which we leave unimpaired, *Fung-ſhin-yn-te* is hereby permitted to ſucceed; we direct, at the ſame time that he ſhall confine himſelf to his family, and not go abroad in order to interfere in the adminiſtration of public affairs.

Fung-ſhin-yee-mien (ſon of *Ho-lin*, and nephew of the miniſter) having been degraded from his title by inheritance, ſhall alſo be removed from his honorary command in the Imperial guards, and we forbid his attendance at the palace-gate *Kan-tſing-men*. As a mark, however, of peculiar conſideration, we confer on him the rank of hereditary *Yun-ky-wee*, and order that he do retire and diſcharge the duties thereof under his native Banner.

Su-lin (ſon of *Foo-chang-gan*) received his rank of hereditary *Yun-ky-wee* by deſcent from *Foo-lin-gan*; and, although we have annulled the hereditary rank of *Foo-chang-gan* in conſequence his crimes, yet as *Foo-lin-gan* was nowiſe implicated

implicated therein, we grant, as a mark of our peculiar favour, our licence to *Su-lin* to inherit the inferior rank of *Yun-ky-wee.*

We remove him, however, from his honorary command in the Imperial guards; we forbid his attendance at the palace gate *Kan-tsing-men*, and desire moreover, that he do retire, and discharge the duties of his station under his native Banner.

The minister of state *Sou-lin-go* is extremely old, and totally deaf, but was nevertheless promoted to that office by *Ho-quen*, on account of his connection by marriage with *Ho-lin*, without any regard to the impropriety of the appointment. For, having passed the eightieth year of his age, and scarcely able to perform a genuflexion, how can he be presumed capable of discharging the duties of his arduous station? *Sou-lin-go* shall therefore, retaining his original rank, retire altogether from office.

With regard to *Oo-sung-lan*, and *Ly-whang*, vice-presidents of supreme courts, and *Ly-quang-yung*, officer of the household, they evidently owe their elevation solely to the interference of *Ho-quen*; *Ly-quang-yung* being incapable from sickness of discharging the duties of his appointment, shall retire from court with his original rank; and although no specific charges have been alleged against *Oo-sung-lan* and *Ly-whang*, yet, as the mode of their elevation cannot be accredited, we degrade them to their former rank, as assistants in the Imperial college; and it is hereby declared, that we dispense with the future attendance of *Oo-sung-lan* at the Imperial southern library. As for the rest, we direct the execution thereof according to the decision of the council.

Khin-Tse.

1. *Translation of an Imperial Edict, declaratory of a general Amnesty to all Persons who had been connected with, or influenced by the Minister* Ho-quen.

AFTER we had issued an extraordinary edict, to give public information of the crimes and charges for which our minister *Ho-quen* had been impeached, we received the report of the deliberate decision thereon of the council of ministers and great officers of state, and ultimately pronounced a definitive sentence on *Ho-quen*, by which he has been favoured with the permission of becoming his own executioner.

For a very considerable period *Ho-quen* held the general administration of public affairs; he was guilty of such a daring usurpation of power, and of such a fraudulent and corrupt interposition of his influence, that the concerns of the subject could not gain admittance to the knowledge of their sovereign. Unless such atrocious guilt had been speedily punished, every principle of an equitable and incorrupt administration of the people in general, and of a due dispensation

ſation of ſalutary ordinances and inſtruction for the guidance of the magiſtrates, muſt have been utterly abandoned. His guilt has been aſcertained with clearneſs and preciſion; the ſentence awarded againſt him has been duly executed.

We have ſtill, however, to conſider, that the tribunals and public boards under the influence and authority of *Ho-quen* were many; and that the appointments and promotions diſtributed by him muſt have been numerous in proportion. The provincial officers and magiſtrates muſt therefore unavoidably have incurred, in many inſtances, the criminality of ſeeking their advancement at the palace of *Ho-quen*, and of obtaining it by means of illicit and corrupt donations.

By a radical and minute inveſtigation, we might find many perſons involved in tranſactions that ſtrict juſtice muſt neceſſarily condemn; but, on the other hand, it is neceſſary to guard againſt too great a propenſity towards ſuggeſting inquiries, which, from their nature and number, it would be difficult to unravel or determine.

We have, it is true, iſſued a public declaration of the criminal charges alleged againſt *Ho-quen*, in which the moſt remarkable inſtances of his guilt are enumerated, in order that every member of the community may poſſeſs competent information of the ſame. But if the officers and magiſtrates of our dominions ſhould miſconceive our views therein, and proceed, in conſequence, to a ſevere ſcrutiny of paſt tranſactions, at the inſtigation of perſonal animoſity and diſlike, expoſing ſecret and concealed actions, and the remote cauſes from which they aroſe, whereby ſuch and ſuch perſons might be ſhewn to have ſhared in ſuch and ſuch tranſactions; although theſe reports ſhould prove juſt and faithful, it would be inexpedient to enter into enquiries which would be almoſt endleſs in themſelves, and but too probably ſuggeſted to us from unworthy motives.

When we deſtroyed this monſtrous contriver of iniquity, we were aware that numerous adherents and connections muſt unavoidably have partaken in his guilt; but it was far from our intention to encourage or permit any malicious or vindictive proceedings. We condemned *Ho-quen* to condign puniſhment for his crimes, more eſpecially on the ground of his having defeated and ſubverted the civil and military operations of the ſtate; in compariſon of which, the guilt he has incurred in various acts of corrupt peculation, and partial infringements of the laws, is indeed but trifling and unimportant. On the former account we determined to enforce the law immediately againſt him, without allowing any excuſe or delay to intervene; but, from the commencement, we reſolved to forbear to implicate in the inveſtigation the perſons who might have concurred in his other acts of criminality, confining ourſelf to ſtrict and corrective admonitions for the future, and by no means intending to recommence an enquiry into abuſes that are now paſt and done away.

The

The greater and lesser magistrates of our dominions may, therefore, cease to harbour any suspicions or uneasiness at a retrospect of their own conduct. We are satisfied that our magistracy still abounds with men of intrinsic worth and ability, to whom it is yet very possible to regain the path of integrity, and to amend their past errors, so as to prove themselves hereafter active and valuable servants to the state. Although in a season of critical difficulty, they may not have withstood the pressure of the times, and may have slipped from the right way, it is still in their power to purify the heart, to cleanse the thoughts, to resolve firmly on an amendment, and finally to become men of approved integrity, evincing that they were very far from having been lost irretrievably in the mazes of error and iniquity.

The present clear and explicit declaration of our pleasure, we therefore issue expressly for the purpose of requiring a strict and respectful obedience, and a diligent co-operation with us in our determination to renovate and rectify the administration, by the discontinuance of all evil habits and abuses, however inveterate. If, after the instructive admonition we have now given, a disposition is not shewn to ameliorate and reform, and the utmost exertions are not made to regain the path of integrity, the transgressors will voluntarily have sought their own ruin and destruction, in a manner which is unworthy of them as men, which will undoubtedly expose them to the consequences of our severe displeasure, and against which they will not be able to plead our having failed to instruct and forewarn them: be this general edict therefore promulgated for their information.

Khin-Tse.

No. IX.

[Referred to from Section VI. Page 9.]

Translation of an Imperial Edict, extracted from the Pekin *Gazette of the 27th of 6th Moon of the 5th Year of* KIA-KING, *or the 18th of August* 1800 *.

WHEN *Quay-lung* was last year appointed to the presidency of the tribunal of civil affairs, he had constant access to our presence, and frequently took occasion to express his desire, that a military command might be given him in

* This is only the last of a series of Edicts relative to the misconduct of the viceroy of the province of *Sechuen*; but it is, at the same time, complete in itself, as it contains a summary of the charges against him, and a declaration of his definitive sentence.

the

the province of *Sechuen*. He ſuggeſted to our recollection, that he had formerly held an active ſituation in that province, during the troubles excited by the rebellious *Miao-tſe*, and had aſſiſted in reducing them to ſubmiſſion by his exertions. He added, that the ſuppreſſion of the rebellion of *Pe-lien-kiao*, actually exiſting, was an undertaking of far leſs difficulty than the reduction of the *Miao-tſe*; the delays by which the preſent conteſt has been for ſeveral years protracted, were, he declared, ſolely to be attributed to the negligence and inactivity of the officers to whom the command of the Imperial Armies had been entruſted. He concluded by obſerving, that if a command againſt the rebels was granted to him, he would engage to accompliſh their total overthrow by an appointed day.

We were, however, fully aware of the egregious vanity that prompted this declaration; and, therefore, did not, at that time, judge it expedient to grant his requeſt.

When *Le-pao*, viceroy and commander in chief of the forces, proved himſelf incapable of tranſacting the united duties of thoſe two ſtations; and had, moreover, been criminally negligent in remaining at *Ta-cheu*, when the invaſion of the province by the rebels, required that he ſhould immediately have taken arms againſt them, we depoſed and committed him for trial, and appointed the General *Ge-le-teng-pao* to take his place as commander in chief of the forces. But as the viceroyalty of the province had likewiſe become vacant by his defection, and as the ſtate was at that time unprovided with an officer duly qualified to ſucceed to the appointment, we conſidered that *Quay-lung*, having ſerved for ſome years in that province, and having ſince held the poſt of viceroy over the united provinces of *Fo-kien* and *Che-kiang*, could not be wholly unexperienced in that department, and we therefore iſſued our orders that he ſhould take upon himſelf the viceroyalty of *Se-chuen*; we did not, however, inveſt him with any expreſs military command.

Towards the cloſe of laſt winter, the rebels of *Se-chuen* paſſed over from that province into *Shen-ſee*, and thence to *Kan-ſoo*; upon which the General *Ge-le-teng-pao*, deſirous to guard againſt falling into the errors of his predeceſſor *Le-pao*, took the field in purſuit of the enemy, on the firſt day of the firſt moon of the preſent year, and left to the care of *Quay-lung* the reduction of the remaining parties of the rebels, which were ſtill lurking in different parts of the province.

If *Quay-lung* had felt himſelf unequal to a charge of ſuch importance, he ought to have prevented the departure of the General *Ge-le-teng-pao*, or immediately have reported to us the real ſituation of affairs, that we might have acted accordingly.

After having, on the contrary, readily accepted the poſt thus aſſigned to him, he loſt eight days in inaction at *Ta-cheu*, under pretence of providing clothes

 and

and accoutrements for the ſoldiers. His ſubſequent operations were alſo tardy and undeciſive; and of this the rebels did not fail to take the advantage, by fording the river *Kia-lin-kiang*; by ſo doing, they at once overwhelmed the inhabitants of the oppoſite diſtrict of *Chuen-ſee* with ruin and devaſtation.

Still, however, *Quay-lung* forebore to take the field in perſon, deeming it ſufficient to direct the officers *O-ho-pao* and *Chu-ſhe-teu* to proceed with a ſmall detachment againſt the rebels. Upon this occaſion his meaſures were ſo injudiciouſly taken, that the objects of the expedition were fruſtrated, and the officer *Chu-ſhe-teu* actually cut off by the enemy.

The apprehenſions of *Quay-lung* were ſo much excited by this diſaſter, that having encamped with his army upon the hill *Fung-whoang-ſhan*, he declined making any further efforts, though he repeatedly declared to us in his addreſſes at that conjuncture, that he was engaged in providing for the defence of the banks of the *Tung-ho*. He had not, however, once perſonally encountered the rebels, at the time that the General *Te-lin-tay*, in obedience to our commands, entered into that country, and engaged the rebels with promptitude and vigour. We confined ourſelves, on this occaſion, to a ſimple declaration to *Quay-lung*, that his life and fortune ſhould depend upon the ſucceſsful defence of the river *Tung-ho*; adding that, as a mark of our eſpecial favour, although we degraded him to the third degree of rank, on account of his criminal negligence in permitting the rebels to gain a paſſage over the *Kia-lin-kiang*, we, at the ſame time, aſſigned him the the poſt of guarding the banks of the *Tung-ho*, to afford him an opportunity of redeeming his credit.

If *Quay-lung* had uſed effectual exertions for the protection of that boundary, *Te-lin-tay* would have been able to have met and engaged the rebels in the eaſtern ſide. The good conduct of the former in a ſucceſsful defence of the banks of the *Tung-ho* would in ſuch a degree have contributed to efface the recollection of his previous neglect at the *Kia-lin-kiang*, that even if we had not reſtored him to the firſt degree of rank, we certainly ſhould not have heſitated to have permitted him to continue to exerciſe his functions in the viceroyalty.

So improvident, however, was *Quay-lung* in his meaſures of defence, that when the petition of *Lieu-tſing*, ſuggeſting the detention of the provincial troops of *Honan* for a further ſecurity, was laid before him, he iſſued orders rejecting their aſſiſtance: ſhortly after, the rebels paſſed the *Tung-ho*, without oppoſition, and after having landed on the weſtern bank, were ſuffered to ſpread rapine and devaſtation throughout that diſtrict, and to ruin or extirpate its unreſiſting inhabitants; even the diſtricts in the vicinity of *Ching-too-fu*, the capital of the province, were laid open to the deſtructive progreſs of the rebels. The arrival of of the General *Te-lin-tay* at this juncture was eminently fortunate. With force and intrepidity he led his troops to the charge, and having firſt checked the progreſs of the aſſailants, he finally drove them back acroſs the *Tung-ho*, and has ſince confined them entirely to its eaſtern banks. *Quay-lung*, in the mean-time, was content with having aſſiſted the General *Le-pao* in one or two engagements with another party of the rebels, and then led off his troops by a circuitous route to the diſtrict of *Lung-gan*. The people of the province are no leſs grateful for the ſervices rendered by *Te-lin-tay*, than diſcontented and exaſperated at the conduct of *Quay-lung*, whoſe daſtardly and ſpiritleſs retreat from the enemy had proved him ſo unworthy of command.

If exemplary puniſhment is not inflicted upon this occaſion, what reſpect will hereafter be ſhewn to martial laws, or ſubmiſſion to military diſcipline. The calamities which the inhabitants of the weſtern diſtricts of the province of *Se-chuen* have experienced are beyond the reach of calculation. Were we to perſiſt in extending to *Quay-lung* our indulgence and compaſſion, the much injured people would look upon him with averted eyes, and lend to his words an unwilling ear; in ſhort, the purpoſes of our adminiſtration would be defeated by committing it to ſuch guilty hands.

Our royal authority was therefore iſſued for his degradation and commitment for trial, at the tribunal of his appointed ſucceſſor *Lee-pao*, and before ſpecial judges whom we named for the purpoſe.

The reſult of their inveſtigation of his crimes, was a ſentence of death by decollation. The princes of the blood and great officers of ſtate were likewiſe convened for the purpoſe of inveſtigating and deliberating upon this ſubject, and have come to a ſimilar deciſion.

Quay-lung, therefore, ought to undergo the unabated rigour of the law, by a public execution in the preſence of the troops.

Upon conſideration, however, of the impending trial and execution of the leaders of the *Pe-lien-kiao*, who are ſubjects of this empire, and have incurred the guilt of rebellion; we were apprehenſive, that the execution of an officer of exalted rank, who had failed in the diſcharge of the duties of his ſtation, might induce an aſſociation in the minds of the inhabitants, derogatory to that reſpect and ſubmiſſion which is due to all magiſtrates, from the people under their juriſdiction.

We iſſued our commands, therefore, for the priſoner to be conveyed to Pekin, and directed the princes of the blood and miniſters of ſtate to renew their inveſtigation for two days, and reviſe the ſentence they had given. The unreſerved acknowledgment obtained from *Quay-lung* of his guilt, has precluded the neceſſity of

 a more

a more ſevere ſcrutiny. The additional charge of having killed the officer *Ma-liang-Cheu*, by a random ſhot from his bow, and which action he had concealed by reporting the deceaſed to have fallen in battle, he now likewiſe confeſſes with equal readineſs. The council of princes and miniſters of ſtate, therefore, perſiſt in ſupporting their former opinion, that puniſhment ſhould be inflicted conformably to the utmoſt rigour of the laws; they have alſo, in obedience to our commands, laid before us a ſtatement of the deciſions that have heretofore been paſſed againſt officers of rank, under ſimilar circumſtances of delinquency.

In reſpect to the caſe of the four officers, *Ma-ur-kiun*, *Na-ching-chang*, *Quang-ſe*, and *Ya-ur-ho-ſhin*, who were executed according to the rigour of the laws, on account of their miſconduct at *Ye-Kin-chuen*, in the exterior provinces; we find, on compariſon, that the conduct of *Quay-lung* is more ſeriouſly criminal.

The ſtatement of the trial of *Lee-che-yao* records, that the ſentence of inſtant execution by decollation was changed to a ſentence of execution in the following autumn, by the favour of our Imperial Father. The guilt of *Lee-che-yao*, in not taking meaſures againſt the rebels called *Whey-fee*, and permitting their leader *Tien-fu* to raiſe the ſtandard of rebellion, and collect his adherents, before he proceeded with his army againſt them, may be compared with the timidity and irreſolution of *Quay-lung* in ſeeking to avoid the rebels, and ſuffering them to ravage the country and ruin the inhabitants of *Se-chuen*; but ſtill the crime of the latter appears of a deeper dye.

With regard to the proceedings againſt *Tang-yng-kiay*, viceroy of the provinces of *Yun-nan* and *Quei-cheu*, during the rebellion of the *Mien-fee*, we find that his circuitous marches in order to avoid an encounter with the enemy, and the deceptive reports which he addreſſed to court, in order to gloſs over his miſconduct, drew upon him a ſentence of immediate death by decollation, according to the law againſt a general who injures the ſtate by miſleading his troops. By our Imperial Father's gracious favour he was neverthelеſs permitted to become his own executioner.

The rank of *Quay-lung* correſponds with that of *Tang-yng-kiay*, each being entruſted with the government of a province. With regard to the circuitous marches which they practiſed in order to avoid the rebels, and prevent a general engagement, they appear equally guilty. The conduct of *Quay-lung*, in reporting himſelf to be engaged in defending the bank of the *Tung-ho*, while actually ſeeking for a pretence to avoid the enemy, and his falſe ſtatement of the circumſtances of the death of the officer *Ma-liang-cheu*, may likewiſe be placed in compariſon with the deceptive reports preſented to court by *Tang-yng-kiay*.

The

The charges ſubſtantiated againſt *Quay-lung*, on the whole, fully juſtify the ſentence which has been awarded againſt him; but as ſome palliation may be conceived to ariſe from the circumſtance of his voluntary offer to ſerve in the war againſt the rebels, we are induced to admit the caſe of *Tang-yng kiay* as a precedent, and ſhall, therefore, ſpare to *Quay-lung* the ignominy of a public execution.

It is our pleaſure that the officers of the ſupreme criminal court make known this our reſolution, and carry it into effect. We grant to *Quay-lung* to become his own executioner; a ſentence to which it would be abſolutely impoſſible for us to admit the moſt trifling alleviation, without becoming ourſelves guilty of dangerous and criminal partiality. It is our firm reſolution never to ſuffer the military diſcipline and martial laws of this realm to be degraded or impaired by the licenſed impunity of any magiſtrate, who fails to protect the people of the diſtrict under his authority from the cruelty and rapine of rebellious invaders.

Yuen-yen and *Cha-la-fen*, the ſons of the magiſtrate *Quay-lung*, ſhall proceed to their place of baniſhment at *Elee* in Tartary, as an expiation for the guilt in which they are involved. Having decided upon this caſe, and explained the cauſes and motives upon which our judgment is founded, we direct that this edict extraordinary may be iſſued throughout all the provinces for general information.

Khin-tſe.

No. X.

[Referred to from Section VI. page 9.]

1. *Tranſlation of the Addreſs of* Pe-ling, *Sub-Viceroy of the Province of* Quang-tung. (1805.)

I HUMBLY addreſs Your Imperial Majeſty for the expreſs purpoſe of charging certain magiſtrates of diſtricts with a flagrant neglect and delay in the execution of juſtice; in conſequence of which the ordinary places of confinement are no longer adequate to contain the multitude of unexamined priſoners. I charge them alſo with connivance at the all-devouring rapacity of their followers and attendants. And, laſtly, with the illegal and improper employment of female curators:

curators *: by which ſeveral offences, the lives of many of Your Majeſty's ſubjects have been ſacrificed. I have accordingly to ſolicit an Order from Your Imperial Majeſty, confirming the degradation and removal of the ſaid magiſtrates; that your ſacred authority may be reſpected and enforced by the due puniſhment of offences of ſuch ſerious magnitude.

My firſt inquiries enabled me to diſcover, that in the hands of the officers of juſtice in this province of *Quang-tung*, the authority of the laws had been, in ſome caſes, abuſed, and, in others, neglected, and relaxed: the priſons were full, and informations had accumulated; but the duſty records of unfiniſhed cauſes ſufficiently evinced that very remote muſt be the day of their final adjuſtment, and no leſs remote the day, on which the wrongs of the injured parties could be redreſſed.

The crafty ſcribes and the lawleſs attendants of the courts of juſtice, had not ſcrupled to combine and concert with thriving profligates in forming plans of deceit and extortion; and the country in general has but too deeply felt the injurious conſequences.

On my arrival at the government allotted to me by Your Majeſty, it was my firſt care to ſeek for, and to remove ſucceſſively, the moſt obnoxious of the official attendants, by whoſe miſconduct the town and country had been diſturbed. Two of the moſt notorious among the attendants of the courts, by name *Me-liang* and *Ly-yue-quang*, have already undergone a rigorous examination and puniſhment.

The removal of the delinquents who had been the moſt diſtinguiſhed by their rapacity and extortion, contributed much to eaſe and tranquillize the minds of the people; I proceeded, nevertheleſs, in my inveſtigation, and had occaſi on to notice, that in the diviſions of the city, under the government of the *Nan-hay-ſien* and *Pun-yu-ſien*, excluſive of the legal priſons already full of perſons in lawful confinement, everal ſubſidiary buildings had been engaged, with the acquieſcence of the ſaid magiſtrates, and under the ſanction of various names, but uniformly for the ſole purpoſe of impriſonment.

The officer whom I appointed to inveſtigate this affair, has reported three ſuch places of confinement in the diſtrict of *Nan-hay*, namely *Tay-hcu-ſo*, *Ky-yun-tſang*, and *Hoei-ſoo-bang*, containing upwards of one hundred priſoners: and in the diſtrict of *Pun-yu* likewiſe, a place denominated *Tay-heu-ſo*, in which alſo above an hundred perſons were found in confinement. Among the priſoners, many had been brought up from the country, under charges of theft, murder, and the like, accompanied by the witneſſes and accuſers reſpectively concerned; the cognizance of their offences having been referred to the magiſtrates of the provincial capital: but, whether the parties were more or leſs implicated, the charges ſerious

* The peculiar ſenſe in which this word is employed will appear from the ſequel.

or

or trifling, it was ufual to expofe them for many months, or even a year, to the hardfhip of a tedious and indifcriminate confinement, in thefe unauthorized places of detention.

Exclufive of the legal and the fubfidiary prifons here defcribed, it has appeared, moreover, that the attendants or officers of police attached to the court of the *Nan-hay-fien*, had not lefs than ten places of private detention, in which alfo, taken together, upwards of an hundred perfons were difcovered. The attendants of the court of the *Pun-yu-fien* were provided in a fimilar manner with twelve places, which were found to contain above ninety perfons.

It was found that thefe places were inclofed with a wooden railing, difpofed like a cage, but at the fame time, attached, on one fide, to the wall of the contiguous building, and fubdivided into cells by means of beams and rafters.

Thus conftructed, thefe dark dungeons have been, in fact, employed to enforce, by oppreffive and arbitrary confinement, nothing lefs than a fyftem of fraud and extortion.

I haftened, after inveftigating, to remedy this grievance, butalready many perfons had perifhed under confinement; and the inhuman, nefarious practice has been fo long eftablifhed, that it is difficult to afcertain the year in which it originated, or to conjecture how many lives have been facrificed by its continuance. The people were either chilled with defpair, or murmuring with indignation at the exiftence of fuch an abufe.

I have, in the next place, to animadvert on the appointment of female curators, under the authority of the faid magiftates, the *Pun-yu-fien* and *Nan-hay-fien*.

Thefe women had become the confidential agents of traders, whom they enabled to carry on a difgraceful and illicit commerce of female flaves, and they often affifted in obtaining a certificate from the magiftrates, when the original right to the flave was not free from fufpicion. To the cuftody of thefe women, all the female prifoners who had not yet received fentence, or been difcharged, were committed; and the younger part of them were not unfrequently let out for proftitution, and the wages thereof received by the curators as a part of their regular profits.

An accurate inveftigation is now taking place, under the direction of an officer efpecially appointed for that fervice, of the feveral prifoners of each denomination, with the view of difcharging at once, all fuch as are able to find fecurity, or againft whom the charges cannot be fubftantiated.

The feveral places of detention, which the officers of the above-mentioned courts, had illegally employed, I have caufed to be appropriated to other ufes, the wooden enclofures to be removed, and the cells rafed from the foundations. The number of the perfons found therein, and the circumftances that occafioned their detention, remains to be afcertained by a fpecific inveftigation, and

and will be accurately recorded for the information of the ſupreme court of judicature at Pekin. The female curators, who had ſo ſhamefully abuſed their truſt, have been diſmiſſed for ever; and the female culprits, formerly under their charge, remanded to the families to which they reſpectively belonged; competent ſecurity having been given for their re-appearance at the period of trial.

Laſtly, after giving the ſubject mature conſideration, I cannot heſitate to declare the uſe and appointment of ſubſidiary places of confinement, altogether illegal; more eſpecially, as the law requires an annual and accurate report to be made of the goal-deliveries in each province, to the ſupreme court.

It having thus appeared that *Vang-Shee*, chief magiſtrate of *Nan-hay-ſien*, and *Tiao-hing-vu*, chief magiſtrate of *Pun-yu-ſien*, to whom theſe, which are in fact, the moſt important diſtricts in the province, have been confided, have proved themſelves unfaithful, and unworthy of their truſt, by audaciouſly erecting ſubſidiary priſons in defiance of the law, and unjuſtly confining divers perſons therein: that they have, in general, ſhewn an utter contempt of the laws of the empire, and the happineſs of the people, by the full licence they have given to the deſtructive rapacity of their followers; by the criminal miſemployment of female curators; and by the falſe impriſonment, and various other grievances, to which they have expoſed the people either directly by their orders, or indirectly by their conſent, or connivance: is it poſſible that their conduct ſhould be tolerated one day longer?

I am in duty bound, therefore, to requeſt that Your Majeſty will ſanction their degradation and removal; and in the mean time, I have made temporary nominations to the vacant offices, and have directed an account of the treaſure and grain for which each of theſe magiſtrates ſtood reſponſible, to be accurately drawn out and compared with the actual ſtate of the treaſuries and granaries, under their reſpective juriſdictions, at the period of their ſuſpenſion; and an exact report in due time will be made of the reſult.

I muſt further ſubmit to Your Majeſty's conſideration, that the *Quang-tcheou-foo*, the *Leang-tao*, and the *An-cha-ſſe*, being the immediate ſuperiors of theſe guilty magiſtrates, are liable to cenſure, for their ſupineneſs and neglect of due examination; which, therefore, ought to become a diſtinct ſubject of inveſtigation, on the part of the ſupreme court: alſo, that as ſoon as the various perſons are aſcertained by reference, who officiated as magiſtrates of the above diſtricts, and as *Quang-tcheou-foo*, *Leang-tao* and *An-cha-ſſe*, when theſe corrupt practices originated, their delinquencies will likewiſe be deſerving of inveſtigation and puniſhment; as indeed, that of any magiſtrate of the province under whoſe juriſdiction ſuch abuſes may be found at any time to have exiſted.—With a view to a comprehenſive enquiry of this nature, I have directed an inveſ-

investigation of all the facts, which it is necessary previously to ascertain; that no measure may be omitted for effectually preventing the repetition of these grievances, and that the feelings of the injured multitude, may be appeased and tranquillized.

These several measures, I have thought it necessary to adopt for the good government of the province; and having respectfully set them forth in this address, they are now humbly submitted to your Majesty's Imperial consideration.

Your Majesty will finally decide upon my conduct; and will be pleased to issue your gracious orders and instructions in regulation of my further proceedings.

2. *Translation of an Imperial Edict, issued in reply to the preceding Address, on the 22d day of the Intercalary 6th Moon of the 10th Year of* KIA KING, (*August the 16th* 1805.)

We have received the addresses of *Na-yen-tching* and *Pe-ling*, charging certain magistrates of districts with neglect and delay in the execution of justice, in consequence of which, the prisons had become inadequate to contain all the culprits successively committed for trial; secondly, with connivance at the rapacity and extortion of their attendants; and lastly, with the illegal employment of female curators: by which several offences, the lives of many of our subjects had been endangered or sacrificed. — We are accordingly solicited to degrade and remove the said magistrates.

The magistrates of districts are undoubtedly forbidden by existing regulations, to employ any subsidiary places of confinement; and in the event of an increase in the number of informations against delinquents in those large districts which include the capital of the province, absolutely requiring such an expedient, it would have been the duty of the magistrates thereof to have represented the exigency to the supreme officers of government, in order that the adoption of the measure, as far as it was necessary, should receive the sanction of the laws.

It has now appeared, upon investigation, that three subsidiary prisons had, nevertheless, been employed in the district of *Nan-hay*; and that the attendants of the tribunal, in the said district, made use of fifty other occasional places of confinement. In the district of *Pun-yu*, one subsidiary prison was found, called *Tay-heu-so*, and also twelve places of occasional confinement. It was moreover discovered, that the attendants had been very culpably suffered to divide those places of confinement into cells, and to enclose them with a railing, whereby dark dungeons were formed, with the view of practising fraud and extortion upon the unfortunate perſons who were confined therein, among whom many became ſick, and died from the ſeverity of the impriſonment.

Laſtly, it has appeared that the female priſoners, previous to their being diſcharged or receiving ſentence, were uſually entruſted to the cuſtody of female curators, by whom it frequently happened that the younger women were expoſed to proſtitution, and the wages thereof received by the curators as a part of their regular profits.

The conduct of the magiſtrates who permitted theſe abuſes is no leſs odious than extraordinary; they ſeem utterly to have neglected the laws of the empire, and the happineſs of the people, with whom, by occaſion of their inferior juriſdiction, they were more intimately connected than other officers of government.

On theſe grounds, the viceroy and ſub-viceroy have ſolicited their degradation and removal; and accordingly we decree that *Vang-ſhy*, magiſtrate of *Nan-hay*; and *Leao-hing-vu*, magiſtrate of *Pun-yu*; be diveſted of their reſpective employments, and expiate their guilt by an immediate baniſhment to *Elee* in Tartary.

And, as it is evident from the exiſtence of theſe abuſes, that the ſuperintending officers of the province have been guilty of ſupineneſs, and neglect of due examination in their reſpective departments, we direct that the ſupreme court do deliberate on the cenſurable conduct of *We-ſhe-poo*, the late viceroy; and on that of *Sun-yu-ting* and *Hoo-tu-lee*, ſucceſſively ſub-viceroys of the province of *Quang-tong*; and likewiſe on the conduct of the *Gan-cha-ſſe* (judge), *Leang-tao*, and *Quang-cheou-foo* (governor of the city), who by virtue of their reſpective offices, poſſeſſed a juriſdiction over, and a power to control the ſaid guilty magiſtrates.

We order that *Na-yen-tching* alſo proceed to aſcertain by inveſtigation, at what period, and under the government of what magiſtrates, theſe abuſes commenced; and that he do ſpeedily report the ſame for our conſideration, ſhewing the degree of miſconduct with which ſuch magiſtrates and their reſpective ſuperiors, are chargeable.

With regard to *Na-yen-tching* and *Pe-ling*, who have ſo lately ſucceeded to the government of the province; we highly applaud the vigour and ability they have ſhewn in the adminiſtration of public affairs, and it is our pleaſure that the ſupreme court for civil affairs, do take their merits into conſideration.

Khin-Tſe.

No. XI.

No. XI.

[Referred to from Section XXXIV. page 36.]

NOTE.

THE application of the laws of China to the case of British subjects trading to, and residing at Canton, concerning which a reference has been made to this article of the appendix, is a subject which might deserve, as well as afford scope for, a distinct treatise. A trade which employs annually, upon an average, upwards of 20,000 tons of English, and 10,000 tons of Indian shipping; which carries off, every year, more than a million sterling in value, of our manufactures and productions; and which alone can supply us with an article so universally in use as to be almost a necessary of life in this country, must, even without estimating how much it contributes to the revenue of the state, as well as to that of the East India Company, be obviously of great national importance.

It is one of the necessary, but embarrassing consequences of the footing upon which foreigners are at present received in China, that they can neither consider themselves as wholly subject to, or as wholly independent of the laws of the country they live in. When unfortunately involved in contentions with the government, there is generally a line, on one side of which submission is disgraceful, and on the other, resistance unjustifiable; but this line being uncertain and undefined, it is not surprising that a want of confidence should sometimes have led to a surrender of just and reasonable privileges; or that at other times, an excess of it should have brought the whole of this valuable trade, and of the property embarked in it, to the brink of destruction.

The plan and limits of this work will not admit of any regular enquiry into a subject of this nature; but it is hoped that the four following translations of public and official documents, will contribute in some degree to illustrate the professed sentiments of the Chinese government in this respect, and be found in other points of view, not uninteresting.

1. The first relates to the Portuguese at Macao. — A Chinese had been killed by a Portuguese subject; and the crime having been fully brought home to the murderer, the authority to which he was amenable under the circumstances of the case, was the only question in dispute. In this instance the Portuguese ultimately prevailed, and the culprit was executed by their authority, and within the limits of their jurisdiction.

2. The second is a translation of an edict issued on the occasion of an attempt made by the Russians, to open a trade at Canton, in the year 1806. The Emperor's interdiction did not arrive in time to prevent the departure of the ships

 with

with full cargoes, but will probable prove effectual in discouraging similar adventures in future.

3. The third relates to a small English vessel, which was stranded in the course of the year preceding, upon the coast of China. The crew were saved, and conveyed to Canton by land; but no part of the cargo was ever recovered.

4. The fourth and last, is a translation of an Imperial Edict issued in the year 1808, and containing the Emperor of China's conclusive and very favourable determination of a question which had previously involved the East India Company's representatives at Canton, in very embarrassing, and for a long time, ineffectual negotiations with the provincial government.

The tenor of this edict, and the circumstances under which it is known to have been published, are calculated, it must be acknowledged, to convey more unfavourable ideas of the administration of the laws in the Chinese empire, than almost any other public act of that government upon record. In this case, all the proceedings were founded on a story fabricated for the purpose; a story, in which the Europeans did not concur, though asserted to have done so; which, in fact, the Chinese magistrates themselves, or the merchants under their influence, invented; which the Chinese witnesses, knowing to be false, adopted; and which, lastly, the sovereign himself appears to have acquiesced in, without examination.

The fact was simply as follows: a number of English seamen had been engaged in a scuffle with the Chinese populace at Canton; in the course of which, one of the natives unluckily received a blow that terminated in his death. The actual perpetrator of the deed not being known, one of the seamen, who had taken an active share in the scuffle, was singled out by the officers of the Chinese government as a proper person to answer for the homicide, and at the same time, this fictitious account of the affair was concerted, in order to justify his acquittal.

In defence of the Chinese government, as far as its general character may be supposed to be affected by these proceedings, it may be said:

First, that the case in question being considered to have been almost unparalleled, cannot justly be made the ground-work of any general inference.

Secondly, that as the Chinese merchant, who, according to the custom of the port, had undertaken a general responsibility for the ship to which the sailors who had been riotous belonged, is said to have purchased the acquiescence of the parties interested, by a division amongst them of a sum little short of 50,000l.; it must be admitted, that the witnesses, and other agents on the occasion, were exposed to more than ordinary temptations, and such as could be but seldom held out to persons in their situations in any country, or under any circumstances.

Thirdly, that the facilities which encouraged an attempt at the subornation of the witnesses, and corruption of the judges, were greater, and the danger of of detection less, in a case in which a foreigner, than in one in which a native, was the object of the prosecution.

Lastly, that although the falsehood in which so many persons concurred, was, no doubt, base and criminal in itself, it neither produced, nor was intended to produce, the slightest deviation from substantial justice in respect to the person accused; he was well known to be innocent, or at least unconvicted, of the murder; but the strictness of the laws unfortunately rendered it impossible for the magistrates to ground a verdict of acquittal upon a true statement of the case, without, at the same time, in some degree implicating and condemning themselves; they, therefore, under these difficult circumstances, contrived to do that which was just in itself, though they certainly resorted to means which were far from defensible.

As to the Emperor's acquiescence in an acquittal, founded upon so plausible and well concerted a story, it certainly cannot be fairly considered as any impeachment of the judgment and impartiality of his government.

1. *Translation of an Edict of the Governor of the Town and District of* Hiang-shan, *addressed to the Chinese and Portuguese Inhabitants of* Macao.

WHEREAS the European Andreas struck and mortally wounded *Chin-a-lien*, a Chinese; although the relations of the deceased, instead of duly reporting, have endeavoured to conceal the fact, I have taken into custody one of the relations *Chin-ky-yen*, together with *Ly-a-voo*, the man who had apprehended the European.

These persons having undergone examination at my office, and the wounds on the body of the deceased having been inspected and legally verified, I proceeded to issue an order to the procurador of Macao to deliver up to me the said Andreas, that his trial might take place according to law; but this procurador deceitfully, and under colour of false pretences, seeks to suppress the enquiry, and is unwilling to give up the culprit.

Considering that these foreigners, who live and reside at Macao, enjoy, through the generous goodness of the Imperial government, the food which they consume, and the ground which they occupy, exactly on the same footing as its natural subjects, it is but just, that they should respectfully obey and submit to the laws and institutions of the country, and comply readily, in this instance, with what our judicial proceedings require.

Now, these foreigners, by persisting to conceal the culprit, do indeed betray such malice and obstinacy, that I ought at once to represent their conduct to the viceroy,

viceroy, preparatory to the meaſure of cutting off all communcaition with them, by cloſing the gates of the diſtrict. Reflecting, however, that there is at Macao a great mixture of Europeans and Chineſe, and that the inhabitants of the latter deſcription are very numerous, ſo as to render the execution of ſuch a meaſure inconvenient, I ſhall only for the preſent addreſs this edict, eſpecially to the the ſaid Chineſe inhabitants, whether traders, labourers, or perſons employed in any other capacity, to inform them, that I hereby prohibit every deſcription of traders from ſupplying the foreigners with their reſpective commodities; and alſo all labourers, carpenters, bricklayers, and other artificers, from working for them in any manner, until the ſaid foreigners conſent to deliver up the culprit, after which permiſſion will be given to reſume and carry on trade and buſineſs with them as heretofore.

Whoever diſregards this prohibition ſhall be taken into cuſtody, and ſeverely puniſhed, without admitting of any mitigation or abatement. All perſons, therefore, will do well to obey and reſpectfully conform thereto.

26th of the 7th Moon of the 10th year of KIA-KING. 18th of September, 1805.

2. *Tranſlation of an Imperial Edict, dated the 9th of the 12th Moon of the 10th Year of* KIA-KING, *addreſſed to the Viceroy of the Provinces of* Quang-tung *and* Quang-ſee.

WE are juſt apprized by the Hoppo *Yen*, that in the courſe of the 10th moon, two Ruſſian ſhips had ſucceſſively anchored in the roads of Macao, and that on board of theſe ſhips two foreign merchants, named Kruſentern and Lyſianſkoy, had arrived, and had brought with them a ſum of money, and a cargo of furs, with the intent of opening a trade at the port of Canton: That the Hong merchants had, upon an inveſtigation, found theſe Ruſſians to belong to the nation termed by the Chineſe *Go-lo-ſe*, and had tranſlated and laid before him their petition for leave to trade at the port; upon which he, the ſaid Hoppo, having conſulted with the viceroy *Na*, and the ſub-viceroy *Sun*, had iſſued the uſual orders, directing the merchants to trade honeſtly and fairly with them.

This is a very negligent and ſummary mode of proceeding; for it ought to have been recollected, that the trade with foreign nations is reſtricted within certain limits, which it is never permitted to violate or tranſgreſs. It is true, that all ſuch foreign nations as are accuſtomed to frequent the ports of Canton and Macao and the neighbouring iſlands, are likewiſe allowed the liberty of trading in thoſe parts, but amongſt theſe, the name of the Ruſſian nation has never yet been obſerved by us: wherefore, their ſudden appearance at this time, and deſign of open-

opening a trade at the port of Canton, cannot be confidered otherwife, than as a very novel and extraordinary circumftance.

Now, all affairs connected with the intercourfe with foreigners, fhould be inveftigated and acted upon with peculiar circumfpection; it was, therefore, the duty of the Hoppo either to have refufed their requeft, not finding it fanctioned by any precedent, and thus at once to have difmiffed them; or at leaft, to have granted a fhort ftay to the firft fhip only. And as there had been a petition received from the foreigners, it ought to have been faithfully reported to us, and no further proceedings allowed until our pleafure was known, inftead of permitting them to trade unconditionally, upon the mere report and ftatement of the Hong merchants. Befides, as the name of Ruffia appears to be nothing more than the foreign pronunciation of *Go-lo-fe*, of which nation there never have been any interpreters employed at Canton, the Hoppo has not fhewn how their petition could have been tranflated, and explained to him; nor do we find in his report, of what fort of furs the cargoes of their fhips confifted; nor the amount of the money they brought with them to trade with; nor laftly, what returning cargoes they were defirous of purchafing. The omiffion of all thefe things, which fhould have been feverally defcribed and explained, is highly reprehenfible; we have therefore directed an enquiry to be held on the conduct of the Hoppo *Yen*, who was principally culpable in this affair; and we have further directed, that the proper board fhould deliberate and report to us, whether the viceroy *Na* and fub-viceroy *Sun*, are not likewife cenfurable for their concurrence.

The viceroy *Vu* and the Hoppo *Oe*, fhall, immediately on the receipt of thefe commands, in the firft inftance, fufpend for a time, all tranfactions at the cuftom-houfe, on behalf of the faid fhips, provided they are not already laden; if they fhall have completed their lading, but not have quitted the port, the viceroy and the Hoppo fhall proceed, without delay, accurately to enquire and inveftigate, whether thefe Ruffians really came from the nation of *Go-lo-fe*; and if fo, how the natives of the *Go-lo-fe* nation, who have hitherto always traded by way of *Ha-ke-htu* (Kiachta) in Tartary, and never before vifited the coaft of *Quang-tung*, have now been able to navigate their fhips thither, and have become acquainted with the fhoals and iflands with which that coaft abounds. Alfo, whether they have not paffed by fome other kingdoms in their way from Ruffia, and what kingdoms; whether they were not from fome, and from what kingdoms, directed and informed how to proceed to this country.

Laftly, they are to enquire whether the Ruffian merchants embarked in thefe fhips, brought their cargoes with them for their own private emolument and advantage, or were difpatched to China to trade, by the orders of their King. The viceroy and Hoppo having taken meafures for collecting full and diftinct information on all

all theſe ſubjects, ſhall tranſmit the ſame to us by expreſs. In reply we ſhall iſſue to them our final inſtructions for their guidance.

But ſhould theſe ſhips, having taken in and completed their cargoes, have been permitted to depart, and no channel remain, through which this ſubject may be inveſtigated, we, in that caſe, do direct that, in the event of any ſhips viſiting for the future the ports of Canton and Macao, or their vicinity, belonging to any other nation beſides thoſe which have cuſtomarily frequented thoſe ports, they ſhall on no account whatever be permitted to trade, but merely ſuffered to remain in port, until the viceroy and Hoppo, having reported to us every circumſtance reſpecting them, ſhall have been appriſed in return of our determination.

We now diſpatch this edict by an expreſs, that the viceroy and the Hoppo may know our pleaſure, and duly conform to it. *Khin-Tſe.*

3. *Tranſlation of an Extract of an Edict of the Viceroy of* Quang-tung *and* Quang-ſee, *communicated to the Senior Captain of His Britannic Majeſty's Ships on the Coaſt of China.*

The Celeſtial Empire (China) is provided with ſtrict and numerous laws, according to which, whenever an act of robbery or theft is committed in the country, orders are immediately iſſued for rigorouſly enquiring after and purſuing the criminals; when they have been taken into cuſtody, it becomes neceſſary, by a legal proceſs, to inveſtigate and verify their guilt, and alſo to identify the property recovered, in order that in the end, a juſt and equitable ſentence may be awarded.

When a ſhip of your nation was ſtranded laſt year, near *Ping-hay*, and you repreſented to this government that it had been afterwards plundered, his excellency, my predeceſſor, immediately iſſued ſtrict orders for the diſcovery and ſeizure of the offending parties.

In like manner, ſince I came into office, I have repeatedly and urgently given inſtructions to the ſame effect; but, on account of the remote and maritime ſituation of the place where the offence is alleged to have been committed, it is impracticable to declare poſitively any preciſe period, within which the guilty individuals may be expected to be traced and brought to juſtice: however, I ſhall again give orders for perſevering in the inveſtigation, and whenever the criminals, and the property plundered by them can be found, a trial and ſentence ſtrictly conformable to law, will undoubtedly follow.

9th of the 8th moon of the 11th year of Kia King. 20th September 1806.

4. *Tranſ-*

4. *Tranflation of an Edict of the Hoppo or Superintendant of the Port of Canton, addreffed to the Chinefe Merchants licenfed to engage in Foreign Trade.*

I have received information from His Excellency the vice-roy to the following effect:

" On the 26th of the firft moon of the 13th year of KIA KING, I received the following difpatch from the fupreme criminal tribunal at Pekin, relating to a cafe that had been tried in this province:

" A decifion having taken place upon a cafe which we had laid before his Imperial Majefty for ratification, it is now fit and neceffary that we fhould communicate the fame to your excellency, as viceroy of *Quang-tung* and *Quang-fee*, to the end that the fame may be duly carried into effect under your excellency's direction.

" His Majefty's inner council having, in the firft inftance, iffued a tranfcript of the report of the vice-roy of *Quang-tung* and *Quang-fee*, ftating his inveftigation of the cafe of a foreigner, Edward Sheen, opening a window-fhutter in an upper ftory, and dropping a ftick fo as to hit and occafion the death of *Leao-a-teng*, a native of this empire; His Majefty was pleafed, on the 8th of the 11th moon of the 12th year, to direct that our tribunal fhould revife the fame and pronounce judgment thereon. — In obedience to orders, we accordingly on the 10th day of the moon, took the faid tranfcript into confideration; and we found that the viceroy's report was grounded, in the firft inftance, on a ftatement of the magiftrate of *Nan-hay-fien*, a diftrict of Canton, which was to the following effect:

" On the 18th day of the firft moon of the prefent year, *Leao-a-teng*, a native " of the diftrict *Pun-yu-fien*, went with his wife's brother *Chao-a-ffe*, to buy " goods in a ftreet within the faid diftrict, called *She-fan-hang*, and happened to " pafs along the ftone pavement under a warehoufe called *Fung-tay-hong*: at the " fame time an Englifhman named Edward Sheen, who was in the upper ftory " of the faid warehoufe, in attempting to open the window, flipped his hand " and dropped a ftick, which, *Leao-a-teng* not expecting, could not avoid, " and was therefore ftruck therewith on the left temple, fo that he fell to the " ground.

" *Chao-a-ffe* acquainted *Leao-a-lun*, the brother of *Leao-a-teng*, with the acci- " dent, who being thus informed of the particulars thereof, came and affifted " the faid *Leao-a-teng* to return to his home, and procured him medical affiftance, " which however had no effect, and the wounded man expired on the evening of " the following day, the 19th of the moon; — the brother of the deceafed then re-

 " ported

" ported the case to the head-man of the district; and by him, information was " laid at the tribunal of the *Nan-hay-sien*, where the witnesses of the fact " having been, in consequence, assembled and examined, the chief of the said " nation was called upon to deliver up the said criminal Edward Sheen, for ex- " amination and trial".

The viceroy proceeded to state, that repeated orders were, in consequence, issued to the *Hong* merchants on the subject, and through them to the chief of the said nation; in reply to which it was alleged, that the said criminal was sick of an ague and fever, and undergoing medical treatment for his recovery: at length, after repeated applications, it was reported that he had recovered from his sickness, whereupon the magistrates of the district confronted the criminal with the relations of the deceased, and having finished the investigation in due form, referred the consideration of the proceedings to the chief judge, by whom the same process was renewed, and the result finally transmitted to the vice-regal office.

His excellency having concluded the enquiry, by personally and strictly examining into the affair himself, ascertained that " that Edward Sheen is a native of England, engaged for hire to perform the duty of a seaman, on board the ship of Captain Buchanan, a merchant of the same nation: the said ship having been laden with a cargo of goods for trade, in the said kingdom of England, had arrived at the port of Canton and anchored in the reach of *Whampoa*, in the course of the 12th moon of the 11th year of KIA KING, after which the cargo was landed, and deposited in a warehouse or factory called *Fung-tay-hong* in the suburbs of the city of Canton: Edward Sheen had immediately thereupon, accompanied captain Buchanan and others to the upper story of the said warehouse or factory, in order to dwell therein, until, the returning cargo having been received, the period of departure should arrive:—This upper story was also contiguous to, and overlooked the street and path-way, towards which a window was opened with moveable shutters.

On the morning of the 18th day of the 1st moon of the 12th year of KIA-KING, Edward Sheen employed a wooden stick in an oblique direction to keep open the shutter of the abovementioned window; but in doing this, the wooden stick slipped and fell downwards:

It happened also, that *Leao-a-teng*, a native of China, accompanied by his wife's brother *Chao-a-sse*, went to the street called *She-san-hong*, to buy goods; and passing at the same moment under the said upper story, was struck and wounded by the end of the stick falling, as aforesaid, upon his left temple; and he thereupon fell to the ground. *Chao-a-sse* acquainted *Leao-a-lun*, the brother of *Leao-a-teng*, with the accident, who, upon being informed thereof, immediately came and assisted *Leao-a-teng* to return to his home; and afterwards procured

cured him medical affiftance; all which, however, proved of no avail; and the wounded man died on the evening of the following day, the 19th of the moon.

"Now, the aforefaid criminal, Edward Sheen, having been repeatedly examined, has acknowledged the truth of all the facts here ftated, without any refervation. — Confequently, in this cafe, there is no appeal againft the conviction of this offender, Edward Sheen; who, having been proved guilty of accidental homicide, may be fentenced to pay the ufual fine, to redeem himfelf from the punifhment of death by ftrangulation".

The foregoing being the fubftance of the report of the viceroy to his Imperial Majefty, we have deliberated thereon, and have afcertained that, according to the preliminary book of the penal code, all perfons from foreign parts, committing offences, fhall undergo trial and receive fentence according to the laws of the empire: — Moreover, we find it declared in the fame code, that any perfon accidentally killing another, fhall be allowed to redeem himfelf from punifhment, by the payment of a fine; laftly, we find, that in the 8th year of KIEN-LUNG (1743) it was ordered, in reply to the addrefs of the viceroy of Canton then in office, that thenceforward, in all cafes of offences by contrivance, defign, or in affrays happening between foreigners and natives, whereby fuch foreigners are liable, according to law, to fuffer death by being ftrangled or beheaded, the magiftrate of the diftrict fhall receive the proofs and evidence thereof, at the period of the preliminary inveftigation, and after having fully and diftinctly inquired into the reality of the circumftances, report the refult to the viceroy and fub-viceroy, who are thereupon ftrictly to repeat and revife the inveftigation. — If the determination of the inferior courts, upon the alleged facts, and upon the application of the laws, is found to have been juft and accurate, the magiftrate of the diftrict fhall laftly receive orders to proceed, in conjunction with the chief of the nation, to take the offender to execution, according to his fentence. *In all other inftances of offences committed under, what the laws declare to be palliating circumftances, and which are therefore not capitally punifhable, the offender fhall be fent away to be punifhed by his countrymen in his own country* *.

The cafe of the Englifhman, Edward Sheen, opening a window-fhutter in an upper ftory, and the wooden ftick which fupported it, flipping and falling down fo as accidentally to hit *Leao-a-teng*, a native, who was paffing by, and by ftriking him to occafion his death, appears to be, in truth, one of thofe acts, of the confequences of which, neither fight, hearing, or reflection could have given a

* This paragraph is particularly important, as it announces an exemption in favour of foreigners, which, however effential to their well-being and fecurity in China, was never before fo diftinctly declared and underftood.

previous warning; there was therefore, no pre-difpofition to injure, and the cafe is evidently agreeable to the conftruction ftated in the commentary upon the law of accidental homicide. The faid Edward Sheen ought therefore, conformably to the provifional fentence fubmitted by the viceroy to his Majefty, to be allowed to redeem himfelf from the punifhment of death by ftrangulation, (to which he would otherwife have been liable, by the law againft homicide by blows,) by the payment of a fine of 12 *leang* 4 *fen* and 2 *lee*, (about 4l. 3s. fterling), to the relations of the deceafed, to defray the expences of burial; and then be difmiffed to be governed in an orderly manner in his own country.

We thus refpectfully laid before his Imperial Majefty, our deliberate judgment upon this cafe, with the confiderations whereupon it is founded, and humbly folicited a declaration of his Majefty's pleafure regarding the fame.

On the 17th day of the 10th moon of the 12th year (January 1808) the addrefs was laid before his Majefty, and received his Majefty's anfwer in thefe words " we ratify your judgment."

The above communication of the fupreme criminal court, having reached the vice-regal office, I, in the firft inftance, directed the provincial judge to attend to the ftrict execution of the Imperial decree, by forthwith taking the faid Edward Sheen and delivering him to the chief of his nation, in order to his being fent back to be governed in an orderly manner in his own country; — the ufual fine being at the fame time duly recovered, for the re-imburfement of the relatives of the deceafed for the expences of his interment: — the exact time of difmiffion of the faid foreigner, and of the reimburfement of the faid relatives, are to be duly afcertained and reported to me; but I think fit, moreover, to communicate thefe things to your excellency, that you likewife may co-operate in attending to the due execution thereof."

His Excellency the viceroy's communication having been tranfmitted to me, as Hoppo, at my office, I determine to make it known to you alfo *Hong* merchants, that you may, agreeably to thefe my orders, attend to the due execution of all things therein required. — May you refpectfully conform to thefe orders.

The 7th of the 2d moon of the 13th year of the Emperor KIA-KING (February 1808).

No. XII.

No. XII.

[Referred to from Section LII. Page 55.]

Translation of an Imperial Edict, extracted from the Pekin Gazette of the 30th of the 3d Moon of the 5th Year of KIA-KING, (*the 23d of April* 1800.)

WHEREAS we have respectfully considered the decisions of our Imperial Father, deceased, on the subject of a petition now presented to us, for permitting the establishment of colleges in various districts of Tartary, where the youth of those provinces might be examined, and receive their literary degrees without the inconvenience of undertaking a journey to Pekin for that purpose. Though we are aware of the advantages that might result from such a measure, yet as the profession of arms is most congenial to the disposition of the inhabitants, as well as of the greatest local necessity in those countries, it would be a matter of just regret, that too great an encouragement given to literary pursuits should ever divert the Tartar youth from the more active employments of the military and equestrian exercises. It might also be reasonably apprehended, that partiality and corruption would gradually insinuate themselves in to examinations, which should be carried on in such remote and unfrequented stations.

It is therefore our pleasure, that the examinations and distribution of literary degrees among the Tartars, should be continued solely at Pekin as heretofore; and at the same time we strongly recommend to the Tartar officers, civil and military, to instruct and exhort their sons, and the younger branches of their families, to consider the art of riding, and the use of the bow, as the most desirable and appropriate objects of their emulation, and which they cannot practice or cultivate with too much assiduity.

Khin-Tse.

No. XII. A.

No. XII. A.

[Referred to from Section LXXVIII. Page 84.]

Translation of an Extract from the Clauses annexed to Section 78.

A Man having no male iſſue, ſhall chuſe an heir and repreſentative from among thoſe who are of the ſame name, and known to be deſcended from the ſame anceſtors, beginning with his father's iſſue, next with his relations in the firſt degree, next with thoſe in the ſecond degree, next with thoſe in the third degree; and, laſtly, with thoſe in the fourth degree; upon the failure of theſe, he is at liberty to chuſe whomſoever he may prefer among thoſe of the ſame name. — If afterwards a ſon ſhould be unexpectedly born to him, ſuch ſon and the appointed heir, ſhall participate equally in the family property.

A widow having no children, and not marrying, ſhall be allowed to remain in poſſeſſion of the family property, but ſhall duly ſummon the next heir to the ſucceſſion.

When there is an open enmity ſubſiſting between a man who has no male iſſue, and the family of his lawful heir, the former ſhall be at liberty to chuſe the one whom he eſteems moſt among his relations, deſcending from the ſame known anceſtors, If, in ſuch a caſe, the excluded heir endeavours to compel the proprietor to admit his claim to the inheritance, the magiſtrates ſhall interfere and protect the right of the heir whom he had elected.

No. XIII.

[Referred to from Section LXXXVIII. Page 92.]

NOTE.

IT has long been a diſputed, and is ſtill perhaps to be conſidered as a doubtful queſtion, whether the tenure by which the land is in general held in China, is of the nature of a freehold, and veſted in the landholder without limitation or controul, or whether the Sovereign is, in fact, the univerſal and excluſive proprietor of the ſoil, while the nominal landholder is like the Zemindar in India, no more than the ſteward or collector of his maſter. The truth probably lies, in this inſtance, between the two extremes. It is well known, that ſeveral of the merchants

merchants who trade with Europeans at Canton have confiderable landed poffeffions, and that they efteem thofe poffeffions to be the moft fecure, if not the moft important portion of their property. The miffionaries refident at Pekin, under the protection of the court, have likewife their eftates in land, granted them by different Emperors, for the fupport of their eftablifhments. Befides; the ordinary contribution of the landholder to the revenue is fuppofed not to exceed one-tenth of the produce; a proportion very different from that which is required from the Ryots, or actual cultivators of the foil in India, and which leaves enough in the hands of the landholder, to enable him to referve a confiderable income to himfelf, after difcharging the wages of the labourer, and the intereft of the capital employed in the cultivation of his property. It is chiefly upon this income that all the fuperannuated, fuperfeded, and unemployed officers of government; all merchants retired from, and no longer engaged in bufinefs; all thofe Tartar families who hold their property in China under a fpecies of feudal vaffalage; and, laftly, all farmers and other not actually labouring agriculturifts, muft be fuppofed to fubfift. — As there are no public funds in China, the purchafe of land is the chief, if not the only mode of rendering capital productive with certainty and regularity, and free from the anxiety and rifk of commercial adventure.

On the other hand, it muft be admitted, that the Penal code clearly evinces that there are confiderable deductions to be made from the advantages juft mentioned; that the proprietorfhip of the landholder is of a very qualified nature, and fubject to a degree of inteference and controul on the part of government, not known or endured under the moft defpotic of the monarchies of Europe. By the LXXVIIIth Section, the proprietor of land feems to be almoft entirely reftricted from difpofing of it by will. By the LXXXVIIIth Section, it appears that the inheritors muft fhare it amongft them in certain eftablifhed proportions. By the XCth Section, thofe lands are forfeited, which the proprietors do not regifter in the public records of government, acknowledging themfelves refponfible for the payment of taxes upon them. Allotments of lands even appear to be in fome cafes liable to forfeiture, merely becaufe they are not cultivated when capable of being fo. — By the XCVth Section, no mortgage is lawful unlefs the mortgagee actually enters into the poffeffion of the lands, has the produce thereof conveyed to him, and makes himfelf perfonally refponfible for the payment of all taxes, until the lands are redeemed by the proprietor. It will alfo be perceived that, except in the cafe of a lawful mortgage, no perfon other than the actual proprietor of the land, is allowed to engage for the payment of taxes upon it, and that therefore fuch engagement is, in fome degree, a teft of property.

No. XIV.

[Referred to from Section XCI. Page 96.]

1. *Extract of a Letter from a Missionary at Pekin, dated the 9th of September* 1801.

" DEPUIS deux mois que j'ai finie mes lettres, il m'a été impossible de les faire partir : une inondation dont on n'a pas d'exemple, ayant rendus les chemins impraticables. A la première cruë d'eau, le gouverneur du district de Pekin a annoncé vingt mille morts, dont il avoit pris connaissance dans l'étendue de son gouvernement, qui n'est qu'une petite partie de la province ; il ajoutoit, ce que tout le monde scait, qu'il devoit nécessairement y en avoir beaucoup d'autres qu'il ignoroit. Ces premières eaux s'étant écoulées en partie, les pluies vinrent derechef, et les eaux allerent toujours en augmentant pendant un mois. — Tous les rapports qui nous viennent de dehors, s'accordent à confirmer qu'il ne reste plus de moisson en terre plate. Depuis un mois, que les pluies ont cesseés, les chemins sont à peine praticables à cheval ; on ne peut pas encore voyager en voiture : heureusement la récolte de bled étoit a peu près finie, mais les autres grains qu'on appelle ici grandes moissons, et qui sont la principale ressource de la province, sont presque tous perdues ; on n'en excepte que les endroits élevés."

2. *Extract of a Letter from a Chinese Christian, dated at* Lu-gan-fu, *in the Province of* Shan-sy, 30*th July*, 1803.

" HIC vitam traho liberam quidem, sed a congressibus hominum alienam ; quid hic aut alibi geratur, me latet omnino : unum scio, penuriam omnium rerum, ob infinitam populi multitudinem, in his regionibus reperiri ; cibaria duplo carius vendi quam venderentur in Europa ; pauperes sustentari, immo rusticos omnes, furfuribus, corticibus arborum et leguminum, vesci panibus rarissime, eosque inter cibos lautissimos habere, carnibus vero nunquam, nisi ad convivium, adhibitos, earum mirandi potius, quam gustandi copiam apponi : quod fames his annis ingentem mortalium stragem non fecerit, fertilis annona auxilio fuit ; ceterum paupertate industriam gignente, hominesque laboribus addictissimos, victum non aliunde magis quam ab agricultura parari ; furta, et homicidia nusquam rarius, quam in hac provincia audiri *."

* This extract is given *verbatim*. — The writer of the letter is the person of whom honourable mention is made in the Authentic Account of the British Embassy, vol. II. p. 594.

No. XV.

No. XV.

[Referred to from Section XCV. Page 101.]

Abſtract of ſome of the principal Clauſes annexed to the XCVth Section.

NO mortgage, or redemption of lands mortgaged, ſhall be reverſed or ſet aſide, after it has been ſigned by all the parties intereſted, or after it has been acquieſced in by them for five years.

When it is expreſsly declared in the preamble of a deed of ſale, that the land is ſold abſolutely, and not by way of pledge or mortgage, and there is no ſubjoined clauſe providing for the contingency of a further payment to the ſeller, as a conſideration for his making the ſale abſolute at a ſubſequent period; ſuch a deed of ſale ſhall be an effectual bar againſt all claims whatſoever of redemption. But if the ſale is not expreſsly declared to be abſolute, or if there is a general clauſe of redemption, or a ſpecific one of redemption at any time after the expiration of a certain period, the original proprietor ſhall, according to the terms of the agreement, be entitled to recover his land, upon repayment of the conſideration for which it was pledged or mortgaged. If the original proprietor, at the end of the period ſpecified in the contract, is ſtill unable to diſcharge the mortgage, it ſhall be at his option, either to retain his right to a recovery of his land, at any future period, or to ſurrender it, and make the ſale abſolute, in conſideration of a receipt of a further ſum to be agreed upon between him and the mortgagee, or between arbitrators duly appointed by the parties. If they cannot agree upon the terms, the mortgagee ſhall have the option of either continuing in poſſeſſion, or of re-imburſing himſelf, by re-mortgaging the land to ſome other perſon, the right of redemption remaining as before with the actual proprietor.

It is however provided, that all deeds of ſale which are doubtful, or imperfect, owing to the tenor of the preamble, but which contain no clauſe of redemption, ſhall, if not queſtioned or objected to for thirty years from the date thereof, become to all intents and purpoſes abſolute.

Thoſe lands which have been allotted on the tenure of military ſervice, cannot be pledged or mortgaged, but may be let for any term, not exceeding three years.

No. XVI.

[Referred to from Section CXXIX. Page 136.]

Tranſlation of an Imperial Edict, extracted from the Pekin Gazette of the 21ſt of the 4th Moon of the 5th Year of KIA-KING, (*25th of April*, 1800.)

WHEREAS the Army Commiſſioner *Tſung-tay* is found guilty of the crime of fraudulently ſuppreſſing part of the ſupplies which had been deſtined for the troops at *Kia-lin*, and of applying the ſame to his private uſe and advantage; it is hereby ordered, that 40 blows with the bamboo ſhall be inflicted upon him, and that he ſhall be baniſhed for life to *Elee* in Tartary.

It is further ordered, that the lieutenant *Tang-lin*, who connived at, and encouraged the corrupt practices of the ſaid commiſſioner, ſhall likewiſe ſuffer 40 blows, but continue to ſerve in his regiment, holding, however, one of moſt laborious and leaſt honourable ſituations in it, as a further mark of diſgrace. *Khin-Tſe.*

No. XVII.

[Referred to from Section CXLIX. Page 158.]

NOTE.

THE exorbitance of the intereſt of three per cent. per menſem, and thirty per cent. per annum, upon either of which rates, according to this code, a contract for a pecuniary loan may be lawfully made, is a peculiarity in the Chineſe laws, which it may be difficult entirely to account for. However, it is by no means to be underſtood, that the ordinary intereſt of money, conſidered ſtrictly as ſuch, in any part of China, ever attains that extent. At Canton, for inſtance, the rate is generally conſidered to be from 12 to 18 per cent.; which, although ſubject to no controul from the laws, does not, it will be perceived, materially exceed, upon an average, the legal rate of 12 per cent. per annum, eſtabliſhed by ourſelves in Britiſh India.

The

The rate of intereſt upon a pecuniary loan muſt, indeed, generally ſpeaking, be influenced by a twofold conſideration. Beſides what is conſidered to be ſtrictly equivalent to the advantage ariſing from the uſe of the money, the lender muſt be ſuppoſed, in moſt caſes, to receive likewiſe a certain compenſation for the riſk to which he expoſes his principal. The former conſideration will always be limited by, and bear a certain ratio to, the peculiar ſtate and degree of the general proſperity of the country; but the latter can evidently be determined by no rule or proportion, which does not include the conſideration of the relative ſituation and circumſtances of the parties intereſted in the tranſaction. In England, indeed, where the ſecurity of property, and the excluſive rights of individuals are ſo well underſtood, and ſo effectually protected by the laws, it may, in general, be almoſt as eaſy to guard againſt riſk, as to compenſate for it. But in China, where the rights connected with property are comparatively vague and undefined, and being diſtinct from the ſource of power and influence, are leſs the object of the law's regard; where, owing to the ſubdiviſion of property, there are few great capitaliſts; and where alſo there is but little individual confidence, except between relations, who, holding their patrimony in ſome degree in common, can ſcarcely be conſidered as borrowers or lenders in the eye of the law; it is not ſo ſurpriſing that it ſhould be deemed expedient to licenſe, in pecuniary tranſactions, the inſertion of ſtipulations for very ample intereſt; and, in point of fact, there is no doubt that the law in this reſpect, indulgent as it is, is frequently infringed upon.

In a ſtate of things ſo unfavourable to the accumulation and transfer of property, there cannot at any time be much floating capital; and the value of that capital, as far as it is denoted by the intereſt which it bears, it is natural to expect, will be high in proportion to its ſcarcity. In other words, where there are many borrowers and few lenders, and where it forms no part of the ſyſtem of the government to grant to the former any peculiar degree of protection or encouragement, it ſeems a neceſſary conſequence, that the latter will both demand and obtain a more than ordinary compenſation in return for the uſe of his property. Trade, therefore, as far as it requires ſuc haid, cannot be ſo extenſively carried on, as it is in thoſe countries, in which there being more available capital, that capital is procurable at a cheaper rate, and accordingly a ſmaller return of profit found adequate to the charges of commercial adventure.

Excluſive of loans made ſimply on perſonal ſecurity, and thoſe which are made upon landed ſecurity, as already noticed under the title "Mortgage," it is a no leſs frequent practice in China, to lend upon pledges; and accordingly, the ſhops of money-lenders, where depoſits may be made of any kind of perſonal property, are extremely numerous in all parts of the empire, and, in general, upon a ſcale of greater reſpectability than eſtabliſhments of a ſimilar nature in Europe.

The intereſt required upon loans thus made is uſually from 1½ to 2 per cent. per menſem; whereas that upon landed ſecurity, eſtimated on an average of the net returns of the land which is pledged or mortgaged, is ſaid not to exceed from 1 to 1½ per cent. per menſem. It is neceſſary, in this place to obſerve, that, in converting monthly into annual intereſt, the Chineſe make it a general rule of computation to exclude the firſt and fixth month of every year, ſo that 1 per cent. per menſem is only equivalent to 10 per cent. per annum, and the reſt in proportion.

When an article offered in pledge has been valued, and the rate of intereſt agreed on, a loan is negotiable, on the condition of the pledge being forfeited, unleſs redeemed while its eſtimated value continues to be ſufficient to cover both the principal and intereſt of the ſum lent. The ſubject of this note is very fully diſcuſſed in the *Memoires ſur les Chinois*, vol. iv. p. 299 to 391.

No. XVIII.

[Referred to from Section CLXII. Page 176.]

Tranſlation of Two Imperial Edicts concerning the Propagation of Chriſtianity in China, dated in the Year 1805.

FIRST EDICT.

THE ſupreme criminal tribunal has reported to us the trial, inveſtigation, and ſentence of that court, upon the caſe of *Chin-yo-vang*, a native of the province of Canton, who had been diſcovered to have received privately a map and ſundry letters from the European *Te-tien-tſe* *; and alſo in regard to ſeveral others, who had been found guilty of teaching and propagating the doctrines of the Chriſtian religion.

The Europeans who adhere to the Chriſtian faith, act conformably to the cuſtoms eſtabliſhed in thoſe countries, and are not prohibited from doing ſo by our laws. Their eſtabliſhments at Pekin were originally founded with a view to the advantage of adopting the weſtern method in our aſtronomical calculations; and Euro-

* The real name of this European was Adeodato. He was a miſſionary of reſpectable character, and had been many years reſident at Pekin in the Imperial ſervice.

peans

peans of every nation, who have been desirous of studying and practising the same at this court, have readily been permitted to come and reside in the above establishments; but, from the beginning, they were restricted from maintaining intercourse with, and exciting troubles among our native subjects.

Nevertheless, *Te-tien-tse* has had the audacity secretly to propagate and teach his doctrines to the various persons mentioned in the report; and he has not only worked on the minds of the simple peasantry and women, but even many of our Tartar subjects have been persuaded to believe and conform to his religion; and it appears, that no less than thirty-one books upon the European religion have been printed in Chinese characters. Unless we act with severity and decision on this occasion, how are these perverse doctrines to be suppressed! how shall we stop their insinuating progress!

The books of the Christian religion were originally composed in the European languages, and, in that state, were incapable of influencing the minds of our subjects, or of propagating their doctrines in this country; but the books lately discovered are all of them printed in the Chinese character, with what view, it is needless to enquire; for it is enough that our simple peasantry, and more especially our Tartar subjects, ought not to be inveigled in this manner; and that such books are capable of producing the most serious effects on the hearts and minds of the people.

With respect to *Chin-yo-vang*, who had taken charge of the letters; *Cheu-ping-te*, a private in the Chinese infantry, who was discovered teaching the doctrine in one of their churches; *Lieu-chao-tung*, *Siao-chin-ting*, *Chu-chang-tay*, and the private soldier *Vang-meu-te*, who severally superintended congregations of Christians; as they have been convicted of conveying letters, or employing other means for extending their sect and doctrine, it is our pleasure to confirm the sentence of the court, according to which they shall severally be sent into banishment to *Elee*, and become slaves among the *Eleuths*; and previous to their departure, wear each of them the heavy cangue for three months, that their chastisement may be both corrective and exemplary.

The conduct of the female peasant *Chin-yang-shee*, who undertook to superintend a congregation of her own sex, is still more odious; she, therefore, shall likewise be banished to *Elee*, and reduced to the condition of a slave at the military station, instead of being indulged with the female privilege of redeeming the punishment. The peasant *Kien-hen*, who was employed in distributing letters for the congregation, and in persuading others to assist in his ministry; and also the soldier *Tung-hen-shen*, who contumaciously resisted the repeated exhortations made to him to renounce his errors, shall respectively wear the common cangue for

for three months; and, after the expiration of that term, be baniſhed to *Elee*, and become ſlaves among the *Eleuths*. The ſoldiers *Cheu-ping-te*, *Vang-meu-te*, and *Tung-hen-ſhen*, who have gone aſtray, and willingly become proſelytes to the European doctrine, are unworthy to be conſidered as men; their names ſhall be eraſed from the liſts of thoſe ſerving under our banners.

The countrymen *Vang-ſhy-ning*, *Ko-tun-ſo*, *Ye-ſe-king*, and *Vu-ſe-man*; and the ſoldiers in the Chineſe infantry, *Tung-ming*, *Tung-ſe*, and *Chee-yung-tung*, have each of them repented, and renounced their errors, and may be diſcharged from confinement; but as the fear of puniſhment may have had more effect than any ſincere deſign to reform, it is neceſſary, notwithſtanding their recantation, that the magiſtrates and military officers, in whoſe juriſdiction they may be, ſhould keep a ſtrict watch over them, and inflict a puniſhment doubly ſevere, if they ſhould relapſe into their former errors.

Te-tien-tſe, who is an European retained in our ſervice at court, having ſo far forgotten his duty, and diſobeyed the laws, as to print books and otherwiſe contrive to diſſeminate his doctrines, is guilty of a very heinous offence. The alternative propoſed by the court, of diſmiſſing him to his native country, or remanding him from the priſon to his ſtation at Pekin, is very inadequate to his crime. We, therefore, direct, that the ſupreme military tribunal appoint an officer to take charge of the ſaid *Te-tien-tſe*, and conduct him to *Ge-ho* in Tartary, where he ſhall remain a priſoner in the guard-houſe of the *Eleuths*, and be ſubject to the ſuperintendence and viſitation of the magiſtrate *King-kie*, who muſt carefully prevent him from having any correſpondence or communication with the Tartars in that neighbourhood.

The noble officer *Chang-ſo*, appointed to ſuperintend the European eſtabliſhments, having been ignorant of what was going forward, and having made no inveſtigation or inquiries during the time that *Te-tien-tſe* was writing letters, printing books, and ſpreading his religion, has proved himſelf incapable and unworthy of his ſtation; wherefore, we direct the interior council of ſtate to take cognizance of his miſconduct.

In like manner, it is our deſire, that the council of ſtate do take cognizance of the neglect and inattention of the military commanders who ſuffered the ſoldiers under their orders to be corrupted with theſe doctrines, and report to us the reſult of their deliberations, in order that we may refer the adjudication of their puniſhment to the proper tribunal.

The council of ſtate ſhall further, in concurrence with the ſupreme criminal court, appoint proper officers to examine all the books of the Chriſtian doctrine which have been diſcovered; after which the ſaid books ſhall, without exception,

be

be committed to the flames, together with the blocks from which the impressions had been taken.

The governor and other magistrates of Pekin, and also the commanders of troops stationed thereat, shall strictly attend to the subject of these instructions, and severally address edicts to the soldiers and people in their respective jurisdictions; they are to inform them, that all persons who frequent the Europeans, in order to learn their doctrine, will, without exception or abatement, be punished with the utmost rigour of the law, for thus acting in defiance of the present prohibition; as for the rest, we confirm the sentence of the court. *Khin-Tse.*

SECOND EDICT.

IT having been discovered, that the European residents at Pekin have maintained a correspondence with our Tartar subjects, for the purpose of instructing them in the doctrines of their religion, and have likewise caused books to be printed in the Chinese and Tartar languages, with a view to facilitate the propagation of their tenets, we issued an edict, strictly prohibiting the same, and also directed that all the books containing their doctrine, which should be found in the different European establishments at Pekin, should be immediately seized for the purpose of being destroyed. The contents of several of their books have been already investigated by our council for state affairs, and having by our desire been submitted to our inspection, we think fit to notice some particular passages.

In "*the useful introduction to the doctrine*" it is said, "*Tien-chu* (i. e.) *the master* " *of heaven, is the great king of all the nations*;" but, in "*the Calendar of Saints*," it is said, that "*Jesus the incarnate is the great king of the earth, and of all crea-* " *tures.*" Again; "*Infidelity is the left road: without meditation it is hardly* " *possible to pursue the strait road, and obey the will of the Lord.*" Is this truth, or good sense? Then we are informed, that "*all creatures are subordinate to the* " *great master of heaven and earth: kings, princes, learned, and the people in* " *general, should all renounce their errors, and seek truth;—when the holy religion* " *prevails, it will soon produce the permanent benefits of order and tranquillity.*" Again; "*The master whom I adore is the true master of heaven and earth, and of* " *all created things;—through him is the way to the kingdom to come; but the* " *ways of this world are the ways of the flesh.—Holy men were desirous of em-* " *bracing the opportunity of propagating the doctrine in China.*"

In the "*Instructions concerning the Institution of Marriage,*" it is said, that " *those who are not of the religion are no better than slaves of the devil.*"

The foregoing passages are sufficiently absurd and extravagant; but this is not all; there are other observations still more false and irrational, making light of the

the obedience due to parents, and declaring, that "*the highest degree of impiety* "*consists in disobeying the will of the Tien-chu*;" a story is related of a *Saint Ursula* *, *who, refusing to obey a command, was killed by the hands of his cruel father, whereupon the Tien-chu being incensed, struck him dead with lightning; and this is announced as a warning to all parents, relations, and friends, who attempt to obstruct the designs of their children; and so forth.*

This is surely as contradictory to reason and social order, as the wild fury of a mad dog.

In another place we are told, that *there was a Pei-tse,* (i. e.) *a Tartar prince, who used to commit many bad actions, and never attended to the expostulations of the Fo-tsin,* (i. e.) *Tartarian princess, his wife, who endeavoured to dissuade him from his wickedness. One day, a legion of devils seized the Pei-tse, and carried him to hell, and the Tien-chu, seeing that the Fo-tsin was a good and virtuous woman, privately informed her, that her husband was suffering everlasting torments in a sea of fire.* From which it is inferred, that those who neglect pious exhortations, cannot possibly escape the everlasting punishment inflicted by the *Tien-chu*.

Now this is absurd and extravagant in the highest degree: where did the Europeans become acquainted with the appellatives *Pei-tse*, and *Fo-tsin*, except it was in their interviews and conversation with the natives of Tartary, from whom they have adopted them in order to fabricate this idle tale!

We do not now mean rigorously to investigate what has been done heretofore; but, it is obvious, that this account of a *Pei-tse* carried to hell by devils, is given without any kind of evidence, and does not possess the least shadow of truth or credibility. It would appear, in short, to be a tale which their ingenuity has contrived; and, upon this principle, what is there that we may not readily expect them to say or to write!

If, instead of an early prohibition, we suffer them to go on diffusing their tenets and fabricating their stories, still more egregious falsehoods and absurdities will be obtruded upon us.

Nothing, indeed, but a severe and exact execution of the laws, can prevent the most dangerous consequences; it is better, therefore, to take salutary and efficient precautions, and we have thought fit to direct *Loo-kang*, the noble officer superintending the European establishments at Pekin, to deliberate with his colleagues on an adequate mode of procedure; as well as to examine and strictly investigate every case of the kind that may occur. In the mean time, we have selected the preceding passages out of their books for general information.

For the future, we earnestly exhort our Tartar subjects, to attend to the language and admonitions of their own country and government; to practise riding and

* The name is here evidently incorrectly stated.

archery;

archery; to ftudy the works of the learned and virtuous, and to obferve the focial duties. If the fects of *Foe* and *Tao-fse* are unworthy of belief, how much more fo is that of the Europeans? Let it be their care to wafh away this foul ftain, and to beware of giving ear to thefe finifter and fallacious doctrines.

Thofe who will not awake from their delufions; who neglect the truth in order to follow what is falfe and perverfe, are unworthy to be confidered as men, and ill requite the care and inftructions anxioufly beftowed on them by their fovereign. We here declare our fentiments, that they may be generally known.

Khin-tfe.

No. XIX.

[Referred to from Section CXCI. page 201.]

Tranflation of an Imperial Edict, iffued in the 8th Year of the Emperor KIA-KING, (1803.)

THE extraordinary council of great officers of ftate appointed by our command on the 20th of the intercalary 2d moon, to try the atrocious malefactor *Chin-te*, have concluded their inveftigation.

When we returned to the palace by the gate *Shun-ching*, on the 20th inftant, in order to obferve the folemn faft appointed for that day, it is unqueftionably true, that fome perfon rufhed forth; although we, being in our palanquin, and already confiderably advanced towards the inner court, did not diftinguifh his features, and only learned the circumftances that had occurred, through the eunuchs of the palace, whom we had fent out to obtain information on the fubject.

On the fame day, we directed the members of the fupreme court of judicature, and of the council for ftate affairs, to inftitute a ftrict and judicial enquiry upon the cafe; but the confeffion which was made to them by the criminal, on that occafion, was highly inconfiftent and unreafonable *. On the following day, we directed the minifters of ftate, and the prefidents of fupreme tribunals, to affift in the inveftigation; but the criminal pertinacioufly refufed to fwerve from his original depofition. We, laftly, added the officers of the nine departments, and the

* It appears that the criminal, upon his examination, endeavoured to charge fome of the principal officers of ftate, and members of the Imperial family, with a participation in a treafonable confpiracy to affaffinate the Emperor, of whom he declared himfelf to have been only the agent.

presidents of the subordinate tribunals, forming, with the other officers of the court, a full council of state; before this council he repeated, without any variation, his original confession.

In a case of this treasonable nature, which both excited our attention and provoked our resentment, we were naturally desirous to discover, by every method of investigation, the original contriver, the confederates, and the nature of the conspiracy, if any, which had been formed on the occasion. The scrutinizing enquiries and examination of the council, and their earnest desire to obtain information, did not certainly exceed a faithful and patriotic discharge of their duty; a duty which required of them to spare no exertion, and to proceed without reserve; and which acquitted them of any imputations arising from the implications or disclosures their enquiries tended to produce.

We, indeed, who hold the universal sovereignty of the earth, (*i. e.* China,) surely have governed with candour and integrity! That our actions are neither equivocal or suspicious, must be obvious to all our subjects, the nearest as well as the most remote from our presence. During these last eight years, though we make no claim to the perfection of political virtue, at least, we have not dared so far to forget ourselves, as to take away a life unjustly. Where, therefore, is there a ground for malice, or an excitement to revenge? The nobles and magistrates who compose our court, are esteemed by us with fraternal regard. Our sons and nephews are united to us by the closest ties of blood: shall we allow a wretched criminal to injure them by his wicked aspersions? In fact, we do not fear or harbour a suspicion against any one. Among the inhabitants of the earth, there may surely be some who rush on wildly like mad dogs, and who commit acts of violence, which no one had previously suggested or contrived. The bird *Chee-kiao* even devours its mother; yet who are its confederates?

If, in consequence of the confession extorted from this criminal, we were to proceed again those, whom, with the blind fury of a mad dog, he has charged with criminality, they would hardly escape with life. We renounce, therefore, altogether, an investigation of such a malignant tendency. Our chief mortification at present arises from observing, that the influence of our government and example is not more effectual; and this leads us to infer that we have been guilty of some failure in our duty, which we must endeavour to rectify, that there may be no blemish in our conduct, to render it inconsistent with our affection for our people.

With regard to the atrocious criminal *Chin-te*, and his two sons, we direct that the council do pronounce the sentence of the law respecting them, and report the same for our ratification. But we direct, at the same time, that all other persons who may have been detained on the same account, be set at liberty, lest the innocent

innocent ſhould be, in any manner, made to participate in the puniſhment of the guilty.

On the other hand, the conduct of *Mien-gen*, Prince of *Ting-ching*, who firſt laid hold of the criminal, and whoſe clothes were torn while exerting himſelf to repel his onſet; the exertions of *La-vang-to-ur-chee*, Prince of *Ku-lun-ge-fu*, and of the officers in waiting *Tan-pa-to-ur-chee*, *Chu-ur-kang-go*, *Cha-ke-ta-ur*, and *Sang-kee-ſe-ta-ur*, by whom the criminal was ultimately ſecured, eſpecially that that of *Tan-pa-to-ur-chee*, who received three wounds in the ſtruggle, all deſerve our warmeſt admiration and praiſe. On the laſt of theſe we confer the dignity of *Pei-le*; and to the two Princes, and the above-mentioned officers in waiting, we ſhall not omit to beſtow diſtinguiſhed marks of our favour and approbation.

But, at the time of this accident, the officers in waiting, together with the other individuals in our train, were certainly not leſs than an hundred perſons; among whom ſix only, regardleſs of danger, ſtepped forward, in order to ſeize the villain. It is true, that the Princes *Mien-gen* and *La-vang-to-ur-chee*, and the four officers in waiting, have long enjoyed our diſtinguiſhed favour; but among ſo many who calmly looked on with their hands in their ſleeves, were there none whom we had in like manner favourably diſtinguiſhed? The Prince *Mien-gen* is indeed our nephew, and the Prince *La-vang-to-ur-chee* our couſin by marriage; and the exertions of thoſe who are ſo nearly connected with us by kindred or alliance is highly grateful to our feelings; but were there not many of the unmoved bye-ſtanders as nearly related to us? Is it thus they teſtify their gratitude and affection to the Sovereign and to the ſtate? If, on ſuch occaſions as this, we experience theſe tokens of indifference and inſincerity, we can have but little reaſon to hope, that on more ordinary occaſions, they will exert themſelves for the good of their country.

It is *this*, and not *that*, (*i. e.* the dagger of the aſſaſſin) which fills us with apprehenſion and uneaſineſs. Heaven has given worth and underſtanding to our nobles and magiſtrates; let them enquire of their own hearts, whether they ought not to feel ſhame and remorſe on this occaſion. This edict we iſſue for general information.

Khin-tſe.

SENTENCE.—By His Majeſty's command, *Chin-te* to ſuffer death by a ſlow and painful execution; his ſons *Lou-eur* and *Fong-eur*, being of a tender age, to be ſtrangled; and the deciſion of the council to be obſerved in all other reſpects.

No. XX.

[Referred to from Section CXCIX. Page 208.]

Translation of an Extract from the Pekin *Gazette of the 23d of April* 1800.

TE-*lin-tay*, general of the Imperial forces, humbly presents his Report to inform His Majesty of the operations of the army against the rebels, during several days successively, in which the enemy was attacked, and the divisions led by *Tsay-tien-yuen* and *Kiay-Ky-siun* entirely routed, and the remainder pursued with great slaughter and effect. The circumstances will be found detailed in the following report, which is forwarded by express: —

The engagements that took place at *Pe-Kia-tsin*, with the five columns of the rebels who attempted to ford the river at that place, the slaughter that ensued, the capture of the leaders *Chin-te-fung* and *Tsay-tien-hiun*, and the subsequent retreat of the enemy, though continuing to watch our motions, have already been stated to Your Majesty.

I lost no time in leading the troops, according to the traces left by the rebels, from *Tse-tung* towards *San-mu-quan*, and reached that station on the 2d of the 3d moon. The scouts whom I had appointed to reconnoitre the position of the enemy then gave us notice, that they were lodged in considerable force in the wood of *Kiang-yeu*. Having advanced thither, pursuant to the information received, we were suddenly attacked by a body of the rebels, consisting of cavalry and infantry, who rushed upon us from four different quarters, with much clamour and impetuosity. The onset was received with firmness and courage by our troops, and upwards of three hundred of the enemy fell in the first encounter. Four hundred suffered the same fate in the skirmishes and partial engagements which ensued, and which lasted for four hours, until the rebels seemed no longer capable of opposing any resistance. In the course of the action, the colonel *Ly-tsung-tsu* was wounded by a spear, and fell from his horse. He nevertheless continued to lead the troops on foot, and greatly contributed towards the victory that ensued The force of the rebels being much broken by this defeat, they hastily dispersed to their fastnesses and concealed stations. During the action, several officers, and one hundred and twenty three privates of the enemy, were taken alive. The officers were put to death in torments, as the law directs; but such of the country people, to the number of several hundred, who appeared to have been forcibly

forcibly detained by the rebels, and on that account to have fallen into our hands, we fuffered to depart unmolefted.

On the following day, I reconducted the troops to their former ftation at *Chung-wha*, and immediately after learned from the reconnoitering party, that a large body of the rebels was collected on the hill *Ma-ti-kang*. I encamped, therefore, the next day, with the army, in a fpot 20 or 30 *lee* (two or three leagues) nearer to the ftation of the rebels, whofe force we now learned to exceed, in cavalry and infantry, taken together, ten thoufand men; this army we found to be regularly difpofed on the oppofite declivity of the hill.

I then determined to divide the Imperial army into four principal divifions; the firft confifting of the Chinefe and Tartar cavalry, under the command of the officers *Tfay-Chung-ho*, *Ly-chao-tfe*, and others, to attack the enemy from the bridge at *Lo-yang*, towards *Tao-kai-keu*. The fecond divifion, confifting exclufively of regular troops, cavalry and infantry, and commanded by *O-ho-pao*, *Ma-ur-quen*, and others, to engage the enemy from *Hay-chang-pu* towards *Ho-fhe-pu*. The third divifion, confifting partly of the regulars and partly of the provincial volunteers, under the command of the officers *Wun-chun*, *O-meu-le-tay*, and others, to engage from the village *Pay-fang-fhy*, towards *Lung-tfe-quan*. The fourth and laft divifion, confifting of the remainder of the regular troops, together with the country militia, and commanded by myfelf, in conjunction with the officers *Ta-le-ching-o*, *O-te-fhe* and others, to attack the enemy by the direct road.

[*After relating in detail the various fkirmifhes and partial encounters that enfued in each divifion, in confequence of the rebels having avoided a regular engagement, the general proceeds to ftate, that*] at this time, a man who announced himfelf to be a native of the diftrict, and to have juft efcaped from the hands of the rebels, profeffed to give information that the rebel poft at *Tfe-lin-koo*, was not defended by more than three hundred and fifty men, and that thofe few were wholly unprovided with fire-arms.

He offered alfo to conduct the army to the fpot. The channel through which we received this intelligence rendering it extremely doubtful and fufpicious, I ordered the informer to be detained, but neverthelefs proceeded with the army towards the place that he had indicated to us.

On a nearer approach to *Tfe-lin-koo*, I fent a detachment to explore the furrounding country, in order to guard againft a furprife from troops in ambufh. The rebels indeed received us with a brifk fire of mufketry and cannon, accompanied with vollies of ftones; and their attack was altogether uncommonly favage and impetuous. Our troops, however, kept their ground, without being in the fmalleft degree difordered or intimidated.

At

At the ſame time, all the other parties of the rebels, whoſe ſtratagems had been likewiſe diſcovered by the troops I had detached for that purpoſe, ruſhed out from their lurking places, and joined in the attack. A ſevere conflict enſued, in which the officers *Ly-chao-tſee, Mey-yn*, and others, behaved with great gallantry and intrepidity. In this action upwards of five hundred of the enemy were killed, ſeveral taken priſoners, and the reſt driven back to the mountains. Upwards of four hundred of thoſe who retreated were afterwards killed in the purſuit. Two or three leaders of rebels, and many others of a meaner rank, were captured, together with two pieces of cannon and a large aſſortment of ſtandards, ſcymetars, ſwords, and the like, and many horſes, aſſes, and other animals. But the moſt important advantage obtained, was that of taking alive the general of the rebels *Tſay-tien-yuen*, whom we afterwards diſcovered to be one of their principal leaders and inſtigators. The priſoner being interrogated, confeſſed that about two months ago, finding his army to be ill ſupplied with the means of ſubſiſtence in the province of *Se-chuen*, he reſolved to paſs over with his adherents into the provinces of *Shen-ſy* and *Kan-ſoo*, and that having collected a ſufficient number of boats for that purpoſe, he had croſſed the intervening river in the night time with an army of between thirty and forty thouſand men, little expecting the vigorous reſiſtance which was afterwards oppoſed to his progreſs. In ſubſequent engagements all his brothers fell in the field of battle, and he was himſelf once wounded with an arrow. He added, that not above five generals of the rebels ſtill kept the field, and that thoſe were deſtitute both of talents and of experience.

By this confeſſion our opinion is confirmed, that this is the ſame leader who has ſo notoriouſly been at the head of the troops of the rebels for theſe laſt five years, to the great detriment and depopulation of the provinces of *Shen-ſy* and *Se-chuen*, and to the ſacrifice of the lives of many valuable officers and men belonging to the Imperial armies. But Heaven no longer permits the perpetration of theſe enormities, and is pleaſed to deliver him up to our hands; an event that muſt have been earneſtly deſired by all ranks of Your Majeſty's faithful ſubjects.

I have not failed repeatedly to publiſh Your Majeſty's Imperial manifeſto, addreſſed to all the well diſpoſed inhabitants, who may have had the misfortune to have been compelled or ſeduced to aſſociate with the rebels, and declaring a free pardon to all ſuch as awake from their deluſion, and renounce their errors; and likewiſe promiſing to furniſh them with the means of returning to their former habitations and profeſſions.

I have

I have, moreover, thought it expedient to ſend the rebel chieftain to *Quay-lung* *, viceroy of the province, that by His Excellency's orders, he might be ſent round with a ſtrong eſcort, and expoſed to public view at all the principal towns and places of public reſort in this part of the empire, in order that on the one hand, Your Majeſty's faithful ſubjects may be henceforward relieved from the terror and alarm which the known cunning and ferocity of this man were calculated to excite; and that on the other hand, the hopes and reliance which the malcontents were wont to place on the talents and ſagacity of their former leader, may every where be blaſted and overthrown.

I finally recommend to Your Majeſty's gracious favor and bounty, all thoſe who have honourably diſtinguiſhed themſelves by their valour and abilities, in the late engagements; and I am happy at the ſame time to obſerve, that the loſs of lives which theſe victories have coſt to Your Majeſty's officers and troops is extremely inconſiderable.

IMPERIAL REPLY.

The gracious favor of Heaven, the protecting influence of our anceſtors, the fidelity and unanimity of our officers, and the valour of our troops, have all conſpired in obtaining for us theſe victories, and in effecting the overthrow of a moſt dangerous and wicked leader of the rebellion: the proſpect this affords of a ſpeedy pacification of the provinces of *Se-chuen* and *Shen-ſy*, is highly conſolatory to us, and diminiſhes our ſelf-condemnation, for the previous ſufferings of our faithful ſubjects in thoſe parts. *Khin-Tſe.*

No. XXI.

[Referred to from Section CCXXV. Page 239.]

Tranſlation of Two of the Clauſes annexed to this Section.

ILLICIT EXPORTATION OF MERCHANDIZE.

1. ALL officers of government, ſoldiers, and private citizens, who clandeſtinely proceed to ſea to trade, or who remove to foreign iſlands for the purpoſe of inhabiting and cultivating the ſame, ſhall be puniſhed according to the law againſt communicating with rebels and enemies, and conſequently ſuffer death by

* An account of the charges ſubſequently brought againſt this officer, and of his condemnation to ſuffer capital puniſhment, is inſerted in the Appendix No. IX.

being

being beheaded. The governors of cities of the fecond and third orders, fhall likewife be beheaded, when found guilty of combining with, or artfully conniving at the conduct of fuch perfons. When only a neglect of their duty, in not taking meafures to prevent the fame, is the offence imputable to them, they fhall not fuffer death, but be degraded and difmiffed for ever from the public fervice. Governors of cities of the firft order, and other officers having the fame rank, when guilty of a fimilar neglect, fhall be degraded three degrees, and removed from their ftations. — Viceroys and other great magiftrates of provinces, fhall in fimilar cafes of imputed neglect, be degraded two degrees, but retain their offices.

Neverthelefs, the neglect of all fuch officers fhall be pardoned, if they afterwards fucceed in fecuring the offenders, and in bringing them to condign punifhment.

2. In general, only a limited number of perfons fhall be admitted into the empire in the fuite of foreign embaffies, excepting in the inftance of the embaffy from Corea. — The embaffy from Siam fhall be limited to twenty-fix perfons; thofe of European nations, in general, to twenty-two perfons; and thofe of any other nation, to twenty perfons only.

Thofe viceroys and fub-viceroys, who, in any cafe, inftead of announcing to the Emperor the arrival of a fhip bringing to the empire an embaffy from a foreign country, and requefting His Majefty's decifion thereon, undertake privately, and of their own accord, to difmifs fuch embaffy, fhall be deprived of their offices.

No. XXII.

[Referred to from Section CCLIV. Page 272.]

The following is a Tranflation of the Claufes annexed to this Section.

HIGH TREASON.

ALL Perfons who are banifhed on account of their connexion, either by blood or by marriage, with perfons convicted of high treafon, fhall be accompanied by their wives: the wives of fuch implicated perfons fhall not, however, be liable to banifhment, when the hufbands happen to die. childlefs, previous to the execution of the principal offender.

The relations of all criminals found guilty of high treafon fhall, in general, be liable to punifhment and execution, conformably to the tenor of the fundamental law;

law; yet, in the inſtance of ignorant or deſigning perſons attempting to eſtabliſh a corrupt ſect and doctrine, for the ſake of obtaining money under falſe and nefarious pretences, and thereby influencing and ſeducing the minds of the people; although this crime is conſtructively high treaſon, and puniſhable accordingly, it does not neceſſarily involve the relations of the criminal, unleſs they are convicted of having been actually concerned in the perpetration of the offence. — Any perſon maliciouſly inventing a charge of high treaſon, with a view to injure particular individuals, is puniſhable according to the law concerning falſe accuſations; but the relations of ſuch perſon ſhall not participate in the puniſhment, as ſuch relations may be endangered, and cannot be benefited by the perpetration of the offence.

All the male relations of criminals guilty of high treaſon, at or above the age of ſixteen, ſhall be executed in the manner directed by the fundamental law; the remaining male children, if proved to be totally innocent of, and unacquainted with the commiſſion of the offence, ſhall be ſuffered to live, but rendered eunuchs, that they may be employed for the public ſervice, in the exterior buildings of the palace. — Among theſe, ſuch as are under ten years of age, ſhall remain in priſon until they attain that age, and then be ſent to court to ſerve as above-ſtated.

No. XXIII.

[Referred to from Section CCLV. page 273.]

The following is a Tranſlation of the Clauſes annexed to this Section.

REBELLION AND RENUNCIATION OF ALLEGIANCE.

THE wives and children of perſons liable to be baniſhed, as relations of criminals convicted of crimes puniſhable by this law, ſhall be baniſhed likewiſe, provided the ſaid perſons are living at the time of conviction, but not otherwiſe.

The grand-children of criminals under this law, when of too tender an age to be ſeparated from their parents, ſhall remain with them, ſubject to the charge and direction of the ſuperintending magiſtrates.

In every trial of offences of this nature, the prefiding magiftrate fhall diligently afcertain the number, refidence, and employment of the relations of the criminal, or criminals, as well as the extent and amount of his or their property within the province; and if it fhall appear that the criminals have any relations, connexions, or property in any other province, notice fhall be immediately given to the chief magiftrate thereof, that he may duly take cognizance of the fame: — All magiftrates failing in this duty, fhall be liable to profecution by an accufation laid before the Emperor.

The Tartarian fubjects of the empire fhall be equally punifhable under this law. — When their property is fubject to confifcation, their flaves fhall be at the difpofal of the fupreme court for affairs of revenue.

All perfons who, without being related or connected by intermarriages, eftablifh a brotherhood or affociation among themfelves, by the ceremonial of tafting blood, and burning incenfe, fhall be held guilty of an intent to commit the crime of rebellion; and the principal or chief leader of fuch an affociation fhall, accordingly, fuffer death by ftrangulation, after remaining for the ufual period in confinement. — The punifhment of the acceffaries fhall be lefs by one degree. — If the brotherhood exceeds twenty perfons in number, the principal offender fhall fuffer death by ftrangulation immediately after conviction; and the acceffaries fhall fuffer the aggravated banifhment into the remoteft provinces. — If the brotherhood be formed without the aforefaid initiatory ceremonies of tafting blood and burning incenfe, and according to the rules of its conftitution, be fubject to the authority and direction of the elders only, but exceed forty perfons in number, then the principal fhall ftill fuffer death by ftrangulation, as in the firft cafe, and the acceffaries a punifhment lefs by one degree.

If the authority and direction of the affociation is found to be vefted in the ftrong and youthful members, that circumftance alone fhall be deemed a fufficient evidence of its criminality; and the principal fhall accordingly fuffer death by ftrangulation immediately after conviction: the acceffaries, as in the preceding cafes, fhall undergo aggravated banifhment.

If the affociation is fubject to the authority and direction of the elder brethren, and confifts of more than twenty, but lefs than forty members, the principals fhall be punifhed with 100 blows, and fent into perpetual banifhment to the diftance of 3000 *lee*. If the affociation under the laft mentioned circumftances, confifts of any number lefs than twenty perfons, the principal fhall fuffer 100 blows, and wear the cangue for three months. — In both cafes, the punifhment of the acceffaries fhall be one degree lefs fevere than that of the principals.

Whenever

Whenever vagrant and diſorderly perſons form themſelves into a brotherhood by the initiation of blood, as aforeſaid, and endeavour to excite factious or leading men to join them, or tamper with the ſoldiers and ſervants of public tribunals, with the ſame intent, having for their ultimate object, to injure the people, and diſturb the peace of the country; and further, when ſuch criminal practices have been duly reported by the country-people and heads of villages, to the magiſtrates and governors of the diviſion or diſtrict; if the ſaid magiſtrates and governors refuſe or neglect to take meaſures for ſuppreſſing ſuch proceedings; or in any other manner countenance or connive at them, ſo that in the end an open ſedition breaks out, and rapine and devaſtation enſue, ſuch culpable officers of government ſhall be forthwith deprived of their dignities and employments, and proſecuted for their miſconduct, by accuſation laid before the ſupreme court of judicature.—Nevertheleſs, if, after ſuch aſſociations had been ſuffered to take place through the neglect or connivance of the magiſtrates, thoſe magiſtrates exert themſelves ſucceſsfully in ſtopping the progreſs of the evil, and in preventing the commiſſion of any act of open violence, ſedition, and rapine, and are, moreover, active in ſeizing the criminals, and bringing them to juſtice, their former neglect and omiſſion ſhall, in ſuch caſes, be pardoned.

All thoſe inhabitants of the neighbourhood, and heads of villages, who, when privy to theſe unlawful practices, omit to give information thereof to government, ſhall be puniſhed according to the degree of their reſponſibility, and the other circumſtances of the caſe; but, on the other hand, thoſe who give timely notice and information, ſhall be proportionably rewarded:—If, however, the charges are found to have been made under frivolous pretexts, the informers will be ſubject to puniſhment as calumniators.

The puniſhment of the brotherhood aſſociated by the initiation with blood, which exiſts in the province of *Fo-kien*, ſhall be conformable to the afore-mentioned regulations; and further, when the perſons thus guilty, take up arms in order to reſiſt the magiſtrates, and a tumult enſues, all who are concerned in ſuch reſiſtance, ſhall, if conſidered as principals, ſuffer death by being beheaded; and by ſtrangulation, if conſidered as acceſſaries to the offence.

All aſſociations connected together by ſecret ſignals, whatever be their extent, are obviouſly inſtituted with the deſign of oppreſſing the weak, and injuring the ſolitary and unprotected.—Wherefore the leaders or principals of all ſuch ſocieties, ſhall be held to be vagabonds and outlaws, and accordingly be baniſhed perpetually to the moſt remote provinces: the other members of ſuch aſſociations ſhall be conſidered as acceſſaries, and puniſhed leſs ſeverely by one degree.

Thoſe perſons who, though not regularly belonging to, had ſuffered themſelves to be ſeduced to accompany ſuch aſſociated perſons, ſhall not be baniſhed,

 but

but ſhall ſuffer the puniſhment of 100 blows, and wear the cangue for three months. — All perſons who, after having been employed as ſoldiers or civil ſervants of government, enter into any of the ſaid unlawful aſſociations, ſhall be puniſhed as principals.

Any inhabitants of the neighbourhood, or heads of villages, who may be convicted of being privy to, and not reporting theſe practices to government, ſhall be puniſhed more or leſs ſeverely, according to the nature of the caſe. — Magiſtrates neglecting to inveſtigate and take cogniſance of the like offences; or from corrupt and ſiniſter motives, liberating and pardoning offenders after examination, ſhall be puniſhed as the law applicable to ſimilar caſes directs.

Notwithſtanding the aforeſaid, perſons aſſembling for the ſole purpoſe of doing honour, or returning thanks to a particular temple or divinity, and immediately afterwards peaceably diſperſing, ſhall not be puniſhed by any conſtruction of theſe prohibitions.

All thoſe vagaband and diſorderly perſons who have been known to aſſemble together, and to commit robberies, and other acts of violence, under the particular deſignation of "*Tien-tee-whee*," or, "the Aſſociation of Heaven and Earth," ſhall, immediately after ſeizure and conviction, ſuffer death by being beheaded; and all thoſe who have been induced to accompany them, and to aid and abet their ſaid practices, ſhall ſuffer death by being ſtrangled.

This law ſhall be put in force whenever this ſect or aſſociation may be revived.

No. XXIV.

[Referred to from Section CCLVI. Page 273.]

The following is a Tranſlation of the Clauſes annexed to this Section.

SORCERY AND MAGIC.

WHOEVER is guilty of editing wicked and corrupt books, with the view of miſleading the people; and whoever attempts to excite ſedition by letters or hand-bills, ſhall ſuffer death by being beheaded: the principals ſhall be executed immediately after conviction, but the acceſſaries ſhall be reſerved for execution at the uſual ſeaſon.

All

All persons who are convicted of printing, distributing, or singing in the streets, such disorderly and seditious compositions, shall be punishable as accessaries.

The constituted authorities at Pekin, and the viceroys or sub-viceroys of the provinces, shall not fail to take due cognizance, in their respective jurisdictions, of the offence of introducing and offering for sale, any species whatever of indecent and immoral publications. — All the copies of such books, and the blocks with which they shall have been printed, shall be destroyed. The author, compiler, or editor thereof, if a magistrate, shall be degraded and deprived of his appointment; and if a private citizen, shall receive 100 blows, and be sent into perpetual banishment to the distance of 3000 *lee*. — The venders of any such book or writing, shall be punished with 100 blows, and banished for three years. — The purchasers and readers thereof shall suffer severally the punishment of 100 blows. — If the magistrates do not take cognisance of, and endeavour to restrain the sale of such unlawful publications, they shall be liable to prosecution, by accusation before the supreme authorities, and punished more or less severely according to the circumstances of the case. Those, however, who charge others with a breach of this law, under frivolous pretexts, shall be punished according to the law against false accusations.

Whoever wilfully publishes a false and malicious report of any public acts and proceedings, which had taken place at Pekin, or in the provinces, shall, if a magistrate, or other officer of government, be forthwith degraded, and dismissed from all his employments; and if a private citizen, shall suffer 100 blows, and be sent into perpetual banishment to the distance 3000 *lee*. — All magistrates of districts, neglecting to take cognisance of such offences, shall be liable to prosecution, by accusation before the supreme authorities.

Whenever the sons, connections, or dependent inmates of the families of any of the great officers of state are convicted of associating with, or in any manner frequenting the company of persons guilty of any of the aforesaid offences, or of persons otherwise criminal and disorderly, they shall be punished according to this law; and the heads of the families shall likewise be brought to trial, for their criminal negligence, in suffering persons under their controul to participate in such unlawful transactions.

No. XXV.

[Referred to from Section CCLXIII. Page 277.]

The following is a Translation of the most material Clauses annexed to this Section.

STEALING TIMBER FROM A BURYING GROUND.

1. ALL civil and military officers, and their attendants, having charge of the Imperial cemetery, shall, whenever approaching the same, dismount from their horses at the distance of one hundred paces. A breach of this regulation, being a great instance of disrespect, shall be punished with 100 blows.

2. Whoever cuts down and removes the cypresses, or other similar trees, growing within the innermost inclosure of the Imperial cemetery, shall, if a principal in the offence, be held guilty of sacrilege, and receive sentence to suffer death by being beheaded; but the case shall be, at the same time, recommended to His Imperial Majesty's consideration; the accessaries shall be banished to the frontiers of the empire. Digging the ground, removing stones, and committing other similar trespasses, shall be punished according to the extent of the offence.

3. Any son or grandson who privately cuts down and sells one or more of the trees which grew in the burying-ground of his father or grandfather, shall receive a punishment of 100 blows, and wear the cangue for three months. When the value of the wood so disposed of is considerable, it shall be estimated, and the unabated punishment of an ordinary theft to the same amount shall be inflicted on the offender. When the number of trees cut down exceeds ten, the offender, if a Tartar, shall be employed in servitude in the district of *Ningouta*; if a Chinese, he shall be perpetually banished beyond the frontier. Any son or grandson, who cuts down the dead or decayed wood belonging to such burying-grounds, without previously giving notice thereof to the magistrate of the district, shall be punished with 80 blows.

Slaves or other persons who, being appointed to watch a burying-ground, steal and sell the timber thereof, shall be punished with 100 blows, and wear the cangue for one month. When the amount stolen is considerable, it shall be estimated, and the offender shall be punished one degree more severely than in the ordinary cases of stealing from a burying-ground. When the purchaser of such fuch timber knows it to have been ftolen, he fhall fuffer the punifhment of ftealing from a burying-ground in ordinary cafes. The purchafer, when ignorant of the property having been ftolen, will not be punifhable.

Stealing grave-ftones, bricks, dry wood, or other articles belonging to, and depofited in a burying-ground, is punifhable in the following manner: if the offender was the flave, fon, or grandfon of the individual whofe tomb or burying-place had been thus violated, the ftolen articles fhall be valued, and the punifhment rated one degree more feverely than in the ordinary cafes of theft.—If the offender was an indifferent perfon, the punifhment fhall be the fame as in ordinary cafes of theft. The purchafer, if aware of the goods having been ftolen, fhall be punifhed one degree lefs feverely than the feller, and the feveral articles fhall be delivered up to the charge of the magiftrate of the diftrict, in order to their being reftored to the owner.

4. Idle perfons and vagrants privately purchafing timber ftolen from burying-grounds, however fmall the quantity, fhall; for the firft offence, be punifhed with 100 blows, and the cangue for one month; for the fecond offence, with 100 blows, and the cangue for three months; and for the third offence, with perpetual banifhment beyond the frontier.

5. All perfons cutting down and ftealing the trees of a burying-ground fhall; for the firft and fecond offence, be punifhed as already ftated; but, for the third offence, fhall be punifhed in the fame manner as for a third offence in a cafe of ordinary theft.

When the offence is repeated fix times within ten days, or twenty or thirty trees are cut down within the fame period, all the parties concerned fhall be perpetually banifhed, according to the law againft theft by combination. — If the theft be committed during three fucceffive days, it fhall be confidered as one offence; and when it is the firft, the punifhment fhall be one degree lefs than it would have have been conformably to the law againft theft by combination. The parties fhall be branded with proper marks, as in ordinary cafes.

No. XXVI.

[Referred to from Section CCLXIV. Page 278.]

The following is a Tranſlation of the firſt Seven Clauſes annexed to this Section.

EMBEZZLEMENT OF PUBLIC PROPERTY.

1. ANY perſon having the charge and ſuperintendance of the grain veſſels of government, when found guilty of embezzling grain to the amount of ſixty ſtone*, ſhall be baniſhed perpetually beyond the Chineſe frontier: if the grain embezzled amounts to ſix hundred ſtone, the offender ſhall ſuffer death by being beheaded, after remaining in priſon until the uſual period.

2. In the different provinces through which the grain veſſels of government are navigated, more eſpecially that of *Kiang-nan*, it ſhall be the duty of all the governors of diſtricts to be on their guard, and to be particularly vigilant in detecting and puniſhing all clandeſtine and fraudulent ſales and purchaſes of grain within their reſpective limits. All perſons offending in theſe reſpects ſhall, when diſcovered, wear the cangue for one month, and be confined until the return of the grain veſſels; upon which the ſuperintending officers of ſuch veſſels ſhall be made acquainted with the circumſtances, and the offenders puniſhed in their preſence with 40 blows each, previous to their being diſmiſſed. All magiſtrates neglecting to take cognizance of ſuch offences, will be ſubject to proſecution by accuſation laid before the ſupreme authorities.

3. All proprietors of the ſmall boats which ſhall be found to have been let out for the purpoſe of ſtealing and clandeſtinely ſelling the grain laden in the Imperial barges as aforeſaid, ſhall wear the cangue for one month, in the ſame manner as the offenders deſcribed in the laſt clauſe; but the ſubſequent puniſhment ſhall be leſs ſevere by two degrees. The pilots of the Imperial barges, when privy to ſuch fraudulent and clandeſtine tranſactions, and failing to inform the officers of government thereof, ſhall be puniſhed with 80 blows; but if they alſo ſhare in the plunder, their puniſhment ſhall be proportionate to the amount, as in other caſes.

4. In caſes of embezzlement of public ſtores or bullion, to the amount or value of one thouſand ounces of ſilver or upwards, the offenders are puniſhable with

* A ſtone weight in China is conſidered to be equal to one hundred and twenty *kin*, or one hundred and ſixty Britiſh pounds.

death,

death, by being beheaded; but when the value does not exceed one thousand ounces, they may be eventually liberated by an act of grace and general pardon.

When the value exceeds the latter sum, the sentence must be executed, unless it is set aside by the Emperor's special command. No civil or military officers of government, when guilty of embezzlement, shall be branded in the manner ordered with respect to other persons.

5. In every case of embezzlement, the names of the wives and unmarried children of the offender shall be registered, that they may be held answerable for the value of the stores embezzled.

If the superintending magistrate is satisfied, after an accurate examination, that the family of the offender possesses no property, applicable to the liquidation of the demands of government, beyond what had been surrendered for that purpose, he shall sign and deliver to them a quittance and full discharge; but such magistrate shall be liable to degradation and other punishment, if it is afterwards discovered that the parties did actually possess other property; all of which, notwithstanding such quittance, shall thereupon be confiscated. No demand or assessment shall, however, be levied, on the more distant relations of any offender; and any magistrate who arbitrarily attempts to enforce the like, shall be degraded. Any magistrate, likewise, who refuses a quittance when due, will be liable to prosecution by accusation laid before the highest authorities.

6. When any offender, after having been convicted under this law, has been pardoned, or indulged with any mitigation of his sentence, the legal punishment shall be aggravated one degree, if he should ever be convicted of a repetition of the offence.

7. Although an officer or magistrate who had been guilty of embezzlement should happen to die before conviction, his sons shall still be answerable for the amount of the loss sustained by government.

No. XXVII.

[Referred to from Section CCLXV. Page 279.]

The following is a Translation of the Clauses annexed to this Section.

THEFT OF PUBLIC PROPERTY.

1. WHOEVER steals rice or other grain from the public barges, to the amount of one hundred stone, will be punishable with death by strangulation, after the usual period of confinement: when the amount is under one hundred

ftone, the punifhment fhall be according to the fcale of ftealing any quantity not exceeding in value one hundred ounces of filver from a public granary.

2. Thieves and their accomplices undermining, or otherwife fecretly attempting to gain accefs to a public ftorehoufe, in order to fteal, fhall be punifhed in the following manner: the principal offender fhall fuffer 100 blows and three years banifhment; and the punifhment of the reft fhall be one degree lefs, as acceffaries.

When the theft is actually committed, and to the extent of one hundred ounces of filver in value, the principal offender fhall fuffer death by ftrangulation: if lefs than one hundred ounces value, he fhall be banifhed to one of the moft remote provinces.

Acceffaries to fuch a theft, when not exceeding eighty ounces in value, fhall be banifhed for five years.

Acceffaries to a theft of eight-five ounces in value fhall fuffer 100 blows, and perpetual banifhment to the diftance of two thoufand *lee*: if ninety ounces in value, the acceffaries fhall fuffer one hundred blows, and perpetual banifhment to the diftance of two thoufand five hundred *lee*: if ninety-five ounces in value, 100 blows, and perpetual banifhment to the diftance of three thoufand *lee*: the punifhment in the cafe of the theft amounting to, or exceeding one hundred ounces, has been already ftated.

No. XXVIII.

[Referred to from Section CCLXVI. Page 281.]

The following is a Tranflation of fome of the moft material Claufes annexed to this Section.

ROBBERY.—HIGHWAY ROBBERY.

1. IF, in attempting to commit a robbery, any individual is killed, a houfe burned, a female violated, a prifon, tribunal, or fortification broken into, or damaged; or, laftly, if an hundred perfons are affembled, and aiding and abetting the fame; in all fuch cafes, each of the criminals fhall be beheaded immediately after conviction; even although the party fhould have obtained no booty;—and the heads of the criminals, as foon as ftruck off, fhall be fixed on pikes, and exhibited as a public fpectacle.

2. Perfons

2. Persons armed, and on horseback, guilty of robbing on the public highways, shall, in all cases, be beheaded immediately after conviction, and their heads exhibited as a public spectacle.

All those who are guilty of committing piracies on the high seas, or on great rivers, shall likewise suffer according to this law.

3. Whereas there are certain practiced villains who frequent taverns for the purpose of administering stupefying drugs to travellers, and afterwards rise by break of day and way-lay them; — whenever such offenders are apprehended, they shall not be removed to a distance, but a diligent search and enquiry shall be immediately made upon the spot, with a view to the seizure and conviction of the whole gang or association; when they are all collected and convicted, they shall be beheaded at the same time; notice of their execution being given by a public edict duly authenticated by the magistrate of the district.

4. Any robber who has been likewise guilty of rapes, murders, burning of houses, severely wounding the person plundered, or any other similar aggravation of his offence, shall derive no benefit or indulgence by surrendering himself. Such robbers as have slightly wounded the person plundered, whether they surrender themselves before the circumstances of the robbery are made public, or after the order had been issued for their apprehension, shall, if principals, still suffer death, by being beheaded; but not until after remaining in prison during the usual period. In cases wherein no person has been wounded, the principals surrendering themselves before the offence has been reported to the magistrates, shall be banished beyond the Chinese frontiers. If, in the latter cases, the offenders do not surrender themselves until after the warrant for their apprehension had been issued, they shall suffer conformably to the law relative to a mere remission of the capital part of the sentence; and accordingly be condemned to perpetual slavery in the garrisoned forts on the banks of the *He-lung-kiang*, near the extreme frontier of Tartary.

If the accessaries to a robbery, when it is their first offence, surrender themselves before information had been given thereof to any magistrate, they shall be pardoned. If they voluntarily surrender themselves, but not before the warrant had been issued for their apprehension, they shall suffer each 100 blows, and three years banishment. If they do not surrender until after having committed the same offence more than once, but previously to the report of the last offence having been made to any magistrate, they shall be banished beyond the Chinese frontier; but if the warrant for their apprehension had been previously issued, they must be banished, and undergo perpetual slavery in the manner aforesaid.

House-breakers surrendering themselves, shall be banished or capitally executed in the same manner as robbers, according to the circumstances stated. The punishment of robbers attempting to escape after condemnation to banishment, shall be aggravated one degree; and if the banishment had been previously decreed to be of the severest kind; that is to say, perpetual slavery on the banks of the *He-lung-kiang*, in Tartary, they shall, in consequence of the aggravation of their guilt, be beheaded, immediately after the sentence pronounced conformably to the law, receives the Emperor's ratification. Persons setting fire to out-houses, and other untenanted buildings, shall suffer banishment according to the law against wilful burning; but if the property destroyed is considerable, the offender shall be banished beyond the Chinese frontier.

5. All persons who, after having been engaged by government as servants of the police, betray their trust, and are concerned in the commission of any robbery, although not actually the principals and instigators thereof, shall, nevertheless, be punished as such, and accordingly be beheaded immediately after conviction. Those magistrates, to whose want of vigilance the opportunity to commit such a crime is imputable, shall be prosecuted by an accusation laid before the Emperor. — If such magistrates attempt to falsify the evidence, and allege that they had previously dismissed from the public service the supposed offenders, their superior officers shall investigate and ascertain the truth of the case, on pain of a similar enquiry being instituted against themselves. — If any of the servants of the police as aforesaid, are convicted of maintaining a correspondence with the robbers, and divulging to them the plan by which they were to have been seized, either by themselves or any other persons in the service of the police, so that the culprits are enabled to defeat such plans, and effect their escape, the persons guilty of such criminal correspondence, whether sharers in the plunder or not, shall suffer the same punishment as had been legally due to those who had fled from justice.

6. Servants of the police, when engaged as aforesaid in the pursuit of the perpetrators of a robbery, shall, in general, suffer equal punishment with the robbers, if convicted of having corresponded with them, and shared their booty. — If only guilty of wilful connivance at the robbery, they shall be punished according to the law against receiving stolen goods, knowing them to have been stolen. If the connivance is not proved, but the police officer is convicted of a designed want of exertion in the pursuit of the criminals, he shall suffer punishment reduced according to the circumstances of the case.

7. The individual who had sustained a robbery, and, in due form, complained of it to a magistrate, shall only be required to attend at the tribunal of government, during the actual trial of the criminals, and the identification of the property recovered; all which property shall, at the conclusion of the trial, be restored to the owner, without subjecting him to delay or molestation: any super-

intending

intending magiſtrate who fails in theſe points, will be liable to an accuſation laid before the Emperor.

8. The individual plundered, when giving in a ſtatement of his loſſes, ſhall deſcribe the ſame in a clear and diſtinct manner: If the loſs has been conſiderable, and he has omitted to inſert any of the articles, through an overſight, he ſhall be allowed a period of five days for preparing a ſupplementary report. The original and ſupplementary reports ſhall remain thenceforward in the cuſtody of the magiſtrate of the diſtrict, that they may be referred to in all the ſucceſſive proceedings, until the criminals are ſeized, and the property recovered. — When any part thereof has been traced and diſcovered, an officer of government ſhall be ſent immediately to the ſpot, for the purpoſe of having the ſame examined and identified in his preſence. — If the police officers preſume of their own accord to condemn property ſeized by them, or, under the pretext of ſearching for and recovering plunder, make vexatious domiciliary viſits; if they maliciouſly ſuggeſt to the robbers in cuſtody, to make falſe depoſitions concerning the places in which, and the perſons by whom, they had been harboured; if they ſeize and condemn as plunder, any articles honeſtly belonging to the priſoners; if they purchaſe articles to be ſubſtituted in the place of thoſe obtained by unlawful means; or, laſtly, if in any caſe, they report the recovery of plunder, falſely or prematurely, they ſhall, in all ſuch caſes, be puniſhed with the utmoſt ſeverity of the law: — The ſuperintending magiſtrate who has neglected to prevent ſuch abuſes, and the viceroys and ſub-viceroys who had omitted to notice them to the Emperor, will be reſpectively liable to an enquiry into their conduct, and to a trial by accuſation before the ſupreme court.

9. When any member of an aſſociation of robbers has been ſeized, the individual who led the way, and ſuggeſted the plan of the robbery, ſhall, in general, be conſidered, and puniſhed, as the principal; and the reſt only as acceſſaries. — Nevertheleſs, if there be one amongſt them, who neither ſuggeſted the plan, nor perſonally aſſiſted in perpetrating the crime, and yet led the way, was poſſeſſed of a previous knowledge of the place intended to be viſited, and of the perſon intended to be plundered, and laſtly, participated in the booty obtained; he alſo ſhall be conſidered, and puniſhed as a principal offender, and accordingly excluded from the benefit of the laws applicable to caſes under palliating circumſtances.

10. If any individual complaining of a robbery, makes a falſe or fraudulent report, by repreſenting that to have been robbery which was merely a theft; or by falſely charging an adulterer with having alſo committed a robbery, ſuch individual ſhall be puniſhed with 100 blows. — If, in a caſe of homicide, or of an

aſſault,

aſſault, a robbery is pretended to have been alſo committed, the accuſing party ſhall be puniſhed with 100 blows, as before; but if he is implicated himſelf in the crime, his puniſhment ſhall be conformable to the utmoſt rigour of the law upon the caſe: — When the crime in which he is implicated, is not conſiderable, his puniſhment ſhall be leſs than that of the chief perpetrator, by one degree. — If any perſons, confiding in their rank and influence, falſely accuſe others of robbery, and deceive the ſuperintending magiſtrates, with the intent to injure and diſtreſs particular individuals by ſuch charges, they ſhall ſuffer the puniſhment to which falſe accuſers of a capital offence are liable, when the charges made by them are diſproved in time to prevent the execution of the innocent perſon. — All perſons aiding and abetting ſuch falſe accuſers, ſhall be puniſhed as acceſſaries.

11. Any civil or military officer of a diſtrict, wiſhing to avoid the difficulties and inconveniencies of carrying the laws into effect in the caſe of a robbery, and with that view, threatening the complainant, and compelling him to ſuppreſs the circumſtances of the robbery, or obliging him to repreſent it as a ſimple theft, ſhall be deprived of his office, and a puniſhment of 100 blows ſhall be inflicted on each of the clerks of the tribunal, who had participated in ſuch miſconduct. — If the compulſion and oppreſſion practiſed, had been carried to ſuch lengths as to occaſion the death of the complainant, or the puniſhment unjuſtly inflicted upon him, had been ſuch as to deprive him of the uſe of his limbs, the magiſtrate guilty thereof, ſhall be puniſhed according to the law applicable to the caſe of an intentionally unjuſt capital condemnation of an innocent perſon. — The magiſtrates of ſuperior tribunals, if they neglect to report ſuch conduct, and the viceroys and ſub-viceroys, if they neglect to accuſe the offenders, as they are bound to do by their office, will reſpectively be liable to be charged with ſuch omiſſion before the Emperor.

12. In every caſe of a theft or robbery, it is the duty of the *Ty-pao*, or head man of the civil diviſion, and of the ſoldier on duty in the military diviſion, to report the occurrence to the civil and military tribunal to which they reſpectively belong, in order that prompt and active meaſures may be jointly purſued by thoſe tribunals for bringing the offenders to juſtice. — If the *Ty-pao* and the ſoldier agree together in concealing the fact, or the *Ty-pao* reports it to the civil magiſtrate, while the ſoldier on duty omits to make a correſponding report to the military officer on the ſtation, or *vicè verſâ*, the parties offending ſhall be puniſhed in the ſame manner as the neighbours of perſons guilty of robbery, when knowing, and failing to report the ſame; namely, with 100 blows. — When only very dilatory in tranſmitting their reports, the puniſhment ſhall be limited to 80 blows.

13. When

13. When any robbers, after having ſurrendered themſelves voluntarily, endeavour to ſatisfy the laws by ſubſtituting borrowed articles in the place of thoſe which they ought to have reſtored; or accuſe innocent perſons of being in league with them; or plot againſt any perſons out of revenge; or, are guilty of any kind of extortion for the purpoſes aforeſaid; they ſhall, on conviction of ſuch practices, whether as principals or as acceſſaries, in poſſeſſion or not, of the plunder, be immediately beheaded.

14. If a leader in a robbery, although he may have wounded ſome perſon and made his eſcape, afterwards voluntarily ſurrenders himſelf, and has likewiſe the merit of delivering into the hands of juſtice ſome other robber, his puniſhment ſhall be one degree leſs than if he had ſimply ſurrendered himſelf at firſt, that is to ſay, he ſhall receive 100 blows, and be baniſhed for a term of three years.

15. When the leader and contriver of a robbery has made his eſcape; but one of the aſſociation who had been taken into cuſtody, offers to indicate the place of the concealment of ſuch leader, ſo that within the period of a year it may be poſſible to trace and apprehend him, the trial of the offenders ſhall ſtand over until the year is expired; when, if the ring-leader is ſtill undiſcovered, the reſt of the gang or aſſociation ſhall be executed, or otherwiſe puniſhed as the laws direct, without further delay; but if the ringleader ſhould have been apprehended in conſequence of the information received, the informer, although by law capitally puniſhable, ſhall ſave his life, but be ſent into baniſhment and perpetual ſlavery in the garriſoned forts on the banks of the *He-lung-kiang*.

If the life of the informer had not been previouſly forfeited by law, he ſhall receive 100 blows, and undergo the ordinary perpetual baniſhment to the diſtance of 3000 *lee*.

16. When reporting the proceedings in caſes of theft and robbery for the Emperor's conſideration, if more than one charge of the kind is under inveſtigation, and more than one perſon has been thereupon capitally convicted, ſeparate reports ſhall be made upon the caſe of each individual; but if the capital part of the charges all center in one perſon, and are ſimilar in their nature, the different charges againſt that perſon ſhall be ſtated in the ſame report, clearly, however, and diſtinctly enumerated.

All the charges againſt the accomplices, and all ſuch other charges as are not capital, ſhall be reſerved for a ſeparate ſtatement, to be communicated in the ordinary manner to the ſupreme court of judicature.

No. XXIX.

[Referred to from Section CCLXXXII. Page 304.]

The following is a Translation of Part of the Claufes and Commentary annexed to this Section.

PRECONCERTED HOMICIDE—MURDER.

1. IN the trial and inveftigation of a cafe of pre-concerted homicide, the artifice and preconcerted plan muft be clearly proved, in order to warrant the condemnation of any perfon to fuffer death by being beheaded, as an original contriver. In like manner, the act of ftriking and wounding muft have been proved againft thofe on whom fentence of death by ftrangulation is pronounced, as acceffaries contributing to the perpetration of the crime. Further, a preconcerted fcheme, and the profpect of booty, muft be proved with the fame certainty, in order to warrant a general fentence of death by being beheaded, againft all the parties, whether principals or acceffaries, in a cafe of premeditated homicide for the fake of obtaining booty.

2. If any magiftrate prefumes to pafs fentence of death in any of the aforefaid cafes of premeditated homicide, without having proof, in each cafe refpectively, of the previous defign, concurrence in the perpetration, or acquifition of booty, as the cafe may be, he fhall be anfwerable for the lives of the individuals whofe condemnation he pronounces.

3. Where a homicide is devifed for the fake of obtaining booty, a diftinction fhall be made between thofe cafes in which a robbery was only attempted, and thofe in which it was accomplifhed.

If the homicide had been perpetrated, and the booty likewife fecured, the principal and all thofe acceffaries who had contributed to the perpetration of the murder, fhall fuffer death by being beheaded immediately after conviction. All the other acceffaries fhall likewife fuffer death by being beheaded, but not till the ufual period of capital executions. Other individuals fubfequently fharing in the booty, fhall be banifhed perpetually to the banks of the river *He-lung-kiang* in Tartary.

When a wound is inflicted with the intent to commit murder, and for the fake of obtaining plunder, the object being alfo accomplifhed; then, although the wound fhould not prove mortal, the principal offender fhall fuffer death by being beheaded immediately after conviction: acceffaries ftriking a blow, or otherwife

wife directly aiding and abetting, shall likewise suffer death by being beheaded at the customary period.

All other accessaries shall, as aforesaid, be banished perpetually to the banks of the *He-lung-kiang* in Tartary. Those who were not concerned in the crime, but subsequently shared in the division of the booty, shall each suffer 100 blows, and be banished perpetually to the distance of 3000 *lee*.

When the murder is effected, but no plunder obtained, the principal offender shall suffer death by being beheaded at the customary period. When the blow struck does not produce a mortal wound, and no plunder is obtained, the principal only, shall suffer death by strangulation at the customary period;—the accessaries shall suffer punishment proportionably reduced, according to the rule already exemplified.

4. When any individual, upon becoming acquainted with a concerted plan against his life, endeavours to escape, but is drowned, or killed by a fall or other accident, in the attempt, the principal agent in such concerted scheme shall be banished perpetually to the distance of 3000 *lee*; and the accessaries shall, each of them, be punished with 100 blows.

If the murder was on the point of being committed when such accident ensued in the manner aforesaid, the principal offender shall suffer death by being strangled at the customary period; and the accessaries, after receiving 100 blows each, shall be banished perpetually to the distance of 3000 *lee*.

5. In all cases of murder committed by the people called *Miao-tse*, for the sake of obtaining booty, all the parties to the crime shall suffer death by being beheaded, immediately after conviction; and their heads shall be exhibited as a public warning.

6. Any person in priest's orders seizing and murdering a child under 12 years of age, shall suffer death by being beheaded, immediately after conviction:—Other persons committing the same crime, shall be punished as in ordinary cases of murder.

7. In all cases of piracy committed by trading vessels belonging to the island of *Tay-wan* (Formosa,) the offenders shall suffer death by being beheaded, immediately after conviction; and their heads shall be exposed to public view at the port of *Hia-men* (Emouy,) together with a written account of their crimes, as a warning to others.

8. Whoever, from an impulse of anger, kills a child under 10 years of age, shall, if a principal in the offence, suffer death by being beheaded, immediately after conviction. The accessaries who were directly aiding and abetting, shall be strangled as soon as convicted; and all other accessaries shall be banished perpetually to the distance of 3000 *lee*.

COMMENTARY.

When a homicide has been planned by a perfon, who was not apparently under the influence, either of refentment or of deep-rooted hatred againft the party whofe life he had defigned to take away, a further object muft have been in view, fuch as the gratification of luft or avarice: — Cafes of the former kind are lefs difficult to inveftigate than the latter, as the actuating motive may fometimes be fo carefully concealed, as to be almoft undifcoverable.

Homicide by device, although refembling the crime of intentional homicide, which is the fubject of another fection of the code, is diftinguifhed by peculiar traits of premeditation and contrivance, whereas the latter is fimply underftood to imply an intent to kill at the time the attempt was made.

When contrivance and premeditation are proved againft any perfon by competent teftimony, fuch proof will be fufficient to convict fuch perfon, as one of the original contrivers, and fuch contrivance will be confidered to amount to a perfonal concurrence in the perpetration of the crime: thofe who afterwards concur in the actual commiffion of the murder, will be feverally punifhable as acceffaries aiding and abetting the previous contrivance, although not perfonally privy thereto: — Thus, under a charge of this nature, for the deftruction of one man, the lives of many may happen to be legally forfeited.

In order to convict any perfon of the crime of a preconcerted homicide, it muft be proved that death has actually enfued; but it fhall make no difference whether death enfued inftantly, or after any lapfe of time, provided there be always fufficient evidence of a previous contrivance.

Although preconcerted homicide neceffarily implies the exiftence of fome previous contrivance, the crime itfelf may be perpetrated in various ways; as by poifoning, burning, drowning, way-laying, ftabbing, or any other mode which admits of a previous defign.

It has been already ftated, that a blow producing a wound muft be proved, in order to convict an individual capitally, as an acceffary directly aiding and abetting the crime: to this it may be added, that any one who menaces the perfon whofe life is attacked, or who defeats the precautions he had taken for his fecurity, is fimply punifhable as an acceffary; whereas, in a cafe of a premeditated homicide effected by poifon, the perfon who prepares and adminifters the fame, is not a fimple acceffary, but capitally punifhable as an acceffary directly aiding and abetting.

If *Kia* confults with *Yee* concerning a plan of murdering a third perfon, againft whom he *Kia* has an enmity, and *Yee*, in confequence, invents or devifes a fcheme for effecting the fame, *Kia* will ftill be deemed, and punifhed as the original contriver.

Acceffaries

Acceſſaries to a homicide by contrivance, cannot redeem by a fine any part of the corporal puniſhment, or baniſhment, to which they may have been condemned by law; nor will the length of the ſurvivance of the deceaſed, after he had been wounded, procure them any indulgence; but as the life of an individual under this charge, may often depend on the diſcovery of the moſt ſecret operations of the mind, more than ordinary care and accuracy ought to be employed in the inveſtigation and elucidation of the facts and circumſtances upon which the conviction of offenders in theſe caſes depends.

No. XXX.

[Referred to from Section CCXCV. Page 317.]

Tranſlation of an Extract from a Volume of Law Reports; containing the Trial, reviſal of Proceedings, and final Sentence, in the Caſe of an Offender charged with Homicide by Gun-firing.

AT a criminal court held in the province of *Kiang-ſee, Whang-chang-whay*, a native of *King-kao-ſien*, was tried upon an information, ſetting forth, that he had fired a muſket at a deer, and by miſchance had mortally wounded a man named *Yao-wun-kuey*.

According to the report of *Mey-ching-tu*, ſub-viceroy of the province of *Kiang-ſee*; it appeared in evidence, that *Whang-chang-whay* and *Yao-wun-kuey* were hunters by profeſſion, and had always lived upon good terms with each other.

On the 21ſt day of the 11th moon of the 38th year of KIEN-LUNG, *Yao-wun-kuey* deſired *Whang-chang-whay* to accompany him, and two others, named *Tang-fung-chiang* and *Kuo-pee-meu*, to hunt on the hills called *Pao-Kiu-ſhan*, and to meet for that purpoſe at the foot of the hills, on the following day.

Whang-chang-whay aſſented to the propoſal, and on the 22d, equipped himſelf with a muſket for the purpoſe, and likewiſe invited *Whang-tien-tſung* to accompany him, and to take a muſket and dogs in order to join in the chace.

Yao-wun-kuey had previouſly ſet out with his dog and a muſket; *Tang-fung-chiang* and *Kuo-py-meu* were alſo ready with their guns and dogs, and ſoon joined the party; ſo that there were five perſons in all, aſſembled upon the hills.

 When

When they opened the chace, *Yao-wun-kuey* took a foutherly ftation, *Whang-chang-whay* took his place to the eaftward in a wood called *Yeu-fhoo-lin*, and *Tang-fung-chiang* with *Kuo-py-meu* watched towards the fummit of the hills; *Whang-fien-tfung* led the dogs upon the fcent; and foon after, a deer was ftarted, and ran to the fouth-eaftward. *Tang-fung-chiang* fired his mufket, but without fuccefs, upon which the animal turned directly fouth, when *Yao-wun-kuey* fired, but having likewife miffed his aim, he took up his gun and ran in purfuit of the animal.

Whang-chang-whay, who ftill remained in the wood of *Yeu-fhoo-lin*, hearing the firing of mufkets in the fouth and fouth-eaft directions, immediately loaded his gun, and made ready for firing. When he advanced from the wood, he faw the deer in the fouth-eaft running leifurely along the hills, and inftantly fired, but perceiving the deer ftill running, found that he had miffed his object.

At the moment that *Whang-chang-whay* fired, *Yao-wun-kuey* accidentally came forward, and in confequence the fhot which had miffed the deer wounded him in the face: on receiving the fhot, he ftaggered, and, falling down, hit his left temple and eye-brow againft the rock. *Whang-chang-whay*, greatly alarmed on the difcovery of the accident, threw down his mufket and fled up the hills. *Tang-fung-chiang* and his companions, being in an elevated fituation, obferved what had paffed below, and immediately came down to give affiftance; but *Yao-wun-kuey* having received a mortal wound, in a fhort time expired.

Upon this, *Tang-fung-chiang* and the others prefent, wifhed to make known the accident to the relations of the deceafed, but *Whang-chang-whay* fearing the confequences of a difcovery of his crime, befought them to conceal the truth, and to report that *Yao-wun-kuey* muft have killed himfelf accidentally, by a fall from the rocks.

Tang-fung-chiang and the others, feeling at the fame time apprehenfive that an enquiry into the affair, might involve them likewife in trouble, agreed to comply with his requeft.

Whang-chang-whay then hid the mufket that had belonged to *Yao-wun-kuey* in the long grafs, and departed with the reft from the fpot, taking with him the dogs that *Yao-wun-kuey* had brought to the chace.

Yao-wun-hing, the elder brother of the deceafed, knew that his younger brother had taken a gun and dogs with him that morning, in order to hunt with *Whang-chang-whay* and *Tang-fung-chiang*. Finding, therefore, in the evening, that he did not return, he went out to make enquiries concerning his brother at different houfes in the neighbourhood. *Whang-chang-whay* and his companions anfwered him according to the deceit which had been concerted between them, and added that they had not feen any thing of the deceafed.

On

On the 25th day of the moon, however, *Yao-wun-king* found the dead body, and immediately reported the affair to the magiſtrates of the diſtrict. A ſtrict enquiry and examination of the circumſtances being made thereupon, *Whang-chang-whay* finally confeſſed the fact of his having ſhot the man by miſtake while hunting, as related above; but it did not appear from the moſt minute inveſtigation, that any diſpute or other previous cauſe had contributed to the event.

It appeared clearly on examination, that *Whang-chang-whay*, upon ſeeing the deer, had taken aim at the animal with his gun, and that, at the ſame inſtant, the deer had ran paſt him, followed by *Yao-wun-kuey*. *Whang-chang-whay* had however already lighted the match of the gun, which accordingly went off, and mortally wounded *Yao-wun-kuey*, before he was able to change its direction. The aim had taken effect before ſight or hearing could notice, or any thought or conſideration ward off the fatal blow. No injury, therefore, to any one, could have been propoſed or thought of by him, when he thus unfortunately gave a mortal wound to *Yao-wun-kuey*.

Whang-chang-whay may be, therefore, eſteemed guilty of homicide by miſchance, which our laws aſſimilate in puniſhment with a homicide committed in an affray, but determine to be redeemable by the payment of 12 *leang*, 4 *tſien*, and 2 *fen*, (4l. 2s. 10d.) to the relations of the deceaſed, in order to defray the expences of his burial.

With regard to *Tang-fung-chiang*, *Kuo-py-meu*, and *Whang-ſien-tſung*; they being privy to the firing of the muſket by *Whang-chang-whay*, and to the conſequences thereof in reſpect to the wound received, as well as in reſpect to the ſubſequent death of *Yao-wun-kuey*, their conduct in acquieſcing in the concealment of the affair, and failing to refer it to the magiſtrates, is highly culpable; though it does not appear, by the inveſtigation, to have been aggravated by the receipt of a bribe, as an inducement to compliance.

They are, therefore, ſeverally puniſhable with 80 blows of the bamboo. The muſkets of *Whang-chang-whay* and *Yao-wun-kuey*, the laws condemn to be deſtroyed and broken up; but the guns of *Tang-fung-chiang*, *Kuo-py-meu*, and *Whang-ſien-tſung*, which were depoſited in the hands of the magiſtrate, may be returned to their reſpective owners.

The trial of *Whang-chang-whay* for mortally wounding *Yao-wun-kuey* by the firing of a muſket, having been reviſed by us, members of the ſupreme court of judicature, we make the amendment in the ſentence, which appears to us requiſite, according to the law in caſes of homicide committed when ſhooting with bows and arrows or otherwiſe; which law directs a puniſhment of 100 blows of the bamboo, and baniſhment for three years; as for the reſt, we confirm the ſub-viceroy's deciſion.

The

The ſupreme court quotes various precedents, and inſtitutes a compariſon between this and former caſes of ſimilar offences, in juſtification of the amendment, and the Emperor finally confirms their deciſion on the 17th day of the 10th moon of the 39th year of KIEN-LUNG, by the following words: —"Purſuant to ſentence be this obeyed."

No. XXXI.

[Referred to from Section CCCXIV. page 341.]

Tranſlation of an Extract from a Collection of Law reports, Book XXI. Page 15, containing the Trial, Reviſal of Proceedings, and final Sentence upon a Caſe of a Maſter charged with the Murder of his Servant.

THE caſe, according to the ſtatement of the ſub-viceroy of *Kiang-ſee*, was as follows:

Lieu-hoey-kuey hired the ſervices of *Pan-kiun-ting*, a ſlave of government, for a period of ten years. — It happened, that on the 9th of the firſt moon of the 45th year of KIEN-LUNG, *Lieu-ſhe*, a married ſiſter of *Lieu-hoey-kuey*, came home to viſit her father *Lieu-kuen-fung* and her mother *Chang-ſhe*; and one day, it being cold weather, her father ſent her into the chamber of the ſervant *Pan-kiun-ting*, to fetch fire-wood. — *Pan-kiun-ting* being at the time intoxicated, laid hold of her clothes, and endeavoured to prevail on her to lie with him—*Lieu-ſhe* reſiſted, but finding herſelf unable to eſcape him, cried out, and was heard by her mother *Chang-ſhe*, who immediately came to her aſſiſtance; upon which the ſlave *Pan-kiun-ting* relinquiſhed his hold, and was ſtruck twice by the mother, *Chang-ſhe*: *Pan-kiun-ting*, fearing puniſhment, ſoon after ran away from the houſe, and took away with him ſome bread and 120 *lee* (about nine-pence) in money.

Lieu-ſhe having complained to her brother of the attempt of the ſlave, and having likewiſe ſolicited him to lay an information before a magiſtrate in order to have the offender puniſhed, returned the next day to her own home, and imparted the circumſtance to her huſband *Puon-kiun-ye*. — As it was a diſgraceful affair, he merely

merely endeavoured to confole her, and took no further notice of the circumftance, until the 14th of the fecond moon, when the abfconded flave *Pan-kiun-ting*, being unable to gain a livelihood elfewhere, returned to his mafter *Lieu-boey-kuey*, acknowledging himfelf guilty. — *Lieu-boey-kuey* did not, however, take any fteps in confequence, until the next day, when his father *Lieu-kuen-fung* ordered him to bind the offending flave, and carry him to a magiftrate, that he might be punifhed. — *Lieu-boey-kuey* fearing that one or two perfons might not be fufficient to accomplifh the object, fent his fervant *Lieu-tfing-ta* the fame evening to his fifter's hufband *Puon-kiun-ye*, begging him to come immediately, and give his counfel and affiftance.

Puon-kiun-ye having arrived, and the flave *Pan-kiun-ting* being again intoxicated and afleep, *Lieu-boey-kuey* took a bamboo cord, and, accompanied by his brother-in-law *Puon-kiun-ye*, and his fervant *Lieu-tfing-ta*, went into the chamber of *Pan-kiun-ting*, before the lamp was extinguifhed: having begun to tie the cord in a knot about the neck of *Pan-kiun-ting*, he awoke; and, difcovering their intention, endeavoured to rife from the bed. Upon this, *Lieu-boey-kuey* defired *Lieu-tfing-ta* to hold him down by the head, and *Puon-kiun-ye* by the feet, while he proceeded himfelf to tie his hands. — At this time *Pan-kiun-ting*, whofe body was uncovered, (having previoufly taken off his clothes,) turned about, and kicked with his legs, abufing them all, in the following terms: " If you carry " me to the magiftrate, I fhall only be beaten or pilloried, and then fent home; " after which, I will furely take your lives in revenge."—*Lieu-boey-kuey* being enraged at this language, took up a fmall knife ufed for cutting tobacco, which happened to lay at the head of the bed, and wounded *Pan-kiun-ting* with it in the lower part of the belly, fo that he died very foon afterwards.

The parties prefent then became fearful of the confequences of the murder, and covered up the body with the bed-clothes. —After the firft watch of the night, *Lieu-boey-kuey* defired *Puon-kiun-ye* and *Lieu-tfing-ta* to take away the corpfe, and throw it into the water, which they did accordingly; but foon after, *Pan-kiung-tching*, and others, related to the deceafed, found the body, and lodged a complaint with the magiftrate of the diftrict. — *Lieu-boey-kuey*, being in confequence brought to trial, and examined, confeffed that the foregoing ftatement of the circumftances was correct.

The facts being thus fubftantiated, the fub-viceroy pronounced the offence to be the wilful murder of an hired flave, and to be equivalent to the wilful murder of a ferving-man, which, according to the penal code, is punifhable with death by ftrangulation, at the next general execution and gaol delivery.

The fupreme criminal court remarks thereupon, that, according to the penal code, if a mafter ftrikes his fervant, fo that he dies in confequence of the blows

blows received, he ſhall be puniſhed with 100 blows, and three years baniſhment :—again, if a maſter deſignedly kills his ſerving-man, he ſhall be ſtrangled : —laſtly, if any man unauthorizedly kills an offender after he has ſeized him, the puniſhment ſhall be conformable to the law in the caſe of killing in an affray.— Now, becauſe unauthorizedly killing, manifeſtly comprehends both deſigned and malicious killing, deſignedly killing an apprehended offender will be puniſhable in the ſame manner as the offence of killing an innocent perſon in an affray, that is to ſay, killing, without a poſitive deſign to kill :—this preciſely applies to the caſe in queſtion ; except that the deceaſed was not the equal, but the ſervant of the perſon who killed him : the puniſhment therefore ought to be conformable to the law againſt a maſter killing his ſervant in an affray, which is 100 blows and three years baniſhment ; or practically, 40 blows inflicted at the place of baniſhment.

The ſub-viceroy altered the ſentence of *Lieu-hoey-kuey* conformably to the ſuggeſtion of the ſupreme court, and added, that as *Puon-kiun-ye* and *Lieu-tſing-ta* threw the corpſe away, they ought to be puniſhed only one degree leſs ſeverely, as acceſſaries ; that is to ſay, with 90 blows, and baniſhment for two years and a half.

The ſupreme court again remarked, that there is a ſpecific regulation applicable to thoſe leſs ſerious caſes of homicide, for which no man is made legally anſwerable with his life; which regulation declares, that whoever throws away the corpſe in ſuch caſes, ſhall only be puniſhed as in any caſe of ſecretly interring a corpſe of an individual whoſe deceaſe has been concealed ; which puniſhment amounts to 80 blows. Now, in the preſent caſe, the offence of killing the ſlave not being determined to be capital, that of throwing away the corpſe cannot be puniſhed with more than 80 blows as aforeſaid :—and as *Lieu-hoey-kuey* directed the corpſe to be thrown away, thoſe who executed the ſame were only acceſſaries to the offence, and, accordingly, ſubject to the puniſhment reduced one degree ; —*Puon-kiun-ye* and *Lieu-tſing-ta* ought therefore to be ſentenced each to receive 70 blows ; or practically, 25 blows.

The ſupreme court laſtly notices the edict of the 38th year of KIEN-LUNG, by which it is ordered that all magiſtrates of cities of the firſt, ſecond, and third order, who concur in pronouncing a ſentence of death, which is afterwards ſet aſide as erroneous, and is exchanged for baniſhment, are ſubjected to a diminution of one degree of rank, and removal to an inferior office. It is thereupon ſuggeſted, that the ſeveral magiſtrates who concurred in the erroneous ſentence adopted and reported by the ſub-viceroy, ſhould be degraded accordingly.

On the 25th day of the 5th moon of the 46th year of KIEN-LUNG, the above proceedings were laid before the Emperor, and on the 29th, they received the ratification of His Imperial Majeſty.

No. XXXII.

[Referred to from Section CCCLXVI. Page 405.]

The following is a Translation of some of the principal Clauses annexed to this Section.

INCEST AND ADULTERY.

ALL persons, whether in official situations or not, when guilty of committing adultery with the principal wife of any civil or military officer of government, shall suffer death by strangulation; the adultress shall likewise suffer death in the same manner.

All civil and military officers committing adultery with the wife of a private individual, shall be degraded, and punished with 100 blows; and shall wear the Cangue for one month.

In all ordinary cases of adultery amongst the people, the guilty parties shall each receive 100 blows, and wear the Cangue for one month.

When the parties to an act of adultery are both slaves, whether in the service of the same master or not, they shall receive 100 blows, but suffer no further punishment.

2. Persons aiding and abetting the parties guilty of the crime of adultery, shall be punished one degree less, as accessaries.

3. Depraved and disorderly persons conspiring together, and seizing on the son or relative of an honest family, in order to commit an unnatural crime, shall, whether their guilt be aggravated by the subsequent crime of murder or not, suffer death, by being beheaded immediately after conviction, as in the case of vagabond outlaws. — Accessaries to such crimes shall suffer death, by being strangled at the usual period of executions, and all other persons concerned in such a criminal association, shall be banished perpetually.

If no conspiracy had been formed, but the additional guilt of murder in curred, or if a boy under ten years of age had been seduced away for such purpose, the criminal shall be punished with death as a vagabond outlaw, by being beheaded immediately after conviction.

Whoever forcibly commits the said crime with a boy under twelve and not above ten years of age, shall suffer death by being beheaded at the usual period for capital executions: and although the party within the age aforefaid, fhould have confented, the crime fhall ftill be punifhed as a rape, that is to fay, with death, by ftrangulation at the ufual period.

An affault, with intent to commit the faid crime, fhall be punifhed with 100 blows, and perpetual banifhment to the diftance of 3000 *lee*.

Perfons committing this crime by mutual confent, fhall be punifhed refpectively, as in ordinary cafes of criminal connexion between different fexes, that is to fay, with 100 blows, and the Cangue for one month.

Endeavouring to injure any perfon by charging him with the commiffion of fuch a crime, is punifhable in the fame degree, as the accufed perfon would have been had he been convicted; neverthelefs, in capital cafes, the punifhment of the falfe accufer fhall be lefs by one degree: — In a cafe punifhable with death by being beheaded immediately after conviction, the falfe accufer fhall be banifhed perpetually beyond the Chinefe frontier.

GENERAL INDEX.

Edicts,

Insurrection,

Quarrel-

Trial

THE END.

Strahan and Preston,
Printers-Street, London.

ERRATA.

Page 4, line 4, *for* adminftering, *r.* adminiftering.
—— 10, — 18, *for* his fituation, *r.* their fituations.
—— —, — 20, *for* his fituation, *r.* their fituations.
—— 27, — 4, *for* orignal. *r.* original.
—— 30, — 8, *for* claue, *r.* claufe.
—— 51, — 16, *dele* he.
—— 53, — 27, *for* tieng, *r.* tien.
—— 54, — 29, *for* enumeration, *r.* enumerations.
—— 104, — 26, *for* drural eities, *r.* rural dieties.
—— 111, — 15, *for* and to other. *r.* and other.
—— 113, — 17, *for* his, *r.* their.
—— 134, — 29, *for* officer, *r.* officers.
—— 209, — 14, *for* a, *r.* their.
—— 313, — 1, *for* texten, *r.* extent.
—— 343, — 1, *for* ftrking, *r.* ftriking.
—— 448, — 20, *for* oi, *r.* or.
—— 474, — 8, *for* has, *r.* have.
—— 510, — 26. *for* everal, *r.* feveral.
—— 522, — 17, *dele* that.
—— 531, — 30, *for* fuc haid, *r.* fuch aid.

THE FOLLOWING VALUABLE WORKS

Are printed for T. CADELL *and* W. DAVIES, *in the Strand.*

1. AN authentic ACCOUNT of an EMBASSY from the King of Great Britain, to the Emperor of CHINA; including curſory Obſervations made, and Information obtained, in travelling through that ancient Empire, and a ſmall part of Chineſe Tartary; together with a Relation of the Voyage undertaken on the Occaſion, by His Majeſty's Ship the Lion, and the Ship Hindoſtan, in the Eaſt India Company's Service, to the Yellow Sea, and Gulf of Pekin; as well as on their Return to Europe; with Notices of the ſeveral Places where they ſtopped in their Way out and home; being the Iſlands of Madeira, Teneriffe, and St. Jago; the Port of Rio de Janeiro, in South America; the Iſlands of St. Helena, Triſtan d'Acunha, and Amſterdam; the Coaſts of Java and Sumatra, the Nanka Iſles, Pulo Condore, and Cochin China. Taken chiefly from the Papers of his Excellency the EARL of MACARTNEY, Knight of the Bath, His Majeſty's Embaſſador Extraordinary and Plenipotentiary to the Emperor of China; Sir Eraſmus Gower, Commander of the Expedition, and of other Gentlemen in the ſeveral Departments of the Embaſſy. By Sir GEORGE STAUNTON, Bart. Honorary Doctor of Laws of the Univerſity of Oxford, F.R.S. of London, His Majeſty's Secretary of Embaſſy to the Emperor of China, and Miniſter Plenipotentiary in the Abſence of the Embaſſador. In Two Vols. 4to. with Engravings; beſides a Folio Volume of Plates, 4l. 4s. in Boards. On Fine Paper, with early Impreſſions of the Plates, 6l. 6s. in Boards. A very few Copies, with Proof Impreſſions of the Plates, may be had, Price 10l. 10s. in boards.

*** Another Edition, in Three Volumes, 8vo. with Three Charts, 1l. 1s. in Boards.

2. Some ACCOUNT of the PUBLIC LIFE, and a SELECTION from the UNPUBLISHED WRITINGS of the EARL of MACARTNEY. The latter conſiſting of Extracts from an Account of the Ruſſian Empire: a Sketch of the Political Hiſtory of Ireland: and a Journal of an Embaſſy from the King of Great Britain to the Emperor of CHINA. By JOHN BARROW, F.R.S. Handſomely printed in 2 vols. 4to. with a Portrait of the Earl of Macartney, engraved by Schiavonnetti, Price 3l. 3s. in Boards.

3. TRAVELS in CHINA, containing Deſcriptions and Compariſons, made and collected in the Courſe of a ſhort Reſidence at the Imperial Palace of Yuen-min-Yuen, and on a ſubſequent Journey through the Country from Pekin to Canton; in which it is attempted to appreciate the Rank that this extraordinary Empire may be conſidered to hold in the Scale of civilized Nations. By the Same. In One Volume 4to. illuſtrated with ſeveral Engravings. Price 2l. 12s. 6d. in Boards.

4. A VOYAGE to COCHIN CHINA in the Years 1792 and 1793: containing a general View of the valuable Productions, and the political Importance of this flouriſhing Kingdom: and alſo of ſuch European Settlements as were viſited on the Voyage: with Sketches of the Manners, Character, and Condition of their ſeveral Inhabitants. To which is annexed, an Account of a Journey, made in the Years 1801 and 1802, to the Reſidence of the Chief of the Booſhuana Nation, being the remoteſt Point in the Interior of Southern Africa to which Europeans have hitherto penetrated. The Facts and Deſcriptions taken from a Manuſcript Journal, with a Chart of the Route. By the Same. Illuſtrated and embelliſhed with ſeveral Engravings, by Medland; coloured after the original Drawings, by Mr. Alexander and Mr. Daniel. 4to. Price 3l. 13d. 6d. in Boards.

5. TRAVELS into the INTERIOR of SOUTHERN AFRICA, in which are deſcribed the Character and Condition of the Dutch Colonies of the Cape of Good Hope, and of the ſeveral Tribes of Natives beyond its Limits. The Natural Hiſtory of ſuch Subjects as occurred in the Animal, Mineral, and Vegetable Kingdoms; and the Geography of the Southern Extremity of Africa. Comprehending alſo a Topographical and Statiſtical Sketch of the Cape Colony; with an Enquiry into its Importance as a Naval and Military Station, as a Commercial Emporium, and as a Territoral Poſſeſſion. By JOHN BARROW, Eſq. Second Edition, in Two Volumes, 4to. with Additions and Alterations, illuſtrated with ſeveral Engravings and Charts. Price 3l. 3s. in Boards.

6. A JOURNEY from MADRAS through the COUNTRIES of MYSORE, CANARA, and MALABAR, performed under the Orders of the Moſt Noble the Marquis Welleſley, Governor-General of India, for the expreſs Purpoſe of inveſtigating the State of Agriculture, Arts, and Commerce, the Religion, Manners, and Cuſtoms, the Hiſtory, Natural and Civil, and Antiquities, in the Dominions of the Rajah of Myſore, and the Countries acquired by the Honourable the Eaſt-India Company, in the late and former War, from

Tippoo Sultaun. By Francis Buchanan, M.D. F.R.S. and F.S.A. Fellow of the Aſiatic Society of Calcutta, and in the Medical Service of the Honourable Company, on the Bengal Eſtabliſhment. Publiſhed under the Authority and Patronage of the Honourable Directors of the Eaſt-India Company. Elegantly printed in Three Volumes, 4to. and illuſtrated by a Map, and numerous other Engravings. Price 6l. 6s. in Boards, or on large Paper, 9l. 9s. in Boards.

7. A TOUR to SHEERAZ, by the Route of KAZROON and FEEROZABAD, with various Remarks on the Manners, Cuſtoms, Laws, Language, and Literature of the Perſians. To which is added, a Hiſtory of Perſia, from the Death of Kureem Khan, to the Subverſion of the Zund Dynaſty. By Edward Scott Waring, Eſq. of the Bengal Civil Eſtabliſhment. Elegantly printed in 4to. and illuſtrated by Two Portraits, from the original Pictures. Price 1l. 5s. or on royal paper, 1l. 16s. in Boards.

8. An ACCOUNT of the GEOGRAPHICAL and ASTRONOMICAL EXPEDITION, undertaken by Order of the late Empreſs of Ruſſia, Catherine the Second, for exploring the Coaſt of the ICY SEA, the Land of the TSHUTSKI, and the Iſlands between ASIA and AMERICA, under the Command of Captain Billings, between the Years 1785 and 1794. By Martin Sauer, Secretary to the Expedition. Dedicated, by permiſſion, to Sir Joseph Banks, Bart. K.B. P.R.S. Elegantly printed in One Volume, 4to. and illuſtrated by Charts, Views of the Countries, the Coſtume of the Inhabitants, &c. &c. 4to. Price 2l. 2s.

9. A TOUR performed in the Years 1795-6, through the TAURIDA or CRIMEA, the ancient Kingdom of Boſphorus, and all the other Countries on the North Shore of the Euxine, ceded to Ruſſia by the Peace of Kainardgi and Jaſſy; by Mrs. Maria Guthrie, formerly acting Directreſs to the Convent for the Education of the Female Nobility of Ruſſia: In a Series of Letters to her Huſband, the Editor, Mathew Guthrie, M.D. F.R. and A.S. of London and Edinburgh, &c. Phyſician to the Firſt and Second Imperial Corps of Noble Cadets, and Counſellor of State to His Imperial Majeſty. Elegantly printed in One Volume Quarto, and illuſtrated by a Map of the Tour along the Euxine Coaſt, from the Dnieſter to the Cuban: with Engravings of a great Number of ancient Coins, Medals, Monuments, Inſcriptions, and other curious Objects. 4to. Price 1l. 11s. 6d.

10. An ACCOUNT of the RUSSIAN DISCOVERIES between ASIA and AMERICA. To which are added, the CONQUEST of SIBERIA, and the HISTORY of the TRANSACTIONS and COMMERCE between RUSSIA and CHINA. By William Coxe, A.M. Prebendary of Saliſbury, illuſtrated with Charts, and a View of a Chineſe Town. 8vo. Price 10s. 6d. in Boards.

11. TRAVELS into Poland, Ruſſia, Sweden, Denmark, &c. Interſperſed with Hiſtorical Relations, and Political Inquiries. By the Same. Illuſtrated with Charts and Engravings. 5 Vols. 8vo. Price 2l. 5s. in Boards.

12. A SURVEY of the TURKISH EMPIRE. In which are conſidered, I. Its Government, Finances, Military and Naval Force, Religion, Hiſtory, Arts, Sciences, Manners, Commerce, and Population. II. The State of the Provinces, including the Ancient Government of the Crim Tartars, the Subjection of the Greeks, their Efforts towards Emancipation, and the Intereſt of other Nations, particularly Great Britain, in their Succeſs. III. The Cauſes of the Decline of Turkey, and thoſe which tend to the Prolongation of its Exiſtence, with a Developement of the Political Syſtem of the late Empreſs of Ruſſia. IV. The Britiſh Commerce with Turkey, the Neceſſity of aboliſhing the Levant Company, and the Danger of our Quarantine Regulations. With many other Important Particulars. By W. Eton, Eſq. many Years reſident in Turkey and Ruſſia. One large Volume, 8vo. Fourth Edition, Price 9s. in Boards.

13. TRAVELS in AFRICA, EGYPT, and SYRIA, from the Year 1792 to 1793. By G. W. Browne. With Maps and other Engravings. 4to. 2d Edit. 1l. 16s. in Boards.

14. TRAVELS in EUROPE, ASIA-MINOR, and ARABIA. By J. Griffiths, M.D. Member of the Royal Medical Society of Edinburgh, and of ſeveral Foreign Literary Societies. Embelliſhed with a Portrait of the Author, and ſeveral Engravings. 4to Price 1l. 1s. 6d. in Boards.

15. The PROGRESS of MARITIME DISCOVERY, from the earlieſt Period to the Cloſe of the Eighteenth Century. Volume the Firſt. By James Stanier Clarke, F.R.S. Domeſtic Chaplain to the Prince, and Vicar of Preſton. Handſomely printed in 4to. and enriched by numerous Engravings from the Drawings of Pocock, and an entire new Set of Charts, by Arrowſmith. Price 3l. 8s. in Boards.

ÖNB
+Z137219001

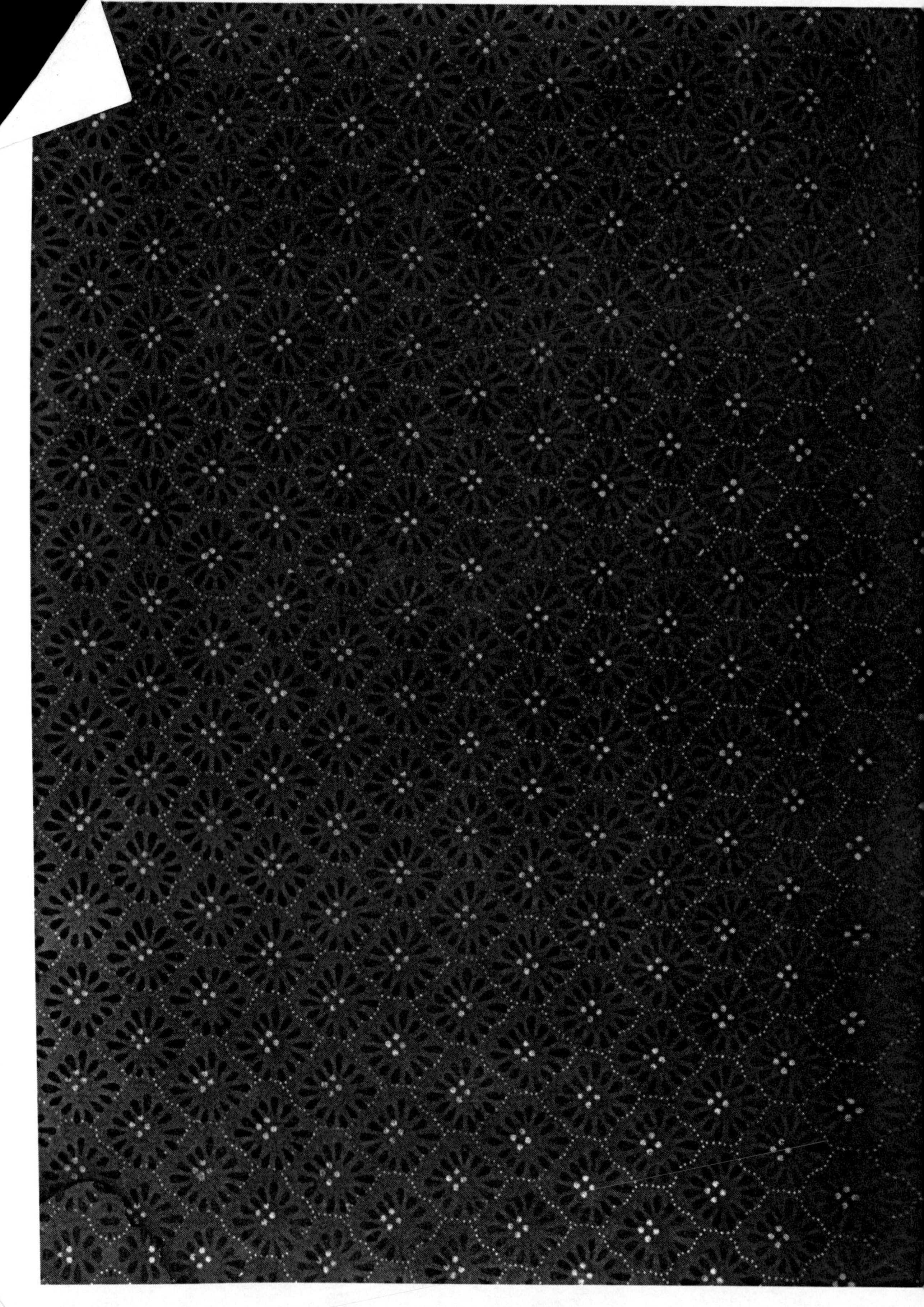

Lightning Source UK Ltd.
Milton Keynes UK
UKOW040322270911

179303UK00002B/131/P